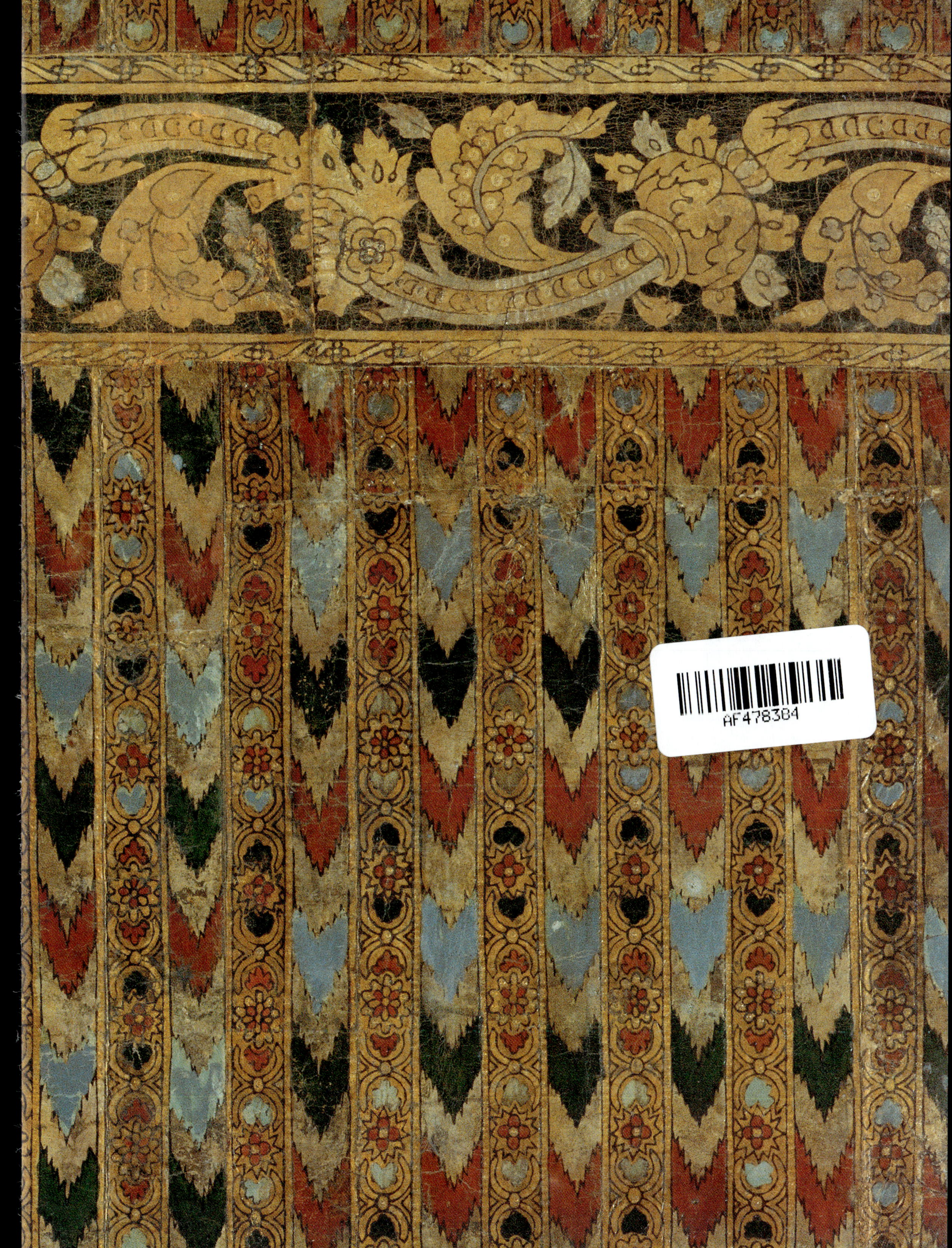

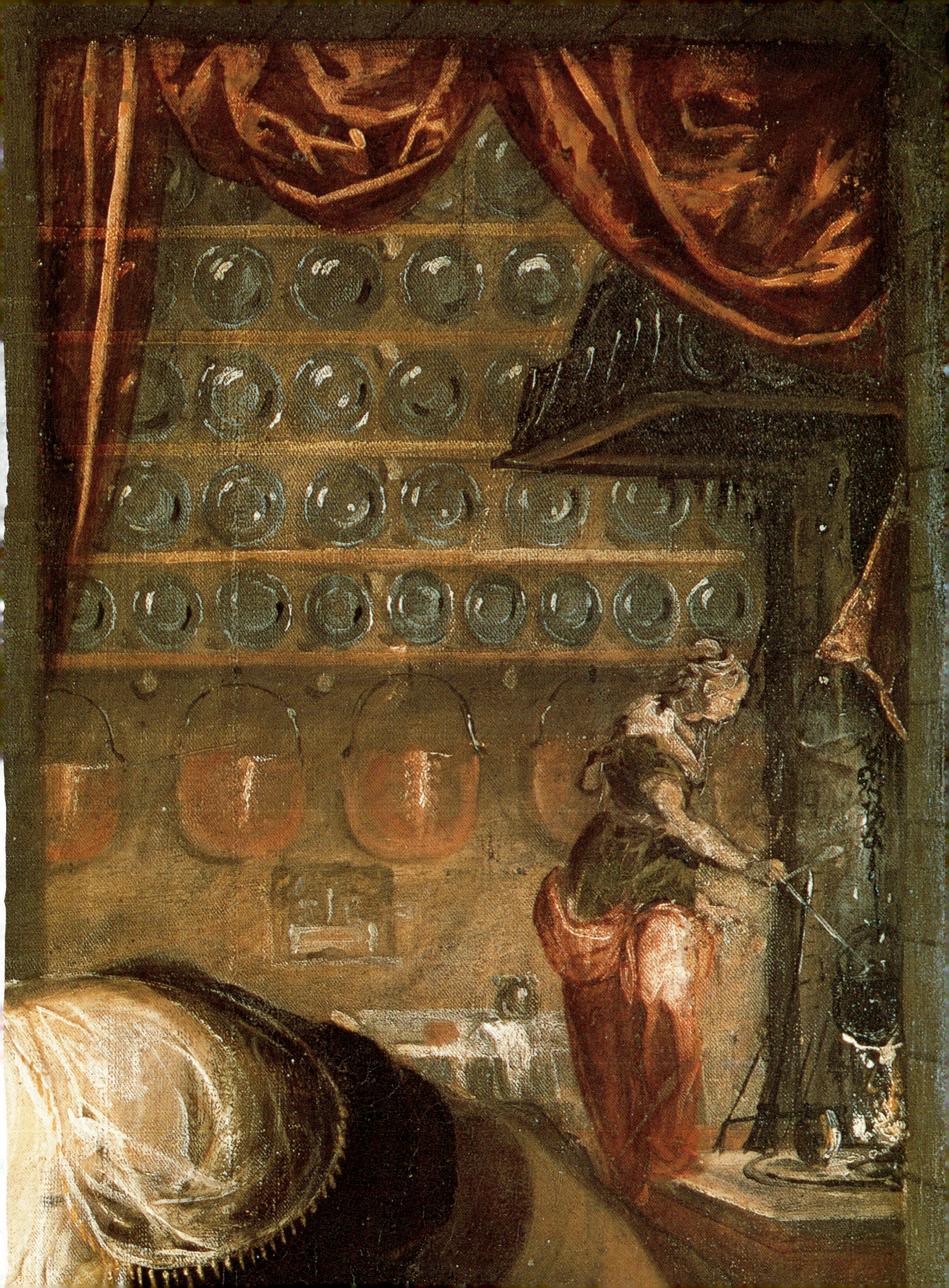

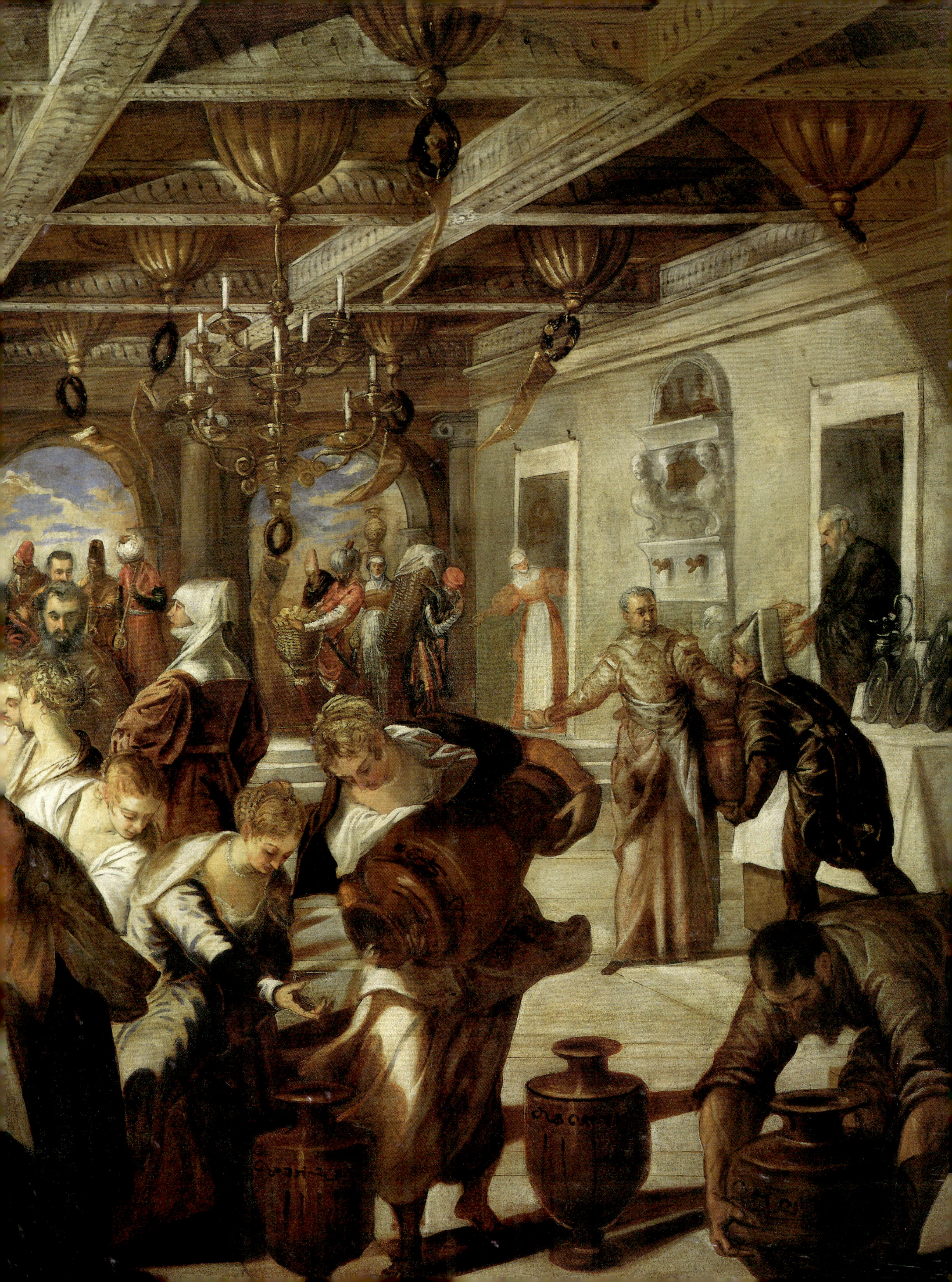

Patricia Fortini Brown

PRIVATE LIVES IN RENAISSANCE VENICE

Art, Architecture, and the Family

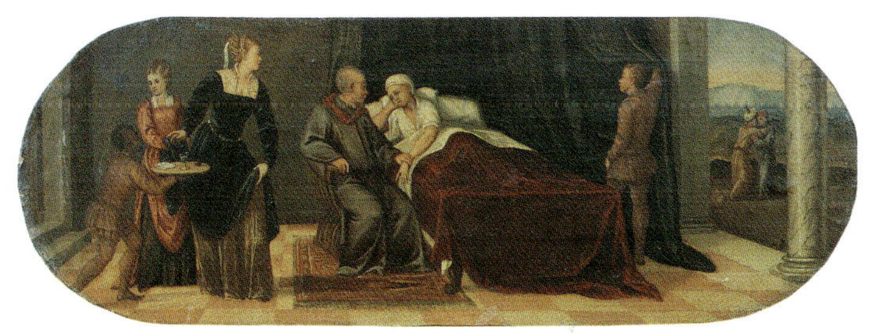

Yale University Press

New Haven & London

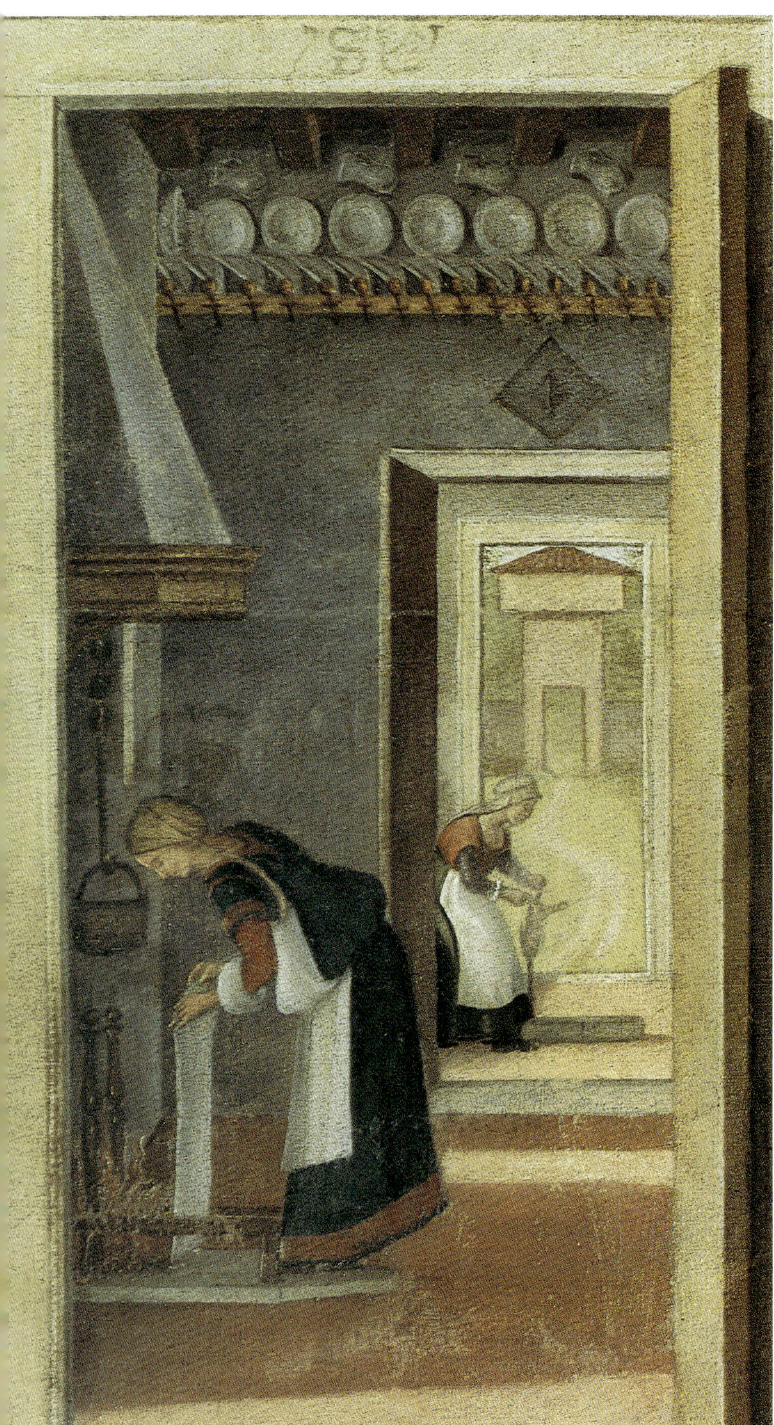

Published with the assistance of
The Publications Committee,
Department of Art and Archaeology,
Princeton University

Designed by Gillian Malpass

Printed in Singapore

Library of Congress Cataloging-in-Publication Number: 2003018889

ISBN 0-300-10236-4 (cl : alk. paper)

A catalogue record for this book is available from the Library of Congress and the British Library

endpapers
Detail from a wall hanging of leather (*bazzana*), with gilding and polychrome decoration, late sixteenth century. Bologna, Museo Civico Medievale. See fig. 83.

page i
Jacopo Tintoretto, *Christ in the House of Martha and Mary*, 1567. Munich, Alte Pinakothek. Detail of fig. 179.

frontispiece
Jacopo Tintoretto, *Marriage Feast at Cana*, 1561. Venice, Church of S. Maria della Salute. Detail of fig. 168.

page iii
Bonifacio Veronese (dei Pitati), *Antiochus and Stratonice*, ca. 1540s. Milan, Museo Poldi Pezzoli. Detail of fig. 103.

this page
Vittore Carpaccio, *The Birth of the Virgin*, 1504. Bergamo, Accademia Carrara. Detail of fig. 104.

Contents

Acknowledgments

One incurs many debts over the course of six years in the research, writing, and preparation of a book. My early research was generously supported by a sabbatical leave in 1998–99 from Princeton University and by a Mellon Postdoctoral Research Fellowship at the Folger Shakespeare Library, where Werner Gundersheimer, then the Director, and his staff offered an ideal environment for scholarly research. I was most fortunate in having fellow colleagues that year – Sue Lanser, Ann Rosalind Jones, Jessie Ann Owens, and Peter Stallybrass – who provided a stimulating intellectual atmosphere when I was in the early phases of developing the lectures that eventually turned into the book. I should like to express my gratitude also to Cambridge University for its generous sponsorship of the Slade Lectures and to St. John's College for its gracious hospitality for Lent term in the winter of 2001. I was fortunate to return to the American Academy in Rome as a resident that spring and am indebted to Lester Little, the staff, and the fellows and other colleagues for offering a setting far from the distractions of Venice to begin recasting the lectures as a book. I am grateful also to the Renaissance Society of America and the Gladys Krieble Delmas Foundation for fellowship support for summer research in Venice, and I acknowledge with thanks the invaluable assistance of the Ione May Spears Fund and the Publication Fund of the Department of Art & Archaeology at Princeton.

My work was greatly facilitated by the staffs of the Marquand, Mudd, and Firestone libraries at Princeton; of the British Library, the Bodleian Library in Oxford, and the University Library in Cambridge; and in Venice, of the Archivio di Stato, the Biblioteca Nazionale Marciana, and the Biblioteca del Museo Correr. I am indebted to them all, as well as to my students at Princeton who continue to challenge and inspire me. Those who participated in my graduate seminar on the Renaissance palace in fall 2000, and gave valuable critiques on a first version of the Slade Lectures, included Dave Daniels, Blake de Maria, Mary Frank, and Christina Stacy, as well as Robert Glass, Kirsten Hammer, Kris Neville. The latter three were also participants in my graduate seminar on Renaissance collecting in spring 2002, along with Alexandra Greist, Jennifer King, Noriko Kotani, Julia Robinson, and Gerald Seid. Their insights and comments helped me to expand and improve the eighth chapter of the book.

A daunting number of individuals helped me in ways too numerous to count and I beg forgiveness from those whom I have neglected to list here. I thank Bernard Aikema, Marta Ajmar, Silvana d'Alessio, Julie Angarone, Malcolm Baker, Cat Bauer, Kate Bentz, Bruce Boucher, Simone Chiarugi, Stan Chojnacki, Monica Chojnacka, Tracy Cooper, Celia Curfman, Michaela Dal Borgo, Martin Durrant, Claire Fontijn-Harris, Alberta Friedenberg, Giorgio (Nubar) Gianighian, Laura Giles, Edoardo Giuffride, James Grubb, Kate Hay, Daniëlle O. Kisluk-Grosheide, the late Patricia Labalme, Stefanie Lew, Rosamond Mack, John Martin, Virginia Mauch, Dulcia Meijers, Starleen Meyer, Reiny and Laura Mueller, Paola Pavanini, Lucia Pini, John Pinto, Janice Powell, Dennis Romano, Amanda Rutherford, Claudio Salsi, Romano Scarpa, Juergen Schulz, Luke Syson, Francesca Tasso, Dora Thornton, Francesca Toffolo, James Yorke, and Marino Zorzi for practical help, advice, and various kinds of assistance; Kirk Alexander, John Blaszewski, David Connelly, Ben Kessler, Jill Moraca, Mark Smith, Janet Temos, and Wolfgang Wolters, as well as Piero Codato and Giorgio Santuzzi of Cameraphoto, Venice, and the staff of the Visual Resources Collection at Princeton, for invaluable help with the photographs and digital imaging; Pietro Scarpa, *antiquariato*, and his wife, for inviting me into their home, the former *casa* of Zuan Matteo Bembo on Campiello Santa Maria Nova, and allowing me to photograph the interior; and the office staff of the Department of Art and Archaeology – Susan Lehre, Diane Schulte, Elayne McCans, Lisa Ball, and Kelly Haffar – for continuing support and secretarial assistance. I was fortunate, indeed, to have Philippa Baker as my copy-editor, whose close reading and attention to the smallest detail was sincerely appreciated.

Finally, I am especially grateful to Deborah Howard, who read the entire manuscript for Yale University Press and offered invaluable criticisms and suggestions for improvement, and to Gillian Malpass, editor *extraordinaire*, for her vision, encouragement, and friendship.

Patricia Fortini Brown
September 1, 2003

Preface

THIS BOOK EXAMINES THE MATERIAL CULTURE of Venetian elites in the context of a changing definition of nobility in the sixteenth century. Among the major themes considered are attitudes toward wealth and display; the articulation of family identity; the emergence of characteristically Venetian decorative practices and styles of art and architecture; the interplay between the public and the private; the equivocal meaning of *politia* – signifying both refinement (as in aesthetic excellence) and civility (as in politic behavior); the private sphere of women; mechanisms of public control over the private acquisition of luxury objects; and, broadly, the attributes of the aristocratic lifestyle in Venice.

As in my earlier books, the methodological approach lies in maintaining a concrete focus on artefact and art object, while setting them within an encompassing contextual frame that embraces both the aspirations and the realities of civic culture in Venice. In *Venetian Narrative Painting in the Age of Carpaccio* (1988) I examined how a Venetian "eyewitness" style of painting functioned in "aesthetic space" to mediate between the ideology and the reality of religious and civic life in Renaissance Venice. This study led me to be concerned with the further problem of how the newly discovered ancient past was perceived by, and rendered present to, the Renaissance viewer, a theme that was the point of departure for my second book, *Venice & Antiquity: The Venetian Sense of the Past* (1996). Here, drawing on a wide range of primary sources, including such remains of vernacular culture as inscriptions, medals and traveler's accounts as well as more learned humanist and antiquarian writings, I sought to weave the visual arts into a tapestry of historical and aesthetic sensibilities that embraced both the public and private spheres. Along the way, life and art behind the palace walls came to the fore as a major focus of interest. And again, my work on this book led to another. In *Art and Life in Renaissance Venice* (1997), along with art in civic and religious life, I dealt with domestic concerns in a summary way in chapters on "private worlds" and on the problem of self-fashioning and representation in the unique political and social context of Venice.

With many unanswered questions about the relationship between the private lives of the Venetians and the visual arts still fresh in my mind from my work on these books, two further encounters informed the present investigation. First, I was struck by Francesco Sansovino's intriguing observation in his *Venetia città nobilissima* (1581) that Venice was a society both frugal and opulent – an ambiguous claim that cried out for explanation. And second, on a visit to the National Gallery in Washington, D.C., I was shown a handsomely carved *cassone* that was said by some scholars to be Venetian, although it was labeled Florentine. The curator asked me what was Venetian about it, and I could not answer. I resolved to find out. The present study was initially sparked by this puzzlement over the *venezianità* of objects and the domestic environment and an aesthetic context that was thought to be both frugal and opulent.

My first attempt to deal with these issues was engendered by a conference held at Syracuse University in the fall of 1997, for which I wrote a paper entitled "Behind the Walls: The Material Culture of Venetian Elites." This paper, eventually published in *Venice Reconsidered: The History and Civilization of an Italian City-State, 1297–1797*, edited by John Martin and Dennis Romano (Baltimore and London: Johns Hopkins University Press, 2000), was my initial formulation of the theme. Several parts of this article have been incorporated into the present book.

In the winter of 1998, upon receiving an invitation to be Slade Professor of Fine Arts at Cambridge University three years hence, I decided to use the Syracuse essay as the foundation for a fuller exploration of the topic to be delivered at the Slade Lectures in winter 2001. The present book represents a reworking and expansion of the eight lectures, written between 1998 and 2000, although the informality of a spoken presentation has been retained whenever possible.

Each chapter was initially inspired by one or more primary sources – voices from the period – that raised a set of issues that could be discussed within the time-frame of a single lecture. While each chapter thus deals with a particular aspect of the engagement of Renaissance Venetians with the visual arts in their private lives, there is no attempt to present a comprehensive view of the topic. Indeed, each of these presentations could well be further expanded into an entire book in itself – an intriguing possibility that I do not intend to pursue at this point, but would like to welcome other scholars to undertake.

Renaissance Venetian painting, sculpture, and architecture – what are considered the fine arts, produced by artists of genius – have been fruitfully (often brilliantly) studied by generations of scholars over the past century. Only recently have the more mundane products of the artisan – furniture, glass, ceramics, metalwork, textiles, and costume – received serious scholarly attention within their full social and historical contexts. Even then, such studies, with a few notable exceptions, tend to isolate the objects within their genre categories, focusing on glass or ceramics or musical instruments, for example, without exploring how they were part of a larger visual culture and the role they played in family life.[1] But I wanted in the lecture series to bring together the high and the low, discovering how the fine arts and the applied arts were integrated in Venetian households both opulent and frugal. It is a subject whose time has clearly come, with major initiatives underway to examine all aspects of Renaissance material culture based upon a belief in – as Marta Ajmar puts it – "the cultural significance of things."[2]

In terms of objects, I aimed at comprehensiveness, within the limits imposed by the lecture format. Mario Praz once wrote that "Furniture is, in origin, of two species: furniture that supports and furniture that contains: the former suggests animal forms; the second, architectonic; the chair is inspired by the horse; the linen chest, like the coffin for that matter, is inspired by the house."[3] But there is a third species of furnishing that Praz's metaphor does not account for, and that is the whole array of essentially flat objects: those meant to lie on the floor or on tables, such as carpets, and those meant to hang on the wall, such as mirrors, whose frames admittedly might take architectural shapes, but not always; tapestries or fabric hangings, whose patterns may include both animal and architectonic forms, but also floral; and paintings and other two-dimensional works of art. If furnishings are positioned along a spectrum that ranges from utilitarian and absolutely essential, such as a bed of some sort, to decorative and a matter of choice, then such pieces would be at the latter end. And it is those pieces that proliferated in particular in the sixteenth century, in number and in type.

Research for the book involved six basic categories of primary-source evidence, ranging from the theoretical to the material: (1) treatises on nobility that grappled with new definitions of what it meant to *be* noble, as well as with the problematic relationship between wealth and class; (2) the *economica* tradition – treatises on the household based upon classical authorities such as Aristotle and Xenophon that defined the home as the most tangible symbol of family identity, continuity and status and discussed what it meant to *live* nobly; (3) sumptuary legislation – the major legal mechanism to control the display of wealth; (4) household inventories in the Archivio di Stato and the Biblioteca Correr in Venice, which offer a wealth of information documenting the actual contents of sixteenth-century Venetian homes at every social level; (5) anecdotal material, including descriptions of domestic space drawn from such sixteenth-century writers as Sansovino, Marcantonio Michiel, Marin Sanudo, Antonfrancesco Doni, Sabba da Castiglione, Carlo Ridolfi, and others; and finally, and most importantly, (6) the furnishings and luxury objects that were assembled to create those luminous interior spaces that the seventeenth-century writer Giustiniano Martinioni described as displaying "refinement without equal, and with rich and honorable furnishings, as much as one can desire in a private house."[4]

The secondary literature on many of these topics is considerable, but there were no direct models for the book. Of particular interest were recent studies by Richard Goldthwaite, Lisa Jardine, Simon Schama, Peter Burke, and Katie Scott, all of whom offer valuable and provocative insights on early modern European material culture.[5] I see the present book, which I am directing toward a broad audience, as part of the discourse set underway in those volumes, but approached from the perspective of an art historian. In the Venetian sphere, Pompeo Molmenti's *La storia di Venezia nella vita privata* was fundamental.[6] A monument of late nineteenth-century scholarship that embedded art and artifacts in a richly articulated historical context, it still provides numerous points of departure for more focused studies. Recent contributions by Dennis Romano, Stanley Chojnacki, and Monica Chojnacka, among others, were also invaluable resources on social relationships in Venetian households.[7]

My goal in this study is to suggest ways in which Venetians attempted to define and defend family identity and social rank through the accumulation of objects and works of art. The first chapter introduces the problem of the Venetian patriciate in the sixteenth century as a nobility that had earned its fortune through trade, but now wanted to be seen as "gentlemen in fact" as well as "gentlemen in name." The focus turns to "the most notable palaces in the city," cited in Francesco Sansovino's *Venetia città nobilissima*, in the second chapter. Here, the public face of the private sphere – the Venetian house, with an emphasis on the facade – is explored as an expression of family identity. The third chapter goes behind the walls, looking at the domestic interior and the tangible accoutrements of a noble lifestyle, including the layout of the house and the use and decoration of various rooms. Remaining inside the home, the fourth chapter considers the issue of gendered space and the objects and activities that relate to women's lives. In the fifth chapter, the narrative turns to entertainments within the home, including games and Venetian rituals of hospitality. At issue are the works of art and luxury objects associated with recreation and festive celebrations, including weddings and the entertainment of distinguished visitors. The sixth chapter turns to another sort of female space and another form of hospitality: the domestic arrangements of the Venetian courtesan, with an exploration of the luxurious lifestyle for which these figures were noted (or notorious). Turning from elites to the more typical experience of Venetians, the seventh chapter examines housing diversity, with a discussion of homes for the middle class and the poor. Finally, in the eighth chapter, the book looks at the emergence of dedicated spaces within the house for studies and collections, where the world is brought into the home, and for entertainments such as gambling, where the world is shut out. The project is thus multifaceted, if not comprehensive. Throughout there is a concern for how Venetians dealt with the tension between the need for communal solidarity and the private aspirations manifested by those modestly named but sumptuously adorned *case*, which not only lined the Grand Canal but were also scattered through every *sestiere* of the city.

following pages Giovanni Antonio Fasolo, *The Dance* (detail), ca. 1570. Fresco. Villa Caldogno, Caldogno (Vicenza).

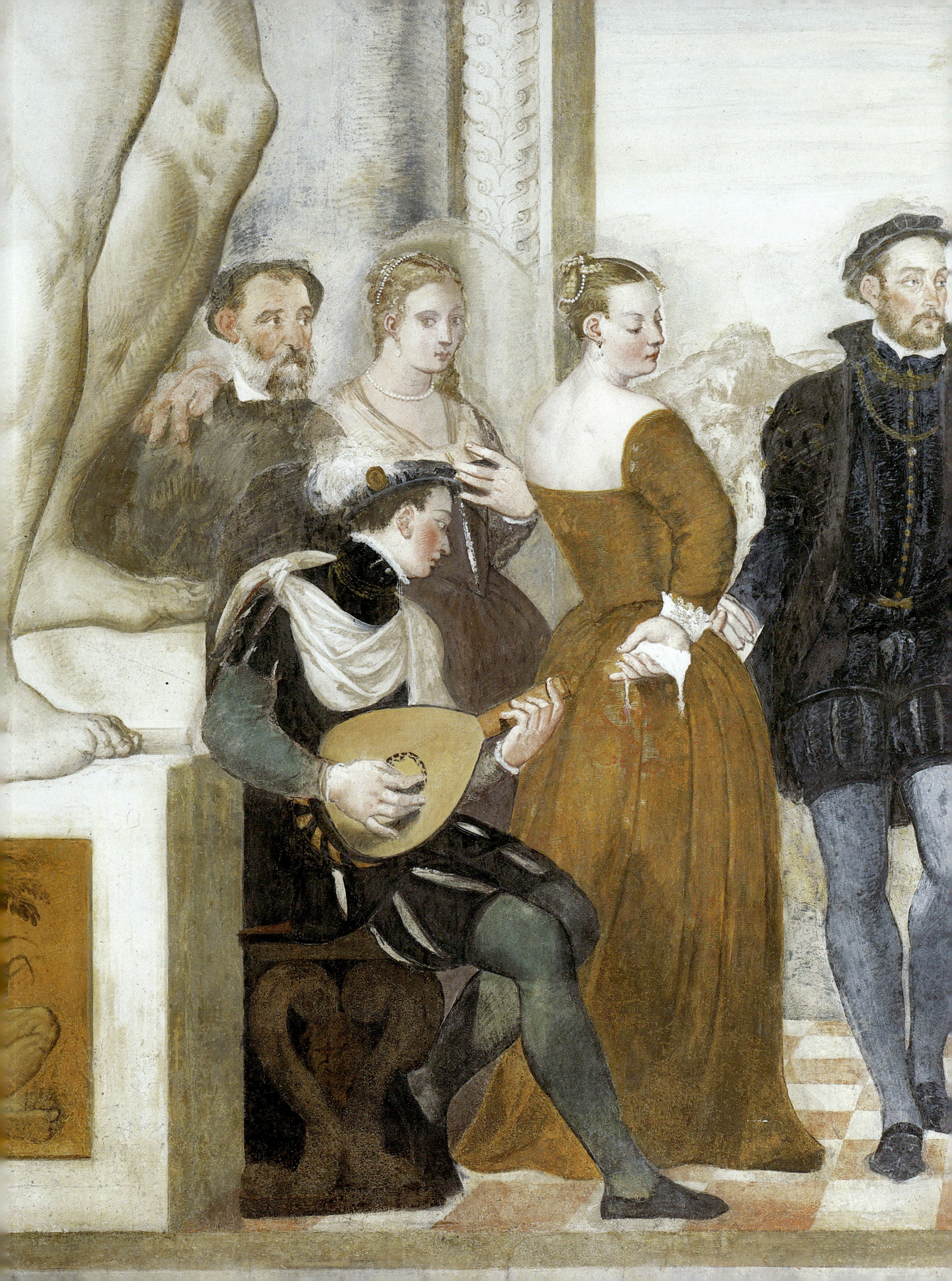

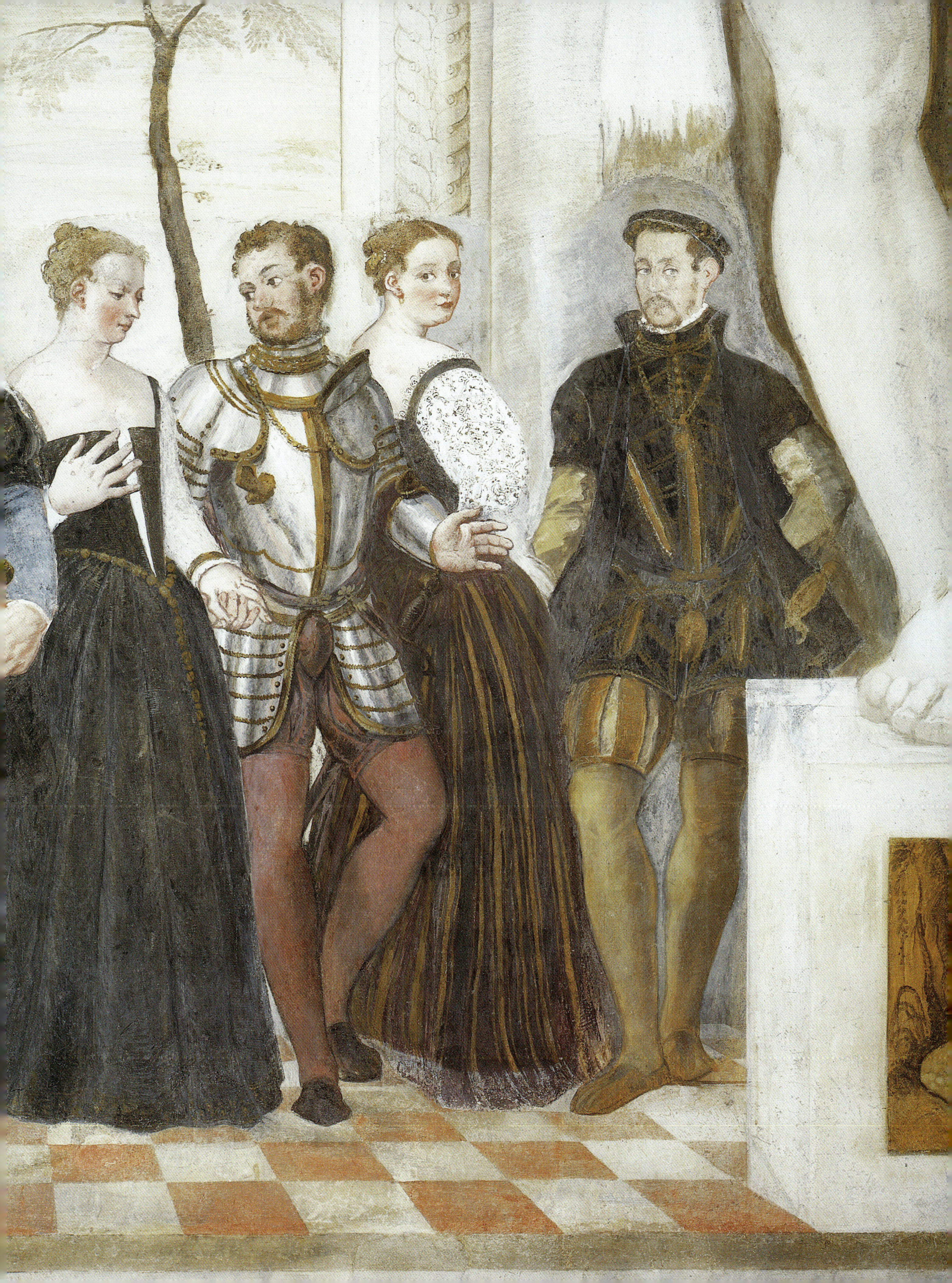

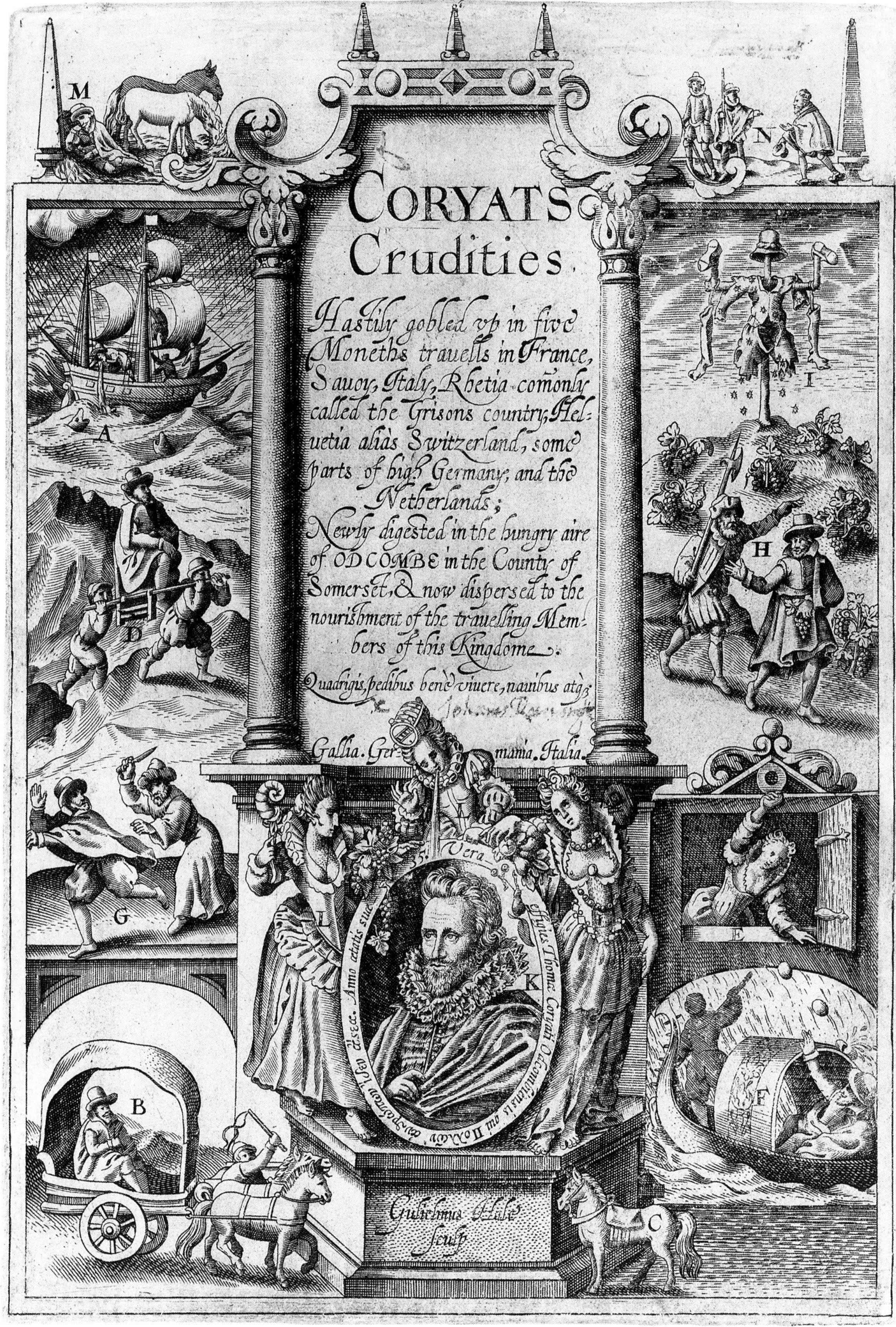

CORYATS
Crudities
Hastily gobled vp in five Moneths trauells in France, Sauoy, Italy, Rhetia comonly called the Grisons country, Helvetia aliàs Switzerland, some parts of high Germany, and the Netherlands;
Newly digested in the hungry aire of ODCOMBE in the County of Somerset, & now dispersed to the nourishment of the trauelling Members of this Kingdome.
Quadrigis, pedibus bene viuere, nauibus atq;
Gallia. Germania. Italia.
Vera effigies Thomæ Coryati Odcombiensis
Anno ætatis suæ 35.
Gulielmus Hole sculp

I

The Title of Their Gentility

IN THE SPRING OF 1608 a young Englishman set off on a five-month tour of Europe and became one of the best eyewitness informants on life and customs in late Renaissance Venice. The son of a country parson in the village of Odcombe in Somerset, Thomas Coryat had attended Gloucester Hall, now Exeter College, Oxford, where he read logic, Greek, and Latin but left without a degree. At the time of his European sojourn he was a member of the household of the young Henry, Prince of Wales, where he seems to have been a sort of unofficial court jester. According to one contemporary, "sweetmeats and Coryat made up the last course at all court entertainments."[1] His quick wit, sharp eye, and inquisitive mind come through in *Coryat's Crudities*, a volume recounting his adventures that he published upon his return to England (fig. 1).[2] His portrait on the frontispiece prompted his friend Laurence Whitaker to write an explanation in rhyming couplets: "These be the three countries with their cornu-copia, That make him as famous, as Moore his Utopia. Or, Here France gives him scabs, Venice a hot Sunne, And Germanie spewes on him out of her Tunne."[3]

Coryat's itinerary was a veritable Cook's Tour. After sailing from Dover to Calais, a trip that took seven hours, he traveled south through France and Savoy and across northern Italy to Venice, returning to England through Switzerland, Germany, and the Netherlands. As the frontispiece illustrates, he traveled by ship, by cart, by horseback, by gondola, and – crossing the Alps – even by a sort of sedan chair, racking up nearly 2,000 miles in all.

In the dedicatory epistle to Prince Henry, Coryat laid out the aim of his arduous journey: first, to encourage the "many noble and generose yong Gallants" who followed the prince's court to "travel into transmarine nations, and to garnish their understanding with the experience of other countries;" and second, to offer the fullest description that had yet been made in the English tongue of the "Virgin Citie of Venice, the Queene of the Christian World, that Diamond set in the ring of the Adriatique gulfe, and the most resplendent mirrour of Europe . . . a subject worthy for the greatest Monarch in the world to reade over."[4]

Indeed, Coryat was dazzled by Venice – by its singular setting, its exceptional beauty, and its great wealth. And the expansive character of his travels through several countries allowed him to make comparisons that reveal some of the particularities of the late Renaissance city to an outside witness. Coryat came well prepared. Having already read a history of Venice by Gasparo Contarini in English translation, he posed a rhetorical question: "Therefore what neede we more descriptions of that Citie?" But then he went on to provide the answer, observing that Contarini had left much out – particularly an account of "the antiquities and monuments of that famous citie."[5]

Like many visitors before and after his time, Coryat was particularly struck by the "hundred and twenty goodly palaces, the greater part whereof is built upon the sides [of the Grand Canal, where they made] a very glorious and beautiful shew" (fig. 2).[6] He went on to give a good account of the exterior aspect of the buildings, describing the characteristic loggias on the facades and the *altane* or terraces on the roofs, but he is less informative about what went on inside their walls.[7] Indeed, aside from the home of his host, an Englishman with a Venetian wife, and the palace of the English ambassador, Sir Henry Wotton, his access to Venetian homes was rather limited.[8] His detailed descriptions of the private spaces of Venetians were confined to what might be considered the extremes of a noble lifestyle: two quasi-public courtyards containing collections of antiquities, and the chambers of a courtesan – two locales that will be revisited in later chapters.

1 (*facing page*) Frontispiece from Thomas Coryat, *Coryat's Crudities: hastily gobled up in five moneths travels* (London: W. S[tansby], 1611). By permission of the Folger Shakespeare Library.

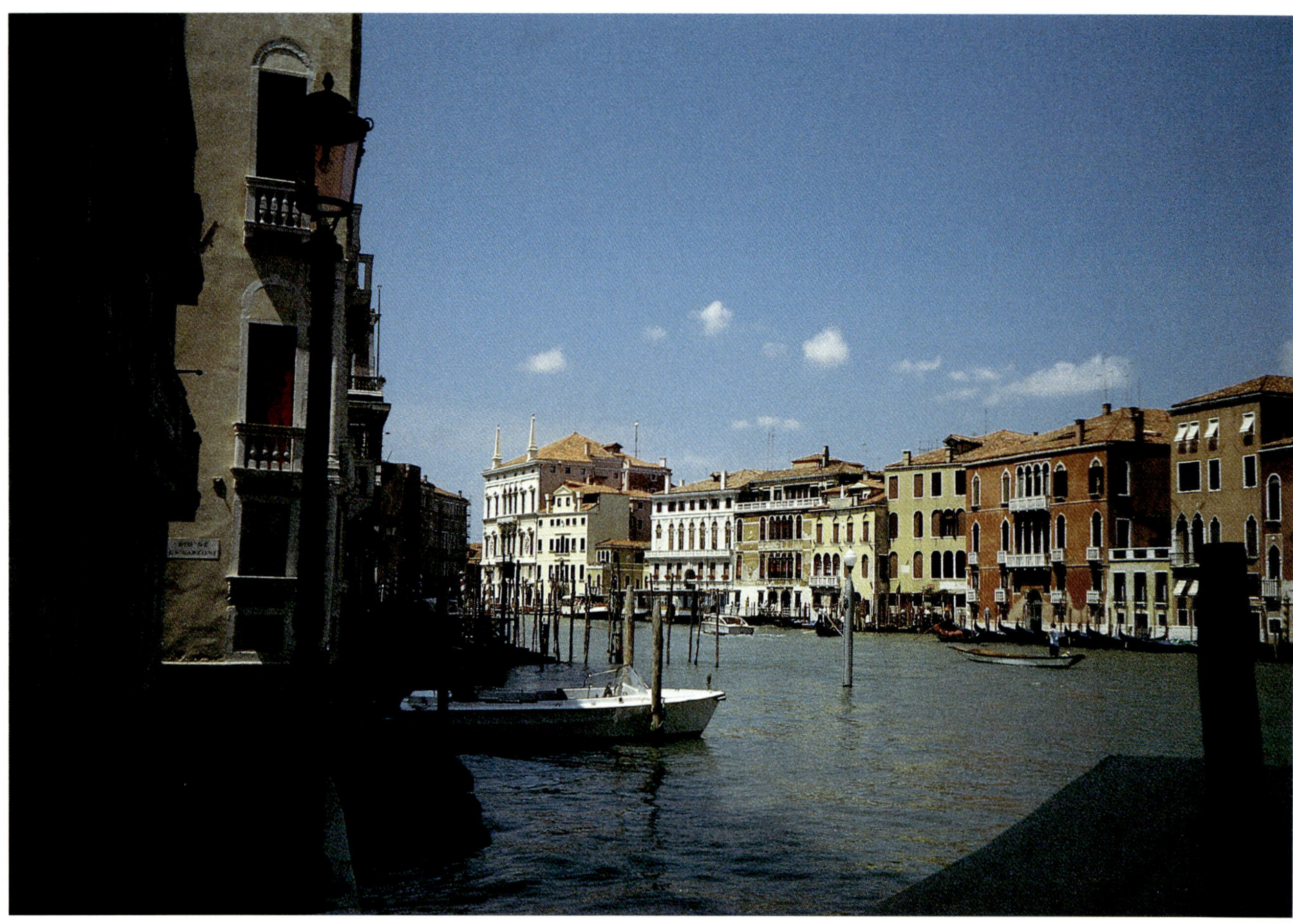

2 Present-day view of the Grand Canal. In the background are Palazzo Balbi, with obelisks defining the upper corners of the facade (attributed to Alessandro Vittoria, ca. 1581–91); Palazzo Caotorta-Angaran (seventeenth century); a small neo-Renaissance house on Rio della Frescada (nineteenth century); Palazzo Civran Grimani (late sixteenth–early seventeenth century with later modifications); Palazzo Dandolo (seventeenth century with the upper floor added in 1924); Palazzo Dolfin, a Gothic house with sixteenth- and seventeenth-century restructuring; Palazzo Marcello dei Leoni (seventeenth century); and the red-hued Ca' Persico-Giustiniani (early sixteenth century).

The Politia *of this City*

But what about the more typical palace of the Venetian patrician? Precious little remains from the interior decoration of the Renaissance period, but the Venetian writer Francesco Sansovino had described such interiors in 1581 in his *Venetia città nobilissima* – a monumental guidebook that laid out the attractions of the city. Son of the renowned sculptor and architect Jacopo Sansovino, he had a fine eye and a fluent pen.[9] He observes that Venetians call their homes "case," or houses, instead of *palazzi* "out of modesty" but then goes on to describe a domestic environment of dazzling opulence. He writes:

> In the past, although our ancestors were frugal they were lavish in the decoration of their houses. There are countless buildings with ceilings of bedchambers and other rooms decorated in gold and other colors and with histories painted by celebrated artists. Almost everyone has his house adorned with noble tapestries, silk drapes and gilded leather, *spalliere* and other things according to the time and season, and most of the bedrooms are furnished with bedsteads and chests, gilded and painted, so the cornices are loaded with gold.[10]

Vivid echoes of such environments are scattered throughout Venice. Palazzo Trevisan in Murano, for example, although it has long been used as a warehouse for a glass factory, still has several rooms with ceilings frescoed with *grotteschi* and the Olympian gods, painted in the sixteenth century (fig. 3). Likewise, a late sixteenth-century

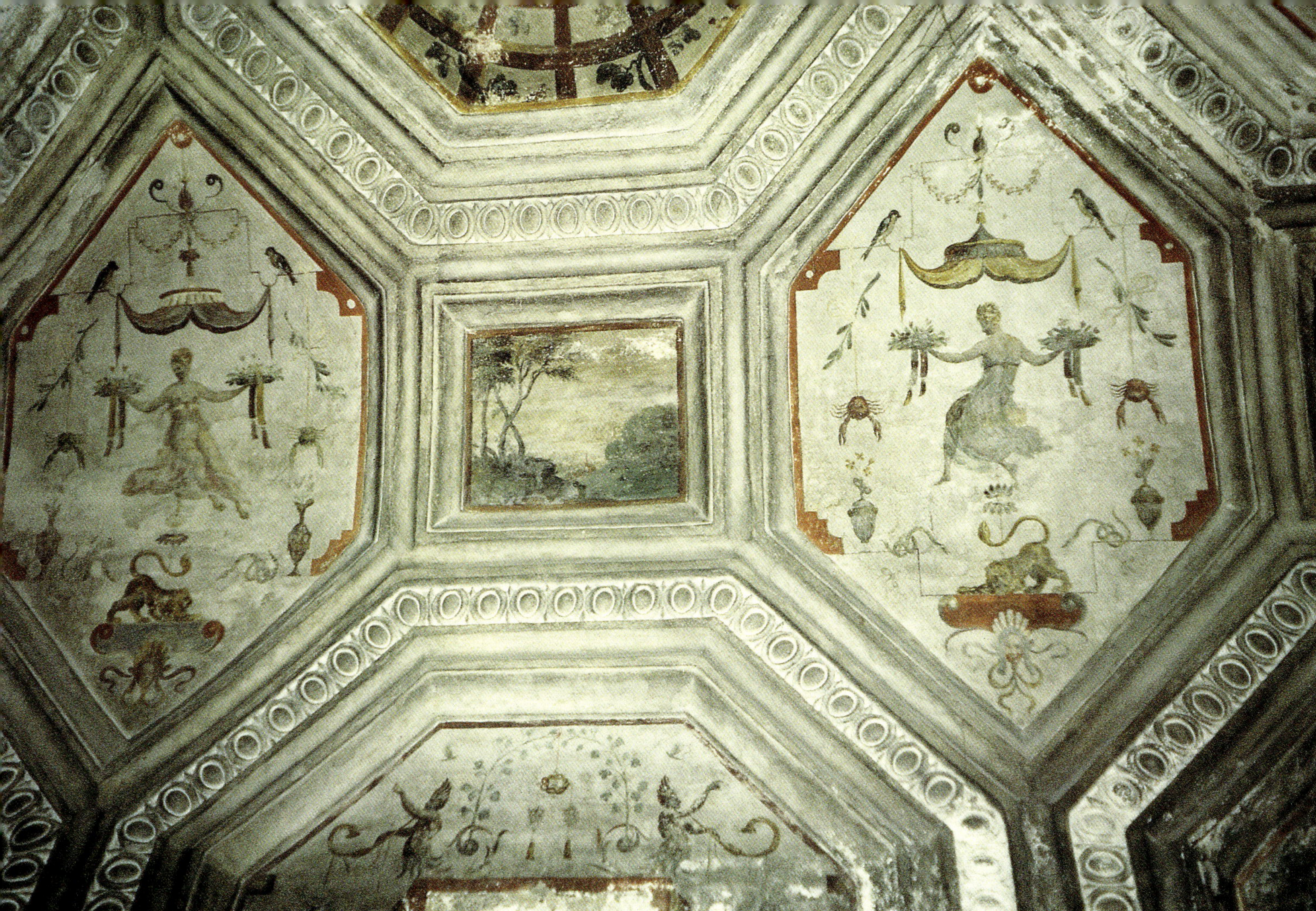

3 Ceiling of a chamber decorated in fresco with *grotteschi* in Palazzo Trevisan, Murano. Built by Camillo Trevisan in the 1560s as an island retreat for intellectual gatherings of literati, the building featured frescoes (of which fragments remain) by Paolo Veronese and Giambattista Zelotti, and was famous for its beautiful garden.

fireplace in Palazzo Contarini delle Figure has a frieze of paintings above its cornices which are, as Sansovino would have put it, loaded with gold (fig. 4).[11]

Sansovino continues:

> The dressers displaying silverware, porcelain, pewter and brass, or damascene bronze are innumerable. In the *Sale* of great families there are racks of arms with the shields and standards of their ancestors who fought for Venice on land and at sea. I have seen sold at auction the home furnishings of a noble condemned by [an] unfortunate incident, that would have been more than a Grand Duke of Italy would wish. The same can be said of the middle and lower classes in proportion. Because there is no person so miserable, with a *casa aperta* [a well-equipped house in which visitors were received[12]] that he would not have chests and bedsteads of walnut [and] green draperies [and] carpets . . . Such is the *politia* of this city.[13]

Turning his attention to household implements, Sansovino cites pewter, copper, chains of gold, and forks and rings of silver. Even the humble domain of the kitchen featured dishes and cooking pots arranged for display, as attested by Jacopo Tintoretto's *Christ in the House of Martha and Mary* (fig. 179). And nowhere is the opulence of the domestic environment more evident than in Paolo Veronese's *Marriage Feast at Cana*, where the table settings and service rival the sumptuous dress of the wedding guests (fig. 171).

Sansovino's choice of the word *politia* was probably no accident. The term had two distinct, if related, meanings in the sixteenth century. One usage derived from the Greek *politeia* and connoted good government, the political life, and civil comportment.[14] Another came from the Latin *politus*, meaning refinement in fashion, politeness of behavior, or the display of luxury.[15] The word is related, as well, to the Italian *polita* or *pulita*: a gleaming cleanliness

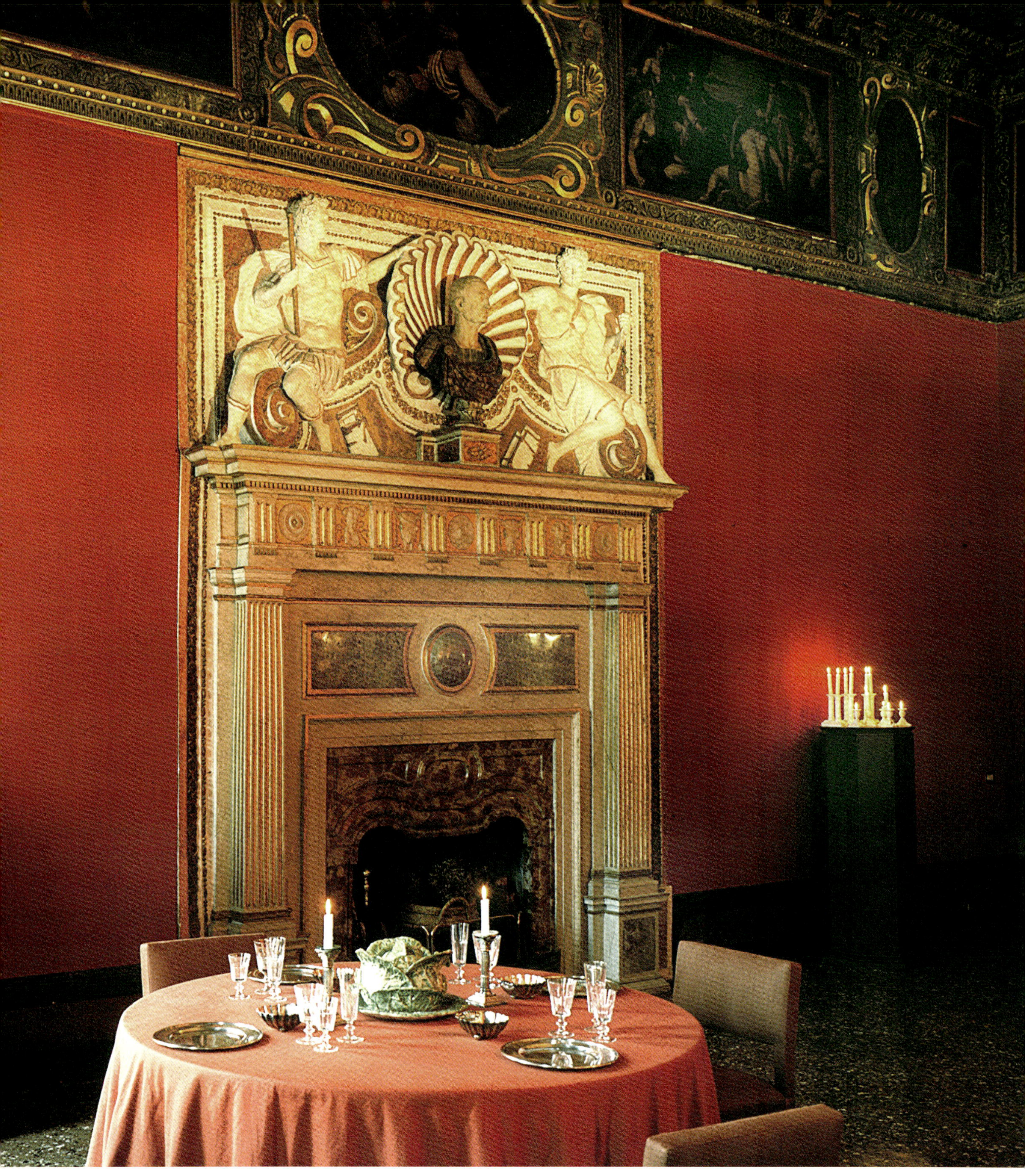

4 Palazzo Contarini delle Figure, chamber adjacent to the *portego* facing the Grand Canal. The fireplace is attributed to the school of Alessandro Vittoria. An elaborate frieze of allegorical paintings with gilded frames runs around the top of the walls.

and orderliness. But here Sansovino was referring to the manners and material goods that added up to an urbane lifestyle of civility and refinement very much bound up with the wise governance of the city. How does he account for the opulence of the Venetian home? Two factors came to mind: first, the city's long history without invasion and pillage; and second, its mercantile activities, which brought in goods from throughout the entire world.

But there is more. Sansovino adds a concluding statement, as follows: "Therefore, with all the foreign nations converging there, the people, who exercise the arts most admirably, participate in this profit so fertile, some more, some less, according to the quality and ingenuity of the person, [but] they are made thereby too soft and licentious."[16]

Incongruities

So, for all his celebration of Venice's material splendor, Sansovino introduces an ambiguous, if not discordant, note on two points. First, the forefathers of his Venetian compatriots were *both* frugal *and* profligate. And second, while his contemporaries enjoyed prosperity from a thriving culture of consumption and display, at least some had become overly addicted to a life of self-indulgence. They were, in short, a frugal people caught up in a sumptuous lifestyle about which he seemingly had mixed feelings. Within this delectable panorama of domestic environments, each richly stocked with worldly goods according to the rank of the owners, there is an uneasy sense of a less harmonious undercurrent of competition and competing values.

Thomas Coryat would also sense incongruities in Venetian society but from the perspective of an outsider. He allows that "the name of a Gentleman of Venice is esteemed a title of . . . eminent dignity and honour," and yet his view of such gentlemen's household arrangements was ambivalent. He asks: "Howbeit these Gentlemen do not maintaine and support the title of their gentility with a quarter of that noble state and magnificence as our English Noblemen and Gentlemen of the better sort doe? For they keepe no honourable hospitality, nor gallant retinue of servants about them, but a very frugall table, though they inhabit the most beautiful Palaces, and are inriched with as ample [means] to keepe a brave port as some of our greatest English Earles."[17] Indeed, as a recent study has shown, the typical patrician family in Venice employed few servants in comparison to their counterparts of the same social rank elsewhere.[18] And a close look at Veronese's banquet table suggests that it is more impressive in its table settings and costumes than in its cuisine, which appears to be a dessert course. While the quality of the wine is unknown, the comestibles are limited to simple dishes of fruit and sweetmeats.

Such restraint was, Coryat learned, due to "a certain kinde of edect made by the Senate, that they should not keepe a retinue beyond their limitation."[19] He was referring to a succession of sumptuary laws that had been passed from time to time to control the display of wealth. While costly women's clothing and jewelry were at the top of the list, banquets and the decoration of private palaces were also favored targets for regulation. But as a later chapter will show, a close look at Venetian initiatives reveals a succession of high hopes, partial successes, and repeated disappointments.[20]

Concordia *and* Unanimitas

Indeed, that anomalous image of frugality amidst material splendor sums up the dilemma of a society in transition. Central to this dilemma was a rigid social hierarchy that had prevailed in Venice (with a few adjustments) since the *Serrata* – the closure of the Great Council – of 1297. The nobility or order of patricians was formed at that time from only those families that had been active on the Great Council during the past four years. All others, even if they had previously played a role in the council, as well as those who would immigrate to the city later, were to be excluded from the governing class. Adjustments were made over the next three decades, with a major infusion of thirty families following the War of Chioggia at the end of the fourteenth century, but from that time forward the nobility had remained stable and virtually impenetrable.[21]

The male members of this noble caste – such as the lordly figure of Nicolò Zen, depicted by Titian in a toga of rich black velvet lined with lynx (fig. 5)[22] – called themselves gentlemen or *zentilhuomini* – Venetian dialect for *gentilhuomini* – and were addressed by the term *clarissimo* or *magnifico*. They all sat on the Great Council, and some in the Senate, where they conducted foreign policy, passed the laws, acted as judge and jury, and elected all public officials, including the doge, from among their ranks. In the early years of the republic most were actively engaged in trade; later on they increasingly lived off their investments.[23] This group comprised about 4.5 percent of the population.

The ideals of *concordia* and *unanimitas* – concord and unanimity – are exemplified by a print of the Great Council, a legislative body to which all adult male patricians belonged (fig. 6). Row after row of anonymous toga-clad gentlemen create a diagram of the long-standing Venetian ethos of

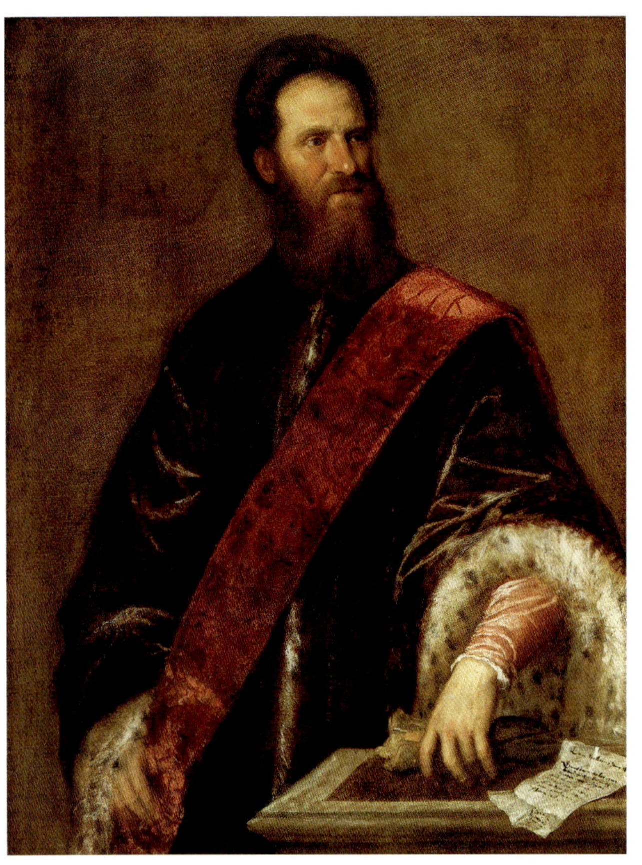

5 (*left*) Titian, *Nicolò Zen*, ca. 1560. Oil on canvas, 123.2 × 96.5 cm. With a life devoted to public service, Nicolò Zen (1515–65) represented the patrician ideal. He held numerous political offices, including membership of the Council of Ten, and was responsible for the reorganization of the Arsenal. Author of several treatises on the origins of Venice, he expounded traditional Venetian values of *mediocritas* – equality amongst the patriciate – and the primacy of commerce in the destiny of the state. Kingston Lacy, The Bankes Collection (The National Trust).

7 (*facing page*) Jacopo Tintoretto, *The Madonna of the Treasurers*, 1566. Oil on canvas, 221 × 521 cm. The painting originally hung in the first room of the Camerlenghi di Comun of the Palazzo dei Camerlenghi, along with Tintoretto's *Saint Mark Seated with the Treasurers* and his *Saint Giustina and the Treasurers* and Vittore Carpaccio's *Lion of Saint Mark*. Venice, Accademia.

6 (*below*) Giacomo Franco, *The Great Council in Session*. Engraving from his *Habiti d'huomeni et donne* (Venice, 1610). The print records the Sala del Maggior Consiglio after the fire of 1577, with Jacopo Tintoretto's *Paradise* covering the end wall. Princeton, Princeton University Library, Department of Rare Books and Special Collections, Marquand Library.

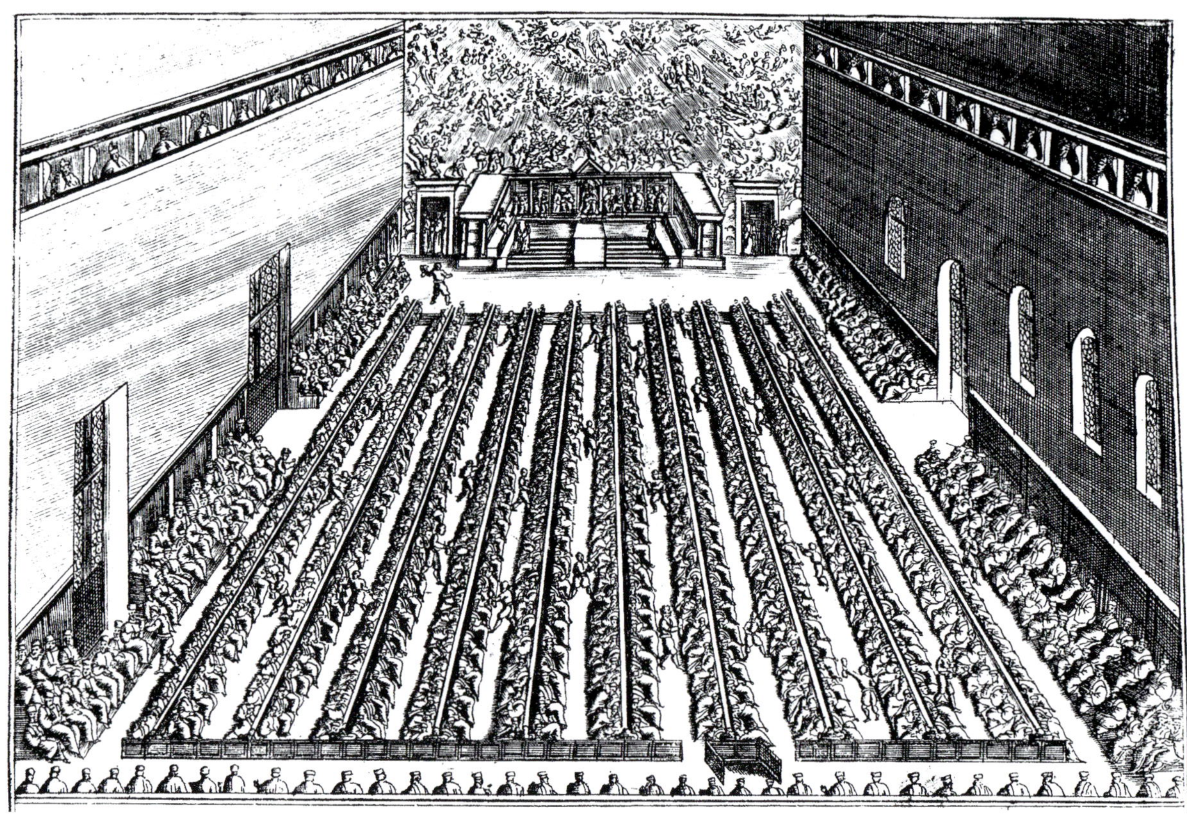

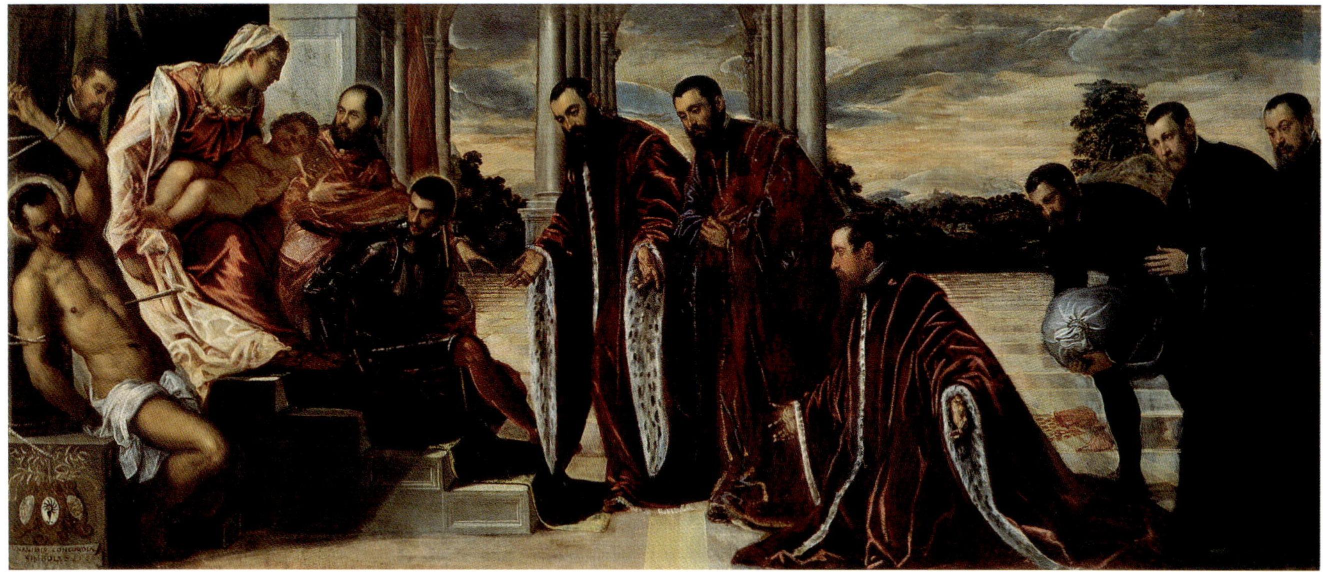

equality and cooperation within the patriciate.[24] Accordingly, discretion in dress and display was strongly encouraged and ostentatious showing off was not.

Below the patriciate was the order of *cittadini* or citizens, and – if less exalted – it was no less exclusive. Membership was either by birth or by privilege upon proof that neither the citizen in question, nor his father nor grandfather, had ever earned his living by working with his hands. While most of these men were merchants, a subset within the group was the order of secretaries who formed the permanent bureaucracy, while their patrician employers rotated in and out of office each year.[25] The relation between the two orders is graphically displayed in a canvas painted for a state office by Tintoretto (fig. 7). The three patrician treasurers, two of them robed in rich crimson velvet lined with lynx, are depicted in the front plane paying their respects to the Virgin and SS. Sebastian, Mark, and Theodore. Their *cittadino* secretaries, dressed in somber black, stand behind them – the supporting cast, so to speak, to the main protagonists in the political drama of the republic. In the lower left corner beneath the coats of arms of the three treasurers – the Pisani, the Dolfin, and the Malipiero – is the legend: UNANIMIS CONCORDIAE SIMBOLUS – symbol of unanimous concord.[26] The highest office open to a *cittadino* was that of grand chancellor – a lifetime position. He ran the State Chancery, staffed with *cittadino* bureaucrats like himself who kept the wheels of government running smoothly.

Cittadini also formed the *banche* – the ruling groups of the rich and powerful Scuole Grandi, comprising six large religious lay confraternities that held considerable property throughout the city. With their families, the *cittadini* accounted for another 5 to 8 percent of the population. Like patricians, the male *cittadini* dressed in long togas in public – usually black, but red if they held certain offices – and visitors to the city would not neasily have distinguished one caste from the other. By the end of the sixteenth century, they too were sometimes addressed by the title *magnifico*.[27]

The remainder of the populace – the *popolani*, close to 90 percent – embraced a wide range of occupations and conditions, from wealthy merchants to artisans and small shopkeepers to unskilled laborers (fig. 8). It should be stressed that each of the three orders included the very rich and the very poor, so these groupings were social and political categories and not economic classes *per se*. And herein lies the rub. Not every nobleman was wealthy, nor was every rich man noble. In short, there was no easy fit between noble rank and wealth. And yet, while social mobility was extremely restricted and political office limited to the patrician caste, domestic peace and concord were maintained by that compelling ethos of group consensus exemplified by the common black toga worn by patricians and *cittadini* alike.

It is interesting to keep in mind, however, a print that captures a moment of politicking outside the Palazzo Ducale, with some great lords currying the favor of those who are even greater (while a ragged beggar sits, ignored, at their feet) (fig. 9).[28] Over the course of the sixteenth century, the myth of concord and unanimity was stretched very thin indeed, with ever greater disparities and concentrations of wealth within the patriciate and disjunctions between economic class and social caste within the society as a whole.

At issue was the public control of private *politia* in a society that privileged civic responsibility over individual or family glory.

A Debate on Nobility

As mentioned, a dialogue between ostentatious display and frugal restraint – the ambiguities implied by both Coryat and Sansovino – was intrinsic to the material culture of Venetian elites in the early modern period. The discourse had been played out in Venetian councils for centuries, but it gained momentum and changed shape in the course of the sixteenth century in the context of a debate on nobility that was taking place throughout Italy.

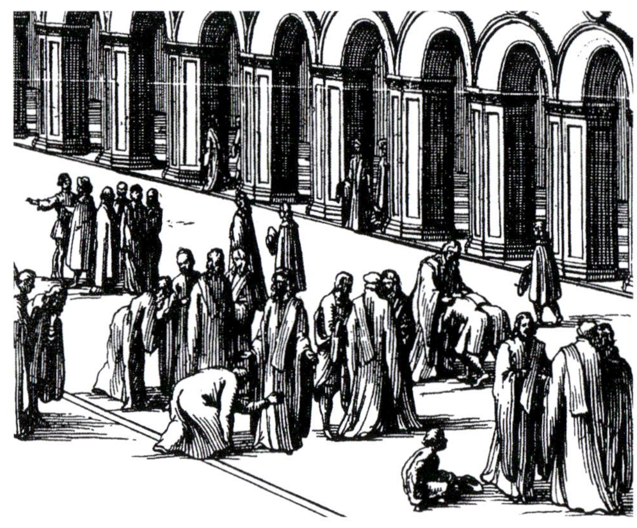

9 Domenico Lovisa, *Broglio* (electoral intrigue). Detail of an engraving from his *Il Gran Teatro di Venezia ovvero raccolta delle principali vedute e pitture che in essa si contengono* (Venice: D. Lovisa, 1717), vol. 1. The term *broglio* derives from *brolo*, meaning orchard, and referred to the area of the Piazzetta next to the Palazzo Ducale, where patricians met and exchanged gossip and bartered for votes before elections. Such activities also took place in the large courtyard inside the palace, as in this detail. Those seeking favors would servilely lower their stoles from their shoulders, shedding a symbol of their patrician dignity to show deference to more influential members of the Great Council, who bowed back in condescension.

8 (*below*) Vittore Carpaccio, *Healing of the Possessed Man* (detail), 1494. Tempera on canvas, whole work 370 × 390 cm. Venice's male population in all its diversity came together at Rialto, the economic hub of the city: toga-clad nobles and *cittadini*, clerks and prelates, Muslim traders and African gondoliers. The *felze* (canopies) of several gondolas are emblazoned with family coats of arms. Venice, Accademia.

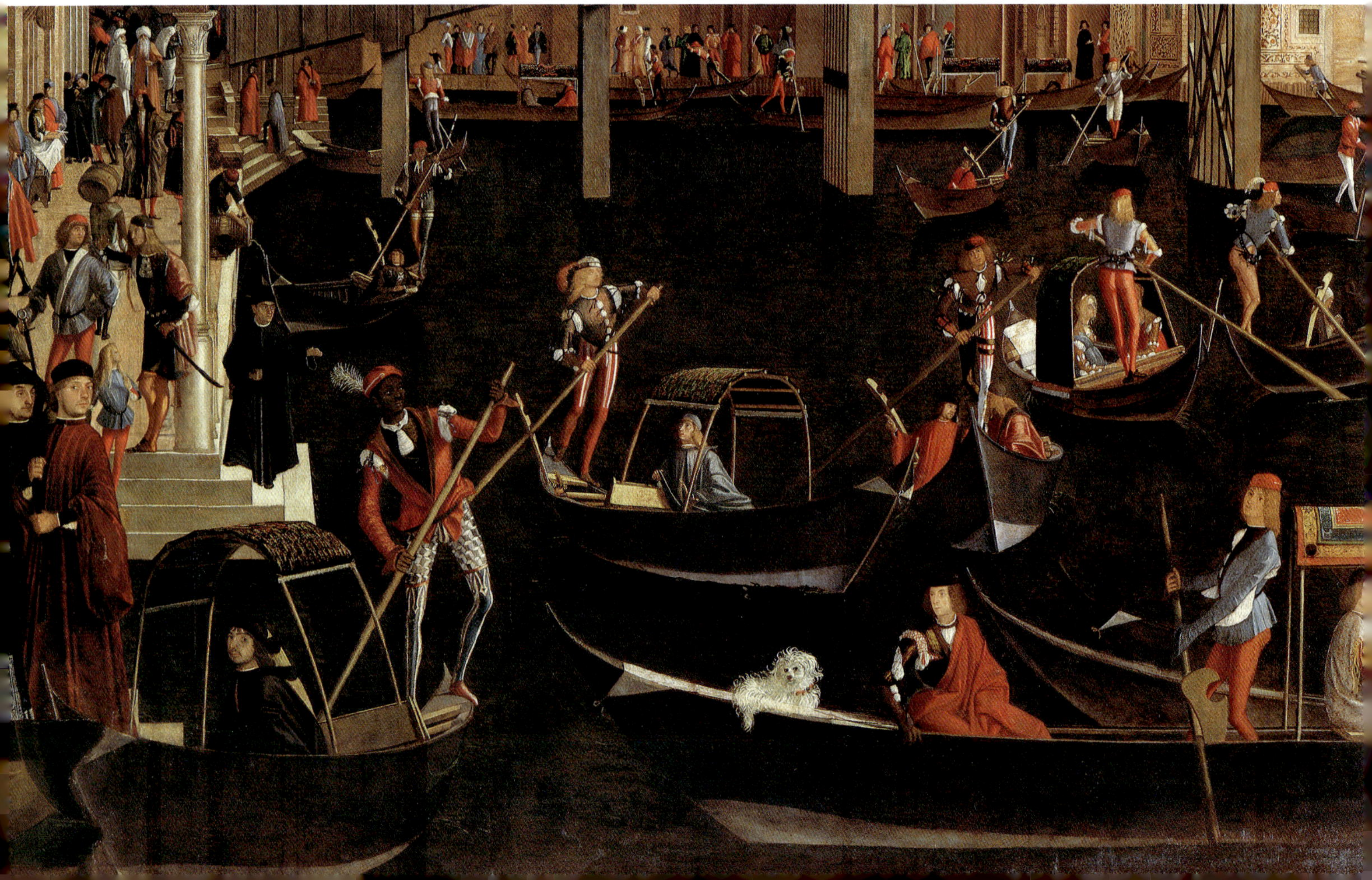

The debate was not new. By the fourteenth century, a new mercantile oligarchy had wrested political power from the ancient military–feudal aristocracy in a number of communities, particularly in central and northern Italy. Accordingly, jurists and humanists would struggle to define the relative importance of blood, wealth, and *virtù* (a term that embraces achievement, fame, and glory, as well as virtue), in defining nobility in the emerging communes and republics. In republics such as Florence in the fourteenth and fifteenth century, to be noble was to be excluded from government. But what about Venice? It was an anomaly. It had never been governed by feudal lords, and with the Serrata it formed its new ruling oligarchy from merchants who sought to be noble. But during the first three decades of the sixteenth century, when class lines were becoming more strictly drawn, this old debate took on new resonance. The presence of foreign armies in Italy, moreover, prompted comparisons with institutions and customs of other nations. A growing body of literature, much of it published in Venice, began to grapple with changing definitions of nobility.[29]

Nicolò Machiavelli, in his *Discourses on the First Decade of Livy*, probably written 1513–17, sought to distinguish between *gentilhuomini* and *cittadini*, that is, gentlemen and citizens. He was not an admirer of nobility and held that, in general, the noble caste was made up of *gentilhuomini* "who without working live in luxury on the returns from their landed possessions, without paying any attention either to agriculture or to any other occupation necessary for making a living." Such men, he charged, were "altogether hostile to all free government." It was, in his view, the hard working *cittadino* who created civility and the civil life.[30] But how, then, did Machiavelli account for Venice, which he "ranked high among modern republics" elsewhere in his treatise[31] and which was ruled by noble gentlemen?

Indeed, in his view an imposing figure such as Nicolò Zen, the Venetian patrician depicted by Titian, was not really a gentleman at all (fig. 5). Machiavelli writes: "The gentlemen in that republic are so rather in name than in fact; they do not have great incomes from landed possessions, but their great riches are based on trade and movable property; moreover none of them holds castles or has any jurisdiction over men. Thus that name of gentleman among them is a name of dignity and reputation, without being founded on any of those things in other cities signified by the word *gentleman*."[32]

And yet, by the mid-1520s, Machiavelli's view, while technically correct, prompted further interpretation. Gasparo Contarini, one of those Venetian gentlemen in name rather than in fact, stepped forth and began to write a treatise entitled *The Commonwealth and Government of Venice* (fig. 10).[33]

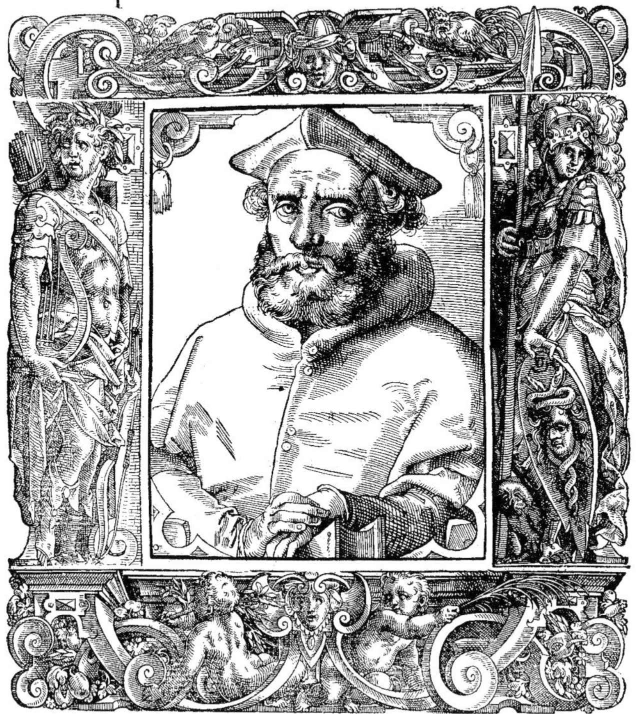

10 Tobias Stimmer, *Gasparo Contarini*. Engraving in Paolo Giovio, *Elogia vivorum literis illustrium*, Basle, 1577, f. 184. Contarini (1483–1542) had studied philosophy in Padua and held a number of Venetian state offices between 1520 and 1534. He was appointed cardinal in 1534 and moved to Rome, where he was active in church reform. Princeton, Princeton University Library.

It was published in dignified Latin in 1543, came out in Italian a year later, and was translated into English in 1599.[34] Thomas Coryat would read it from cover to cover before his visit to Venice. The English translation, though somewhat stilted, captures the unabashed certainty of a privileged elite, and is worth repeating here. Like Machiavelli, Contarini observed that all political authority was vested in a Great Council made up of a company of citizens (by which he too meant the patriciate). But he went further, explaining; "Now first I am to yeeld you a reckoning how and with what wisedome it was ordayned by our auncestors, that the common people should not bee admitted into this company of citizens."[35]

And he went on to make a critical point. He allowed that *some* of the founding fathers had proposed that this "company of citizens" should be defined by ability and the abundance of riches, but, he argued, this was totally wrongheaded: "for it happeneth often that those of the basest sort, yea of the very skum of the people, do scrape together great wealth, as those that apply themselves to filthy artes, and illiberall occupations . . . defrauding themselves of the comforts of life, thereby to increase their substance." Conversely, the well brought up, in other words patricians, often fell into poverty either through adverse fortune or through spending their time on liberal studies rather than on increasing their wealth. In consequence, Contarini continues, if "ill mannerd men favouring of nothing but gaine, utterly ignorant of good artes" came to govern, disaster would ensue. Overlooking the mercantile activities of most of the Venetian patriciate that Machiavelli had praised, he concludes: "Therefore our wise and prudent ancestors, lest their commonwealth should happen into these calamities, ordered that this definition of publike rule, should go rather by the nobility of lineage, than by the estimation of wealth."[36]

In fact, the purity of the noble bloodline received special attention in Venice during this period. A law passed in 1506 requiring registration of all noble births with the state was strengthened in 1526 by legislation calling for marriages to be officially recorded as well. These would henceforth be inscribed in a Libro d'Oro – a Book of Gold – that was zealously guarded in the State Attorney's Office of the Ducal Palace. While marriages between patrician men and commoner wives that conferred nobility on their offspring were not completely forbidden, they were now to be carefully scrutinized. On a page documenting the Condulmer family's inductions into the Great Council, the first entry is crossed out, canceling the record of an unfortunate young noble born before the new laws took effect and already admitted to the council (fig. 11). The large x tells the tale. Failing to prove his noble birth when challenged, he was thereby stripped of his nobility.[37] These laws were intended, the legislators declared, "to keep immaculate and pure the rank and order of the nobility," on which rested "the honor, peace, and preservation of our state."[38] The integrity of the male bloodline was crucial. The illegitimate daughter of a fully proven noble was held to be a more suitable match for a noble youth than the legitimate daughter of a well-respected (and wealthy) commoner. The illegitimate son of a nobleman, however, was barred forever from the nobility and a seat on the Great Council.[39]

In short, wealth did not matter so long as one was nobly born. But this is taken for granted in many traditional societies. Why did Contarini make such a point of it? The hard edge on his words suggests that wealth did matter, and that resentment of wealthy commoners among the poorer members of the patriciate, and rivalries within the patriciate, were tendencies that were becoming increasingly troublesome and must be held in check. Contarini did this by stressing the membership of all patricians in a community of noble equals who shared political privilege. Although he did not explicitly criticize the mercantile activities that had been the basis for the long-lasting commercial – and even political – success of the republic, he was implicitly distancing himself and his peers from the active management required by those activities that had produced such disparities in wealth. In sum, he was expressing the desire of a growing portion of the patriciate to be considered gentlemen in fact as well as in name.

11 (*facing page*) Page from the Libro d'Oro, with proofs of nobility for the Condulmer family. The entry on Zuan Francesco Condulmer, son of Girolamo, was crossed out when he failed to prove his noble status. Venice, Archivio di Stato, Avogaria di Comun, Reg. 165 (Balla d'Oro, 1498–1544), f. 113v.

But old reputations change slowly. And the mercantile nobility of Venice continued to be an anomaly often remarked upon by writers of the period. In 1543, the year in which Contarini's treatise appeared, Giovambattista Nenna da Bari published his own treatise on nobility. Nenna was struck by the diverse ways in which nobility was defined in different communities: "We see in the magnanimous and signorial city of Naples that the practice of trade – *mercadantia* – is alien to the noble caste." There, as in ancient Thebes, he observes, merchants are not allowed to hold public office. In Venice, by contrast, "it is completely contrary: since not only plebes, but [also] nobles, including their senators, are engaged in trade. The purity of the blood of their ancestors is what distinguishes noble from non-noble, not their profession."[40]

A Stratified Patriciate

There was thus a toga-clad mercantile nobility whose pure bloodlines were acknowledged throughout Italy and whose wealth was regarded with wonder and envy, but whose honor was somewhat impaired by their mercantile activities. How did they overcome their essentially ignoble origins to express the "title of their gentility," as Coryat had put it? And how did any one stand out in this community of equals?

First, there were important distinctions of dress that reinforced the political hierarchy. Aside from the doge, who, as Contarini put it, "represent[ed] in all thinges the glory, gravitie and dignity of a king," there was also a special group of office-holders elected by, and elevated above, their patrician

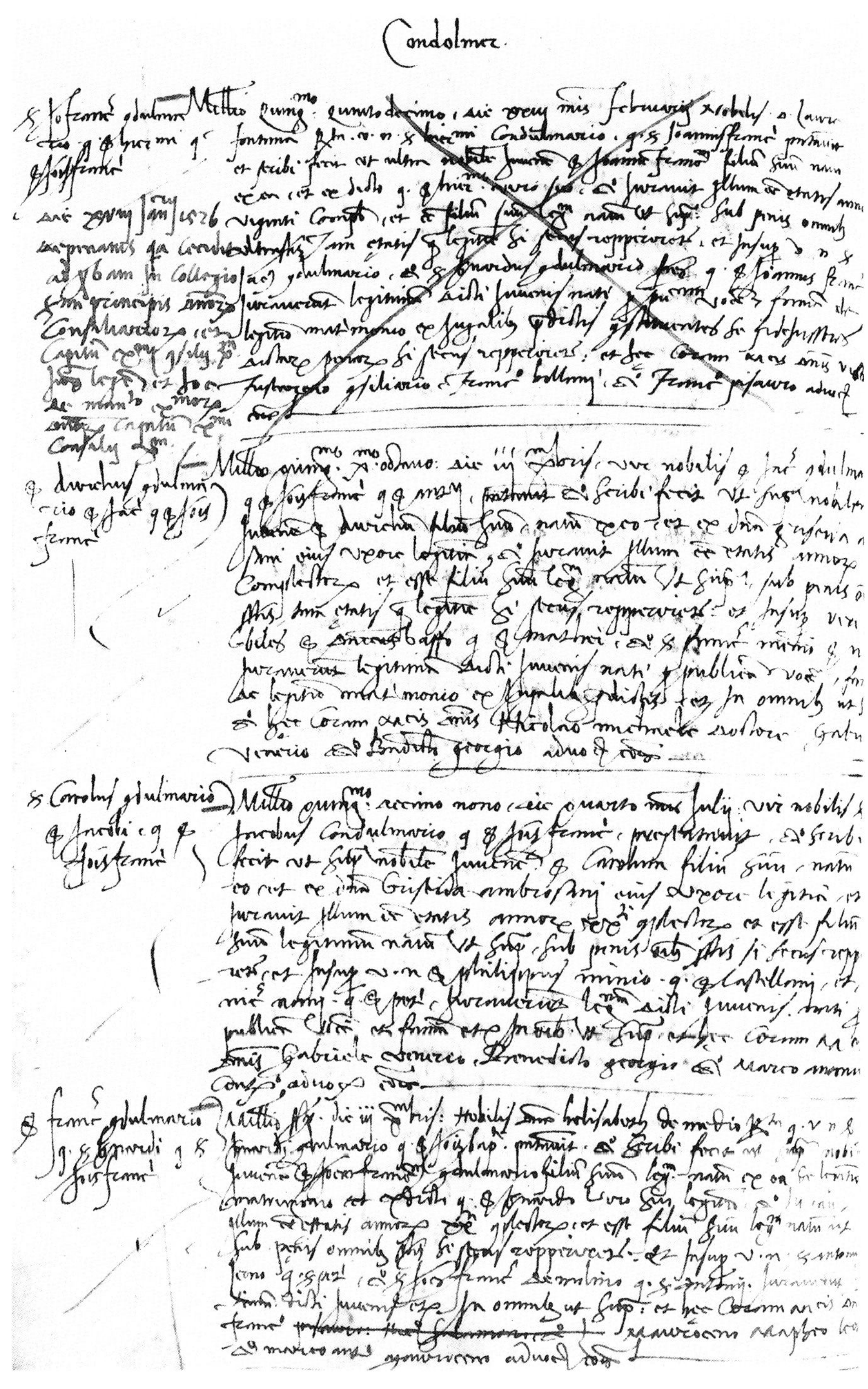

Condolmer.

peers. Those in the Senate, the Council of Ten, and the Signoria, consisting of the Doge and his chief councilors, "carry with them a certaine shew of an Aristocracy or government of the nobilitie" (fig. 12).[41] This "aristocracy of the nobility" wore togas, but of special colors or with a cut of the sleeve that set them apart. Senators and members of councils were required to wear togas of scarlet cloth for official business and something more grand like crimson on special occasions. Procurators were allowed to wear wide-open sleeves called *dogali*, a privilege also given to doctors of medicine and to ambassadors and heads of regiments returning from service abroad (fig. 23). The assiduous attention accorded by the patrician diarist Marin Sanudo to the color of dress and the cut of the sleeve on ceremonial occasions is an index of

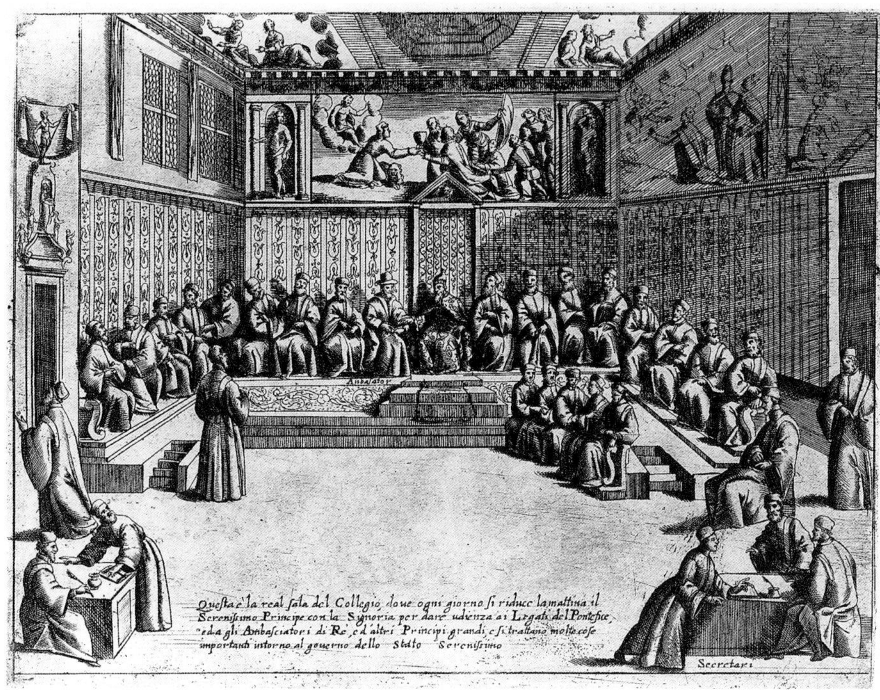

12 Giacomo Franco, *The Collegio in Session*, with the doge and his councilors meeting the papal legate and foreign ambassadors. Engraving from his *Habiti d'huomeni et donne* (Venice, 1610). The *cittadini* secretaries in the foreground are clad in togas similar to those of their patrician employers. Princeton, Princeton University Library, Department of Rare Books and Special Collections, Marquand Library.

the value accorded dress as a sign. These costumes displayed a hierarchy of office and not a hierarchy of wealth.[42]

Contarini's stratified patriciate, with some nobles more equal than others, reflected a political reality. But he chose to overlook an additional reality: that wealth and power – that is the holding of high office – often went hand in hand, an inconvenient fact that would become increasingly divisive as the century progressed. And while the uniformity of male dress in public space tended to level the playing field for those above the artisan level, the attentive viewer would have noted subtle distinctions in the quality of the cloth, the fineness of the weave and the costliness of fur linings that created a hierarchy of dress that *was* based upon the financial resources of the wearer.

But beyond the wearing of colors and a prestigious sleeve, how did the patrician define himself? As Contarini had stressed, the most precious possession of the Venetian patrician was his birthright. And after the establishment of the Libro d'Oro in the early years of the century, a written certification was right there in the Ducal Palace for all to see, attesting to his legitimate birth to a patrician father and his right to sit on the Great Council. Indeed, one observer, Girolamo Muzio of Constantinople, had written of Venice: "for antiquity of blood there is no city in Italy that has more noble families. Both from their order of magistrates and for the memory that they keep of their lineages, one can distinguish nobles from others better here than in any other part."[43] Ancient roots were so important in establishing a hierarchy within this patriciate of equals that some noble families hired genealogists to trace their lineage back beyond the foundation of the republic, in some cases all the way back to Rome.[44]

Still, there was only one Libro d'Oro. How could this distinction be displayed outside the Ducal Palace, in and around the more intimate environment of the family home? One such vehicle was the illustrated genealogy or Book of Arms – a new literary genre that appeared around the same time, not just in Venice but throughout Italy.[45] Most of these volumes were compiled to celebrate a particular family, but – and this is the key point – they typically included the arms of every patrician house with a short caption declaring the antiquity or origins of the family – and often, the important offices that its members had held (fig. 13).

* * *

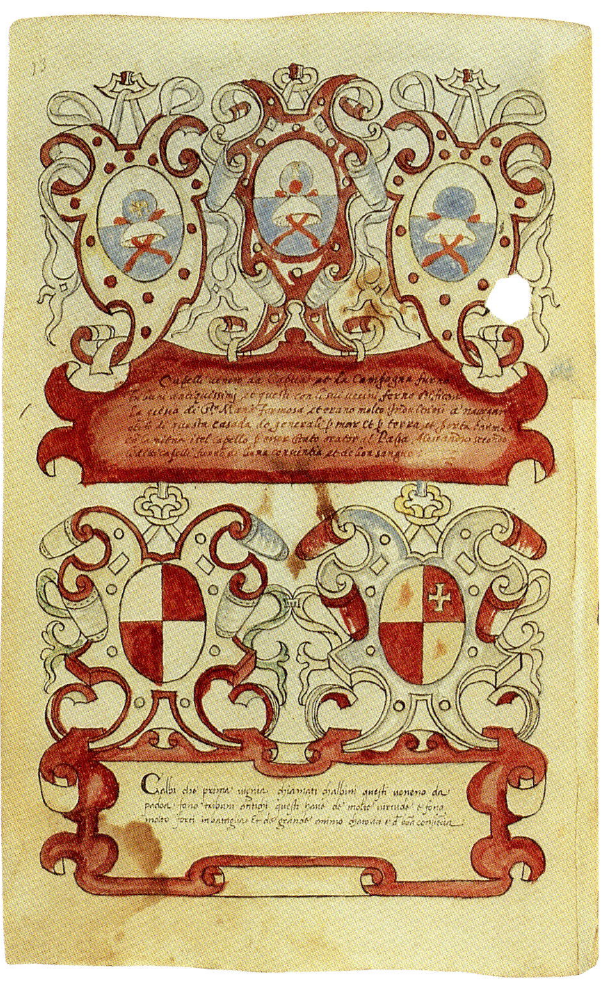

13 Coats of arms of the Cappello and Calbi families. Each *stemma* is accompanied by a mini-history of the family, both claiming descent from ancient tribunes of the city. The Cappelli, who originated in Capua and the Campagna, helped build the church of Santa Maria Formosa and were distinguished by two generals of the sea and the land. Their coat of arms features a mitre inside a broad-brimmed hat in recognition of an ancestor who served as Venetian ambassador to Pope Alexander II: "The hats signify good conscience and good blood." The Calbi came from Padua and were previously called di Albini. They, too, "had many virtues and were strong in battle and great in spirit, Catholics, and of good conscience." Venice, Archivio di Stato, Misc. Cod. ser. I, Storia Veneta, B. 37.

Arms and Insignia

Heraldry was part of the language of medieval chivalry that had expanded into the mercantile classes in the early Renaissance, with the coat of arms the most direct and visually powerful assertion of the antiquity and social rank of the family. But in Italy the complex rules in use in northern Europe, with dividing and quartering of bloodlines on the coat of arms, were ignored in favor of personally invented insignia and *impresa*. For while in some states north of the Alps the coat of arms was considered a prerogative of the titled nobility, in Italy the use of arms would be extended to cities in the twelfth century, to merchants and officials in the thirteenth, and to Jews and peasants in the fourteenth. Bartolo da Sassoferrato, whose mid-fourteenth century *Tract on Insignia and Coats of Arms* remained the authoritative work on the subject throughout the period, allowed that some coats of arms were proper to a particular rank or office and that some were granted to private persons by emperors or other lords. But he continued: "Some assume coats of arms and insignia on their own initiative, and we should consider whether they are permitted to do it. I think that they are permitted. Just as names are created to identify persons, so insignia and coats of arms are devised for this purpose. Anyone is permitted to use such names for himself, and thus anyone can bear these insignia and depict them on his own belongings, but not on another's."[46] And this was true even in Venice, with its juridically defined – and essentially closed – patrician caste. Display of a coat of arms – popularly called a *stemma* or *scudo* – was thus no proof of nobility but was simply the sign of a certain level of *politia* as Sansovino would have understood it.[47] But it did denote the family's *politia* in an immediately comprehensible way, like an icon on a computer screen, distinguishing it from all others to a public that was largely non-literate. And so the *stemmi* proliferated.

Outside the palace, the *stemma* was often embedded in walls or attached to portals to proclaim and delimit the space of the *casa*. An angel supported by two shields or *scudi* with coats of arms on the exterior wall of Ca' Soranzo at Ponte dell'Angelo celebrates the piety of the noble Soranzo family while protecting their household (fig. 14). And for good measure there is yet another *stemma* of another family in the wall above. Likewise, a portal leading to a courtyard in Castello is topped by another guardian angel flanked by the *stemmi* of the *cittadino* Rizzo family (fig. 15).[48]

Or the *stemma* might be carved onto a well-head, proclaiming the public domain of a wealthy family; or it may provide a mobile insignia on the canopy of a gondola, as in a painting by Vittore Carpaccio (fig. 8). Or it could document a marriage, as on the Gothic arch that unites two rows of houses flanking Calle del Paradiso (fig. 16). When Pellegrina Foscari married Alvise Mocenigo in 1491, her dowry included twenty-six houses that ran down both sides of the *calle*. These were rental units that would continue to produce income which her husband could use to support the family or to invest in a business of his own. The arch is carved in relief on both sides with a Madonna of Mercy. That on the outside appears to date from the late fourteenth

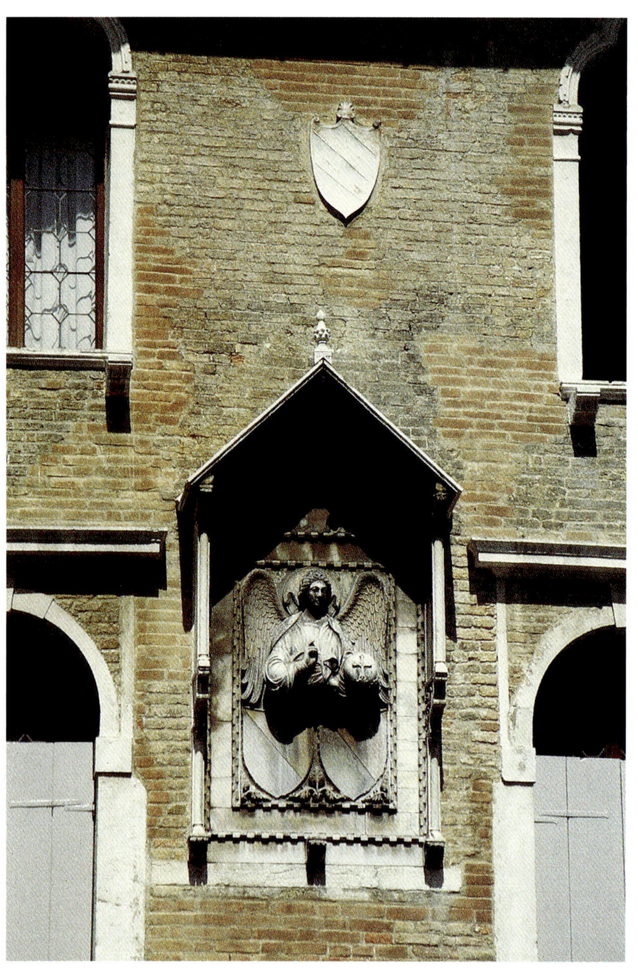

14 (*left*) Tabernacle with a blessing angel surmounting two coats of arms of the Soranzo family, fourteenth century. Istrian stone and Greek marble, 120 × 80 cm (relief) and 250 × 120 cm (tabernacle). Canal facade of Ca' Soranzo at Ponte dell'Angelo near San Zaccaria, Castello 4419. The facade of this palace was once decorated with *trompe-l'oeil* frescoes by Jacopo Tintoretto.

16 (*facing page left*) *Madonna della Misericordia with Patron*. Sculptural relief above the entrance to Calle del Paradiso near Santa Maria Formosa, third quarter of fourteenth century. Istrian stone.

17 (*facing page right*) *Madonna della Misericordia* with two patrons, late fifteenth century. Reverse of the sculptural relief illustrated in figure 16. The kneeling figures may be Pellegrina Foscari and Alvise Mocenigo, who were married in 1491, with their respective coats of arms.

15 (*below*) *Blessing Angel* (thirteenth century) with two coats of arms of the Rizzo family (fourteenth century). Angel: marble, height 80 cm, base 25 cm. Coats of arms: Istrian stone, 55 × 45 cm each. The group is above the entrance arch of the *sotoportego* leading to Corte de l'Anzolo. The word *rizzo* in Venetian dialect means spine, as in porcupines or sea urchins, and the device was a pun on the family name. Venice, Calle Magno, Castello 2691A.

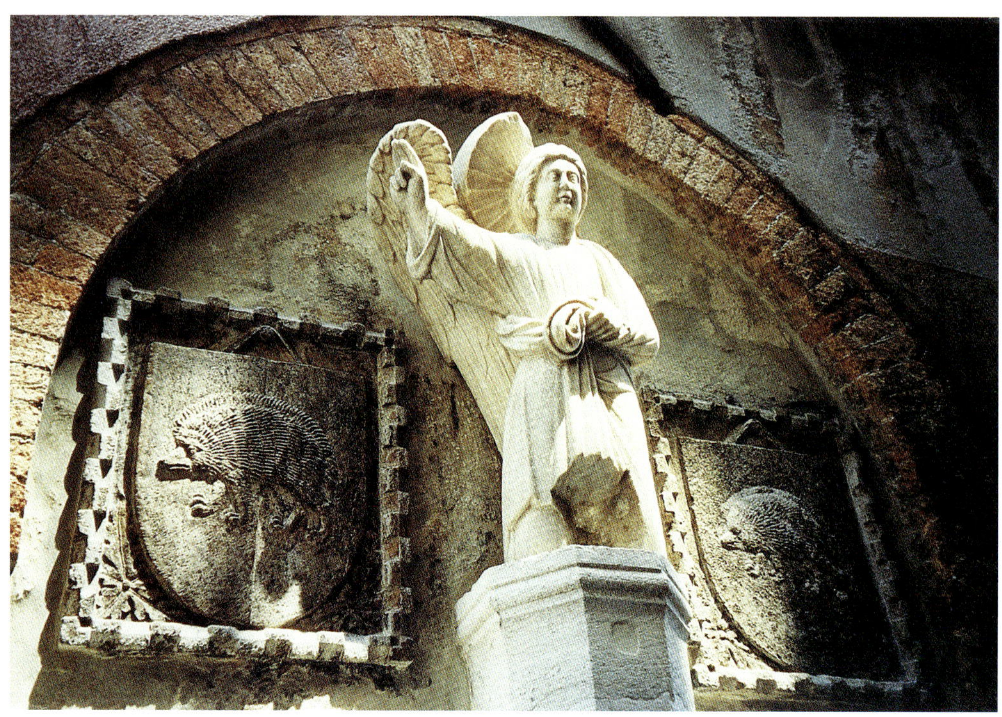

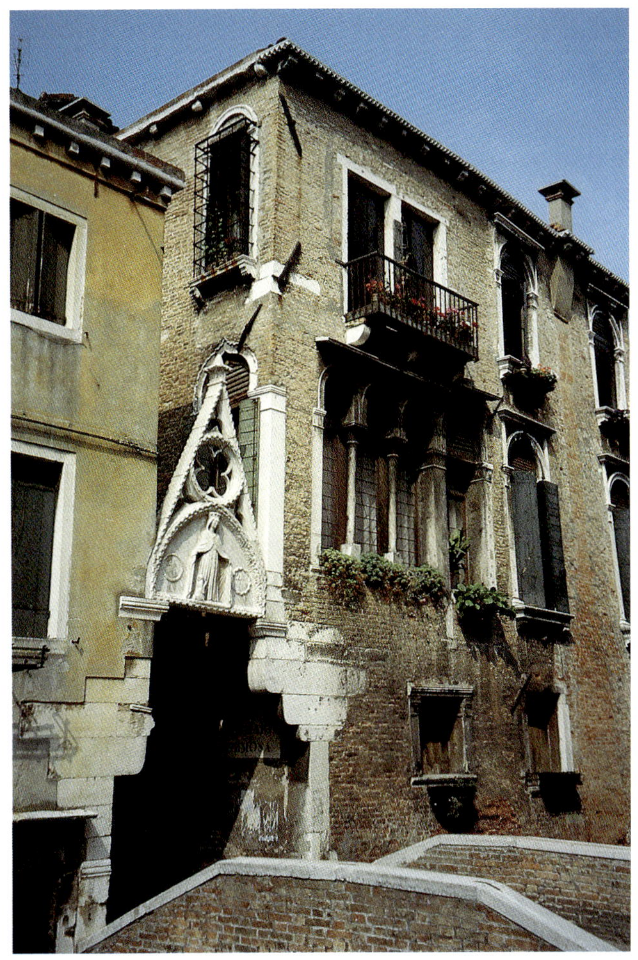

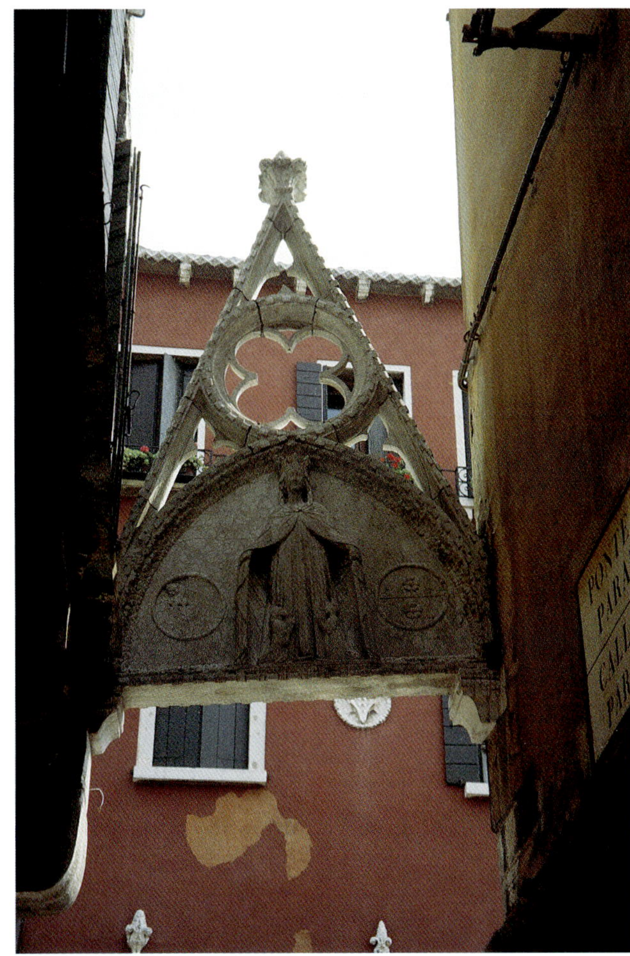

century, with a single donor, who was probably responsible for the original building project. But the relief on the reverse, seen from inside the *calle*, has two kneeling figures – male and female – dressed in late quattrocento style, flanked by the Foscari and Mocenigo coats of arms (fig. 17). In all likelihood it is Pellegrina and Alvise themselves, the bride and the husband to whom she brought this handsome property in her dowry.[49] The pair are sheltered by the Madonna in a visual promise that this union of two great Venetian families would indeed have "a good beginning, a better middle, and a most perfect end" as stated in the typical marriage contract, under the protection of the Virgin and all the celestial court.[50]

Inside the palace walls, the *stemma* could be woven into a tapestry, like those being aired on the *altana* in Carpaccio's *Healing of the Possessed Man* (fig. 18), or embroidered onto a backrest of padded silk fabric, or carved on a fireplace hood as in Giovanni Mansueti's *Healing of the Daughter of Ser Nicolo Benvegnudo of San Polo* (fig. 85).[51] Or the *stemma* might be carved onto a chair back or on the frames of mirrors or paintings, or painted or carved on a chest, or incised on bronze bells or the handles of cutlery, or tooled on book covers, or painted onto a ceramic or a glass dish (fig. 19). The inventory of the rich patrician Domenico Cappello was typical in its listing of "an hourglass with its colonettes and the Cappello arms . . . a damascene basin with the Cappello and Bernardo arms . . . nine tapestries, that is *spalliere*, with beautiful figures, and five others with the Cappello and Bernardo arms."[52]

While the *stemma* outside the house was clearly a statement of ownership or magnificence, what did it mean within the more private environs of the palace? Who was the audience and what was the message? There is no single answer. In the case of Cappello's damascene basin and tapestries, which carried the coats of arms of his wife as well as himself (as on the arch at Calle del Paradiso), it documents the joining of two lineages – and probably marks objects that were made at the time of the marriage. The serving dishes played a role in hospitality, advertising the level of affluence and good breeding of the hosts to the guests. But

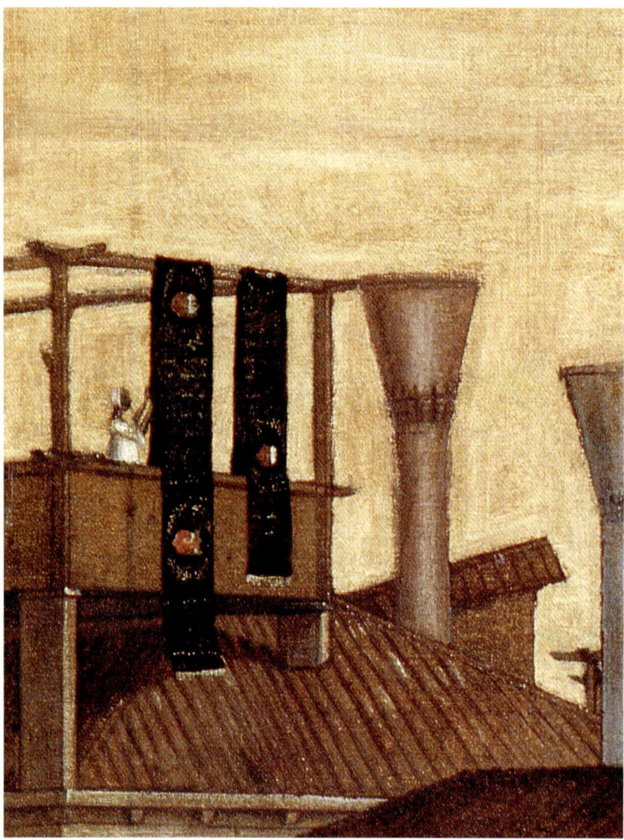

18 Vittore Carpaccio, *Healing of the Possessed Man* (detail), 1494. Tempera on canvas, whole work 370 × 390 cm. A black maid is airing two *spalliere a verdure*, woven with a vegetal pattern and coats of arms, on an *altana* on the roof of Ca' Civran. Venice, Accademia.

these objects were also made not only for their own time but also to be passed down through the lineage, thus providing continuity between the generations. The term *stemma* itself tells the story. John Florio, in the first comprehensive Italian–English dictionary to be published – *Queen Anna's New World of Words* of 1611 – defines *stemma* as "any stem or branching stalke. Also the stocke, race or blood of a house or familie."[53]

Renewing the Names

By the mid-sixteenth century, two other traditions – one verbal and the other visual – had developed to reinforce family identity and preserve the memory of those who had passed on. The verbal strategy soon becomes apparent to anyone who tries to sort out the lineages of various branches of a Venetian family, with the same first names appearing and reappearing – both vertically and laterally – throughout the generations.[54] It was customary to name the oldest son after his paternal grandfather, but beyond that naming was based upon family custom, genuine affection, and – perhaps most importantly – personal virtues that the family wished to perpetuate. Consider the Della Torre family, mainland nobility that Giulia, daughter of the Venetian patrician Zuan Matteo Bembo, would join when she married Count Girolamo Della Torre at the age of eighteen. She was a woman of such sterling qualities of character and breeding that Francesco Sansovino would later write a book about her. Celebrating that Giulia had given birth to five sons and five daughters with the count, Sansovino observed that she had thus "renewed, both men and women, the major part of the ancestors and herself." Their first born son, Ludovico, was named after the count's father and brother, who shared the same name and were known for their "saintly habits and truly exemplary kindness." The second son, Sigismondo, was named to "to renew the names" of both the Patriarch of Aquileia and another illustrious brother of the count. Then came Taddea, the first daughter, who was named after the count's mother. She was followed by Giulio, who was named after his mother, Giulia, at her own request "because this would perpetuate her name in the house of the Torre." The next child, Marcella, was named after Giulia's mother, "out of respect for her grandmother who was . . . a matron of the highest virtue." Two sons and a daughter then followed, Giovanni, Luigi, and Ginevra, who were named after three siblings of the count. Helena, the next born, was named after the wife of the count's brother, and finally came little Giulia, whose birth brought about her mother's death and who "renewed the maternal name."[55] Centuries later, when the singular virtues of the principals involved have been long forgotten, genealogical research in Venice can thus be a linguistic minefield, with homonyms easily leading to cases of mistaken identity.[56]

Portrayals of the Lineage

As to the visual strategy, with the proliferation of paintings in the home, portraits would become an important emblem of an aristocratic lifestyle. Crediting the painter Giovanni Bellini with starting the custom, Vasari wrote that "there are many portraits in all the houses of Venice, and in many gentlemen's homes one may see their fathers and grandfathers back to the fourth generation, and in some of the more noble houses back further still."[57]

The noble Soranzo family went one step further, commissioning Tintoretto to paint a huge panel, around 5 feet high and 16 feet wide, of three generations of the family for their splendid Gothic palace on Campo San Polo (figs. 20 and 21). Described by one art historian as an "aesthetically disastrous group portrait,"[58] it is, nonetheless, a powerful statement of the lineage at one point in time.

Now cut down into three separate panels, the work depicts the paterfamilias, the procurator Jacopo Soranzo (1467–1551), on the central panel and was probably painted shortly after his death. Once a full-length figure, he is now shown in the traditional bust-length format used for individual portraits, thanks to a drastic trimming of the top and bottom edges. But on the intact panel Jacopo was bracketed by his only son Francesco and his dark-haired daughter-in-law, Chiara Cappello, whose inward-facing positions on the edges of the two side panels now give an awkward sense of facing into a void (for the Soranzo family tree, see Appendix, p. 260).[59] They are flanked by their five sons and three daughters who had survived to adulthood, along with the latter's spouses – twelve figures in all.

Three sons, all in the front row, have been convincingly identified through comparisons with other known portraits. Next to Francesco on the left-hand panel is his oldest son, Jacopo (b. 1518), who was named after his grandfather following Venetian custom. On his wide fur lapels he wears a double-rose gold necklace given to him by Mary Tudor in 1554 after a three-year tour of duty as Venetian ambassador to England. Allowed by special permission of the Senate to keep the decoration rather than consigning it, as required by law, to the state, he served on other important diplomatic missions and eventually became a procurator himself, earning the nickname "tocco d'oro" – the golden touch.[60]

Two of the junior Jacopo's brothers appear on the right-hand panel: the bearded Lorenzo (b. 1519), standing next to his mother, and clean-shaven Benedetto (b. 1522) beside him to the viewer's right. The other brothers are probably depicted on the left-hand panel – Giovanni (b. 1520) in the front row and the young Vettore (b. 1532) on the left end. The two blonde women in the front row – one on each panel – are probably their sisters, Elisabetta and Cecilia, both wearing the pearl necklace and bound hair of recent brides. Although Cecilia had married in 1539 and would have been considered a matron by this time, it is plausible that she would still be wearing pearls for a portrait made in the 1550s. Sumptuary legislation was passed in 1562 prohibiting women from wearing pearls more than twelve years "after giving their hand" in marriage, suggesting that this was a common practice. The dark-haired woman at the far right is probably Elena, who never married. The remaining figures in the second row would be husbands and wives who had married into the lineage.[61] Infrared reflectography reveals the traces of two *stemmi* at the lower margins of the

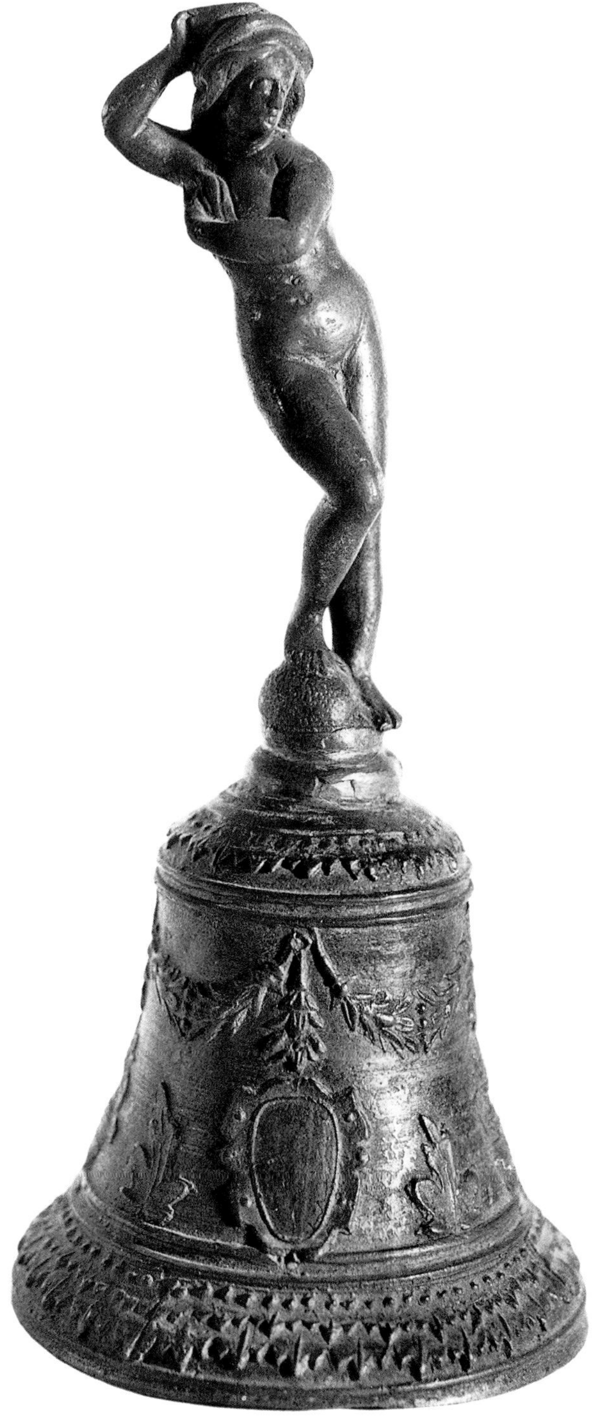

19 Paduan artist, bell with a handle in the form of Venus, sixteenth century. Bronze, height 18 cm, diameter at base, 8 cm. The bell is decorated with festoons and a cartouche for a *stemma*. Venice, Museo Civico Correr.

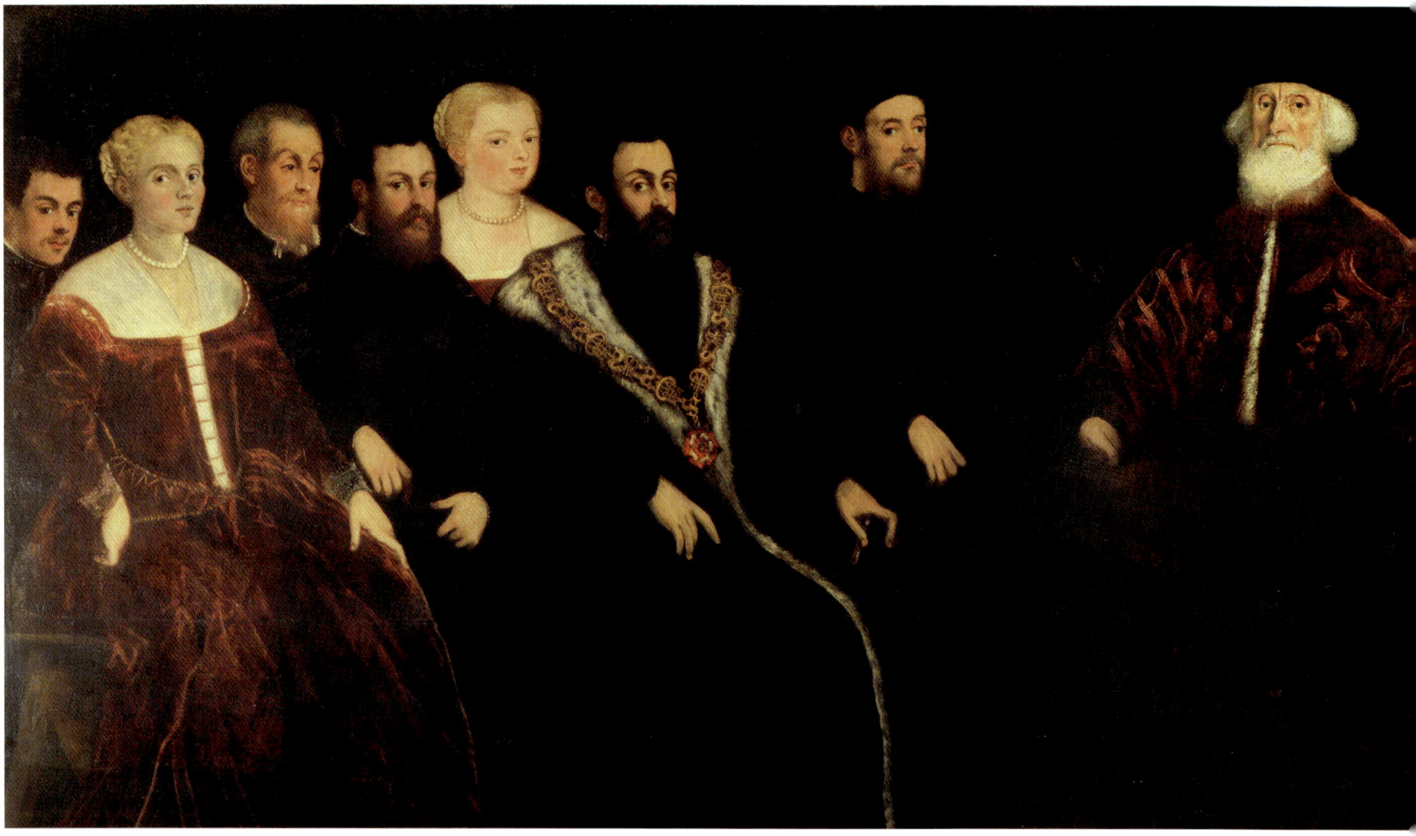

20 Jacopo Tintoretto, *Portrait of Jacopo Soranzo and Group Portrait of Fourteen Members of the Soranzo Family* (composite), ca. 1555. Oil on canvas; central panel 75 × 60 cm; left panel 152 × 216 cm; right panel 153 × 215 cm. On the assumption that those born into the Soranzo family would be seated prominently in the front row, a hypothesis as to the identities of the figures drawing upon archival information can be constructed (see Appendix, p. 260). The figures flanking Jacopo Soranzo would be, from left to right: on the left panel, his grandson Vettore; his granddaughter Elizabeth and her husband, Giovanni Vendramin (m. 1544); his grandson Giovanni and his wife, Marietta Zane (m. 1555); his grandson Jacopo; and his son Francesco; and on the right panel, his daughter-in-law Chiara Cappello; Marina Cappello – who married his grandson Lorenzo (m. 1548), who is next on the right; his grandson Benedetto; Marco Giustinian – who married his granddaughter Cecilia (m. 1539), who is next on the right; and his granddaughter Elena. Milan, Pinacoteca del Castello Sforzesco.

side panels, the Soranzo on the left and the Cappello on the right.[62]

The parents, Francesco and Chiara, also had no fewer than three sons named Bernardo, who may well have died in childhood: Bernardo Natale, his middle name commemorating his birth just before Christmas on 23 December 1524; Bernardo Caterino, born in 1530, whose middle name honored his great grandmother, Caterina; and Bernardo

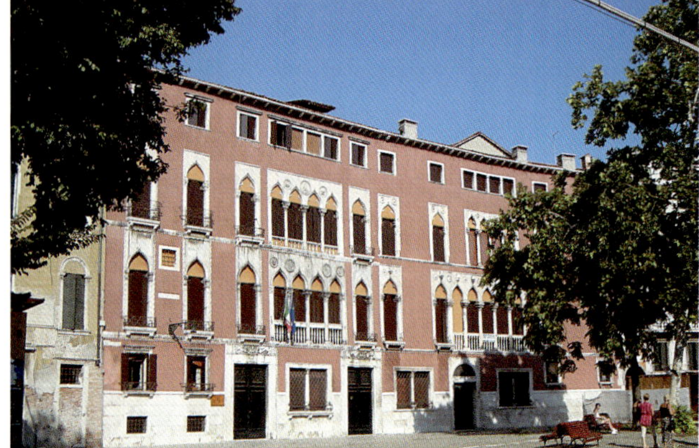

21 (*right*) Palazzo Soranzo, late fourteenth to early fifteenth century, on Campo San Polo.

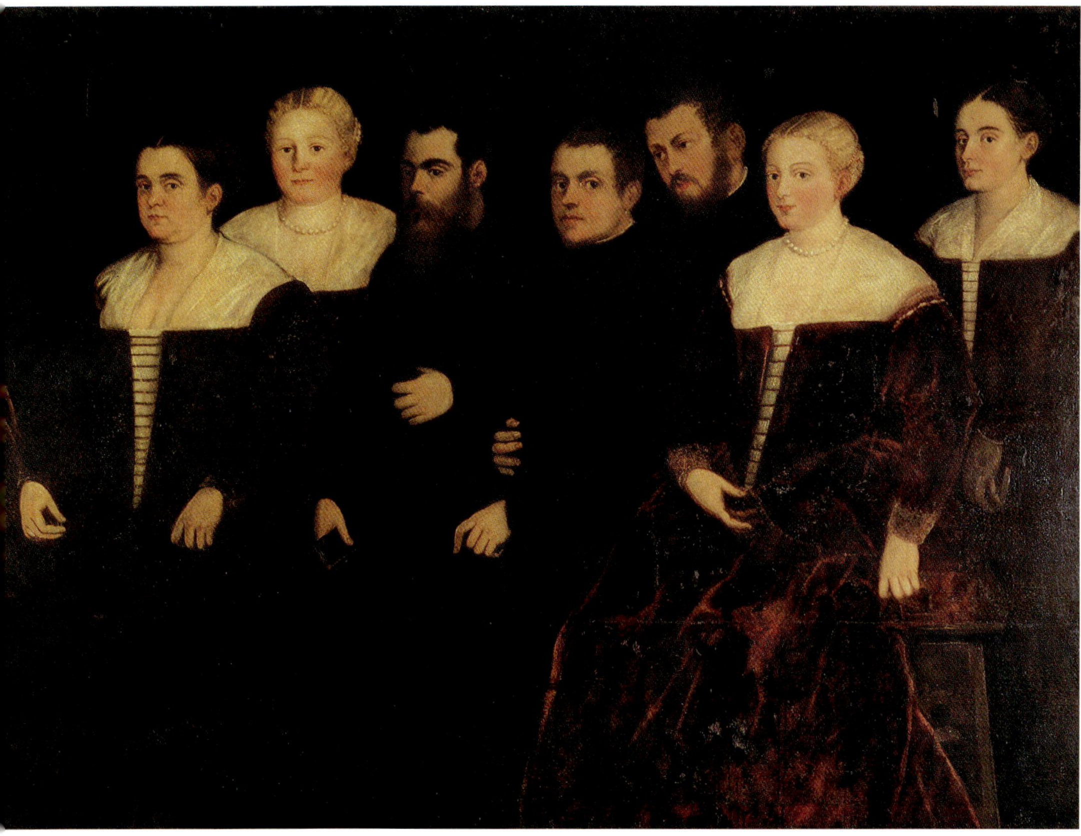

Gaspare, born in 1534 on 6 January, the feast day of the Epiphany, whose middle name commemorated one of the Magi. It is also worth considering the fact that the next generation – Lorenzo's first son Jacopo, born in 1549, and Cecilia's three sons, born by 1550 – was not included in the picture. While the exclusion of Cecilia's children is not surprising, since they did not carry the Soranzo name, in all likelihood the intent of Francesco and his adult children was to celebrate not their posterity but their relationship to a distinguished ancestor, as well as the close lateral bonds of the *familia*, as evinced by loving evocations in their testaments.[63]

Tintoretto's painting is virtually unique in his own repertoire and in the genre of Venetian family portraits. Although individual portraits, particularly of men, became common – indeed, essential – even in homes of modest means, few included the family as a whole. Those which do survive, such as Veronese's *Madonna of the Coccina Family*, seem to have been commissioned either by *cittadino* families in Venice or by patrician families on the Terraferma, a term denoting mainland territories under Venetian political control, including the cities of Padua, Verona, Vicenza, Treviso, Bergamo, and Brescia.[64] And yet, if a gallery of family portraits and a coat of arms were no guarantors of nobility, neither was the family name. For virtually all the surnames mentioned – the Cappello, the Bernardo, the Barbarigo, the Trevisan, the Cornaro, the Foscari, the Mocenigo, the Soranzo – were shared by patrician and commoner alike.

Chivalric Fictions

But there was another marker that might be considered the quintessential emblem of noble identity in Venice: a display of weapons called the *lanziera di arme*, installed in the *portego* – the Venetian term for salon or living room or *sala* – of the family palace (fig. 22).[65] In the aftermath of the disastrous events of the War of Cambrai of 1509, when Venice had lost nearly all her possessions on the Terraferma to the combined armies of the pope, the emperor, France, and Spain, Doge Leonardo Loredan had castigated himself and his peers for removing weapons from his *portego* to accommodate guests at large banquets and saw the growth in luxurious living as an offense to God.[66] But other houses had maintained, or restored, the traditional arrangement, for not only did Sansovino describe them as typical items in the

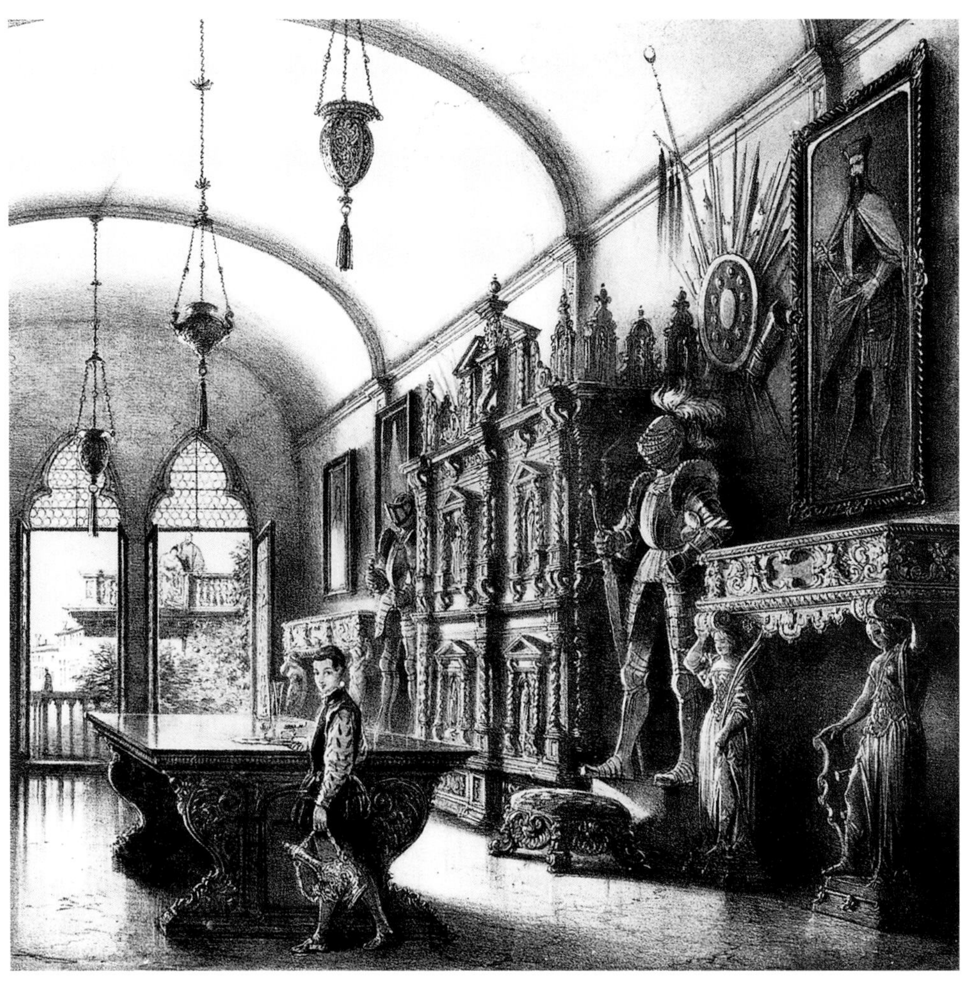

22 "Palazzo Capello on the Grand Canal" (detail), from Lake Price, *Interiors and Exteriors in Venice* (London, 1843). The family *lanziera di arme* was still in place in the *portego* of the palace when Lake Price visited it in the early nineteenth century. Palazzo Barbarigo della Terrazza can be seen through the window in the background.

Venetian *sala* in 1581, but a number of inventories of the period include them as well.[67] Indeed, among a respectable but far from opulent list of household goods belonging to the recently deceased Magnifico Michele Memo, the sole furnishings in his sparsely furnished *portego* were twenty-four well worn benches, twelve rush-bottomed chairs of walnut, and the *lanziera di arme*. In this case, the display comprised a gilded shield with a helmet bearing the Memo arms, a standard, a *restelliera* – a rack of spears fanned out like a rake – and a regimental banner.[68] It should be noted that relics of battles fought by ancestors on land or sea were not often found in the home of a non-noble merchant, no matter how wealthy.[69]

The taste for assemblages of weaponry in patrician homes points to another peculiarity of the Venetian experience – the absence of a true and proper chivalric past. There was no landed nobility in their ancestry because there was no land. For the most part, these were arms of noble citizens and not of knights. But chivalric display did play a significant role in Venetian public life in the Renaissance period, and it tended to reinforce the distinctiveness of noble status. Jousts were occasionally held on Piazza San Marco, and youth brigades, called the Compagnie della Calza, were the principal organizers of citizen entertainments up to the middle of the sixteenth century. They took their name from the colored tights – *calze*, often particolored – that were distinctive to the various companies.[70]

Calza members were also highly visible protagonists in a number of Carpaccio's paintings, where they were usually positioned to display their fine apparel and resplendent coats of arms. But these groups were not ongoing and permanent. Each was formed by a group of adolescents for a limited time period – anywhere from a few years up to a decade or so – and by the time a young man was in his mid-twenties he was expected to hang up his embroidered jackets and particolored *calze* and assume the toga of a Venetian gentlemen. Although there is evidence of at least one *cittadino* company in the fifteenth century, by the sixteenth the members were virtually all patrician. It was one more sign of the growing stratification within Venetian society, with the separating out of a distinctly noble order.

There were also two orders of knights in Venice, but of a peculiarly Venetian sort, who grew in importance particularly in the last half of the sixteenth century. One of these – the Knights of San Marco – was made up almost entirely of foreigners who had been honored by the Venetian government for their particular service to the republic, so they played no significant role in the Venetian nobility. The other order was called the Knights of the Stola d'Oro, and here the title did pertain to Venetians. The name comes from a stole or sash of gold cloth that was worn over one shoulder on ceremonial occasions (fig. 23). Permission to wear it and other knightly insignia, and admission to the order, was granted by the Senate to a select group of patricians who had served as ambassadors at foreign courts and had been granted knighthood by foreign sovereigns for their service. It is important to remember that the title was not hereditary. It was granted for meritorious service and it disappeared with the death of the recipient.[71] And yet, since most such embassies were headed by rich gentlemen who could afford the expenses of high office, the Stola d'Oro tended to reinforce a hierarchy of wealth within the patrician caste. Aristotle's theory of magnificence, which sanctioned, indeed required, great expenditures and appropriate display by the wealthy, had been part of the aristocratic rationale in Italy since the fifteenth century.[72] And it ran head on against the age-old Venetian ideal of *mediocritas* – of not standing out above one's noble peers.[73] Contarini's acclaim for rule "rather by the nobility of lineage, than by the estimation of wealth" was fine in theory, but small comfort in real life. As Antonio Colluraffi later wrote in his *Il Nobile Veneto*, "It is not enough then for our noble to say: I am born *Nobile*; but he should also say: I want to live *Nobile*; I want to die *Nobile*."[74] At issue was personal identity. For by the later sixteenth century, great riches were necessary to live in a noble manner.[75] And the famed solidarity of the Venetian patriciate was becoming less a miracle and more a mirage. But that mirage had a compelling force, and the republic would last another two hundred years without serious internal strife, until the armies of Napoleon brought the thousand-year-old institution to an end in 1797.

This chapter has offered a brief look at the impact on republican Venice of new notions of nobility that were becoming dominant in Italy, and at a few ways in which honor was asserted and the "title of gentility" defined in visual terms. Future chapters will explore what it meant for both men and women to live *nobile* – in a noble manner – and how patrician ideals and identities were expressed through domestic architecture, dress, and the accumulation of objects and works of art.

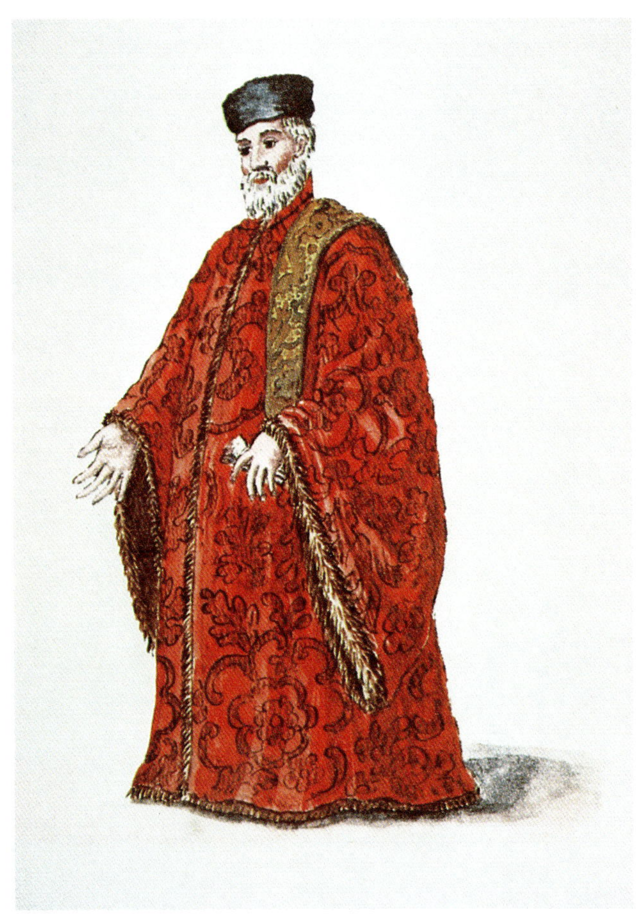

23 Giovanni Grevembroch, *Knight of the Stola d'Oro*, eighteenth century. Watercolor. Grevembroch (1731–1807), a painter of Flemish extraction, was commissioned by the nobleman Pietro Gradenigo in 1754 to record the costumes of the Venetians, both contemporary and historical – a labor that eventually resulted in *Gli abiti de' Veneziani di quasi ogni età . . .*, a four-volume compendium of 648 watercolors of costumes, notable personages, genre scenes and tradespeople. Under Gradenigo's patronage, Grevembroch recorded a variety of curiosities, antiquities, and architectural details, including well-heads and door knockers, throughout the city. The historian Gian Antonio Moschini, in his *Guida di Venezia* of 1815, wrote: "with this collection our Pietro Gradenigo conserved precious drawings of many things, that by now are no more." Venice, Museo Civico Correr.

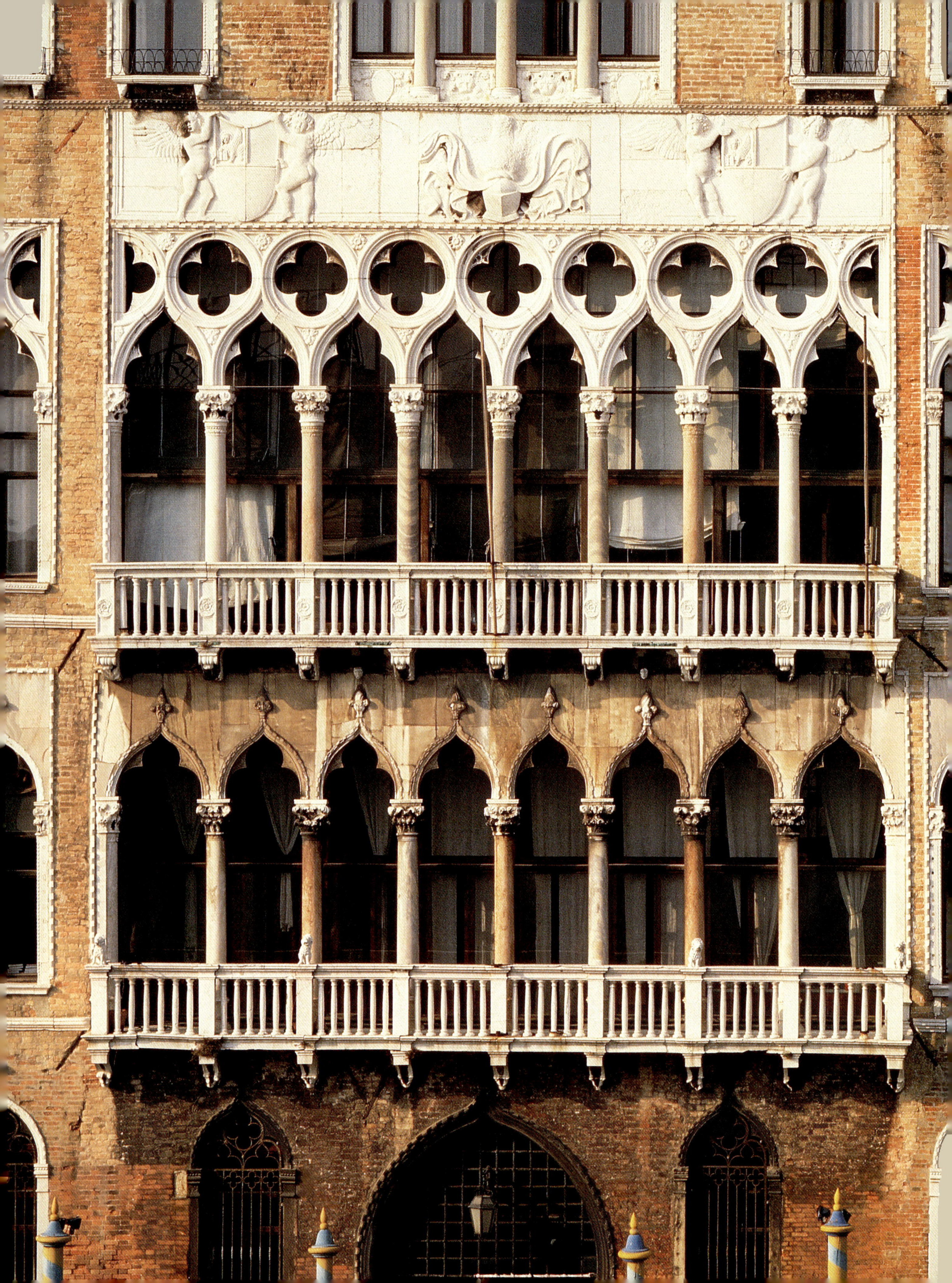

2

Not Having the Name of Palazzo

SIXTEENTH-CENTURY VENICE was a society caught in a paradox. Observers described the city as opulent in terms of its material culture, and yet its leading citizens proclaimed an ideal of frugality and restraint. As Francesco Sansovino noted in 1581, the Venetians called their magnificent residences *case*, "not having the name of *palazzo*, out of modesty."[1] Some noble families were rich and powerful; others had little more than a noble title and the right to sit on the Great Council; but all, whether rich or poor, lived in *case*. Even a structure as palatial as Ca' Foscari, with the term *casa* abbreviated in Venetian dialect, was simply a "house" (figs. 24 and 25).[2] These houses were also homes –

24 (*facing page*) Detail of the marble relief on the facade of Ca' Foscari (fig. 25).

25 (*below*) The two Case Giustiniani (left) and Ca' Foscari (right) on the Grand Canal. The site of Ca' Foscari was originally occupied by a Veneto–Byzantine-style palace. Called "the House with the Two Towers," it was bought by the republic in 1429 to give as a gift to the *condottiere* Gian Francesco Gonzaga, Marquis of Mantua, for his service to the republic in the war with Milan. After he changed sides, the palace was taken away and given instead to Francesco Sforza, Gonzaga's replacement as *capitano generale* of the Venetian armies in 1439. When he in turn wrested power in Milan in 1450, the building was again confiscated. Doge Francesco Foscari bought it at auction in 1452, had it rebuilt, and lived there until his death in 1457. The two adjacent Giustiniani palaces were also rebuilt in those years and exhibit a remarkably close stylistic affinity to Ca' Foscari, balancing its height with their combined width. Ca' Foscari remained in the Foscari family until 1845 when it was sold to the Congregazione Municipale di Venezia.

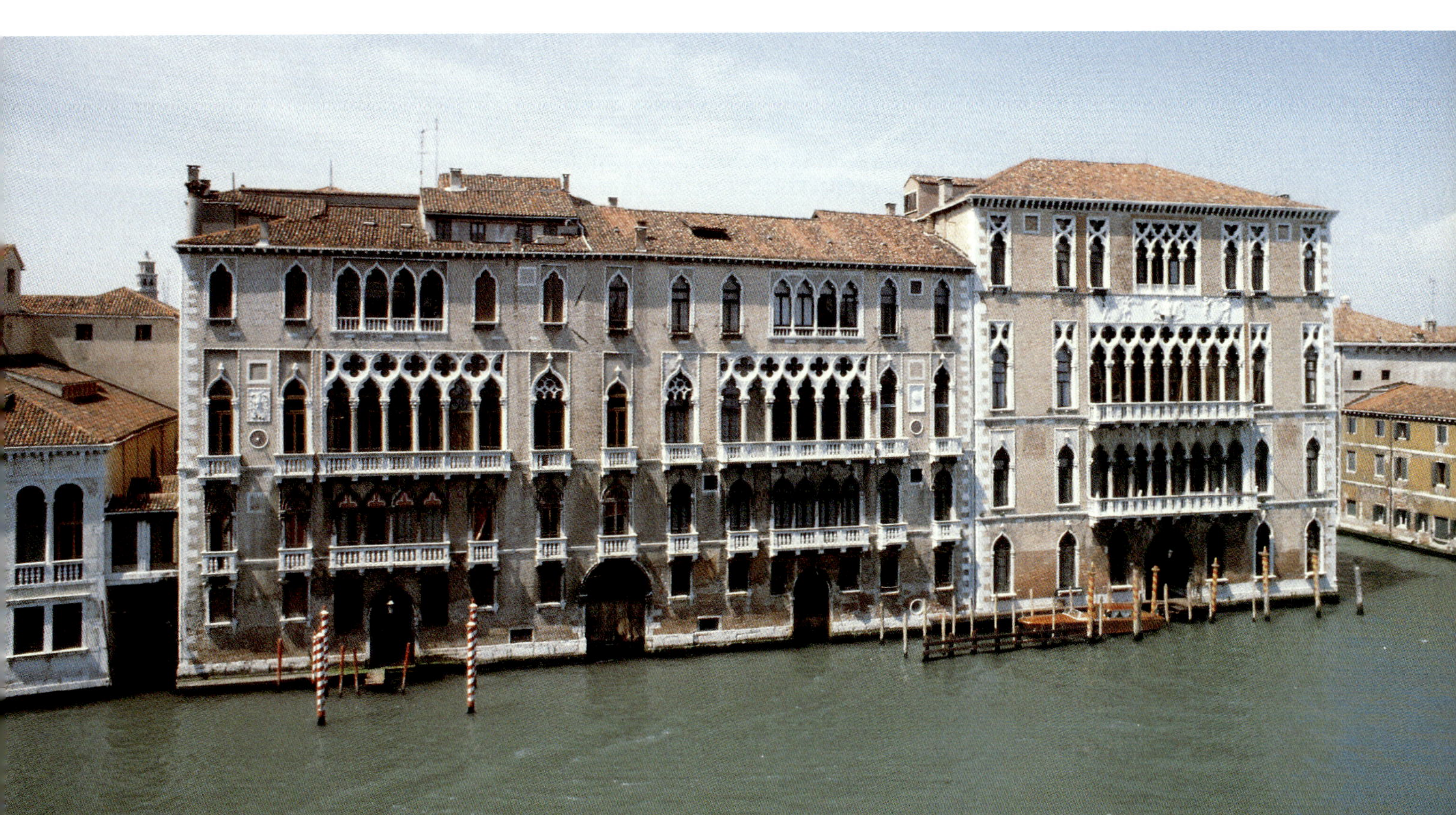

the primary locus of personal identity in any society. On a basic level, their size or grandeur, as well as their style, convey silent messages of family values and status.[3]

An Embodiment of the Family

In the case of Venice, the fundamental meaning of the home may be summed up in the government's response to what has come to be called the Querini–Tiepolo conspiracy of 1310. It was the first of two attempts, both made in the fourteenth century, to overthrow the duly constituted government. There were to be no others. On the first occasion, two patricians, Marco Querini and his son-in-law Baiamonte Tiepolo, conspired to remove Doge Pietro Gradenigo from his lifetime appointment by force.[4] History credited Gradenigo with the Serrata and the eternal foundation of the republic.[5] But he was not universally popular in his own time. Blaming him for a ruinous war and generally bad times, Querini and Tiepolo garnered popular support and formed an elaborate plot to march on the ducal palace at dawn on Sunday, 15 June, shouting "freedom . . . and death to Doge Gradenigo!" Their plans went awry thanks to a violent storm and an informant in their ranks who tipped off the doge, whose palace guards were waiting. The insurrection was put down by force, Querini and others were killed, and Tiepolo, who happened to be the son of the doge's nephew, was exiled.[6]

But out of sight might be out of mind. A permanent visible reminder of this day of infamy was in order, not just to celebrate the survival of the republic but also to warn future generations against such acts of treason. The celebration of the feast day of San Vito on 15 June suggested the appropriate response. Ten days later three sculpted reliefs of Greek marble were stripped from the exterior wall of Tiepolo's house, as well as the wooden door and jambs from the main portal, and installed in the church of San Vito in the *sestiere* of Dorsoduro (figs. 26 and 29). That was not all. Even though Tiepolo's house was associated with his grandfather, Lorenzo Tiepolo, a previous and popular doge, it was razed to the ground. As one scholar put it, "By destroying its palace, the government hoped to exorcize the spirit of the family."[7] Henceforth 15 June was declared a public holiday and each year thereafter until the end of the republic a temporary bridge was thrown across the Grand Canal and the doge and his magistrates made a solemn procession to the church. The confiscated objects did not lose their resonance over time; after the church was torn down in the nineteenth century, the door frame and reliefs were transferred to an oratory newly built near the site.[8]

Nor was the Querini palace forgotten, although it posed a conundrum. It was owned by three brothers *in fraterna* – a typical Venetian arrangement whereby the property was held in common – but only two of them were involved in the conspiracy. So two-thirds of the building was demolished and the other third, owned by a brother who had not taken part in the rebellion, was bought by the state. This truncated remnant was thereupon transformed into the *beccaria*, the public slaughterhouse, also called the *Stalon* (or large stall). When it was torn down, its Gothic windows were incorporated into Venice's fish market where they remain today (fig. 27). The Balduin, a third family involved in the affair, were ordered by public decree to keep the door of their home always open day and night, a penalty that prevailed for more than one hundred years.[9] The image of the lion of San Marco was affixed to the houses of other guilty families.

Some fifty years after the Querini–Tiepolo affair, with the failure of a second and final attempt to overthrow the government – this time by the doge, Marin Falier, himself – a column of infamy was erected on the site where the Tiepolo house had once stood (fig. 28). The inscription states: "Of Baiamonte was this land, and now for his iniquitous betrayal, it is held by the commune for others to fear, and to show to everyone it will always prevail."[10]

What can be learned from this event and its aftermath? For one thing, that the house was not a neutral shell; it was an embodiment of the family. Expropriation was not enough; only through its destruction would the family's presence be removed from the site. For another, in Venice a man's *casa* was not his castle. The state held the right of eminent domains, even to the extent of insisting that the doors of a private home remain open. And for another, images such as the marble reliefs taken from the Tiepolo palace were powerful signs (fig. 29). Two of the reliefs (upper left and bottom) embedded in the wall of the church of San Vito depict eagles triumphing over hares – classic symbols of virtue overcoming vice. A third, on the upper right, shows a prowling lion. In the twelfth and thirteenth centuries such reliefs, carved with Christian, oriental, and classical imagery such as figures of Hercules, were a popular form of exterior ornament on family palaces.[11]

Such images were more than just decoration. While they served to define the *casa* – to distinguish a house from its neighbors and to express family values – they may also have been amulets of protection, preventing evil from entering the house.[12] The removal of the *paterae* from the walls of the Tiepolo palace, where they were apparently less than efficacious, served three purposes beyond the simple appropriation or preservation of objects of aesthetic value *per se*: it

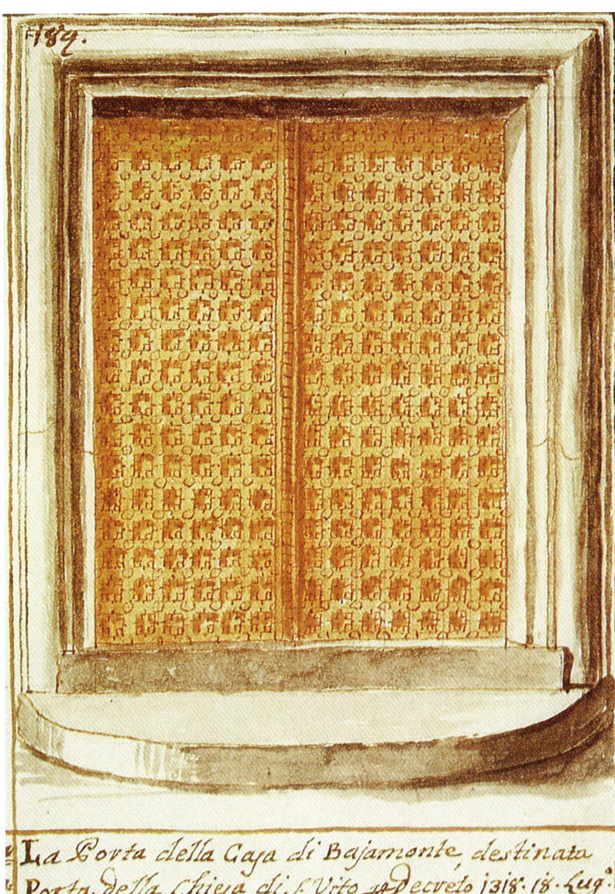

26 (*left*) Giovanni Grevembroch, doors removed from the house of Baiamonte Tiepolo and installed in the church of San Vito. Watercolor, eighteenth century. The Council of Ten also forbade anyone to wear, keep, or have painted the arms of the Tiepolo or the Querini anywhere in Venice. Venice, Museo Civico Correr.

28 (*below*) Column of infamy. Venice, Museo Civico Correr.

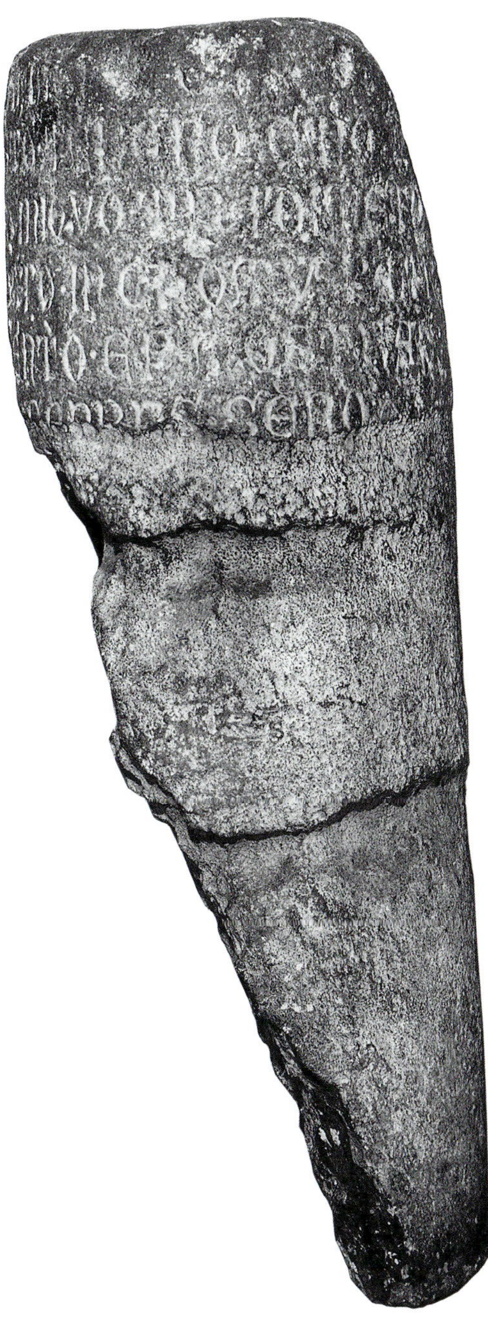

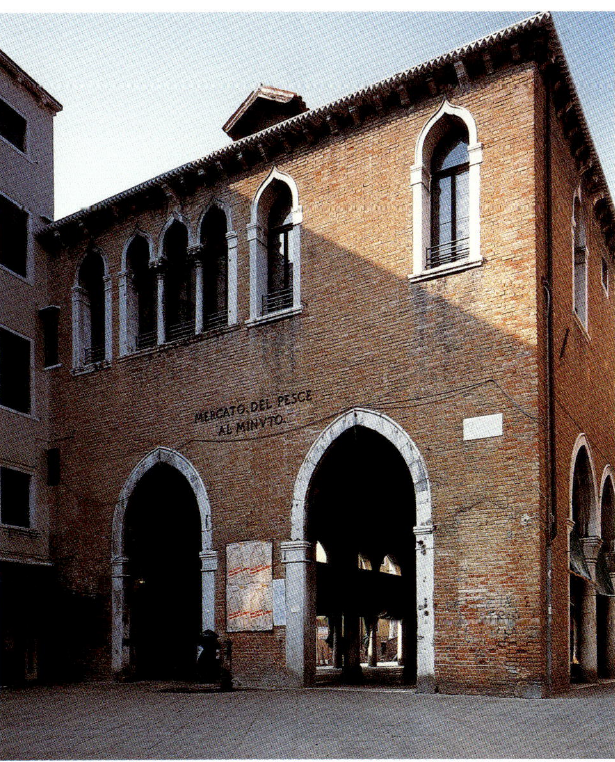

27 (*left*) The Pescheria (fish market) with Gothic windows from the thirteenth-century house of Marco Querini. Campo delle Beccarie.

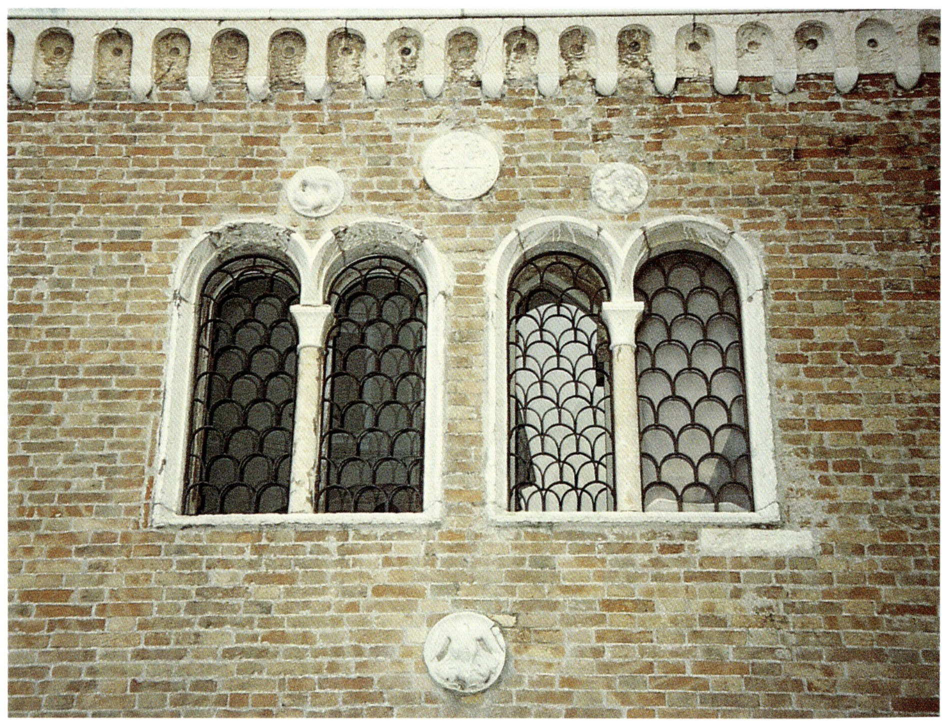

29 Oratory of San Vito, west wall. The round plaques (twelfth–thirteenth century) taken from the Tiepolo home are called *paterae*. The cross (fifteenth century) is a later addition.

deprived the home of their protection; it re-sacralized and perhaps recharged the power of the objects through their transfer from secular to sacred space; and it completed the public humiliation of the family.[13]

During the centuries that followed, the great merchants of Venice, whether noble or not, earned huge profits from their trading activities. While the prevailing ethos of the patriciate, right to the end of the republic, counseled moderation in all things – *mediocritas* – and public service over private advantage, the *casa* remained the primary venue in which a family could display its taste, its prosperity, and its prominence.

Houses Worthy of Note

The patrician Marin Sanudo, writing in the last decade of the fifteenth century, was aware of the role played by the home in the civic magnificence of Venice. He declared: "It is, then, a very big and beautiful city, excelling over all others, with houses and *piazze* founded upon salt water, and it has a Grand Canal . . . On either side there are houses of patricians and others; they are very beautiful, costing from 20,000 ducats downwards."[14] Most ranged in value from 3,000 to 10,000 ducats, with some even more, and – as he puts it – "a few, but very few, of less value, which are being rebuilt." Sanudo singled out just two examples of these dwellings by name, from "the many others which would take too long to record." Ca' Foscari, the late Gothic palace built by Doge Francesco Foscari in 1452, was, Sanudo observed, "of the greatest value" (fig. 25). Also worthy of note was the *casa* of "the magnificent Zorzi Corner, most worshipful knight and brother of the Queen of Cyprus [Caterina Corner]."[15] It had been built several decades earlier by a wealthy *cittadino*, who was thereafter called Bartolomeo Malombra *della bella casa* – "of the beautiful house." Zorzi Corner purchased it for around 22,000 ducats in the late fifteenth century and spent another 10,000 to remodel it in a suitably grand manner. The palace, recorded in Jacopo de' Barbari's woodcut view of Venice of 1500, no longer stands (fig. 30).[16]

What is it about these two *case* that distinguished them from numerous other fine examples of Gothic architecture that lined the Grand Canal? In all probability, their ownership by the exceedingly rich and politically powerful. That they were on the Grand Canal was itself significant; it was the only waterway worthy of the title "Canal," while each of those that separated the little islands that made up the city was called a *rio*. It is difficult to judge Ca' Corner's visual

31 (*right*) Ca' Corner Piscopia-Loredan, probably thirteenth century, with later additions. Above the arcade of the *piano nobile* a series of figural reliefs alternating with roundels proclaims the glory of the Corner family. Reliefs of David and Goliath bracket the facade, with the Corner coat of arms above the second column in on each side. In the center are the Lusignan coat of arms, a royal crest, and the Corner coat of arms containing the quartered insignia of the knighthood of Cyprus, flanked by the figures of Justice and Fortitude under small tabernacles. The house passed to the Loredan family through a marriage in 1703.

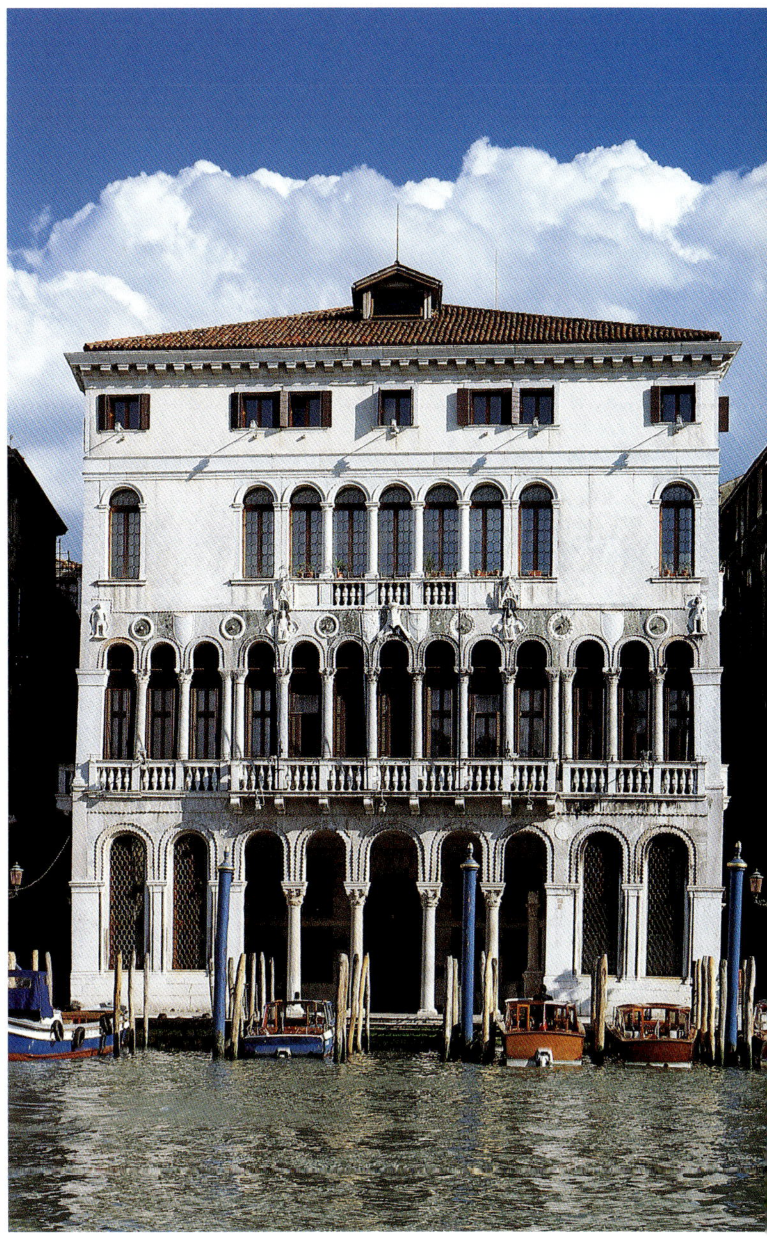

effect from the woodcut, but in the case of Ca' Foscari, Sanudo's high appraisal would have been inspired by its combination of tradition and restrained innovation.[17] On the one hand, it retained the rigorous symmetry that was characteristic of the Veneto–Byzantine palaces of the twelfth and thirteenth centuries, such as Ca' Corner Piscopia-Loredan (fig. 31).[18] Furthermore, like Ca' d'Oro, built in the third and fourth decades of the fifteenth century in the Gothic style (fig. 32), Ca' Foscari adopted the quatrefoil tracery pattern of the Palazzo Ducale for the windows of the central bay.[19] Here the quotation was perhaps even more appropriate, for it associated the doge's private family palace with the prestige of the republic. On the other hand, it rejected the expansive waterside arcade – a portal through which merchandise could be carried for storage on the ground floor – which had long been a hallmark of the great merchant's palace type now called the *casa-fondaco*.[20] But then so did other palaces built in the same period.[21]

30 Jacopo de' Barbari, *View of Venice*, detail of Ca' Corner *della bella casa*, 1500. Woodcut. The palace was destroyed by fire in 1532.

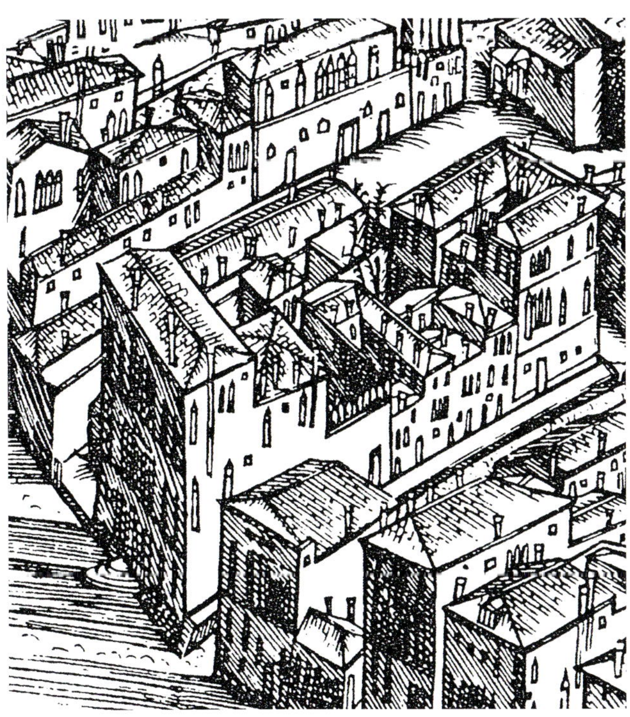

What was truly unique about Ca' Foscari was its size and assertiveness. Situated at the junction of a wide *rio* and the bend of the Grand Canal, it was taller, more massive, and more visible than its neighbors (fig. 33). It also featured a central loggia expanded from six to eight lights, recalling the full arcades that spanned the entire width of earlier palaces like Ca' Corner Piscopia-Loredan. Yet it remained firmly within the prevailing Gothic style. The result was a sump-

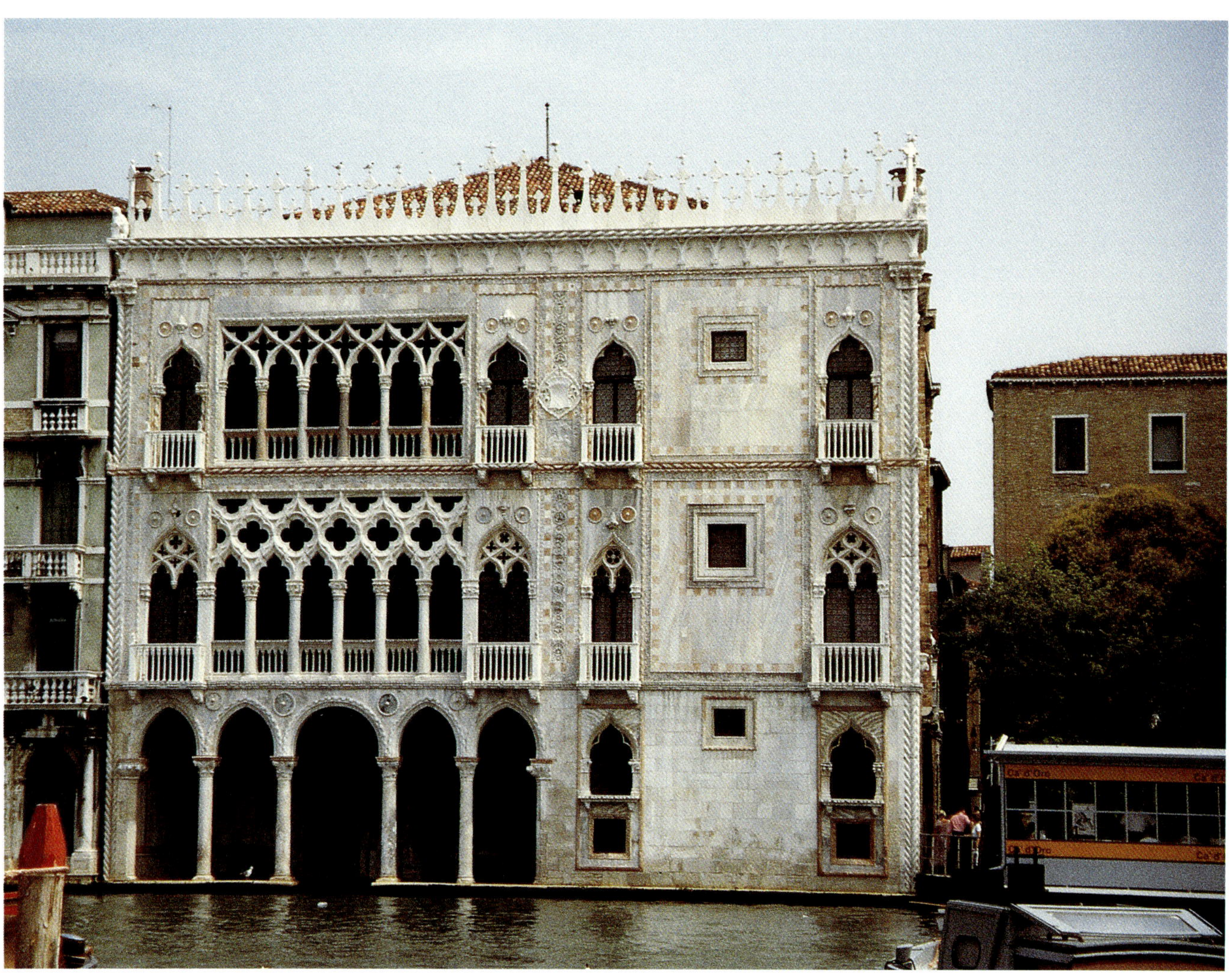

32 (*above*) Ca' d'Oro, begun 1424. The palace, built by Marino Contarini, incorporated decorative fragments from the Veneto–Byzantine Palazzo Zen, which it replaced. The palace is presently the site of the Galleria Giorgio Franchetti.

33 (*facing page*) G. B. Arzenti, *View of Venice*, detail showing the Grand Canal from the Canale di Cannaregio to San Marco. Watercolor, seventeenth century. The three-story, white marble facade of Ca' Loredan-Vendramin-Calergi dominates the upper end of the canal. At the eastward bend on the right, the Rialto Bridge provides the only land-link between the two sides of the city at that time. On the left, Ca' Foscari and the Case Giustiniani anchor the westward bend of the canal. Across the *rio* to their right is the gleaming facade of Palazzo Balbi, built in the 1580s, of which Padre Stringa wrote in his revised edition of Sansovino's *Venetia nobilissima* in 1604: "it is built in the modern style, decorated with marbles, with the windows *alla romana*." Further to the right is the similar, even larger, white facade of Palazzo Coccina, built by a *cittadino* family in the 1560s. At the bottom of the detail is the island of Giudecca, separated by water from Palladio's church of San Giorgio Maggiore on the far right. Venice, Museo Correr.

tuously imposing facade contained by the quoining on the corners in a well-calibrated balance of elegance and solidity.

Foscari was the first doge to advance the notion of an imperial Venice as a new Rome, and the *bas-relief* above the upper *piano nobile* was an announcement of new values, about as subtle as a great banner stretched across the facade of an exhibition hall. Here, in a mixture of chivalric and Renaissance humanist values, classical *putti* support the Foscari arms on a strip of brilliant white marble (fig. 24). And yet its rather awkward insertion here is not classical at all. It recalls that age-old taste in Venice for the architectural pastiche, as with the *paterae* on the house of Baiamonte Tiepolo.[22] But as visible and polemical as Ca' Foscari may have been, it was still only first among equals. It did not challenge the established late Gothic decorative idiom as such.[23] The successful incorporation of classical antique values into a Venetian aesthetic would come to fruition in architectural terms only in the next century.

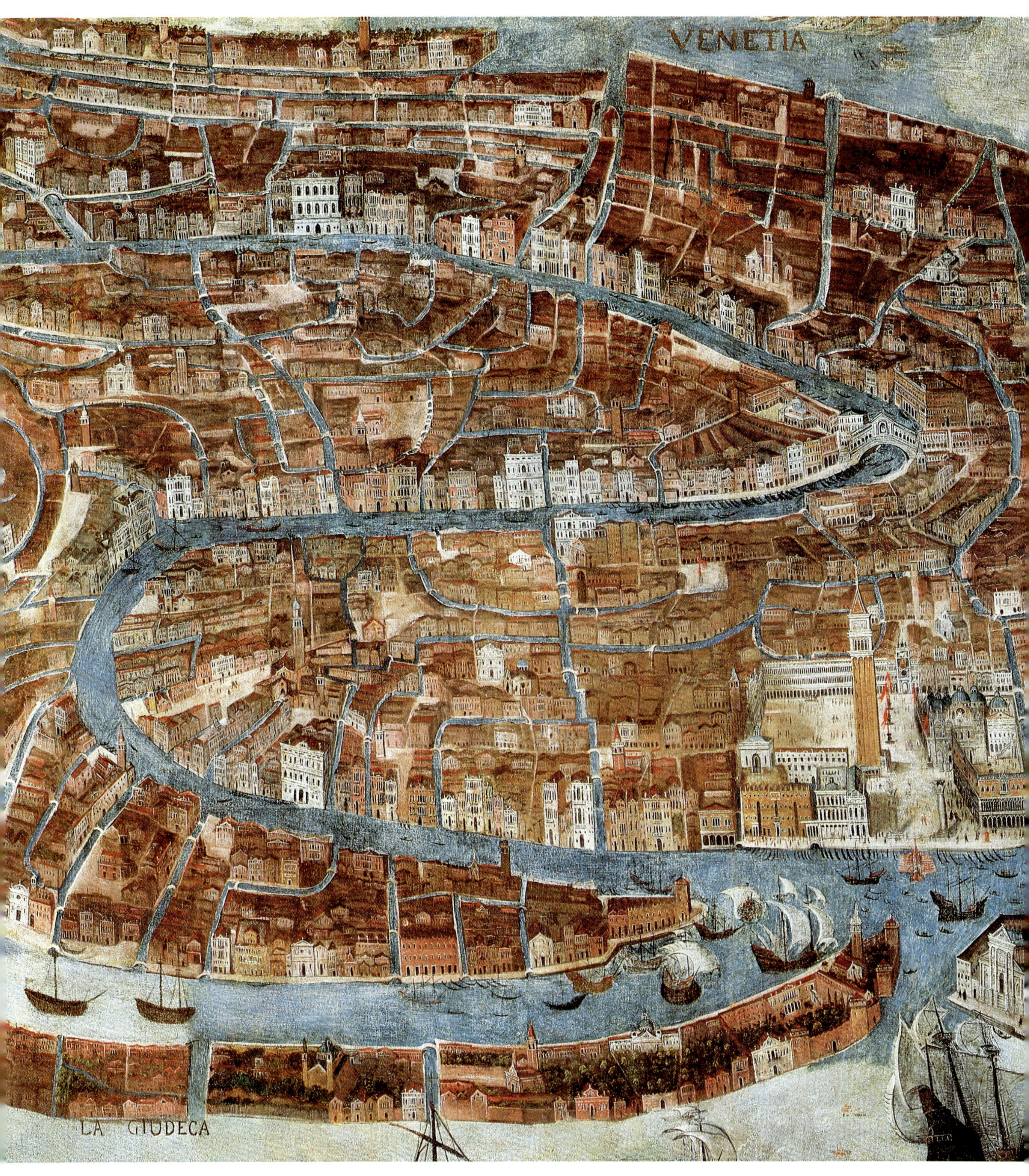
VENETIA
LA GIUDECA

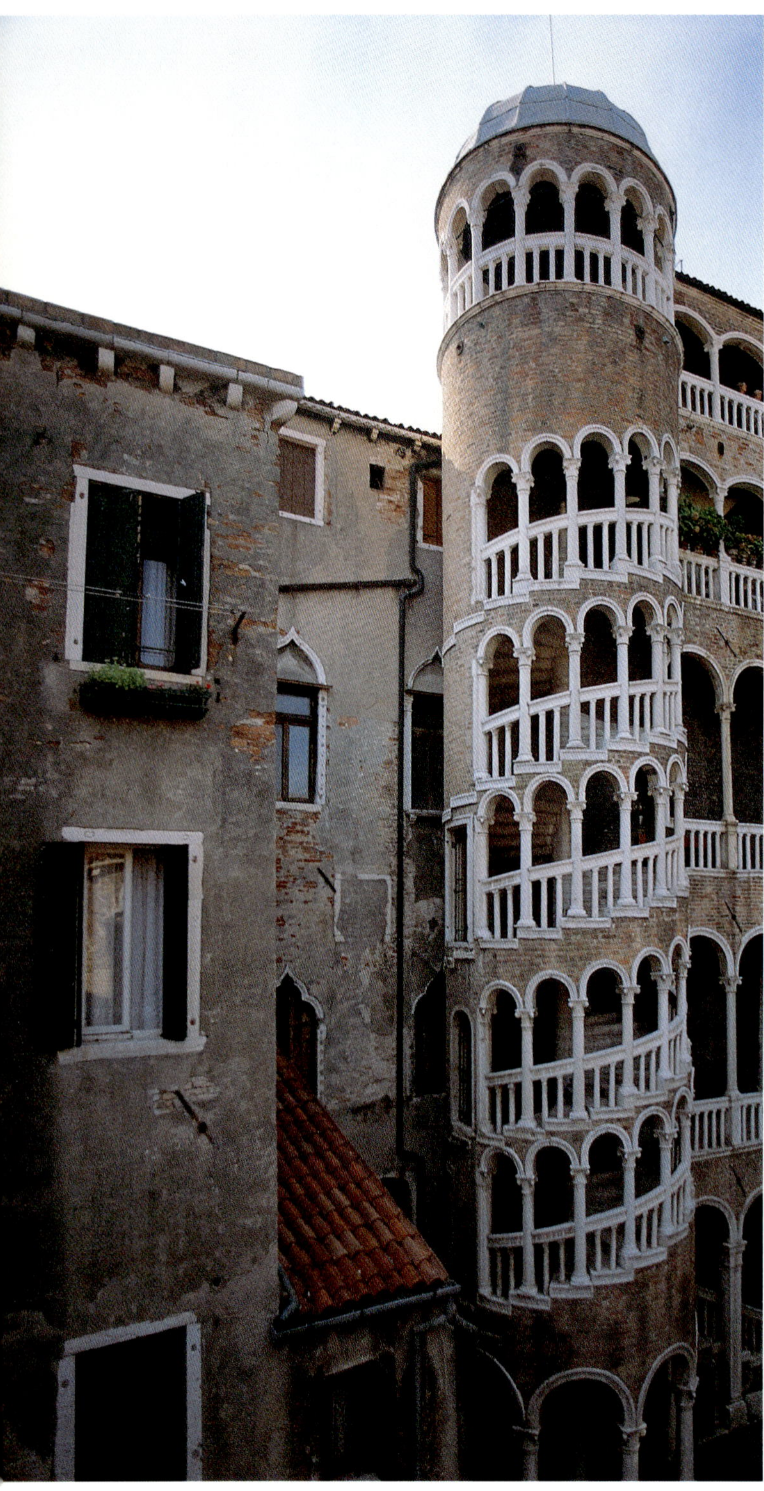

34 (*left*) Ca' Contarini del Bovolo at San Paternian, ca. 1499. Although the beautiful spiral staircase to the rear is the most notable feature of the palace today, the main facade faces Rio di S. Luca.

35 (*facing page*) Ca' Dario, begun ca. 1487. Elected secretary of the Council of Ten in 1487, Giovanni Dario left the house in his will to his natural daughter, Marietta, who married the patrician Vincenzo Barbaro. The house passed to her son, Gasparo, upon her death and remained in the Barbaro family until the nineteenth century.

New Initiatives

In the prosperous final decades of the quattrocento, a growing urge for family self-expression and the desire to participate in a *renovatio* of the antique produced a number of experiments, with influences ranging from Byzantine to Islamic to Lombard to Tuscan to Roman, and these began to break up the Gothic hegemony of the Grand Canal and neighborhoods throughout the city. One strand of innovation looked toward the sensual chromatic values of the East, with colored marble incrustation and large-scale figures painted on facades; another toward the more cerebral, Vitruvian ideal of classical Rome and Greece. Within an essentially anarchical situation, the hallmark of modernity was the roundheaded arch.[24]

The new initiatives included exotic flights of fancy like the circular staircase of Ca' Contarini del Bovolo and the marble encrusted facade of Ca' Dario (figs. 34 and 35). Giovanni Dario, the *cittadino* owner of the latter palace, celebrated a diplomatic career in Persia and the Near East with a polychrome radial motif that he must have seen in Cairo. He tempered possible criticisms of vainglorious display with an inscription dedicating the house to the genius of the city: URBIS GENIO IOHANNES DARIUS.[25] What was particularly Venetian and unthreatening about all this was its seemingly random, idiosyncratic quality. Now it was not just the erratic classical *fragment* that was incorporated into the facade of a staidly traditional Gothic building: it was the erratic *building* that was inserted into the unitary fabric of the Veneto-Byzantine and Gothic *case* that lined the Grand Canal.

Perhaps the most long-lasting results of the drive to be different can be seen in two palaces designed by Mauro Codussi. A native of a small town near Bergamo, he introduced Lombard and Tuscan forms that offered the first serious challenge to local Venetian traditions and a viable model for the future. Ca' Corner-Spinelli was built for a member of the Lando family around 1490 (fig. 36). The fully rusticated ground floor was virtually a novelty in residential Venice and looked across the lagoon to mainland

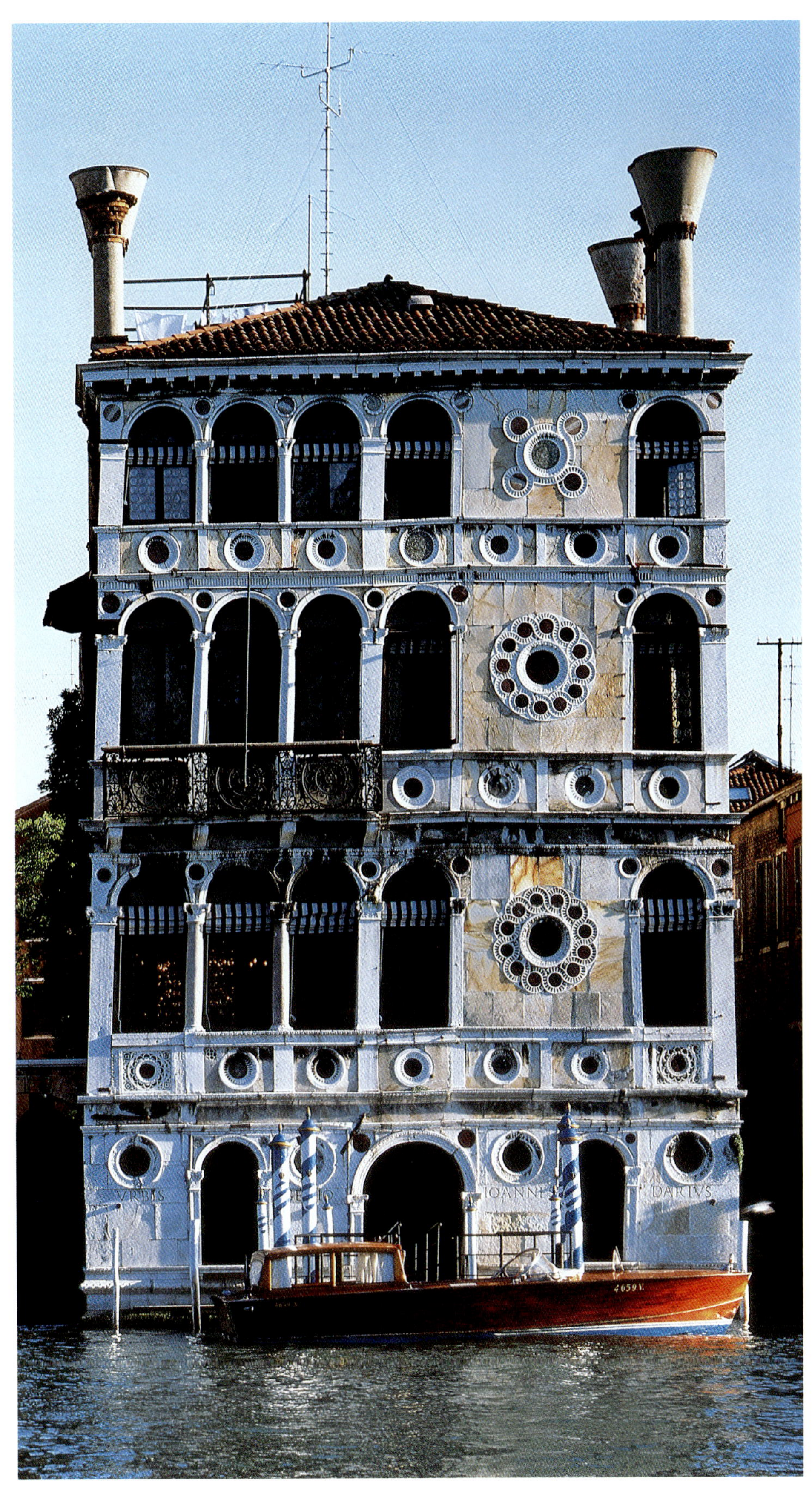
VRBIS
IOANNES
DARIVS
4659 V.

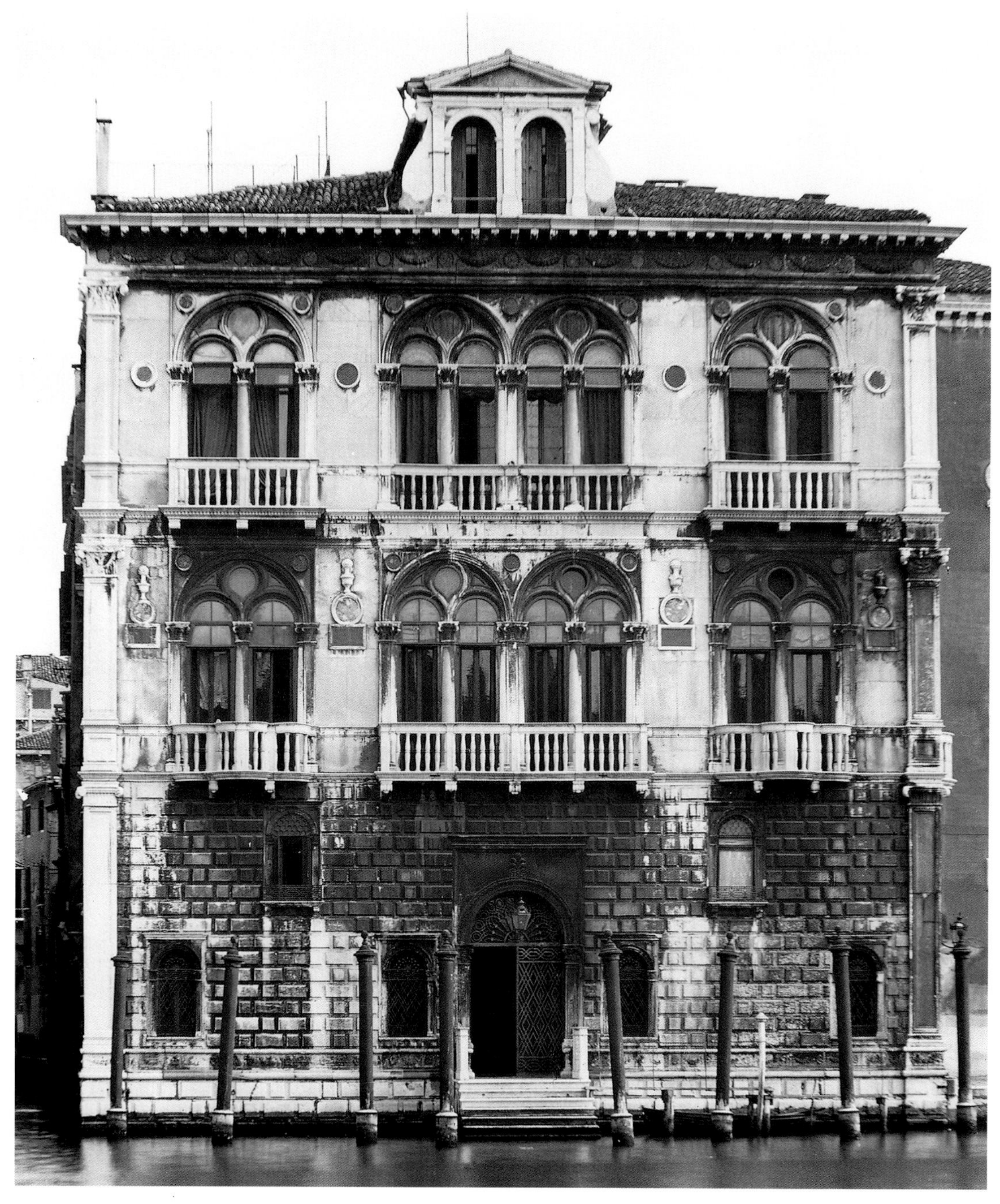

36 Ca' Corner-Spinelli, begun ca. 1490. Zuane Corner bought the palace, designed by Mauro Codussi, from Pietro Lando, then doge, in 1542. Corner had it enlarged and redecorated by Michele Sanmicheli. The architect designed a ceiling with carved frames for one of the rooms and persuaded Corner to hire Giorgio Vasari to complete it with paintings. Representing a seemingly homogenous space unified by a foreshortened balustrade, the illusionistic ceiling featured nine large oil paintings: the figure of Charity occupied a central octagon, flanked by four long oval paintings of Patience, Justice, Hope, and Faith at the sides and four panels with *putti* in the corners.

prototypes, particularly in Tuscany. Even more than Ca' Foscari, it suggests that a fortress mentality, with the family closed off from the city, was replacing the welcoming openness of Ca' d'Oro and the earlier palaces with ground-floor arcades.[26]

But it was Ca' Loredan, now known as Vendramin-Calergi, built by Codussi for Andrea Loredan in the first decade of the sixteenth century, that marked the debut of full patrician magnificence in recognizably classical terms

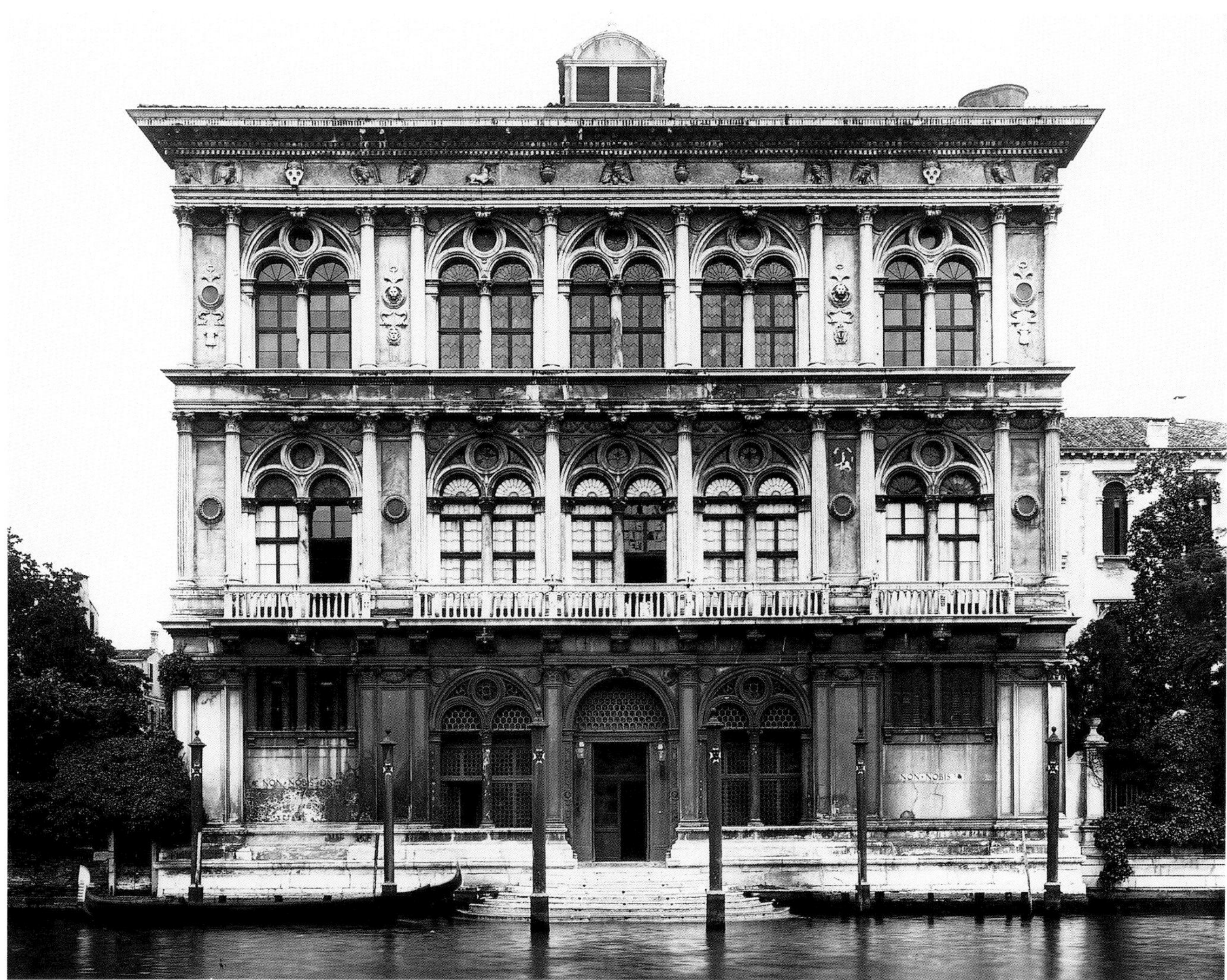

37 Ca' Loredan-Vendramin-Calergi, begun ca. 1502. Designed by Mauro Codussi, the palace was sold by the Loredan family to the Duke of Brunswick in 1581. It then passed through several hands before being bought at auction by Vittore Calergi in 1589. His daughter, Marina, wife of the patrician Vincenzo Grimani, inherited it in 1595 and added a left wing and garden in the back. The property passed down through her male heirs, eventually going to a Vendramin nephew of Marina's daughter in 1738. The palace is presently the Casinò Municipale of Venice.

(fig. 37).[27] Even though it could not be mistaken for a Roman, or even a Tuscan, palace, it is probably the first Renaissance residence built in Venice that the Roman architect Vitruvius would have looked upon with some favor. For this is a *legible* facade. The trademark Codussian windows are set into a framework formed of double flat pilaster strips on the ground floor, fluted columns on the first *piano nobile* and smooth columns on the second. Corinthian capitals are used throughout. Passing through that triumphal watergate, a visitor would have entered not a grubby storage room for merchandise but the Venetian version of a classical atrium, decorated with frescoes by Giorgione depicting allegorical figures of Diligence and Prudence (fig. 38).[28]

This expression of traditional Venetian virtues in a building that was a *casa* in name only, was reinforced by the biblical passage inscribed on the facade: NON NOBIS D[OMI]NE NON NOBIS – Not unto us Lord, Not unto us. Pious spectators could turn to Psalms 115 to complete the message: "But unto Thy name be the glory given."[29] Indeed, public inscriptions on private palaces declaring a personal credo or seeking to legitimize ambitious building campaigns that stretched the parameters of Venetian *mediocritas* were not uncommon in this period.[30]

The Trevisan family had dedicated *their* marble-encrusted palace, built around 1500 on the canal behind the Ducal

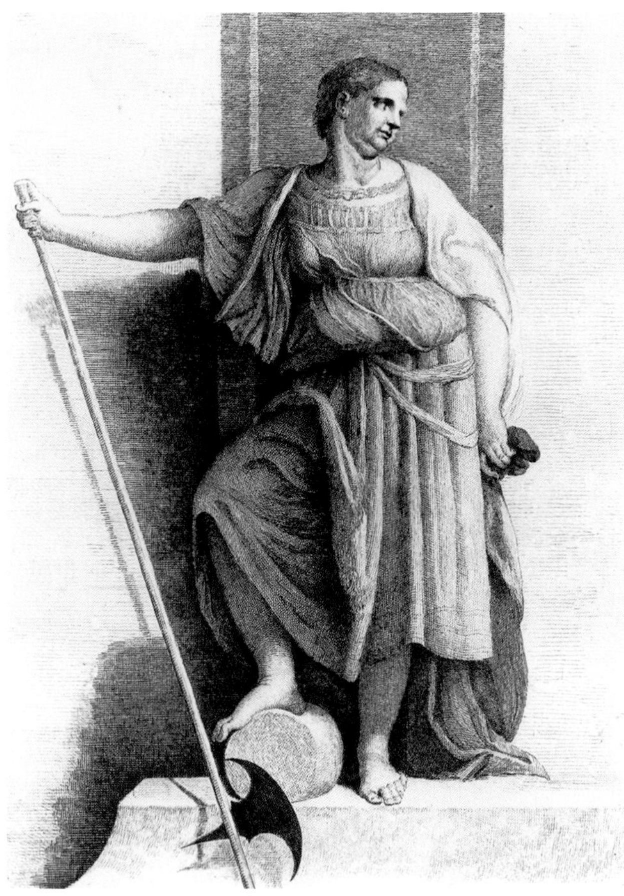

38 Antonio Maria Zanetti, *Diligence*, engraving after Giorgione, from his *Varie pitture a fresco de' principali maestri veneziani ora la prima volta con le stampe pubblicate* (Venice, 1760). The work was once frescoed in the courtyard of Ca' Loredan-Vendramin-Calergi. Princeton, Princeton University Library Special Collections, Marquand Library.

Palace, with the inscriptions SOLI DEO and HONOR ET GLORIA – To God alone, Honor and Glory. The Della Torre used exactly the same phrase above the main door of their far more modest house behind SS Apostoli and, for good measure, added another inscription on a window embrasure on a side wall around the corner: SPES MEA IN DEO EST – My hope is in God. And in the enclosed courtyard there was a well-head carved with the family arms and another inscription, now in the Venetian vernacular, summing up a basic tenet of patrician ideology: SERVENDO SE AQUISTA – By serving, one acquires.[31] Above the main water portal of Palazzo Barbarigo della Terrazza the owners expressed hopes for a heavenly reward: IN TE DOMINE SPERAVI NON CONFUNDAR IN AETERNUM – I have put my hope in you, Lord, so as not to be confounded in eternity (fig. 39).[32]

The exuberance of this residential building boom was dampened by the Wars of Cambrai and Venice's military defeat at Agnadello in 1509. The city without walls that had survived unviolated for more than eight centuries lost almost all her mainland territories in a matter of a few weeks. It was a time for reflection and considerable soul-searching. Many expressed the view that Venice's defeats were due to the pursuit of private goals at the expense of the common good: the rejection, in short, of the traditional values of *mediocritas* and restraint expressed in the Della Torre inscriptions. Among the pejorative expressions that appeared frequently in sumptuary legislation of the period were *ambizioso*, meaning ambitious, and *superbo*, meaning proud, with repeated admonitions against superfluous expenditures. It should be noted, however, that there were never any legislative efforts to restrict palace building *per se*, only their interior decoration.[33] In any event, the calls for moral renewal of the second decade of the sixteenth century were followed by calls for an architectural renewal in the third.

Indeed, in the late 1520s Doge Andrea Gritti virtually transformed the Piazzetta of San Marco into a second Rome in a campaign of urban renewal that came to be known as the Roman *renovatio*, resulting in a bold expression of *Romanitas* in the heart of the city. Three buildings carried the symbolic message: the Loggetta in front of the *campanile*; the Biblioteca Marciana; and, facing the lagoon, the new mint. The term *renovatio* had a special meaning in Venice – different from Rome, for example, with its deep

39 Inscription on the portal of the water entrance of Palazzo Barbarigo della Terrazza on Rio San Polo, sixteenth century.

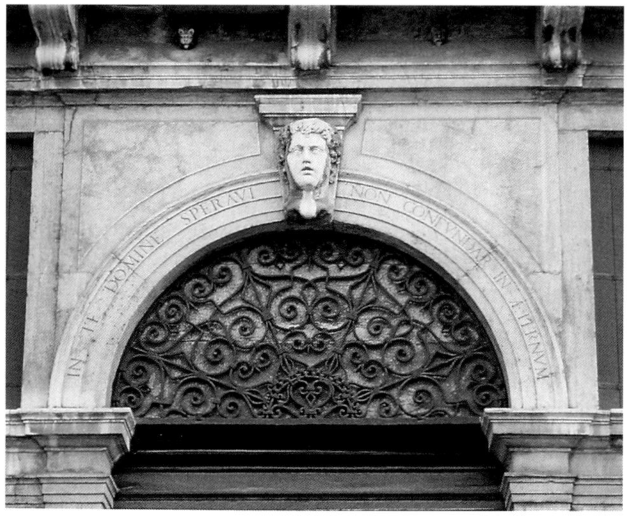

classical roots. The Venetian *renovatio* was grounded in the idea that the city was born in perfection and that all returns were to that original perfection and not to the borrowed glory of another civilization such as Rome.[34] It was a deeply conservative – and conserving – notion, and one that allowed the incorporation of modern – that is, antique – elements into the prevailing Byzantine–Islamic–Gothic scheme, without rejecting what was already there.[35]

And yet while Gritti was striving toward a more universalizing statement in public buildings, it was inevitable that pretensions toward grandeur would spread into the private sphere. Indeed, it was precisely during these years that Venetian patricians were beginning to withdraw from active participation in trade and desiring to be gentlemen in fact as well as in name.[36] Two competing ethical models were in play: on the one hand, that espoused by the traditionalists, who sought to preserve the deeply rooted principle of *mediocritas*; and on the other, that practiced by the proponents of a new trend toward private magnificence.

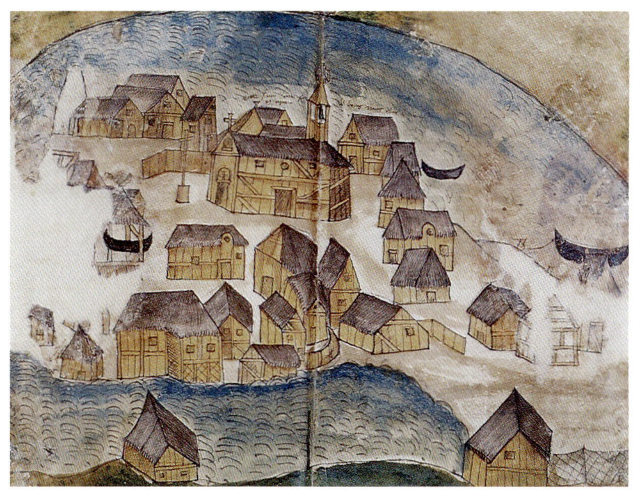

40 View of early Venice near San Lio, from Tommaso Diplovatazio, *Tractatus de Venetae urbis libertate et eiusdem Imperii dignitate et privilegiis*. Cod. Lat XIV 72 (2991), ff. 22 v–23 r. Venice, Biblioteca Nazionale Marciana.

Without Concern for Vainglory

The traditionalists were supported by Venetian chroniclers who, inspired by Andrea Gritti's call for *renovatio*, were looking back to the origins of the city to recast the Venetian myth of equality and republican liberty in terms that responded to the needs of the present. The earliest written source, and a fundamental text, was the sixth-century account of Cassiodorus, who had described small settlements of fishermen, with rich and poor living side by side in similar houses.[37]

One chronicler, writing in 1524, augmented Cassiodorus's text with an imaginary watercolor view of the area around San Lio filled with modest wooden dwellings with thatched roofs (fig. 40). The patrician Nicolò Zen (see fig. 5), writing about fifteen years later, asked why some great civilizations that had – like Venice – begun "without pomp, without concern for vainglory or needless expenses," lost their reputations and fell into decadence. He answered: "They think only of idleness and pleasure, and then they come to value architects, songs, sounds, players, palaces, clothes, and having put arms aside, they scorn furthermore those who enjoy them, and certain other follies are valued, that are commonly called courtiers' arts."[38] But it was not architecture *per se* that he condemned. It was *private* magnificence.

In a second treatise, Zen invented further particulars to supplement Cassiodorus's cryptic account. One of the early settlers called Daulus, he wrote, had proposed that the wealthy immigrants who were taking refuge in the lagoon from the raids of Attila should leave behind their "palaces and magnificent habitations in order for one not to exceed the other; fixing by law, that all residences should be equal, alike, of similar size and ornamentation."[39] Daulus thus supplied mythic authority for the collective ethos of *mediocritas* that had ensured the liberty of the republic from its origins to his own time. Accordingly, Nicolò's uncle, Francesco Zen, embraced the notion of a classical *renovatio* in the civic sphere, but resisted the push toward private magnificence in the construction of a new family palace, beginning in 1533.

The *casa* that Francesco designed for himself and his three brothers was situated in the far reaches of Cannaregio near the church of the Gesuiti (fig. 41). This fact alone may account for a certain restraint of opulence, but Francesco's intentions are documented by the palace itself and the treatises written by his nephew Nicolò during the course of the construction. It featured a very long facade facing the Rio di Santa Caterina, fronting a commodious rectangular building originally intended to accommodate the families of four brothers in separate apartments. It looks unexceptional but for the alternating roundheaded and ogee arches on the *piano nobile* – an unusual combination in a period of stylistic consistency. It was as if Francesco Zen either did not know the difference between Gothic and Renaissance or could not decide between them and decided to use both. But a recent study makes a convincing case that he was well informed on architectural principles, with close ties to the theorist Sebastiano Serlio, who advised on the interior

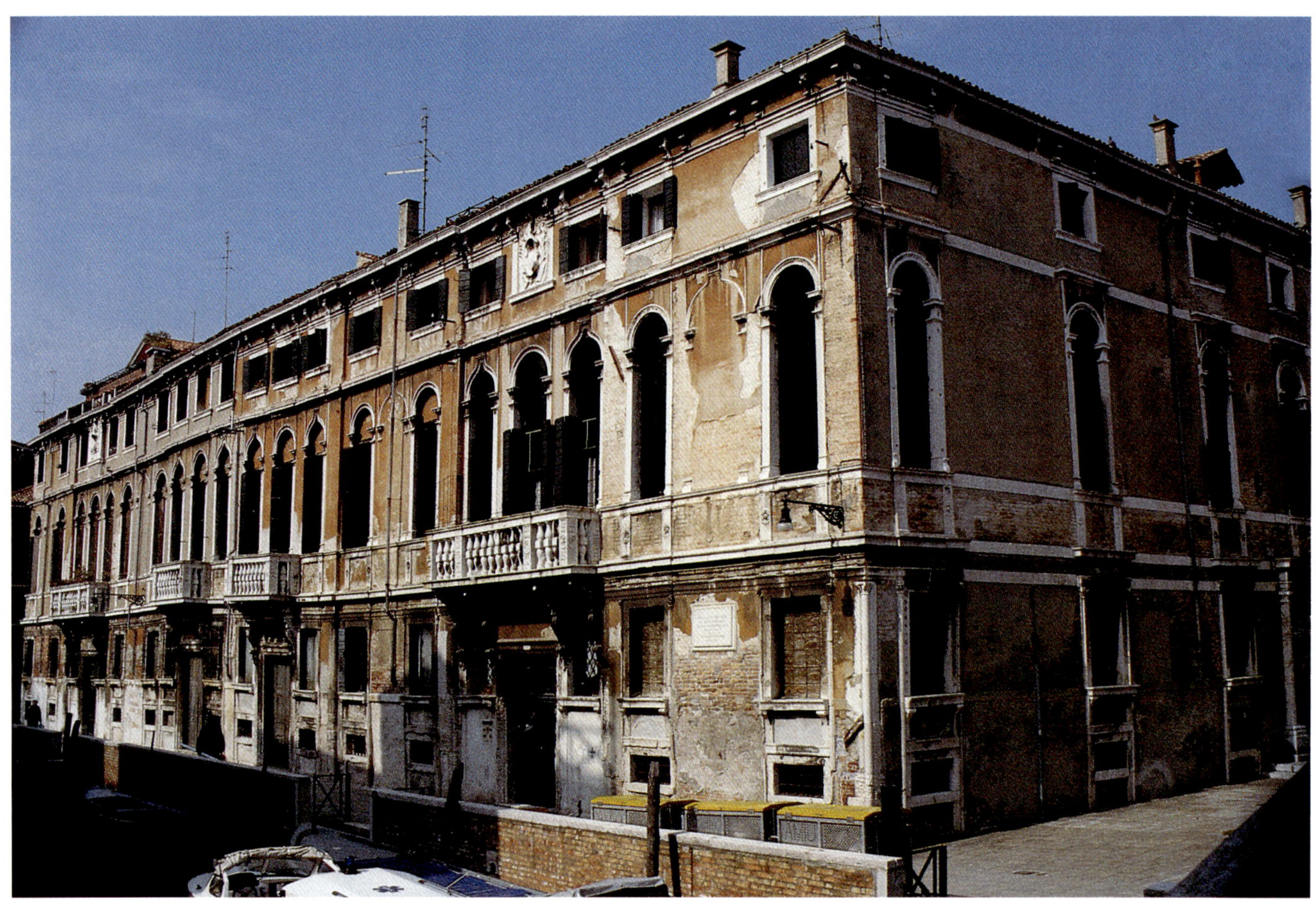

41 Palazzo Zen, 1533–53. Francesco Zen, author of the project, died before it was completed. The palace was then reduced to three apartments but four portals remained, the two in the center opening to a single residence, that of his brother Vincenzo. In his will, Francesco asked to be conducted to his tomb "by the workers, between masons, carpenters, and stonecutters," accompanied by the architect Sebastiano Serlio and the foreman Innocenzo Lombardo.

layout and decoration of the palace. Francesco, in short, would have known full well what he was doing.[40]

Similar combinations of alternating round and pointed arches had been used in Venetian paintings of the preceding period to denote architecture of the Levant, particularly in works by Vittore Carpaccio. By adopting this strategy of architectural "contamination," Francesco could refer to age-old family interests in the Mediterranean and Middle East, in trade, arms, and diplomacy, as well as his cognizance of Serlio's rules of modern architecture.[41] These suggestive allusions were reinforced by *bas-reliefs* decorating the lower plane of the cresting cornice and depicting oriental scenes including city gates, camels, and palm trees. The reliefs were augmented, moreover, by frescoes on the main facade that had been specified in the testament of Francesco Zen's father, Pietro, and portrayed the notable deeds of their ancestor, Carlo Zen, hero in the War of Chioggia at the end of the fourteenth century.

Such a display may seem as blatant a demonstration of family self-promotion as might be imagined, but it was, in fact, well within the norms of Venetian architectural decorum. Indeed, the palace – as large as it was – had a low and modest profile, with only one *piano nobile* – and this for a family with great wealth, culture, and political prominence. Most families were building *up* in that period, but the Zen were not on the Grand Canal, where land was costly and in short supply, and they had the option of building *out*. Frescoed walls were common already in the fifteenth century, responding to the Venetian taste for polychrome decoration, and they remained popular in this period as an alternative to more costly marbles. Since most such painted facades in the cinquecento featured allegorical figures or scenes from Roman history, the subject matter of the Zen frescoes was unusually personal.[42] And yet it was fitting. For the history of the Zen family was at one with the history of the republic right up to the present.

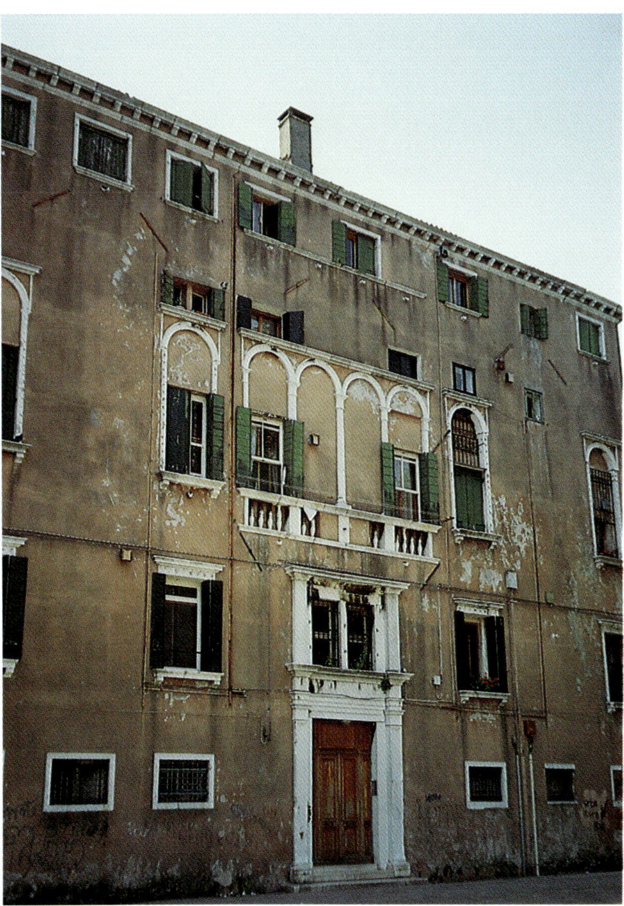

42 Palazzo Gritti at San Francesco della Vigna, begun ca. 1525. The palace was bought in 1586 from Andrea Gritti's heirs for 20,000 ducats by the Venetian Senate, who gave it to the Pope as a residence for papal legates. With the windows of the *piano nobile* filled in, the present building is a sad remnant of a once dignified, if unornate, residence deemed suitable for ambassadorial use.

Doge Andrea Gritti also adopted an ostentatiously austere mode for his own monumental *casa* at San Francesco della Vigna, built in 1525 for his eventual retirement and, like Ca' Zen, situated in an outlying area of the city (fig. 42).[43] But his vision of *renovatio* in the public sphere, being carried out by the architect Jacopo Sansovino at the time of Gritti's death in 1538, had consequences in the private sphere about which he would probably have had deep reservations. And this brings us to the second ethical model, championed for the most part by families with connections to the papal court in Rome. It was a model of unabashed classical magnificence, not just in public sites, but also in domestic architecture.

* * *

Mediocritas *and* Romanitas

A comparison of the two palaces designed by Sansovino on the Grand Canal reveals the changing sensibility (figs. 43 and 44).[44] The first palace was commissioned by the patrician Zuanne Dolfin, presumably in 1536, just months after the Council of Ten had approved Sansovino's revolutionary model for a new mint, called the Zecca, which featured a mixture of rustication and the Doric order. Dolfin was sole heir to a considerable shipping fortune and was actively engaged in trade himself. He was one of those "gentlemen in name rather than in fact" of whom Machiavelli would have approved. Dolfin's new *casa*, with its clear geometry and hierarchy of the Doric, Ionic, and Corinthian orders, effected the translation of Gothic into a classicizing language in a manner that Vitruvius would not only have looked upon with favor – as with Ca' Loredan-Vendramin-Calergi of about thirty years earlier – but would have positively embraced.[45]

And yet, although Dolfin's palace echoes the continuous ground-floor arcade and some internal features of the Zecca, in its *public* persona it was discreet and even traditional in spirit. With the familiar tripartite arrangement of the facade, it did not really look Roman at all. The arcade functioned as a public walkway – and still does – while sustaining the living quarters of the family above it. Behind it were the ground-floor warehouses characteristic of the *casa-fondaco* of the Venetian merchant since the Middle Ages.[46] Furthermore, this *casa* was deliberately built to conform to the scale and character of its neighbors, most notably Ca' Bembo, the large Gothic palace next door. Well embedded in its surroundings, Ca' Dolfin offers a striking demonstration of Sansovino's singular ability to honor the precepts of *mediocritas* while building something big, modern, and subtly magnificent, with a price tag of no fewer than 30,000 ducats.[47]

Sansovino's second palace on the Grand Canal was another matter altogether (fig. 44). The story begins with the palace of Zorzi Corner that had attracted the attention of Marin Sanudo at the end of the fifteenth century (fig. 30). In 1527, Zorzi died and left a huge fortune to his four surviving sons. In his will he ordered that the palace on the Grand Canal should remain in the Corner family forever, never to be sold, divided, or given away. Two of the sons, Zuane and Giacomo, remained in the palace, but in 1532 it burned to the ground and they moved into another Corner palace across town. This branch of the Corner family was one of the wealthiest in Venice. If there were ever four sons who could afford the cost of rebuilding the old palace, thus honoring the wishes of their father, it was them. Nonethe-

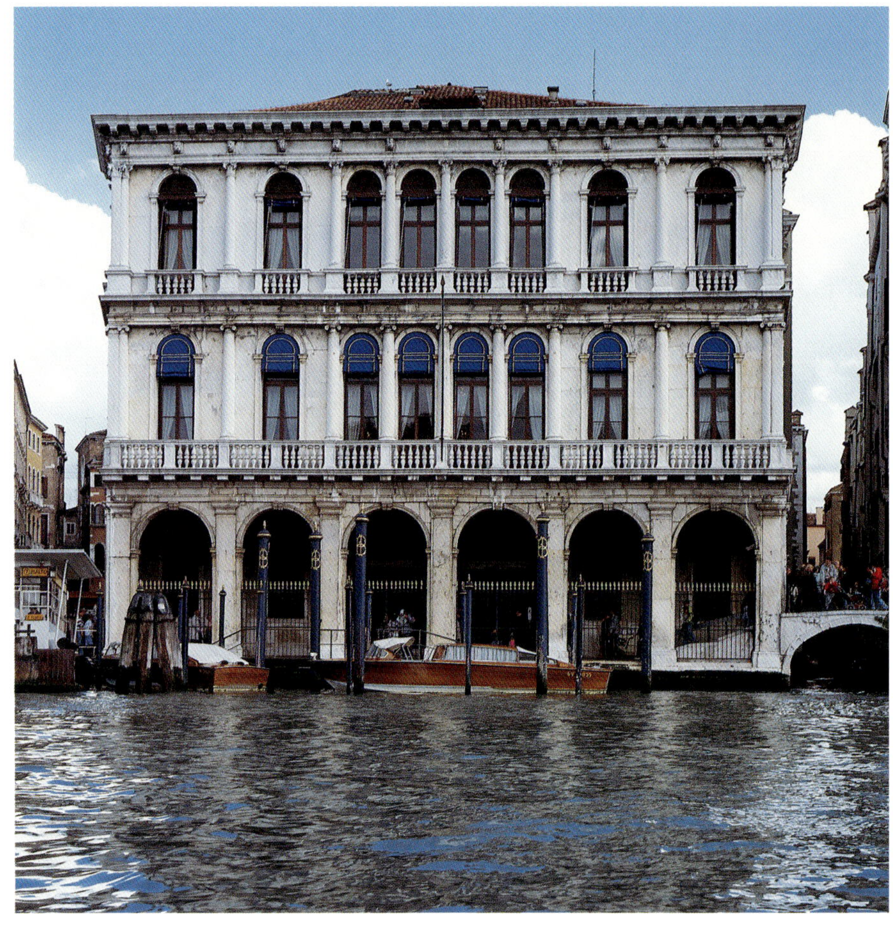

43 Ca' Dolfin on the Grand Canal, begun 1538. The symmetrical facade masks a trapezoidal floor plan that splays out at the back. Because of the pedestrian walkway in front, the water entrance is on the canal to the right. Like Ca' Corner della Ca' Grande, the building features a Roman-style central courtyard, unusual in Venetian residences. The interior was completely rebuilt in the late eighteenth century for Ludovico Manin, the last doge of Venice.

less, they wasted no time in petitioning the state for disaster relief. They cited the fact that three of the brothers had eight daughters, who would eventually need dowries, and many sons, and that the fourth brother was a cardinal with a high-maintenance lifestyle. A new palace suitable to their needs would cost at least 50,000 ducats and they reminded the republic that it had supported others who had suffered similar misfortunes in the past. In a rationale for private magnificence that went back at least as far as Aristotle, they argued that the city itself would benefit most from such a beautiful structure. Finally, there was a clinching argument: the brothers belatedly laid claim to the 61,000-ducat dowry of their aunt, Caterina Corner, once queen of Cyprus, which had been deposited with the republic when her kingdom was handed over to Venetian rule in 1489. At the time of her death in 1510, Venice was involved in the Wars of Cambrai and the family did not seek restitution. But now it was the state's turn to be generous to its most loyal citizens. The Council of Ten agreed, at least in part, and supplied 30,000 ducats as seed money for the new project. That it was situated on the Grand Canal, which was becoming a grand state ceremonial route to welcome distinguished visitors to the city, would have been a major incentive for an aristocracy ever more concerned to show its nobility in fact as well as in name.[48]

And what a project it would be. After Giacomo, one of the sons, died in 1542 the *fraterna* was broken up and his son – named Zorzi after his grandfather and called Zorzetto – inherited the ruins of the great burnt-down *casa* on the Grand Canal. Shortly after 1545 he began construction of a new residence, Ca' Corner della Ca' Grande, with Jacopo

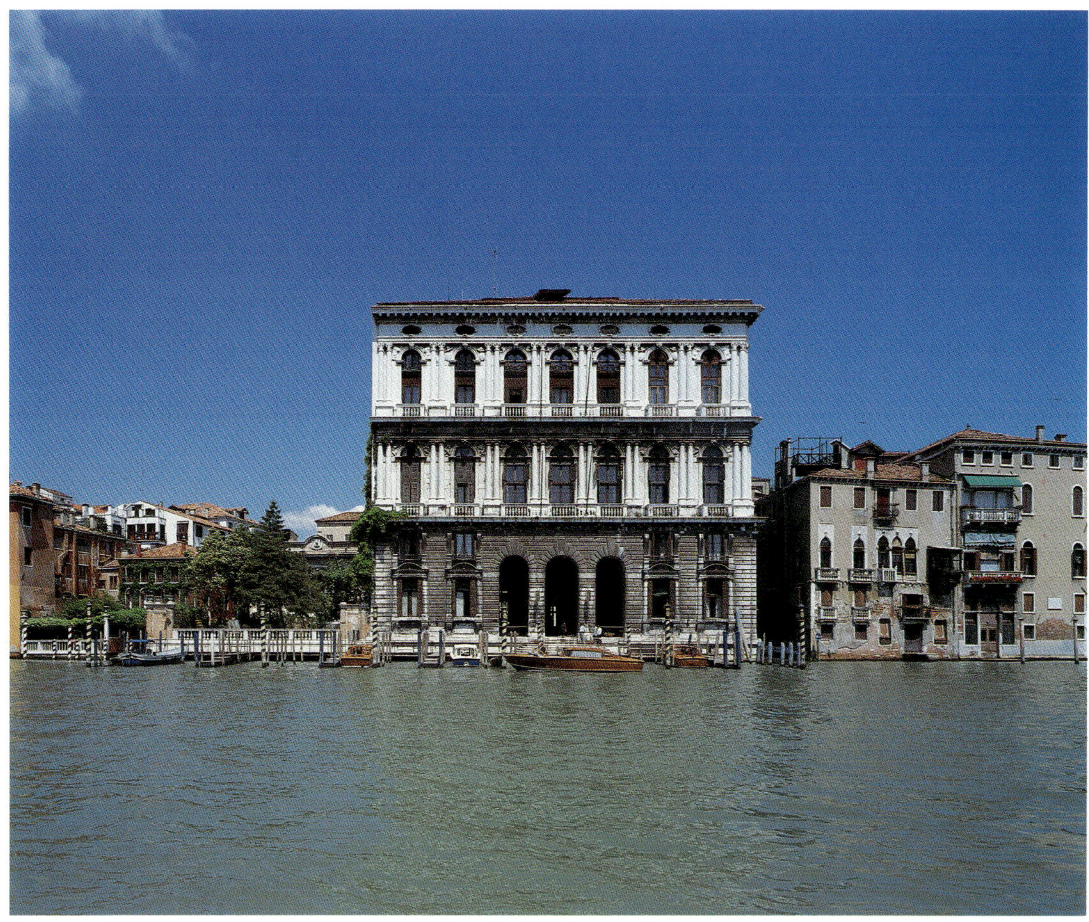

44 Ca' Corner della Ca' Grande, begun ca. 1545. The massive size and gleaming marble facade of the palace, sited on the north bank of the Grand Canal approaching Piazza San Marco, are clearly visible in the detail of Barzenti's map in figure 33.

Sansovino as architect, and by the 1560s he was living there. To the untutored eye, it appears to incorporate features of all three of Sansovino's key projects for the Piazzetta San Marco – the Zecca, the Biblioteca, and the Loggetta.[49]

The combined influences of the stunning new *Romanitas* borrowed from the Piazzetta complex, of family connections with Rome through a succession of cardinals, of wealth beyond imagination, and of an empty lot on the Grand Canal where Ca' Corner *della bella casa* had once stood, added up to an opportunity for blatant self-glorification that pushed the limits of the traditional Venetian model of *mediocritas*. Among the new palace's most notable features were its height and mass. Unlike Sansovino's Ca' Dolfin, it stood apart from, and in front of, its neighbors and towered over them. It was also distinctive in its formal language, moving toward an assertive Roman antique style and breaking more definitively with local traditions. Decorated with *bas-reliefs* of cuirasses, shields, war trumpets, and Roman armor in the spandrels of the arches on the two *piani nobili*, it reminded the onlooker of the Corner family's claims of descent from the Roman clan of the Scipios.[50] The palace was to be, in the words of a contemporary writer, "*magnificentiae exemplar*" (an example of magnificence) and "*nobilitatis theatrum*" (a theater of nobility).[51]

From all appearances, Zorzi Corner (and Sansovino for that matter) cared little for the law of Daulus, as hallowed as it may have been in Venetian rhetoric of the time. But he did not have to look far afield to find a theoretical rationale for his spectacular building activities. Two new literary genres emerged in those years that played a crucial role in sanctioning a new ethos for residential architecture in Venice: the *economica* treatise, which dealt with the manner of living *nobile*,[52] and the architectural treatise, most notably

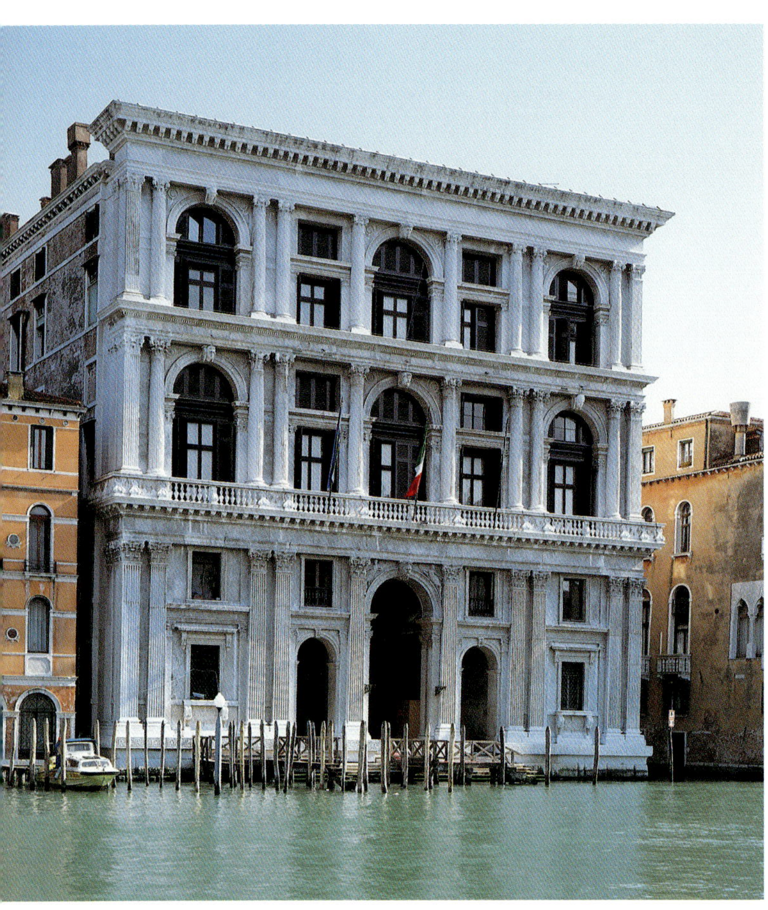

45 Ca' Grimani at San Luca on the Grand Canal, begun 1559. In accordance with its triumphalist architecture, the palace was the site of notable celebrations. In 1576 the dukes of Mantua were sumptuously entertained there. A generation later, it was again the site of luxurious festivities when Girolamo Grimani's son, Marino, rose to the dogeship in 1595, and in 1597 when the Dogaressa Morosina Morosini Grimani made a triumphal entry and was "crowned."

that of Serlio, whose first volume, Book IV, which dealt with the Roman orders, was published in Venice in 1537.[53]

The point of departure for the *economica* treatises was Alessandro Piccolomini's translation of Xenophon's *Oeconomicus*, a fourth-century treatise on the art of governing the home, published in Venice in 1540.[54] Two years later, Piccolomini brought out his own treatise, entitled (in translation), *The principles of the happy life of the man born noble and in a free city*.[55] Similar works followed by other writers, who depended on Aristotle as well as Xenophon. The central premise was that the house, as the most tangible symbol of family identity and continuity, should balance *comodità* (convenience) with *decoro* (honor) in its design. Its dimensions, its floor plan, its decorations, and its furnishings were all eloquent signs of the family's status and quality of life. Although some writers were more oriented toward rural than city life, they all presented principles and norms shared by the new aristocratic elite that had taken over most of the old citizen republics of Italy.[56]

For Venice's mercantile nobility, the demands of honor and convenience had traditionally been balanced between a magnificent facade facing the Grand Canal and a ground floor inside that served as a repository for merchandise.[57] The palace of Zuanne Dolfin is a case in point. He still lived according to the precepts of Prudence and Diligence, as exemplified by a ground-floor hallway flanked by warehouses for his own use that might also be rented out to others. But as wealthy merchants like Zorzi Corner began to refashion themselves into nobles in fact as well as in name, their homes were refashioned as well, with presentation taking precedence over parsimony.

By the time Ca' Corner della Ca' Grande was begun, Serlio had already moved to France and was writing his Book VI, which dealt specifically with domestic architecture.[58] He was concerned not only with the proper neighborhood, but also the proper house for the various social and economic levels, and he organized the book according to a hierarchical structure of society with houses for the rich, the middling, and the poor. The concept, already articulated by Leon Battista Alberti and Il Filarete in the fifteenth century, was by now part of the noble consciousness of the period, even in Republican Venice.[59] Giovanni Maria Memmo, the author of an *economica* treatise, considered the issue from a Venetian perspective. He warned that many a patrician had come to ruin for building a princely palace beyond his means and subjecting his family to shame and distress. The palace should also, he concludes, "be decorated and furnished according to the condition of the patron and the custom of the city."[60] At stake was the order of society.

Ca' Corner della Ca' Grande soon inspired emulation. In 1556, Girolamo Grimani, a Procurator of San Marco whose family credentials and balance sheets were equal to those of the Corner, acquired a ruined house on the Grand Canal, hired the architect Michele Sanmicheli and broke ground for a new palace of his own. It too was oversized in respect to its neighbors, but it presented a different notion of classical grandeur (fig. 45). Although it adopted Mauro Codussi's Ca' Corner-Spinelli as its starting point, it is *polemically* Roman with a triumphal arch scheme that informs the ground floor and a monumental framework of tall, fluted Corinthian pilasters and columns.[61]

Such displays of family self-aggrandizement as the palaces of the Grimani and the Corner made a mockery of the ethos of *mediocritas*. The precepts of the treatise writers on architecture and *economica* had taken hold, and a legitimizing theory to support the new ventures in Venetian terms was required. Not surprisingly, it was Jacopo Sansovino's son, Francesco, who would articulate a complementary rationale of architectural magnificence. It may be no coincidence that he was the illegitimate son of an immigrant – a *cittadino* at best – who was unencumbered with the weight of ethical baggage that every patrician took as his birthright.

As discussed earlier, Francesco gave a good account in his 1581 *Venetia città nobilissima* of the opulent interior decoration and appointments of the *case* of his time.[62] But he also wrote at length about the structures themselves. He observed that the outlying neighborhoods had been built up in the infancy of Venice and that they still showed the "parsimony of the early founders." Facing the influential writings of Nicolò Zen head on, he allowed "one reads that in the early times, our ancestors, wishing to demonstrate union and parity in all things, built their houses all equal in height according to the law of Daulus. But after the wealth had increased through trade, that was always the vigor of this republic, the [houses] were raised and lowered according to the taste of the builders,"[63] and the people built "palaces and houses of much grandeur."[64] Thus, residential building was not properly the domain of ethics; it fell into the purview of taste.

One Part by Which to Grasp the Whole

And it is clear where Sansovino stood on matters aesthetic. He observed that as the city grew through the centuries, barbaric Gothic architecture had filled it up, almost extinguishing the beauties of Rome – a situation that was now being rectified. He went on to single out those palaces or *case* that were "the most prominent and important," thus "noting to foreigners – desirous of seeing everything – one part by which they would grasp the whole." Seventy were cited by name: twenty-three on the Grand Canal, forty-five elsewhere in the city proper, and two on the island of Giudecca.[65]

Looking at the Grand Canal, Sansovino praised four *case* that stood out above the others according to four criteria: architecture (that is, good design according to the Vitruvian model), craftsmanship, size, and expense. The total cost of these homes, he noted with approval, amounted to 200,000 ducats. He began with Ca' Loredan-Vendramin-Calergi, "of great mass and of great height, and prior in time to the others . . . [It] is very noble, since in addition to the great number of rooms inside, the facade is covered with Greek marbles and [has] large windows all with Corinthian columns" (fig. 37).[66] Then came Sanmicheli's Ca' Grimani, "which excels in great length of regal rooms and of every other thing [and] is most rich in craftsmanship, since the stone carving, the carved foliage, and other delicacies made almost down to the foundations are of excessive expense" (fig. 45).[67]

He concluded his list of honor with the two palaces designed by his father. Ca' Dolfin was, he intoned, "the first [palace] after the Loredan that was built in Venice with the rules of architecture [that] is worthy of praise" (fig. 43). Why is this? "Since it occupies a great space of land, with a courtyard in the middle surrounded by loggias in the Roman manner, the exterior has a well-designed facade and inside it has very large and comfortable rooms."[68] But his greatest enthusiasm was reserved for Ca' Corner della Ca' Grande: "for site, for magnificence, for capacity, for richness of stones, for structure, and for symmetry, and among all the others memorable . . . And it looks out at the lagoon and is in open view all around by its height . . . [appearing] to the spectator full of majesty" (fig. 44).[69]

Sansovino had a clear preference for buildings designed according to the precepts of Vitruvius, but good Venetian that he was, he did not ignore tradition. Echoing the words of Marin Sanudo of nearly a century before, he wrote: "But all these four are surpassed in the site and size of the edifice by Ca' Foscari, very old in fabric and [built] according to the German custom" (fig. 25).[70] How had this home overcome its Gothic style to play such a distinguished role in Sansovino's inventory? Aside from a grandeur that could be claimed by many such palaces, it is largely a question of size, location, and visibility. Situated at the bend of the Grand Canal, its inhabitants enjoyed a sweeping view and were viewed in return from the Rialto Bridge all the way down to Palazzo Contarini dal Zaffo, just beyond the moorings of the present Accademia Bridge (see fig. 33).

The massive double palace of the Giustiniani next door to Ca' Foscari shared in its reflected glory and was mentioned by Sansovino in passing, but several other early buildings also met with his approval as representative parts of the urban fabric by which one might grasp the whole. The oldest were two Veneto–Byzantine palaces once connected with foreign royalty and also used by the republic to house visiting dignitaries: Ca' Corner Piscopia-Loredan given to the Corner family by the King of Cyprus in the fourteenth century (fig. 31); and the palace of the Duke of Ferrara (now known as the Fondaco dei Turchi), the latter described as "ancient and built in the form of a castle with a German structure" (fig. 46).[71] For the Gothic era Sansovino cites five palaces in addition to those of the Foscari and the Giustiniani. These include the massive Ca' Pisani, now the Gritti Palace Hotel, "of the German style, but with a

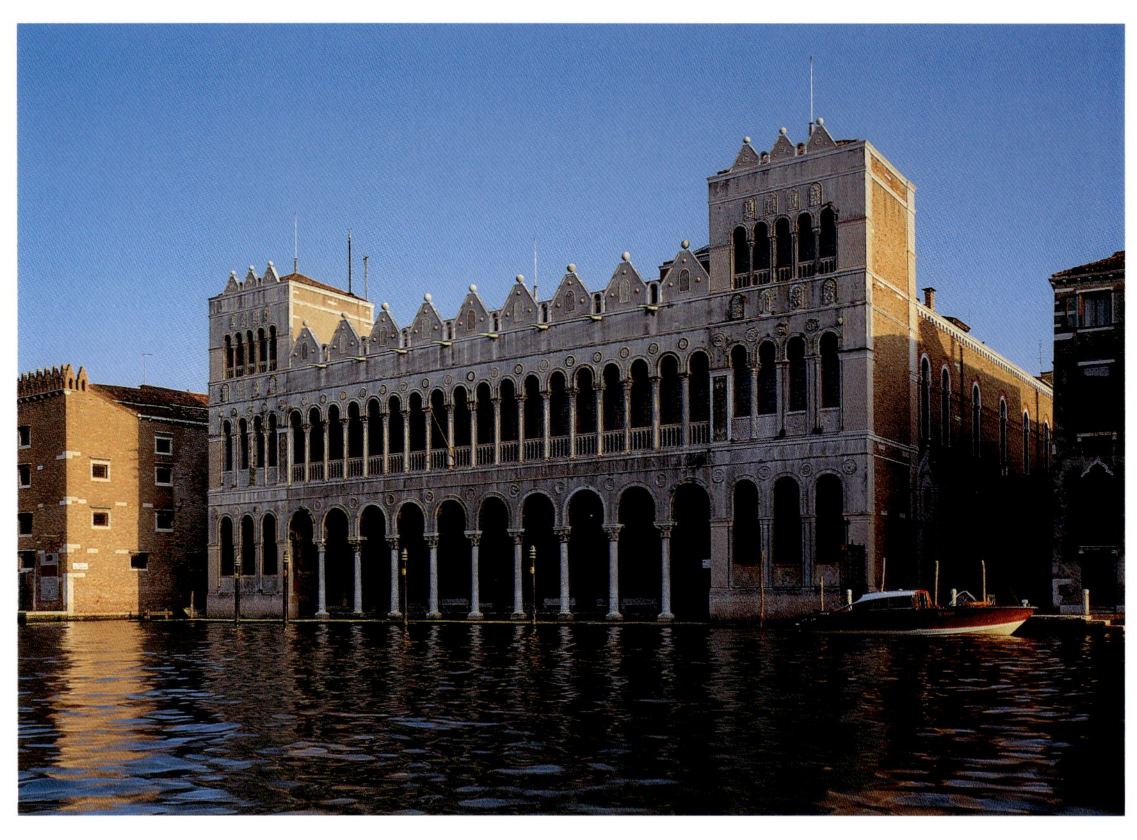

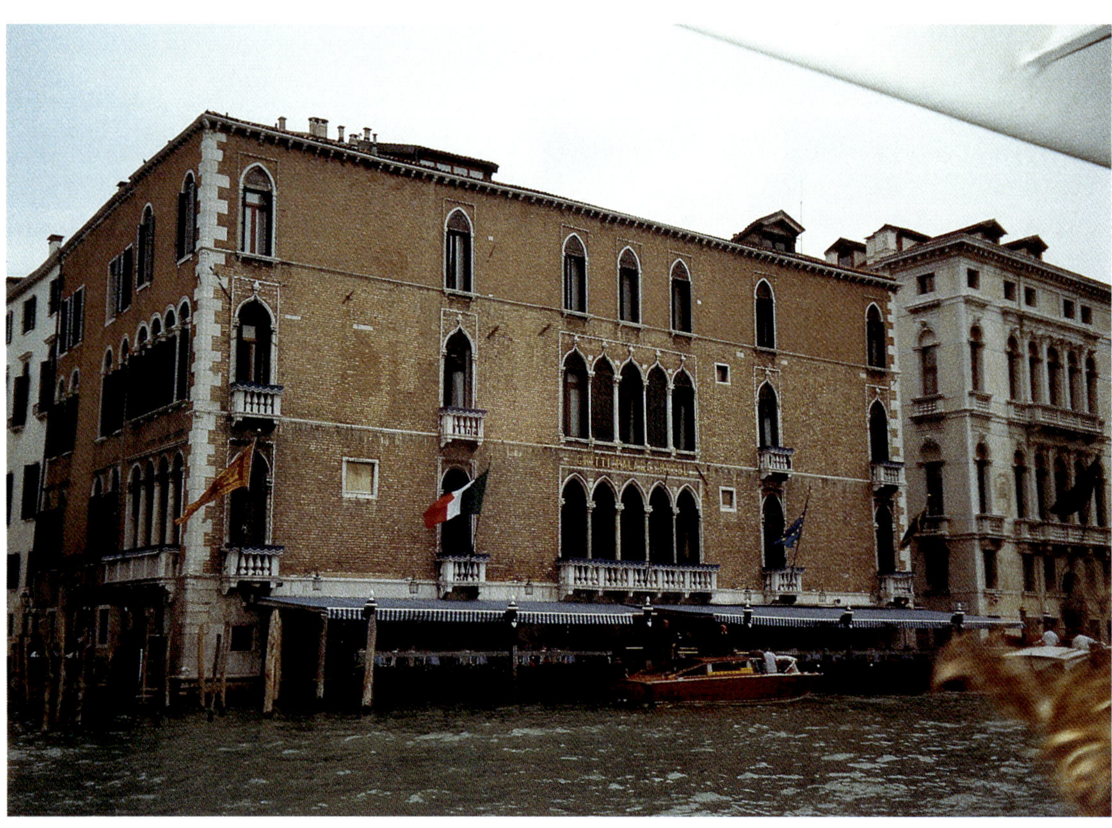

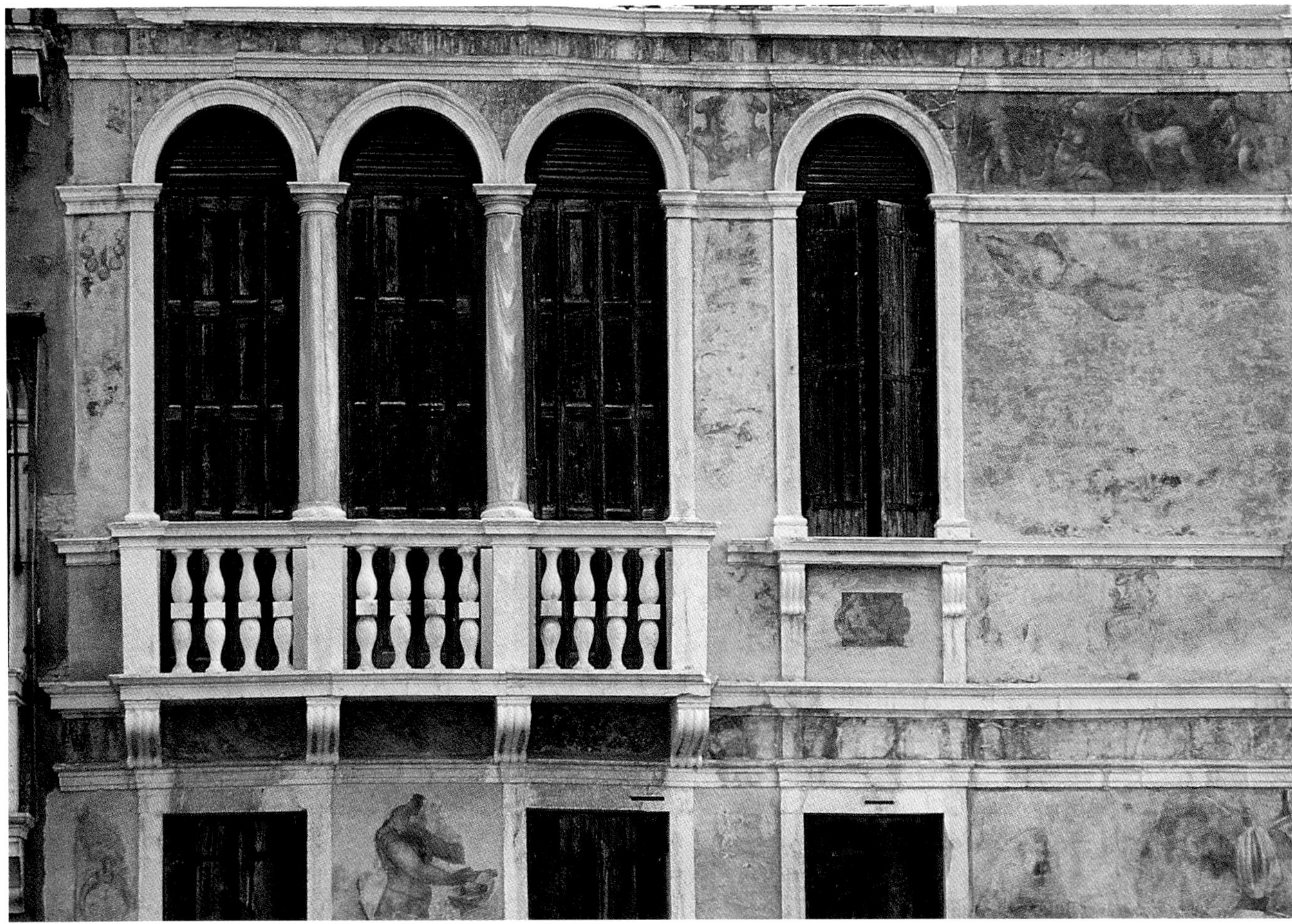

46 (*facing page top*) Fondaco dei Turchi, late twelfth century. Originally built as a palace for the Pesaro family, this Veneto–Byzantine palace represents a building type destined to have a long life in Venice. It featured a porticoed facade on the waterfront with a ground-floor area for merchandise and storage and the living quarters above. It was sold to the Venetian Signoria – an important deliberative body of state, comprising the Doge, his six councilors, and the three heads of the judicial courts – which gave it as a gift to the marchese of Ferrara in 1381 for services in the War of Chioggia. Aside from two confiscations during wars in which Ferrara opposed Venice, it remained in possession of the dukes of Ferrara for most of the period until it was ceded to Cardinal Aldobrandini, the nephew of Pope Clement VIII in 1602. In 1618 the palace was sold to Doge Antonio Priuli, who rented it to Ottoman merchants as living quarters and a warehouse for merchandise and it became known as the Fondaco dei Turchi. In 1648, through a dowry, it was given to the Pesaro family. It was heavily (some would say overly) restored in the nineteenth century.

47 (*facing page bottom*) Ca' Pisani-Gritti at S. M. Giglio, beginning fifteenth century. The building is now the Gritti Palace Hotel.

48 (*above*) Ca' Barbarigo, Cannaregio 2256, Corte Bragadin, second half sixteenth century. The facade has deteriorated considerably since 1930, when an observer described the fresco decoration as divided into eighteen compartments, with figures including War, Peace, and Minerva.

durable and solid form" (fig. 47).[72] During his time it was adorned with resplendent frescoes. The critic Marco Boschini wrote in the seventeenth century that the large mural surfaces of the facade were "painted by the hand of Giorgione with many friezes of chiaroscuro, of red on red, yellow on yellow, and green on green, with various caprices of little *putti*, in the middle of which are painted four half-sized figures [of] Bacchus, Venus, Mars, and Mercury, colored *al naturale*."[73] A glimpse of the original multi-hued richness of the city is captured by the faded fragments still visible on Ca' Barbarigo on the Grand Canal near the Maddalena in Cannaregio (fig. 48). Painted around 1565–70 by Camillo Ballini, it was praised by Boschini for its frescoes of "Ceres on her chariot, Fame, Time, and various other figures."[74]

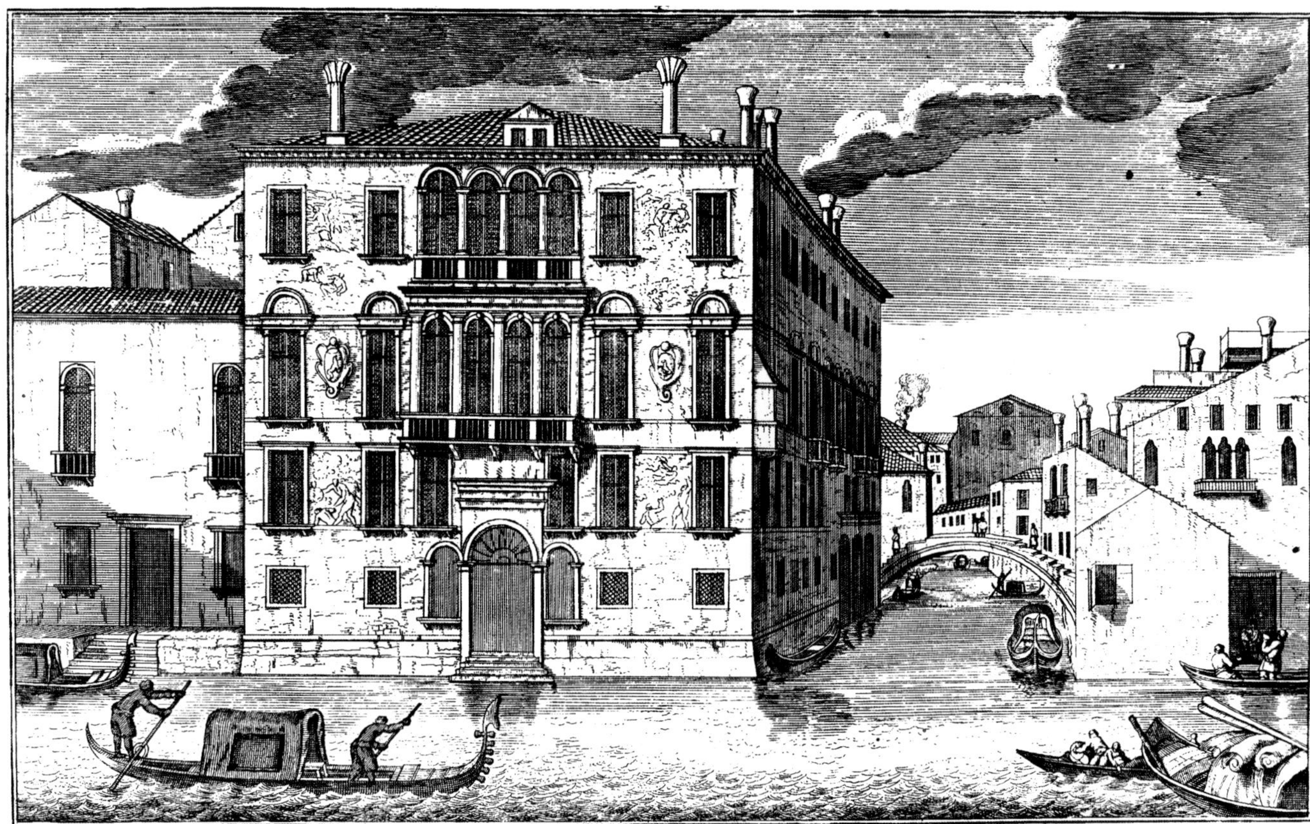

49 Luca Carlevarijs, *Facade of Ca' Gussoni-Grimani*, 1703. Engraving. According to a chronicle, the Archduke Carlo of Austria, brother of the Emperor Maximilian, watched a regatta in his honor from the balconies of the palace in 1569. From 1647 to ca. 1690, it was the seat of the Accademia Delfica Gussonia, a society devoted to exercises of extemporary eloquence.

Greater Pleasure to the Eyes

The Venetian taste for figures in living color on these classicizing facades was well articulated by Ludovico Dolce in his *Dialogue on Painting*. Putting words into the mouth of the writer Pietro Aretino, he asks:

> Is there a man, finally, who does not understand the ornament that painting offers to any object at all? For though their interior walls be dressed in extremely fine tapestries, and though the chests and tables be covered with most beautiful cloths, both public and private buildings suffer a marked loss of beauty and charm without some painting to ornament them. Outside, too, the facades of houses and palaces give far greater pleasure to the eyes of other men when painted by the hand of a master of quality than they do with incrustations of white marble and porphyry and serpentine embellished with gold.[75]

Dolce's taste for facades frescoed "by the hand of a master of quality" was a narrow polemical view, perhaps a pointed criticism of such confections as Ca' d'Oro, whose red Verona marble and white Istrian stone facade was overpainted with oil and varnish to bring out the colors and polychrome detailing in gold, ultramarine blue, and black on white veining to imitate marble (fig. 32). The Venetian delight in multicolored marble facades was noted by many visitors to the city, manifest not only in the red, white, and gray lozenge pattern of the Palazzo Ducale, but also on less exalted facades of homes where fictive brickwork was created by painting over real bricks, reinforcing the normal courses or creating a new masonry pattern.[76]

But of the remaining palaces on the Grand Canal that Sansovino had cited as the "most prominent and important," it is significant that no fewer than four featured facades frescoed with large-scale figures – a way for a family without the financial resources of the Grimani or the Corner to define a distinctive visual persona. In an earlier book that came out in 1556, Sansovino had already praised Ca' Gussoni for its beauty and the comfort of its interior appointments (fig. 49).[77] It would have been shortly after this that Jacopo Tintoretto painted the facade with a mixture of biblical and allegorical figures, thus fulfilling Dolce's dictum for parity between interior and exterior chromatic magnificence. These frescoes have long disappeared, but *Adam and Eve* and *Cain Slaying Abel* were still observable in the 1660s, and *Dusk* and *Dawn* were recorded in engravings by Anton Maria Zanetti a century later (fig. 50). Tintoretto drew them from relief copies that he kept in his studio of Michelangelo's sculptures in the New Sacristy in Florence. The interior courtyard was painted with images of classical statues – "giants in chiaroscuro" as Boschini put it – artful surrogates for the real antiques that had disappeared into the great collections by this time and were rarely available on the market. Whether a homage to Michelangelo or a challenge in the *paragone* debate, intended to prove that painting was superior to sculpture, the fresco program showed the culture of the patron and his piety as well.[78]

Despite his classical orientation, Sebastiano Serlio was also sensitive to the Venetian taste for chromatic facades. But, following Alberti – who objected to illusionism in wall-painting – he also counseled moderation:

> Therefore, if you have to decorate the facade of a building with painting, what is certain is that any opening which simulates sky or landscapes will not be suitable. These things break up the building – a solid and corporeal form – and transform it into a transparent one, without solidity, like a building that is unfinished or ruined. Similarly, neither human figures nor animals in colour are suitable unless one is simulating a window with people at it – and even these in calm postures rather than in bold movements.[79]

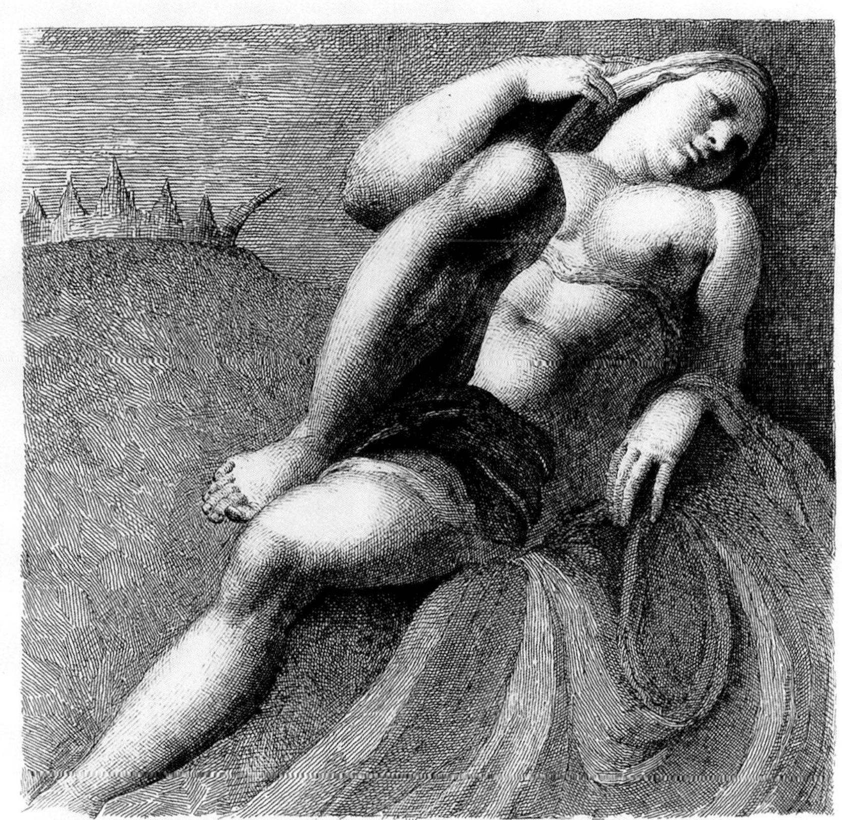

50 Anton Maria Zanetti, *Dawn*, engraving after Jacopo Tintoretto, from his *Varie pitture a fresco* (1760). The figure was once frescoed on the facade of Ca' Gussoni-Grimani on the Grand Canal (as in fig. 49). Princeton, Princeton University Library Special Collections.

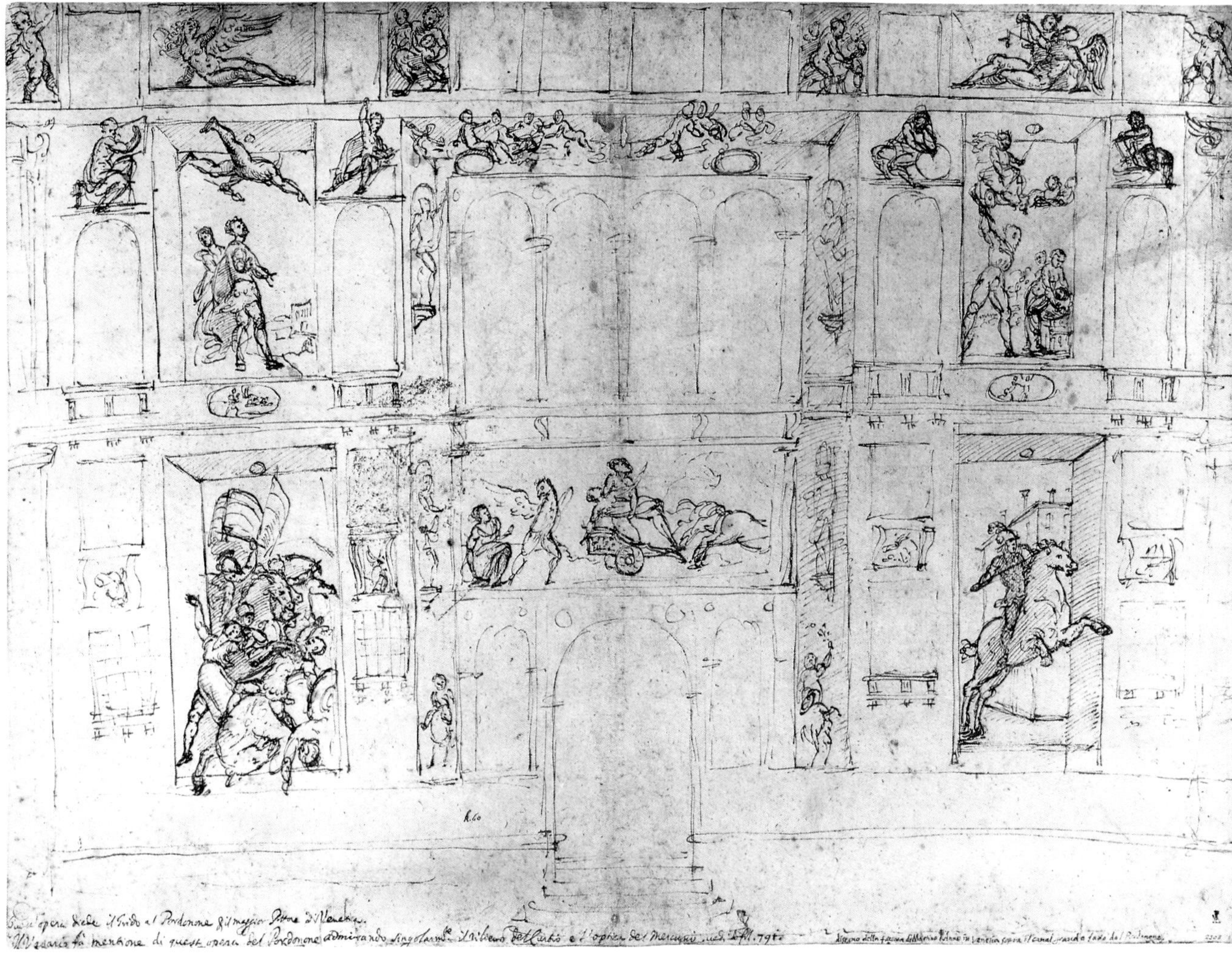

51 Giovanni Antonio da Pordenone, *Facade of the Palazzo Talenti-d'Anna*, 1531–32. Pen and brown ink, 412 × 559 mm. London, Victoria and Albert Museum.

Tintoretto's strongly foreshortened figures, silhouetted against the sky within the fictive "windows" allotted to them on the Gussoni facade, were probably a breach of Serlio's decorum. While Giorgio Vasari had greatly admired Pordenone's fresco of Mercury on the facade of Palazzo Talenti-d'Anna, "who flies freely through the air" (fig. 51),[80] Serlio wanted something that passed for real. He writes further, that if "you are to decorate a facade with painting and do it with sound judgement, you could simulate marble or some other stone, 'carving' whatever you wanted into it. You could also simulate niches containing bronze figures in high relief and even some *istoriette*, also simulating bronze, because making objects in this way will keep the work solid and worthy of praise by those who can tell real from false."[81]

What Serlio ultimately envisioned was something like the palace of Camillo Trevisan on Murano, with its sixteenth-century frescoes by Prospero Bresciano, later recorded in a wash drawing (fig. 52). Bresciano created a feigned masonry facade in yellow ochre chiaroscuro to serve as an armature for a program of fictive sculpture: statues of Hercules and Neptune in the niches and *bas-reliefs* of mythological and genre scenes and figures in the zone above the balcony level.[82] The chromatic richness and natural forms of the figured facades tended to provide a transition between the architectural character of the built environment and a physical setting of sky and water in constant movement.

* * *

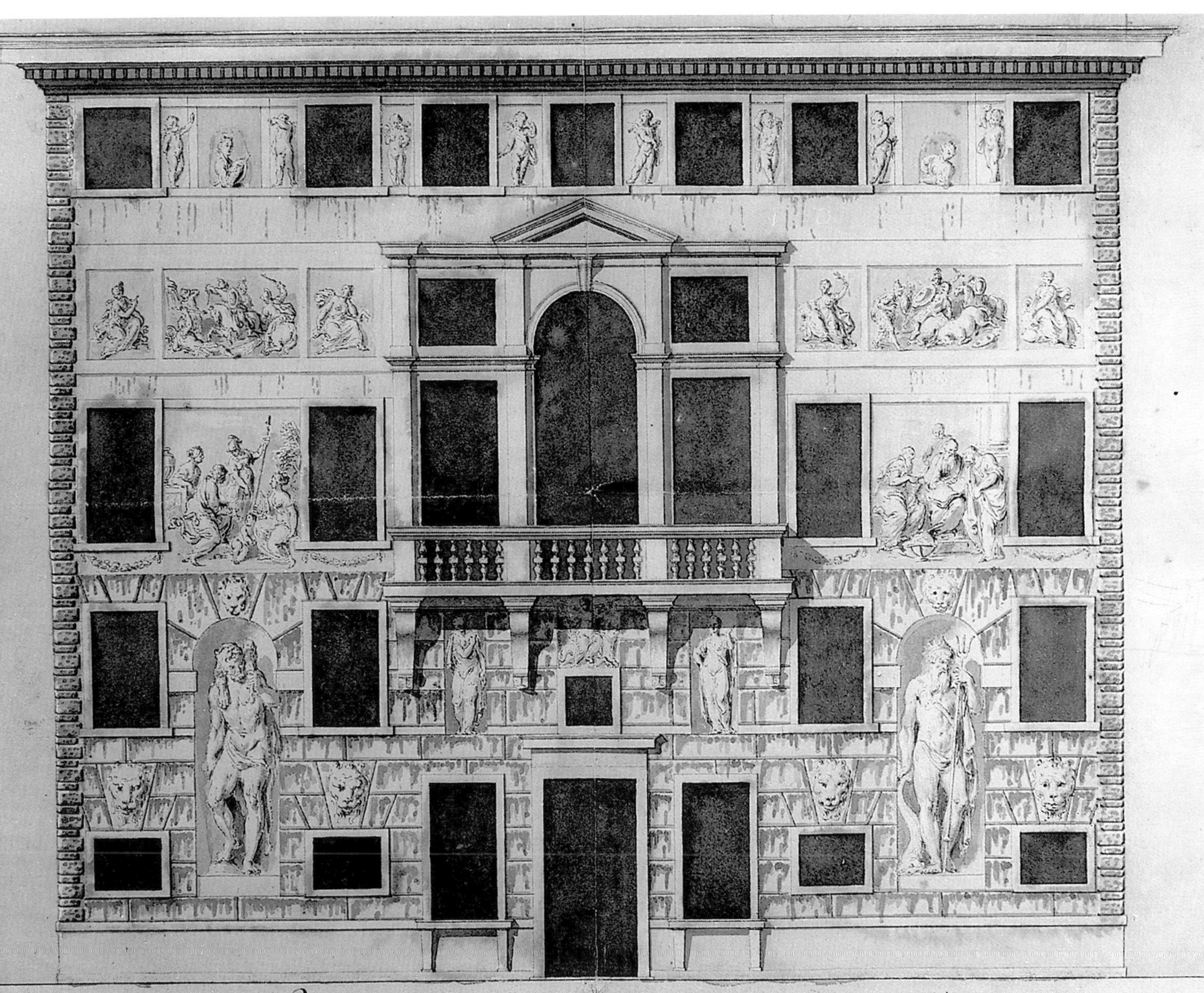

52 Pietro Uberti, *Facade of Palazzo Trevisan at Murano*, late seventeenth–early eighteenth century. Pen and ink with sepia watercolor, 462 × 330 mm. The fictive architecture of the facade was painted by Prospero Bresciano in chiaroscuro fresco with a feigned rusticated basement punctuated by lion heads. In addition to the monumental figures of Hercules and Neptune with a trident, and dolphins frescoed in the niches, battle scenes, mythologies, and allegorical figures were painted on the facade in the guise of antique low reliefs. Venice, Museo Civico Correr, c. III, n. 7337.

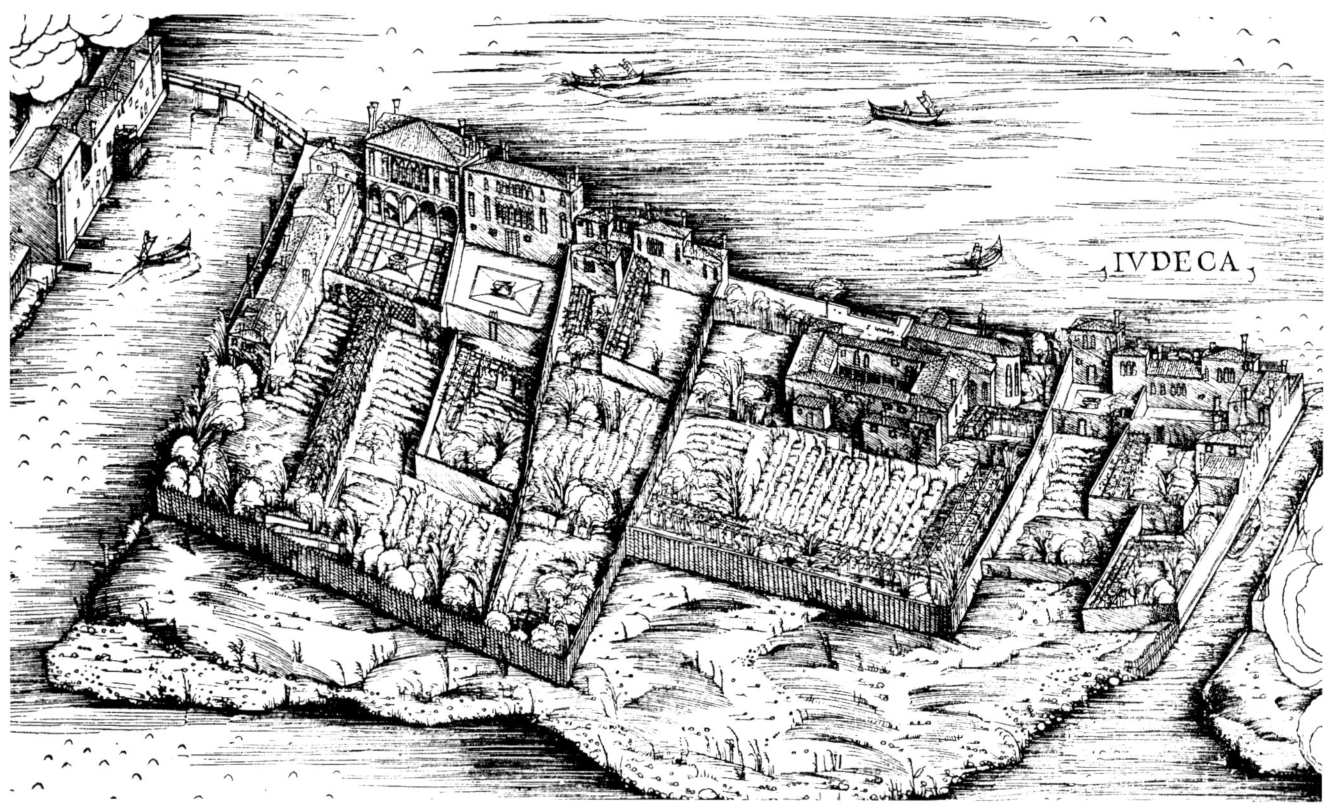

53 (*above*) Jacopo de' Barbari, *View of Venice*, detail of gardens on the Giudecca, 1500. Woodcut.

54 (*facing page*) Garden of Palazzo Nani-Luccheschi on the Grand Canal.

Nature Overcome by Human Artifice

Serlio had observed that since Venice was built on water and the land was very costly, most of the houses had neither gardens nor courtyards, a fact that he regretted.[83] But he understated the ingenuity of those who were determined to maintain a noble lifestyle that included the outdoor living space taken for granted by mainland aristocrats. Within the city itself, courtyards – often with a well-head – were ubiquitous (though not of the centralized Roman type to which Serlio probably referred), and well-planted gardens were not all that unusual, particularly on the periphery of the city.[84] As Francesco Sansovino would later write in *Venetia città nobilissima:* "There are also diverse gardens, aside from the common ones of simples, that are notable and famous for noble and rare plants, an incredible thing to foreigners, since they think that the salt water could not be overcome by human artifice."[85] He named twenty as particularly worthy of praise, five of them on the Giudecca. Although such gardens are truly gone forever, a sense of how they looked at the beginning of the sixteenth century is provided by a detail from the Barbari view (fig. 53).[86] Many must have resembled that of Palazzo Nani-Luccheschi today (fig. 54). The treatise writer Memmo saw such spaces as particularly essential to the man of letters and counseled:

> Try to have a large and spacious courtyard, and a beautiful garden adorned with various and delicate fruits, herbs, and flowers of many kinds, qualities, and fragrances, because for the citizen, who spends a good part of his life in the palace, such things will be of no small enjoyment and recreation, and he will be especially delighted in agriculture so located, appreciated and used by the ancient sages: the garden, the loggia, and the courtyard will take away a great part of worries and boredom that are part of human affairs. And delighting in the study of good literature, [the citizen] will find infinite recreation each time, when tired from study, he enters the garden and with a little knife in his hand will choose some fragrant and delicate flower; he will capture a salad leaf in his own hand, he will pick a mature fruit; and enjoying such a pastime and recreation, he will create the highest and divine concepts, with which he will then fill learned and honored pages upon returning to his study.[87]

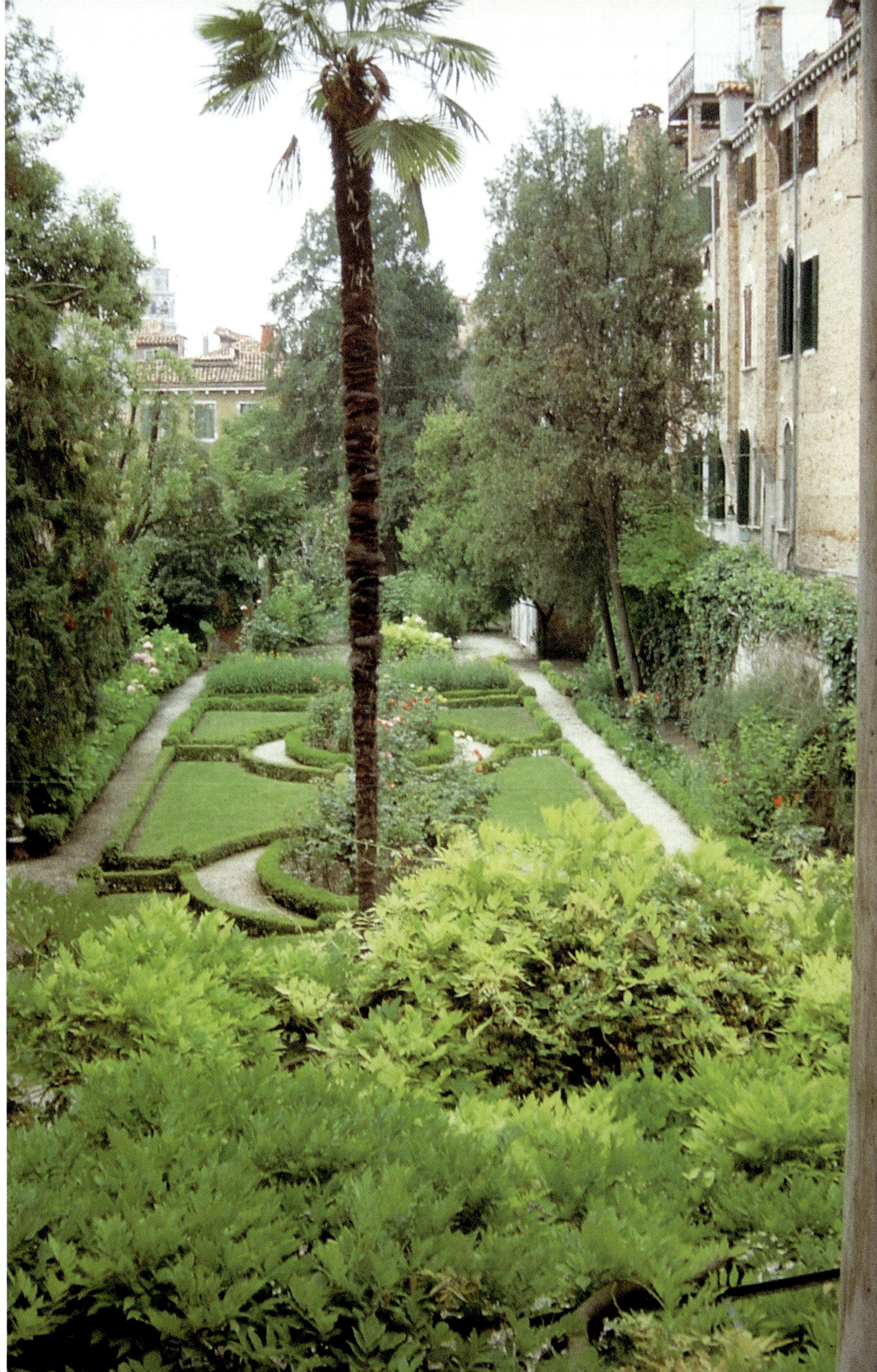

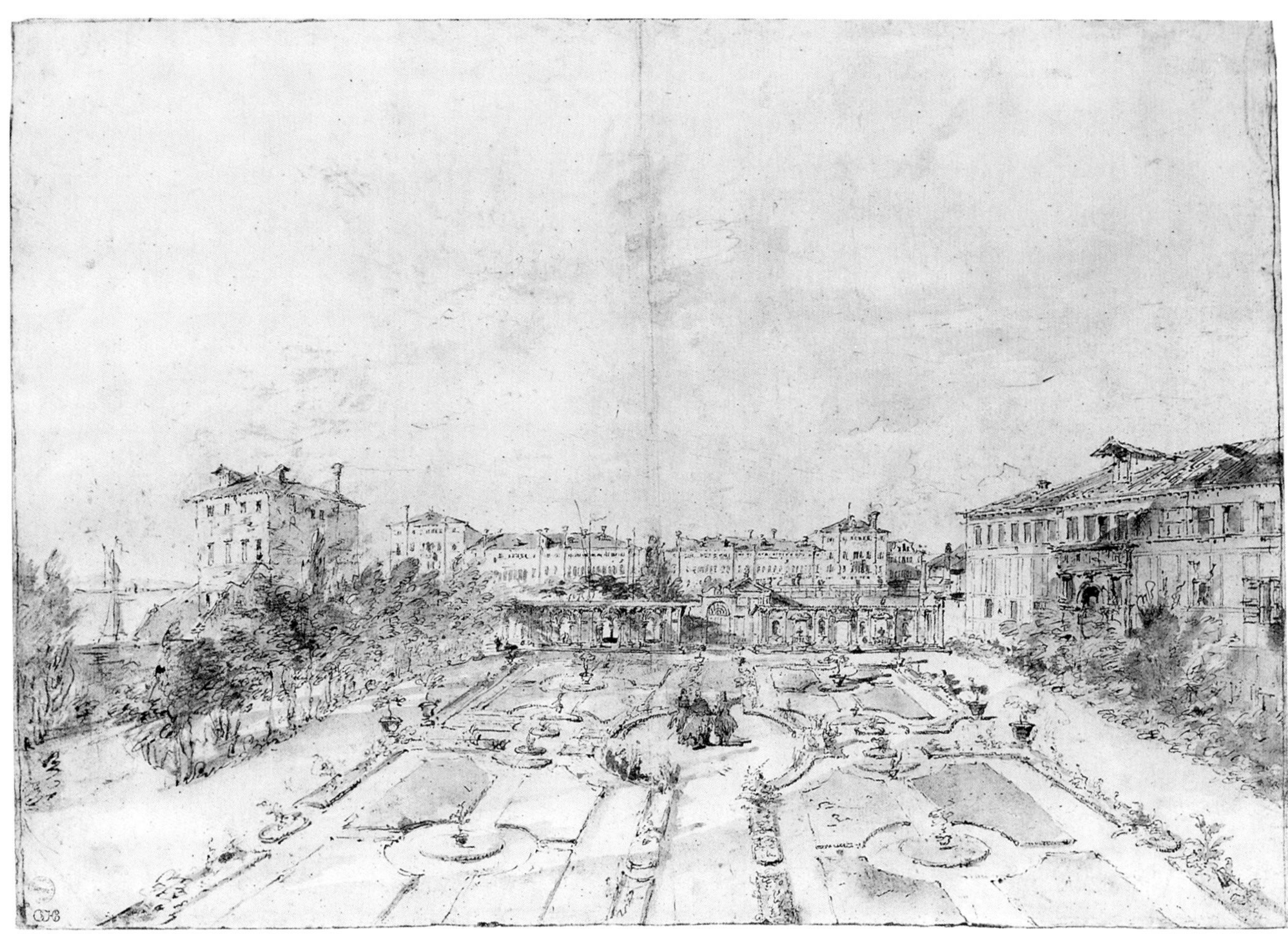

55 Francesco Guardi, *Garden of Palazzo Contarini dal Zaffo*, eighteenth century. Pen and ink, gray watercolor, with traces of black pencil, 355 × 510 mm. Oxford, Ashmolean Museum.

The garden of Palazzo Contarini dal Zaffo, one of those singled out by Sansovino, grew to grandiose proportions by the eighteenth century, as attested by a drawing by Francesco Guardi (fig. 55). It was of a scale possible only because it was situated on the northern edge of Venice proper. In contrast to the kitchen plots of the Giudecca, the Contarini garden, with its elaborately laid-out parterres decorated with sculpture, was for representation and recreation rather than utility. There is no more eloquent testimony of the transformation of the Venetian patriciate from a nobility in name to a nobility in fact.

Over the course of the sixteenth century, the fabric of parity within the patriciate was stretched exceedingly thin as some of the wealthiest sought to define and defend their nobility by building palaces that challenged the traditional stylistic norms of *mediocritas*.

Ca' Loredan on Campo San Stefano may be said to sum up the aesthetic and ideological debates of the sixteenth century (fig. 56). Sansovino observed that the main facade had been frescoed by 1581 in multi-hued allegories of the cardinal virtues, grotesques, and Roman heroes and heroines. But in 1618, a ballroom was added to the north end of the palace with its own facade, completely faced in stone – a proper classical frontispiece.[88] The family could thus project two personae: on the one hand, it honored the Venetian past both aesthetically and morally with the didactic painted face on the east; on the other, it recognized the present with an up-to-date *all'antica* facade of gleaming white stone on the north, harkening back to ancient Rome. In essence, the family had it both ways.

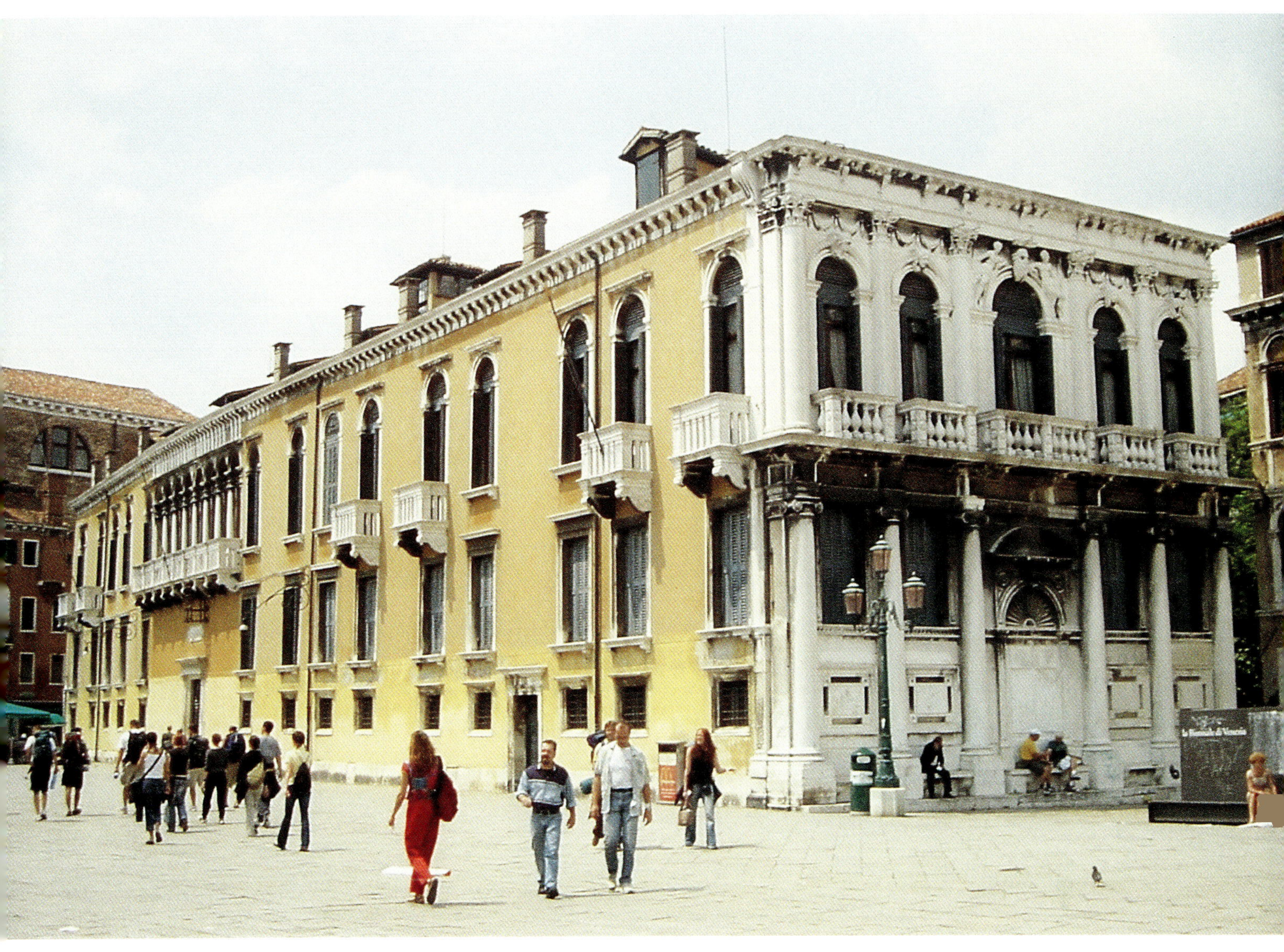

56 Ca' Loredan on Campo San Stefano, begun after 1536. Originally a Gothic palace, of which vestiges remain on the *rio* facade and in the interior, the building was purchased by the Loredan family in 1536. Antonio Scarpagnino, the architect of the east wing of the Palazzo Ducale and the Scuola di San Rocco, was commissioned to carry out a drastic remodeling. He deliberately left the main facade unembellished to accommodate frescoes. The interior features an unusual plan with two monumental doorways opening from the *campo* and the *rio* to an extended square atrium, from which a double-ramped staircase embellished with columns and arches rises to the *piano nobile*. The building now houses the Istituto Veneto delle Scienze, Lettere ed Arti.

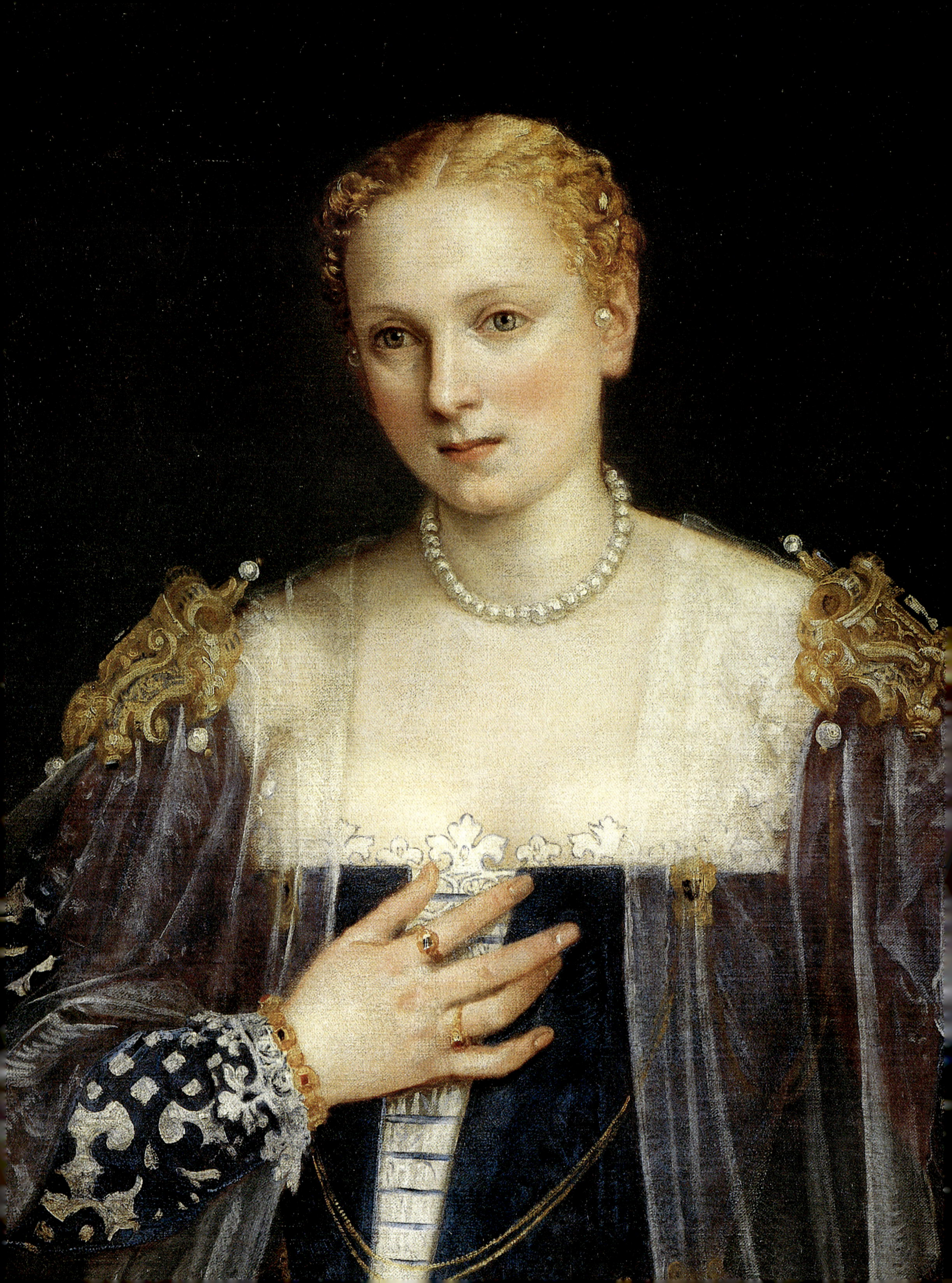

3

To Live Nobile

IN 1494, CANON PIETRO CASOLA, an elderly Milanese priest of noble background, set out on a pilgrimage to the Holy Land. His first stop was Venice, the embarkation point for the pilgrim galleys, and he toured the city while waiting for his ship to set sail. After reporting on the churches, the Ducal Palace, and other public buildings, Casola describes a bustling commercial emporium that survives to the present day (fig. 57): "And who could count the many shops so well furnished that they also seem warehouses, with so many cloths of every make – tapestry, brocades, and hangings of every design, carpets of every sort, camlets of every color and texture, silks of every kind."[1] But this was only the public face of the city. A further exploration of Venetian life must continue inside the luminous interior spaces that Casola and others described so intriguingly and must look at how the *casa* was arranged and to learn what it meant to live *nobile*, expressing status in a manner legible to all.

Worthy Frontispieces

Sebastiano Serlio had observed that "the most noble entrance to these houses is by water," but the landward portal also offered opportunities for grandeur.[2] The first expression of a family's gentility, as well as its Venetian identity, might be made at the entrance door of its *casa*, whether on land or at the water's edge. As we have seen, pious inscriptions were often carved onto facades or into the frames of entry portals (see fig. 39), but architraves and tympanums above doorways also provided an opportunity to make a powerful visual statement of family values. A sculpted relief above the entry portal of Ca' Soranzo-Pisani at San Boldù, datable to the early fifteenth century, features enthroned personifications of Faith/Temperance and Justice flanking the family coats of arms, surmounted by a guardian angel (fig. 58; cf. figs. 14–15). This was originally the land entrance to the home, located on a corner at the foot of a bridge spanning the intersection of two canals joined at right angles.[3] Passersby, as well as those who entered, would thus have a constant reminder of the nobility, not only of birth but also of spirit, of those who lived in the house.

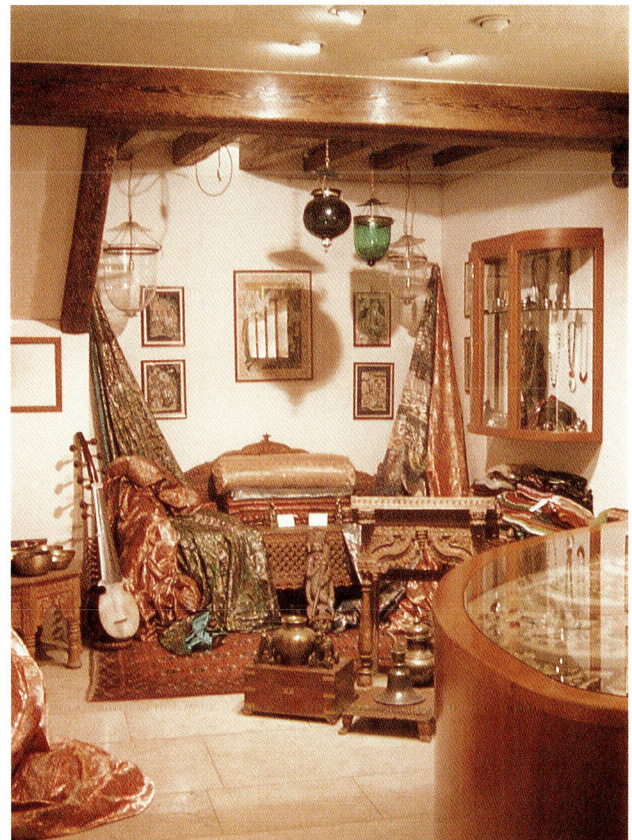

57 (*right*) Venetian shop on Ruga Ravana between San Polo and Rialto.

facing page Paolo Veronese, *La Belle Nani*, ca.1560 (detail of fig. 77).

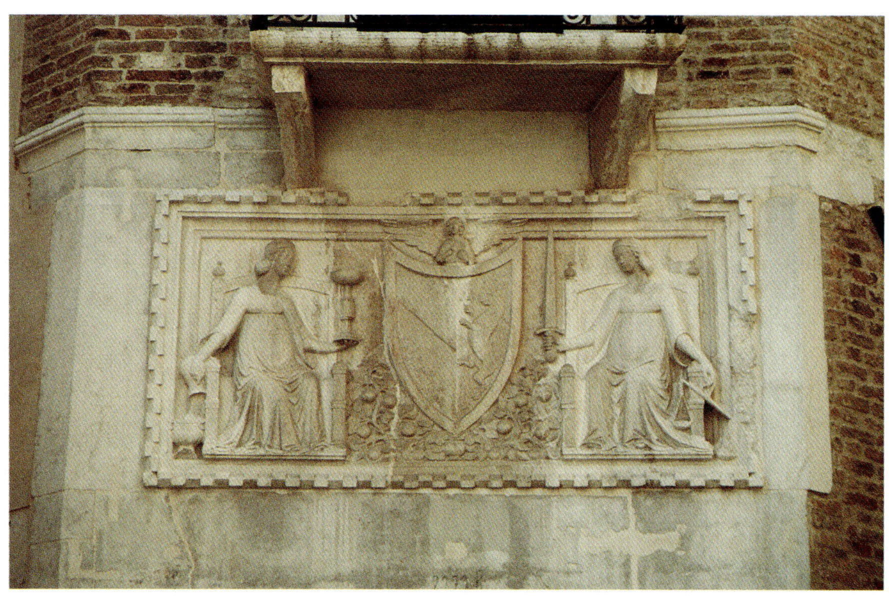

58 *Faith/Temperance and Justice* with the coats of arms of the Soranzo and Pisani families. Marble relief. Ca' Soranzo-Pisani, San Polo 2279.

The door itself was also worthy of attention, and in the course of the sixteenth century, elaborate bronze door knockers began to appear on palace portals throughout the city. One handsome example designed by Jacopo Sansovino, or an artist close to him, features two sea creatures – a nereid and a triton – rising out of a bed of acanthus leaves in an affectionate embrace (fig. 59).[4] Their tails curve upward in a lyre shape to culminate in a leafy swag of fruit and foliage at the top, where a hinge in the form of a grotesque mask once attached the object to the door. Three robust *putti* standing on the heads and chests of their elders animate a perfectly calibrated but dynamic ensemble. The piece was meant to impress: with its cost, for bronze was expensive; with its fine artistry, for it is vigorously modeled and skillfully cast; and with its ingenuity, for it transforms a utilitarian necessity into a work of art. That it was actually used is revealed by the worn-away patina on the acanthus at the base, burnished from the touch of many hands. What better way could the family allude to love and fertility, as well as to its maritime interests, on the door to its home?

The challenge to produce ever more artful introductions to the interior delights of the *casa* stimulated the imagination of other leading artists. A striking piece from the same period, probably designed by Alessandro Vittoria, features the magisterial figure of Neptune, balancing himself on the crossed forelegs of two hippocampi and raising his trident to subdue the turbulent waters of the sea contained within a seashell (fig. 60).[5] The invention would have appealed to the learned, for it derives from an episode in the *Aeneid* (I,135), beginning with the words "Quos Ego," when Neptune calms a tempest called forth by Juno to impede the safe progress of Aeneas, son of her great rival Venus, on his voyage to Italy. But the sculptor need not have known the story at all. His design was based upon a drawing by Leonardo da Vinci that had a wide circulation in engravings and medals (fig. 61).[6] And indeed, it enjoyed extraordinary good fortune on Venetian door knockers: no fewer than forty examples of the genre survive today.[7]

The lyre shape offered endless possibilities for creative adaptation, as demonstrated by a door knocker that ended up in the Victoria and Albert Museum (fig. 62). While the

59 (*facing page top left*) Jacopo Sansovino, or an artist close to him, door knocker with nereid, triton and putti, ca. 1550. Bronze. Washington, National Gallery of Art [Pepita Millmore Fund A-1820].

60 (*facing page top right*) Venetian sculptor, door knocker with Neptune between two hippocampi, ca. 1560. Bronze, height 37.4 cm, width 30.3 cm. The piece was probably designed by Alessandro Vittoria who, along with Jacopo Sansovino, may be considered one of the two great Venetian sculptors of the mid- to late sixteenth century. Similar examples survive at Palazzo Pisani and Palazzo Loredan. Vienna, Kunsthistorisches Museum.

61 (*facing page bottom*) Leonardo da Vinci, *The Sea God Neptune Commanding his Quadriga of Four Sea Horses*, ca. 1503–4. Black chalk, 251 × 391 mm. It is not known whether Leonardo had a copy of Virgil's *Aeneid*, but he did own Ovid's *Metamorphoses*, which also describes the destructive powers of the sea god. Windsor Castle. The Royal Collection © 2003, Her Majesty Queen Elizabeth II.

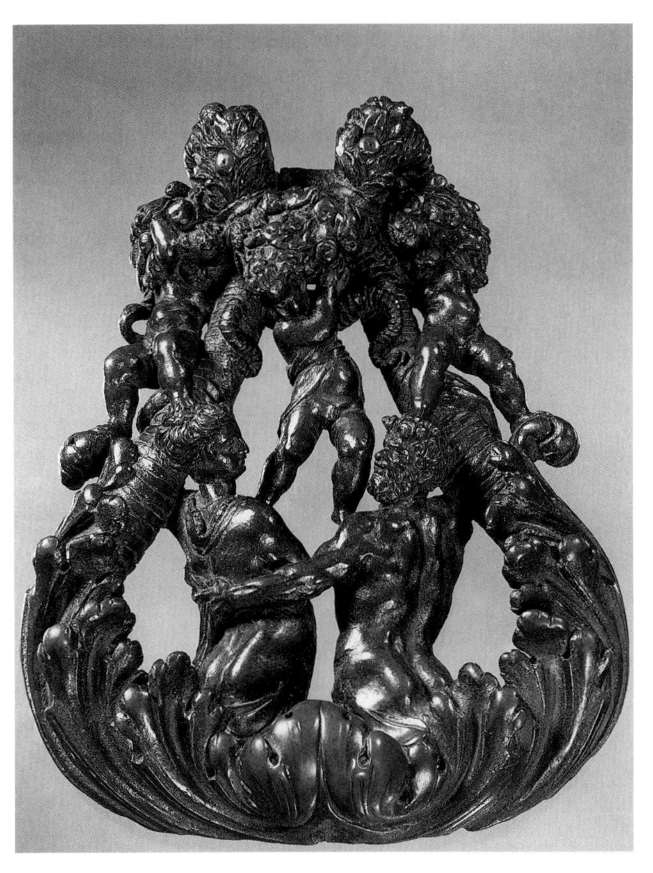

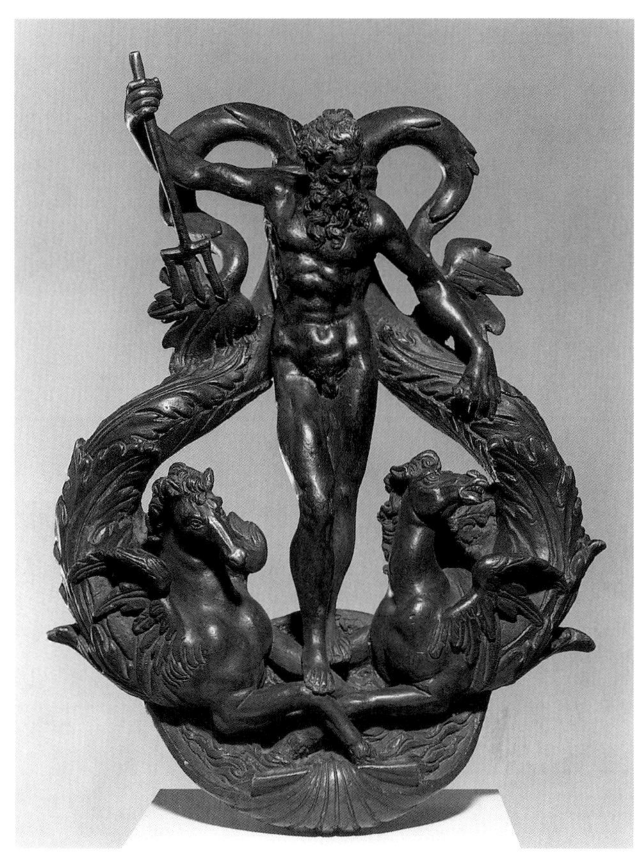

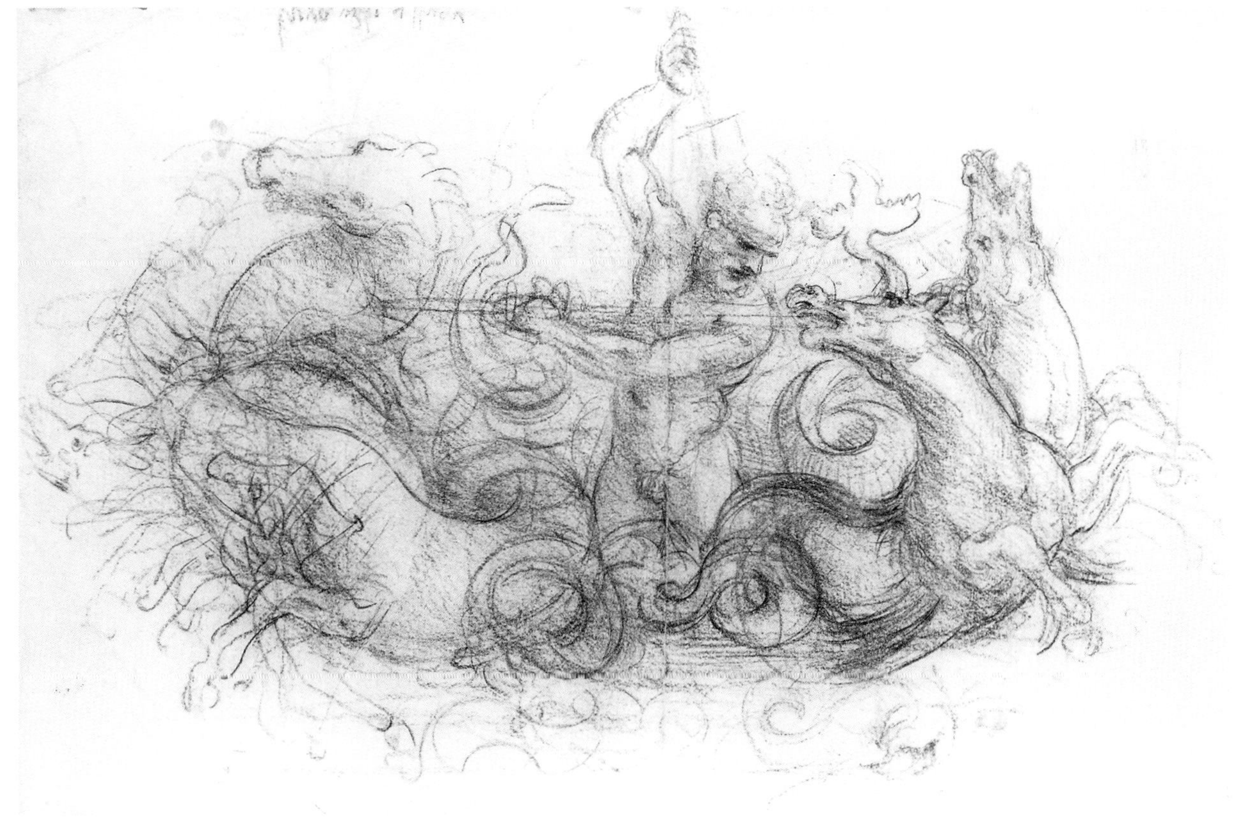

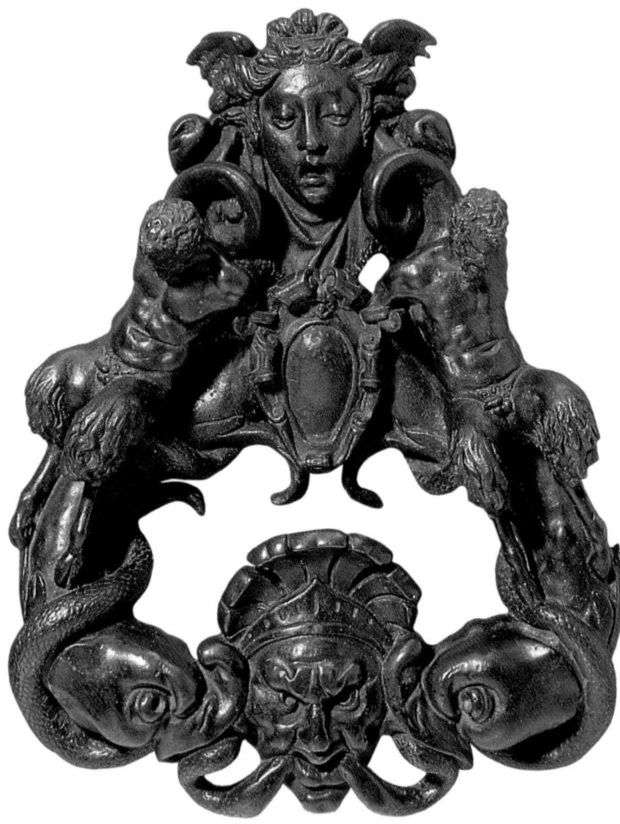

62 Door knocker with masks, sixteenth century. Bronze. London, Victoria and Albert Museum.

sculptor retained a maritime theme, with stylized dolphins forming the arms of the piece, featuring a decorative vocabulary, with grotesque masks, it is less naturalistic and more mannered than the Neptune door knocker.[8] It is also a subtle, witty, and sophisticated updating of the more direct assertions of family virtue afforded by reliefs of the early fifteenth century, such as that on Ca' Soranzo-Pisani (fig. 58). The bound satyrs, signifying vice overcome by the virtue of the house – represented by the coat of arms in the center – provided the rationale, if one were needed. By the end of the sixteenth century, objects such as these were one of the sure signs of a family's gentility, visible to passersby as well as to those who entered the house.

When the bronze door knockers came to be seen as true and proper works of art they disappeared into museums and private collections, and few remain on Venetian doors today. Nor do many of the doors themselves endure, with wood a material subject to assault by the elements if not by collectors. However, there are survivals, including a great coffered wood affair that still prefaces the Palazzo Soranzo Van Axel near the church of Santa Maria dei Miracoli (fig. 63).[9] Equipped with a peephole, it was built to last and to protect. It thus belies a stereotype of Venetian homes, with all their windows, as open and inviting places. For everyday life in the Serenissima was not always serene, and theft in particular was not uncommon.[10] The threshold thus had to function as a barrier as much as a portal. It had symbolic resonance; it is no coincidence that the front doors of the family palace of one of the perpetrators of the Querini–Tiepolo conspiracy of 1310 were seized by the state and installed on a votive church.[11]

Once through the outer door, the visitor entered an intermediate space – no longer public, but not yet fully private. Whether entering through the water portal and walking through the ground-floor *androne* where the gondola was stored, or arriving by land where one might proceed through a covered passageway, the visitor to a *casa da statio* (a term denoting a substantial family palace) usually ended up in a spacious courtyard containing a well-head above a cistern to collect rainwater.[12]

As the Venetian writer Giovanni Maria Memmo counseled in his treatise on the household, the noble residence "above every other thing should be abundant in sweet, clear, and fresh water, either from fountains or cisterns."[13] Accordingly, the well-head offered yet another occasion to define the family. The courtyard of Ca' d'Oro, now Galleria Giorgio Franchetti, is dominated by a magnificent well-head carved in red Verona marble by Bartolomeo Bon in the 1420s (fig. 64).[14] Following Venetian tradition, it is shaped like a large capital, with one face featuring the Contarini coat of arms. The other three sides are carved with personified virtues – Fortitude, Justice, and Charity – each sitting on a leonine throne and framed by Gothic foliage. These were among the most cherished virtues of the Venetian family, at one with the virtues of the state, and the fifteenth-century visitor would know that this was a house where virtue was esteemed and perhaps even practiced.

But let us imagine that our caller could be transported through time to the mid-sixteenth century and the grand romanizing courtyard of Ca' Corner della Ca' Grande. The silent message on its well-head was significantly different

63 (*facing page*) Ca' Soranzo van Axel, entrance portal on Fondamenta Sanudo next to Rio della Panada. Beyond the carved larchwood door, with a door knocker (upper right) in the shape of a fish, is a spacious courtyard. It features an external staircase that rises in two flights to the second *piano nobile*. Built in the fifteenth century by the Soranzo family, the palace was purchased in the seventeenth century by the van Axels, wealthy Flemish merchants who bought their way into the Venetian patriciate in the mid-seventeenth century.

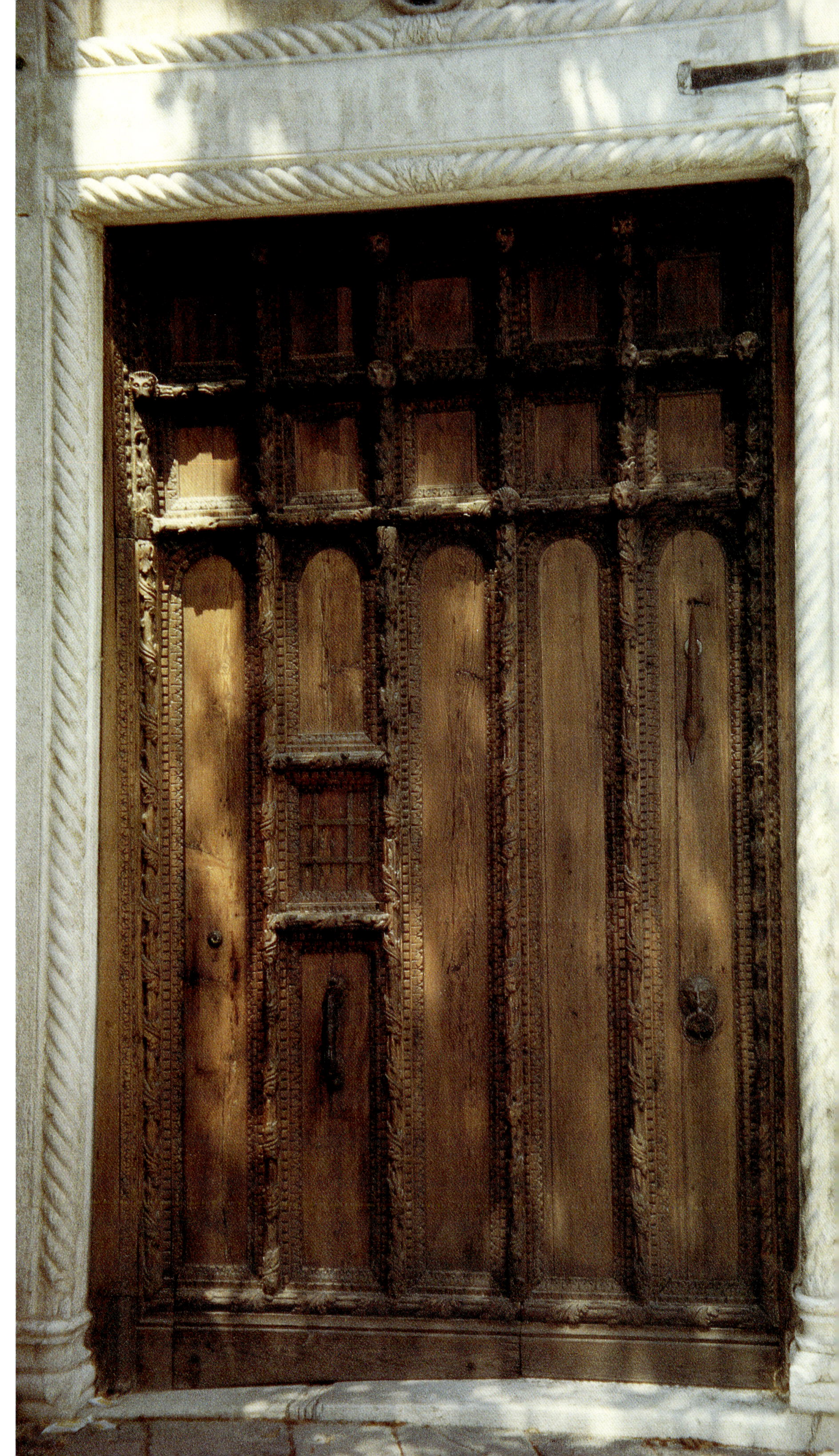

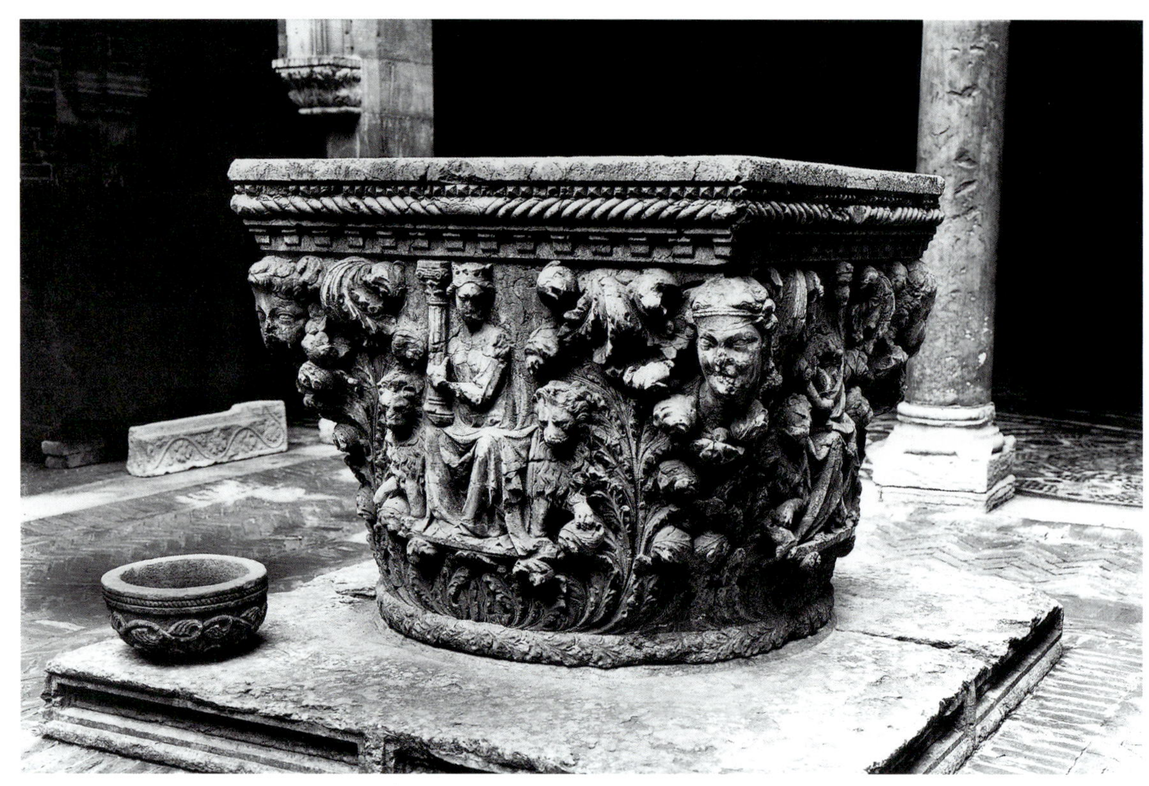

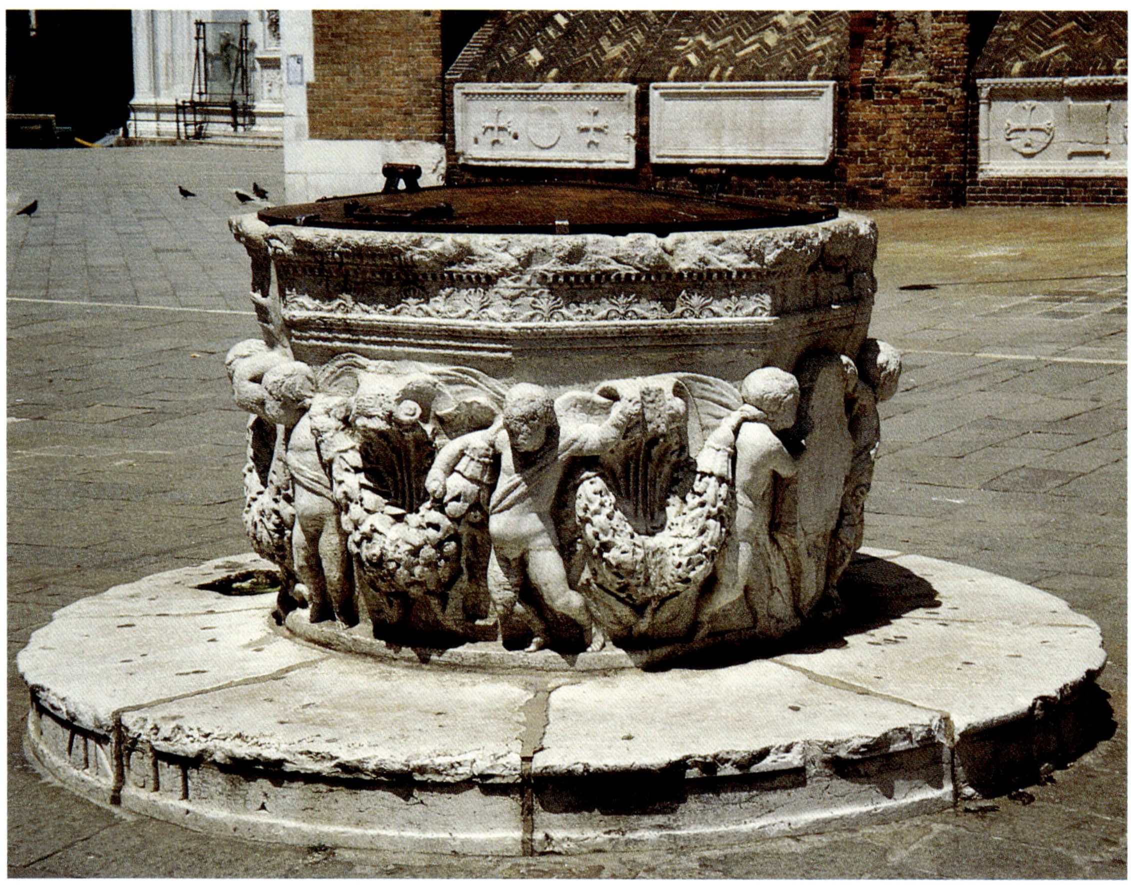

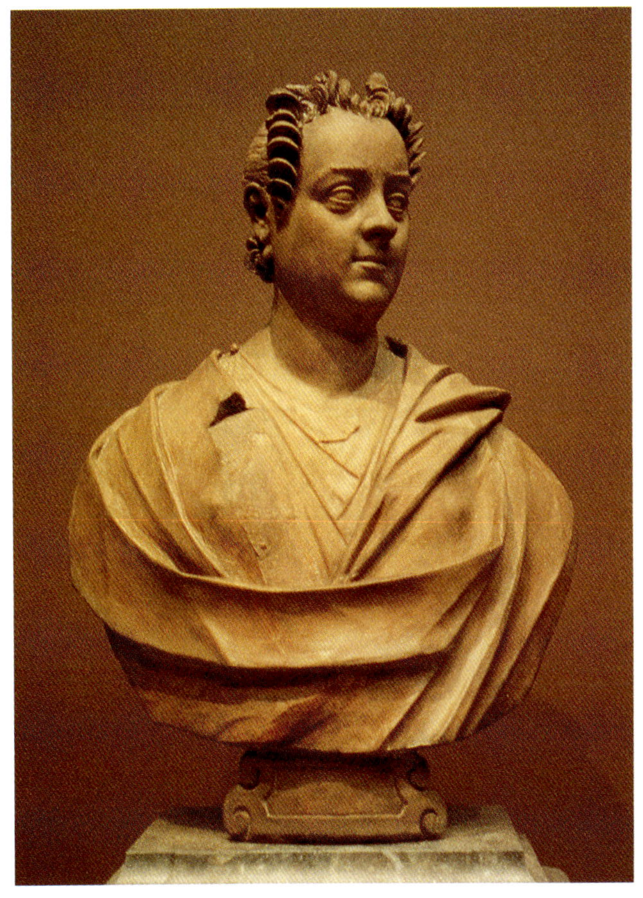

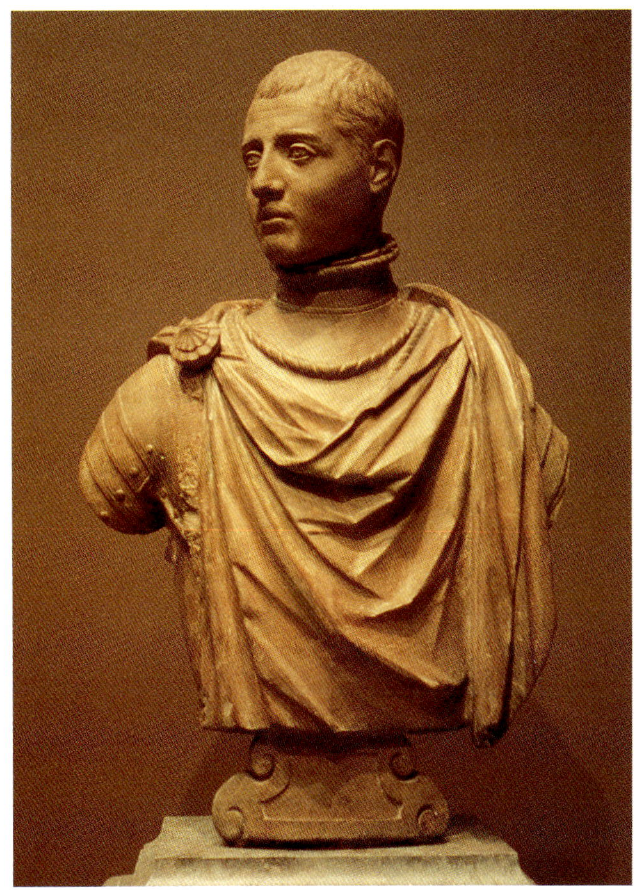

from that at Ca' d'Oro (fig. 65). Opulently massive, with eight sides, it is ringed with robustly carved *putti*. Two present the Corner coat of arms, while the others stagger under the weight of great swags of fruit and foliage – symbols of triumph and celebration. The difference is not just a question of style or the emergence of an *all'antica* vocabulary in sculpture. What is now expressed are not the moral values of the patrician family, but rather its elevated taste, capable of appreciating the aesthetic, and presumably the moral, qualities of classical culture.

At around the same time that the well-head was installed at Ca' Corner, another family had its courtyard remodeled to express its humanistic culture, its dedication to Roman republican ideals, and its dynastic identity. This was at Ca' Zorzi on Rio San Lorenzo, one of those palaces cited as worthy of note by Francesco Sansovino in 1581, featuring, as he put it, "a number of handsome busts and figural sculptures in marble as well as in stucco [his term for terracotta] by Alessandro Vittoria."[15] When the artist had remodeled the courtyard loggia several decades earlier, he seems to have flanked the entrance to the house with bracket consoles, designed to hold portrait busts in the manner of ancient Roman palaces. As Pliny had written: "Round the doorways . . . in the halls of our ancestors, portraits were the objects displayed, each on a separate support to furnish likenesses of the family."[16]

66 (*above left*) Alessandro Vittoria, portrait bust of a young woman (?Cristina Zorzi), late sixteenth century. Terracotta, height 81 cm. Washington, National Gallery of Art.

67 (*above right*) Alessandro Vittoria, portrait bust of a young man (?Alvise Zorzi) ca. 1570s. Terracotta, height 90.2 cm. Vittoria was particularly noted for busts with draperies *all'antica* for funerary monuments. Washington, National Gallery of Art.

64 (*facing page top*) Well-head with a personification of Fortitude, 1420s. Red Verona marble. The well-head was removed from the courtyard in the mid-nineteenth century and restored and returned to its original location by Baron Giorgio Franchetti in 1896. Venice, Galleria Giorgio Franchetti (Ca d'Oro).

65 (*facing page bottom*) Well-head from Ca' Corner della Ca' Grande, mid-sixteenth century, now on Campo SS Giovanni e Paolo.

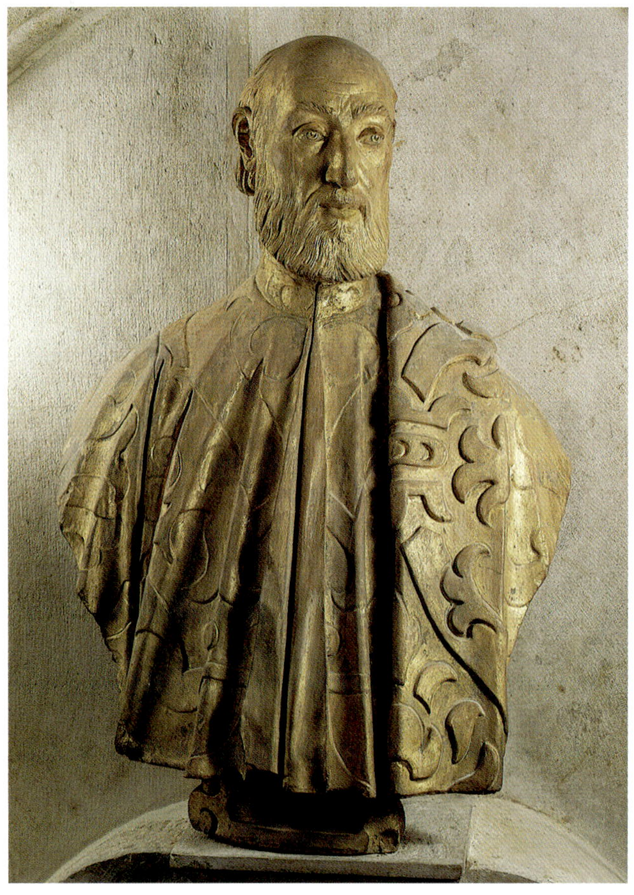

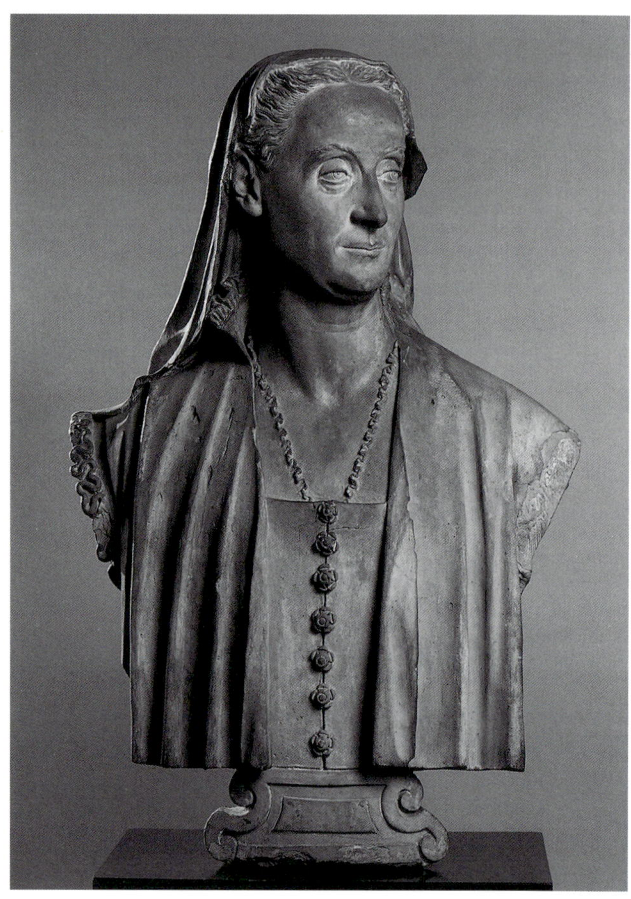

68 (*above left*) Alessandro Vittoria workshop, portrait bust of Antonio Zorzi, last third sixteenth century. Terracotta, gilded, lifesize. The bust is on Zorzi's tomb monument. The proliferation of portrait busts in the last half of the sixteenth century in Venice was largely owing to Alessandro Vittoria. Venice, Church of San Stefano.

69 (*above right*) Alessandro Vittoria, portrait bust of a woman (?Angela Loredan Zorzi), early 1570s?. Terracotta, height 83 cm. Vienna, Kunsthistorisches Museum.

The sculptures were subsequently dispersed, but four terracotta busts survive that have been identified as part of the original integrated program. Two are clad in classicizing dress: a young male in military armor, draped with a toga in the Roman manner, and a female wearing draperies *all'antica* – an affectation characteristic of medallic portraits of the period (figs. 66 and 67). However, the other two busts are clothed not *all'antica* but *alla veneziana*, without classical pretensions (figs. 68 and 69).[17] The juxtaposition of the traditional (that is, contemporary Venetian) and the novel (that is, classicizing), is not accidental. Indeed, it is what makes the program quintessentially Venetian. As with the palace that is Gothic, and the entrance that is Roman, the old is not discarded nor is it displaced. It is simply augmented and, indeed, validated by the new.[18]

Although there were many variations of the palace entrance, Ca' Zorzi was exceptional. Returning to the more typical residence, it is fair to say that over the course of the sixteenth century ostentation and display increasingly took precedence over utility. The one constant is that people of means did not live on the ground floor. The staircase thus provided another opportunity to create an introduction to the house and to become a place of presentation. The shortage of building space meant that every square meter counted, and in the Gothic period even the great palaces often located the main entry staircase outside in the courtyard (figs. 70a and b). There it could be as wide and as grand as desired and adorned with a colonnaded banister and sculpted decorations such as lions, foliage clusters, pine cones, or human heads – the latter more than likely portraits of the family and perhaps medieval precursors to the *all'antica* portrait busts displayed in the Zorzi courtyard. With the earliest-known examples dating to the twelfth century, the exterior staircase continued on through the

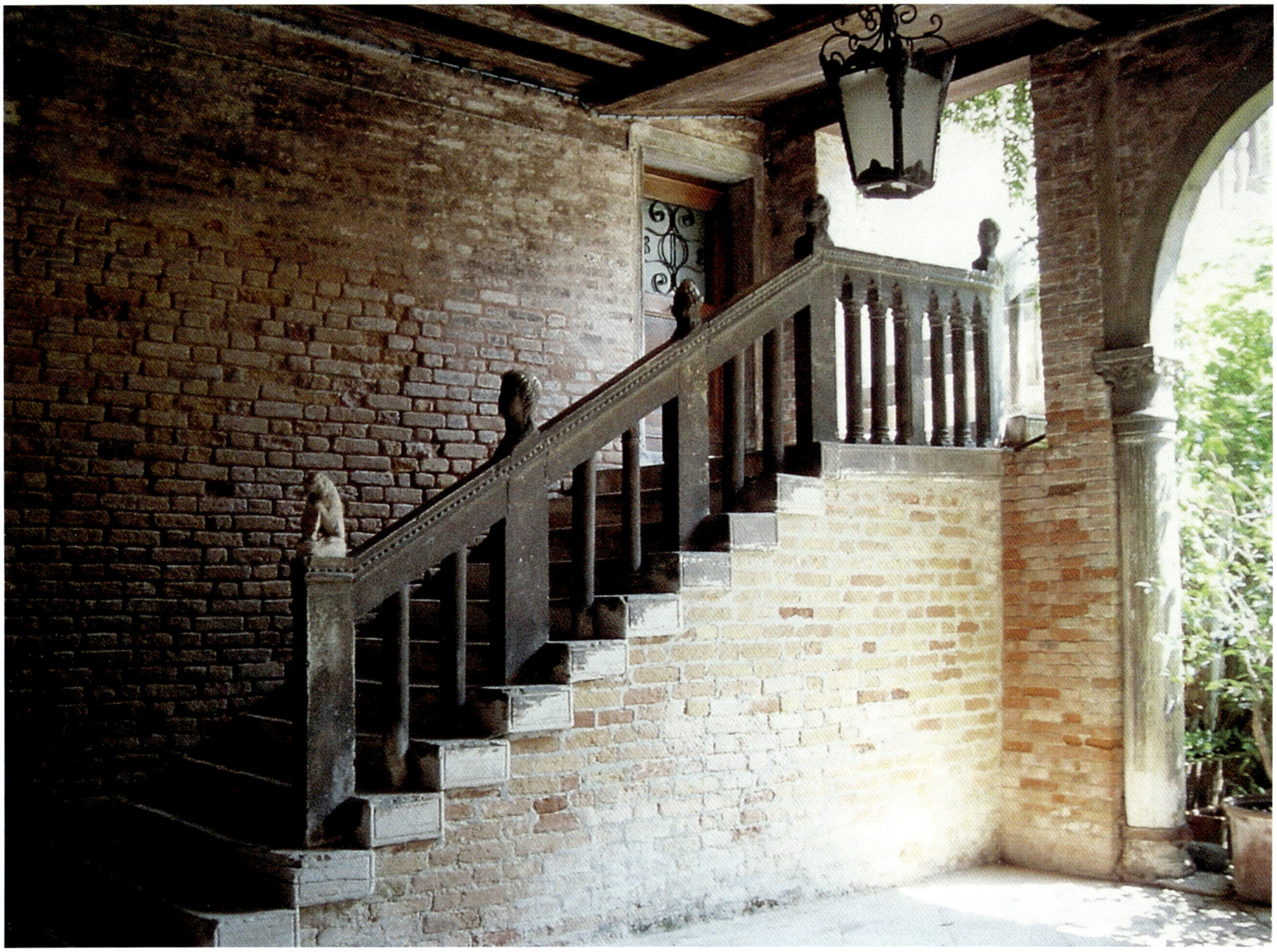

70a (*above*) Staircase in Palazzo Grifalconi-Loredan near SS. Giovanni e Paolo, fifteenth century (now reconstructed). In a typically Venetian confusion of motifs, the balustrade is decorated with romanizing heads crowned *all'antica* with laurel, alternating with late Gothic fleurons.

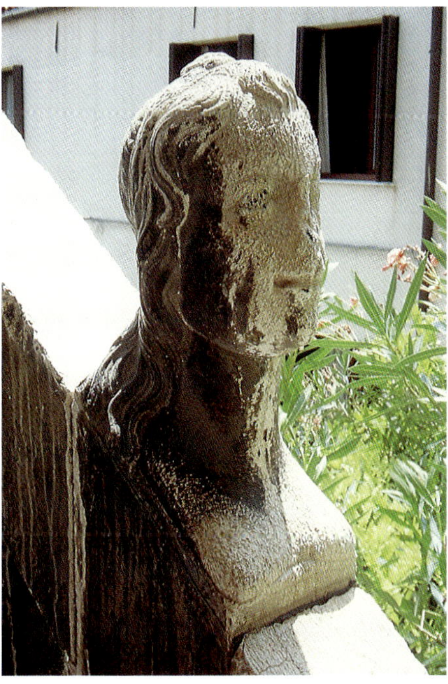

70b (*left*) A female head from the balustrade illustrated in figure 70a.

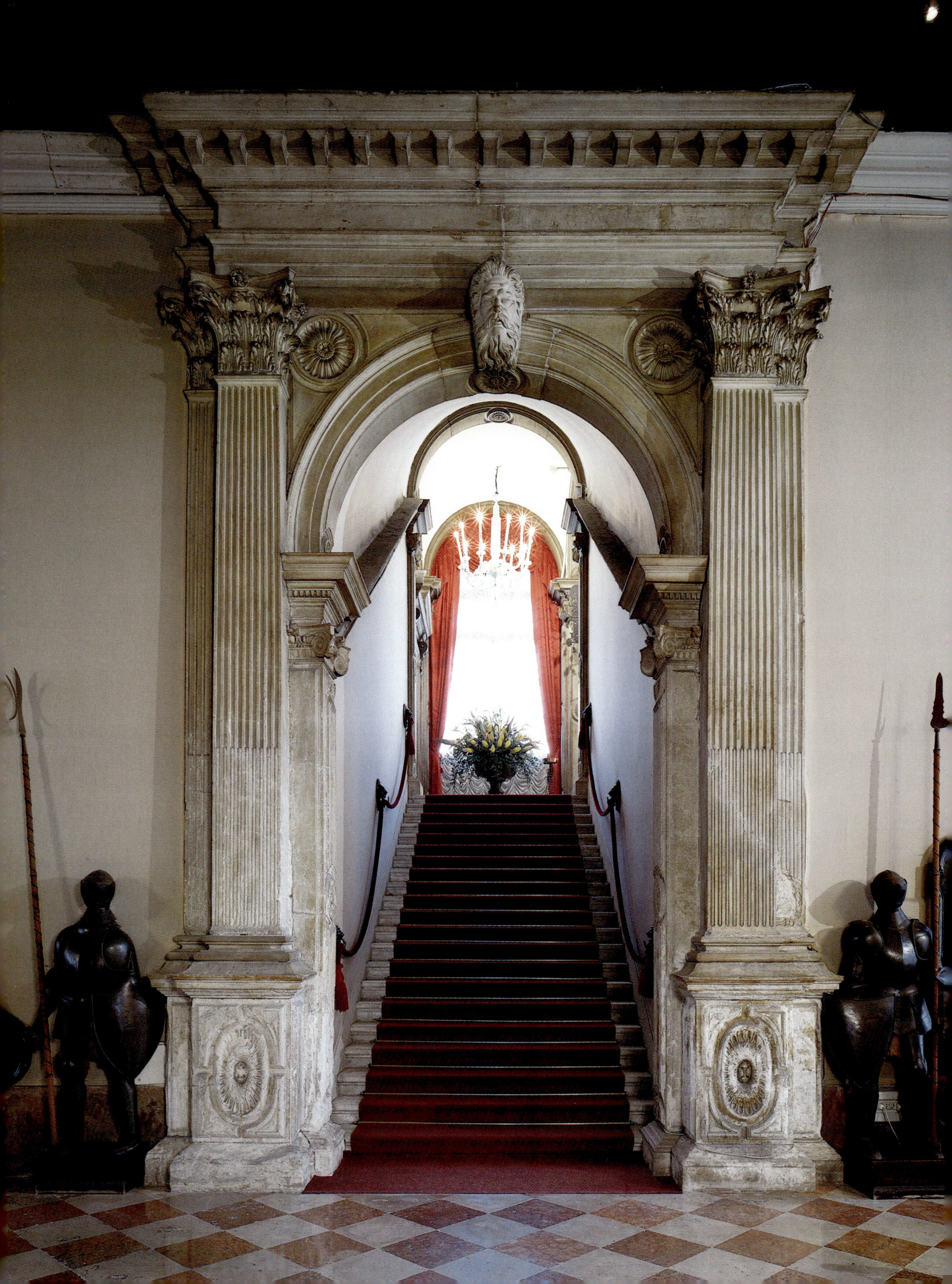

Baroque period in the more modest aristocratic homes.[19] As is evident with the spectacular Scala del Bovolo or even the more modest Ca' Goldoni, grand scenographic effects were part of the equation (fig. 34). While the user is exposed to the elements with the exterior staircase, a dignified and visible ascent (and descent) is possible along the way. Anticipation propels one upward toward a refuge and a welcome.

The sixteenth-century writer Pietro Aretino was well aware of the metaphorical charge of the staircase, recalling that his friend, Giulio Camillo, "used to take a delight in remarking to me that the entrance to my house from the landside, being a dark one and with a beastly stair, was like the terrible name I had acquired by revealing the truth. And then, he would add that anyone who came to know me would find in my pure, plain, and natural friendship the same tranquil contentment that was felt on reaching the portico and coming out on the balconies above."[20]

Such enclosed staircases, deprived of natural scenographic effects, posed a challenge, which Mauro Codussi (and the romanizing architects of the sixteenth century who followed) tackled with enthusiasm and imagination. In great block-like palaces such as Ca' Loredan-Vendramin-Calergi, suitably – sometimes astonishingly – grand staircases were incorporated into the fabric of the building (fig. 71).[21] With these interior staircases, the visitor, having arrived in the courtyard, would enter (or re-enter if they had arrived by water) the *androne*, and from there ascend to the family living space protected from the outside world, drawn upward by a sense of luxuriousness rather than (as in the case of Aretino's friend) discomfort. In any case, once the visitor was inside the home, nature was excluded, and the domestic experience had begun.

The Domestic Experience

The layout of the Venetian palace was determined by the urban fabric. At the beginning of the sixteenth century, Venice was already a crowded city. Building lots were expensive and hard to come by, especially in the main centers around Piazza San Marco and Rialto and along the Grand Canal. In order to build, one often had to tear down something else first. The standard rectangular lot of today was rare in the medieval city and particularly rare on land that had been reclaimed from a cluster of islands. So builders had to be flexible. They were often forced to adapt the house plan to a plot that typically had an irregular shape and was tightly wedged in between two other palaces or next to a curving canal.

As a result, a virtually symmetrical facade quite often masked an interior with rooms laid out according to their function and the exigencies of nature, rather than a pre-existing notion of ideal form. This is evident in the slightly trapezoidal, and certainly asymmetrical plan of Ca' Foscari (fig. 72; see fig. 25 for the facade). It is also true of the double palace of the Giustiniani next door. Behind each facade was a deep hallway running from front to back, flanked by rooms that, when possible, opened one into the other. These were bedchambers and sitting rooms for the most part. Each house featured a small courtyard – the *corticella* (the central house had two) – that interrupted the sequence of rooms on one side in the central block. And each had a much larger courtyard – the *cortile* – to the rear. Both palaces here are four stories high, with the *piano terra* at ground level, two *piani nobili* above – which would have had essentially the same floor plan – and a lower-ceilinged floor at the top. Most large Venetian residences of the Byzantine and Gothic periods featured a version of this plan, though more often with just three stories, despite the varying constraints of the site.[22]

So even before the arrival of Serlio and other followers of Vitruvian principles, the floor plan of the Venetian house had a certain logic and a certain consistency. One constant that distinguished it from those in other cities was that great hall, called the *portego* or *sala*, that typically ran from front to back on each *piano nobile*. It was functionally a circulation space – in smaller homes often not much more than a spacious corridor – that gave access to the rooms at the sides. Combined with a gallery or loggia with glazed windows on the front, it was also a breezeway and solarium of sorts, bringing light and air into the interior of the house.[23]

These multi-floored palaces were the homes that defined the *politia* of which Venetians were so proud. But many of the large palaces also functioned as apartment houses. Increasingly, in order to prevent dispersion of the family patrimony, only one or two of the sons married. With brothers often staying in the household, three or even four generations of a family might live in a single palace. Indeed, the dominant form of business association in Venice was a family partnership called the *fraterna* – loosely translated as "brotherhood." All the property inherited from the father would be entered into the account books of the *fraterna*, along with household expenses, and shared jointly. Thus the sense of cooperation that characterized political life was also present in families, by necessity if not by choice.[24] Each of the sons, particularly those with wives and children, might occupy a single, separate floor or part of a floor in a palace, or in the case of bachelors, perhaps simply a single room. These secondary living spaces might also be located on a

71 (*facing page*) Interior staircase in Ca' Loredan-Vendramin-Calergi, now the Casino Municipale of Venice.

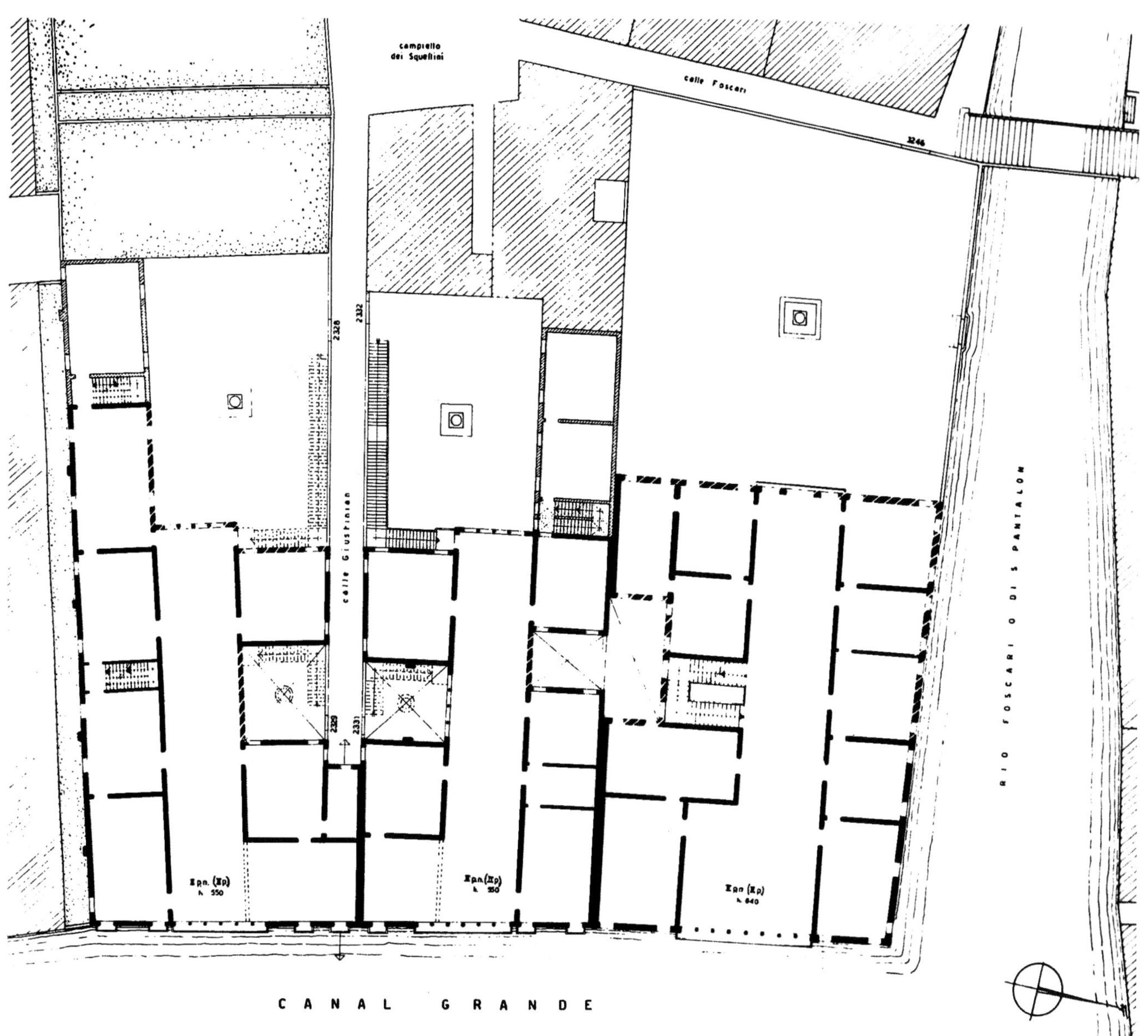

72 Case Giustiniani (left) and Ca' Foscari (right), floor plans of the second *piano nobile* of each palace (after Paolo Maretto, *L'edilizia gotica veneziana*, Rome, 1961, 105).

mezzanine level, between the floors, where the kitchen, business offices, and utility rooms were also often found.[25] All would share the entry ways and storage rooms on the ground floor and possibly the rooms for servants and additional storage in the attic – called the *soffita* – at the top.

It should be noted that one of the main virtues of the traditional T-shaped plan, with all its variants, was its great flexibility. Doors could kept be kept open or locked, creating different units within the same floor-plan configuration, thus adapting to different family situations over the generations.[26] Also, in many cases, a floor or a suite of rooms was rented out to unrelated families or individuals. Privacy must have been hard to come by with rooms arranged like these, with one opening into the next and all opening into the *portego*, and by the middle of the sixteenth century the treatise writers were strongly recommending that houses be arranged so as to ensure more seclusion.[27] Even so, Sir Henry Wotton, writing at the beginning of the seventeenth century, remarked: "for I observe in no Nation in the World, by Nature more private and reserved then the Italian, and on the other side, in no Habitations lesse privacie, so as there is a kind of Conflict, betweene their Dwelling and their Being."[28]

Palladio would later compare the house to the human body, which has noble and beautiful parts, but also ugly and ignoble but necessary parts that are best kept covered. In the house, also, the most beautiful parts should be placed in areas of greatest visibility, to be seen immediately; the less beautiful places should be hidden away.[29] This chapter will attempt to rediscover the most beautiful parts of the Venetian domestic interior, those that defined what it meant to live *nobile*, focusing in particular on the *portego* and the chambers that served as places of presentation.

Traces of Lost Interiors

Those sixteenth-century interiors are elusive. Even when the architectural shell is still intact, tastes have changed over the centuries and little remains in place from the early period, with the exception of door frames, window moldings, ceilings, and an occasional fireplace that can no longer be used. For example, the *portego* on the *piano nobile* of Ca' d'Oro maintains its Renaissance structure, but is now a museum with Renaissance furnishings arranged for display rather than use.

What is there to work with? In the category of visual evidence, a few paintings and prints of interiors survive, such as Giovanni Mansueti's *Healing of the Daughter of Ser Nicolo Benvegnudo of San Polo* or Jacopo Tintoretto's *Marriage Feast at Cana*, which will be looked at later. These stage sets for biblical, historical, or legendary narratives must have been based upon typical rooms, but as seen through the correcting lens – and the *fantasia* – of the artist. There is also the actual, tangible *stuff*: the objects themselves, such as chairs and chests, detached from their original settings, that survive by chance. Turning to written evidence, at the high end there is theory – those ideal prescriptions by the treatise writers on home economics, such as Memmo, or on domestic architecture, such as Serlio, who had much to say on how families should arrange their living spaces. But such admonitions often reflect what was not the case rather than what was. Moving to the lower plane of eyewitness accounts, there are a handful of descriptions, usually maddeningly brief, by contemporary observers, and some literary references to domestic life. These probably stand somewhere between the ideal and the real situation. And then there are inventories – very real, but very opaque, with puzzling terms for furnishings and no drawings to help us interpret them.

But to explore beyond artistic ingenuity and pure speculation and to recapture a concrete sense of the actual Venetian home, the quest leads inevitably to the inventories. These were drawn up by notaries and listed virtually all the objects (no matter how modest) in a house – in most cases room by room (fig. 73). The notary often distinguished between new and old objects, and "old" was further divided between *antico*, which meant venerable, *vecchio*, which meant well worn, and *triste* which meant worn out. Such documentation offers reliable evidence of a material culture that was truly sumptuous at the high end and dismal indeed at the lowest. It also provides a check on the ideal prescriptions of Serlio and the writers of treatises like Memmo. Because of the random nature of the inventories that survive, ranging from lengthy catalogs of affluent houses to the poignantly meager lists of the relatively poor, they offer a reasonably representative cross-section of the different levels of wealth and consumption in Venetian society.[30] And from them we can begin to define the decorative principles of the Venetian home.

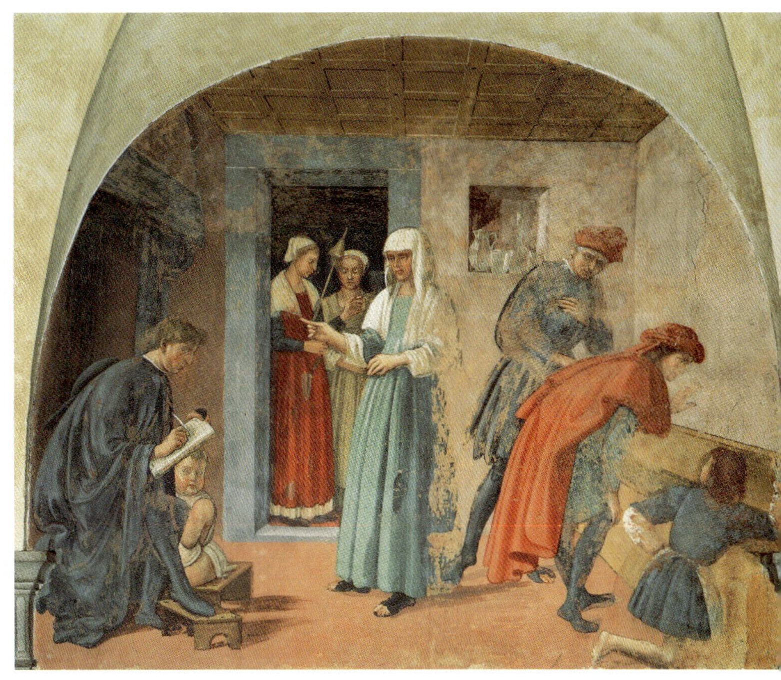

73 Workshop of Domenico Ghirlandaio, *Notary Making an Inventory of a Household*, late fifteenth century. Fresco. Inventories were most often made upon the death of an individual with minor-age children or for a widow who was reclaiming her dowry. Florence, Oratory of the Buonuomini of San Martino del Vescovo.

To put these disparate genres together to reconstruct the Venetian Renaissance interior requires a bit of scholarly license along with the reader's indulgence. It is necessary to cut and paste, juxtaposing descriptions of actual rooms with prescriptions for ideal ones. And to illuminate textual

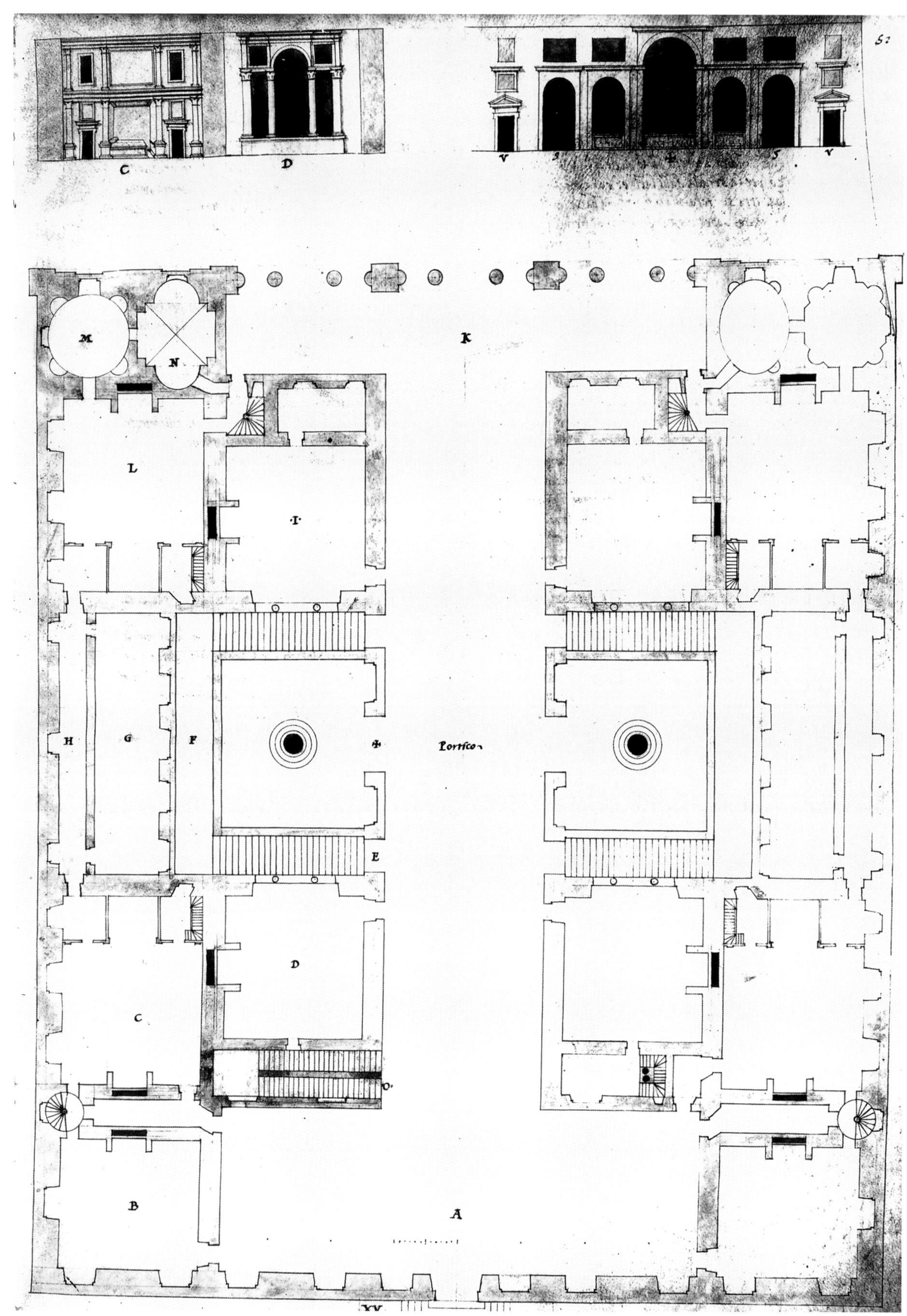

74 Sebastiano Serlio, floor plan of a palace for a Venetian gentleman, 1547–50. Ink on parchment. Munich, Bayerische Staatsbibliothek (Codex Icon. 189, f. 52).

descriptions, typical objects may be considered – that is, items that could have been in the rooms in a given time period – but not, alas, the actual objects. And these, in turn, may be further understood by referring back to the verbal material.

A House for a Noble Gentleman

Beginning with the ideal, let us call Sebastiano Serlio as our first witness. He wrote two drafts of his Book VI, which dealt with domestic architecture, in the 1540s, shortly after he moved to France, but he was greatly influenced by the thirteen years he had spent in Venice.[31] It is in his treatise that Vitruvian principles are codified specifically for Venetian domestic architecture. Serlio observed in the earlier draft that "the major part of the ornaments of the houses of this city are licentious, also with things disordered," and offered two plans specifically tailored to the needs of the Venetian gentleman.[32] One of these is a Romanizing layout, with the rooms arranged around a central courtyard; this will not concern us here. But the other demonstrates Serlio's sensitivity to local tradition, for it is simply an elegant updating of the old T-shaped plan – a perfecting, if you will – rather than a rejection of Venetian practice. Although few building sites in Venice would actually have accommodated such a well-ordered, symmetrical configuration, Serlio's T-shaped plan serves as a useful point of departure to explore an ideal layout for a Venetian palace. The plan used here is from Serlio's second draft of Book VI and shows some significant changes from the earlier version, which will be pointed out (figs. 74 and 75).[33]

In the text accompanying his floor plan, Serlio acknowledges "the universal custom of the city" and retains the *portego* beloved to Venetians. But as a corrective to a length that he found excessive, he added a luminous *sala* in front and a loggia in the rear. He proposed, moreover, not just one but two large courtyards at the sides – each containing a cistern with its well-head – to provide more light to the interior. This latter arrangement was employed already, if in a more *ad hoc* manner and on a more modest scale, in the Giustiniani palaces and many others. The *portego*, in its capacity as reception hall, passageway, and neutral zone, might be considered a permeable membrane. In Serlio's plan it divides the floor into two essentially equal apartments, thus responding to the needs of at least two nuclear families sharing the same floor. More symmetrical than most Venetian homes, it is also most unusual in having two rows of rooms (rather than one) on each side of the central *portego*.

How would Serlio's house have been lived in? Using his text as a guide to the *piano nobile* – one of two identical elevated floors – we enter the house on the ground floor through the watergate, "the most noble entrance to these houses." Using staircase **O**, which leads all the way up to the attic, where the granary is located, one ascends to the sala (**A**), at the front of the house. The small stairwells at the other end of the floor, connecting the loggia (**E**) to chamber **L** and a chapel (**N**), contain spiral staircases. They service the land entrance "for those not wishing to ascend by the uncovered steps," the grand ceremonial staircase of stone which rises at the sides of the large central courtyard that in turn leads to the *portego* on the *piano nobile*.[34]

Focusing on the left-hand suite in the plan, we find two chambers – **D** and **I** – open only to the *portego*, which were probably used as day rooms, perhaps for dining and entertaining. Like the other chambers – excluding the *portego* – they were provided with fireplaces. Next to each, but without a connecting door, are chambers of a similar size – **C** and **L** – each with an *albergo* – "as the place for the bed is called" – on one wall, flanked by two closets, one containing "a staircase by which one climbs above the bed."[35] The elevation on the upper left of the page depicts the *albergo* wall for chamber **C**. Serlio explains that the staircase in the right-hand closet leads up to a mezzanine room, which might contain three beds for the children and their nurse.[36] Writing fifty years later, the architectural theorist Vincenzo Scamozzi wrote: "Here in Venice, they use certain mezzanine rooms which they call *sopraletti* – above the beds – so that with one step they can see and give orders when [the children] are healthy and take care of their needs when they are sick."[37] The elevation next to it on the right shows the large window, called a Serliana, facing the open courtyard, which illuminates chambers **D** and **I**. Further to the right, a section depicts the large Serliana overlooking the courtyard that opens to the *portego*.

Chamber **C** at the bottom of the plan connects at the lower left-hand corner through a hallway with a spiral staircase to chamber **B** at the front of the house. This staircase would lead up to a mezzanine level above. The corresponding room at the top (**L**) connects to a round room (**M**), which might serve as a study, with a chapel (**N**) next to it. Beneath **M** and **N**, Serlio advises, "one could have the ovens and bathroom." The nearby spiral staircases opening to the loggia would, in any case, lead down to the garden and ground-floor rooms where the washing was done and the kitchen might have been located.[38]

The hallway on the far left, marked **H**, is, Serlio writes, "a secret passageway through which one passes from room to room without going through the *portego*."[39] Here we get our first clear sense of gendered spaces within the house. But there is more. To the left of the courtyard, between the "secret passageway" and a mezzanine hallway (**F**) is a "loggietta segreta" (**G**), in which "the daughters remained in order not to be seen from any side."[40] Serlio adds: "Above this and the secret passageway will be an uncovered terrace, a very comfortable thing in these houses."[41]

Scamozzi offered the same advice on the separation of male and female space, but he is more specific than Serlio. He counsels that the father of the family should be given rooms in the front part of the house, while the mother's rooms should be further inside so that she could – as he put it – take care of the family more comfortably. The bedrooms of husband and wife should be linked "as parts that unite together the entire body" of the house, and the mother's rooms should be near those of her small children.[42] Likewise, Giacomo Lanteri, the Brescian writer on *economica* or home economics, had held that the women's rooms should be the furthest from the entrance and connected to the garden and the places of washing and storage so that the women could go freely from one place to the other "without passing through the rest of the house where they can be seen."[43]

According to these precepts, how, then, would Serlio's family have occupied these rooms? The evidence is ambiguous. Chamber **C**, near the front of the house, would seem to be most appropriate for the husband, while his wife should occupy chamber **I** in the rear, next to the spiral staircase "which leads to the garden and the places of washing and storage," as Lanteri had recommended. But what use would she make of the round chamber (**M**), which looks more suitable for a study than a sewing room? The uneasy fit suggests a disjunction between the ideal and reality. In any case, the plan was intended to control access and order traffic, with degrees of separation between private and not-so-private space.[44] Using Serlio's ideal plan as an annotated

75 Sebastiano Serlio, elevation of a palace for a Venetian gentleman, 1547–50. Ink on parchment. Munich, Bayerische Staatsbibliothek (Codex Icon. 189, f. 53).

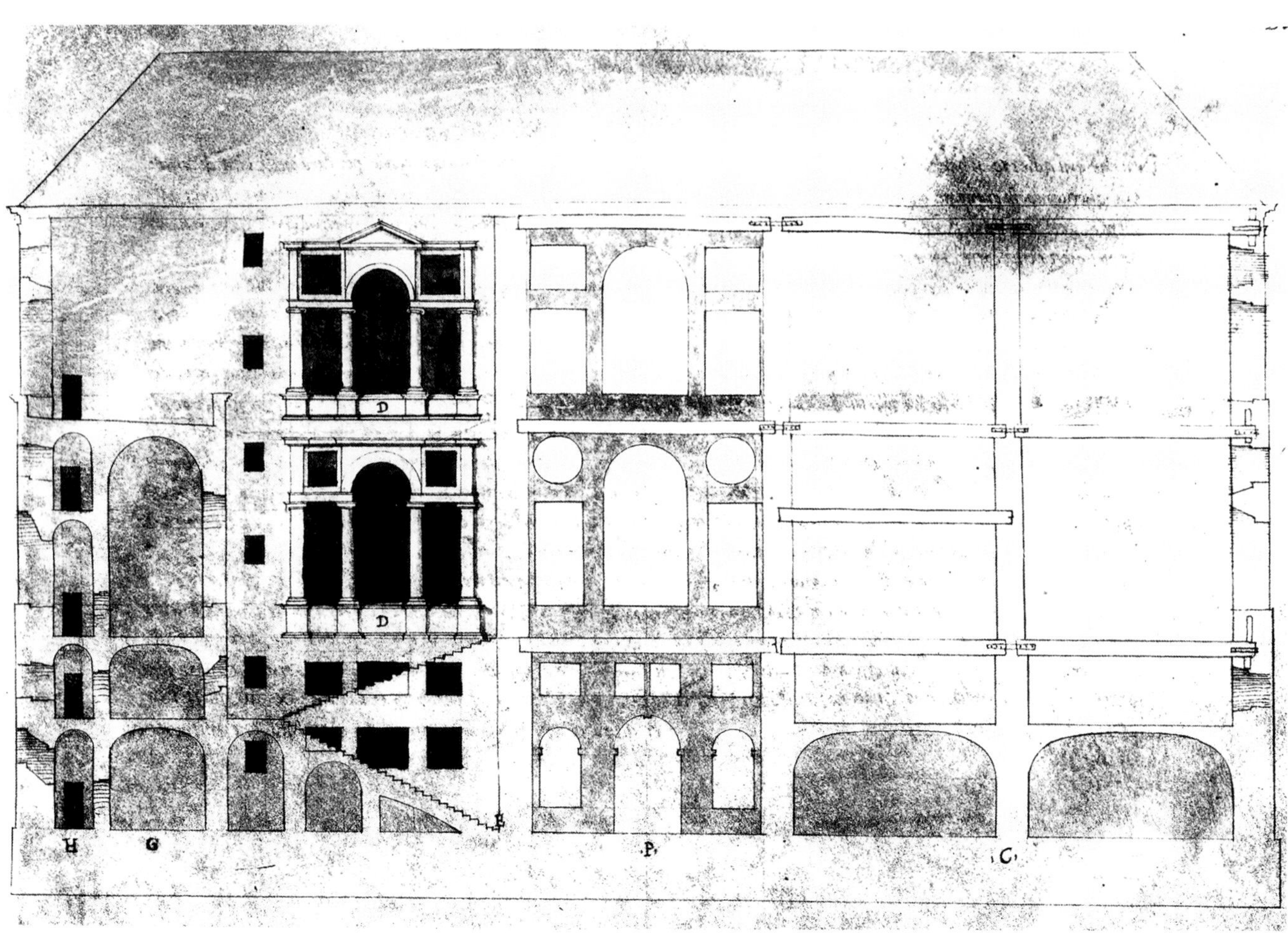

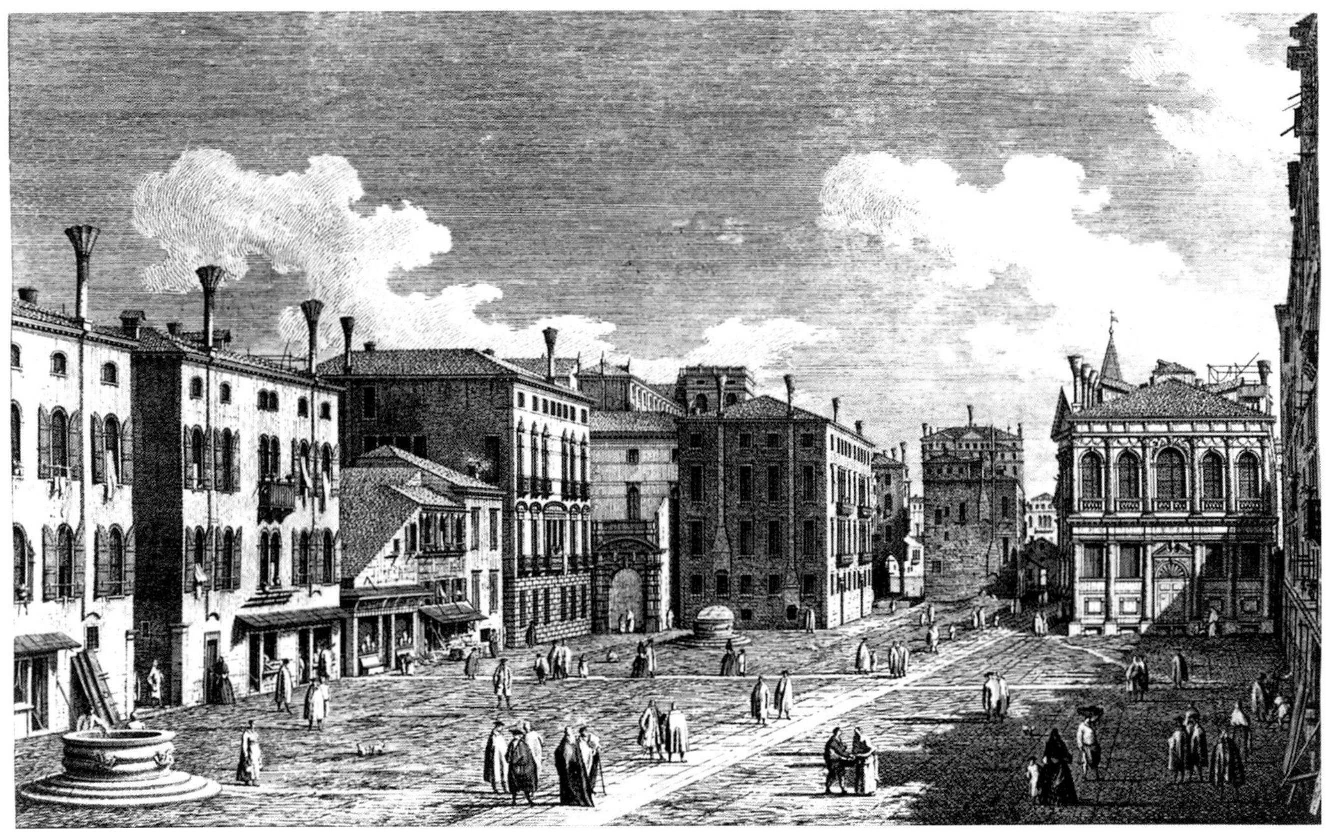

76 *View of Campo San Stefano*, eighteenth century. Engraving. The view is toward the south, with the seventeenth-century rusticated facade and portal of Palazzo Morosini on the left and the classicizing end facade of Palazzo Loredan on the right.

template, we will now try to find our way through an actual house with only the unillustrated pages of archival documents as our guide.

A Venetian Family

Matching up an inventory with wills and tax declarations allows us to get a good sense of the overall domestic arrangements of a specific family at a given point in time. And yet the variations that come through in such documents soon reveal that each household is different and that none can really be considered typical. With that caveat in mind, let us consider the family home of the patrician Donado Da Lezze as a point of departure for a more general discussion of what it meant to live *nobile*. Born in 1546, he lost his father at the age of five and was raised by his mother, Lucrezia, soon remarried, and a stepfather, Zorzi Marcello (for the Da Lezze family tree, see Appendix, p. 259). In 1573, at the age of twenty-seven, Donado was married to a patrician bride, Chiara Morosini. She brought with her a respectable dowry of around 5,000 ducats, which included an expensive wardrobe.[45] But like his own father, Donado would die young, just nine years later, of quartan fever (probably malaria) at the age of thirty-six. He left Chiara with seven young children, the oldest just eight years old and the youngest not yet two.

However, Chiara's widowed mother, Marietta, was living with them at the time, and the family was not without resources. At the time of his death, Donado owned a *casa da statio* – the family palace – on Campo San Stefano (fig. 76), plus another thirty houses in Venice that he rented out – one of these to his stepfather – as well as properties on Murano and the mainland. His income from the rental housing alone was a comfortable 816 ducats per year shortly before he died in 1582.[46] In his will, Donado named his wife, mother, and stepfather as his executors. He asked that his wife be repaid a loan of 500 ducats, a sum that she "had lent to him more than once," without a promissory note. She was also to receive back the entire cash portion of her dowry so long as she did not remarry, and not just the two-thirds to which she was entitled by law.[47]

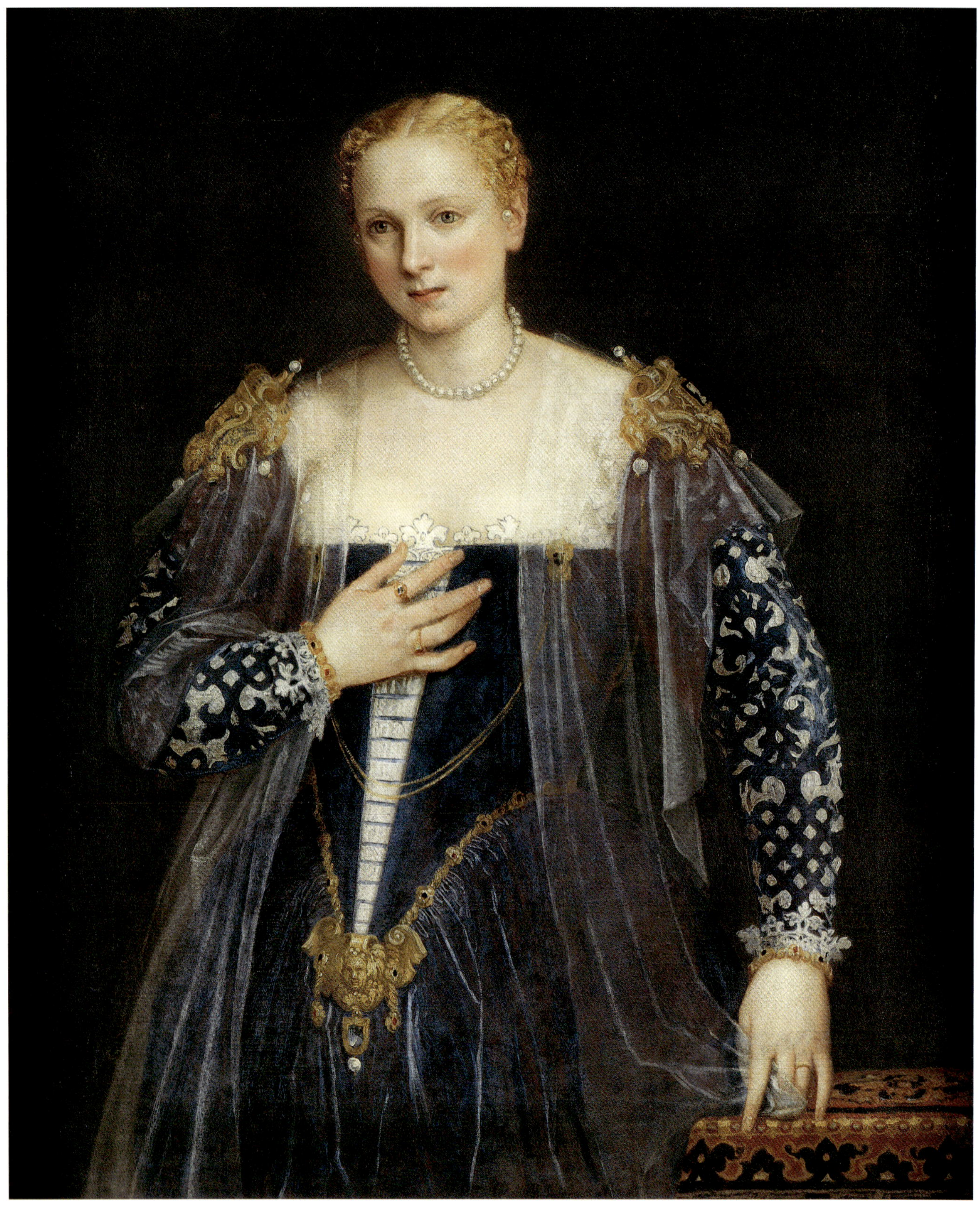

77 Paolo Veronese, *La Belle Nani*, ca. 1560. Oil on canvas, 119 × 103 cm. The painting takes its name from a portrait seen by Marco Boschini in Ca' Nani in 1660, but there is no evidence that it is the same work. The lady's pearl necklace and bound hair suggest that she is a recent bride. Paris, Musée du Louvre.

Aside from the properties in Murano and on the mainland, which were to go to his sons, all of Donado's worldly goods, including the houses in Venice, were to be divided among his four daughters and three sons, according to the judgement of the executors. And it was the executors – wife, mother, and stepfather – who were to raise the children whether Donado survived or not. For although he was gravely ill, Donado allowed that he might recover, and if so he wished to enter a monastery to serve God; he counseled his children to remain obedient to their mother and grandparents. If he should die, his body was to be buried outside Venice, either in Padua or Verona, according to the wishes of his wife and his mother, 12 feet under ground in a tomb with a cover of plain red stone at little expense.[48] A number of attitudes can be inferred from Donado's testament: loyalty to the lineage, with respect for his wealthy wife and a strong attachment to his mother; an even-handedness with his children as far as property distribution was concerned; unusual piety; and perhaps a weariness with family life.

And how did the young Da Lezze family live, before Donado's final illness? Their palace on Campo San Stefano consisted of two main living floors comprising a *portego*, five chambers – one with a studio and another with a *sopraletto* (mezzanine or loft) – and a *salvarobba* (closet or storeroom), kitchen, and laundry. On the mezzanine and the ground floors below were storage rooms and a courtyard with a well. The household probably included at least one servant – more likely two or three – along with the married couple, mother-in-law and seven children.[49] Although Chiara is now only a name without a face, Paolo Veronese's portrait – probably idealized – of an aristocratic young wife now known as *La Belle Nani*, may serve as her surrogate as we accompany the notary through her house (fig. 77).[50]

The Portego

To enter the aristocratic house, as we have seen, the visitor invariably climbed a staircase. Whether it is inside or outside, narrow and dark, or broad and bright, it led in most cases directly to the *portego* – the spine of the house. The Venetian *portego* was typically a room of reflections and hard edges. Light streaming in through the windows in front, or flickering from a glass lamp or chandelier, glanced off floors of gleaming *paston* or *terrazzo* (fig. 78). Sansovino claimed that in entering such rooms you would seem to find yourself in a "very reverend and spotless church of nuns," and that *terrazzo* floors could be given such a high polish "that a man could see himself mirrored in it."[51] As Scamozzi later confirmed, "The cleanliness of the homes of nobles, has no equal anywhere else in the world . . . every footstep [on] the terraces of the houses is cleaned by servants, so that they appear to be lustrous stones."[52] The gleaming, multicolored *terrazzo* floor was one of the hallmarks of luxury in the sixteenth-century Venetian home.[53]

The ceiling might be coffered, but more often it was constructed of parallel beams, called *travi*, which were often gorgeously painted, and even papered, with decorative patterns.[54] In 1542 Giorgio Vasari would paint a *soffito* in Ca' Corner-Spinelli with an illusionistic program of personified virtues set into wood-framed compartments. Lavish coffered ceilings that served as picture frames for a cycle of paintings were already becoming fashionable in public buildings such as the Palazzo Ducale and a number of churches. But although Tintoretto and a few other artists also completed several such commissions, these extravagantly expensive ceilings remained the exception in domestic architecture.[55]

The Da Lezze *portego*, following Venetian custom, asserted noble lineage with portraits of Donado and of his Da Lezze grandfather in gilded frames, but was otherwise furnished with abundant seating and not much else. Arranged around the room were twenty-four walnut stools, both carved and plain, and six rush-bottomed chairs, of a type called *da donna* – for the woman – which were more comfortable than bare wooden seats in a time when upholstery had not yet become commonplace (see fig. 124). The *portego* was also provided with sixteen folding walnut chairs. As with much of the furniture of the period, these were designed to be portable (figs. 79 and 80).[56] Alternatively, some homes had large suites of elaborately carved chairs designed specifically for the *portego* (fig. 81). Stored in another room of the Da Lezze residence were 28 meters of crimson damask in thirteen pieces, to be hung around the walls of the *portego* on special occasions.[57]

Aside from its function as an elegant corridor with seating for nearly fifty guests, how was the *portego* actually used? Written accounts suggest that this was the most public room in the house, a space for grand entertaining: as Scamozzi put it, "to receive relatives at the time of weddings, and to have banquets, and celebrations."[58] It was almost certainly not used for everyday family meals. While modern writers sometimes define the *portego* as the symbolic heart of domestic space, inventories such as the Da Lezze's tell another story.

Their experience is replicated by many others, such as the very wealthy Domenico Cappello, who died in 1532, leaving a widow, Lucia, and at least six children in his palace on Rio San Lorenzo – a Gothic-style building later praised by Sansovino as one of the hundred or so *palazzi* in the city worthy of the name. Elected capo of the Council of Ten *per*

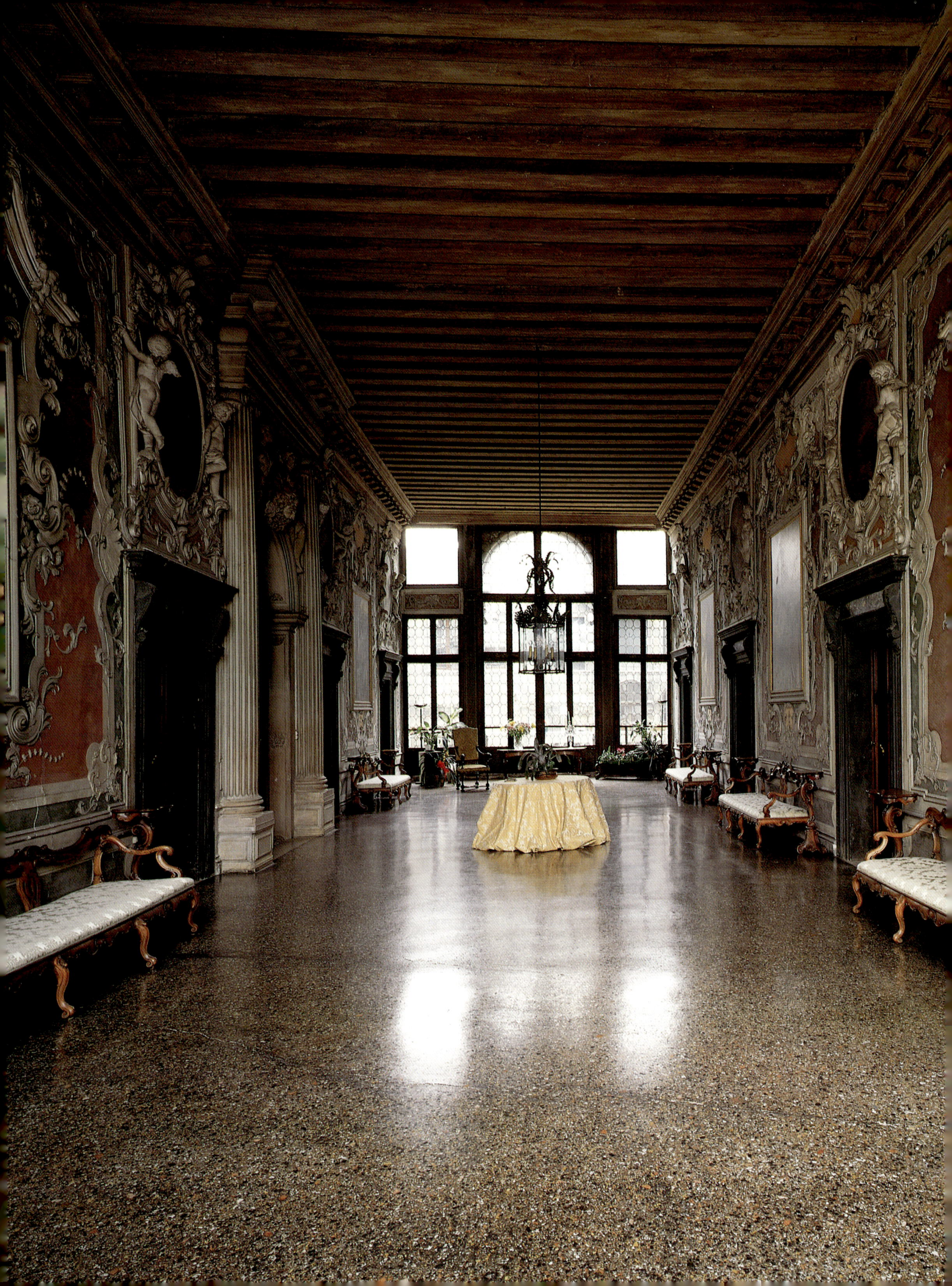

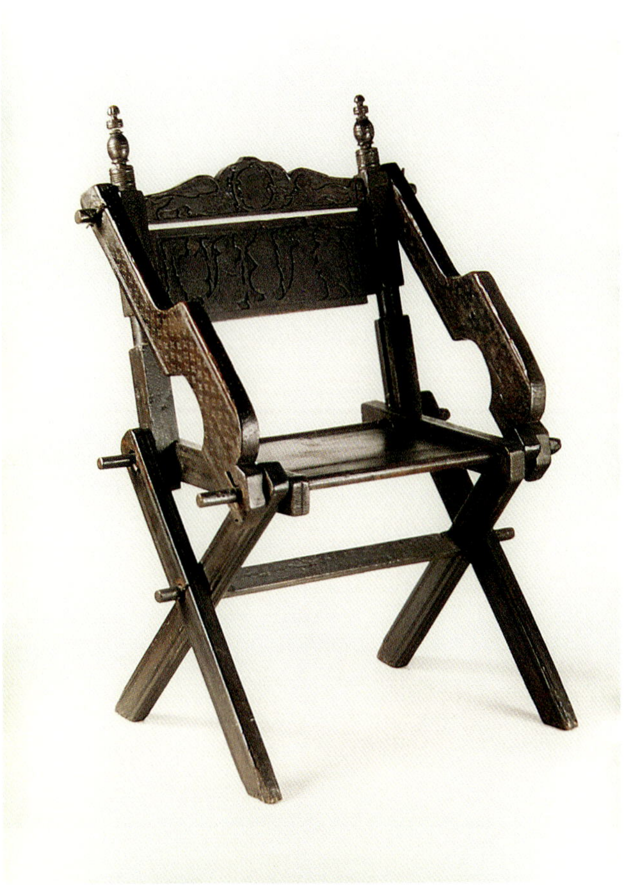

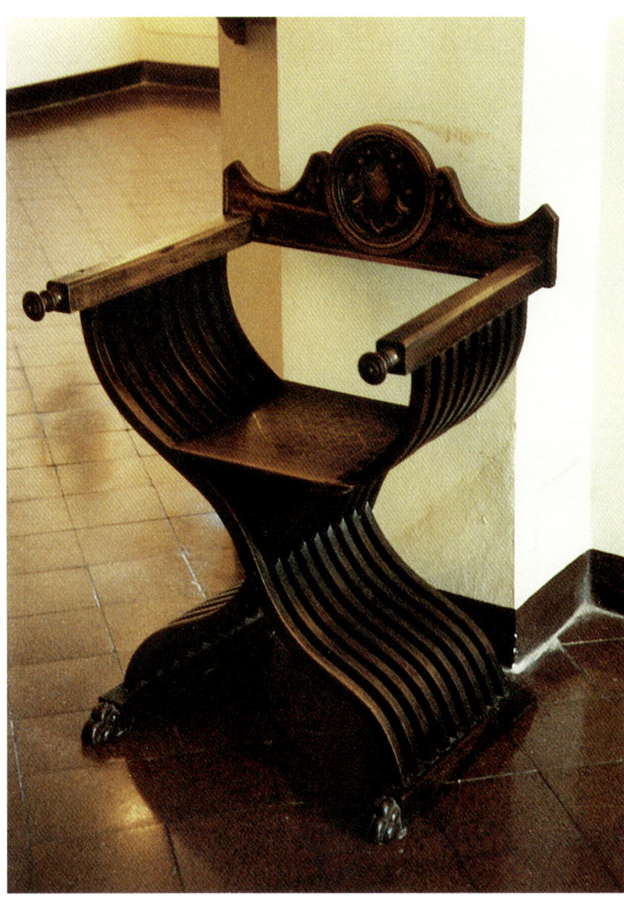

79 (*above left*) Folding chair (*sedia smontabile*), also called a camp chair or *cariega da campo*, (?)second half fifteenth and nineteenth century. Cypress, height 110 cm, width 78 cm, depth 52 cm. The camp chair was a common type of portable seat in northern Italy. On this example, the backrest is carved with a heraldic shield flanked by stylized animals on the top and lords and ladies at the fountain of youth – a chivalric motif – on the bar below. The arms of the chair are carved with a lozenge pattern, probably of Islamic origin. Although parts of the chair were remade in the nineteenth century, the type corresponds to the *sedia del Petrarca*, preserved in Petrarch's house in Arquà Petrarca, and similar examples survive in other collections. Milan, Museo Bagatti-Valsecchi, inv. n. 241.

80 (*above right*) Folding chair (Savonarola chair), sixteenth century. Walnut. The chair is composed of curved slats held together in an X-frame construction that folds like scissors. Of antique origin, the type was revived in Florence and became popular throughout Italy in the fifteenth and sixteenth centuries. The backrest of this example is carved with the ubiquitous coat of arms or *stemma* – a silent statement of the family's aristocratic credentials. Siena, Pinacoteca.

78 (*facing page*) *Portego* on the upper *piano nobile* of Ca' da Mosto. Pietro Aretino lived in the building in the sixteenth century. It later became one of the city's finest hotels, known as Leon Bianco (or White Lion). The wall decoration dates to the eighteenth century.

danari (that is, for money), as Marin Sanudo noted, Capello was active in political life and far richer than the Da Lezze.[59] And yet, while Domenico's *portego* was decorated with eight paintings, including a portrait of his son Nicolò, already deceased, it was furnished with little more than fifteen painted benches that lined the sides of the room. His inventory also listed six dining tables, all of them on trestles, but their placement in the house is not noted and it is probable that they were moved around, like the Da Lezze's folding chairs, as the occasion demanded.

Inventories place a variety of objects in the Venetian *portego* but, as with the Da Lezze and Cappello families, there were two constants: paintings and an ample number of chairs or benches. In addition, a good number of noble *porteghi* contained at least a few weapons or trophies of a military nature, often arranged in the traditional display called the *restelliera* (see fig. 22).[60]

The portego was seldom provided with a fireplace. These sources of warmth were usually limited to the *camere* or chambers at the sides where they were the focal point of each room (see fig. 4). In fact, it is no coincidence that in Italian the same word – *fuoco* (*foco* in Venetian dialect) –

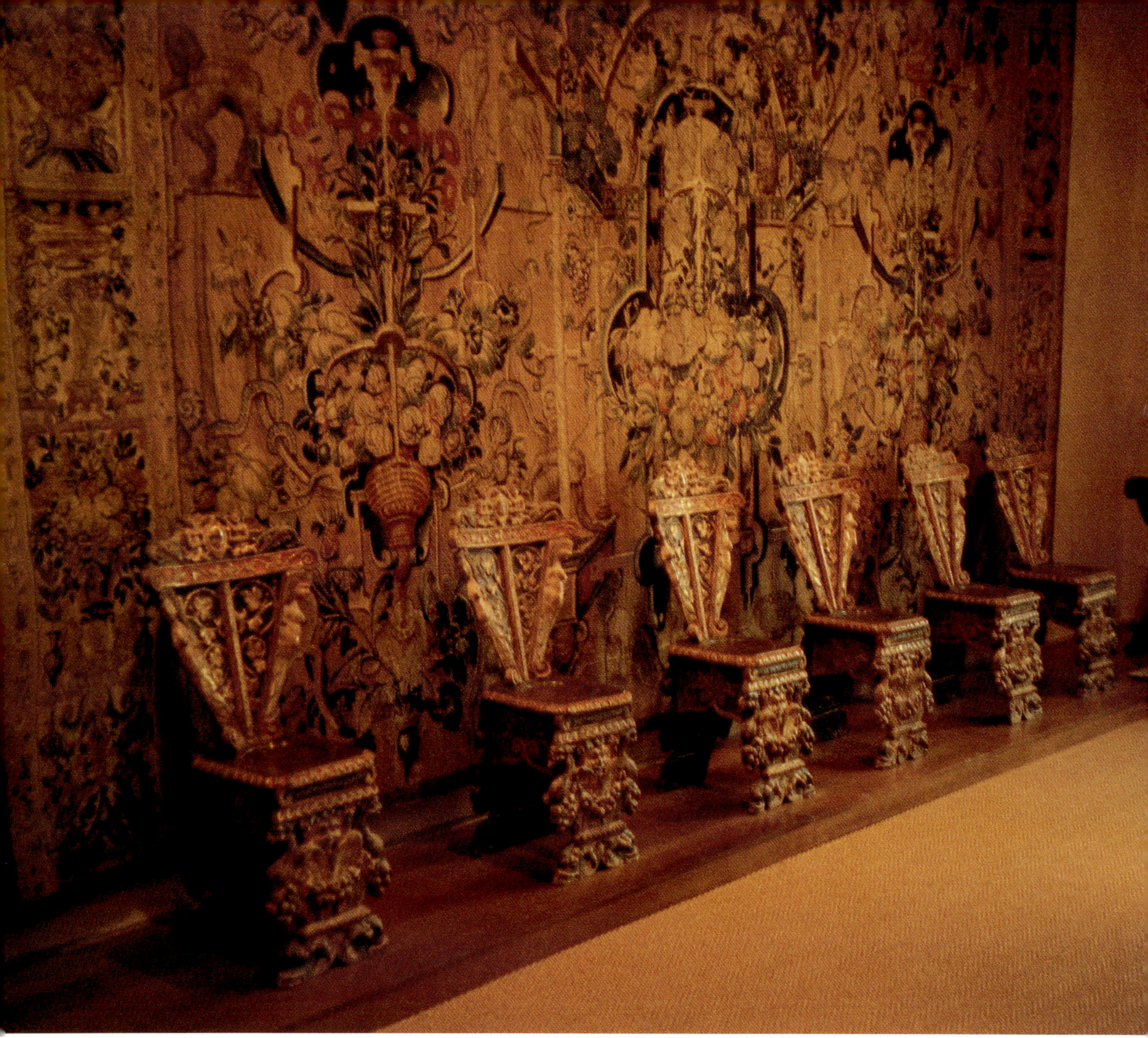

81 Six side chairs (*sgabelli*), Venice, sixteenth century. Wood, painted and gilded. Paris, Musée des Arts Decoratifs.

means both fire and focal point. But the *portego* did have a focal point, and that was the loggia on the facade at the end of the room – both focal point and frontispiece. For the family within, the loggia gave visual access to the world beyond the walls (fig. 82). And, conversely, to all those outside the *casa*, friend and stranger alike, the loggia windows made legible the presence of this room so central to family representation.[61] As Sansovino put it, "the windows of the *sala* are placed in the middle of the facade so that onlookers can easily recognize where [it is] located."[62] The semi-public function of the *portego*, where

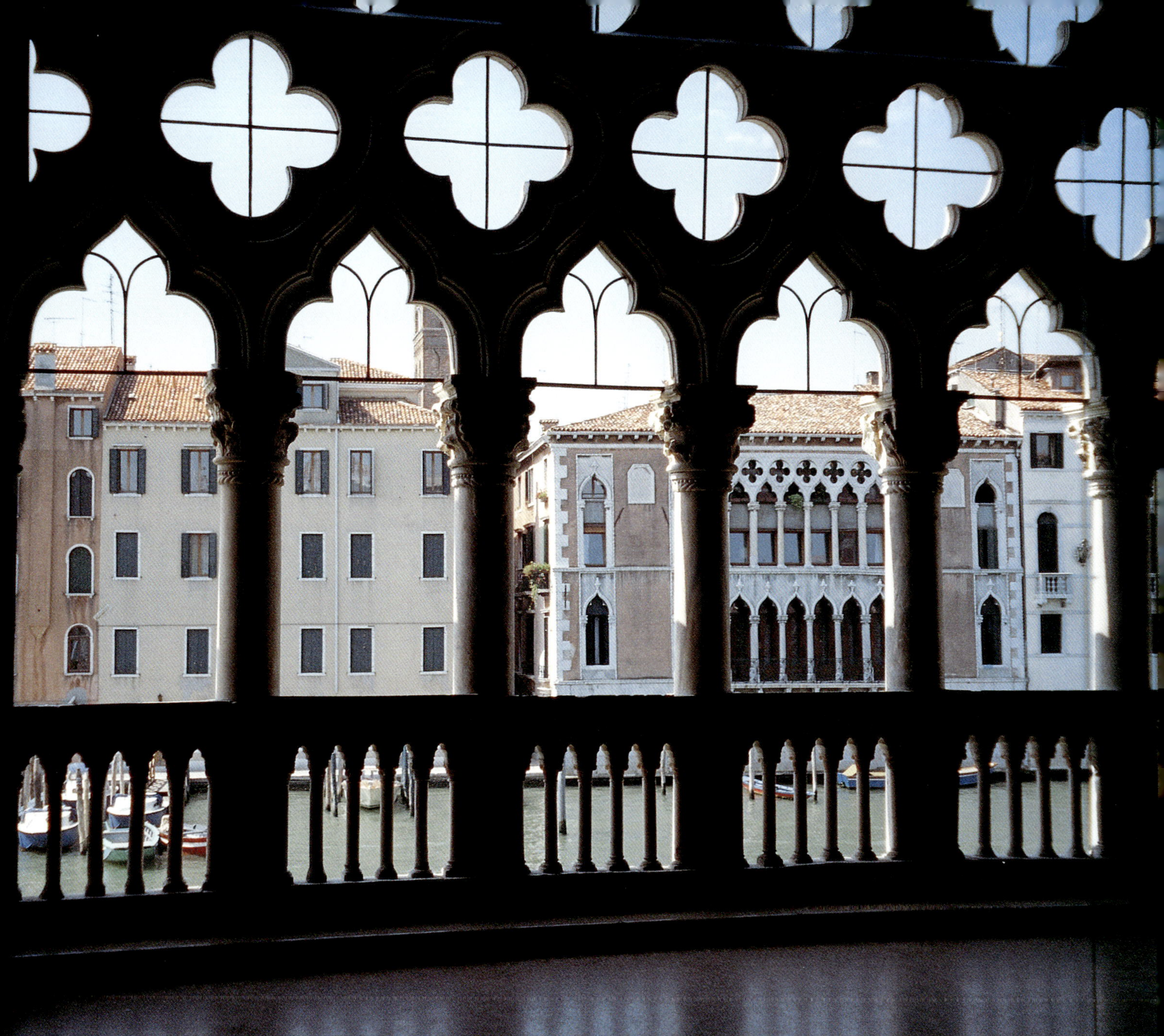

82 View from the loggia of Ca' d'Oro. Documentation shows that the windows were originally glazed, although the present glass screen at the head of the *portego* is modern.

the head of the house might receive business clients who would not be invited into the more private rooms, is suggested by this degree of visibility from the outside. Anyone passing by in a gondola could admire the beamed, coffered, and often painted ceilings and Murano glass chandeliers. Indeed, the function of the *portego* was, first and foremost, display. This was a privileged space that defined the family. It expressed their values, with paintings of suitably moralizing content, and their achievements, with relics of exploits on the sea.

* * *

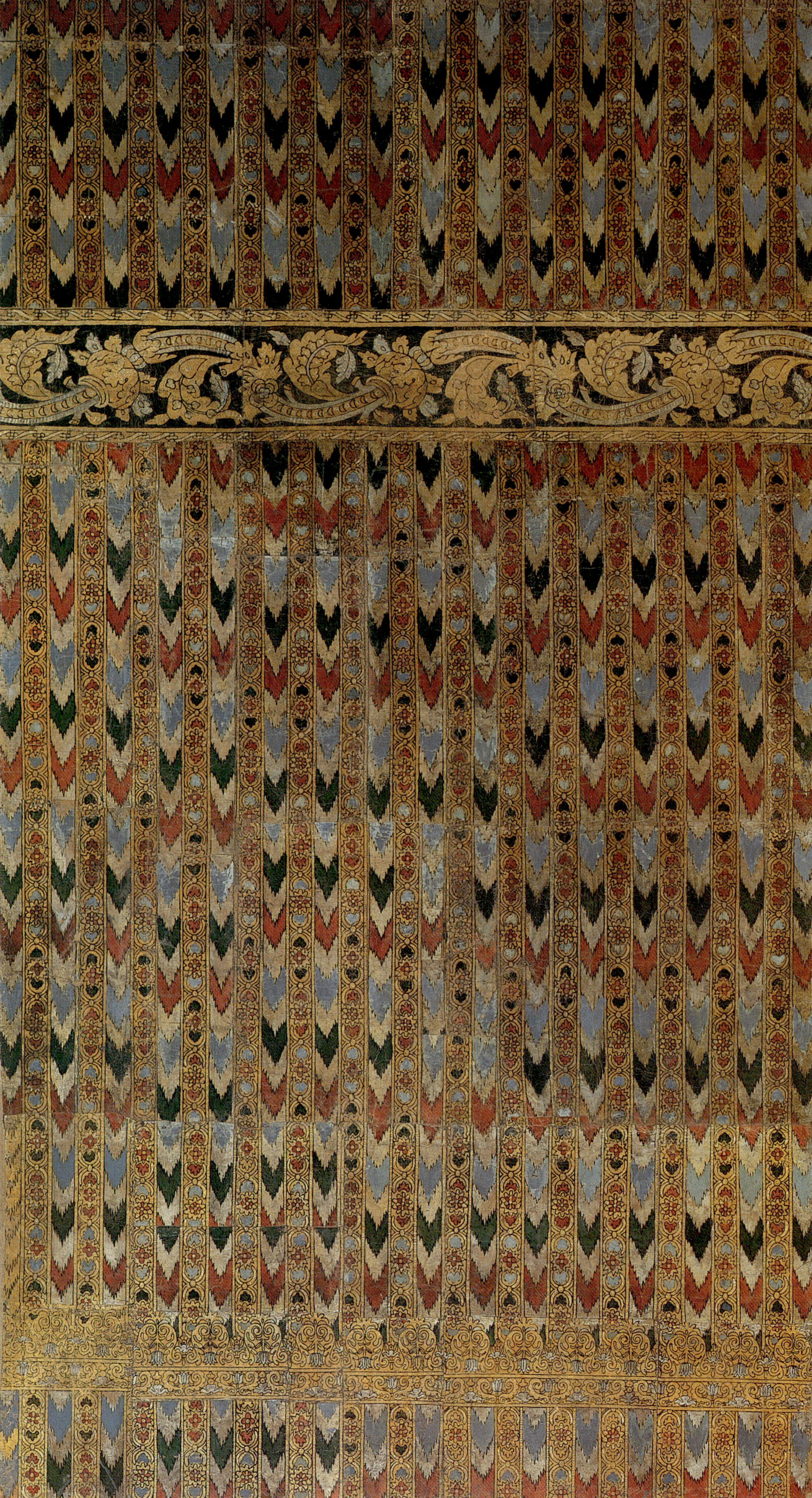

The Camera d'Oro

But it is in the various chambers at the sides that signs of domesticity and comfort are most evident. Two such rooms, probably flanking the Da Lezze *portego* on the *piano nobile*, looked out on the *campo*. The first of these was called the *camera d'oro* – chamber of gold – a term that referred to the ceiling and wall decoration, since none of the furniture in the room was described as gilded. While some such rooms might be lined with hangings of gilded leather, there is no evidence that the Da Lezze walls were decorated in this sumptuous manner (fig. 83).[63] Nor were they adorned with paintings or tapestries, even though this was probably the de facto living room of the house. More intimate than the bare *portego*, it was equipped with a fireplace and furnished with a harpsichord, five rush-bottomed chairs, and *un scagno de noghera da lavorar suso* – a walnut stool for Chiara or her mother-in-law to sit on when doing needlework. The room also held a walnut *cassone* that must have been very large indeed, for it contained eleven women's dresses made of bulky luxury fabrics, such as brocades, velvets, and silks, that would not have been worn every day, particularly by a wife who must have been in a perpetual state of pre- or post-partum. It was in this room that the family treasures were kept. Aside from the gowns, which Chiara later reclaimed as part of her dowry, there were two locked *scrigneti*: cabinets filled with jewelry, silver cutlery, and hollowware, including a little basin with the Da Lezze coat of arms and important legal documents – wills, lawsuits, marriage contracts. With its luxurious appointments, the room recalls the chamber described by Canon Pietro Casola, who had attended a childbirth celebration for a lady of the Dolfin family in 1494. In his journal, Casola spoke of a fireplace of Carrara marble in her bedchamber with "so much gold everywhere" that he was certain its decoration must have cost 2,000 ducats or more.[64]

The Da Lezze *camera d'oro* might also have been used for sleeping, for the notary listed *una carruola da campo de noghera* – a movable camp bed on wheels – provided with mattresses, though he described it as "unfurnished." It was, perhaps, used by a servant or even for the childbirth celebrations that had occurred with all too frequent regularity in the Da Lezze household. But there might also have been a bed built into the wall, which would not have been recorded by the notary since it was considered part of the house rather than a piece of furniture. Such built-in beds were common in Venice, with inventories listing mattresses of down, wool, and cotton, along with luxurious silk draperies and bedding, but no true and proper bedstead (fig. 84; see also fig. 191). Casola had described the bed in the Dolfin bedroom as "fixed in the room in the Venetian fashion," adding, "I had better not try and describe the ornaments of the bed . . . that is the covering and the cushions, which were six in number, and the curtains, as I fear I should not be believed. They were in truth most wonderful."[65] In a *sopraletto* above the Da Lezze *camera d'oro* was a cradle and at least one bed, along with baskets, some pieces of cloth, and large pieces of majolica. Serving as both storeroom and bedroom, this was probably – in accordance with the prescriptive texts of Serlio and Scamozzi – a space in which a nurse and some of the children slept.[66]

Visitors to Venetian homes in this period who left written accounts rarely mention the *portego* but what did strike them were these golden chambers at the sides, like the Da Lezze's *camera d'oro*, perhaps similar to the room depicted in Mansueti's *Healing of the Daughter of Ser Nicolo Benvegnudo of San Polo* (fig. 85). As early as 1384, a Florentine traveler described the interior of Remigio Soranzo's palace as a "house of gold, and he had many rooms in which little was to be seen except gold and azure," an impression that was repeated in different homes by other visitors in the fifteenth century.[67] Writing in 1495, Philippe de Commynes, the French ambassador to Venice, was more specific. He exclaimed that most houses "have at least two rooms which have gilded ceilings, rich mantlepieces of cut marble, gilded

83 (*facing page*) Wall hanging of leather (*bazzana*), with gilding and polychrome decoration, late sixteenth century. 283 × 156 cm. Bologna, Museo Civico Medievale, inv. no. 2014.

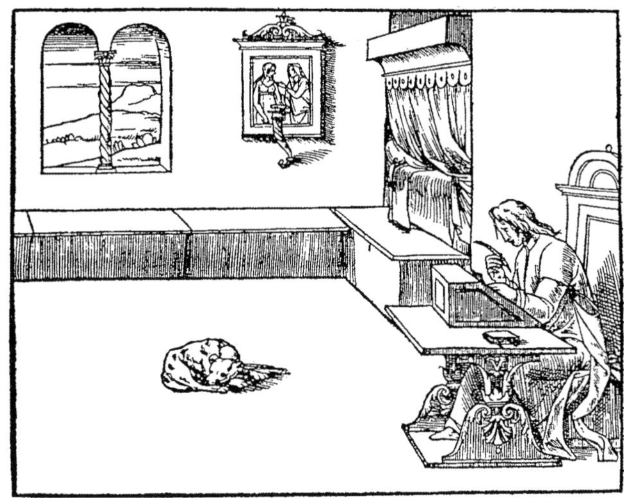

84 Polifilo's bedroom, from the *Hypnerotomachia Poliphili* (Venice: Aldine Press, 1499).

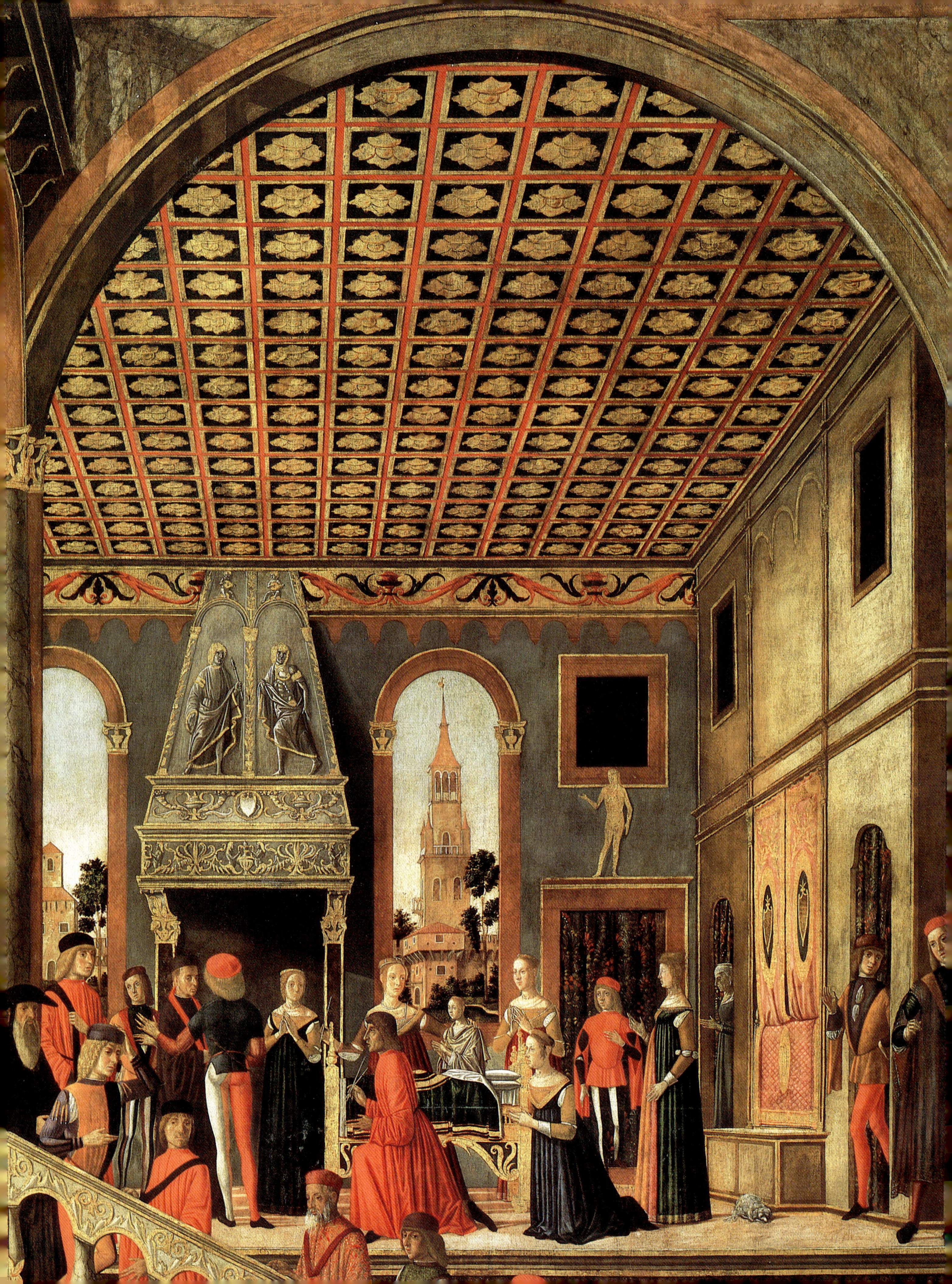

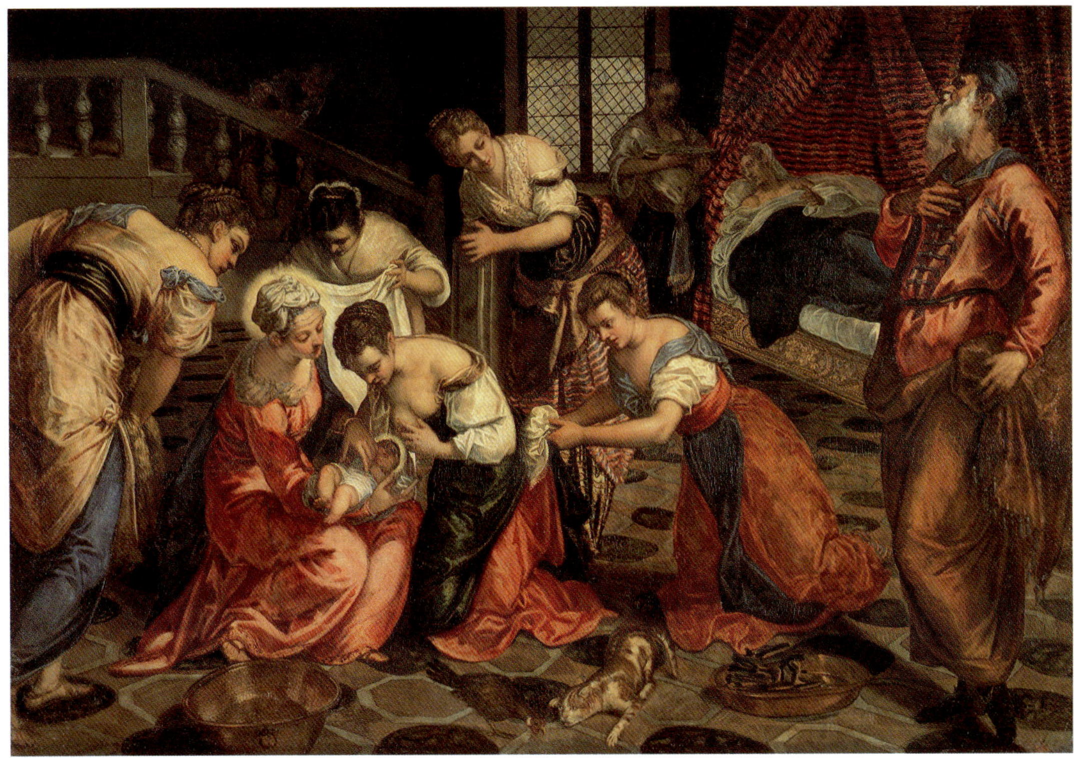

86 (*above*) Jacopo Tintoretto, *Birth of St. John the Baptist*, 1583–87. Oil on canvas, 422 × 545 cm. St. Petersburg, Hermitage.

85 (*facing page*) Giovanni Mansueti, *Healing of the Daughter of Ser Nicolo Benvegnudo of San Polo* (detail), ca. 1506. Oil on canvas, whole work 369 × 296 cm. The painting depicts the miraculous recovery of a three-year-old girl who had been blind since birth, through the agency of the relic of the True Cross, owned by the Scuola Grande di San Giovanni Evangelista. The windows of the *sopraletto* are visible above the built-in bed on the right. Venice, Accademia.

bedsteads, and painted and gilded screens, and very fine furniture inside. It is the most sumptuous city which I have ever seen."[68] He was seconded by the local historian, Marcantonio Sabellico, who wrote in a short guide to the city that Venetian homes were "more ornate inside than outside" and asserted that "one does not see any new house that does not have golden chambers, and there are few who would not have covered their houses with gold if the laws did not restrict [such] luxury."[69]

But such reports – like those of Marin Sanudo and Sansovino – are hearsay at best, and myth creation at least. Returning once again to the *casa* of Domenico Cappello, his death inventory designated three rooms as "golden," outdoing the Da Lezze threefold.[70] This suggests a ceiling and wood moldings with a generous coating of gold leaf, such as in Mansueti's painting, but among the furnishings of Cappello's *camera d'oro grande* were also a large gilded writing desk of walnut, a mirror with a gilt frame, and no fewer than ten painted and gilded chests.

The Bedchamber

However the *camera d'oro* might have been used, the second chamber in the Da Lezze house that looked out on the *campo* was a true and proper bedroom, although according to the custom of the day it would also have been used as a day room and for receiving guests. Here the gold was on the furniture, including a gilded iron bedstead, a painting of Our Lady *alla greca* – "antique" as the inventory put it, probably referring to a Byzantine-style icon – with a gold-leaf background, and five gilded walnut chests. The fireplace was furnished with brass andirons and bellows of green velvet with a walnut handle and a nozzle of gilded bronze. The canopied bed was of the *da pavion* (pavilion or tent) type, with the bed curtains supported by a little cap of gilded walnut suspended from the ceiling (as in fig. 86). The accoutrements were sumptuous, but most of them were stored away inside the chests. There, the notary listed a green damask canopy with a matching coverlet; a bedskirt of crimson silk; two large and two small cushions and fine

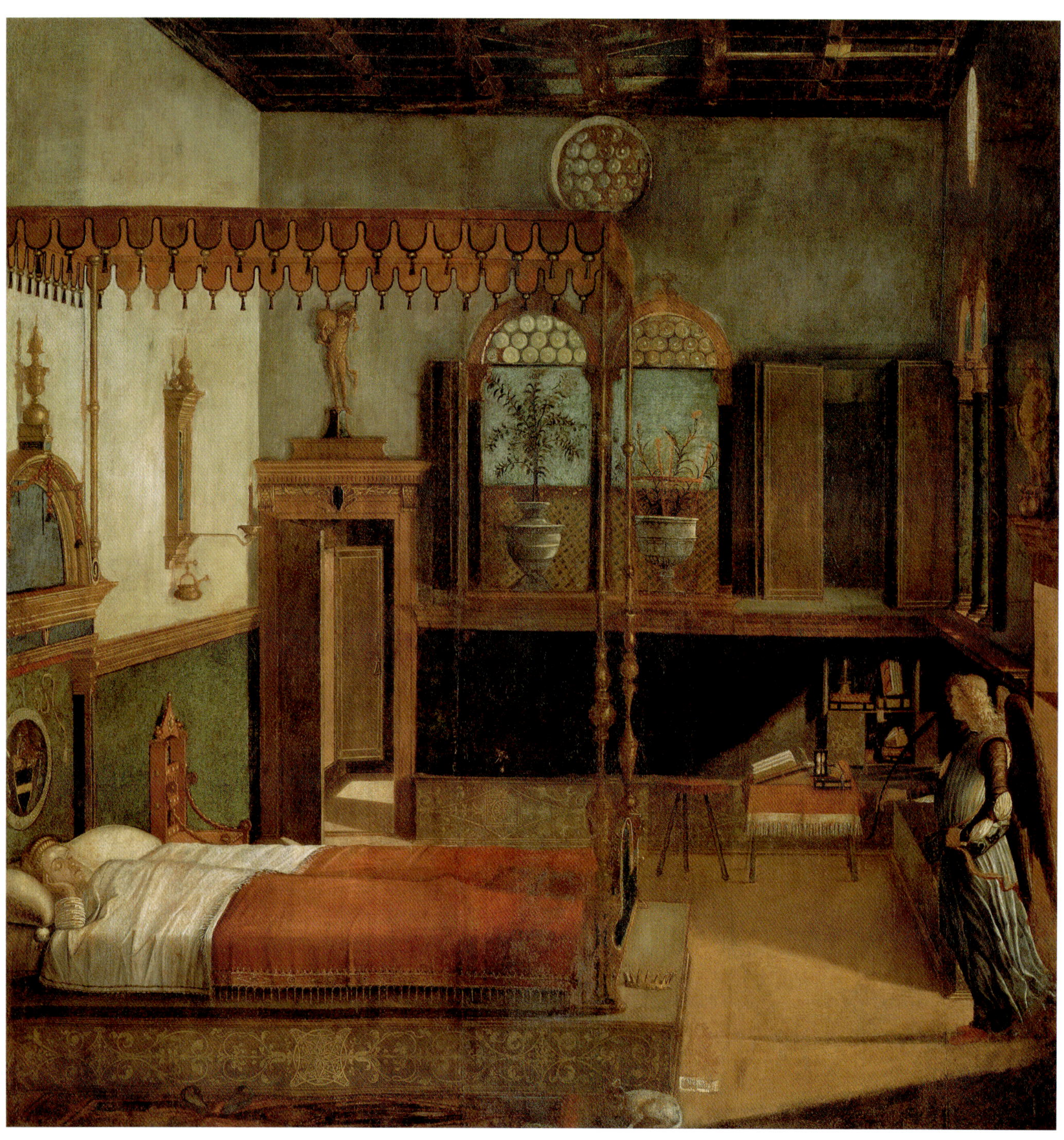

87 Vittore Carpaccio, *The Dream of St. Ursula*, 1500. Canvas, 274 × 267 cm. Chests aligned along the back wall of the room, as well as the base of the bed, appear to be decorated with an intarsia inlay. Venice, Accademia.

linen pillowcases with gold embroidered borders; two sets of sheets with lace trim; and four window curtains of green taffeta. Two sets of wall hangings for the room were stored in a chamber above: a *spalliera a boschaia* – a tapestry with a verdant, or leafy, pattern – in six pieces, about 22 meters in length; and an old *spalliera* with the arms of the family of Donado's mother, the Contarini.[71] The green-and-red color scheme emerges from inventories in general as the most prevalent combination in Venetian homes of this period.[72]

The room also held four rush-bottomed chairs, the *carieghe da donna*, and two tables. Clothing for men, women, and children was also stored in the gilded chests. A maternity dress, labeled "used," of white satin (*raso*) with gold ribbons, and two cradles, one of carved walnut and the other of fir, indicate that the room served in part as a nursery. And yet an armoire containing books and unspecified writings also reveals the presence of the man of the house. While the contents suggest that this might have been the bedroom of the married couple, or perhaps that of Chiara alone – a room from which the husband was all too ready to flee – there was a room called the *camera grande* further back in the house, away from the *campo*. It too contained a gilded iron bed – possibly with a rectangular canopy frame or tester to hold up the curtains (fig. 87) – a fireplace with bronze andirons, a painting of the Magi, and chests that held twenty-three ladies' chemises, "part used, part old and part torn," as well as men's shirts. A room where sewing was done, it also contained a basket of yarn and a *homo de legno* – a wood mannequin. An adjacent studio was dedicated to activities both sacred and profane. Furnished with a little altar below a carved wood crucifix and another painting of the Magi, "with its gold framing according to custom," the studio also contained a cushion to make bobbin lace.[73] Were this chamber and studio the lodgings of the married couple, or of Donado alone, or did they belong to Chiara's widowed mother, who would have occupied herself with needlework and prayer? We will never know for sure.

According to Scamozzi, the husband's rooms should have been those in the front of the house with Chiara's further back. And yet it is clear that each of these chambers contained items pertaining to both male and female members of the household, and two held objects suggesting the presence of children and perhaps a servant or nurse. With such rooms usually multi-purpose in use, specialization of function had not yet become part of the domestic canon. Whether male or female, few people in this period, even the rich, had the luxury of a room of their own. The chambers on the floor above also contained beds and clothing and must have accommodated at least some of the children and perhaps a servant.

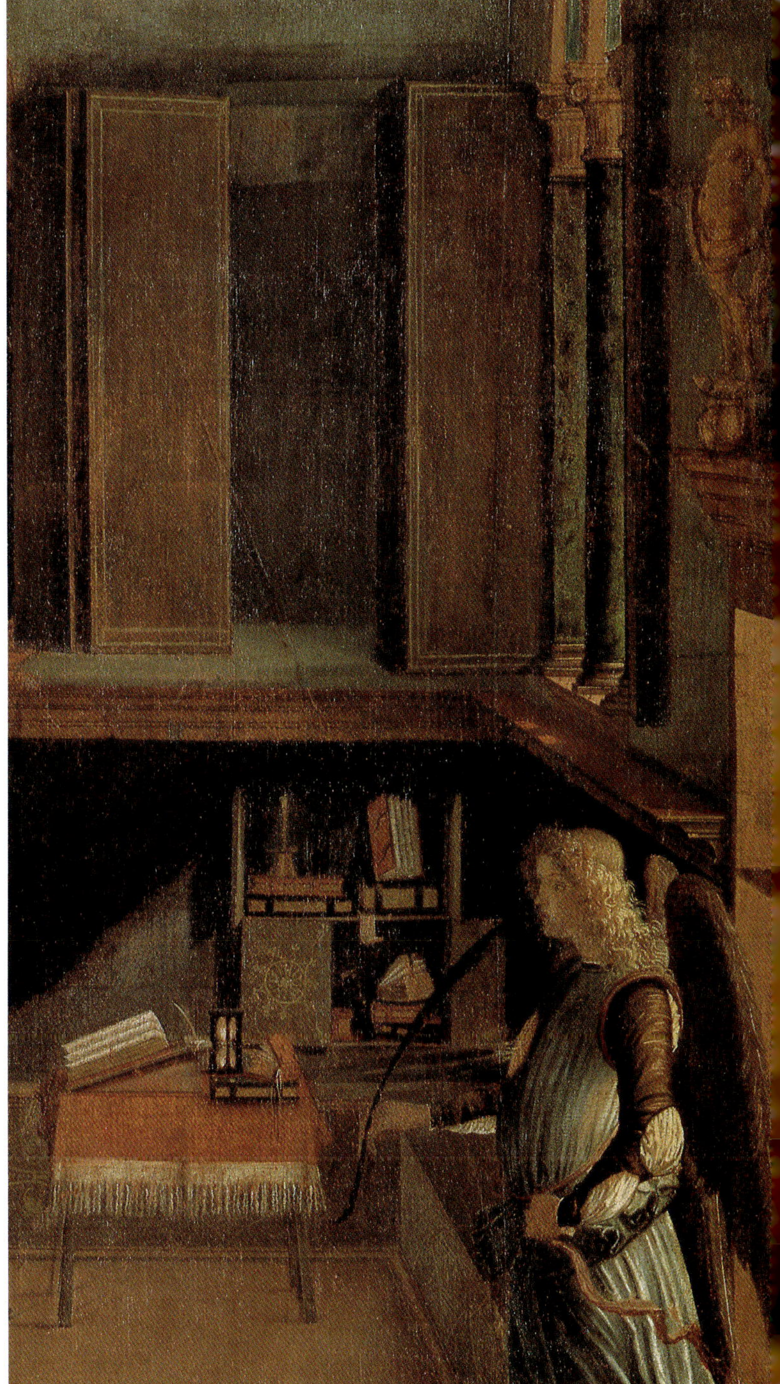

above Detail of fig. 87, with a table and a small cabinet, making this corner a miniature *studiolo*.

To round out the snapshot of the Da Lezze home, it should be noted that the kitchen contained cooking utensils of all sorts – among them mortars, cauldrons, pots, and

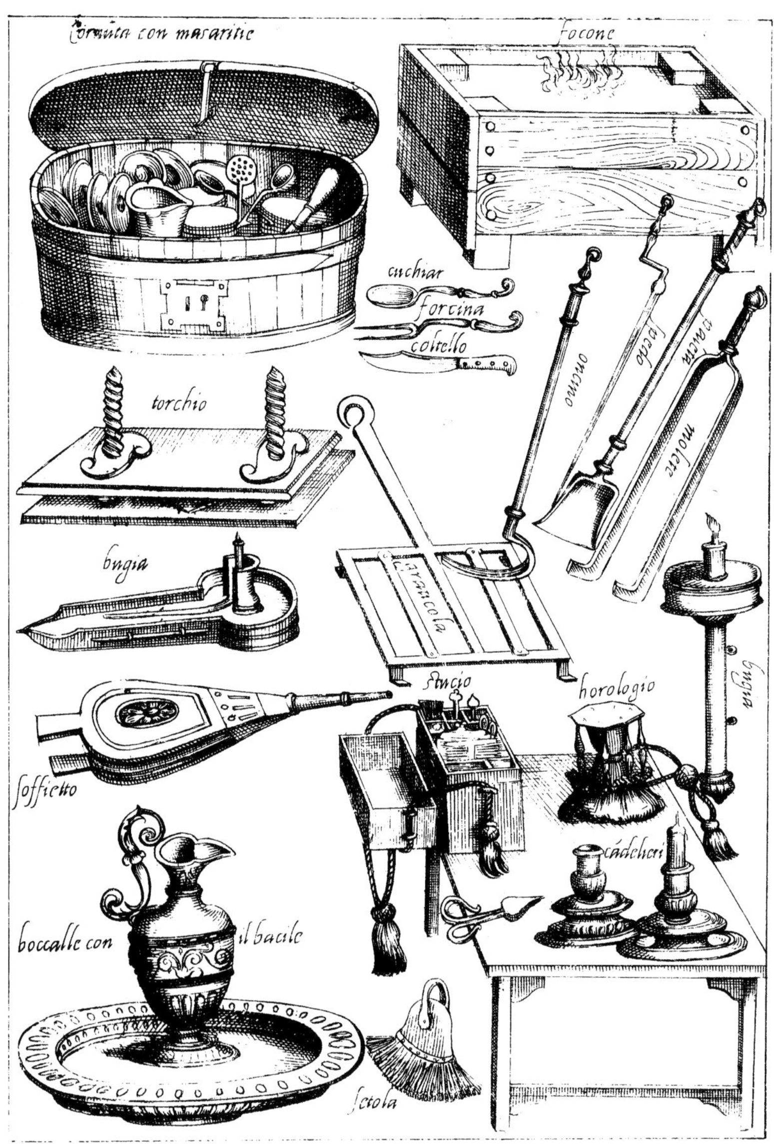

88 Household implements, engraving from Bartolomeo Scappi, *Opera* (Venice: Michele Tramezzino, 1570). Most of the items in the print were found in the Da Lezze family kitchen. Pottery and majolicaware were often stored in baskets or chests such as the one at the upper left. The *torchio* beneath it is a linen press. On the table are a sewing kit, shears, an hourglass, and two candlesticks.

pans – as well as 147 pieces of pewter of "diverse types and sizes," such as those illustrated in Bartolomeo Scappi's treatise on cooking (fig. 88).[74] That the family exemplified the virtue of prudence, with an ample supply of provisions, there is no doubt. However, the location of the kitchen is not certain. Assuming that the notary went to each room in order, the placement of a room in the sequence may reveal its location. In this case it is suggestive, but not conclusive. The inventory listed the *portego*, a small *salvarobba* (storage closet), the kitchen, the *sopraletto* above the *camera d'oro*, the laundry, the *caneva* (wine storage room), and the courtyard with the well, in that order. The *salvarobba* contained such items as a walnut *credenza*, and a pewter mortar, suggesting that it functioned as a pantry adjacent to a kitchen on the *piano nobile*, with a nearby staircase leading up to the *sopraletto* and down to the laundry, a space normally located near the well in the courtyard. In the storerooms on the ground floor and mezzanine level were pieces of cast-off furniture, barrels of wine, boxes, chests filled with clothing, and "several scraps of wood," among other things. Intriguingly, in the courtyard doorway, stowed along with jugs of wine, was "a preaching bench with its benches all around."[75]

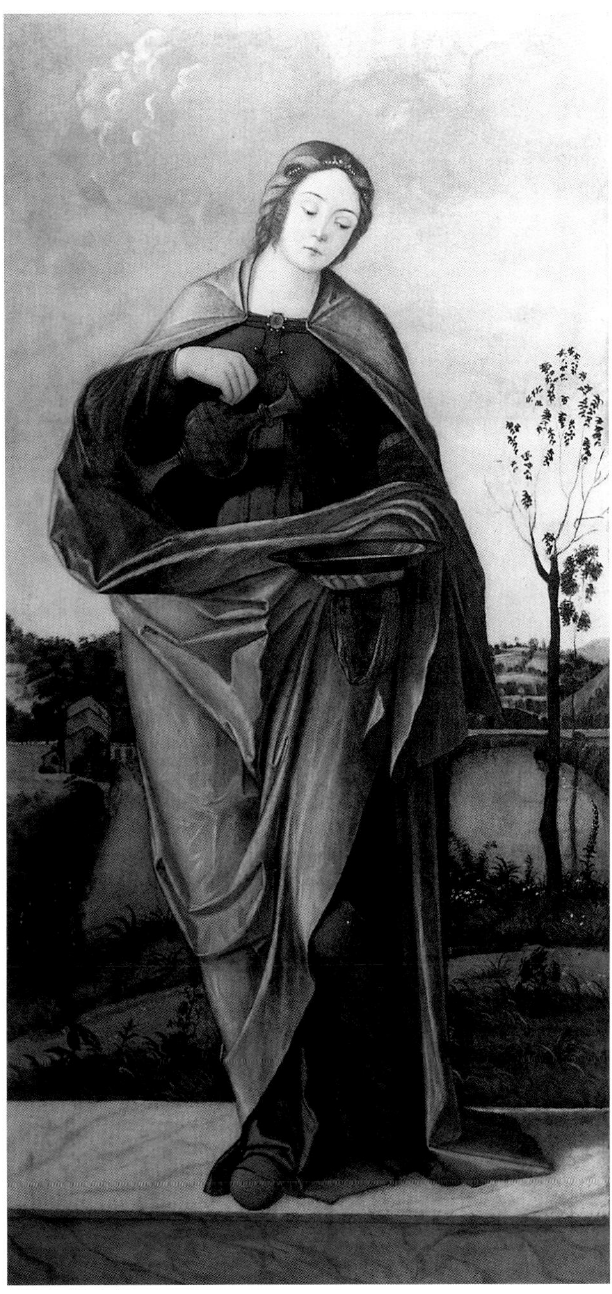

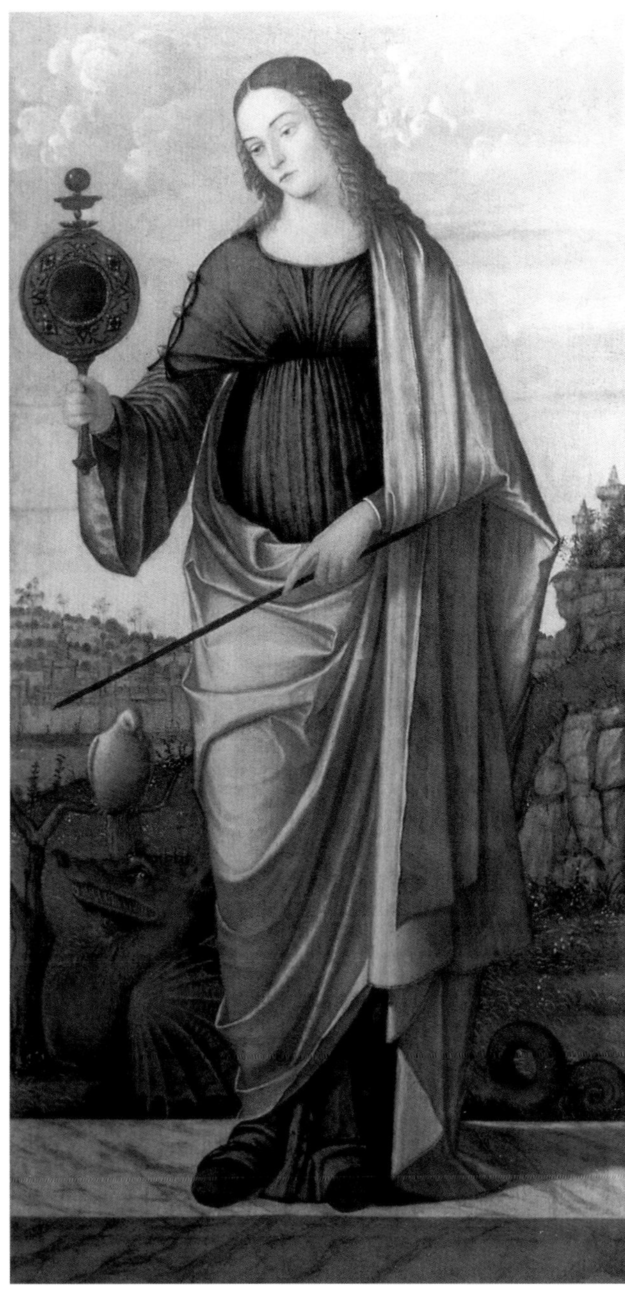

89 (*above left*) Vittore Carpaccio, *Temperance*, ca. 1500. Oil on panel, 108 × 55 cm. Atlanta, Georgia, High Museum of Art. Gift of the Samuel H. Kress Foundation, 58.35.

90 (*above right*) Vittore Carpaccio, *Prudence*, ca. 1500. Oil on panel, 108 × 55 cm. Atlanta, Georgia, High Museum of Art. Gift of the Samuel H. Kress Foundation, 58.35.

Family Values

The impulse to articulate cherished values of the mercantile nobility seen in the public environs of the threshold of the home continued its momentum in the more private spaces within. The walls of Domenico Capello's *camera d'oro grande* were decorated with four paintings: a *Madonna with Saints Peter and John* in a frame with gilded colonettes, and painted images of *Prudence*, *Temperance*, and *Justice*, each in its own gilt frame. Although the fate of Cappello's paintings is unknown, two works by Vittore Carpaccio may serve as surrogate examples of the *Prudence* and *Temperance* (figs. 89 and 90). While *Temperance* dilutes wine with water, *Prudence* regards herself in the mirror, not because of vanity but to see herself as she really is.

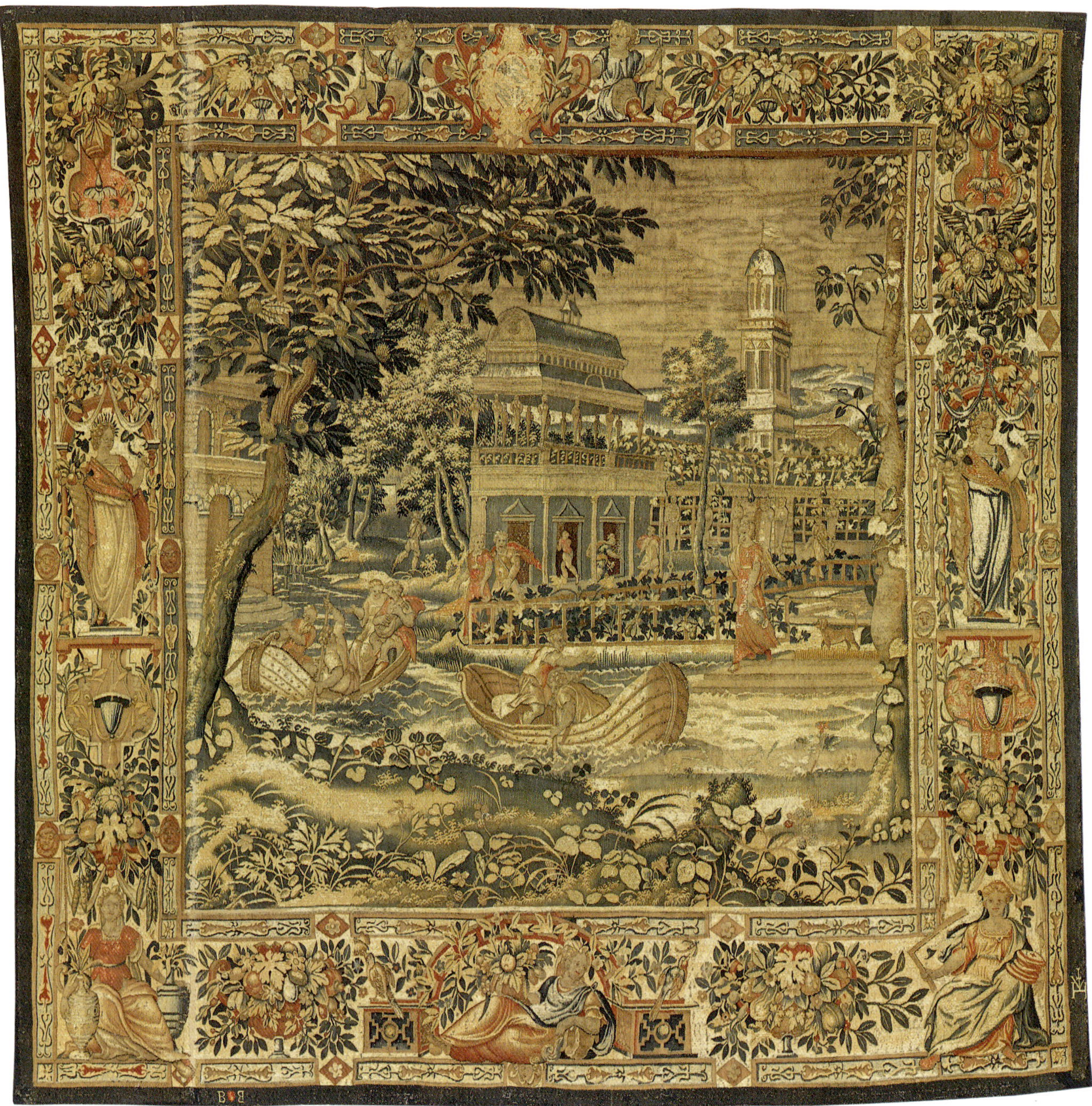

91 Tapestry. Brussels, late sixteenth–early seventeenth century. Wool and silk, 2.335 × 2.36 m. One of a set of five tapestries depicting lush landscapes and pleasurable activities of the countryside, this piece features a palace with pavilions and a pergola overlooking a river where figures are fishing and playing the lute. The borders of each piece are decorated with bouquets of flowers, fruit, foliage, and trophies. The coat of arms of the Contarini family of Venice is woven into the top border with the allegorical figures of Ceres, Flora, and Arithmetic at the sides and bottom. London, Victoria and Albert Museum (130–1869).

Personified virtues were the secular patron saints of the Venetian household, and their images in painting and sculpture were constant presences in Renaissance palaces. Indeed, the earliest wall decoration to survive from a Venetian house consists of two large fresco fragments of personifications of Temperance, Charity, Constancy, and Hope, dating to the mid-fourteenth century. These appear to have been part of a comprehensive program that included both the cardinal and theological virtues.[76] Usually, however, such displays consisted of just a few selected virtues that held particular meaning for the family, as on the well-head at Cà d'Oro and the relief above the entry portal of Ca' Soranzo-Pisani (figs. 64 and 58).

That Justice seems to have been present in nearly all these programs, while her companions changed according to the personal preferences of the patron is not surprising.[77] An essential component of the ethical canon over the course of three centuries, justice was the fundamental value that justified the hereditary nobility of Venice and ensured republican liberty.[78] But sixteenth-century debates on the nature of nobility placed a new emphasis on prudence as a significant ingredient of the patrician ethos. Sebastiano Venier, writing in the 1590s, summed up previous pronouncements on the subject by Alessandro Piccolomini and others in his treatise *De nobilitate*. He stressed two virtues as essential to patrician honor: justice and, above all, prudence. Among Venier's few original contributions to the argument was an insistence that prudence was the necessary bridge between the intellectual and the moral virtues. Prudence, based as it was upon *experientia*, ensured proper comportment and the attainment of the cherished *mediocritas*, and, indeed, was essential to the righteous exercise of justice.[79]

Prudence did not, however, preclude golden *camere* in the palaces of the wealthy. The chambers, whether golden or not, were more intimate and comfortable environments than the *portego*. But even if they were used for sleeping, they were also quasi-public spaces, open to friends not only for childbirth celebrations but for marriage banquets and other entertaining too.[80] They were meant to be seen.

Aesthetic Values

Amid this glistening refulgence of gold leaf – whether on woodwork, ceilings, or furniture – illuminated by windows of real glass and the reflections of light on mirrors and floors, was a kaleidoscopic array of color and pattern. The Venetian engagement with color, which still animates shop windows, illuminates the austere pages of inventories. The green damasks and taffetas, crimson silks, and linens trimmed with gold recorded in one of the Da Lezze bedchambers were not exceptional. An inventory of 1582 reveals that Procurator Lorenzo Correr had a choice of no fewer than six coverlets to make up his bed. The possibilities included crimson silk with a green lining; columbine silk satin lined with yellow cloth; and sky-blue and white satin lined with red. The fluid prose of the notary attests to an eye well practiced in distinguishing not only colors, but also silk fabrics of various sorts.[81]

And within the chromatic splendor of the Venetian palace a garden flourished. Here again, the Da Lezze family was no exception. For the inventories tell us that walls of chambers throughout Venice were adorned with *spalliere a verdure* – tapestries woven with vegetal or *mille fleurs* designs, such as those hung out to air on an *altana* in Carpaccio's *Healing of the Possessed Man* (fig. 91; cf. fig. 18). Consider, for example, the inventory made in 1530 of the worldly goods of Nicolò Duodo, a wealthy *cittadino* merchant. No fewer than sixteen walnut chests in the *camera grande* facing the garden in his palace at San Marziale were filled with *spalliere*, mostly *a verdure*, in pieces about 4 feet high ranging from 6 to 24 feet long. All together, they added up to around 68 meters or 222 running feet – enough to adorn the walls of a fair-sized room several times around.[82] The death inventory of Domenico Cappello of the same year listed both *antiporte* (door curtains), such as those seen in Mansueti's painting, and *spallieri a verdure*, as well as *spallieri a verdure con paesi* – probably tapestries with pastoral or rustic scenes.[83] By the middle of the sixteenth century, frescoed landscapes *all'antica* following the mode of ancient Roman wall painting would decorate the walls not only of villas on the Terraferma, but also of homes such as Palazzo Trevisan on Murano (fig. 92).[84]

92 Paolo Veronese, landscape fresco in Palazzo Trevisan on Murano, after 1556.

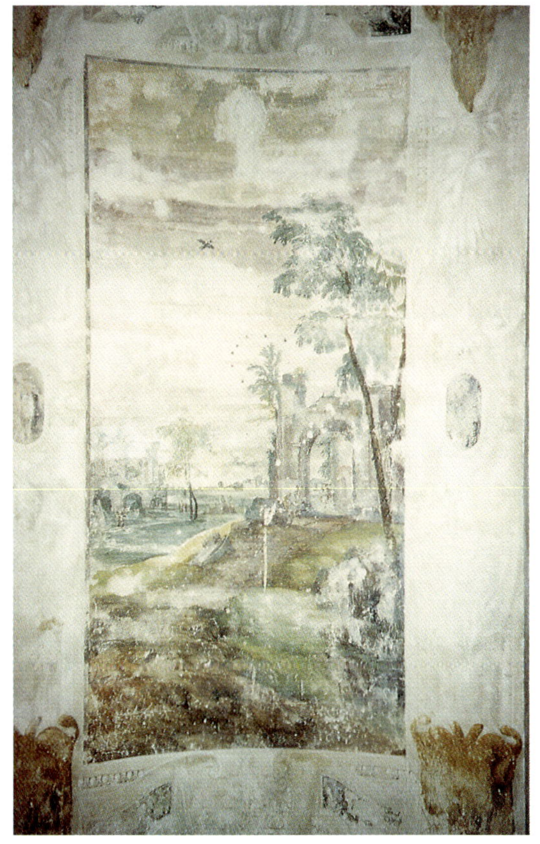

Monetary Values

That the *portego* was not considered worthy of note by visitors to the city may have been a direct reflection of how it was furnished, in addition to the absence of resplendent golden surfaces. Paintings and chairs were not the most valued items in the house. What were? Those inventories that do list appraised values are revealing. On a scale of relative cost, the decorative arts were far more expensive than what are now considered the fine arts – paintings, sculptures, and so on. The names of artists, like those of artisans, were rarely mentioned in the lists until the seventeenth century. The point is that, unlike today, easel paintings were situated at the low end of a family's movable material wealth. So where did the money go?

The death inventory of Pietro Gritti, drawn up in 1557, is instructive, for it assigns an appraised value for each item. A second cousin of Doge Andrea Gritti, Piero lived with his wife and children on the upper two floors of a four-story palace facing the Grand Canal at San Salvador. The single most expensive items of furnishing in the house were two sets of *spalliere* for the two *camere d'oro* – one appraised at 60 ducats and the other at 80. How costly *was* this? A master carpenter of that time made about 50 ducats per year. For a university professor, who earned anywhere from 100 to 400 ducats a year, one set of such *spalliere* could cost him well over half his yearly earnings. But the Gritti residence had no fewer than fourteen sets of *spalliere* in all, plus nine tapestries and eleven door curtains.[85]

Gritti's golden chambers also held beds, equipped with woolen mattresses, bolsters, and pillows, that were valued at 11 and 16 ducats. A bed ensemble of the *da pavion* or pavilion type, featuring a tent-like canopy (fig. 86), with two matching curtains and a satin coverlet, was estimated at the handsome price of 16 ducats, even though described as "used," a term denoting items that were not in pristine condition. And a similar ensemble, made of a less costly purple silk lined with fur,[86] was set at only 8 ducats, the same price given to a gilded walnut globe of the world on a platform. Andirons of bronze and brass, dispersed throughout the house, were put as high as 12 ducats and as low as 2.5. Two dozen oriental carpets – more likely to be placed on tables than on floors – were appraised at 2 to 6 ducats each, and walnut chairs upholstered with *pavonazzo* velvet at 3. But such delectable-sounding items as six gilded chests, two painted with lions and landscapes and four with gilded *tondi* in the center, merited a price of only 1 ducat apiece, the same as a *profumego alla damaschina*, an incised bronze incense ball (fig. 93).[87]

But what about paintings? There were fourteen in all. The most expensive was described as "a large painting of the *Judgment of Solomon* with a gilded walnut frame," appraised at 15 ducats. The others ranged from an icon of the Madonna at 6 ducats, to portraits of Doge Andrea Gritti and Piero's brother, Alvise, at 5 and 3, to a Flemish painting of Lucrezia at 1. So on a scale of relative values, paintings stood somewhere between storage chests and bed furnishings. Aside from the silver and jewelry, appraised at a total of more than 1,000 ducats, the aggregate value placed on the goods of the Gritti household was around 1,400 ducats, of which paintings accounted for less than 38.[88] Gritti's material comforts can be considered representative of the affluent classes. If jewelry and silver are excluded, the most costly items in his house were textiles, most notably *spalliere*, tapestries, and wall hangings, and the inventories suggest that these typically adorned the walls of the chambers rather than the *portego*. The wealthiest homes had multiple sets to be changed, as Sansovino said, "according to the time and season."[89]

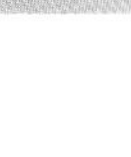

93 (*right*) Incense ball, Syrian, late fourteenth century. Bronze. The piece is just one example of the many exotic objects of Middle Eastern provenance found in the Venetian house. Venice, Galleria Giorgio Franchetti (Ca' d'oro).

facing page Detail of fig. 86.

A Culture of Consumers

How and when were these objects acquired? Dowries of wealthy girls were almost always made up of cash, real property, and a portion designated for their *corredo* – what would now be called a trousseau – which included clothing as well as household furnishings. While furniture was passed down through the family, there is evidence suggesting that an entire household might be provided by the *corredo* portion of the wife's dowry at the time of a marriage. The Da Lezze

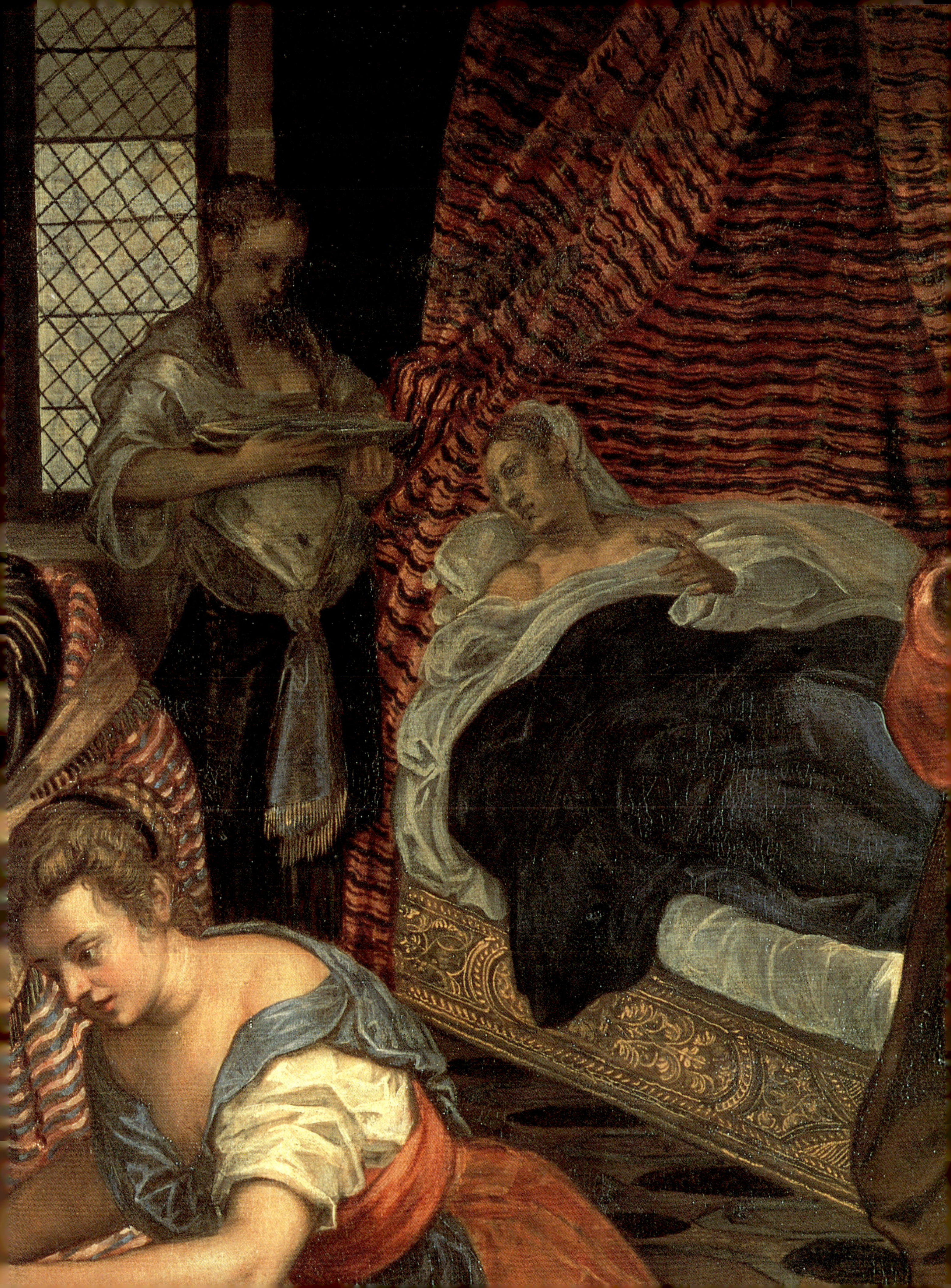

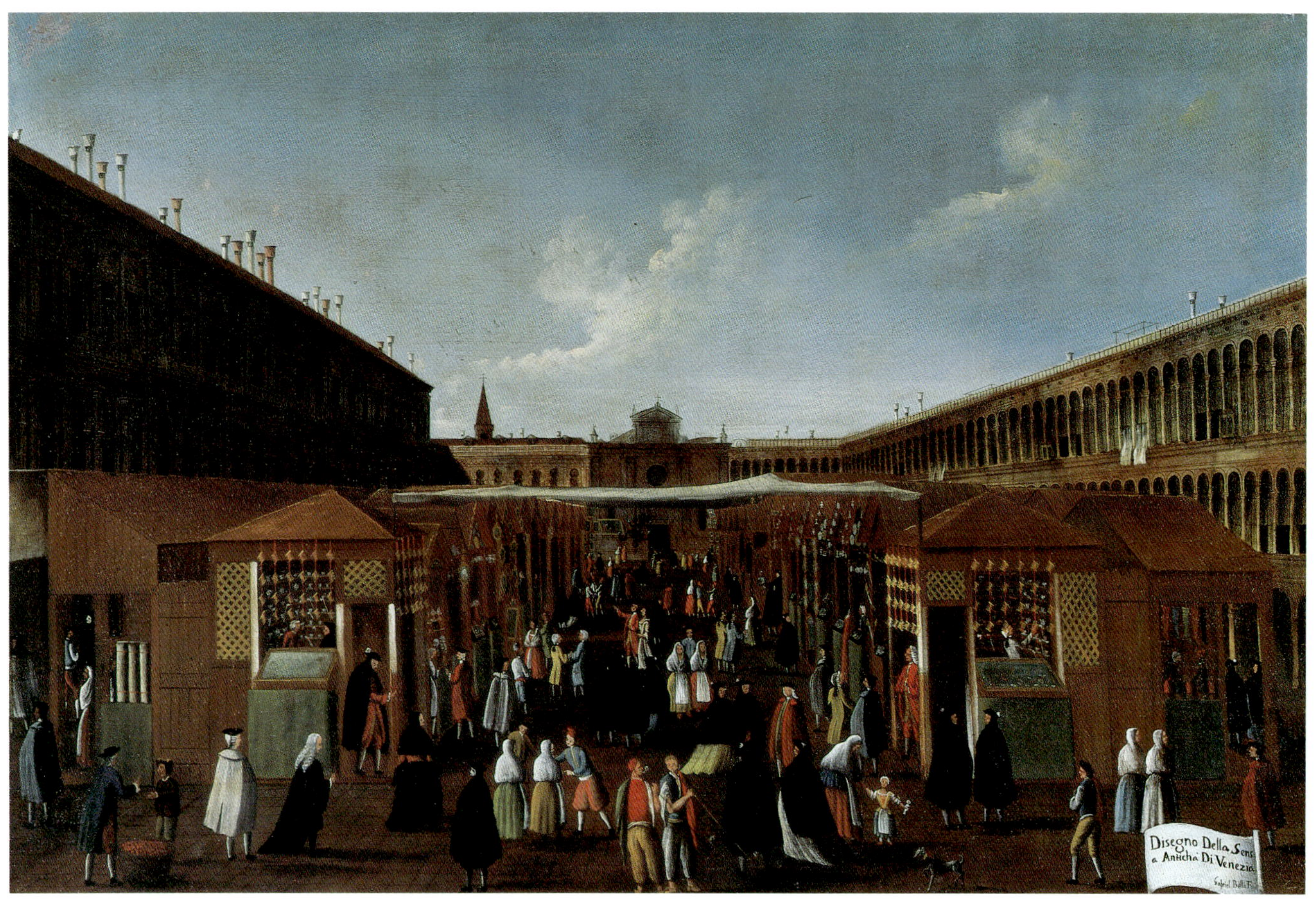

94 Giacomo Bella, *The Ancient Feast of the Sensa*, ca. 1790. Oil on canvas, 98 × 48.5 cm. In the background is the church of San Gimignano, torn down to build the Ala Napoleonica, now part of the Correr Museum. The painting offers a three-dimensional representation of the stalls indicated in the diagram in figure 95. Venice, Pinacoteca della Querini-Stampalia.

family is a case in point. After her husband Donado's untimely death at the age of 36, Chiara Da Lezze reclaimed nearly her entire dowry of 5,000 ducats. When Donado's death inventory is compared to Chiara's claim for restitution, it transpires that nearly every piece of furniture in the house came back to her as the share in her own family's patrimony that she had brought into the marriage: the gilded iron bedsteads and their furnishings, the gilded walnut storage chests and chests *alla marmorina*, the *spalliere*, the harpsichord, even the paintings in the *portego*. Thus, she was reimbursed in kind. In addition to 640 ducats that she received in cash, she was left with household goods appraised at 4,000 ducats – this is what it took to furnish the home of a high-maintenance bride.[90]

Where would these goods have been obtained? The central market place was at Rialto. It was there that merchandise was sold wholesale and then moved to retail outlets throughout the city. Mercers gave their name to the Merceria, which led from Rialto to Piazza San Marco and is still the most important shopping street in Venice. The business was lucrative. Sanudo, in his *Diaries*, records the death of a rich mercer in 1506. A commoner, he died without children and left 60,000 ducats to charities and the state: "In sum, he made a wise testament, but lived miserably."[91]

Then, as now, there were also special sales at certain times of year. Most notable was the Feast of the Sensa, a fifteen-day trade fair on Piazza San Marco that took place every spring on the feast of the Assumption (fig. 94). Such fairs coincided with major religious festivals right across Europe in this period, and markets were set up near important devotional centers. Thus the Sensa was not unusual in that sense, but the Venetians added a quasi-sacred political dimension as well. By joining it to the traditional ceremony when the doge cast a ring into the Adriatic, they confirmed the republic's marriage to, and their dominion over, the sea. The entire piazza was covered with stalls displaying the best that Venetian merchants had to offer, and foreigners flocked to the city (fig. 95).[92]

The less affluent, a constituency that included the vast majority of the population, also bought their goods second-hand and found their way to the Ghetto to do their shopping (see figs. 236–38). The Jews of Venice had been moved here in 1516 by government decree and set up banks, pawnshops, and second-hand stores on the ground floors of these buildings.[93] Second-hand dealers enjoyed considerable prestige and dealt in such household furnishings as beds, mattresses, bedding, rugs, wall hangings, and lengths of used cloth, as well as clothing. There were also auctions of goods from the deceased and the financially distressed, and an important rental business that included luxury furnishings.[94] The English ambassador, Sir Henry Wotton, rented furnishings for an entire palace from the Jewish dealer Isaac Luzzatto in 1604. The goods supplied included figured tapestry wall hangings for the audience chamber, leather wall furnishings for the main reception area, tapestries for the dining room, thirteen beds with bedding, velvet covered seats, a bed canopy for his bedroom, a billiard table, and a gondola.[95] Thus luxury could be hired and face maintained.

Writers of the time knew that a person's character could be read from his residence, and good taste was to be associated with urbanity. Aristotle had counseled: "A magnificent man will also furnish his house suitably to his wealth . . . and in every class of things he will spend what is becoming."[96] Writing in the late fifteenth century, the Neapolitan humanist Giovanni Pontano refined the notion, finding "splendor" a more suitable term to refer to ornaments and furnishings within the household: "We call objects ornamental if we acquire them not so much for use as for embellishment and polish such as seals, paintings, tapestries, divans, ivory seats, cloth woven with gems, cases and caskets variously painted in the Arabic manner, little vases of crystal, and other things of this type with which the house is adorned according to one's circumstances . . . The sight of these things brings prestige to the owner of the house."[97] The exotic and the unfamiliar might count for as much as the cost. By the mid-sixteenth century, the writer Sabba da Castiglione could admire those who decorated their halls with "beautiful and artistic things from the Levant or

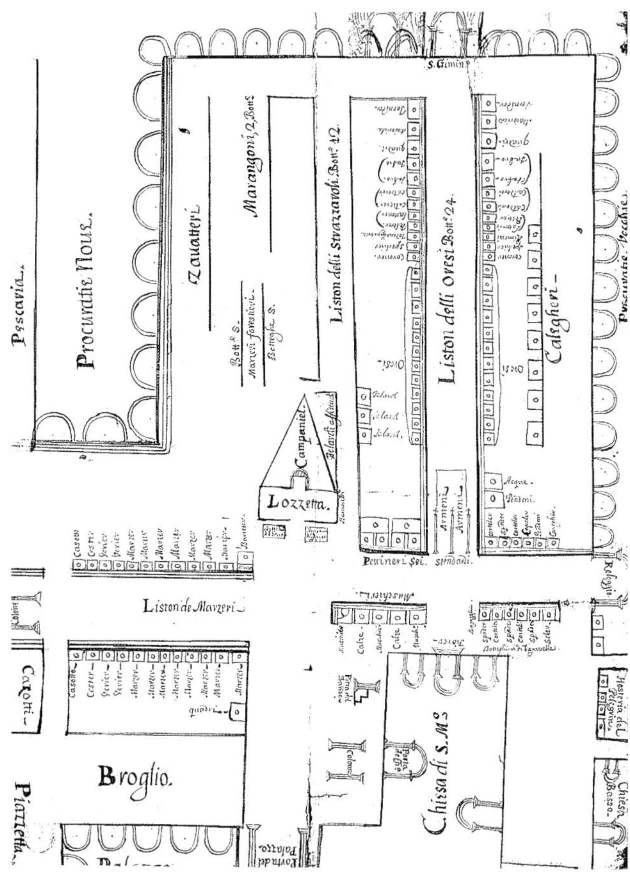

95 Diagram of the shops in Piazza San Marco for the Feast of the Sensa, eighteenth century. The major booths on the piazza are occupied by the *zavatteri* (cobblers), *marangoni* (woodworkers), *strazzaroli* (used-clothing sellers), *oresi* (goldsmiths), *calegheri* (shoemakers). The *marzeri* (mercers) fill the piazzetta. Venice, Archivio di Stato, Procuratori di S. Marco de Supra, Chiesa, B. 53 (or ASV, Miscellanea Mappe 1396).

Germany," or with "Spanish leather ingeniously wrought" or hangings of Arras and tapestries of Flanders. He intoned: "I favour and praise all these ornaments, too, because they are a sign of judgement, culture, education, and distinction."[98]

Indeed, as Renaissance Venetians knew full well, the home has a metaphorical character, with its arrangement and appointments expressing the tastes, attitudes, and hierarchy of values of those who lived in it.[99]

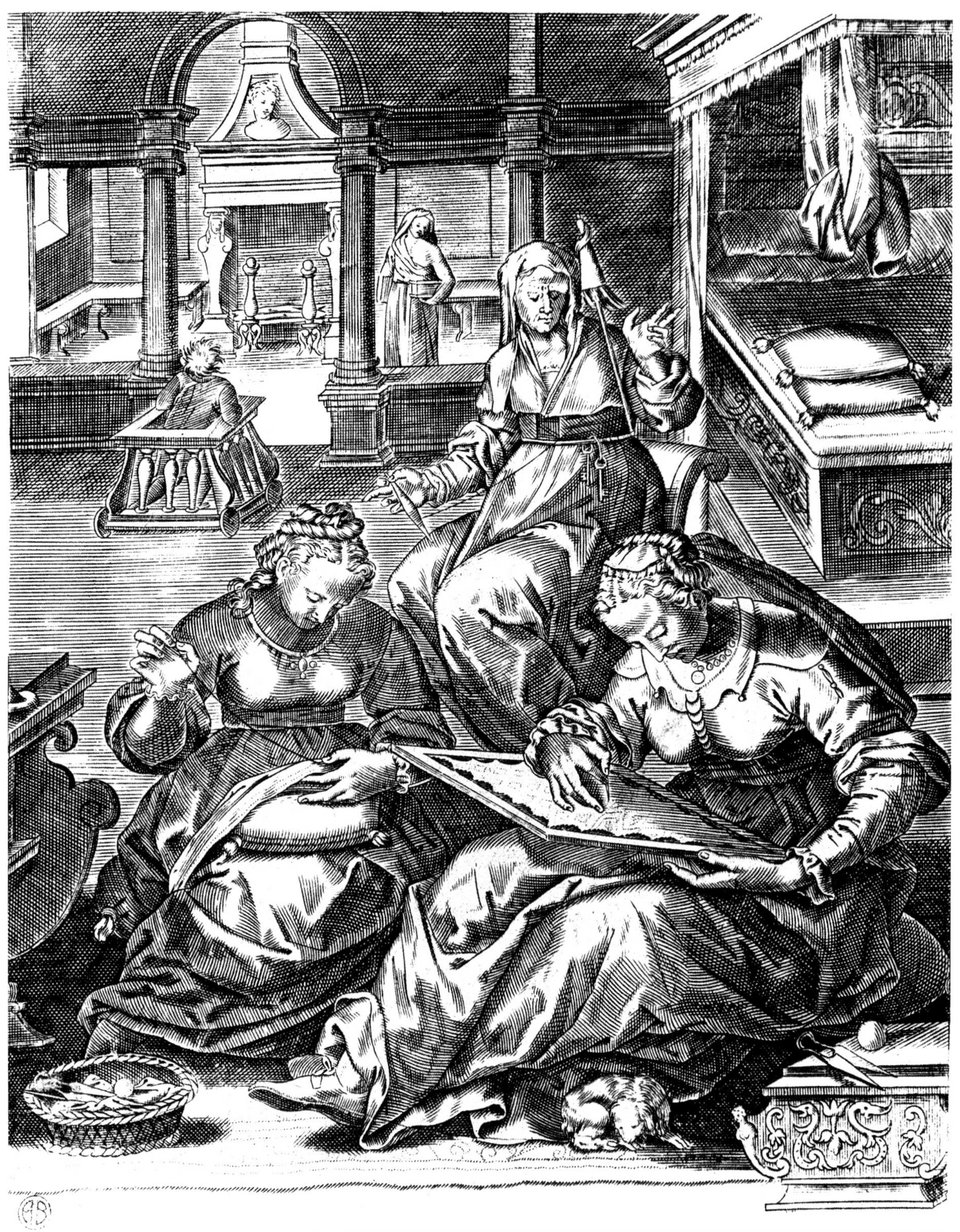

Si come di beltà sete adornate
Donne gentil, e di uirtute amiche,
Conuien ch'ogn'hora le uirtù cercate,
Et ecco il specchio delle Donne antiche

Lucretia illustre in futtura Ettate,
Con le compagnie de l'otio inimiche
Tal siate sempre acciò per molti Lustri
Il bel nome di uoi, uoi stesse illustri

Lucæ Bertelli formis.

4

The Mirror of Ancient Ladies

As in beauty they are adorned, gentle ladies are friends of virtue. They gather to seek virtue from every hour; here they are, the mirror of ancient ladies. Lucretia and her companions, renowned for handiwork, were enemies of sloth. You are ever the same, so that by many glories, your beautiful names [and] you yourselves are renowned.

INVOKING THE EXAMPLE OF AN ancient Roman heroine, the printmaker Luca Bertelli thus captioned his engraving of Venetian women bent over their needlework in a bedchamber of the family palace (fig. 96).[1] One spins, a second sews, and a third embroiders a piece of linen stretched on a frame. A small dog is curled at their feet, and a toddler scoots through a doorway in his *girello* or walker, attended by a maidservant in the rear. It is an image of wholesome domesticity that gives visual form to the admonishments of sixteenth-century treatises on the household and on the education of women. Casual visitors to the palace might not meet these women, for ideally their domain was a world apart or, to put it more accurately, apart from the world.

And just what was the woman's place within the Venetian house? Although Vincenzo Scamozzi and other writers had counseled that the wife's rooms should be furthest from the entrance and linked but separate from her husband's, is it correct to speak of gendered space within the Venetian home? Usage of Sebastiano Serlio's secret passageways and galleries, mentioned in the previous chapter, must have been a matter of occasion – in force only when certain categories of visitors were in the house – and not a permanent state of affairs. And on some occasions, such as lying-in celebrations for the birth of a baby, friends and relatives of both sexes – and even perfect strangers – were allowed into the mother's bedchamber, if Canon Pietro Casola is a reliable witness.[2] It may also have been not so much a matter of gender as of age and status. The evidence suggests that by the end of the sixteenth century unmarried daughters were kept hidden away and were heavily veiled when they left the house, but that wives enjoyed considerable freedom. Scamozzi implies this when he writes: "The male servants never go into the women's apartments when they do not know for certain if there are daughters of marriageable age [damsels] in the house, and likewise the young female servants do not appear, or do so only rarely, in the apartments of their masters, but they serve in the apartments of their mistresses . . . and they go there through very secret staircases."[3] It was not by accident that Serlio situated a private terrace immediately above the secret galleries reserved for the unmarried daughters of the house.

And yet, as Vittore Carpaccio's painting of *Two Ladies on a Terrace* suggests, aristocratic wives, freed from duties of daily shopping – a responsibility assumed by husbands – experienced the outdoors primarily on *altane* and terraces and not on the streets of the city, unless going to church (fig. 97).[4] Here a young bride, identifiable as such by her pearl necklace, sits with an older woman – perhaps her mother or elder sister – in decorous elegance on the terrace of the family palace. Surrounded by symbols of chastity, nobility, wealth, and marriage, they become allegories of female virtue in their modest comportment and restrained voluptuousness.[5]

Wives and Daughters

Through inventories we have traced the movements of women within domestic space. As noted in Chapter 3, Chiara Da Lezze's clothing and personal adornments were found throughout the family palace on Campo San Stefano. Her dowry had furnished virtually the entire house, for

96 (*facing page*) Luca Bertelli, *Lucretia and Her Companions*, sixteenth century. Engraving. Milan, Civica Raccolta delle Stampe Achille Bertarelli (SPP p 17B-1).

upon her husband's death she had reclaimed almost every item there, and the goods were appraised at nearly 4,000 ducats – evidence of a luxurious standard of living made possible by the bride's contribution from her own family patrimony.[6] Recent scholarship has shown that dowry inflation in the sixteenth century gave Venetian women considerable economic power.[7] In the absence of male heirs in the direct line (and sometimes in spite of them), they often inherited entire estates.

The testamentary strategy of Zuan Alvise, the wealthy son of Procurator Girolamo Bragadin, is instructive. Though a bachelor, he was surrounded by young women.[8] He was raising Catarina and Elena, the two daughters of his deceased brother Tomaso, as if they were his own, probably in his home at San Samuele. He was also supporting Prudencia, the daughter of another deceased brother, Angelo, in the convent of the Ognissanti, as well as an orphan named Catarina, but called Imperia, whom Tomaso had adopted from the Pietà – a foundling home – in memory of his wife Lucrezia. Zuan Alvise provided for all these girls in his will of 1566 and died the following year (for the Bragadin family tree, see Appendix, p. 257).[9]

At the time of her marriage, Prudencia would be given a modest dowry of 1,000 ducats, including cash and goods. If she decided to enter a convent instead, her dowry would consist of 500 ducats and her *cassa* – a chest full of her clothing and necessities. Imperia was being raised by a noblewoman in the Terraferma city of Piove di Sacco. Zuan Alvise hoped that she would be married to "some good artisan." In such case her dowry would consist of 100 ducats cash and 50 ducats in goods. The orphaned Imperia was perhaps being trained in household skills by working as a maid in a noble house.

The household at San Samuele also included four servants in addition to Zuan Alvise and his two nieces. The housekeeper, Dona Margarita, was given 15 ducats and a bed furnished with a coverlet and linens for the marriage of her daughter. A male servant, Marcantonio, had already been left 20 ducats from Tomaso Bragadin's will. To this Zuan Alvise added another 30 from his own for a total of 50 ducats. Two slaves whom Zuan Alvise had inherited from Tomaso were to be freed upon Zuan Alvise's death and each provided with a legacy to give them a new start in life. The female slave, Zuana, was to receive a dowry of 50 ducats, plus a bed, cushion, and bolster, two pairs of sheets and a coverlet, and her clothing. The male, Zuane, by contrast, would be given "my coach [*cocchio*] and horses to support himself" – valuable possessions that must have been kept at a property on the mainland.[10] Zuan Alvise's settlement on his two slaves was generous by standards of the time. Many children of artisans did not get as much. It is interesting to note what means were considered sufficient for their subsistence: for Zuane, a way to earn a living; for Zuana, a well-furnished bed and a dowry to find herself a husband.

After all such bequests were paid, the remainder of an ample estate consisting of property in Venice and the Terraferma was to be divided equally for the dowries of Catarina and Elena, the daughters of Tomaso. If Zuan Alvise should die before they reached marriageable age, they were to be raised in the monastery of the Ognissanti. If Elena decided to become a nun (the possibility was not envisioned for Catarina) she would receive 1,000 ducats. Her sister would receive the remainder of the estate for her dowry and be obligated to pay Elena an allowance of 12 ducats per year for her needs. However, Zuan Alvise's fondest wish was that the girls should marry Camillo and Giulio Ziliol, both sons of the ducal notary, Alessandro Ziliol. And this they did.

Fifteen years later, in 1582, Catarina was living with Camillo in Ca' Duodo at Sant'Angelo with her husband's uncles, but the couple also had a residence at Piove di Sacco that Caterina had inherited from the Bragadin estate.[11] Eventually they would have at least eleven children, named in Catarina's will written in 1614: four sons and seven daughters, four of whom became nuns, as she put it, "so that they would not grow old in the house."[12] When Catarina's sister Elena wrote her own will in 1634, her husband Giulio had already died. She was then living in the *contrada* (the Venetian term for parish) of San Luca and left most of her estate to two children, Alessandro and Catarina, to be divided equally. She also made a bequest of furniture and money to "my most beloved grandchildren," Giulio and Elena Ziliol, "in sign of love."[13] Such arrangements and dispositions were not unusual. In various ways, though respectable women were excluded from public life, the female presence was thus ubiquitous throughout the Venetian house.

Francesco Barbaro had written the earliest treatise on Venetian family life back in the early years of the fifteenth century, but the principles he enunciated held true in general until the end of the sixteenth. According to him, the wife must observe three things in a praiseworthy marriage.

97 *(facing page)* Vittore Carpaccio, *Two Ladies on a Terrace*, ca. 1500. Oil on wood, 94 × 64 cm. The bride in the background is flanked by vases containing lilies and myrtle, symbols of purity and marriage. The upper part of the panel was cut off at some point and is now in the J. Paul Getty Museum. Depicting a scene of young men hunting in the lagoon, it underlines the different leisure activities of men and women. Venice, Museo Civico Correr.

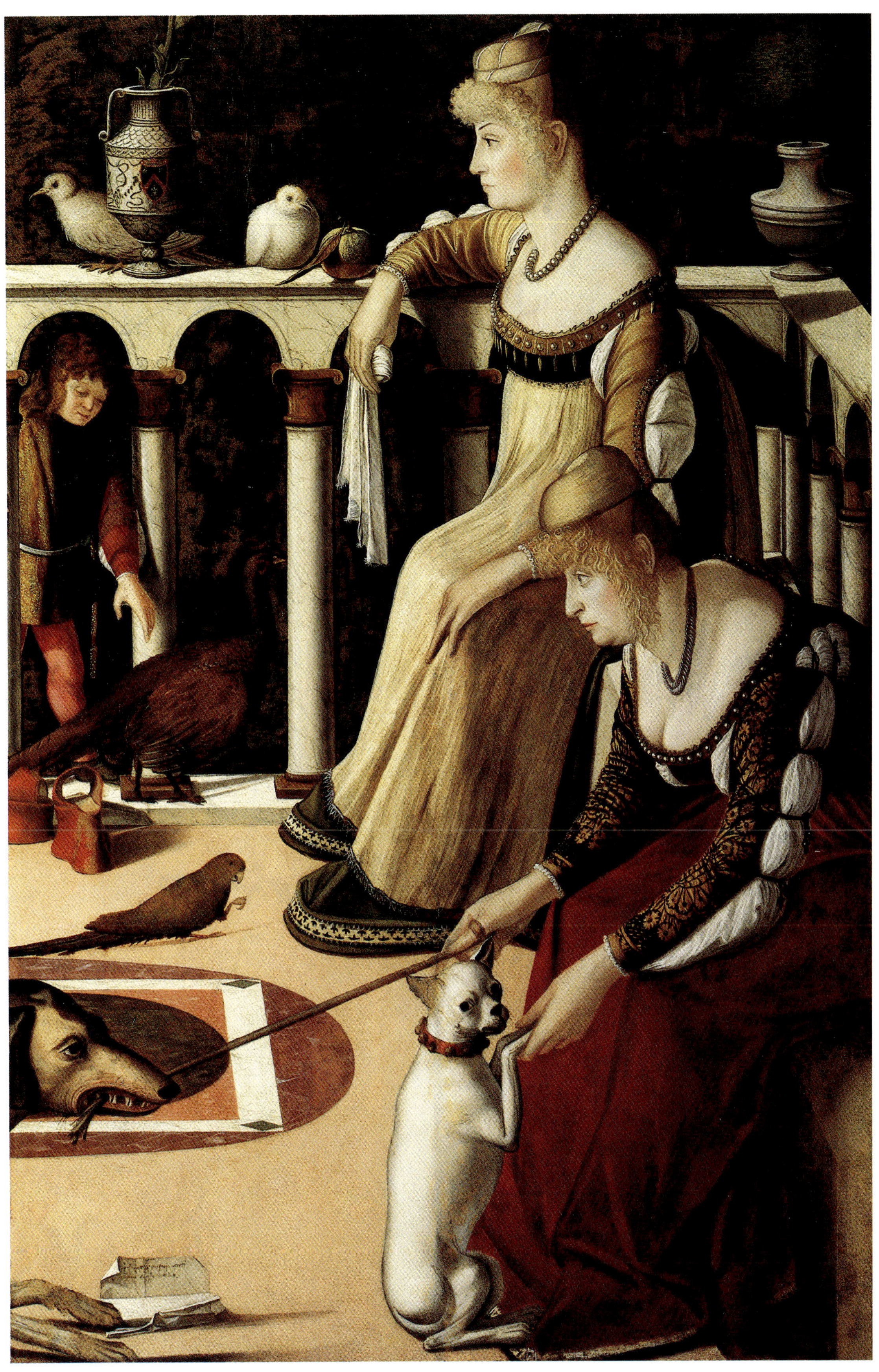

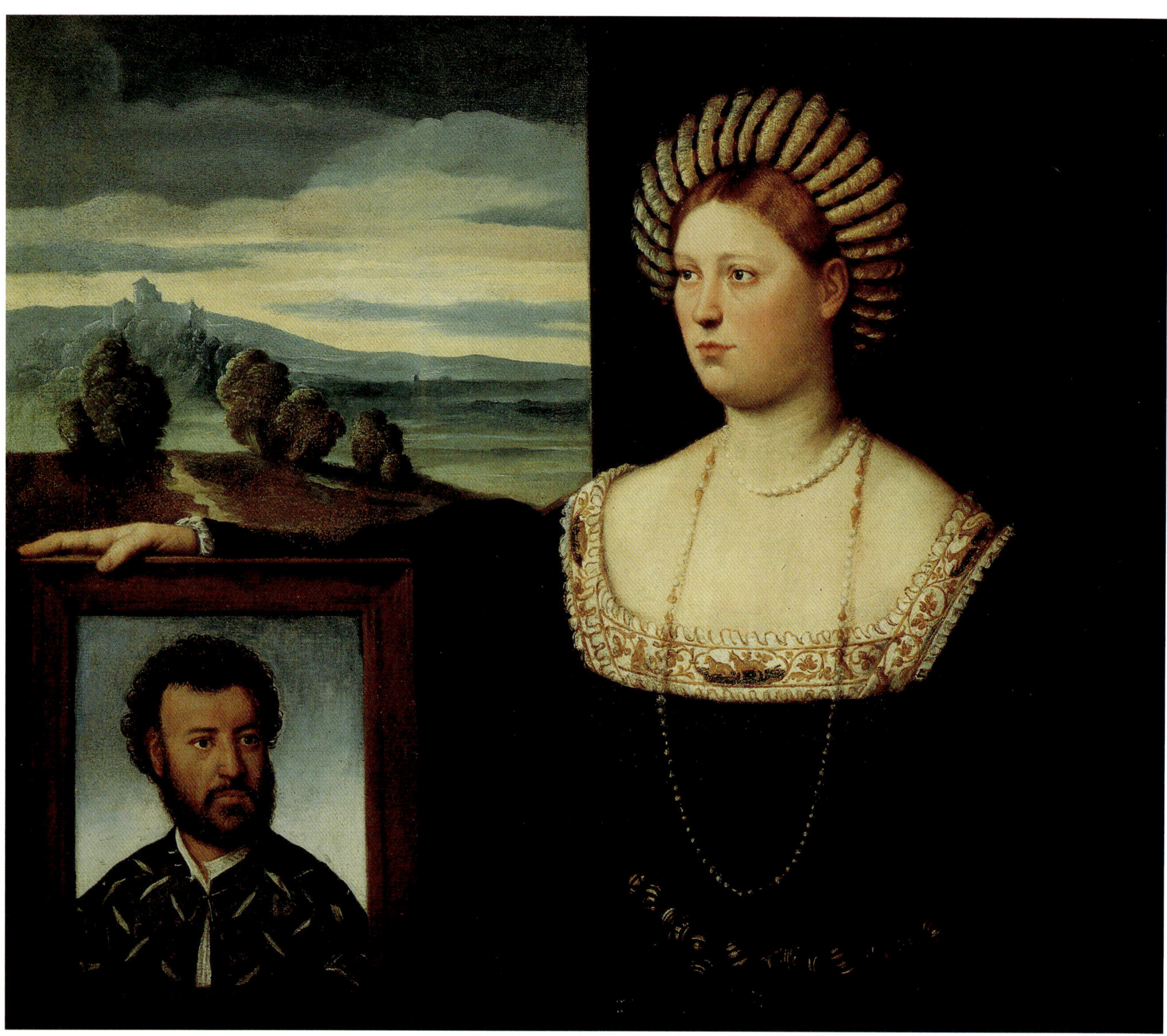

98 Bernardino Licinio, *A Wife with her Husband's Portrait*, sixteenth century. Bergamo, Private Collection.

First, she must be devoted to her husband: obedient, respectful, loving. A portrait by the Venetian artist Bernardino Licinio offers eloquent testimony of the matrimonial ideal (fig. 98). Second, she, like her husband, must observe moderation in all things: speech, gesture, dress, behavior. And third, she should be diligent in domestic matters.[14]

* * *

Well Provided with Heirs

The wife's first responsibility was to bear and raise children. Pietro Bembo's letters to Zuan Matteo Bembo offer a unique glimpse into the life of a family and the affective relationships between men and women. Zuan Matteo was married to Marcella Marcello, the daughter of Pietro Bembo's sister Antonia. Already esteemed as a man of letters, Pietro would later be named a cardinal. Zuan Matteo came from a distant branch of the Bembo family, and the two men soon developed a close relationship, with a correspondence that continued over many years. The letters offer poignant testimony to Pietro's ongoing concern for Marcella's welfare and that of her children.[15]

Zuan Matteo married Marcella in 1519 and she became pregnant immediately. On 28 July 1520, when the birth of her first child was imminent, Pietro wrote to Zuan Matteo: "I am pleased that your Marcella has entered the ninth month because she will be over that burdensome labor so much sooner. The name of the child who is born, if male, I would like to be called Quintilio, if female, Lucina" (for the Bembo family tree, see Appendix, p. 256).[16] A month later Pietro wrote again:

> I rejoice with you for the son who has made you a father, with good health and little annoyance to Marcella, his mother, and my daughter [a term which he used figuratively]. Nor do I demur in celebrating with you that she is a valiant woman, [and] that our lord God would make both you and all your house and ours (that is one alone, both in love and in name) happy with this baby boy. Take care of him well and kiss him in my name many times, and also his mother.[17]

Judiciously acceding to the great-uncle's request, the young couple gave the baby two names: Lorenzo Quintilio, although the child was known from then on simply as Lorenzo.[18]

Less than six months later, Marcella was pregnant again, and Pietro was concerned. On 6 January 1521 he admonishes Zuan Matteo: "I am pleased that Marcella is expecting [again] in that children will not be lacking. [But] for her, I am worried that she will grow old too quickly. Take care of yourself, and refrain from those bad practices that take away or shorten or weaken, and ruin old age."[19] A daughter, Augusta, was born later that year, to be followed by sons Alvise in 1523 and Marc'Antonio in 1524 and another daughter and five more sons between 1528 and 1537 – a total of ten.[20]

Pietro showed continuing concern for the well-being of the family throughout this period, calling the children "part of my health" and frequently sending kisses to them and to Marcella. In June 1530 he hoped that Zuan Matteo would "stay well in this heat together with my Marcella and your *brigatella*."[21] In July 1531 he was thinking of Marcella, again pregnant, during another heat wave, "who with her great body would be faring badly in her prison."[22] When a daughter, Giulia, was born two months later, he rejoiced: "I am happy that Marcella has fared well, and also that she has given birth to a girl, since by now you have too many males."[23] However, three years later, in 1534, he was again congratulating Marcella on the birth of another boy, and complimenting Zuan Matteo: "you have increased the number of male children, of which there can never be too many in my house."[24] In 1537 another male child appeared on the scene. Pietro worried that Marcella's health was being compromised by so many pregnancies, and suggested that the couple now had enough children, "you being well provided with heirs and family."[25] In June 1541, Pietro wrote from Rome that he had always regarded Marcella as a daughter, and praised her as "prudent, patient, and wise"[26] – virtues to which every patrician male aspired.

But Marcella was more than just a mother. She accompanied Zuan Matteo on political assignments in Istria and Crete and even found time for intellectual pursuits. Francesco Sansovino would later write: "in the true religion and in the virtues of mind she was quite equal to her husband and endowed with such a happy genius, that much to her credit she learned both Latin and Greek."[27] Marcella belies the general impression that patrician women were poorly educated and caught up either in domestic concerns or frivolous pursuits, and it seems probable that, while exceptional, she was not alone.

Indeed, Marcella's daughter Giulia followed her mother's pattern both in fecundity and virtue. She married into mainland nobility at the age of eighteen and, after giving Count Girolamo Della Torre ten children, died at the age of thirty giving birth to a daughter, who was named Giulia in her memory. In his biography of Giulia, Francesco Sansovino praised her "grandeur of mind, nobility of habits, and most prudent governance of family affairs, as well as true zeal for the holy faith, noble desire of virtue, and an elevated spirit." She was, in short, "a shining example to our times."[28] Sansovino wrote that Della Torre had chosen Giulia as his bride over three other women "of the most noble condition in Italy," whom his dearest friends and relatives had favored. His choice was providential: "since it happened that none of those three ladies, after they married, was ever favored with children, a defect that is the principal cause for unhappiness in a marriage."[29]

What physical traces of the lives of such treasured children survive outside the pages of inventories and treatises? Individual portraits of fathers, sons, and grandfathers often found their way onto the walls of the *portego* or the *camere* over the course of the sixteenth century. But, unlike Florence, in Venice patrician brides and wives were seldom portrayed in individual portraits, if surviving works are a valid measure.[30] The male contingent of the family group was sometimes celebrated collectively, as in Titian's altarpiece, the *Madonna of the Pesaro Family*, as well as in his *Vendramin Family and the Reliquary of the True Cross*. Very occasionally the full family, with both males and females, is commemorated, and relationships idealized in a most positive way. Jacopo Tintoretto's *Soranzo Family*, discussed in Chapter 1 is one such exception. Paolo Veronese's *Supper at*

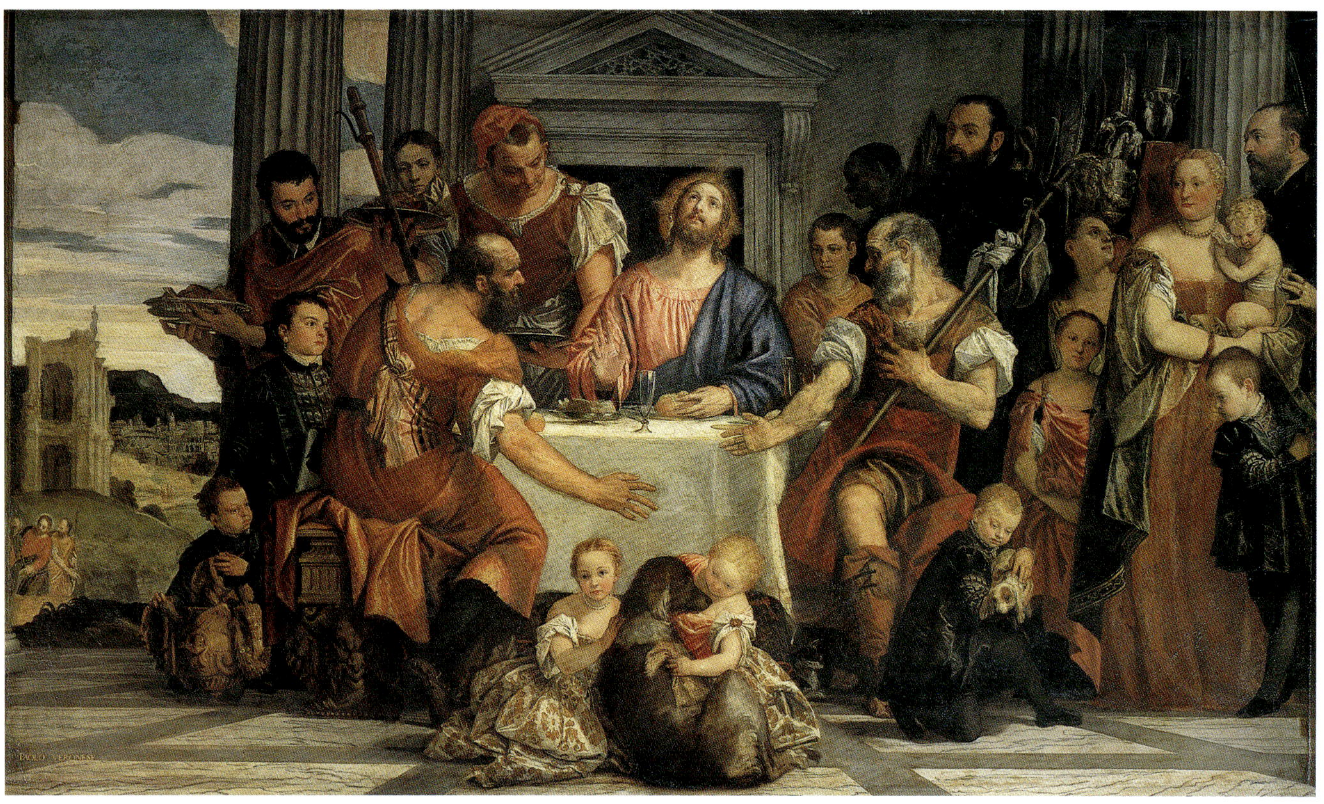

99 (*above and facing page*) Paolo Veronese, *Supper at Emmaus*, ca. 1559–60. Oil on canvas, 241 × 416 cm. The identity of the family is unknown, and it may well have been of *cittadino* rather than patrician rank. Paris, Musée du Louvre.

Emmaus, painted ca. 1559–60, is another (fig. 99). Here, Christ's meeting with two pilgrims in the countryside is embedded in the landscape to the left, while the miraculous revelation of his identity to them is shown front and center. The patron stands at the far right, his wife at his side, surrounded by well-behaved children who had seemingly arrived on a yearly basis: four girls, dressed in fine silks, four boys elegantly clad in black, and a babe in arms. In all likelihood, the wife's unmarried brother-in-law is the man to her right, separated from the other witnesses to the sacred event by the pilgrim's staff, but part of the extended family nonetheless. Despite the sacred theme of the scene, it is difficult not to see it as a celebration of the family's prosperity and fecundity as well. It is as much family portrait as pious act, for the holy figures exist in a world apart, unaware of the family that has invited them into the classicizing loggia of their palace. As one observer has noted, it is a painting within a painting.[31] In Veronese's later *Madonna of the Coccina Family*, modeled on votive paintings in the Ducal Palace, the family became active participants rather than just a reverent honor guard.[32]

Furniture designed specifically for children is another physical remnant of their presence in the household, and a few pieces have found their way into museums. The square *girello* in Bertelli's domestic scene, for example, has its counterpart in a round device now in Museo Bagatti Valsecchi in Milan (fig. 100). As with most household objects in this period, the hand of the artisan has made it a thing of beauty as well as utility. The top is carefully carved with a cut-through design of leaves and clusters of grapes, including two babies in swaddling clothes, that would surely have formed a taste for ornament in the eleven-month-old wheeling around in it.[33]

Likewise, a cradle was not just a place for the baby to sleep. It was also an occasion to display the good taste and affluence of the family. In one handsome example, the infant would have been protected by head- and footboards decorated with a cross flanked by peacocks, whose plumed tails are echoed by the dolphin's snouts on the rockers at the base (fig. 102).[34] Such furniture often displays an artful combination of motifs from disparate sources. In this instance, the sides of the cradle are carved in a striated design originally taken from Roman sarcophagi and often used on storage chests.

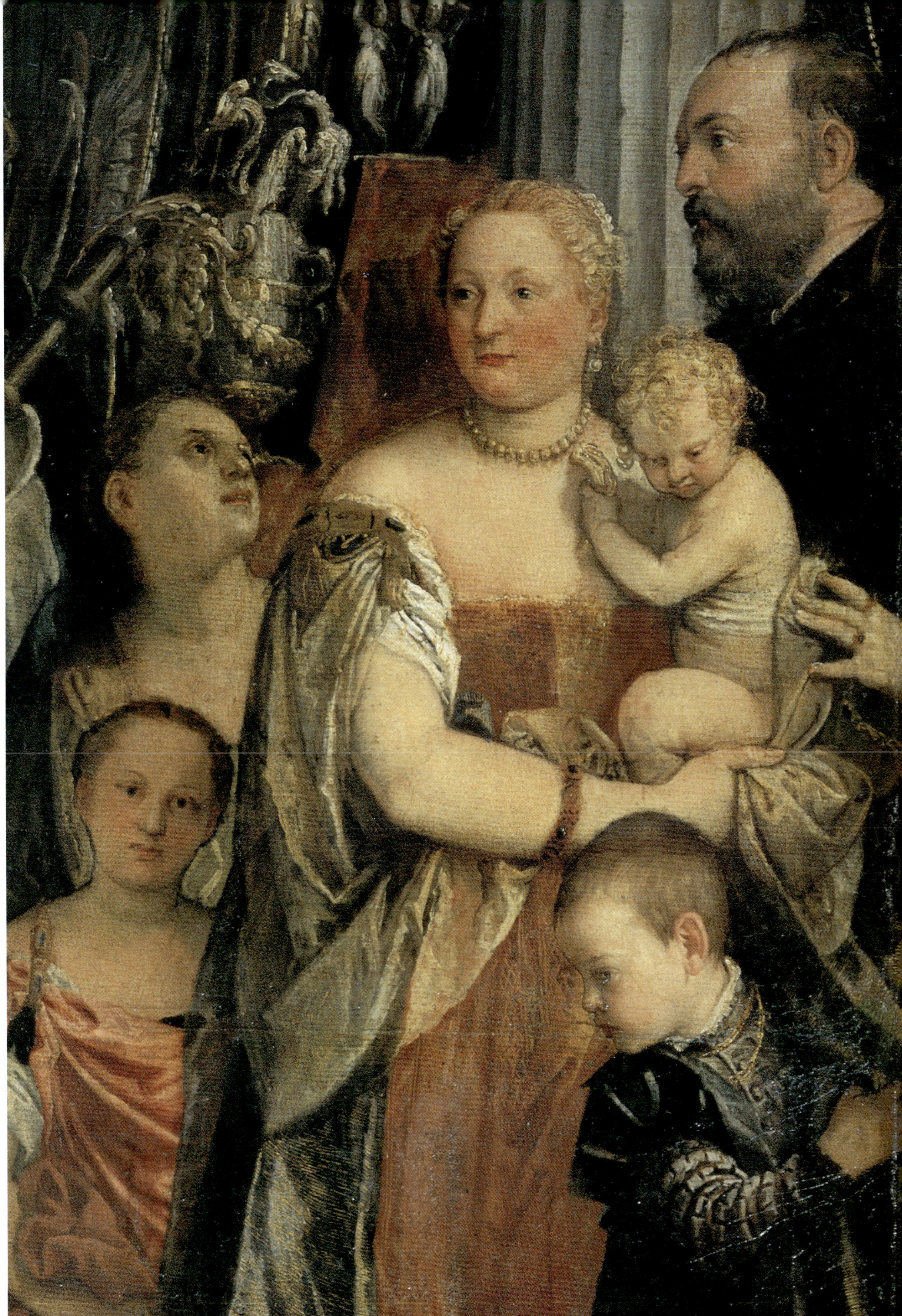

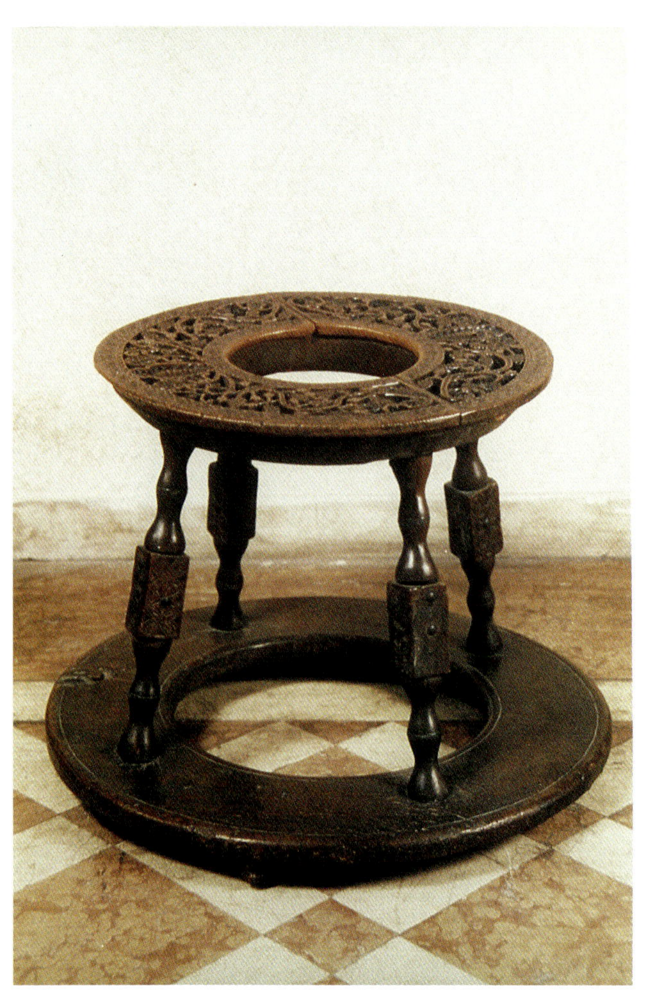

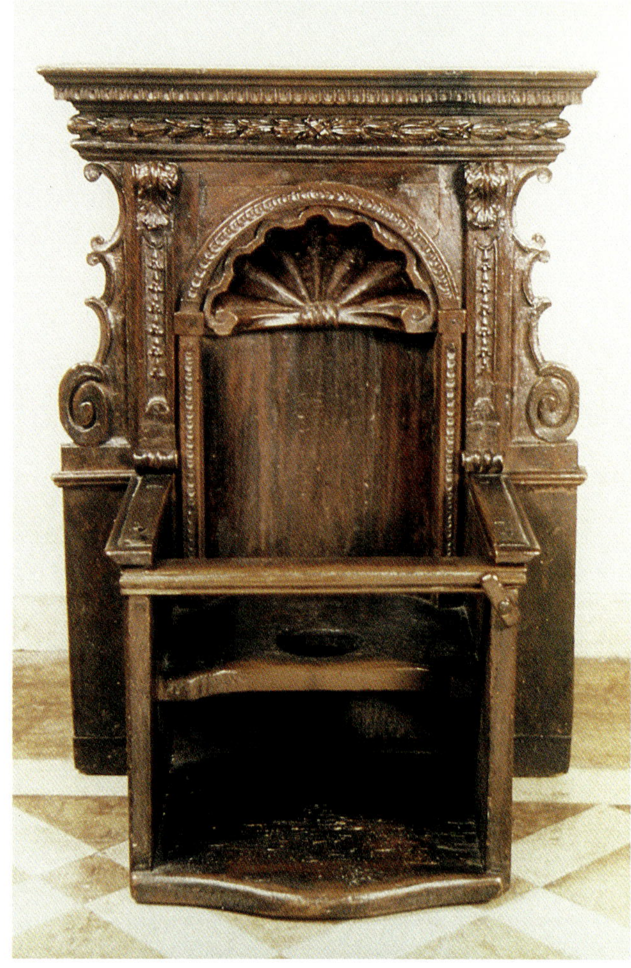

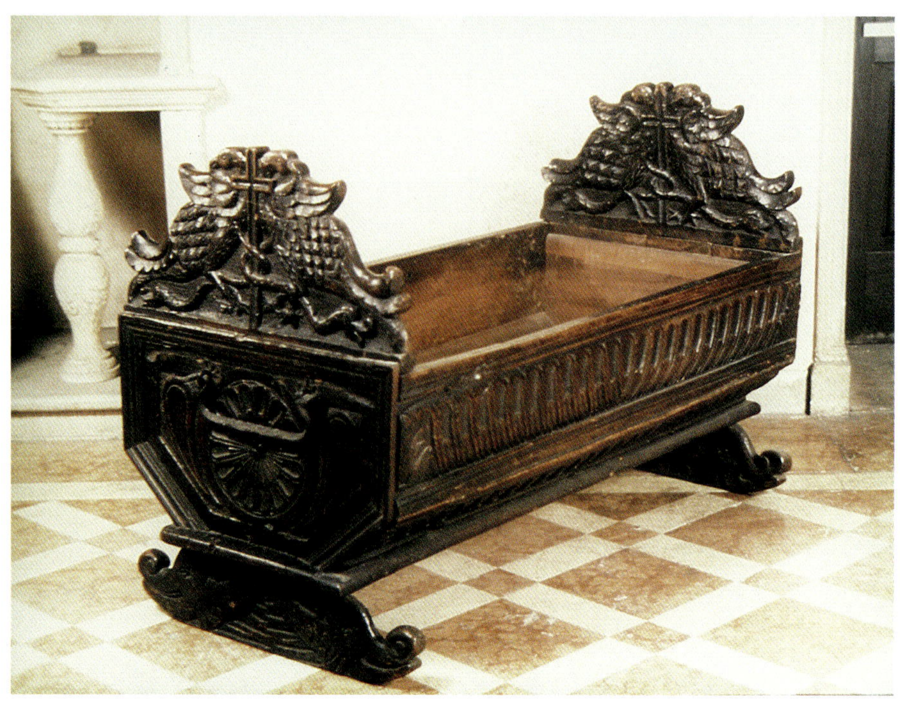

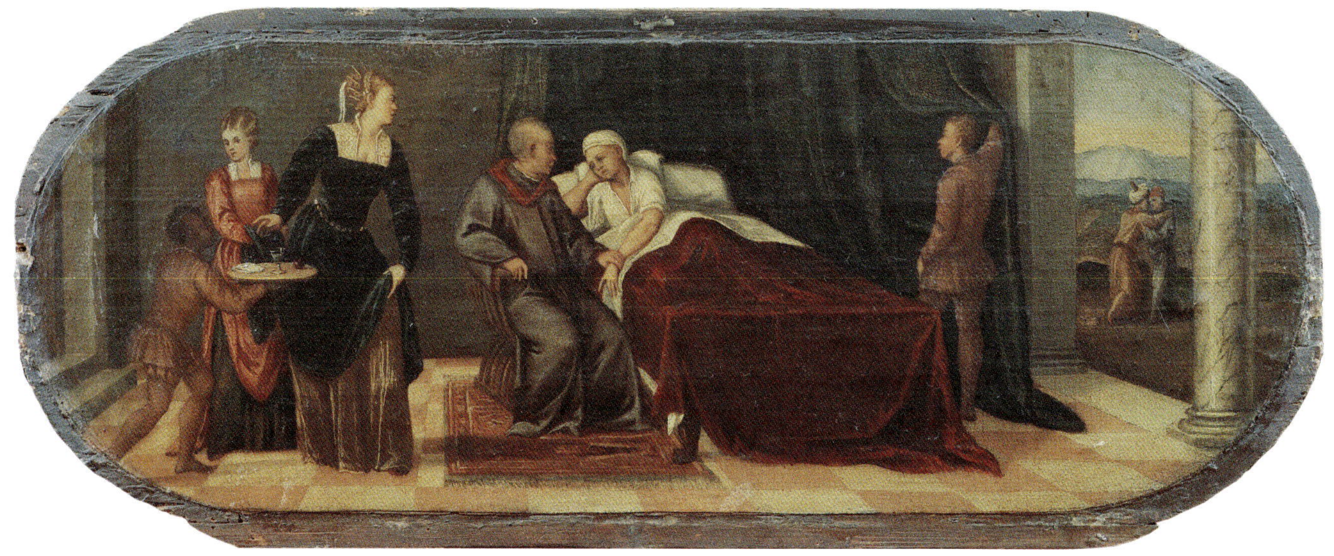

103 (*above*) Bonifacio Veronese (dei Pitati), *Antiochus and Stratonice*, ca. 1540s. Oil on wood panel, 21 × 54 cm. An aristocratic wife hovers anxiously while a doctor attends to her sick husband. Although the domestic interior is typically Venetian or North Italian, according to one interpretation the scene depicts an episode in the story of Antiochus and Stratonice, from Plutarch's *Life of Demetrius*. Antiochus, son of Seleucus, fell in love with his father's second wife, Stratonice. When the son was on the point of death because of his passion, which could never be consummated, his father parted with Stratonice and gave her to Antiochus in marriage to save his son, thus ensuring the future of his empire. The panel would originally have been inlaid in a piece of furniture. Milan, Museo Poldi Pezzoli.

100 (*facing page top left*) *Girello* (baby walker), (?)Lombardy, sixteenth–seventeenth century. Walnut, height 40 cm, depth 54.5 cm. Children's clothing sometimes had tapes sewn to the backs so that they could be held up when learning to walk (and to function as leashes to keep them from wandering off). Milan, Museo Bagatti Valsecchi, inv. n. 314.

101 (*facing page top right*) *Comoda per bambini* (child's commode), Italy (possibly Veneto), end of the nineteenth century, with fragments of the sixteenth and seventeenth century. Walnut, beech and fir, height 126 cm, width 58 cm, × depth 34.5 cm. John Russell's *Boke of Nurture*, a fifteen-century English treatise on childcare, counsels parents: "Look there be blankit cotyn or lynyn to wipe the nether ende." Milan, Museo Bagatti Valsecchi, inv. n. 313.

102 (*facing page bottom*) *Culla* (cradle), (?)Lombardy, (?)sixteenth century, with nineteenth-century interventions. Walnut, height 66 cm, width 95 cm, × depth 51 cm. Although most cradles of the period were made to rock from side to side like this one, those that rocked forward and backward (from head to toe) were also popular. Milan, Museo Bagatti Valsecchi, inv. n. 68.

But perhaps the focal point of the aristocratic nursery would have been a commode – what we would call a potty chair (fig. 101).[35] Sitting on such a splendid throne, complete with a classicizing scallop-shell niche, would surely have given a nobly born baby a sense of his destiny as a ruler of the Venetian Republic.

The Governance of Women

But let us return to his mother, for it is she who was responsible for the smooth running of the household (fig. 103). Barbaro writes: "wives ought not to lack praise if they merely organize, as is their duty, the wealth that has collected in the home. They ought to attend, therefore, to governing their households just as Pericles daily attended to the affairs of Athens."[36] The model of the good marriage that comes through in such treatises, while it may well be patriarchal and civic, is that of a partnership. For the diligence of both husband and wife was held to be necessary for the well-being of the family. The husband's role was to acquire and provide; the wife's to conserve. While the aristocratic home typically had a servant or two to do the laundry and other manual labor, it was the wife's charge to arrange the house and keep the household in good order.[37]

Sansovino had praised Giulia Bembo for "maintaining the house with the most beautiful order" and for her "noble industry . . . in advantageously procuring the provisions necessary for a house which gave the impression of great magnificence and was always full of illustrious personages, and for her great prudence in using [such provisions] and her diligence in conserving them." Most laudable was her success in outfitting and maintaining households "in many and diverse places, that is in Udine, in Ceneda and in Villalta . . . three palaces which she left not only well furnished with the comforts of living, but also adorned with rich ornaments . . . more appropriate to the grandeur of the Torriana family." This achievement was all the more impressive "because when she became the wife of the illustrious Lord Count, she found few and worn-out ornaments, both because the house had been for many years without the governance of women, as well as from dire and cruel events of civil discord, accompanied by fires, thefts, and deaths."[38]

A constant theme in the treatises, and one that is closely related to the ideals of separation and specialization seen in Serlio's proposed plan for a Venetian house, is that of the primacy of order. Barbaro had written: "Indeed, there is surely nothing more excellent in household affairs than that everything be put in its place, because there is nothing more beautiful, more useful than order, which is always of the greatest importance."[39] Although furniture was typically moved around, most of the objects in the house, whether a basket of fruit or a sack of grain, a kitchen implement, a tablecloth, or a pillowcase, had their proper location. Alessandro Piccolomini, who was particularly eloquent on this matter, wrote: "And the clothing of each has to have a different place – one place for the children's, another for the husband's, and finally another for that of his consort. As to [the wife's] ornaments, one place is appropriate for her dresses, another for a ring, or jewel, or necklace, or bracelet, or similar expensive things which should be kept in the most secret place in the lady's bedchamber."[40] The lesson was clear: the beauty of a space – including that of the *casa* – lay in the order and legible arrangement of the objects it contained.

While household inventories, most notably that of the Da Lezze, suggest that such perfect order was more an ideal than a reality, they also indicate that the necessities and adornments of everyday life were arranged in markedly similar ways in a wide variety of homes from the artisan to the patrician caste.

Instruments of Orderliness

One of the most striking features of the inventories is the number and diversity of containers. These architectonic forms, inspired in turn by the form of a house, as Mario Praz would have it, were the primary instruments of orderliness in the Renaissance house. Ranging from the precious to the serviceable, they became increasingly specialized throughout the period, with the lexicon expanding to distinguish between them: the armoire, the bookshelf, and the *stipo* or *studiolo* – a cabinet with drawers and doors – were invented in this period. But the basic piece of furniture in these houses without closets was the chest – in Venice called a *cassa* – such as those depicted in Titian's *Venus of Urbino* (figs. 193 and 194).[41] Particularly in the early period, chests were sometimes called *cofani*, or *forzieri*, or *capsa*, but throughout the sixteenth century, *cassa* was the term most often used. Only late in the sixteenth century did the term *cassone* appear in Venetian inventories, referring to a particularly large *cassa*.

In 1582, the Da Lezze palace, for example, was provided with three *cassoni*: one in the *camera d'oro* for Chiara Da Lezze's best dresses; another near the kitchen for the storage of grain; and a third, particularly capacious one in the mezzanine, which held four walnut chairs and four folding stools. There were also twelve walnut *casse* or chests; four *casse alla marmorina*, presumably with a *faux marbre* finish; and sixteen pine *casse*. Furthermore, there were two locked cabinets called *scrignetti*, filled with jewelry, silver, and legal documents; four horsehair-covered strongboxes called *forzieri*; a walnut *credenza*; three little walnut *scatole*, or boxes; and two pyramid-lidded *caseli da pavion*, one intaglioed and the other of pine. In sum, forty-four storage containers of different types – a plethora of possibilities, their character and specificity of function sometimes difficult for us to distinguish now. All were designed to ensure the good order of the household.[42]

During the fifteenth century, the *cassa* was typically multi-purpose. As in Carpaccio's depiction of St. Anne's bedroom it was often placed below the built-in bed (fig. 104). Or there might be several aligned against a long wall as in the bedchamber of Titian's *Venus of Urbino*. Flat on top, it could serve not only as a container but also as a seat, a step, or even a table. Although the painted *cassoni* of Florence seem to have come in pairs, Venetian inventories more often list larger ensembles of chests. The *camera d'oro* in the Da Lezze palace was furnished with five walnut chests that appear to be a matched set. In another chamber were four chests of gilded walnut, also described as similar to one another; and in the *camera grande* were the four chests painted *alla marmorina*.[43] In the *camera grande* of Tommaso Michiel and his wife Elisabetta Contarini were no fewer than six walnut chests belonging to Elisabetta, which the notary described as decorated with intarsia squares, and four large old chests, brought from the chamber above, which were decorated "with two coats of arms, the one Michiel and the other Contarini."[44] The *camera grande* facing the garden of Nicolo Duodo at San Marziale contained sixteen walnut chests described as *simile*.[45]

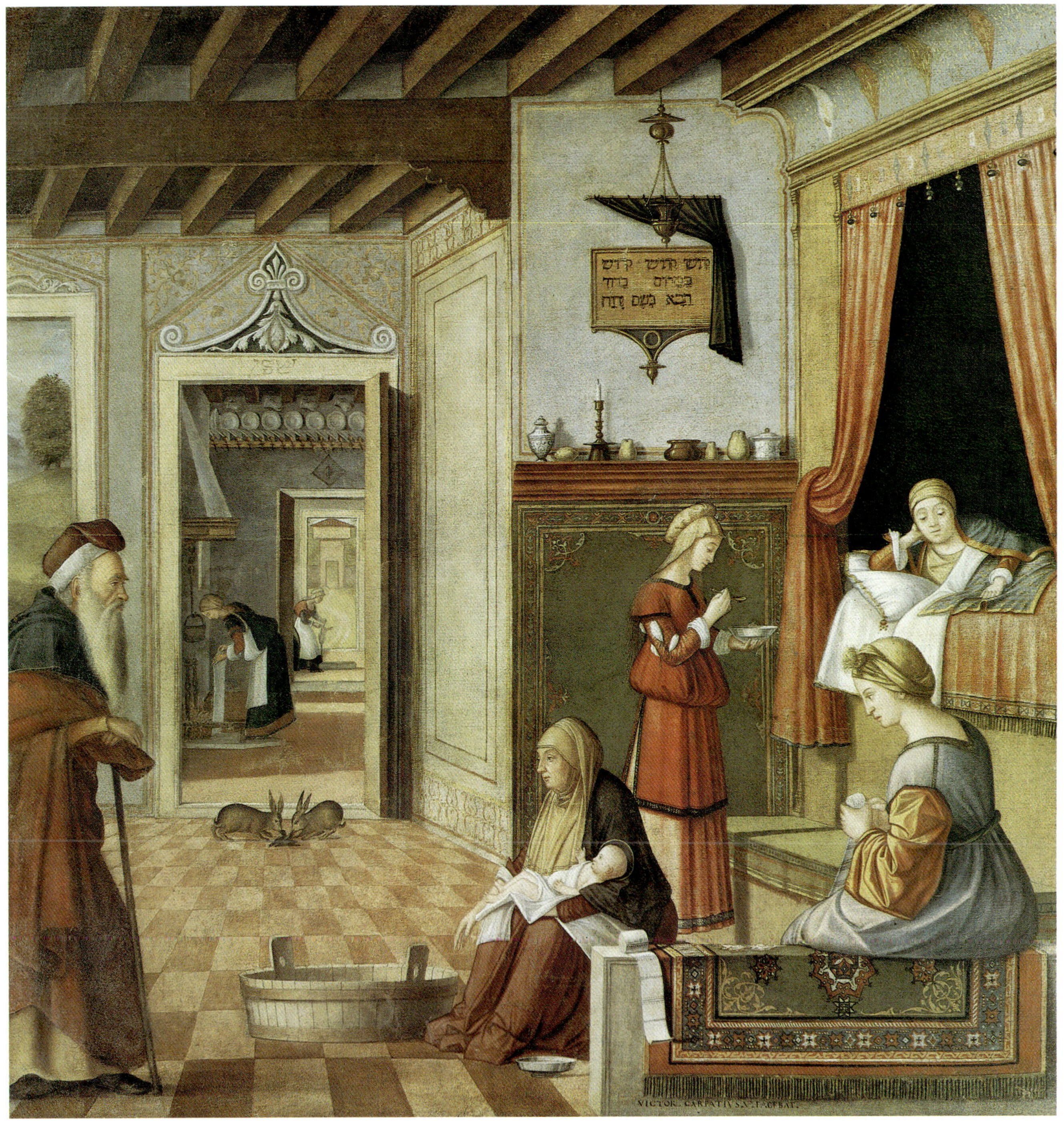

104 Vittore Carpaccio, *The Birth of the Virgin*, 1504. Oil on canvas, 126 × 129 cm. Originally part of a cycle of six paintings of the Life of the Virgin, the work was made for the Scuola di Santa Maria degli Albanesi. Bergamo, Accademia Carrara.

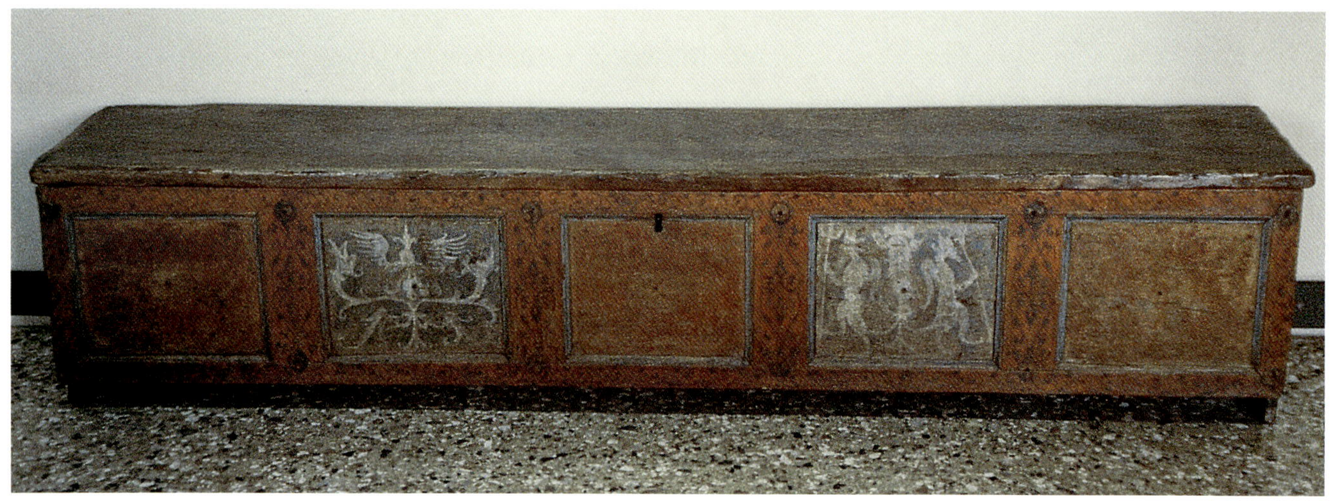

Although chests were often covered with a carpet or special runners called *bancali*, the surfaces were decorated in a number of ways, and tastes changed over the course of the fifteenth and sixteenth centuries. Several tendencies are apparent: in shape, a development from planar to sculptural; in surface treatment, from color and pattern to unadorned wood or gilding; and in stylistic vocabulary, from motifs inspired by oriental textiles and ceramics to a classical aesthetic inspired by antique sarocophagi.

Among the surviving examples from the fifteenth century is a *cassapanca* in Ca' d'Oro (fig. 105). Long and low, it could be used as a bench as well as a capacious box. It is badly damaged, with some of the original decoration apparently removed from the panels, but the borders reveal the original decoration of arabesques and rinceaux: that is, tendrils of leafy vines curving around in a scroll-like pattern. These are painted in black on a red background and probably derive from textile designs. It is, however, a fairly crude work.

Far more costly is a cypress chest in Treviso, datable to the mid-fifteenth century (fig. 106). Decorated on the front with courtly scenes in an International Gothic style recalling Antonio Pisanello, it is framed by a border with hunting motifs and stylized foliage, again in a rinceaux pattern.

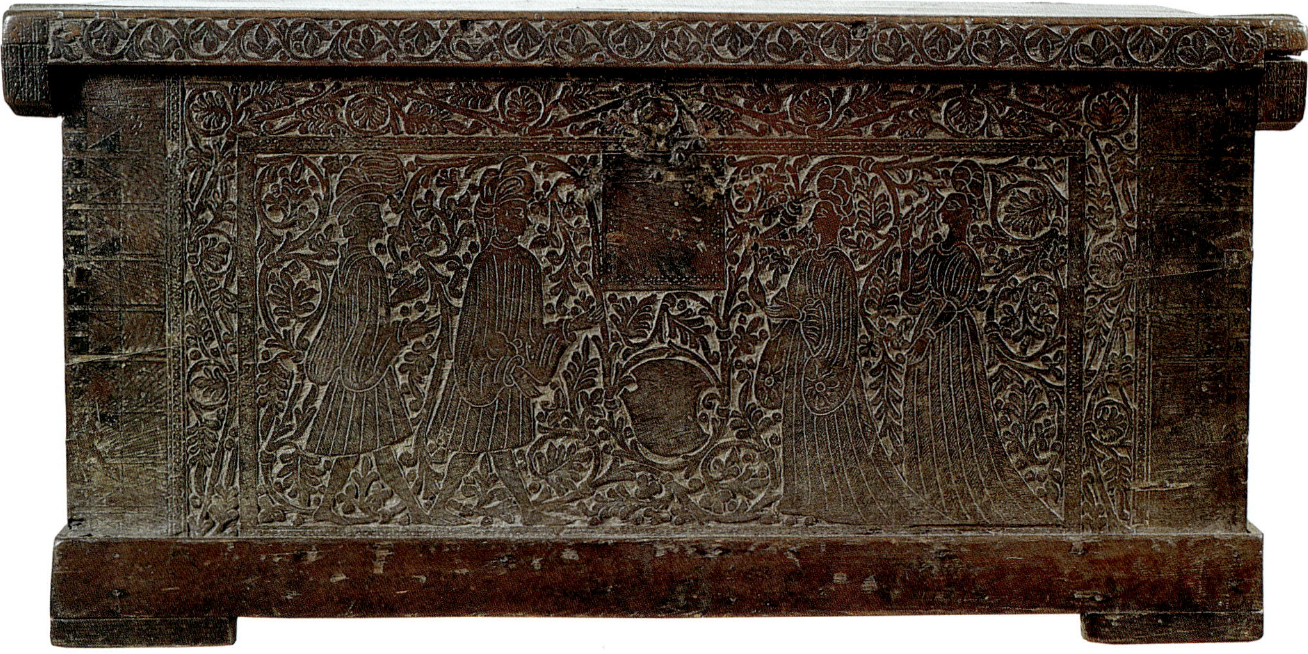

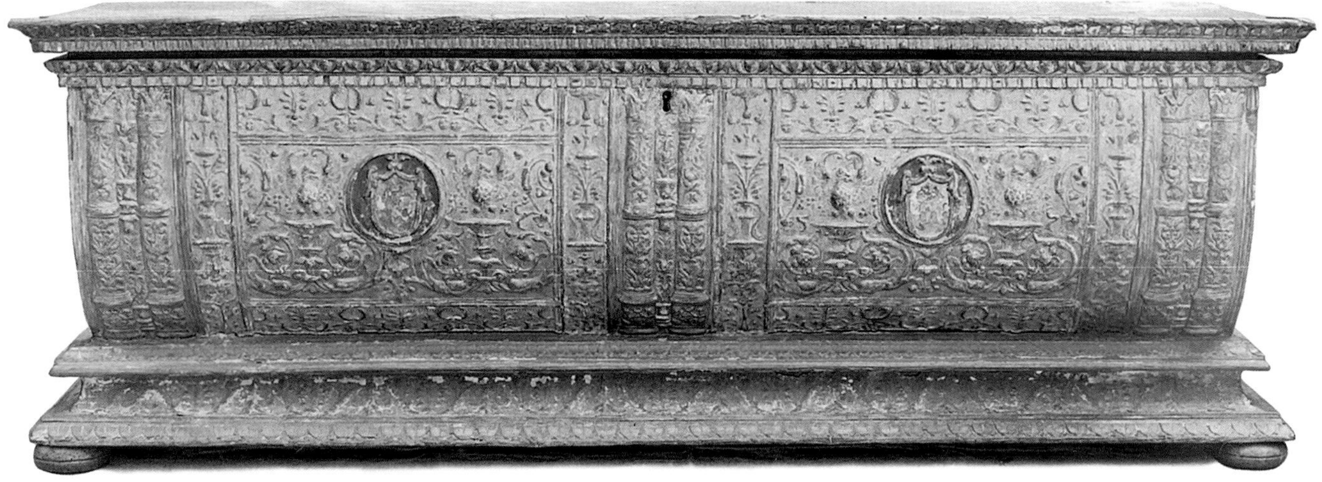

107 (*above*) *Cassone*, North Italian, late fifteenth century. Wood covered with stucco ornament in relief of columns, balusters, foliage, and gilt, with two painted coats of arms, height 63.5 cm, length 175.25 cm, width 53.3 cm. One of the coats of arms belongs to the Dondi dell'Orologio family of Padua. London, Victoria and Albert Museum.

105 (*facing page top*) *Cassapanca*, fifteenth century. Wood, painted. Venice, Galleria Giorgio Franchetti (Ca' d'Oro), M. 5.

106 (*facing page bottom*) *Cassa*, Veneto, mid-fifteenth century. Cypress wood. In a romantic scene, two gentlemen face two ladies against a foliate background. Treviso, Museo Civico Bailo.

108 (*below*) *Cassa*, Venice, first half fifteenth century. Wood, painted and gilded with *pastiglia* decoration. Using the *pastiglia* technique, the artisan first applied a thick white paste and then stamped, molded or carved it in low relief with a stylus. He then finished it with painting and gilding. Venice, Galleria Giorgio Franchetti (Ca' d'Oro).

The planarity of the fifteenth-century *cassa* was softened in two ways. First, the artisan could complicate the overall shape. A chest in the Victoria and Albert Museum retains the traditional flat lid, but it has a double basement with a bulging convex panel supported by a recessed straight base (fig. 107). The surface is painted with a delicate vegetal pattern of gold on black that may have been inspired by goldsmith work or Islamic textile designs. The two coats of arms indicate that it is a marriage chest.[46]

Another way of relieving the severe lines of the rectangular box was through texture, with a surface treatment called "pastiglia," as in a fifteenth-century *cassa* in the Galleria Giorgio Franchetti in Venice (fig. 108). The front of this chest is divided into four sections, the two in the center featuring two different coats of arms surrounded by *pastiglia* arabesques, and those at the ends painted to simulate a brocade pattern. With two additional coats of arms

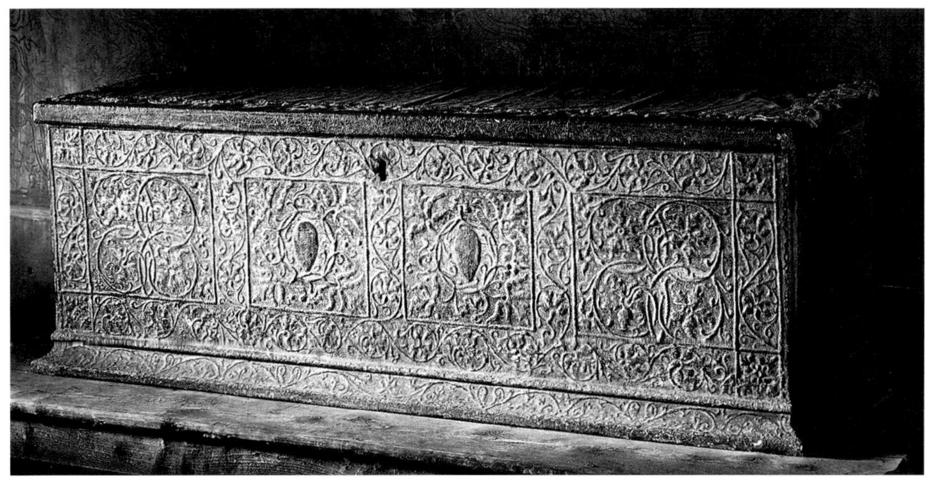

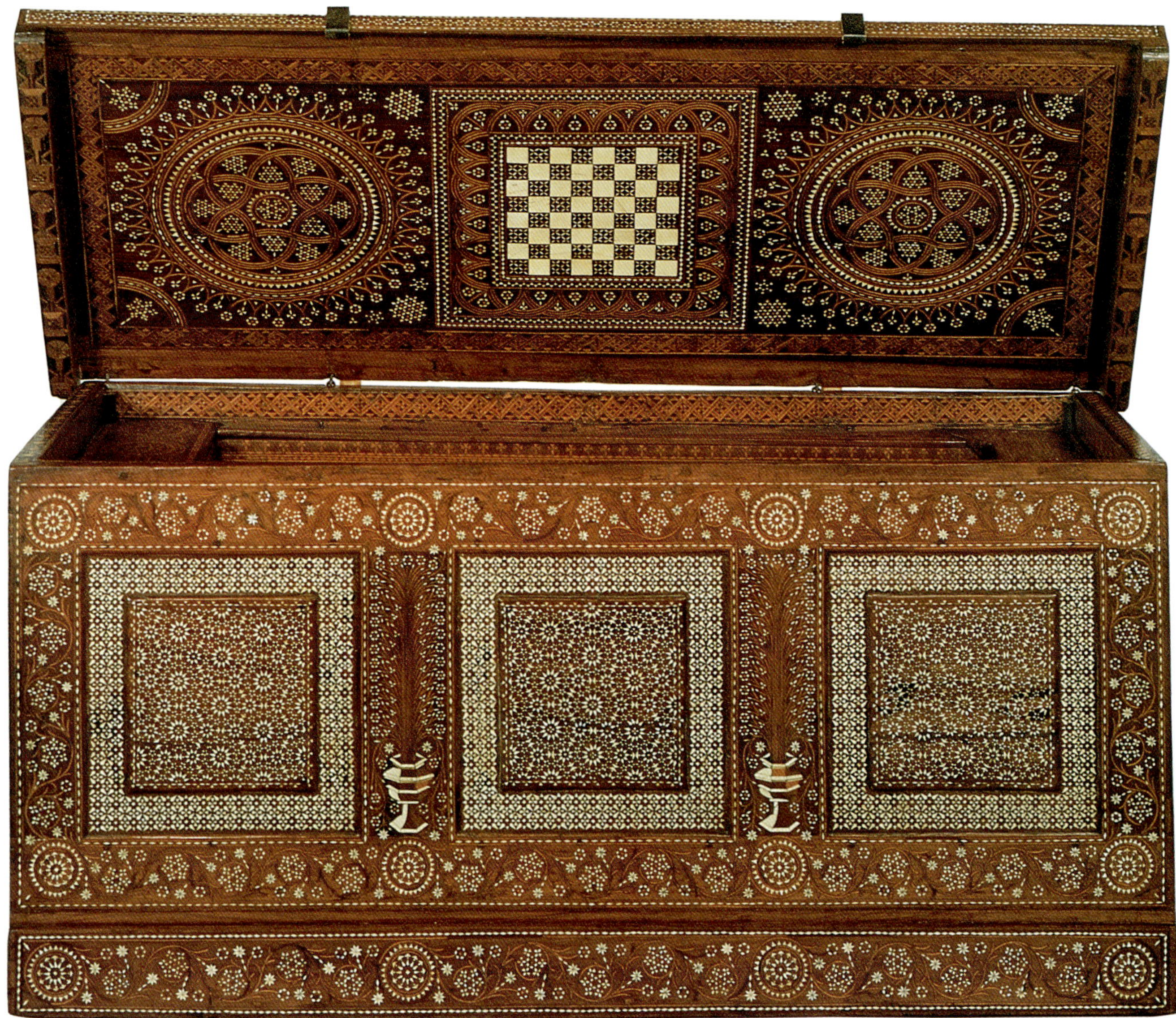

109 *Cassa*, Venice, ca. 1500. Walnut inlaid with marquetry of ivory and colored woods in a finish called *intarsia alla certosina*. The checkerboard inlay in the inside lid, suitable for games of chess or tric-trac (checkers), suggests that the piece might have served for entertainment as well as for storage. London, Victoria and Albert Museum.

on the ends of the chest, the full lineage of husband and wife, both paternal and maternal, could be displayed in the bridal chamber.

But the most luxurious treatment in this early period was intarsia or inlay work, now called *alla certosina* (fig. 109). The finish is thought to take its name from Carthusian monasteries in northern Italy, which specialized in the technique, but it is of near Eastern origin. Venice became a major center for its production, and this was probably the type of decoration referred to elsewhere as *alla veneziana*.[47] It speaks of a trading nation with close connections to the Islamic world and a taste born of a mosaic aesthetic, with geometric motifs in bone, ivory, and mother-of-pearl, inlaid in a wood support – in this case walnut and rosewood.[48] But if a patron could not afford the full treatment, then there was always the fake – a venerable Venetian tradition. A chest in Ca' d'Oro looks at first glance to be *intarsia alla certosina*, but is, in fact, only painted to look like it (fig. 110). The little paw feet are early evidence of a taste for zoomorphic elements in furniture design that would flourish in the sixteenth century.

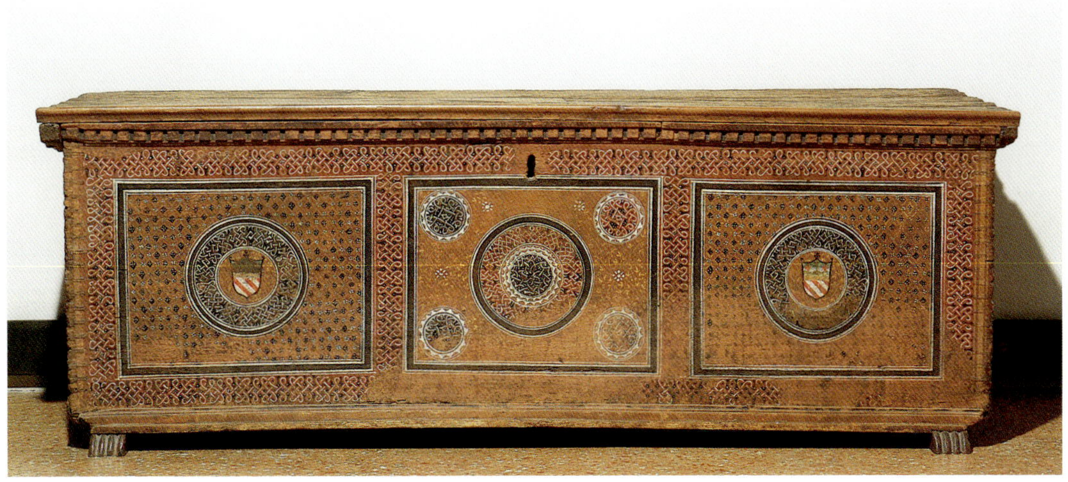

110 *Cassa*, Venice, first half fifteenth century. Wood painted with tempera to look like *intarsia alla certosina*. Venice, Galleria Giorgio Franchetti (Ca' d'Oro).

111 *Cassa*, Venice, first half sixteenth century. Wood covered with gilded stucco ornament. Paris, Musée des Arts Decoratifs.

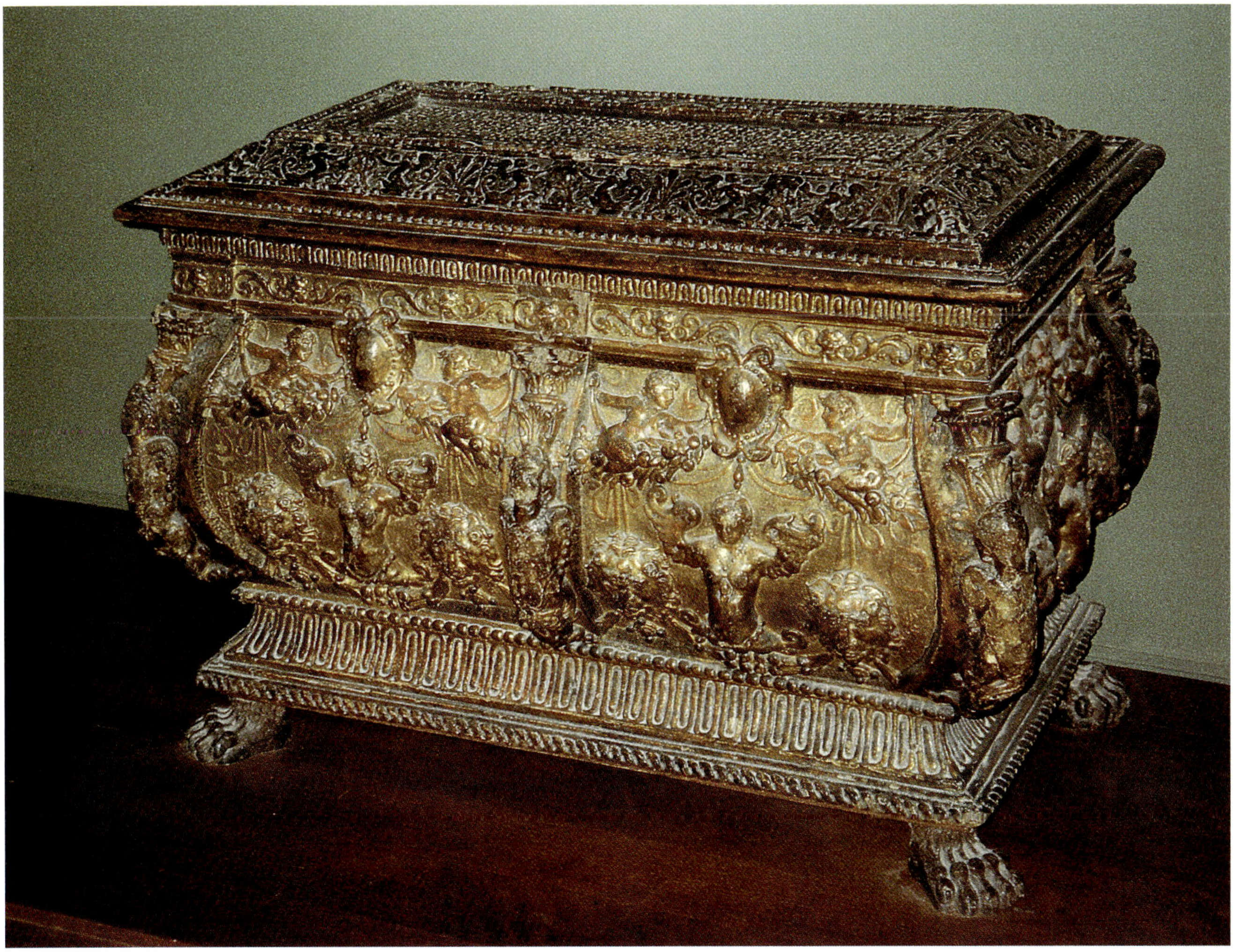

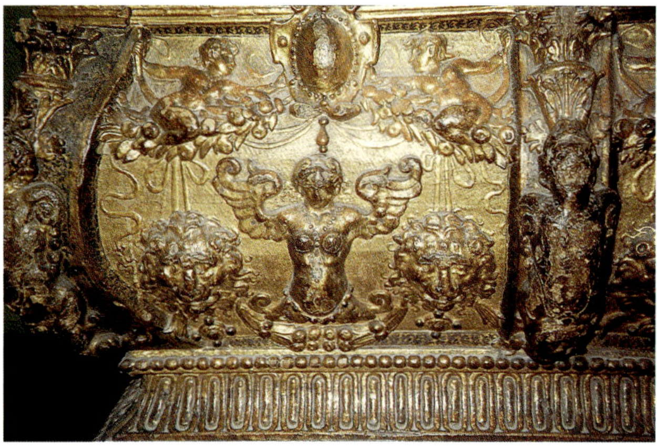

above Detail of fig. 111.

In the sixteenth century, when furniture became more specialized, the *cassa* took on a sculptural shape derived from Roman sarcophagi. Chests were no longer needed for seating as chairs became more common in the house, and lids began to take on a truncated pyramid profile. A sumptuous gilded chest in the Musée des Arts Decoratifs in Paris, would surely have been in violation of the much-abused sumptuary laws that specifically forbade such costly items (fig. 111). It reveals the shift to *all'antica* decoration, with winged sea creatures flanked by lions' heads positioned at the center of each panel beneath swags of fruit and flowers that support frolicking nudes who hold aloft a shield. With caryatid harpies defining the corners, there is no surface left untouched.[49]

A carved walnut chest, now in Ecouen, slows the progression to a fully resolved classicizing coffin-type casket that has become at once architecture and sculpture (fig. 112). Voluptuous caryatids supported by grotesque masks now define all four corners of the piece. On the front panel, a prominent coat of arms with a winged San Marco separates scenes of Jason and Medea on the left and Poseidon and Amphitrite on the right, all carved in high relief. The ensemble is tied together by a frieze of festoons of foliage and fruit at the top and an apron at the bottom with shells and volutes, each punctuated by a grotesque mask in the center. The ends are decorated with robustly carved *putti* riding sea creatures. A coved molding makes a graceful transition between the raised lid and the chest below. The marine themes, along with its structure and carving, point to a Venetian provenance.[50]

Although Venice is not usually associated with the historiated painted *cassoni* that were common in Florentine aristocratic homes in the fifteenth century, there is evidence that they were made there as well, even as late as the mid-

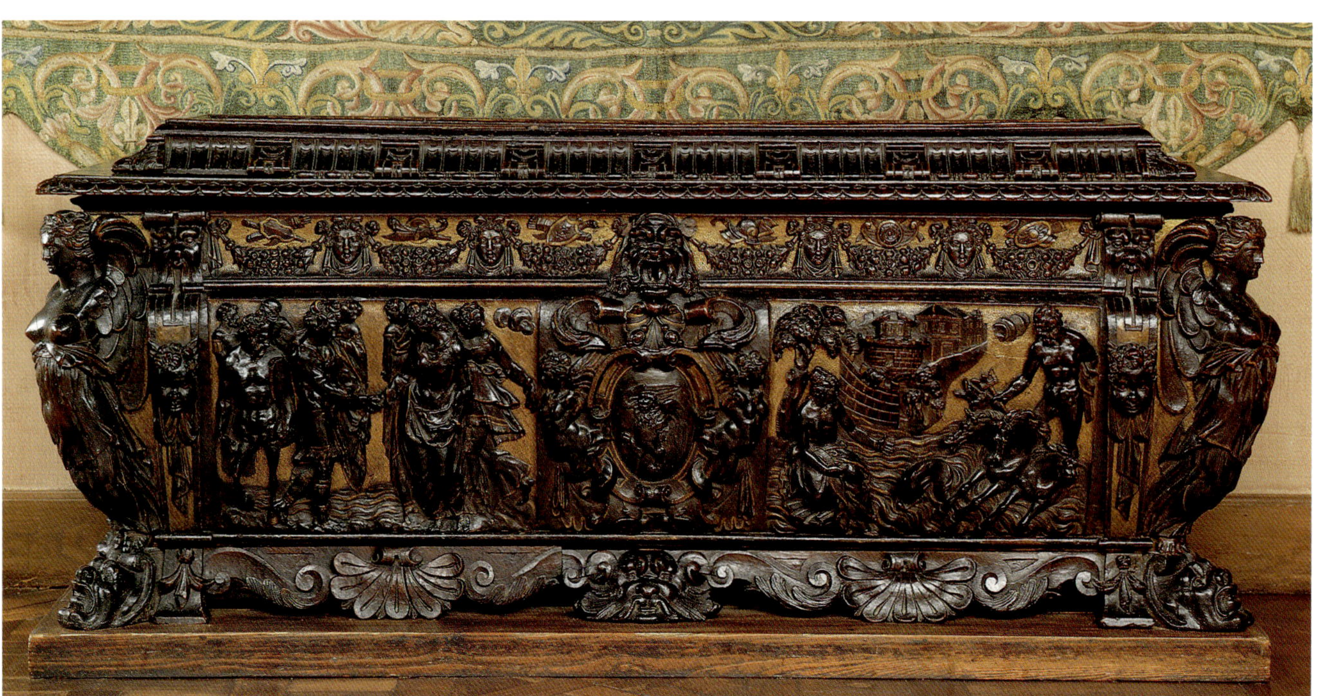

112 *Cassa*, Venice, mid-sixteenth century. Walnut, carved. The grotesques on this coffin-style chest are similar to those on numerous pieces of Venetian furniture. Niccolo dei Conti's bronze well-heads in the courtyard of the Palazzo Ducale, dated 1556, are decorated with ovals containing nude reclining figures alternating with marine motifs, similar to those on the chest. Ecouen, Musée Nationale de la Renaissance., Inv. 20402.

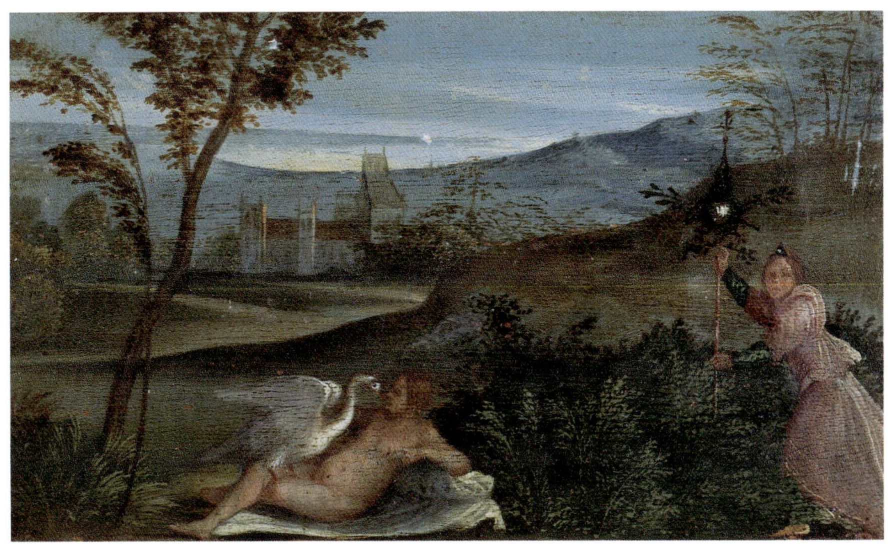

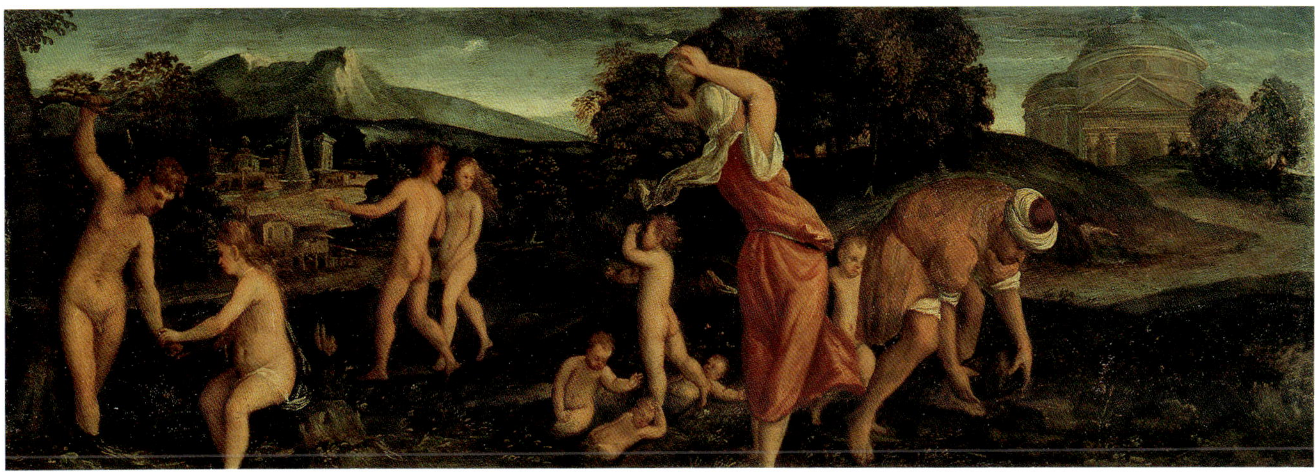

sixteenth century when they had fallen out of fashion in Florence.[51] Carlo Ridolfi wrote in 1648 that Giorgione had painted cupboards, headboards, and coffers, usually with stories from Ovid.[52] Remnants of this activity may survive in a number of little wood panels painted with allegorical and mythological scenes, dispersed in museums throughout the world (fig. 113). Ridolfi also named Andrea Schiavone as a painter of sacred and profane stories on beds, chests, and other furniture (fig. 114).[53] A few years later, the critic Marco Boschini explained that when the artist did not have other commissions he painted chests for a certain Rocco della Carità, who had his *bottega* beneath the Procuratie Vecchie on Piazza San Marco. Rocco's son recalled that his father had paid Schiavone 24 soldi daily for painting up to two *casse* per day "with histories, fables, foliage, arabesques, grotesques, and similar things." He further noted, not without irony, that "today these chests are sold for up to 100 ducats each, and one does not find them on sale any more;

113 (*top*) Circle of Giorgione, *Leda and the Swan*, early sixteenth century. Wood panel, 12 × 19 cm. This popular story was depicted by some of the greatest artists of the time, including Leonardo da Vinci, Michelangelo, and Antonio Correggio. Padua, Museo Civico.

114 (*above*) Andrea Schiavone, *Deucalion and Pyrrha Repopulating the World*, sixteenth century. Wood panel, 41 × 118 cm. Ovid (*Metamorphoses* 1:348–415) recounts a pagan version of a great flood that destroyed all of mankind except for the righteous Deucalion, son of Prometheus, and his wife Pyrrha. Adrift in a small boat for nine days, they ran aground on Mount Parnassus and were left alone "as samples of mankind." An oracle ordered them to veil their heads and "throw behind you the bones of your great mother," which they understood to mean "the stones in the body of the earth." Doing this, they saw the stones thrown by Deucalion turning into men and those by Pyrrha into women. Ovid concluded: "So it comes about that we are a hardy race, well accustomed to toil, giving evidence of the origin from which we sprang." The theme would have had exemplary import in a society that placed a high value on human fertility. See figure 265 for a watercolor copy of another version of the subject by Schiavone in the collection of Andrea Vendramin. Accademia, Venice.

rather one sees them decorating many galleries, as precious things, and of this there is no doubt."[54]

Several such works by Schiavone and other artists ended up in the painting collection of the Venetian collector Andrea Vendramin, not as pieces of furniture, but as independent works of art (fig. 265).[55] The rise in value of the little wood panels painted with mythologies or biblical scenes would help explain their detachment from the chests and their entry into museums and private collections as separate pieces. And, as Peter Thornton has noted, "the split between Fine Art and Decorative Art becomes apparent to us with hindsight, although it may not have been so clear-cut at the time."[56]

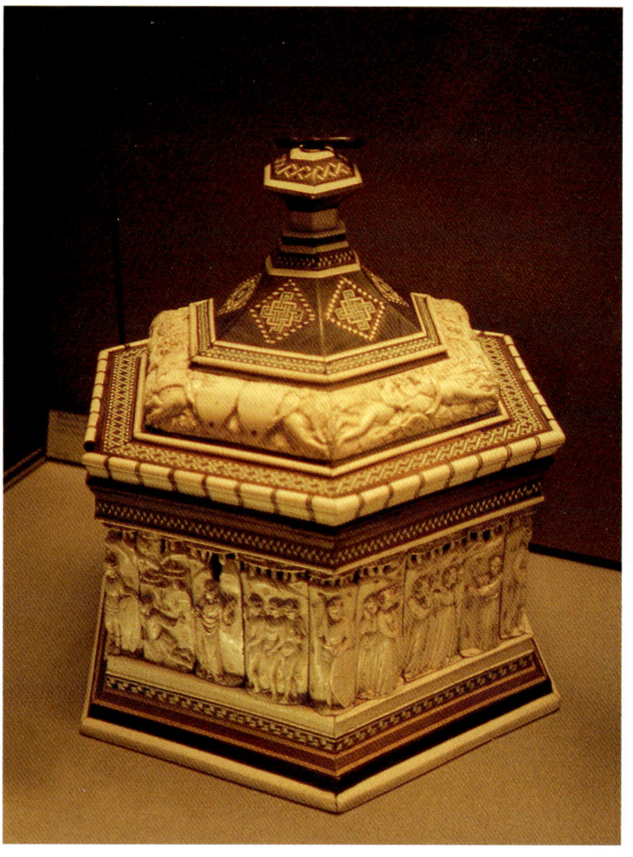

Larger objects might be stored in a *credenza*, but small treasures were kept in small boxes – the *cassetta*, the *cassetina*, the *cassella*, the *casselletta*, the *cofanetto*, the *stipetto*. Quite often the smaller the chest, the more precious the surface treatment. In the early quattrocento little ivory chests, either six-sided or casket-shaped, were popular wedding gifts for the affluent. Featuring a distinctive surface treatment associated with the Embriachi workshop in Venice, these costly *cassette* were covered with wood inlay and ivory or bone plaques, carved with courtly scenes or episodes from Greek mythology, like the Florentine *cassone* (fig. 115).[57] By the end of the century, a bride might also keep her jewels in a *cofanetto*, covered with embossed leather, or in one of metal with gold and silver decorations *alla damaschina*, or in a precious box decorated with *pastiglia* work (figs. 116 and 117).[58]

Presentation boxes became ever more elaborate, with luxurious caskets of silver-gilt and lacquered wood set with rock-crystal inserts appearing at the end of the sixteenth century. Filled with baby linen blessed by the pope (called *fascie*), some of these were presented as luxurious gifts to noble parents. But they were also available in the market place. Francesco Sansovino reported seeing a "casket of pure

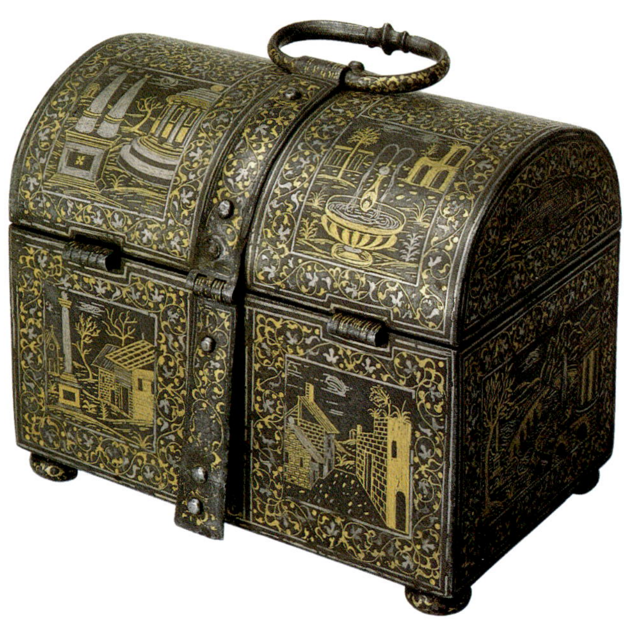

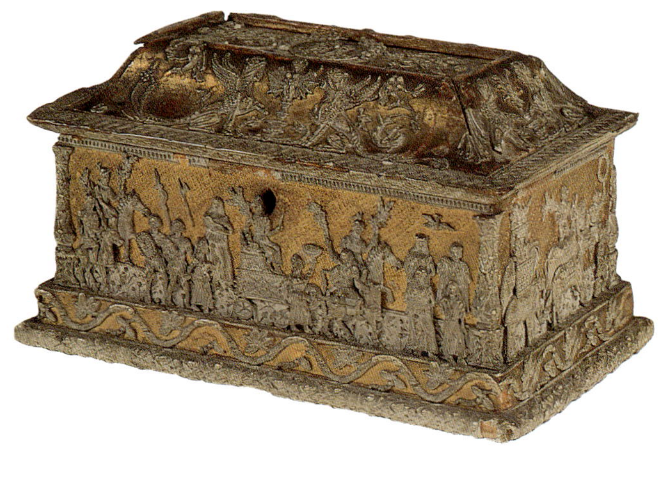

115 (*facing page top*) Embriachi Workshop, *cassetta*, beginning of the fifteenth century. Bone with traces of polychrome, height 32 cm. The exploits of Paris, the Trojan prince who was also a shepherd and whose capture of Helen caused the Trojan War, is depicted in the delicately carved relief plaques on the sides. The three female nudes on the lower right must represent Juno, Minerva, and Venus; the hero awarded a golden apple to the latter in the beauty contest known as the Judgment of Paris. Paris, Louvre.

116 (*facing page bottom left*) *Cofanetto*, Venetian, beginning of sixteenth century. Damascene bronze. Ecouen, Musée du la Renaissance.

117 (*facing page bottom right*) Workshop of the Roman Triumphs, *cofanetto*, Venetian, ca. 1500. Pastiglia. The little casket is decorated with scenes from Roman history, with a Triumph, probably of Caesar, on the front. The truncated pyramid-shaped lid features sphinxes and other grotesques and foliated designs. The upper part, decorated with a portrait medallion of Gaius Mucius Scaevola, slides open to reveal a small rectangular compartment. The white lead *pastiglia* surface, probably intended to imitate more costly ivory or bone, has darkened over time to a brownish color. Ecouen, Musée du la Renaissance.

118 (*below*) *Cofanetto* or *scrigno*, probably for toilet articles, Venetian, 1570–90. Beechwood, lacquered and painted in gold on a dark brown background, with silver-gilt mounts. Height 18.26 cm, length 41.6 cm, depth 28.9 cm. The decorative treatment, inspired by the Middle Eastern technique of embossed metal called "alla damaschina," is adapted here to create arabesques and vegetal motifs by applying powdered gold with accents of red, green, and blue. New York, The Metropolitan Museum of Art, 57.25 ab.

crystal" in the shop of the jeweler Anton Maria Fuga in the Ruga dei Orefici at Rialto. It was, he wrote, "very large, made in such a manner that the items placed inside looked at from the outside appeared as if they were sculptured."[59]

By the late sixteenth century, an equally luxurious mode appeared in the form of a fitted casket, which might be called a *cofanetto*, a *cassettina*, or possibly a *scrigno*. Two particularly precious examples are also in the Metropolitan Museum. Each had a mirror inside the cover, indicating that they were used as vanity cases. One piece is decorated inside and out with tiny glass plaques painted with figures and miniature versions of contemporary paintings (figs. 119 and 120). These alternate with mother-of-pearl plaques painted with Moorish motifs that carry over to the wood case. The cornices feature ivory intarsia incrustations. The inside is divided into several small compartments covered with embroidered silk.[60]

The other piece, made of lacquered beechwood, has a more distinctly Islamic flavor (fig. 118). Inspired by Venice's commerce with the East, it is painted with gold and silver arabesques, or moresques, on a dark-brown background, with touches of red, green, and blue. Similar motifs appear on ceramic jugs and pitchers, with arabesques and palmettes connected in a continuous motif according to classical Islamic schemes. The decorative treatment is inspired by

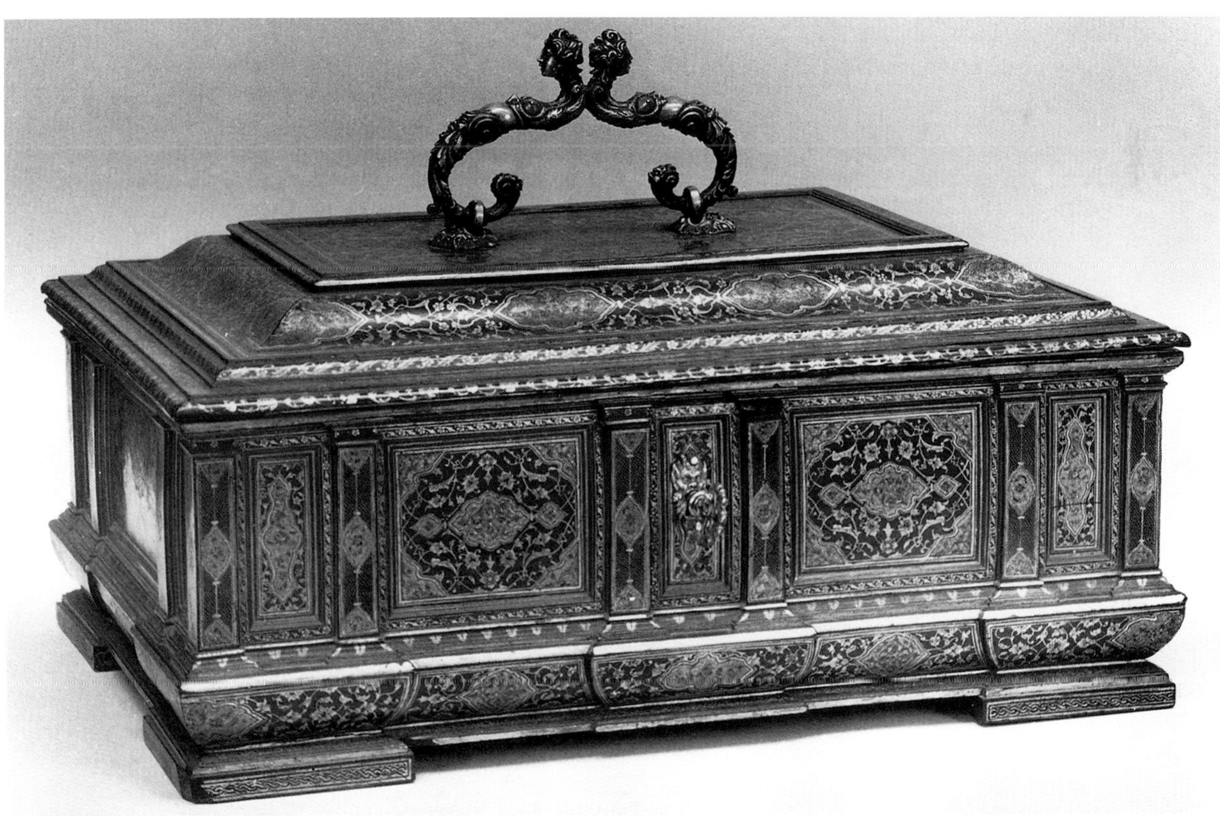

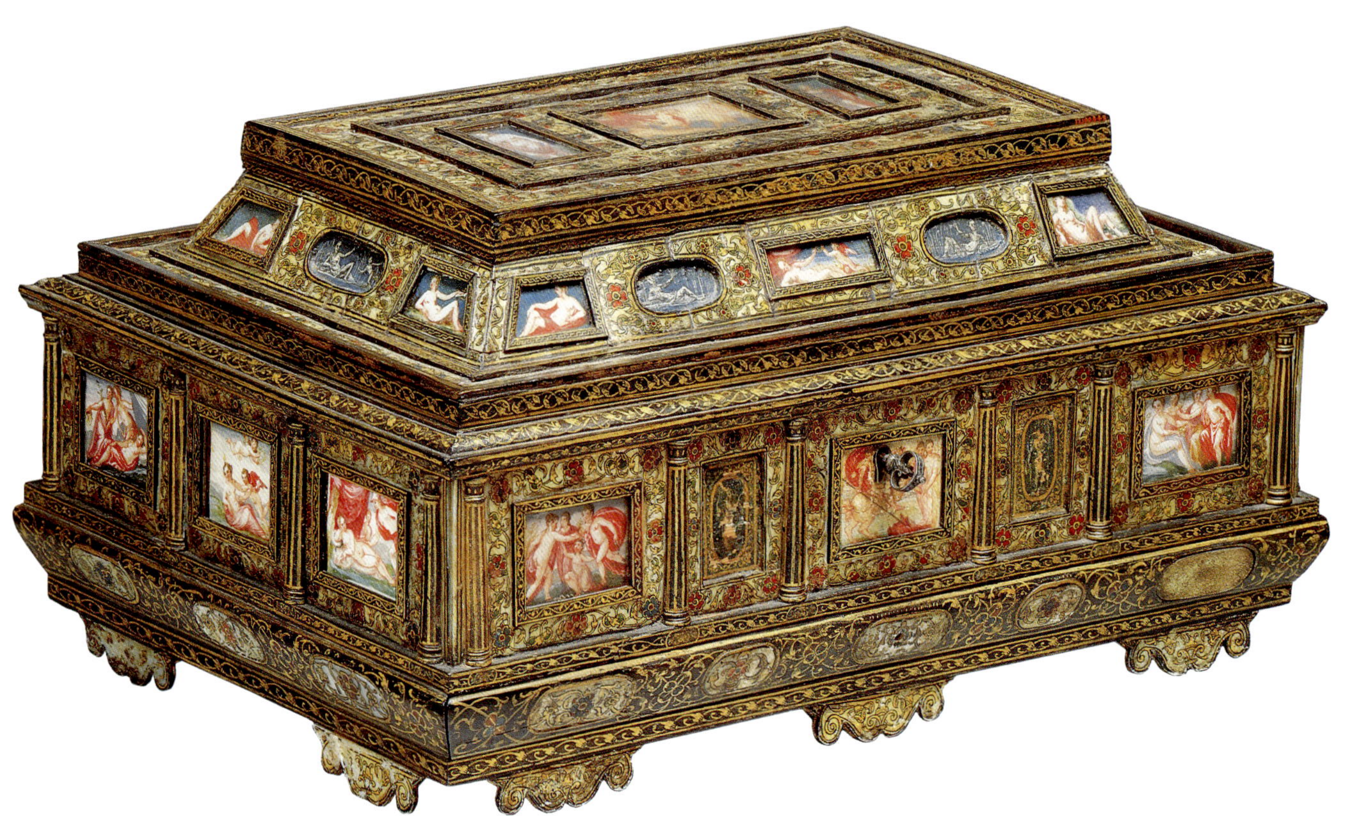

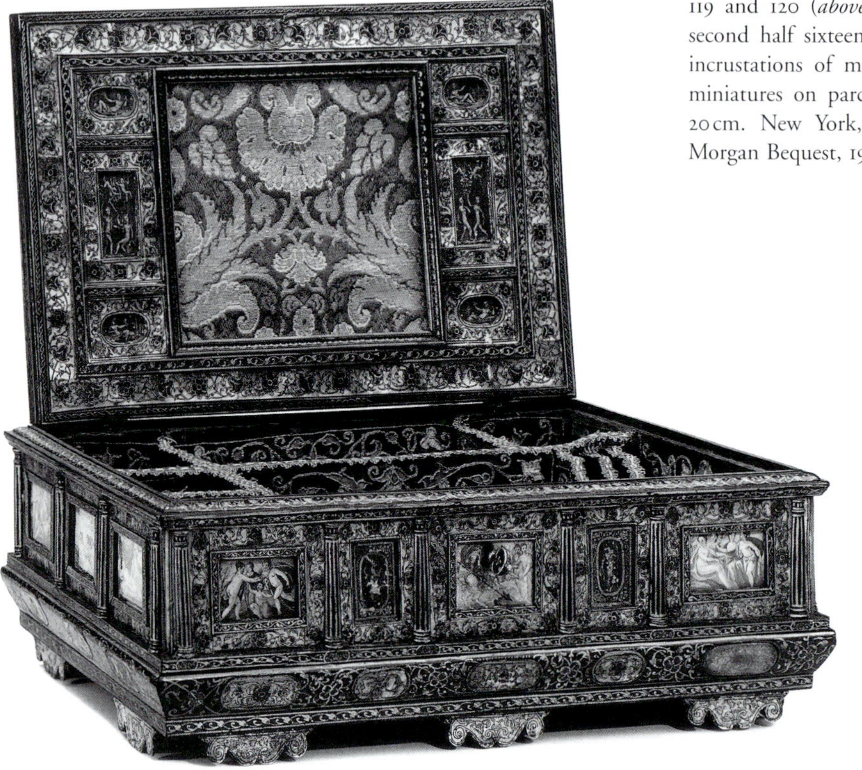

119 and 120 (*above and left*) *Cofanetto* for toilet articles, Venice, second half sixteenth century. Ebony, painted and decorated with incrustations of mother-of-pearl, ivory with gilding, and gouache miniatures on parchment under glass, length 39.69 cm and depth 20 cm. New York, The Metropolitan Museum of Art, Pierpont Morgan Bequest, 1917. (17.190.848).

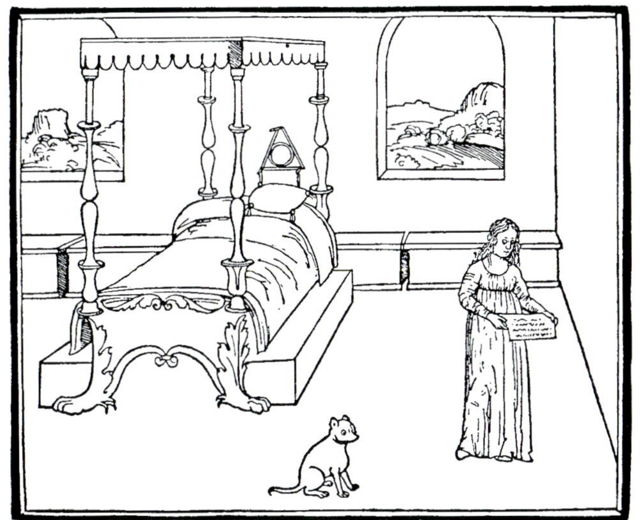

121 (*left*) *Polia's Bedroom*, woodcut from the *Hypnerotomachia Poliphili* (Venice, 1499). The frame of a triangular mirror mounted above the headboard of the bed is provided with pegs in each corner to hold toilet articles. Princeton, Princeton University Library.

122 (*below*) Carved and gilt tabernacle mirror frame, early sixteenth century. Wood with gilding, *pastiglia*, and polychrome decoration, 8.7 × 72.4 cm (frame); 25.8 × 25.4 cm (mirror). The frame features candelabrum-style columns, a lintel, a base strip decorated with a vegetal design, and a dentilated cornice with blue recesses. It is also decorated with acanthus leaves on the top and sides of the frame and on the antependium at the bottom. Vestiges of a coat of arms and four plugged peg holes on the base strip are still visible. New York, The Metropolitan Museum of Art, Robert Lehman Collection, 1975 (1975.1.2104).

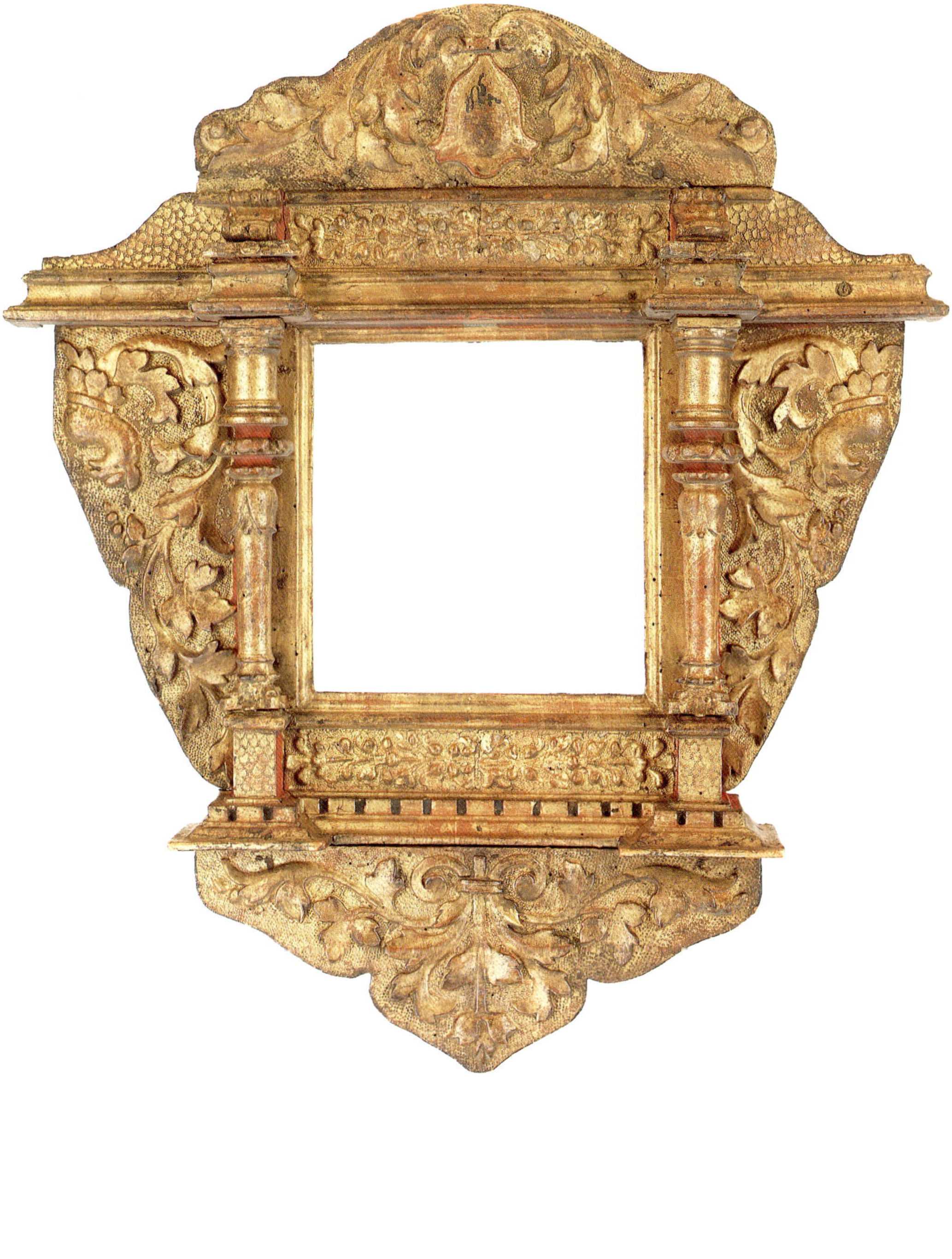

the metal finish called "alla damaschina," but the silver-gilt handles are finely worked in a Renaissance style.[61]

It has often been noted that the Renaissance was a period when every object of utility became a work of art. The Venetian *restello* is a case in point. This is a piece of furniture that first appears in inventories in the mid-fifteenth century, but virtually disappears by the end of the sixteenth. The term *restello* derives from the Latin *restellus*, denoting a small rack with protruding nails or hooks from which to hang various objects. At some point, artisans had the idea of making a wall mirror serve double duty as both reflective device and rack with pegs, and the *restello* was born. A modest example hangs above the bed in Polia's bedroom, depicted in a wood-cut in the *Hypnerotomachia Poliphili* of 1499 (fig. 121). *Restelli* became so luxurious that their production was banned by a sumptuary law of 1488, but they continued to be made.[62] A fine example in the Metropolitan Museum in New York features a round mirror with a carved, wood frame richly decorated with gilding, *pastiglia*, and paint – the type of object that would be listed in an inventory as "a *restello* of gold with its mirror" (fig. 122).[63] It has plugged holes in the base molding that once held hooks for toilet articles, as in the woodcut. These would have been small, often costly objects, such as an ivory comb, a silver perfume flask, a hairbrush, a *scriminal* – that is, a stylus or needle of bone, glass, or silver to part the hair – and perhaps a *coda*, a horsehair switch to clean the comb. Indeed, with the *restello*, the organizer and the objects organized together became a work of art.Such objects can be said to define the level of "refinement without equal" claimed by Venetians of this period.

123 *Venetian Lady Doing Needlework*, from Anton Francesco Doni, *I marmi del Doni, academico peregrino* (Venice: F. Marcolini, 1552–53), 138. The print is adapted from a series of forty-two moral allegories etched by Enea Vico (1541–67), where it is entitled *Industria*. Princeton, Princeton University Library Special Collections.

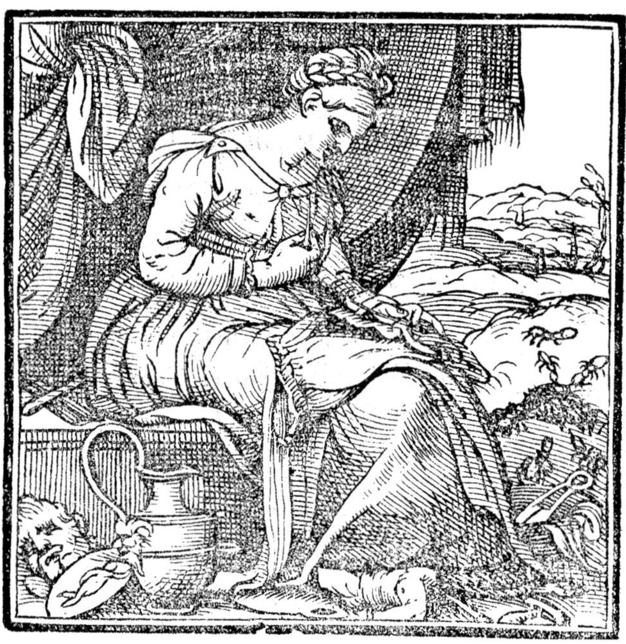

Fatta in Casa

But what activities occupied the good wife when she was not tending the children or storing away the linens and clothing in her numerous chests and organizing her *restello* or her *cofanetto*? In all likelihood she was emulating Lucretia and her companions, with whom this chapter began. The Florentine writer and critic Anton Francesco Doni published his *Ragionamenti* in Venice in 1552. It included an engraving by Enea Vico depicting a Venetian matron absorbed in her needlework next to a large window (fig. 123).[64] The image accompanies a description of a room in a Venetian palace, although the artist situates the scene in the countryside. Doni writes that the ladies sit beneath the windows because of the light, to embroider and make fine things with the needle, while the family eats on one table at the end of the room and plays games on another at the side. He further notes, in accordance with the family values set forth in treatises of the period: "Some stroll around, others stand at the fire, and so there is a place for everyone."[65]

The print bears further examination, for it also makes a moral point. The attentive viewer will notice a swarm of ants just outside the window behind the sewing basket on the right, their industriousness echoing that of the lady. Lying around on the floor are the cast-off appurtenances of a lifestyle of luxury and leisure. The mirror is a traditional symbol of vanity, while the dish painted with a nude figure and the broken torso and bust are probably signs of classical interests appropriate for a gentleman but of little relevance to the gentle lady. Indeed, as attested by Sansovino's praise of Giulia Bembo's industriousness, women – of whatever caste or class – were supposed to keep busy. The *Magnifica* Marina, widow of Michele Memo of San Marcuola, would have been the model wife. An inventory taken in 1572 just after her husband's death included twenty-three bed sheets, four pillowcases, twenty handkerchiefs, and seventy chemises for men, women, and children, all designated as "fatta in casa" – made in the house.[66]

In his treatise on the education of women, published in 1547, the Venetian writer Ludovico Dolce counseled that the activities of little girls be carefully supervised. They should, moreover, play only with one another and not with boys. Furthermore, he tells parents to take away the dolls that their young daughters like to dress up with jewelry and various costumes, since they resemble idols and can only "teach them to value ornaments and pomp." For these frivolities they should substitute miniature household tools of wood and metal, "so that they will learn with delight the name and function of each."[67]

Dolce further laments that spinning and weaving, both honored activities for noblewomen in antiquity, were now the province of women of low rank, and he exclaims: "O vapid vanity and damaging delicacy of the noble ladies of our century." Such activities were, as numerous images attest, good enough for the Virgin and her mother St. Anne. Dolce adds: "and certainly needlework is necessary not only for private ladies, but also for princesses and queens; and so much more for them since they are free from the burdens of caring for the family, so what else will they do? Simply while away the hours among a multitude of damsels and court ladies?" As to his own daughter, she should at least be taught to sew.[68] Dorothea, his respondent in the dialogue, allows that "Truly all embroidery is a beautiful and ingenious work, not being as necessary as sewing, it carries no shame in not knowing how to do it . . . but to tell the truth, knowing how to sew for women is equivalent to knowing how to write for men."[69] Dolce replies that his daughter should learn not only "activities particular to the house (which are many) such as how to decorate a chamber [or] to outfit a bed, but also to have all the family furnishings arranged in order in their [proper] place, so that it appears that all the house in every part would . . . be filled with happiness."[70]

Dolce might not have approved of the vapid vanity of one lady, depicted in a print sitting in the open air in the privacy of her *altana*, her wide-brimmed, crownless hat protecting her fair skin while exposing her hair to the bleaching rays of the sun (fig. 124).[71] But a closer look reveals that these hands are not idle. For on her lap is a cushion on which she is making lace.

Over the course of the sixteenth century, lacemaking, in particular, would become the noble ladies' activity *par excellence*. The first pattern books of lace and embroidery designs were published in the 1520s in Germany and Venice in the only sector in the publishing industry dedicated to the applied arts.[72] These little manuals were revised and reprinted repeatedly, but with a noticeable change in authorship, audience, and ideological stance over time. The two earliest Italian manuals were published in Venice in 1527. Giovanni Antonio Tagliente, a calligrapher in the employ of the Venetian Republic, put together a collection of drawings of embroidery designs already in circulation as loose leafs and entitled it "Exemplar of Embroidery." The frontispiece announces it as an "opera nuova" – a new work – that teaches women to sew, to embroider, and to design, and adds that it will be of great utility to artists as well. The illustration depicts women engaged in a variety of needlework activities.[73]

Alessandro Paganino went a step further. His manual, published the same year, has two frontispieces, one showing women weaving on a table loom and a floor loom – an artisan occupation – and the other featuring four women engaged in embroidery – a more genteel activity (figs. 125 and 126). The first image betrays a northern origin, with women in German rather than Italian dress. And although it features classical motifs such as profile heads of Roman emperors, the tone of the manual is strictly utilitarian and didactic in a practical sense. Paganino includes not only patterns, many of them influenced by woven textile and tapes-

124 Luca Bertelli, *Lady Bleaching her Hair*, sixteenth century. Engraving. London, British Library.

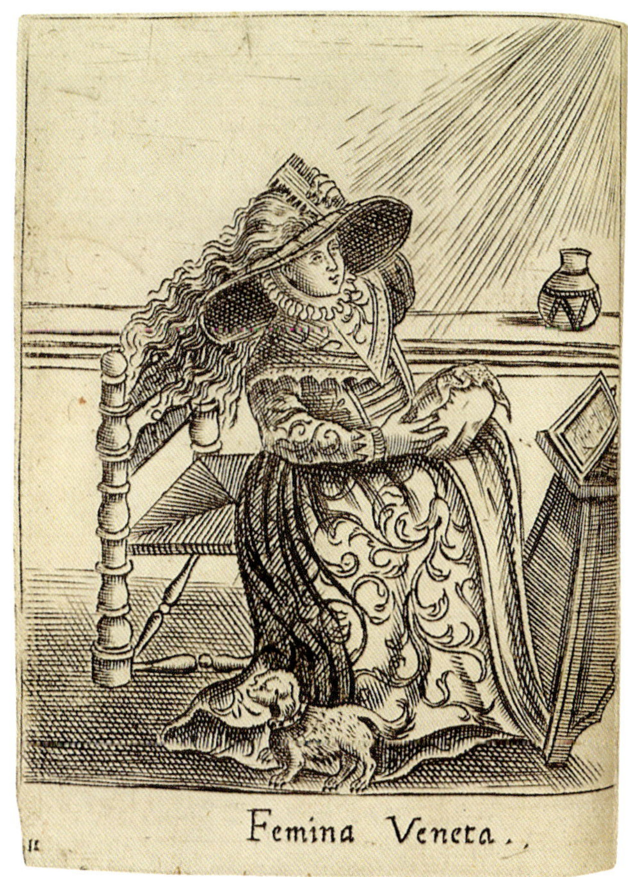

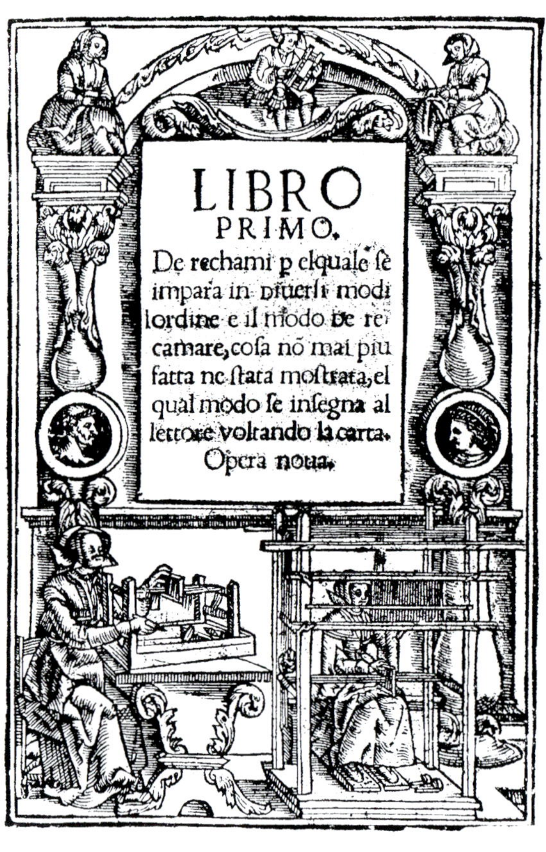
LIBRO
PRIMO.
De rechami p elquale se
impara in diuersi modi
lordine e il modo de re-
camare, cosa nō mai piu
fatta ne stata mostrata, el
qual modo se insegna al
lettore voltando la carta.
Opera noua.

E auertisse con el disegno insieme ti apportiamo vn porfilo bellissimo e vago a locchio cosa non mancho da tenerse cara che esso disegno: laquale cosa da noi sono stata con grandissima fatica composta e ordinata a tua vtilita e pochissima spesa. Vale.

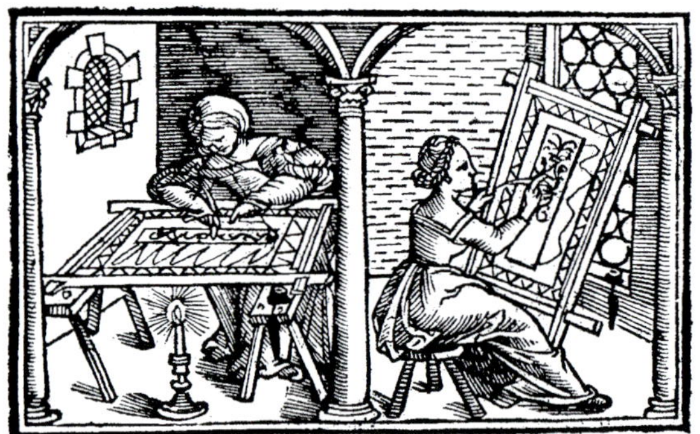

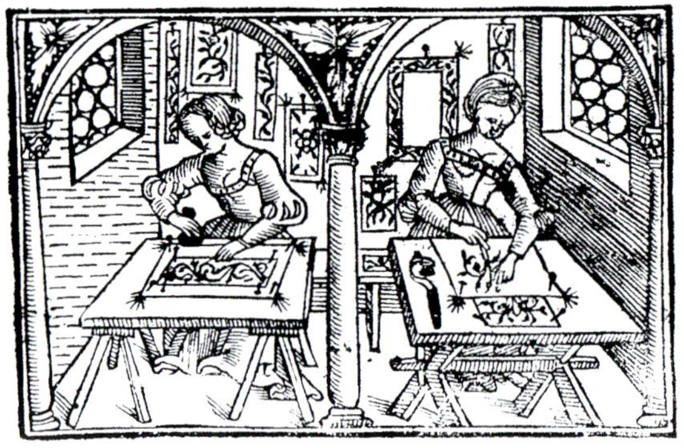

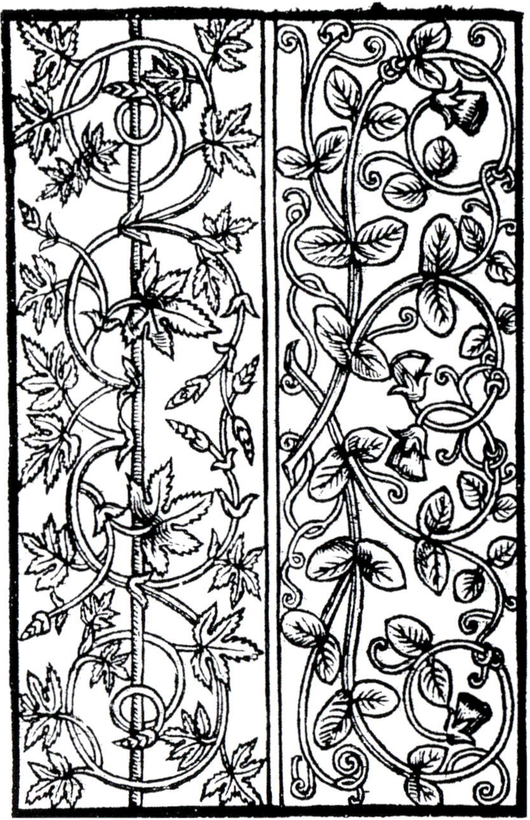

125 (*facing page top left*) Left frontispiece from *De rechami per el quale se impara in diversi modi lordine e il modo de recamare . . . Opera nuova*. (Venice: Alessandro Paganino, 1527). Venice, Museo Civico Correr.

126 (*facing page top right*) Right frontispiece from *De rechami per el quale se impara in diversi modi lordine e il modo de recamare . . . Opera nuova.* (Venice: Alessandro Paganino, 1527). Venice, Museo Civico Correr.

127 (*facing page bottom left*) Embroidery pattern from *De rechami per el quale se impara in diversi modi lordine e il modo de recamare . . . Opera nuova*. (Venice: Alessandro Paganino, 1527). Venice, Museo Civico Correr.

128 (*facing page bottom right*) *Tappezzaria* (tapestry) with S-shaped pattern similar to those found in Paganino's book, Venice, late sixteenth century. Venice, Palazzo Pisani Moretta.

try designs (figs. 127 and 128), but also detailed instructions for transferring them. "And first I say that you should choose the design that pleases you, and then take a fine needle and perforate all the outlines of the drawing, so that the holes would be a little distance one from the other."[74] Carbon or pumice would then be pounced through the holes onto the cloth, creating a pattern for the needleworker to follow in stitching the design.

In the 1530s, a printer called Zoppino published no fewer than ten such manuals, which now included lace patterns. These introduced a new, more elevated tone. The *Convivio* – or Banquet – *of Beautiful Women*, promised "new works with just measure . . . not seen before, with which they can

129 (*below left*) Frontispiece from *Convivio delle belle donne* (Venice: Nicolo d'Aristotile detto Zoppino, 1532) (from Lotz, *Bibliographie der Modelbücher*, fig. 97). While the social benefits of needlework are emphasized in the vignette at the bottom, the compartments above feature a mountain landscape and the cardinal virtues of Justice, Temperance, Prudence, and Fortitude. Princeton, Princeton University Library.

130 (*below right*) Frontispiece from *Gli universali de i belli Recami antichi, e moderni: ne i quali un pellegrino ingegno, si di huomo come di donna, potra in questa nostra età con l'ago vertuosamente esercitar si. Non anchora da alcuni altri dati in luce* (Venice: Nicolo d'Aristotile detto Zoppino, 1537), fol. A (1) verso (from Lotz, *Bibliographie der Modelbücher*, fig. 108). One of the vignettes at the top of the page depicts ladies purchasing embroidered braid from a mercer. The scene at the bottom appears to show a school with a lady instructing a group of young girls in the art of embroidery and lacemaking. Princeton, Princeton University Library.

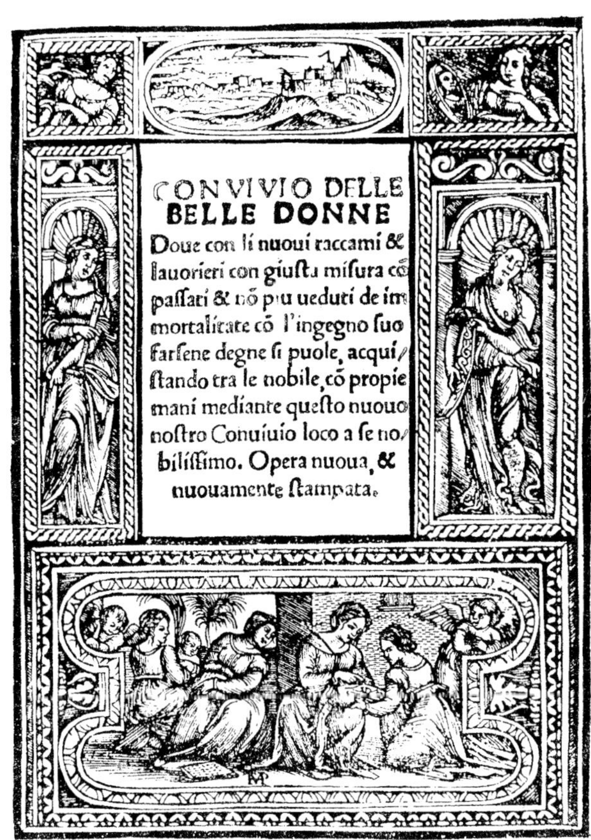

CONVIVIO DELLE
BELLE DONNE
Doue con li nuoui raccami &
lauorieri con giusta misura cō
passati & nō piu ueduti de im
mortalitate cō l'ingegno suo
farsene degne si puole, acqui/
stando tra le nobile, cō propie
mani mediante questo nuouo
nostro Conuiuio loco a se no/
bilissimo. Opera nuoua, &
nuouamente stampata.

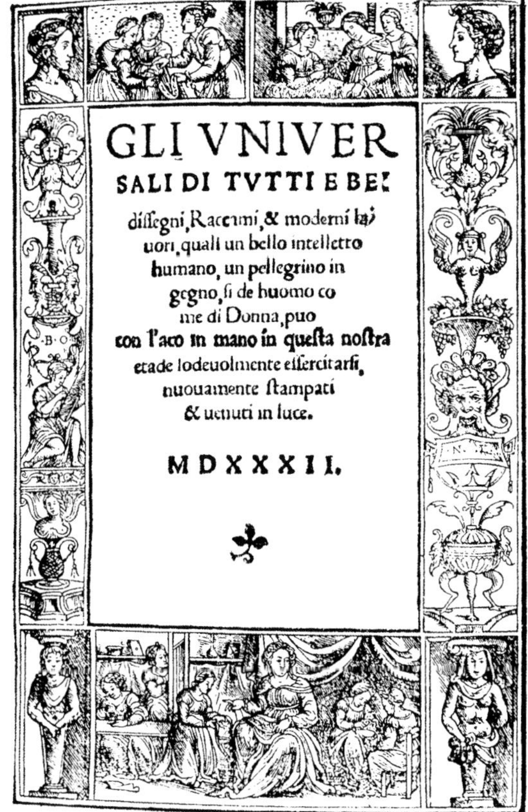

GLI VNIVER
SALI DI TVTTI E BE!
dissegni, Raccami, & moderni la/
uori, quali un bello intelletto
humano, un pellegrino in
gegno, si de huomo co
me di Donna, puo
con l'aco in mano in questa nostra
etade lodeuolmente essercitarsi,
nuouamente stampati
& uenuti in luce.
MDXXXII.

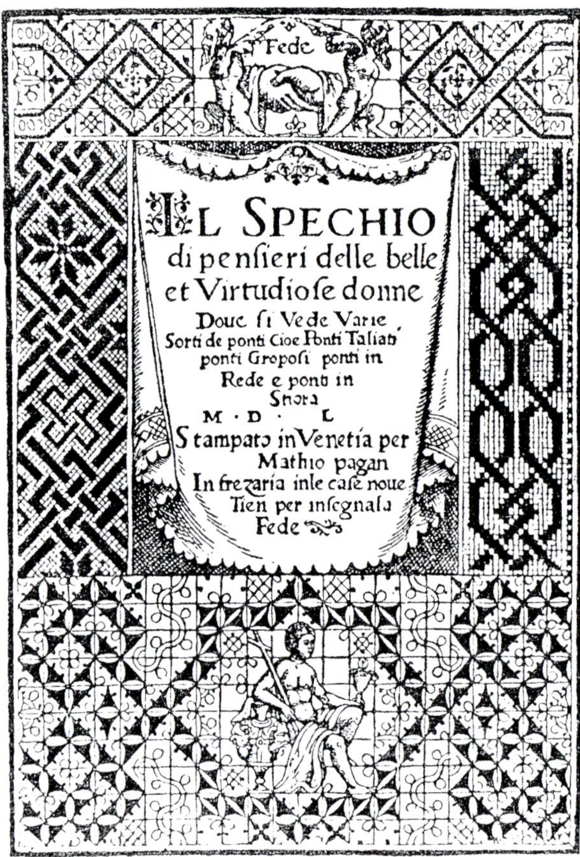

Fede

IL SPECHIO
di pensieri delle belle
et Virtudiose donne
Doue si Vede Varie
Sorti de ponti Cioe Ponti Taliati
ponti Groposi ponti in
Rede e ponti in
Stuora
M · D · L
Stampato in Venetia per
Mathio pagan
In frezaria inle case noue
Tien per insegna la
Fede

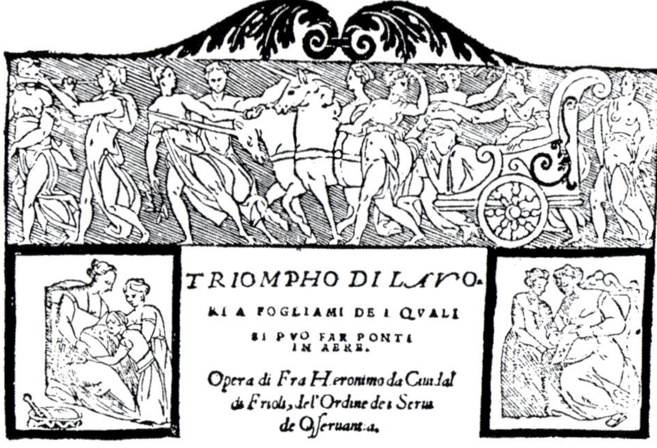

TRIOMPHO DI LAVO-
RI A FOGLIAMI DE I QVALI
SI PVO FAR PONTI
IN AERE.
Opera di Fra Heronimo da Ciuidal
di Frioli, del'Ordine dei Serui
de Osseruantia.
CVM GRATIA ET PRIVILEGIO PER ANNI.

131 (*above*) Frontispiece from *Specchio di pensieri delle belle et virtuose donne* (Venice: Mathio Pagan, in Frezaria in le case nove tien per insegna la Fede, 1550) (from Lotz, *Bibliographie der Modelbücher*, fig. 116). The page features examples of the embroidery and lace patterns offered within. Pagan's shop sign of two clasped hands is at the top of the page and the figure of Faith holding a cross and chalice is embedded in the lace pattern at the bottom. Princeton, Princeton University Library.

132 (*above right*) Frontispiece from *Triompho di lavori a fogliami* (Venice: Hieronimo da Cividal di Frioli, 1555) (from Lotz, *Bibliographie der Modelbücher*, fig. 122). The vignettes below the scene of triumph show ladies with a *tombolo* – or cushion – in their laps making lace. Princeton, Princeton University Library.

achieve immortality with their own hands" (fig. 129).[75] In his preface to the *Universals of All Beautiful Designs*, he vowed to "satisfy every high intellect," having imitated the ancient painter Zeuxis in choosing the most beautiful patterns that were worn by women in his time and creating a new synthesis that exceeded the beauty of any one of his models (fig. 130). The volume, he boasts, is "the most refined book, that was ever composed in our times."[76]

Increasingly, the audience for these books was women rather than artisans – women who were becoming ever more literate. Many noble ladies established small schools of embroidery and lace in their homes, a fact reflected in the frontispieces, which emphasize conviviality. One writer observed that the needle belonged to "all women both high and low, but where the poor find only utility in these arts, the rich, the noble, and beautiful lady wins honor also."[77]

Mathio Pagan was another prolific publisher of lace patterns, producing nearly thirty editions in the 1550s and 1560s. Like Zoppino, he continued the shift in emphasis from the handiwork itself to the practitioner, and now from intellect to virtue. In 1550 he published a tract entitled "The honorable example of the virtuous desire that is held by women of noble mind to learn to make needle lace [*I punti tagliati a fogliami*]."[78] Two other editions are addressed to beautiful and virtuous ladies: in one, to their ornament, and in the other, as the mirror of their thoughts (fig. 131).

133 (*left*) Border of needle lace (*punto in aria*), Venetian, 1600–50. To make needle lace, threads are laid down over a pattern drawn on parchment and the piece is made with a needle and thread in a buttonhole stitch. For bobbin (or pillow) lace, a pricked parchment pattern is attached to a pillow called a *tombolo*. The threads, wound on bobbins, are braided, twisted, or woven together around pins inserted in the pillow. Burano, Museo dei Merletti.

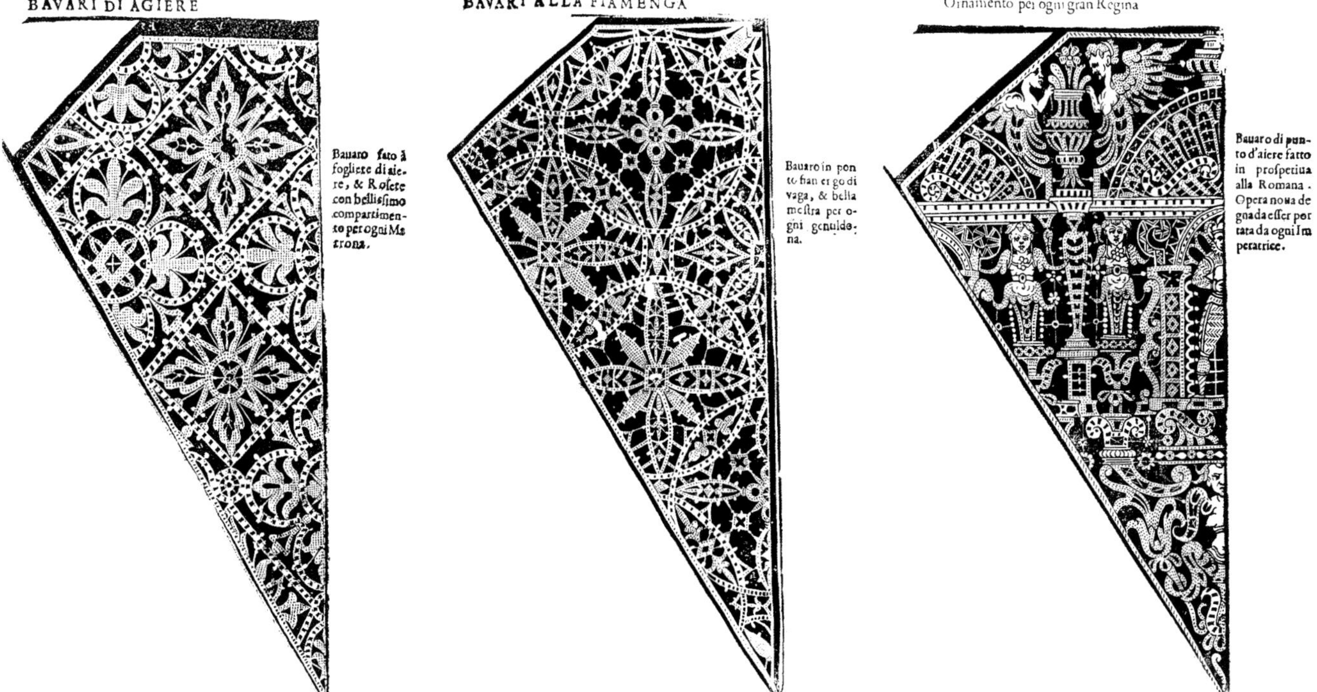

Hieronimo da Cividal di Frioli introduced similar material the following year with a new triumphalist tone (fig. 132). But Pagan was not to be outdone. Three years later he responded with *La gloria e l'honore de ponti tagliati et ponti in aere* ("The Glory and Honor of Bobbin and Needle Lace") (see fig. 133).

As the century progressed, the relationship between manual activity and spiritual well-being was clearly spelled out, and the moral message prevailed over production. How can the promotion of needlework as the ideal occupation for the gentlelady be explained? One scholar makes a compelling argument that "no other activity so successfully promoted the qualities that Renaissance men, anxious to define gender difference, wanted in a wife. Embroidery combined the humility of needlework with rich stitchery. It connoted opulence and obedience. It ensured that women spent long hours at home, retired in private, yet it made a public statement about the household's position and economic standing."[79] The case for embroidery was even stronger for lacemaking.

Ornaments Suitable to Her Condition

During the last decades of the sixteenth century, lace was used extravagantly on both male and female clothing as well as on all kinds of linens: collars, cuffs, shirts, sheets, handkerchiefs. The collar in particular became an object of gift and symbolic exchange (see figs. 138 and 184). The implications of this are evident in a pattern book by a certain Lucrezia Romana. Not surprisingly, she dedicated her fifth volume of patterns, published in 1620, to "virtuous ladies."[80] For each caste or estate there was an appropriate design, the complexity increasing with ascent of the social ladder. One *bàvero* – a lace collar – featuring a foliate design and rosettes was held to be suitable "for every matron." Another –

134 (*above left*) *Bavari di agiere.* Pattern for a collar with a foliate and rosette design "for every matron," from [Lucretia Romana], *Ornamento nobile per ogni gentil matrona, dove si contiene bavari, frisi d'infinita bellezza, Lavori, per Linzuoli Traverse, e Fazuoli, Piena di Figure, Ninfe, Satiri, Grotesche, Fontane, Musiche, Caccie di Cervi, Uccelli, & altri Animali, con ponti in aria fiamenghi, et tagliati con Adornamenti bellissimi, da imparare, per ogni virtuosa Donna, che si diletta di perfettamente cucire* (Venice: Appresso Lessandro de' Vecchi, 1620).

135 (*above center*) *Bavari alla fiamenga.* Pattern in the Flemish manner for a collar with circles and a snowflake design "for every gentle lady," from [Lucretia Romana], *Ornamento nobile per ogni gentil matrona* (1620).

136 (*above right*) *Ornamento per ogni gran Regina.* Pattern for a collar with grotesques and a "perspective in the Roman manner: a new work worthy to be worn by every empress," from [Lucretia Romana], *Ornamento nobile per ogni gentil matrona* (1620).

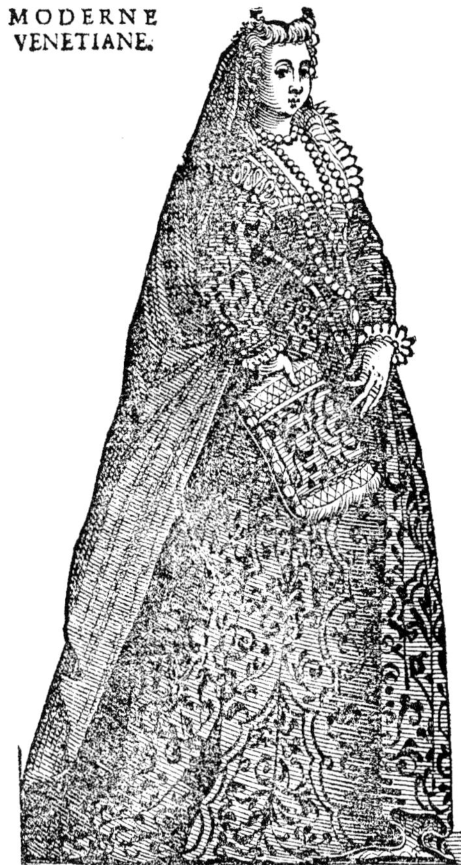

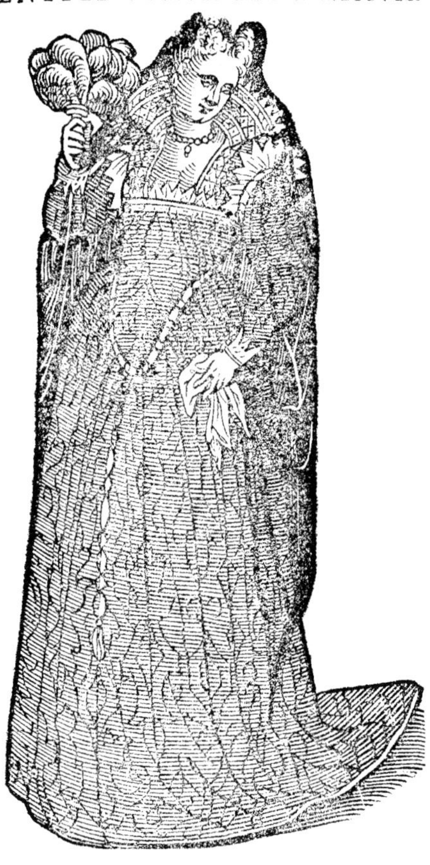

137 (*above left*) Cesare Vecellio, *Modern Venetian Lady*. From his *Habiti d'huomeni et donne* (Venice: 1590), 129v. Vecellio writes: "In the habit shown here, one sees how Venetian ladies adorn themselves with ornaments of precious gold, rich with pearls and other jewels, and with how much study and diligence they adorn their heads, arranging their hair with certain curls that make the form of a half moon with the points like horns." By permission of the Folger Shakespeare Library.

138 (*above right*) Cesare Vecellio, *Modern Venetian Gentlelady*. From his *Habiti d'huomeni et donne*, 140r. According to Vecellio, "Because women's costumes are very subject to change and variability, more than the phases of the moon, it is not possible in a single description to say all that one can about them." By permission of the Folger Shakespeare Library.

somewhat more complex – was held to be appropriate "for every gentle lady." And yet another was defined as an ornament for every great queen or empress. It features more elaborate figural motifs, including harpies and caryatids within an architectural structure that makes full use of the classical vocabulary (figs. 134–36). Lacemaking was by now an activity that had a strong moral component as a symbol of feminine virtue. But it was also a metaphor for a crystallized social hierarchy.

And yet, around this time, the great demand for Venetian lace throughout Europe led to the rise of an industrial model of the large workshop making piecework. Hospices and orphanages, which provided cheap labor, increasingly became the site of lace production, and lacemaking lost its prestige as an elegant activity for noble ladies. Patterns became proprietary property of a business concern, and the model books disappeared.[81]

And what of those noble ladies with their precious lace collars? The woman dressed was the bridge between private and public space, the tangible signature of her husband's status. And the treatise writers admonished the wife to dress according to her station. Piccolomini held that "if the lady is joined as a consort to a noble gentleman, it is a most ugly and odious thing to see her appear outside in clothing that would be more appropriate for a duchess or a queen than a great gentlelady; for she would be dressing in brocade and cloth of gold, embroidered and bordered with pearls and gems and other similar ornaments unsuitable to her condition."[82]

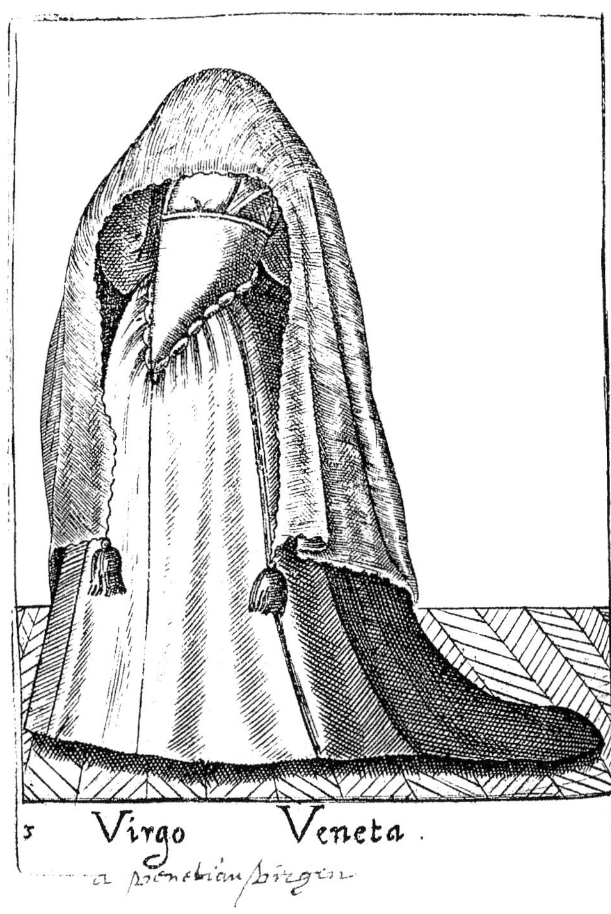

139 Luca Bertelli, *Venetian Virgin*, sixteenth century. Engraving. British Library.

But Venetians, as conscious as they were of noble privilege, deliberately controverted caste-based distinctions in dress with sumptuary laws that applied to patrician and commoner alike.[83] And women of all classes took full advantage of the prerogatives of wealth to dress as grandly as their husbands or their own resources would allow. The writer Pietro Aretino once observed to a friend: "I had to laugh at a Florentine who, seeing in a richly fitted gondola a most beautiful housewife, was astonished at the crimson, jewels, and gold with which she was bedecked and exclaimed, 'Why, we are a mountain of rags!' Nor was he so far wrong, for here, the wives of bakers and tailors go dressed in more pomp than do gentlewomen in other lands."[84] It would take a discerning eye indeed to detect the difference between Cesare Vecellio's *Modern Venetian Lady* and *Modern Venetian Gentlelady* (figs. 137 and 138).[85]

The real distinctions in women's dress were made according to marital status. Thomas Coryat soon became aware of the code. He wrote: "Most of the women when they walke abroad, especially to Church, are vailed with long vailes, whereof some doe reache almost to the ground behinde. These vailes are eyther blacke, or white, or yellowish. The blacke eyther wives or widowes do weare: the white maides, and so the yellowish also."[86]

On the other hand, Coryat noted a strange paradox with some bemusement: "Almost all the wives, widowes and maydes do walke abroad with their breastes all naked . . . a fashion me thinkes very uncivill and unseemely, especially if the beholder might plainly see them."[87] Thus, while the face was covered, the breast was not (fig. 139). It is worth considering why. Is it that pulchritude could be displayed so long as identity was concealed? This calls to mind the masks worn by both Venetian ladies and gentlemen by the end of the century that allowed them to move freely throughout the city without being recognized (see fig. 208).

Free movement could be limited, however. Coryat also looked with wonder at the high platform clogs – *pianelle* – worn by most ladies of quality (see fig. 206). Such footware, he observed, "maketh many of their women that are very short, seeme much taller than the tallest women we have in England . . . All their Gentlewomen, and most of their wives and widowes that are of any wealth, are assisted and supported eyther by men or women when they walke abroad, to the end they may not fall." Judging the clogs to be "dangerous instruments," he adds: "Many of them are curiously painted; some also I have seene fairely gilt: so uncomely a thing (in my opinion) that it is a pitty this foolish custom is not cleane banished and exterminated out of the citie. . . ."[88] The platforms had the effect of making women, who were industrious household managers in private space, into precious objects in public space – requiring care and handling like the worldly goods in their homes. When some daughters of a seventeenth-century doge introduced a new fashion of platforms with a reduced height, a French visitor observed to the doge and his councilors that these lower clogs were undoubtedly more comfortable. One of the councilors responded with an austere expression and without humor: "Only too comfortable; only too comfortable!"[89] And yet, Luciano Bursati da Crema, in his *La vittoria delle donne* published in Venice in 1621, charged that Venetian women adopted platform soles "to make themselves equal and even superior in stature to men."[90] He was seconded several decades later by the Venetian nun Arcangela Tarabotti in her *Antisatira*, who saw the *pianelle* as a sign of the dignity of women: "Grand and magnificent things are never at ground level: they are always exposed on high, as objects of wonder and reverence."[91]

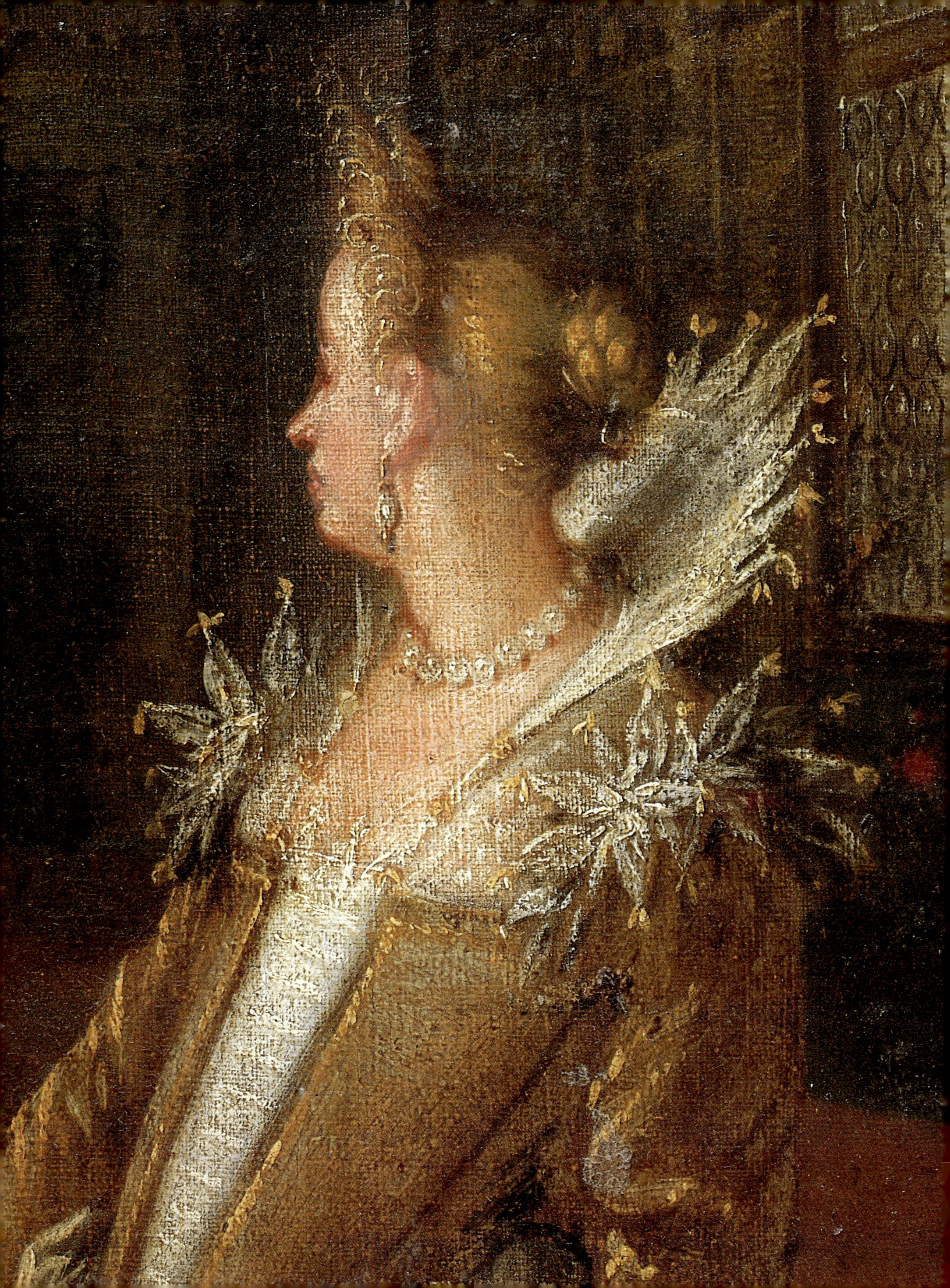

This chapter has touched upon a few aspects of the domestic experience of the virtuous wives of Venice, focusing in part on the objects that allowed them to maintain order in a smoothly run household, and in part on activities that gave order to a smoothly run life. Let us conclude with just one more example: a case of mosaic leather (fig. 140). Painted and gilded with an intricate interlace pattern and a little vignette with a landscape, it was especially designed to hold personal cutlery: a knife, fork, and spoon. At the banquets and other entertainments to be considered in the next chapter, an aristocratic lady, whose life was built around order, would have worn it suspended from her belt. Wearing it, she was, in effect, a walking *restello*:[92] a place for everything and everything in its place.

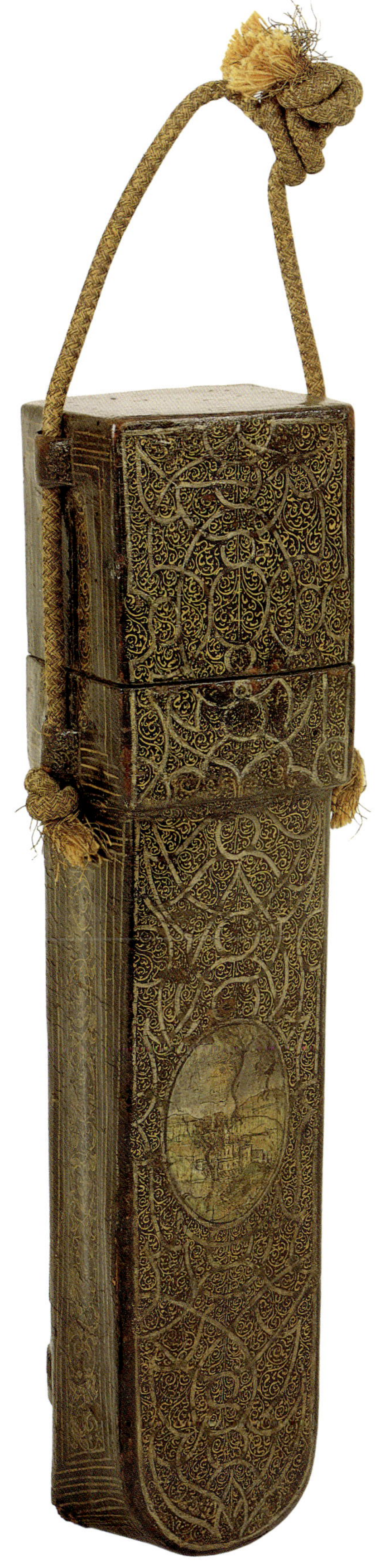

140 (*right*) Case for cutlery, Venice, early sixteenth century. Mosaic leather, painted and gilded. Offenbach am Main © Deutsches Ledermuseum.

facing page Detail of fig. 197.

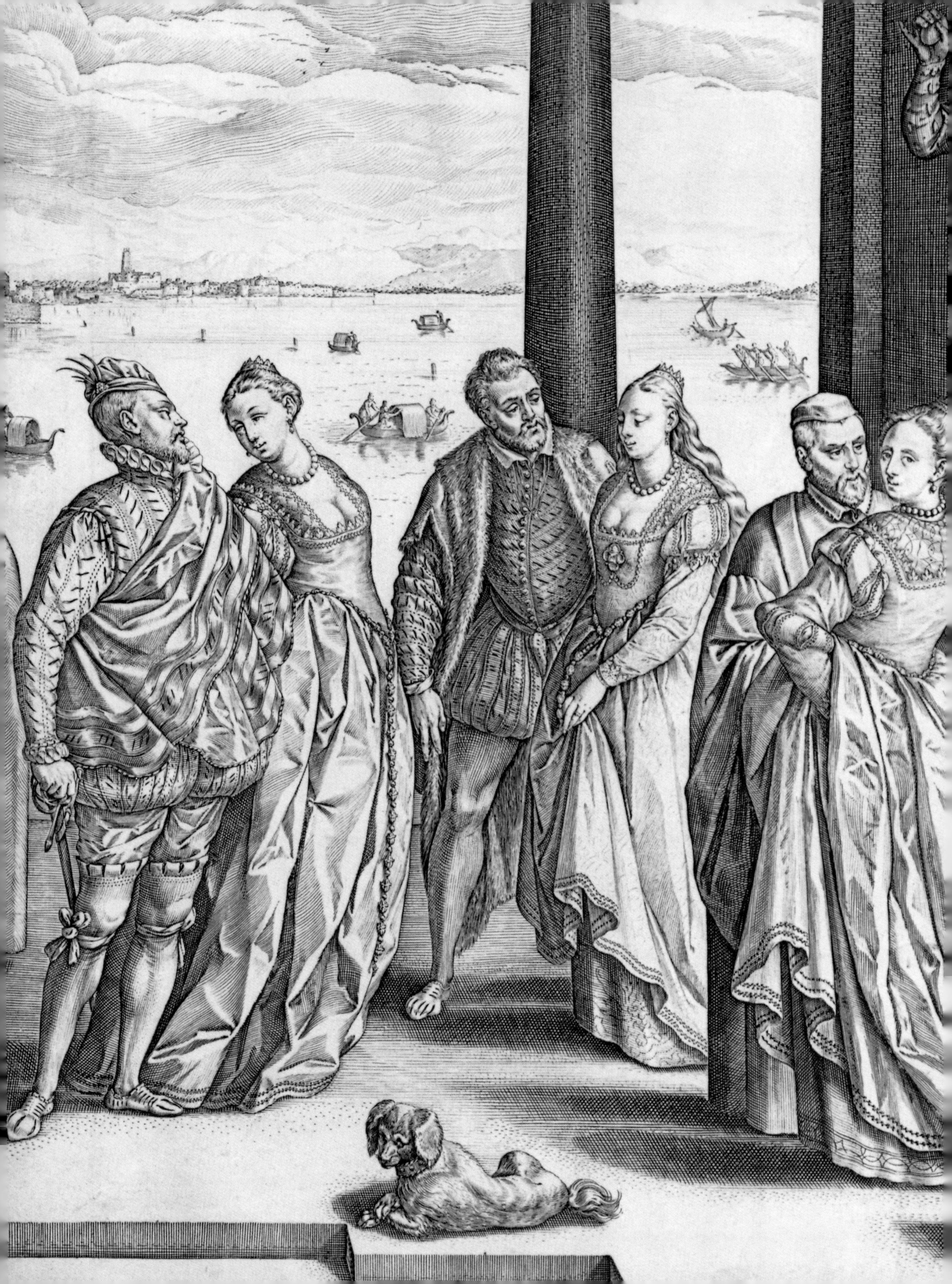

5

The Game of Life

How did Venetians amuse themselves when not doing needlework if female or, if male, when not looking after their business affairs? At times the home became a theater. Marin Sanudo wrote of the "beautiful show" in Ca' Pesaro at San Beneto in the dead of winter in 1515, when the courtyard was covered with a "sky" – some kind of awning – and "magnificently dressed" actors drawn from the membership of the Immortali, a Compagnia della Calza, performed a play. Between the acts a professional actor named Zuan Polo

> put on a new *comedia*, pretending to be a wizard who had been to hell, and he made a hell with fire and devils appear. Then he pretended to be a cupid, and he was taken to hell, where he found Domenego Taiacalze chasing wethers [men dressed as castrated rams]. Taiacalze came out with the wethers and they danced together. Next came a chorus of nymphs on a float who were singing a song, each one beating a hammer in time on an anvil, pretending they were beating a heart. And when the principal comedia was over, they also had a tableau of Paris and the goddesses [who competed for the apple which] he gave to Venus. It was a beautiful show . . . [and] many women were present, showing off their rich clothing. . . . The entertainment wound up at seven hours after sunset [around 1:00 A.M.]; then there was supper for the women and their husbands, and a ball.[1]

Such occasions animate the pages of Sanudo's diaries, providing relief from his relentless focus on political life and meriting attention because they were exceptional – worthy of note, as he would have said – and not everyday events. But the Venetian home was also the site for more mundane entertainments. This chapter will explore what went on inside the walls in terms of recreation and hospitality. Beginning with the more private, family-centered diversions, it moves on to banquets, receptions, and wedding celebrations – events that are both public and private – and finally touches briefly on the princely reception, when public festivities were brought into private space.

The Rarest Music

Music was probably the major entertainment in the Venetian home. From concerts held in the aristocratic *portego* to more intimate family musicals, the houses of noble and *popolani* alike were filled with the harmonious sounds of the human voice and instrumental music.[2] According to one study, less than a third of wealthy *cittadino* merchant families owned books, but all had at least two musical instruments.[3] The same was true for the artisan classes, while patrician families had as many or more. The painter Leandro Bassano depicted two young women, one playing the spinet and the other the lute, accompanying the rest of the family in an evening chorale (fig. 141). A more compelling statement of domestic solidarity and harmony could not be found. The aging father and mother are front and center, flanked by their children and spouses, grandchildren and probably (on the upper right) the father's brother and sister-in-law. There is even room for the family dog. The open books suggest that literacy in Venice included an ability to read musical scores, here shared by all three generations.[4]

Concerts in the home could be quite elaborate, with professional musicians hired to perform before a group of guests. In a book dedicated to Elena Barozzi, the beautiful wife of Antonio Zantani – a connoisseur of painting and sculpture and collector of antiquities and ancient coins, who lived near Campo San Tomà – the writer Orazio Toscanella noted: "Then it is very well known that she so delighted in music that for a long time he paid the Compagnia de' Fabbretti et Fruttaruoli [blacksmiths and fruit sellers], the most excellent singers and players, who made in the house the rarest music."[5]

facing page Hendrik Goltzius, *A Venetian Wedding*, after Dirck Barendszen, 1584 (detail of fig. 167).

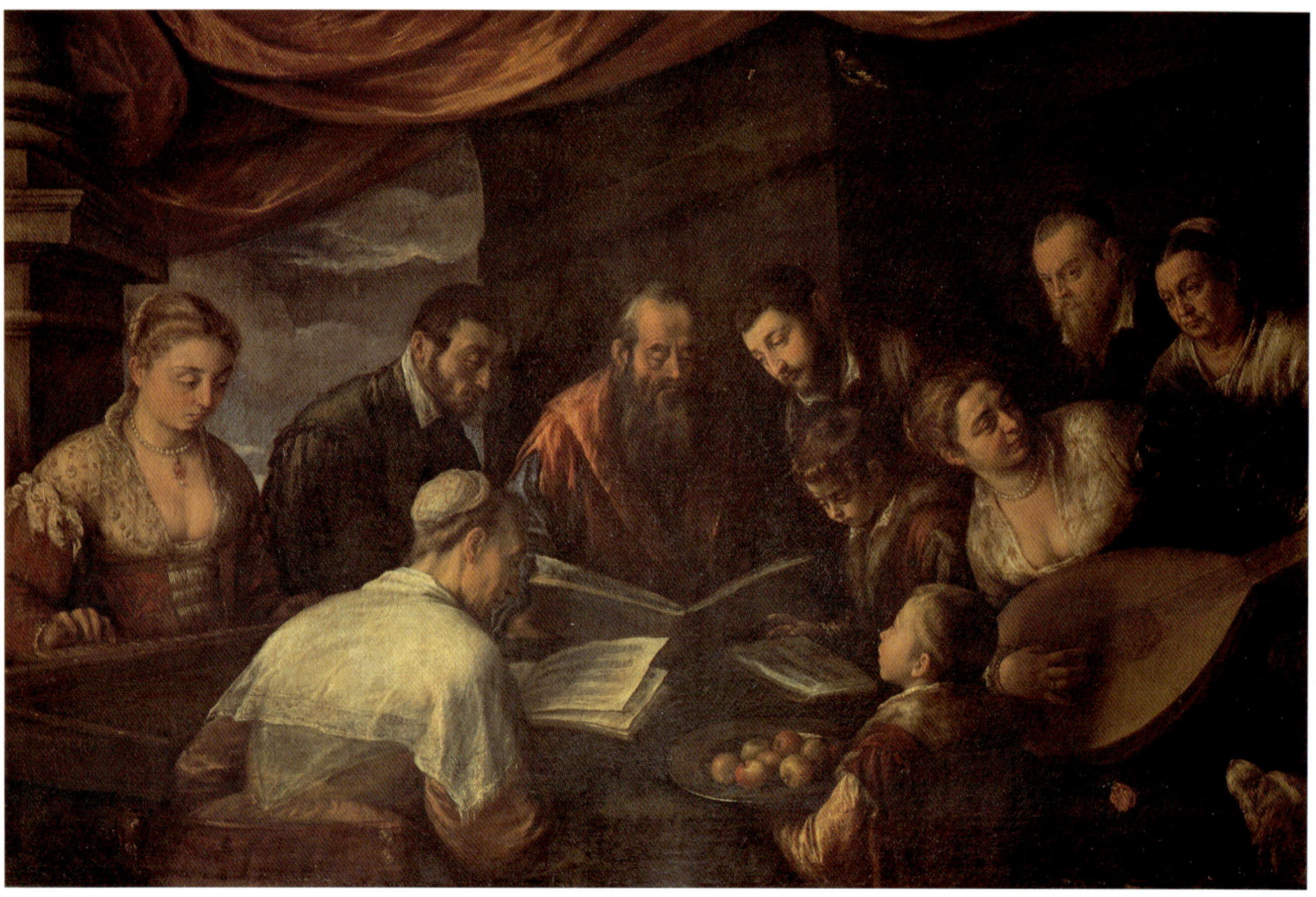

141 Leandro Bassano, *Concert*, 1592. Oil on canvas, 114 × 178 cm. Florence, Gallerie degli Uffizi.

Music was also a part of villa life, and concerts in the open air are recorded by artists and writers (fig. 142). In a treatise celebrating country living, Agostino Gallo recounts a discussion between two noble gentlemen, one telling the other how he spends his days at his villa: after a morning spent hawking in the countryside followed by the midday meal, "we often find ourselves getting together again to read, play cards or board games or chess, sing or play musical instruments [and] sometimes at the same hour, we come across our ladies in the midst of their own amusements . . . Sometimes one of us sits down to play the lute or the viol or some other instrument of that sort." Likewise, the poet Alberto Lollio describes the charms of *villegiatura* – the custom of leaving behind the cares of the city for leisurely holidays in a rural setting: "As for private pleasure . . . in our house music of various sorts is played every day. And we engage in every sort of proper and delightful game. Sometimes we dance for recreation and to delight the company. Here we read books with pleasure and we discuss various matters. In sum, one has here all those entertainments and diversions that one can decently desire."[6]

Given the Venetian love of music and the city's rich artisan tradition, it is not surprising that Venice was a major center for the production of musical instruments. A handsome spinet made by Antonio Baffo in Venice in 1570 confirms that the virtuosity of the musician was often matched by the virtuosity of the artisan (fig. 143). The case is richly decorated with gilding and a polychrome wood inlay that features stars and a precious arabesque pattern of intertwining tendrils and defines the instrument's structure. The motifs are based upon Islamic prototypes, possibly inspired by Ottoman ceramics.[7] No surface was left untouched, the pattern being carried over to adorn even the ends of the ivory-topped keys.[8]

Well-crafted musical instruments also became objects for display (fig. 144). The cultivated Milanese noblemen Sabba da Castiglione wrote a series of essays to his grandnephew on how to become the perfect Christian knight, with opinions on topics as wide-ranging as marriage, religion, politics, and home decoration. He observed that rich and clever gentlemen delighted in adorning and refining their palaces, their houses, and especially their chambers and studies with various and diverse ornaments, according to the variety and diversity of their intelligence and imagination, so that it happens that some adorn them with musical instruments, such as organs, harpsichords, monochords, psalteries, harps, dulcimers, *baldose*, and other similar things; and others with lutes, violas, violins, lyres, flutes, cornets, tubas, bagpipes, *dianoni*, and other similar things, which ornaments I certainly commend very much, since such instruments are most delightful to the ear and greatly refresh the mind, for, as Plato said, they record the harmony that is born from the movements of the celestial spheres, also they are very pleasing to the eye.[9]

Francesco Sansovino cited notable collections in homes throughout the city: the lawyer Luigi Balbi at Santa Maria Zobenigo; the cavalier Sanudo at San Giovanni Decollato; Agostino Amadi at Santa Croce, who "had enriched his father's artistic collections with rare specimens of musical instruments; and Caterino Zeno at the Crociferi, who possessed an organ with four rows of pipes built in 1494 by Lorenzo da Pavia for Mathias Corvinus, King of Hungary."[10]

Ornaments of Literacy

What else did aristocratic Venetians do with their leisure time? Many read. With Venice a major center of printing, about 150 titles were printed there each year, with press runs averaging around 1,000 each. A good number of these editions were in the *volgare* (vernacular Italian) – chivalric poems, novels, and theatrical works and accessible to the

142 (*below*) Ludovico Pozzoserrato (Lodwijck Toeput), *View of a Villa*, ca. 1580s. Oil on canvas, 73 × 96 cm. Venice, Galleria Giorgio Franchetti (Ca' d'Oro).

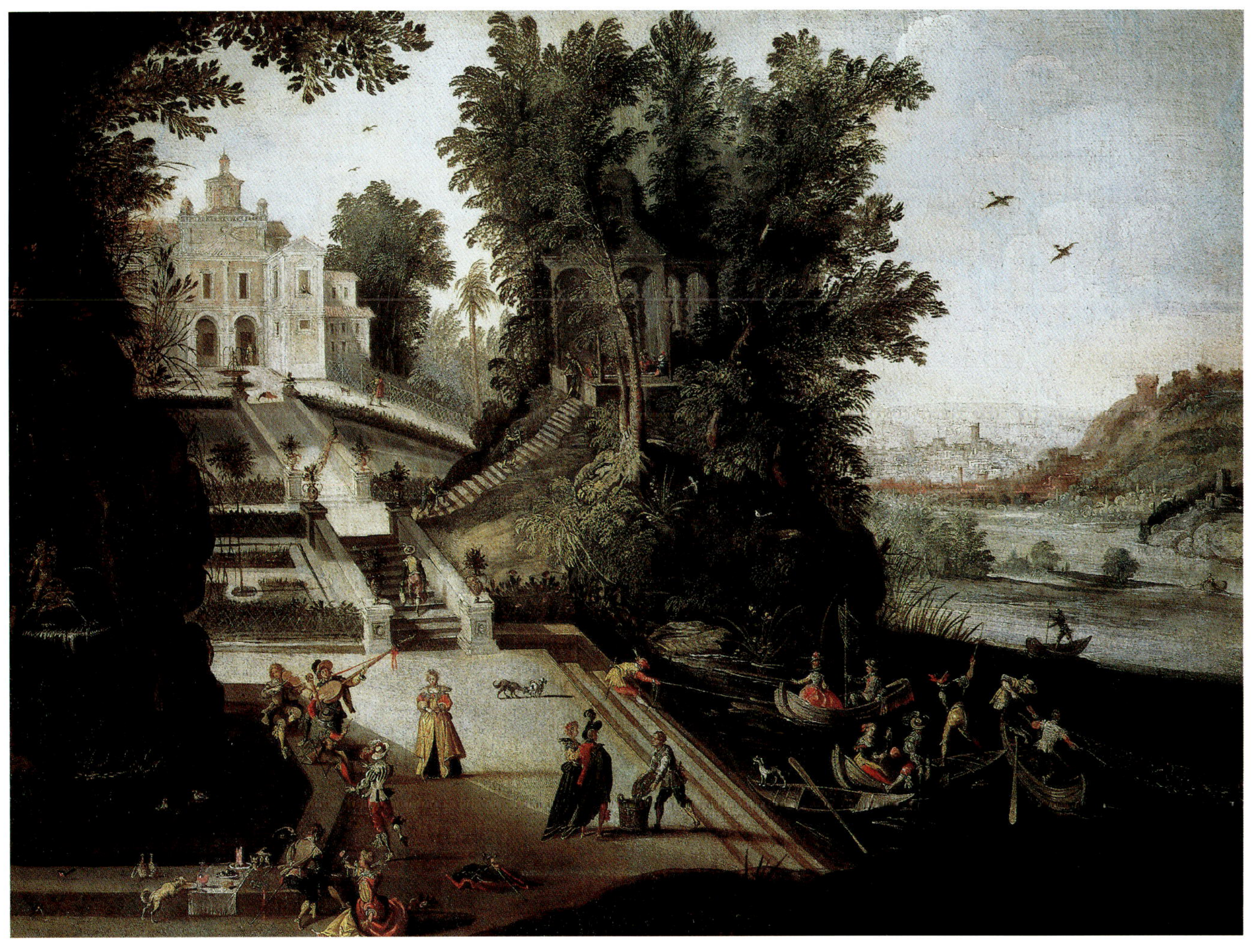

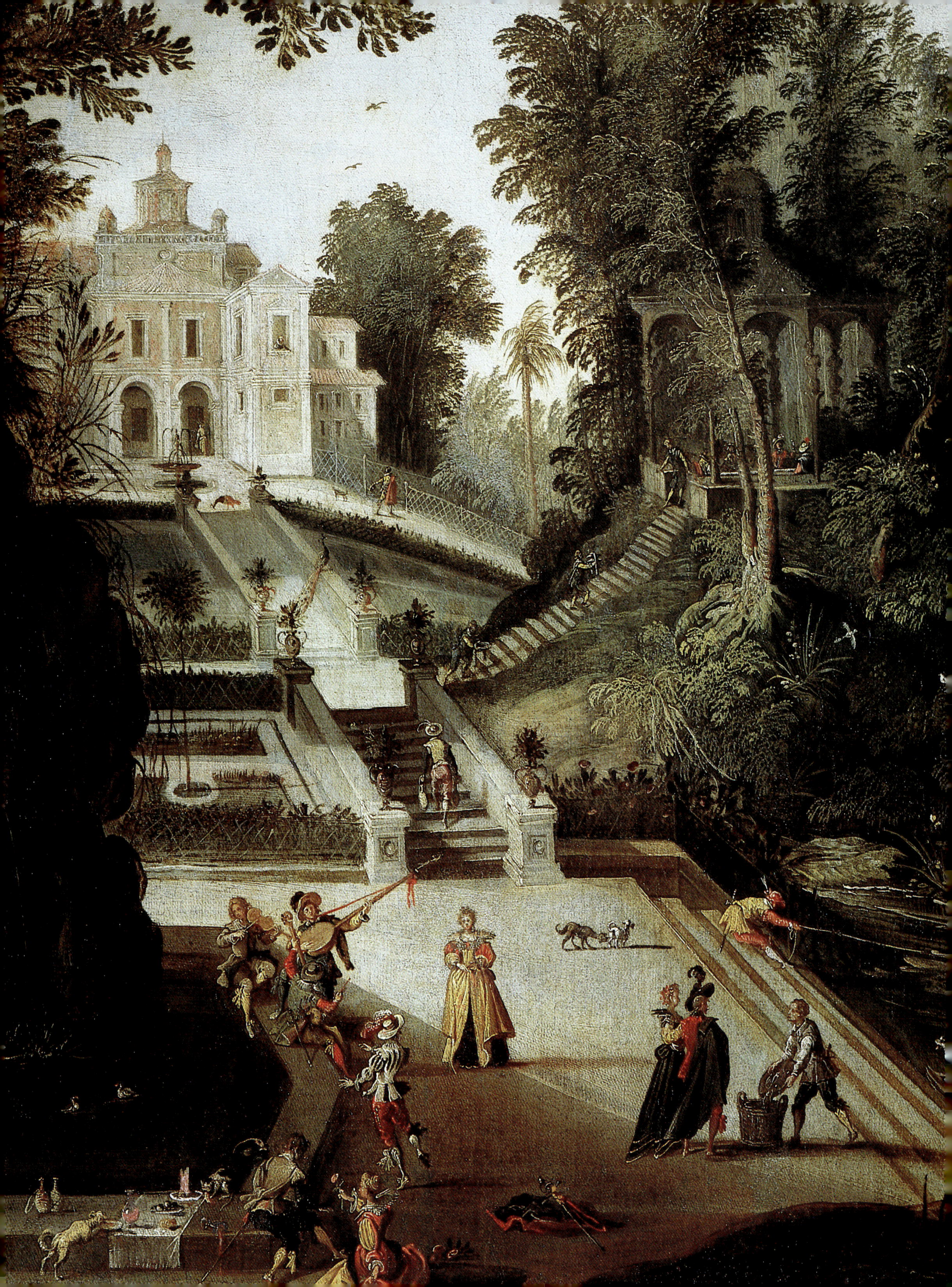

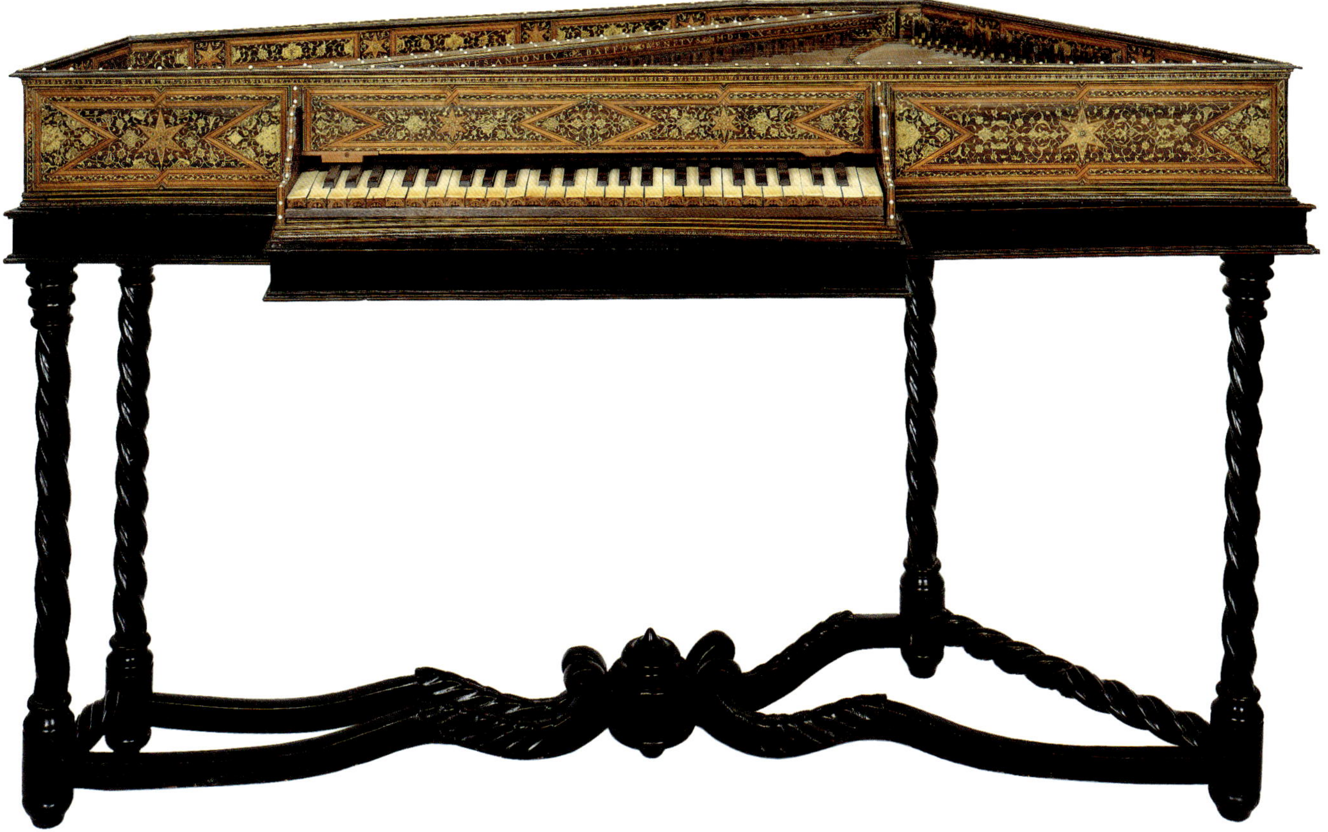

143 Antonio Baffo, spinet, Venice, 1570. Gilded wood with marquetry inlay. A spinet is a type of harpsichord, with the sounds made by little points of leather or metal that pluck strings running parallel to the keyboard. Ecouen, Musée Nationale de la Renaissance.

generally literate and not just those with a classical humanist education.[11] Writing in 1581, Francesco Sansovino singled out twenty private libraries "of singular esteem and truly worthy of being recorded and seen."[12] Greek and Latin classics, as well as history, theology, and the sciences, had a strong presence in patrician libraries, along with some literature. One study of sixteenth-century inventories found books in 70 percent of patrician homes, both rich and poor, with many volumes – particularly prayer books, poetry, and romances – belonging to women.[13] Studies indicate that virtually all male nobles and professional men, as well as the average merchant, could read and write well, while their wives and daughters had attained at least rudimentary literacy skills.[14]

facing page Ludovico Pozzoserrato (Lodwijck Toeput), *View of a Villa*, ca. 1580s (detail of fig. 142). The villa in the painting has not been identified and may have been invented by the artist. Pozzoserrato moved from Antwerp to Italy some time after 1573 and became known there by the Italianized version of his name. After working in Venice, Florence, and Rome, he settled in Treviso, near Venice, around 1582 and collaborated with Benedetto Caliari on several fresco campaigns to decorate Veneto villas.

144 Vittore Carpaccio, *Musicians*, ca. 1518. Pen and wash drawing on blue paper, 189 × 277 mm. London, © British Museum.

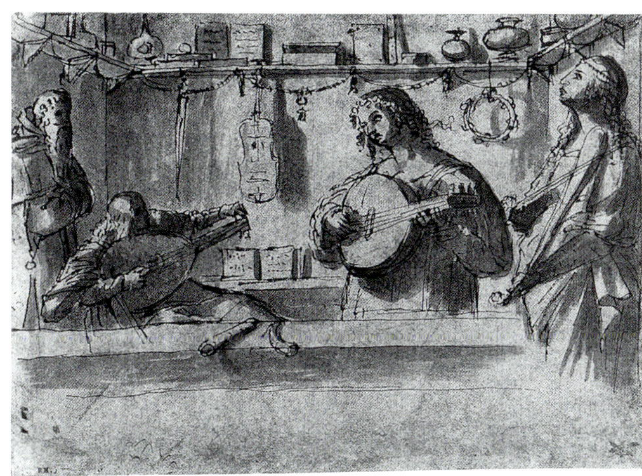

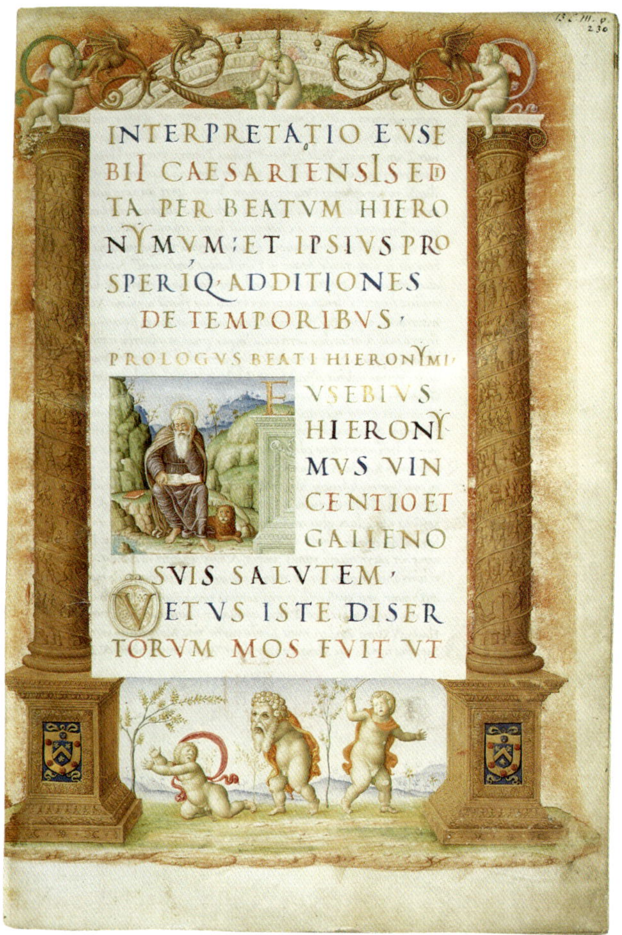

145 Eusebius, *Chronica*, translated from Greek by St. Jerome, British Library, ca. 1485–88. The manuscript was made in Rome, with the script attributed to the Paduan Bartolomeo Sanvito and the illumination to Gaspare da Padova. Bernardo Bembo probably obtained the manuscript on one of three missions to Rome for the Venetian state in that period. The father of Pietro Bembo, who later became cardinal, Bernardo was the grandfather of Marcella Marcello, discussed elsewhere in this book. London, British Library. Royal MS. 14 C.III. fol. 2r.

Sabba da Castiglione wrote: "If you should ask me which ornaments above all others I would desire in my house, I would respond without thinking, arms and books . . . The books I would like to be by serious authors, mature, proven, and authentic, but used and turned over, not dusty so that one could write with the finger on the covers, because to have books and not use them is not to have them at all."[15]

The love of books had implications not just for the verbal, but also for the visual culture of the time. While a rediscovered classical manuscript might be prized simply for its text by a humanist scholar, it could serve as a point of departure for further embellishment by a wealthy owner. In the latter case the text would be hand-copied or, by the later fifteenth century, printed and provided with an illuminated frontispiece, such as that prefacing a volume of Eusebius's *Chronica*, made for the learned Venetian humanist and diplomat Bernardo Bembo and bearing his coat of arms (fig. 145). In a *tour de force* of spatial ambiguity, the miniaturist creates a fictive manuscript page, inscribed with the incipit and featuring a miniature suspended from a columned gateway and depicting St. Jerome and his lion in a Veneto landscape. With a free-standing initial E placed on the altar next to Jerome in the miniature, and yet another landscape below the depicted page, here showing frolicking *putti* – one wearing a bearded mask to tease his companions – the image plays with the reader's faculties of perception. In such instances, the ancient texts were turned into works of art in themselves – emblems of an ever more luxurious lifestyle, but also collectors' items and ultimately precious commodities.[16]

Tooled leather bookbindings offered yet another opportunity to display refinement and good taste. Giovanni Francesco Condulmer had his *commissione* as *podesta* of Oderzo in 1577 bound in a handsome tooled and gilt-leather binding (fig. 146).[17] It combined two styles: the recessed center and cornerpieces were decorated with Ottoman-style gilt filigree over satin, while the area in between was filled with a tooled and gilt French fanfare design. As Baffo's harpsichord suggests, Moorish tracery – which came into the West on ceramics, textiles, bookbindings, and damascene objects and was disseminated through prints – provided an important vocabulary of motifs, particularly in Venice with its strong ties with the East.[18]

Serious Play

In addition to enjoying music, reading, and conversation, Venetians also played a wide variety of games: board games, word games, memory games, riddles, ciphers, rebuses, games of skill, and games of chance. Chess had the most distinguished lineage, dating back to the Middle Ages, and Renaissance chessboards and chess pieces made of ivory, crystal, gems, and exotic woods were often works of genuine artistry if not true and proper works of art. Sanudo reported seeing a particularly costly chessboard in the Senate

146 (*facing page*) Book cover. Leather. *Commissione* of Giovanni Francesco Condulmer as *podesta* of Oderzo in 1577. Giovanni Francesco was the first cousin of the unfortunate gentleman of the same name who was expelled from the Great Council in 1528 (see fig. 11). Baltimore, Walters Art Museum, MS. W. 492.

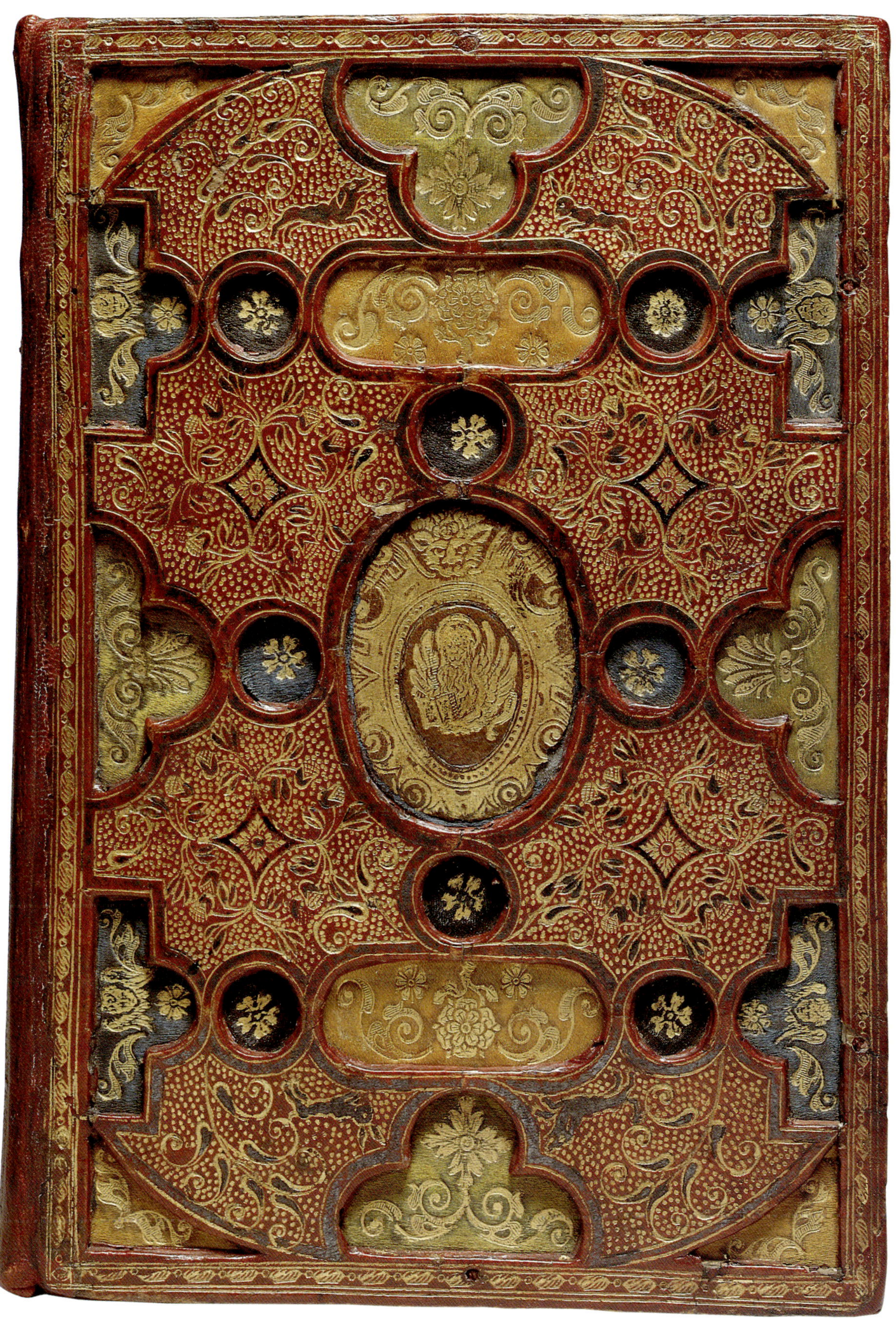

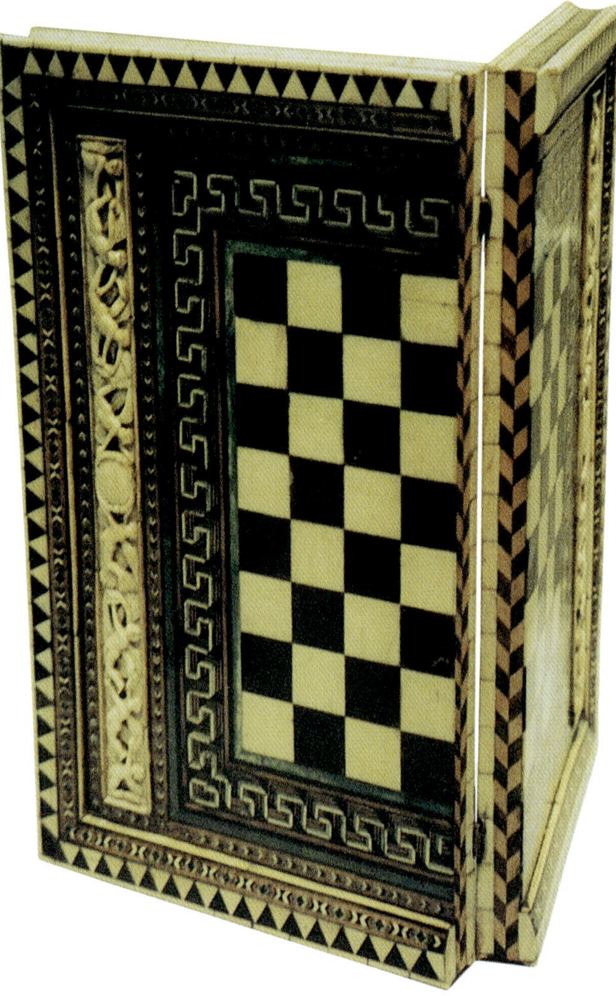

147 (*above*) Attrib. School of Baldassare Embriochi, chessboard, ca. 1500. Wood inlaid with geometric marquetry of bone and chestnut. New York, The Metropolitan Museum of Art, Anonymous loan. 1983.54.1.

chamber of the Ducal Palace in 1527: "It was a round, high chessboard, large and very beautiful . . . wrought of gold and silver and inlaid with chalcedony, jasper, and other jewels. The chess pieces were made of the purest crystal." The patrician Jacopo Loredan had given it as a dowry gift to two of his daughters who had married two brothers of the Donado family. The girls' uncle brought it to the Ducal Palace to see if the government would buy it as a gift for the Venetian ambassador to take to the Turkish sultan in Constantinople. The price tag was 5,000 ducats – a true king's ransom in a time when a palace on the Grand Canal could be purchased for less.[19]

The fate of the Loredan chessboard is unknown. More typical is a piece made of bone and chestnut in the Metropolitan Museum of Art in New York (fig. 147). A masterpiece of the intarsia-worker's art, it features several levels of illusionism. The flat surface is framed with a meander motif, intended to look three-dimensional, and strips of bone *Embriachi* work deeply carved with *putti* or cupids are inset on each side. Such pieces were often crafted to serve a double use, with a backgammon board on the reverse.[20]

Two chess players in a painting by Paris Bordone make do with a less costly model, which appears to be made only of wood, albeit on a table covered with a luxurious oriental carpet (fig. 148). Chess had a political dimension in Renaissance culture. The game was regarded as an allegory of the civil life, with the chess pieces – kings, queens, knights, bishops, and pawns – standing for the several orders of society. A well-known treatise on chess, written by the Dominican friar Jacopo da Cessole, was subtitled "A new work in which one teaches the true regiment of men and women of whatever degree, status or condition one wishes to be." The chess pieces falling onto the lap of the man on the right suggest that even well-ordered hierarchies can be disturbed by the indifferent hand of fortune.[21]

Unique pieces of special luxury furniture, such as a table in the Museé Jacquemart-André in Paris, were made specifically for playing games, (figs. 149 and 150). The top is a single slab of marble, with the coats of arms of the Giustiniani and Emo families in the center. At the ends are gameboards for backgammon and chess, defined by incrustations of lead. The table surface is further embellished with images of *putti* playing with a deer and hounds, and with arabesques and rinceaux, which also form the border. The supports of Istrian stone are sculpted in the form of lions' legs, each pair enclosing a figural relief that continues the imagery of the table top. One support features, on the outer face, an infant Hercules wrestling with the hydra between an eagle and a chimera, and on the reverse a sleeping Eros. On the other support, the Giustiniani *stemma* adorns the more prominent outer face, while just visible beneath the table, an elegant greyhound is carved on the inner side. A piece of mannered elegance carved in the style of Alessandro Vittoria, the table celebrates a patrician matrimonial alliance and ennobles the family's leisure-time activities.[22]

In the background of Bordone's painting four men sit around a table playing cards – a pastime that combines skill and chance. Playing cards were in use in Europe from the fourteenth century on. The earliest were hand painted and thus expensive and a prerogative of the wealthy. But with the invention of woodblock printing in Germany they were mass produced and became quite popular in all classes.[23] The European deck was always divided into suits, which varied in different countries. In Italy, the suits were chalices,

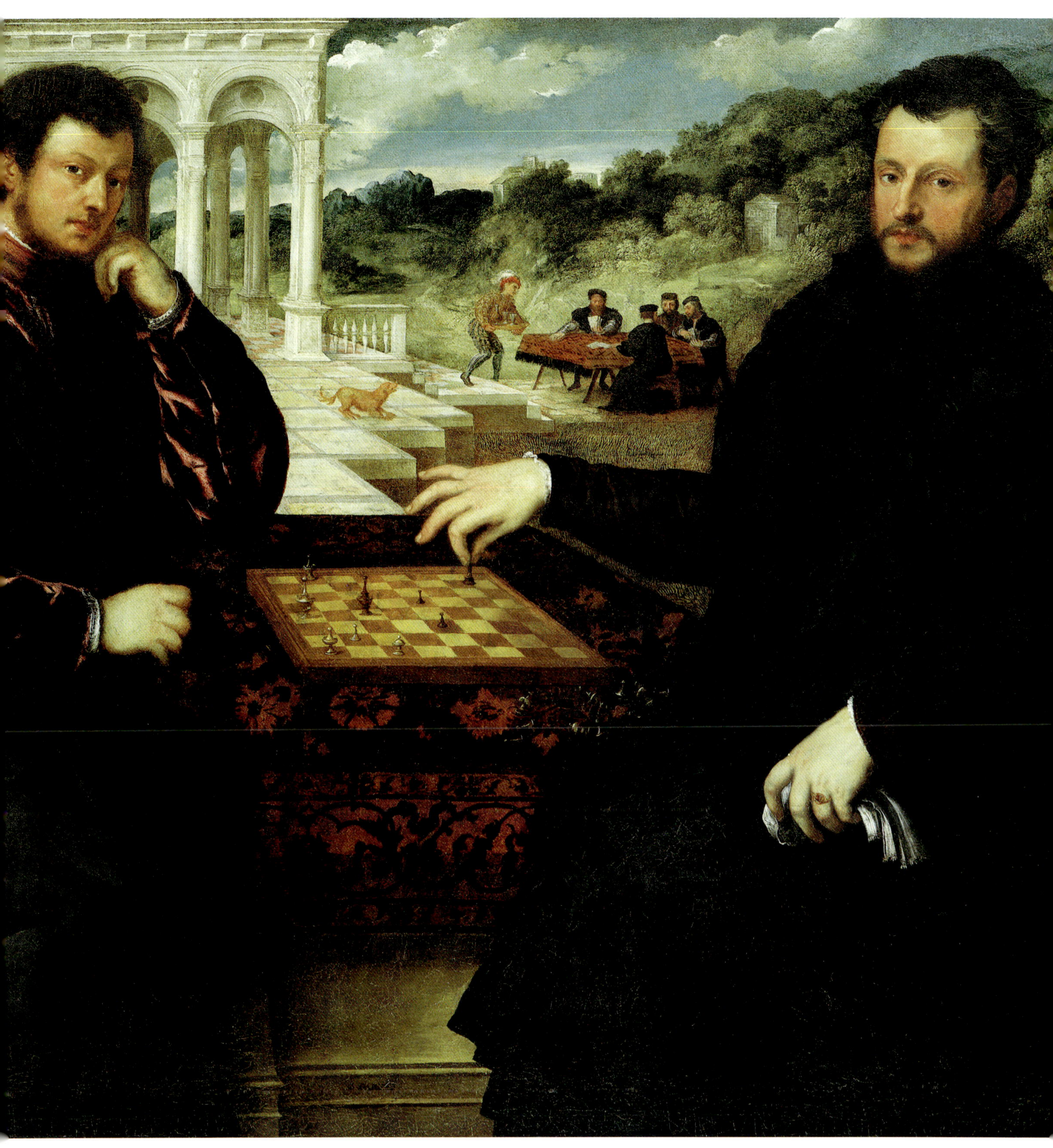

148 Paris Bordone, *The Chess Players* (detail), 1550–55. Oil on canvas, whole work 112 × 181 cm. The landscape is similar to the foothills around Bassano and Conegliano northwest of Venice, where many Venetian families owned villas. Berlin, Staatliche Museen Preussischer Kulturbesitz.

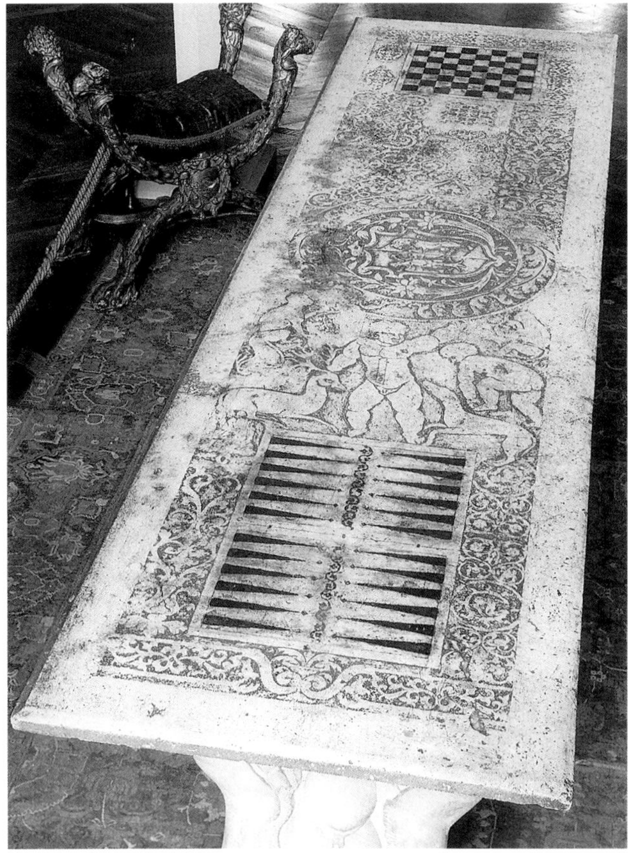

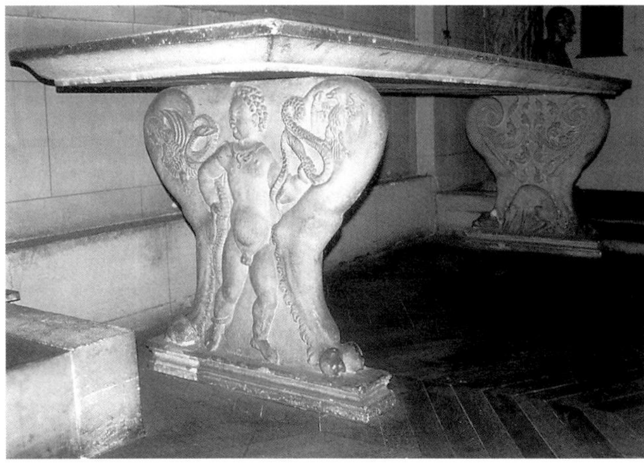

149 and 150 (*left*) Game table, Venice, ca. 1550–60. Marble top with supports of Istrian stone. The form and decorative carving is modeled after wooden types. The table has been attributed to Alessandro Vittoria on the basis of similarities with his stuccoes on the vault of the Scala d'Oro in the Palazzo Ducale and on the staircase of the Biblioteca Marciana. Paris, Musée Jacquemart-André.

swords, coins, and cudgels or batons, representing, respectively, the four estates: the church, the aristocracy, the merchants, and the peasantry (fig. 151). The early decks had four courts or trump cards: King, Queen, Knight, and Valet or foot soldier (now called the Jack), with fourteen cards in each suit. This was an inconvenient number for games like whist, where tie scores were possible. So one of the courts was dropped, and a fifty-two-card pack, with four suits of thirteen cards each, became standard. The French and British retained the queen and dropped the knight, but the Italians, the Germans, and the Swiss disposed of the Queen and ended up with an all-male court (fig. 152).[24] What such choices reveal about national character one would not venture to say. In any case, as with chess, the iconography of the playing card had chivalric roots that tended to reinforce the aristocratic social hierarchy.

Tarot cards first appeared in the 1430s in the courts of northern Italy. The tarot deck consisted of seventy-eight cards in four suits with twenty-two trump cards whose obscure imagery was based upon an arcane symbolism. The game required a skilled interpreter to predict future fortunes from their relative positions. Like chess and other card games, tarot was not just amusement: it might be considered serious play. Emanuele Tesauro wrote that the game represented not only the different conditions but also the desires of men, "as if a player holding a deck of cards has the world in his hand and, metaphorically, playing is nothing less than making confusion in the universe."[25]

It may be asked if decorated playing cards can be considered art. Before the days of mechanical reproduction, the answer could well be yes. The tarot card, in particular, attracted the talents of some of the most gifted artists of the time. An especially luxurious deck created by the Milanese artist Bonifacio Bembo around 1450 was virtually a set of manuscript illuminations, finely painted in the International Gothic style with tooled gold-leaf backgrounds and expensive colors (fig. 153).[26] By contrast, less than a generation later, an artist close to Andrea Mantegna responded to a new humanist-inspired taste for correct proportions and mastery of *disegno* with a deck of *tarocchi* cards that was attractive more for its display of creative ingenuity than its preciousness of materials (fig. 154).[27]

In Venice, playing-card makers constituted a branch (or *colonnello*) of the painters' guild. They enjoyed the same privileges and voting rights as fresco and panel painters,

151 (*facing page*) Playing cards, Ferrara, end of the fifteenth century. Woodcut with hand coloring, 180 × 93 mm each. The four number cards, each from a different suit, were part of a *tarocchi* deck: the ace of spades (swords), two of clubs (cudgels), four of cups, and four of coins. Venice, Museo Civico Correr (cl. XXX, 80).

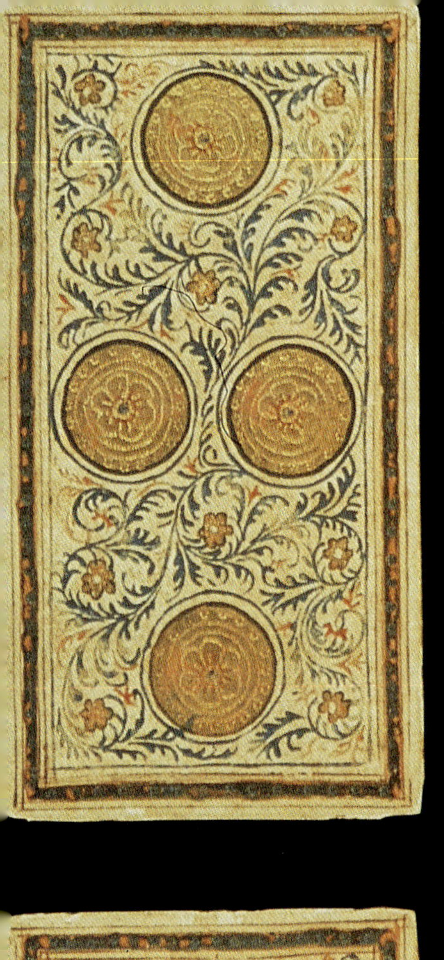
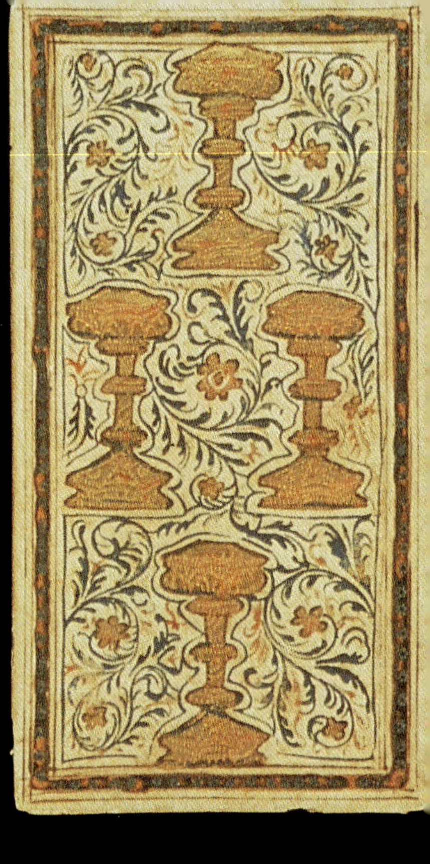
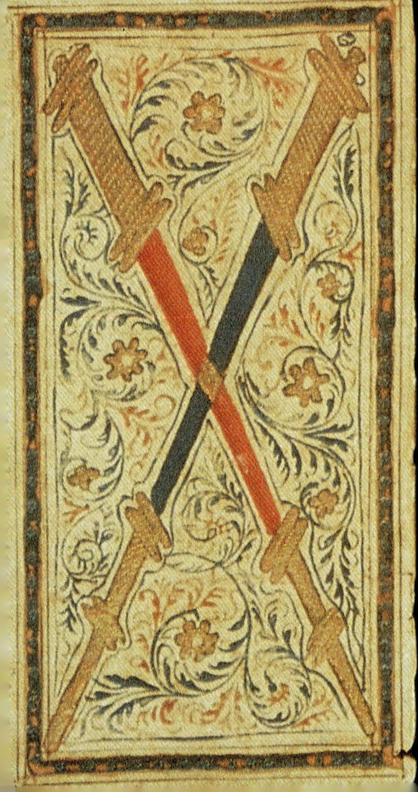
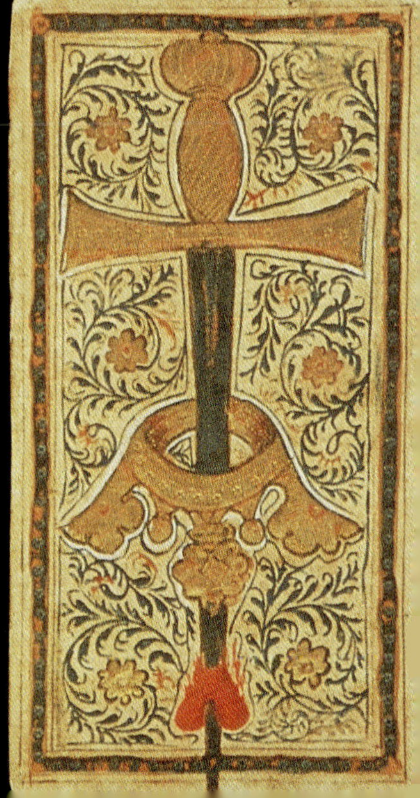

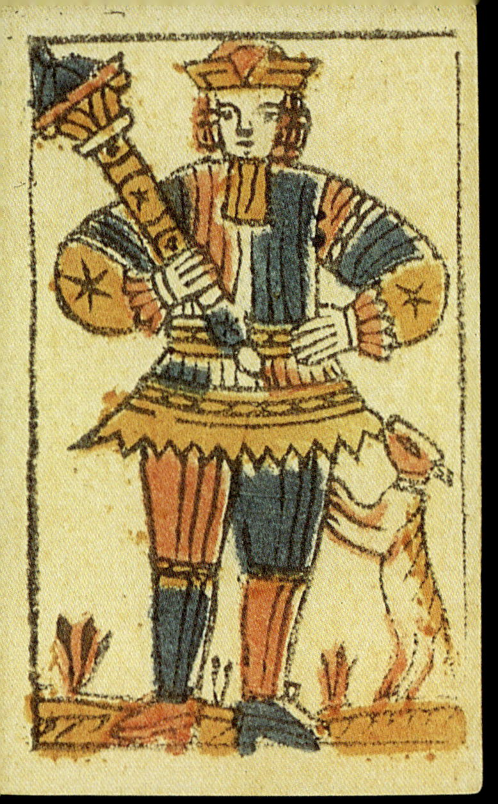

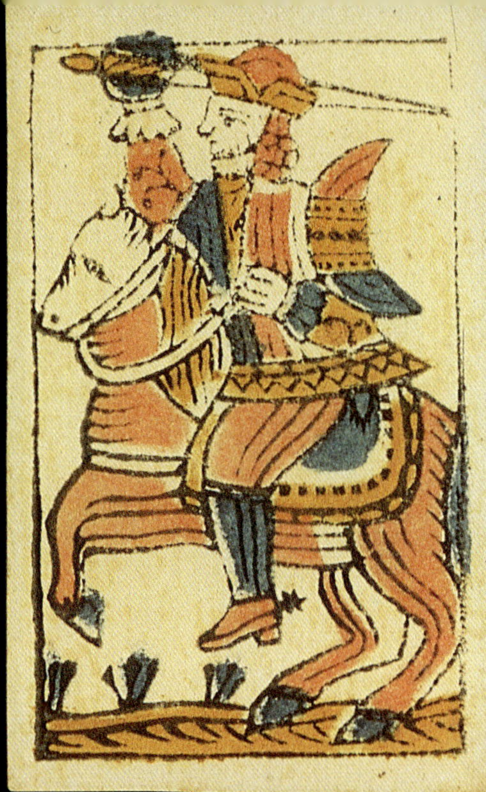

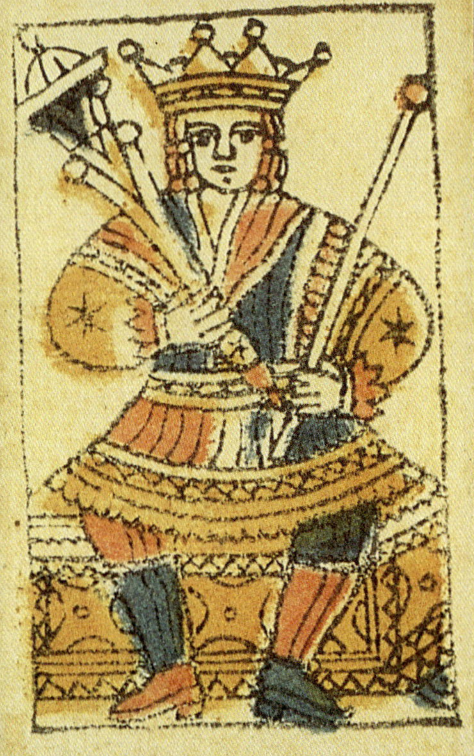

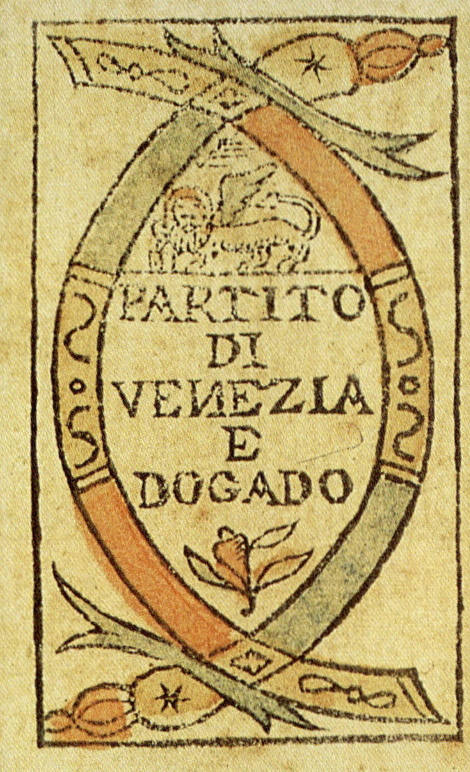
PARTITO
DI
VENEZIA
E
DOGADO

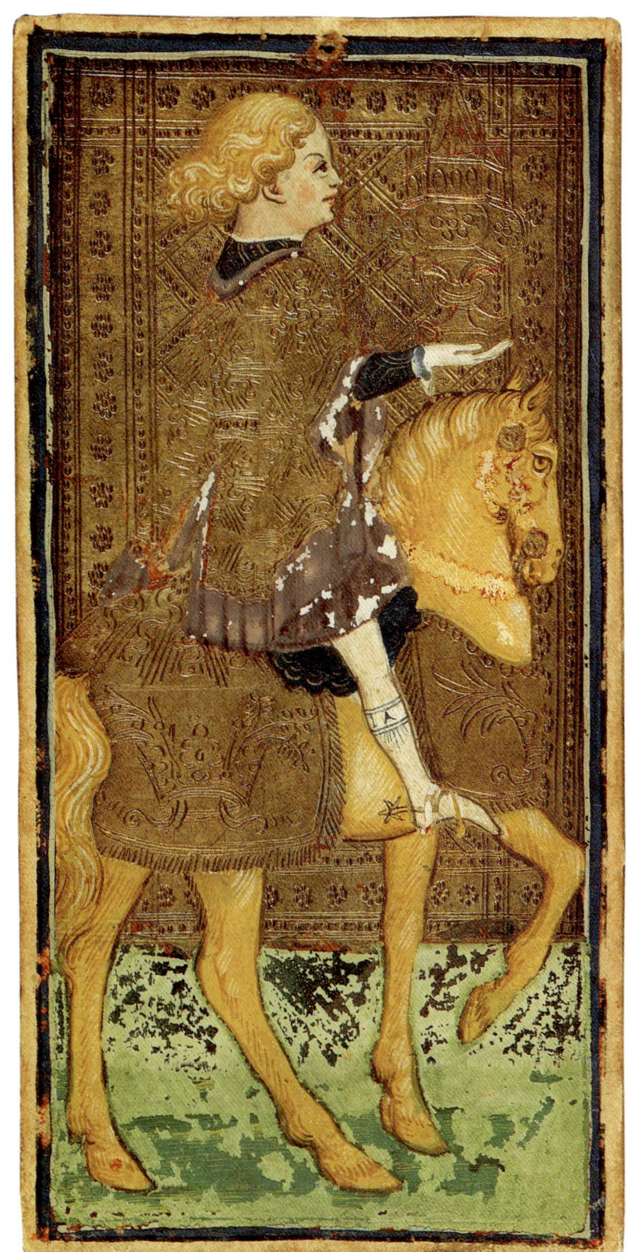

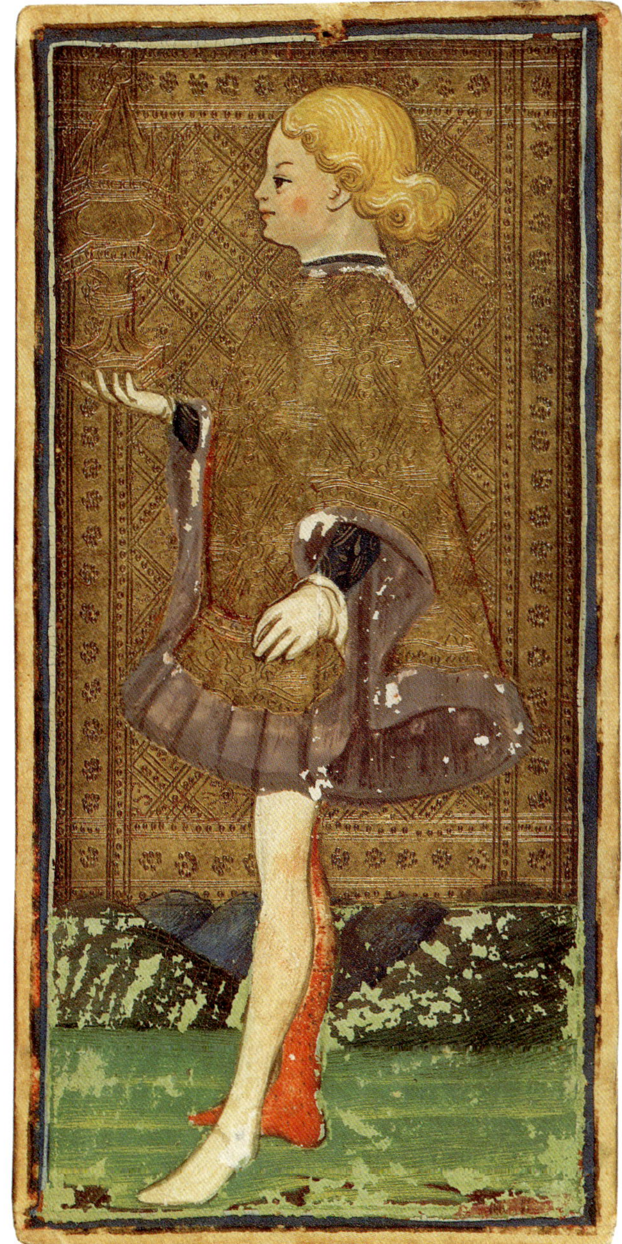

152 (*facing page*) Playing cards with Italian suits, eighteenth century. Woodcut with color, 95 × 53 mm. The cards are the valet (jack) of clubs, knight of spades, king of clubs, and a title card identifying the deck as a "Game of Venice and the Dogate." Venice, Museo Civico Correr (cl. xxx, 84).

153 Bonifacio Bembo, *Knight of Cups* (on horseback) and *Page of Cups* (standing), ca. 1450. Heavy cardboard, 173 × 87 mm. These illuminated tarot cards were made for the Visconti-Sforza family of Milan. The thirty-five cards in the Pierpont Morgan Library, together with twenty-six in the Accademia Carrara in Bergamo, and thirteen owned by the Colleoni family of Bergamo (seventy-eight in all) make up one of the few complete extant sets of Italian painted tarot cards. The illuminations on some of the other cards in the deck are attributed to Zavattari of Milan and Antonio Cicognara of Cremona. New York, The Pierpont Morgan Library, M. 630.

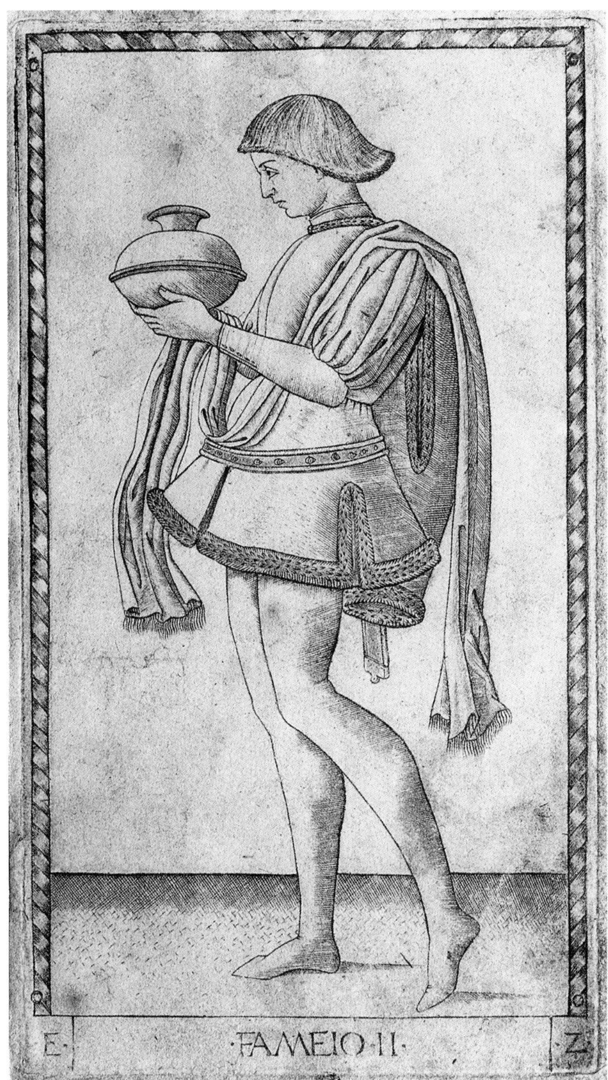

154 Master of the Tarocchi, *Fameio (Servant)*, *tarocchi* card, Ferrara, early 1460s. Woodcut with traces of gilding, 185 × 105 mm. *Tarocchi* cards, which lack pip cards and suit honors, do not make up a true and proper tarot deck. It is unknown whether they were used as a game or merely as a series of didactic images. Washington, National Gallery of Art, B-3505A.

along with gilders, miniaturists, textile designers, workers in gilded leather, mask makers, and painters of shields.[28] The guild's charter of 1441 records legislation that banned the importing of painted or printed playing cards in order to protect local masters against unfair competition from foreign imports.[29]

Books of fortune, based upon astrology, were another favored pastime. The writer Andrea Calmo bought three books as a gift for a lady friend: a volume of Petrarch, because of her love of the poet's Laura; Boccaccio's *One hundred novelle* as "a recipe book for all lovers"; and a "pleasant Book of Fortune to play a game with the family or with a company of ladies and gentlemen, [for] throwing those three dice one sees through the longest fables, the greatest bagatelles, the greatest falsehoods in the world."[30] Here Calmo was referring to an astrological lottery book/game such as Lorenzo Spirto's *Libro de la ventura* – a popular form of home entertainment in the sixteenth century that combined reading and fortune-telling (fig. 155).[31] The frontispiece shows how the game is played, with a convivial group of well-dressed ladies and gentlemen gathered around a table with the book in the middle flanked by dice on one side and an armillary sphere on the other.

The frontispiece of Sigismondo Fanti's *Triompho di Fortuna* is more elaborate (fig. 156).[32] The woodcut, made from a drawing by Dosso Dossi (or by Baldassare Peruzzi, according to some) sums up a world view. In the center, an Atlas figure supports a celestial globe by grasping two crank handles. The pope is seated atop the globe, accompanied by two figures: Virtus on the left, pointing up, and Voluptas

155 Frontispiece from Lorenzo Spirto, *Libro de la ventura. Con somma diligentia revisto: et corretto: & novanecche [sic] ristampate* (Venice: Mattio Pagan, 1557).

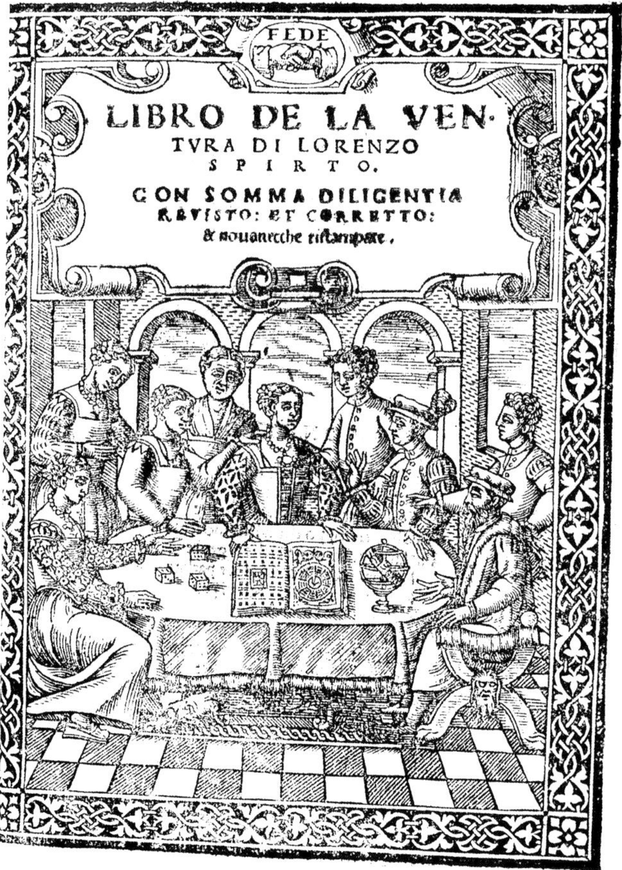

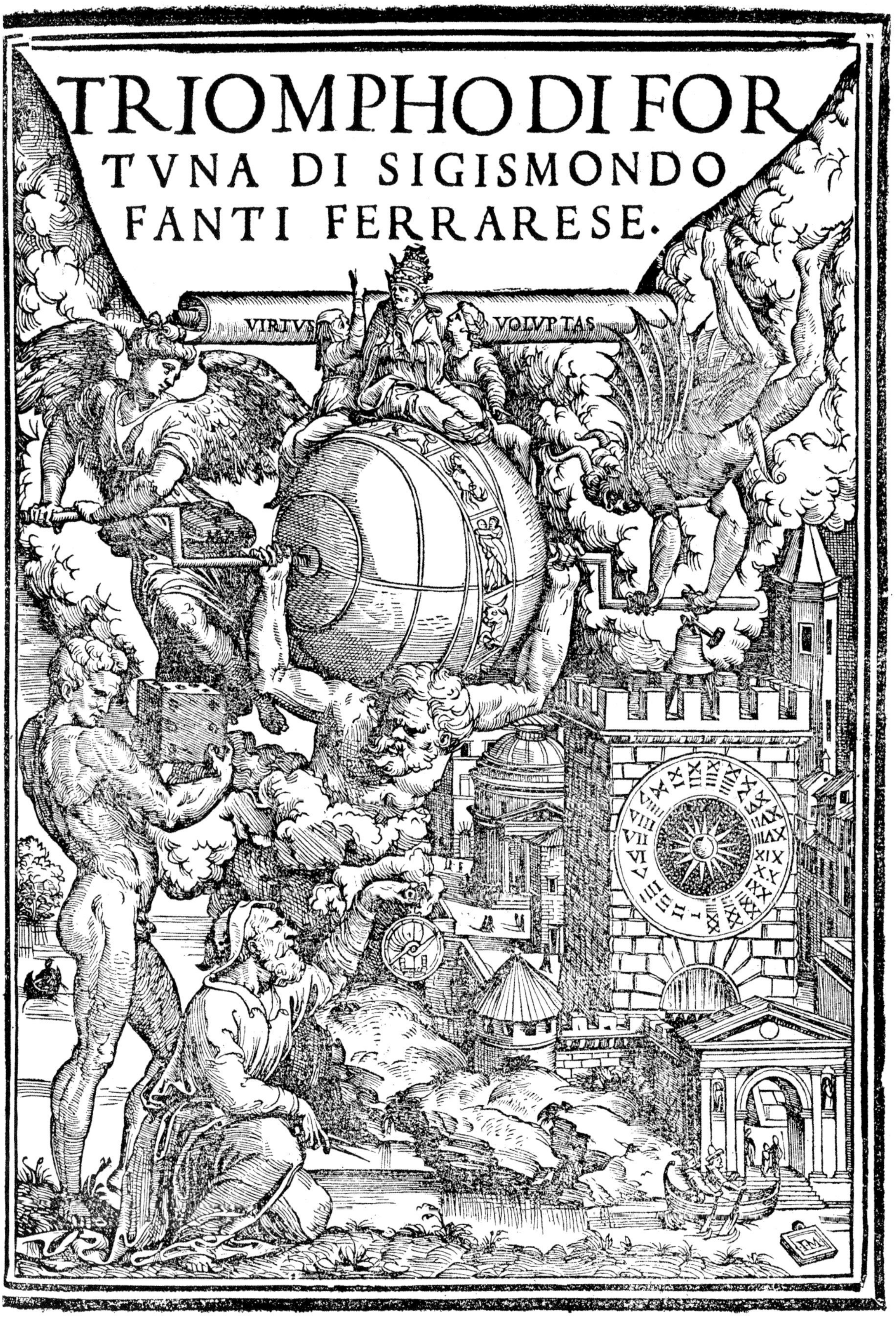

156 Frontispiece from Sigismondo Fanti, *Triompho di Fortuna* (Venice: Agostino da Portese, 1527). Height 35 cm. By permission of the Folger Shakespeare Library.

vna dõna, douendo esser tenuta perfettamente bella.

DOMANDA XXIIII

Quando si de cominciar una fabrica, Et per farla eccelentissima: quai sono le cose di che si de far prouigione.

Va alla Fortuna di Borea alla lettera E

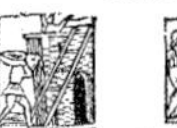
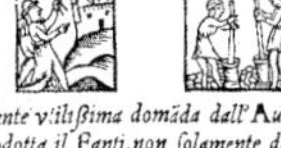

NElla presente vtilissima domãda dall'Auttore introdotta, il Fanti, non solamente da l'hora e'l pũto quãdo ogni fabbrica si de prĩcipiare, Ma insegna anchora a conoscere & preparare tutte le cose necessarie. Et come per farla eccellentissima si debbano disporre.

DOMANDA XXV

Quanti mariti hauera la donna

Va alla Fortuna d'Oriente alla lettera C

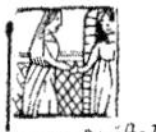
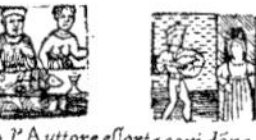

IN q̃sto luogo, l'Auttore essorta ogni dõna, a non douer pigliar che due mariti, o tre al piu, quãdo no puo fare altramẽte, volẽdo cõseruar l'honore, pche a torne piu, dà assai manifesto segno d'esser impudica, Et tanto maggiormẽte, quãdo p lo nuouo sposo abadona i piccoli figliuoli. Onde il Fanti dice, che l'amor del padre verso de figliuoli e molto maggiore, che q̃llo della madre, pche il padre non gli abandona mai, come fa lei, per sodisfare al suo dishonesto appetito.

DOMANDA XXVI

Se un'auersita si de terminare

Va alla Fortuna d'Occidente alla lettera A

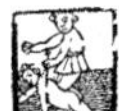
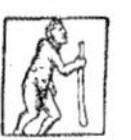
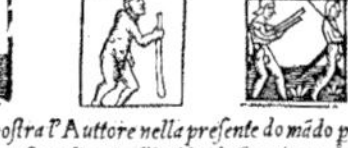

DImostra l'Auttore nella presente domãdo p diuersi modi, come l'huõ ha da fare, se vuole vscire, o veramente entrare in vn dispiacere, con descriuer la cagiõe e'l fine di tal dispiacere, soggiongendo, q̃sto mõdo essere vna gabbia da stolti, Et vn'arca d'affanni, perche prima che l'huõ esca d'vna auersita entra in vn'altra maggiore, & cosi pcede in infinito, sperando sempre di meglio.

DOMANDA XXVII

Quello che fra'l marito & la moglie de auenire, Et quello, che il marito de auertire prima che se la meni a casa.

Va alla Fortuna di Settentrione alla lr̃a D

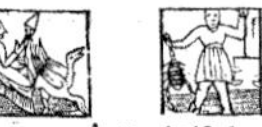
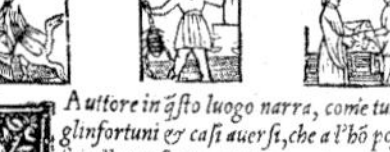

LAuttore in q̃sto luogo narra, come tutti glinfortuni & casi auersi, che a l'hõ possa nella presente vita interuenire, nascono quasi sempre dalle femie. Onde il Fãti, fa cauti glibuomini a nõ cosi leggiermente vnirsi cõ q̃lle dicẽdo, che anchor che l'huõ la pigliasse a proua, sarebbe simplicita la sua, quãdo poi credesse di potersene interamẽte fidare, pche quasi tutte sono di tãto piggior natura delle mule, di quãto, che q̃ste, hauẽdo il loro signore assicurato, cõ vn solo calcio si fanno conoscer. Et q̃lle, assicurati che hãno gli sciocchi mariti, ne trã mille, che in fatto piu dogliono, prima che da essi mariti possino esser conosciute. Ma douẽdola pur torre ricorda, che p nõ gionger male al male, & fastidio all'affanni, debba ritrar la dota prima che in casa se la lassi entrare. Et cosi indiuersi casi auenuti, va diligentemẽte narrãdo, molte delle fraudi loro, come nel procedere dell'opora vedremo.

DOMANDA XXVIII

Se gl'e bene a far uiaggio & a che tempo

Va alla Fortuna d'Austro alla lettera A

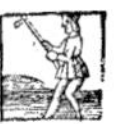
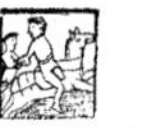
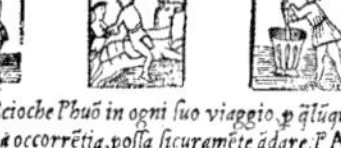

ACcioche l'huõ in ogni suo viaggio, p q̃lũque sua occorrẽtia, possa sicuramẽte ãdare, l'Autore ĩ q̃sta sua domãda, da il tẽpo & l'hora, che egli de partire, Et pche il Fãti dice, che in q̃sti tal viaggi puo seguire di molti casi, & qualche volta la ruina, nõ solamẽte di se stesso ma della ppria patria anchora, narra la cagione de contrari accidenti, che possono & sogliono auenire, adducendone molti, in diuersi luoghi, & a piu persone auenuti.

DOMANDA XXIX

Se l'huomo hauera figliuoli

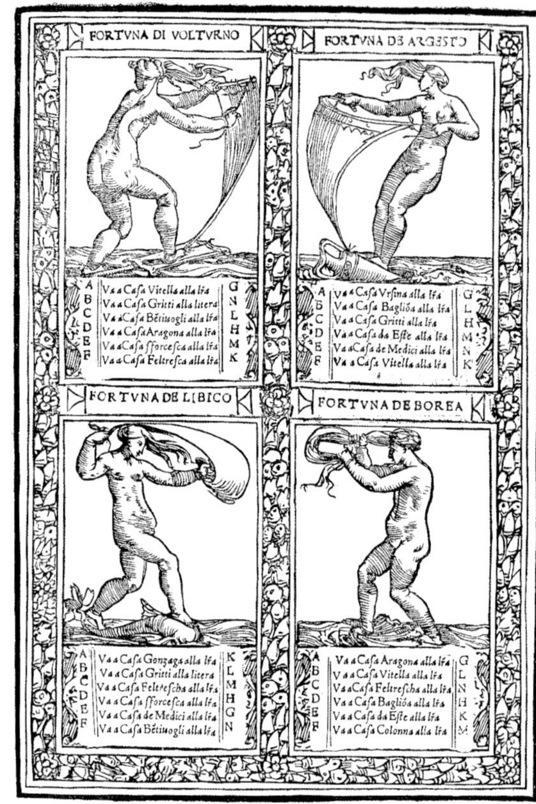

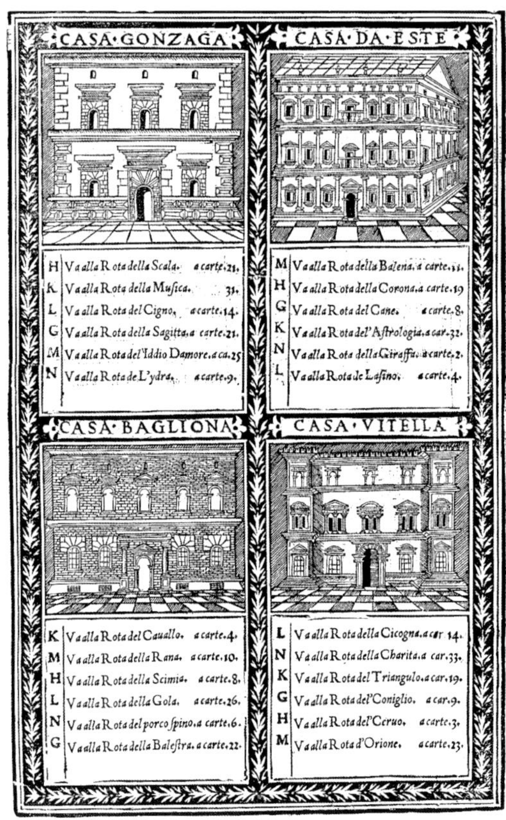

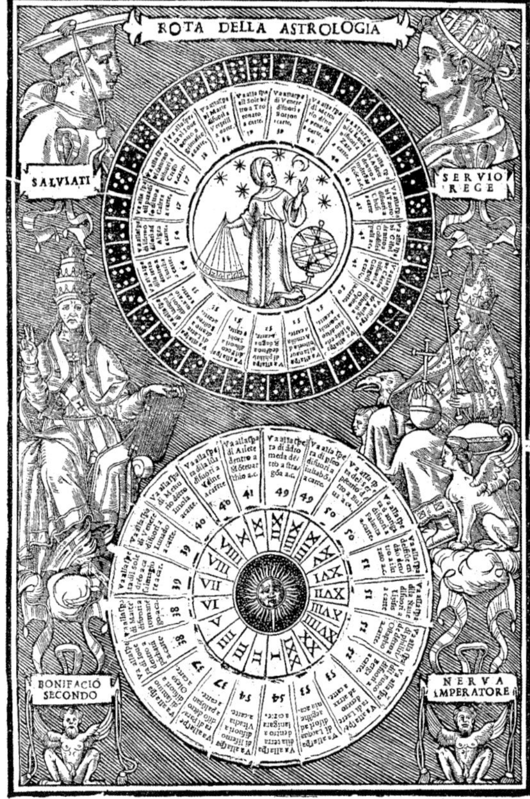

157 (*facing page top left*) Table of *domande* (questions), from Fanti, *Triompho di Fortuna*. The questions include: how many husbands a woman will have; how a man gets into and out of adversity; what will happen between a husband and wife and what the husband should be aware of before taking [his wife] into his house; and if and when one should make a journey. By permission of the Folger Shakespeare Library.

158 (*facing page top right*) Table of fortunes (winds), from Fanti, *Triompho di Fortuna*. The winds on this page include Vulturnus (a Roman east wind, equal to the Greek Eurus); Argestus (the Greek surname for Eurus, denoting the east or southeast wind); Libico (Italian Libeccio – a southwest wind, coming from Libya); and Boreas (a Greek north wind). By permission of the Folger Shakespeare Library.

159 (*facing page bottom left*) Table of houses, from Fanti, *Triompho di Fortuna*. Each house was associated with a ruling family in one of the many principalities or cities in Italy: the Gonzaga of Mantua, the Este of Ferrara, the Baglioni of Perugia, and the Vitelli of Città di Castello. By permission of the Folger Shakespeare Library.

160 (*facing page bottom right*) Wheel of astrology, from Fanti, *Triompho di Fortuna*. By permission of the Folger Shakespeare Library.

on the right, pointing down. On the side of Virtus, an angelic winged figure, most likely *Bona Fortuna (Good Fortune)*, turns the crank in one direction; but next to Voluptas, a diabolical horned monster with dragon wings, probably *Malus Genius (Evil Genius)*, tries to turn the crank in the other. It is the eternal struggle between good and evil. Below on the left, in front of a watery landscape, stand a nude youth displaying a dice cube and a bearded astrologer holding a compass and astrolabe. To the right is Rome, symbolized by the Pantheon, and a medieval crenellated tower with a twenty-four-hour clock, signifying Time. The scene as a whole is emblematic of the Renaissance debate over whether Fortune or Divine Providence controls the affairs of men.[33] A few pages later a sonnet promises that "herein one will learn much of what noble nature retains in itself and at the same time enjoy a magnificent game."[34]

Let us open the book and see how the game is played. The first section consists of tables of *domande* or questions, seventy-two in all (fig. 157). The one at the upper left asks: "When should one begin a building? And to make it most excellent, what are those things for which one should make provision?"[35] The question is illustrated with three vignettes of building construction activities, the text below promising: "In this most useful question introduced by the author, Fanti, [it teaches] not only the hour and point when every building should be started, but also how to understand and prepare all necessary things. And what one must do to make it as excellent as it can be." To find the answer, the reader is instructed to "go to the Fortuna of Borea at the letter E," and now the quest begins.[36]

We then turn several pages to the next set of tables (twelve iconographic figures of fortune) and the Fortuna of Borea – that is, the north wind – where the letter E instructs us to go to the House of Este and find the letter K (fig. 158). So we turn the pages again, and come to a section with the twelve houses of Italy (fig. 159). Here the letter K under the House of Este directs us to a page with the Wheel of Astrology, where we come to the heart of the matter (fig. 160). One of seventy-two wheels featuring the great figures of antiquity and modern times, it shows Pope Boniface II and Cardinal Salviati, representing spiritual authority, and the Roman Emperor Nerva and King Servius, standing for temporal power. Now the dice are thrown for the first time, and Fortune – to which both pope and emperor are subject – is brought into the equation. Throwing a double five, for example, takes us to the ten o'clock position on the upper left, where the text directs us to the Sphere of Jove, one of thirty-six spheres, where we will receive further instructions under the name Grimasco (fig. 161). There, at the bottom of the page, Michelangelo, heroically chiseling a reclining

161 Sphere of Jove, from Fanti, *Triompho di Fortuna*. By permission of the Folger Shakespeare Library.

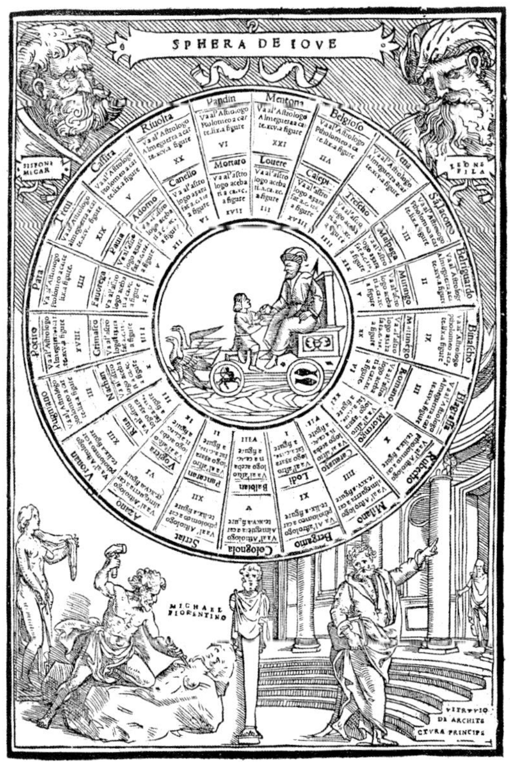

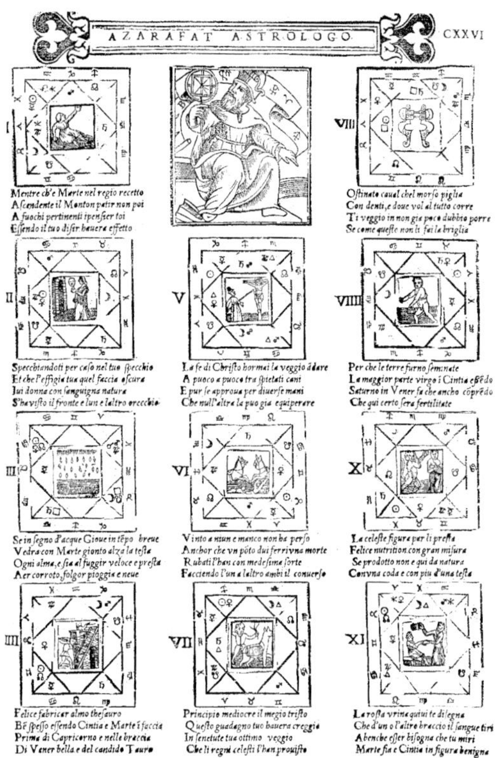

AZARAFAT ASTROLOGO CXXVI

I
Mentre ch'e Marte nel regio recetto
Ascendente il Monton patir non poi
A fuochi pertinenti ipensier toi
Essendo il tuo disir hauera effetto

VIII
Ostinato caual chel morso piglia
Con denti, e doue vol al tutto corre
Ti veggio in non gia poco dubbio porre
Se come queste non li fei la briglia

II
Specchiandoti per caso nel tuo specchio
Et che l'effigia tua quel faccia oscura
Jui donna con sanguigna natura
S'ha visto il fronte e lun e laltro orecchio

V
La fe di Christo hormai la veggio ădare
A puoco a puoco tra spietati cani
E pur se approua per diuerse mani
Che null'altra la puo gia equiperare

VIIII
Per che le terre furno seminate
La maggior parte virgo ĩ Cintia essẽdo
Saturno in Vener fa che ancho cõprẽdo
Che qui certo sera fertilitate

III
Se in segno d'acque Gioue in tẽpo breue
Vedra con Marte gionto alza la testa
Ogni alma, e sta al fuggir veloce e presta
Aer corroto, folgor pioggia e neue

VI
Vinto a niun e manco non ha perso
Anchor che vn põto dui ferri vna morte
Rubati l'han con medesime sorte
Facciendo l'un a laltro ambi il conuerso

X
La celeste figura per li presta
Felice nutrition con gran misura
Se prodotto non e qui da natura
Con vna coda e con piu d'una testa

IIII
Felice fabricar almo thesauro
Bẽ spesso essendo Cintia e Marte ĩ faccia
Prima di Capricorno e nelle braccia
Di Vener bella e del candido Tauro

VII
Principio mediocre il megio tristo
Questo guadagno tuo hauera creggia
In senetute tua ottimo veggio
Che li regni celesti l'han prouisto

XI
La rossa vrina quiui te disegna
Che d'un o l'altro braccio il sangue tiri
Abenche esser bisogna che tu miri
Marte sia e Cintia in figura benigna

162 Table of Azarafat, astrologer, from Fanti, *Triompho di Fortuna*. By permission of the Folger Shakespeare Library.

figure, is paired with Vitruvius. Contemporary sculptor and legendary architect, they function as representatives of Jove, the supreme maker in the pantheon of the ancients.[37] Grimasco is found at the nine o'clock position, where we are directed to proceed to the astrologer Azarafat at figure four.

And now flipping through the pages again, we come to the final section of the book, where each page is governed by a sibyl or a renowned astrologer and, finally, the answer that we have been seeking (fig. 162). Beneath Azarafat, at figure four, one of the small vignettes from the original *domande* reappears, along with astrological coordinates in the form of a quatrain that will allow us "to build happily a gracious treasure." The text counsels that the moon should be in opposition to Capricorn (that is, in Cancer) and Mars in opposition to Taurus, one of the two signs ruled by Venus. This may be interpreted to mean that one builds while the moon is in Cancer, opposing Capricorn, as a way of integrating the home and preservation with construction and innovation. Mars should be in opposition to Taurus for the combination of stability and beauty and for an amalgamation of energy and decay. What is sought is a kind of permanence created by integrating opposing factors that might undermine the project or cause it to be unstable.[38]

The basic process of divination thus involves two acts – throwing dice and astrological calculation – allowing both fortune and human erudition to determine the outcome. In the course of the game the cosmos and the whole of man's knowledge are taken apart, put into ciphers, and then reassembled. Of course, this was a game to play with friends, and thus an amusement. As one historian has noted, "the oracles of antiquity, stripped of every solemn and public form, were transformed into a literary pastime in a social game."[39] And yet, in a culture where astrology was regarded as a science, it was the game of life and thus a serious matter indeed.[40]

And astrology governed even the most serious contract a Venetian was likely to make: the marriage. In 1526 the feast day of the Conversion of St. Paul, 25 January, was chosen as the wedding day for Viena, the granddaughter of Doge Andrea Gritti, not because it was an important Christian feast day, but because it was *punto di stella* – "when the stars make a special aspect." It was also thought that the weather on that day would last for the rest of the year.[41]

Francesco Marcolini's *Le sorti intitulate giardino di pensieri*, a book of divinations subtitled *The Garden of Thought*, published in Venice in 1540 and republished in 1550, enjoyed a success similar to Fanti's *Triumpho*. It also combined choice and chance, the player choosing from among a group of questions – thirteen each for men and women and twenty-four for either sex – with the course determined by drawing from a deck of cards. Here, too, the player follows a path of words and images toward final answer, now in the form of a tercet. A type of memory theater, this complex and subtle game looks to both past and present, arranging words and images like flowers in a garden (hence the subtitle) on the model of the anthology, or *florilegium*. Marcolini writes that "even though they ask the same question, the lines of poetry come out varied, and when they ask different questions, they will encounter the same tercets in response to them."[42] As a form of *ars combinatoria*, the game became a vehicle to reveal and represent the hidden structure of reality.[43] The intent was to balance unity and variety, thus replicating the workings of fortune itself in the lives of men and women – creating, in short, "an amusing, ingenious duplicate of the world."[44]

To be enjoyed fully, such sophisticated and witty games of word and image, played by both men and women, required (and developed) excellent visual memories and a good knowledge of literature. Judging from their wide dissemination in the sixteenth century, they were not just pastimes for the court but also found their way into homes in Venice and other cities.

* * *

Special occasions engendered other forms of hospitality. Just as games were serious play, grand entertainments were not to be taken lightly. Banquets and receptions were costly and required considerable organization. The youthful members of the Compagnie della Calza often staged such events for their own enjoyment, but also functioned as impresarios for wedding celebrations and other festivities in private homes. The Ortolani put on a lavish *festa honoratissima* – a most honorable celebration – at Ca' Venier at Sant'Angelo on the Grand Canal in 1522 in honor of Pier Antonio di Sanseverino, Prince of Bisignano, who had just joined their group. The courtyard, *portego*, and chambers were hung with carpets, tapestries, and paintings, and a throne was covered with a costly strip of cloth of gold, fashioned for the prince. Silver valued at 5,000 ducats was displayed on a *credenza*. Many patrician ladies were in attendance, elegantly attired in dresses of gold cloth, and the guests danced to the sounds of *trombe, pifferi, pive, cornette, flauti*, and the jests of buffoons until dinner was announced.[45]

Like such receptions, the wedding celebration was an event that stood at the intersection between public and private life. As such, it represented the high end of Venetian hospitality. Festivities were often prolonged over several days and varied according to the financial resources and social ambitions of the families. But the proper wedding as celebrated by wealthy families was expected to have the same basic components: the signing of the marriage contract; an announcement of the engagement to the families; the ritual showing of the bride in her home and in public; receptions at the houses of the bride and groom; the public declaration of the marriage vows; and a banquet, usually in the bride's home. Finally, the groom took his bride back to their new home and the marriage was consummated. During the course of these events there would be feasting, dancing, and other entertainments, and, not least, a display of wealth. The extended wedding ritual summed up in an emblematic way the close bond between familial and civic interests in Venice and deeply influenced the material culture of the Venetian home.[46]

The signing of the marriage contract was the result of negotiations between the two families, usually with the help of a mediator. The bride was not present; she was represented only by a male relative – her father or, if he was deceased, an uncle or a brother – in the State Attorney's Office, where contracts for noble marriages were recorded. But the groom appeared himself, in company with his kinsmen. The contract, duly agreed to, was signed by both men. Also present were witnesses and the *compare dell'anello* or ring sponsor, the equivalent of today's best man.[47]

For the bride, the announcement of the betrothal was truly a coming-out party in the most specific sense of the term. Unmarried girls of aristocratic rank were secluded, closely guarded and seldom if ever seen (figs. 163 and 164). In a typical announcement scenario, the *parentado* – the

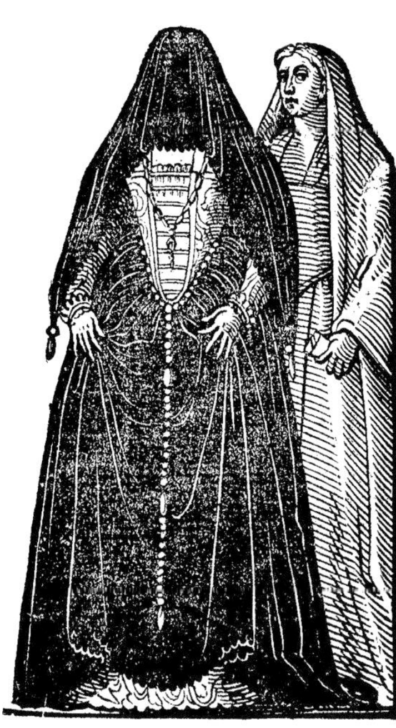

163 Cesare Vecellio, *Spose non sposate* (*Bride not yet Married*). Engraving from his *De gli habiti antichi, et moderni* (1590). Height 18 cm. According to Vecellio, "For some time now it is customary for brides, before they say their vows (give the faith) or receive the ring from their husband, to be visited on one day by all their male friends and relations and on another by the women, and then they go well accompanied to some entertainments." By permission of the Folger Shakespeare Library.

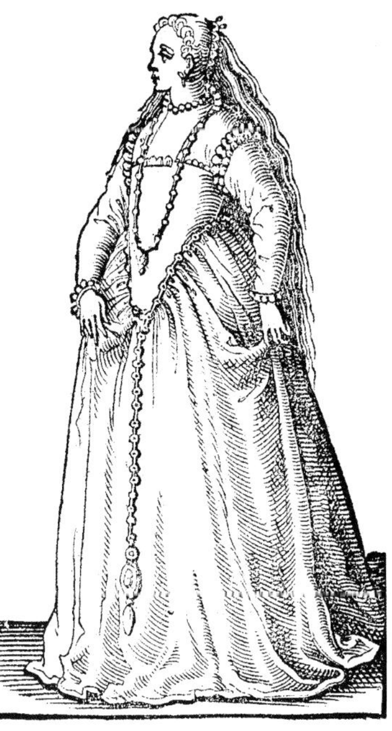

164 Cesare Vecellio, *Spose sposate* (*Bride Married*). Engraving from his *De gli habiti antichi, et moderni* (1590). Height 18 cm. Vecellio reports that the dresses worn by brides at the reception were usually made of white *raso* (satin), "adorned with pearls, gold, and jewels of great value." By permission of the Folger Shakespeare Library.

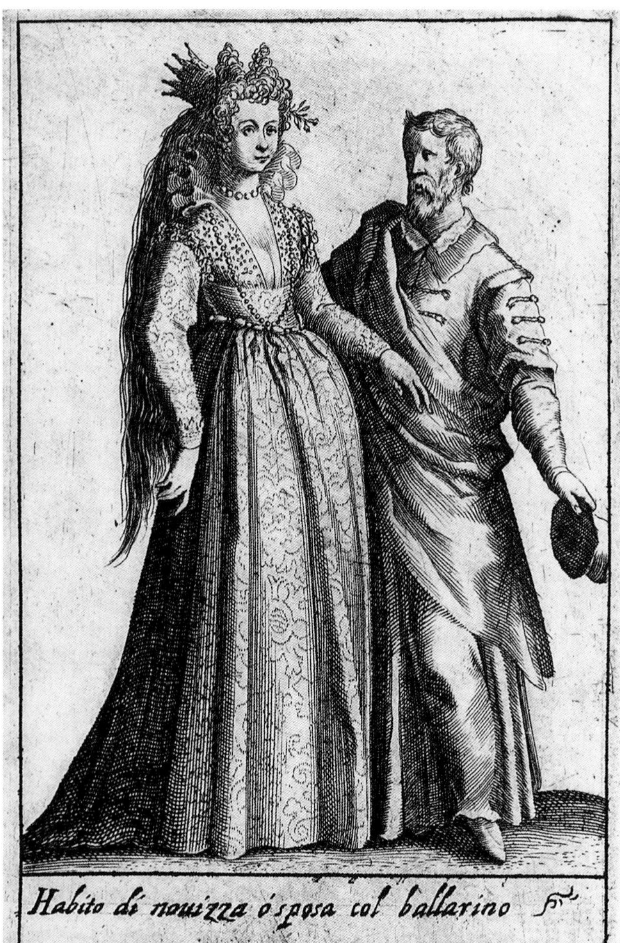

165 Giacomo Franco, *Venetian Bride with her Ballarino* (dance master). Engraving from his *Habiti d'huomeni et donne* (Venice, 1626), 26. Cesare Vecellio observes: "These brides are accustomed to be trained in dancing, and toward this end they have some dance masters who serve them on those days, and they are elderly men; and these, at the time of the *parentado* [reception for the family], typically lead the bride from the *camera* into the *portego* in the presence of relatives and a circle of friends that are sitting there; and so, to the sound of diverse instruments, they perform some dances, and then return to the *camera*, where there are many ladies who adorn them, and change their dress often." By permission of the Folger Shakespeare Library.

extended family on both sides – were invited to the home of the bride. According to Sansovino they sat themselves in the *sala* or *portego*, and a dance master led the bride out of one of the chambers, "dressed in white by ancient custom, and with her hair falling loose onto her shoulders, interwoven with golden thread" (fig. 165). Her dance master leads her around the room, Sansovino continued,

> to the sound of *pifferi*, of trumpets, and other harmonic instruments . . . always dancing in a stately manner and making bows to the guests. And so having shown herself and been viewed by everyone, she leaves the room, and when new persons come in, she returns to the *sala* and leaves again. This having been done many times in the space of an hour or a little more, she descends to the ground floor, and accompanied then by diverse gentle ladies who were waiting in various chambers, she boards a gondola, and is seated outside the canopy on a chair that is elevated and all covered with carpets [fig. 166].
>
> Followed by a great number of other gondolas, she goes to visit the monasteries of nuns, where she has either sisters or other relatives and kin. All these things are done for a purpose. Since having to increase the begetting of the family which she has entered, she displays herself at home, and outside to the city, almost as to so many witnesses to the marriage contract. And the people all around go to the ceremony, as if they were celebrating their own, since by order of the government, they are joined together forever, as if they would be of the same family.[48]

166 Giacomo Franco, *Venetian Brides in Gondolas*. Engraving from his *Habiti d'huomeni et donne* (1610). Height 29 cm. The inscription explains: "In this manner the brides go in gondolas to visit their relatives in monasteries accompanied by a great number of gondolas." Princeton, Princeton University Library, Department of Rare Books and Special Collections, Marquand Library.

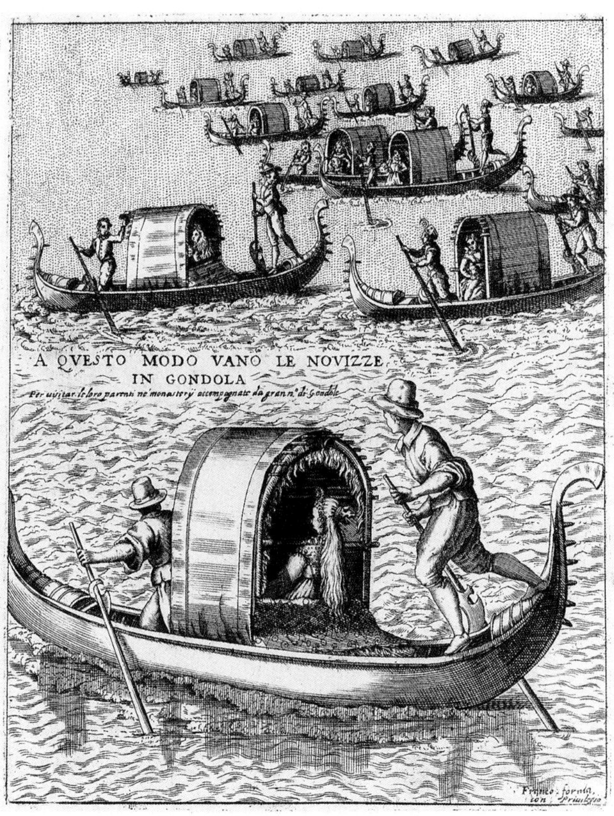

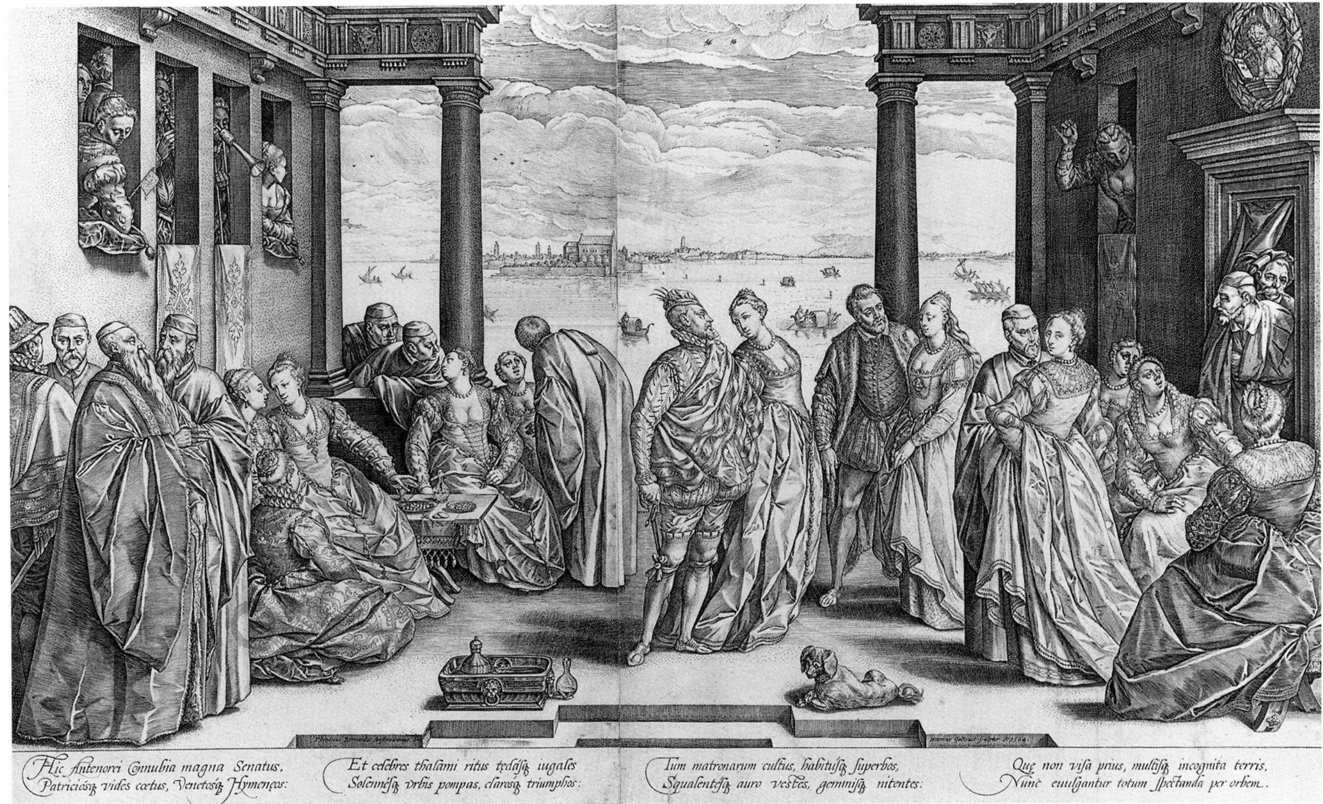

167 Hendrik Goltzius, *A Venetian Wedding*, after Dirck Barendszen, 1584. Engraving, 433 × 740 mm. Barendszen studied in Venice with Titian, and the view out from the *portego* over the lagoon toward the north, with the island of San Cristoforo in the background, may have been taken from drawings made in Titian's home, which was located on the northern edge of the city. Princeton, Princeton University Art Museum. © Trustees of Princeton University.

At no other single point in Venetian life are the fortunes of private families joined with the public good in such an explicit manner. The emblematic power of concealment and dramatic revelation should not be underestimated. It is like the showing of a holy relic – sequestered under lock and key for most of the year and then brought out on high holidays and revealed to the faithful.

The dinners, balls, theatrical performances, and other festivities that typically followed the betrothal reception would have been orchestrated by the ring sponsors or, during the early sixteenth century, by a Compagnia della Calza if the groom was a member. The actual wedding, the *sposalizio*, typically came several days later. Although in earlier times it was often held at home, in the later sixteenth century it usually took place in church and, like the bride's epiphany in the gondola, provided another moment when private life spilled into public space. On the day of the wedding, the windows of the family palaces of the bride and groom were hung with carpets and tapestries. The bride rose at dawn and, dressed in white silk or crimson velvet, with her flowing locks still unbound, went to church, preceded by fifers and trumpeters and followed by a procession of female friends and relatives. After the nuptial rites, the entourage returned to the bride's home for yet another reception and the marriage banquet – the culminating event (but one) of the wedding ritual.

An engraving dated 1584 by Hendrik Goltzius after a drawing by the Dutch artist Dirck Barendszen is a fine rendition of a wedding celebration (fig. 167).[49] Note that the bride, easily distinguished by her unbound hair, is not front and center, but placed over to the right in a compositional strategy that is characteristic of Venetian, as well as northern, aesthetic taste.[50] The Latin inscription proclaims: "Behold the great nuptial rites of Antenor, in the manner of the patricians of the Venetian Senate: the crowded fete at the site of the wedding, the ceremonial torches, the solemn triumphal procession through the city, and moreover, the magnificent vestments of the ladies, imbricated with gold and radiant with precious stones, as never before seen and unknown in other lands. Now it all can be seen and admired

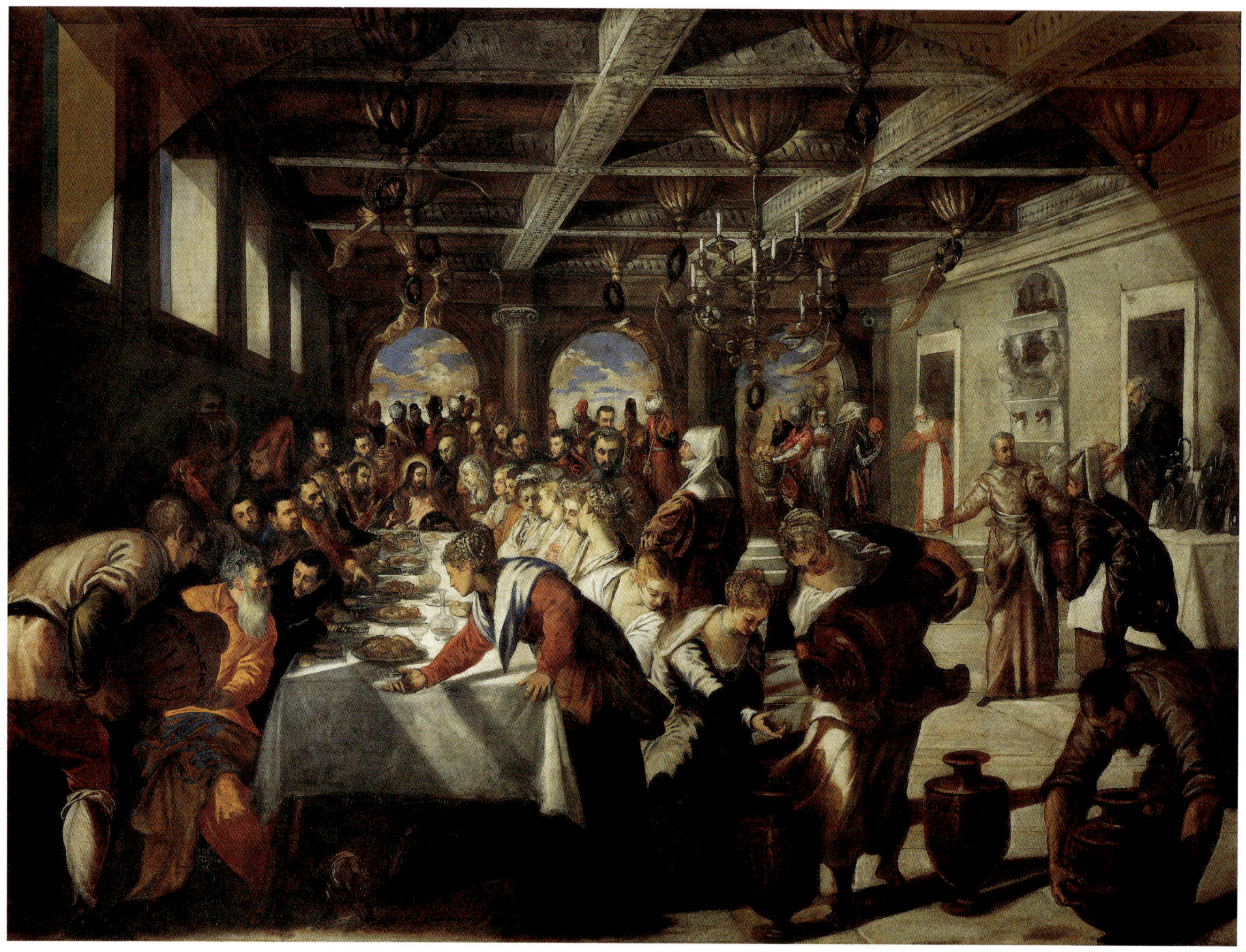

168 Jacopo Tintoretto, *Marriage Feast at Cana*, 1561. Oil on canvas, 435 × 545 cm. Venice, Church of S. Maria della Salute.

throughout the world."[51] The reference to Antenor refers to Venice's proud claim of a Trojan ancestry pre-dating the foundation of Rome.[52]

And what about the banquet itself? It would have been held, Sansovino wrote, "with pomp and notable expense, since the guests ordinarily invited to common marriages often amount to three hundred persons, with offerings of exquisite and diverse refreshments, but regulated however by laws."[53] The laws will be discussed later, but first Jacopo Tintoretto's *Marriage Feast at Cana* is worth considering (fig. 168) for it offers a credible depiction of one of the smaller wedding banquets, more modest than those cited by Sansovino. Blown glass was the Venetian craft *par excellence*, and Tintoretto has set his tables with fine crystal goblets and serving carafes called *inghistere*. Thomas Coryat had praised the Venetian wines, particularly "their Lagryme di Christo; which is so toothsome and delectable to the taste." He added: "These wines are alwayes brought up into the roome wherein the ghests doe make their meale, in certaine great glasses called Ingistera'es . . . out of which glasse the servants that attend at table, doe use to poure their wine into lesser glasses, and so to deliver them to the guests. This word Ingistera I therefore name, because the etymologie of it is very pretty." He explained that the term comes from the Greek word *gaster*, signifying belly: "for the middle part of it doth truly represent the shape of a bellie."[54] The word also calls to mind the Latin *ingerere*, meaning to carry, the root of *ingest* in English. The basic shape, consisting of a spherical receptacle on a footed base with a tall narrow neck, is documented in written sources as early as the thirteenth century, and it persisted throughout the Renaissance period. In the seventeenth century, apprentice glass blowers were required to blow an *inghistera all'antica* before being granted journeyman status. There were also variant shapes. An *inghistera* ringed with two strips of white glass to make it easier to grasp, now in the Metropolitan Museum, features a bowl flattened at the bottom to form its own base (fig. 169). With the narrow neck of the *inghistere* reducing the exposure of their contents to air or contamination, they were used for wine, oil, and water.[55]

Fine glassware was an insignia of aristocratic status.[56] Turning to Paolo Veronese's more ostentatious *Marriage Feast at Cana*, held in an outdoor loggia, one finds a wide shallow goblet now called a *tazza* on the tables (see fig. 171). This was made specifically for red wine – and for drinking rather than storage purposes – to maximize the exposure of the wine to oxygen. As a 1997 exhibition catalogue noted, the goblet's shape "also makes it almost impossible to drink from without spilling."[57] But then we are not Renaissance Venetians, and presumably the noble guests at the banquet would have mastered the technique of artful imbibing. Another way to express a refined taste was through a more ornate piece of glass, such as a set of goblets decorated with gilt and raised enamel dots in color – a popular decorative motif for which Venetian artisans were famous (fig. 170).[58]

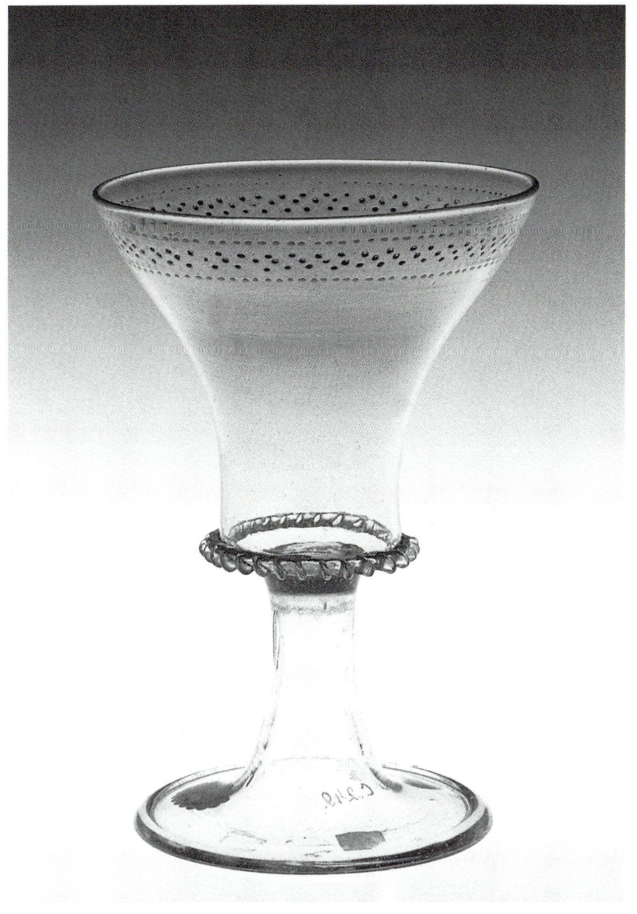

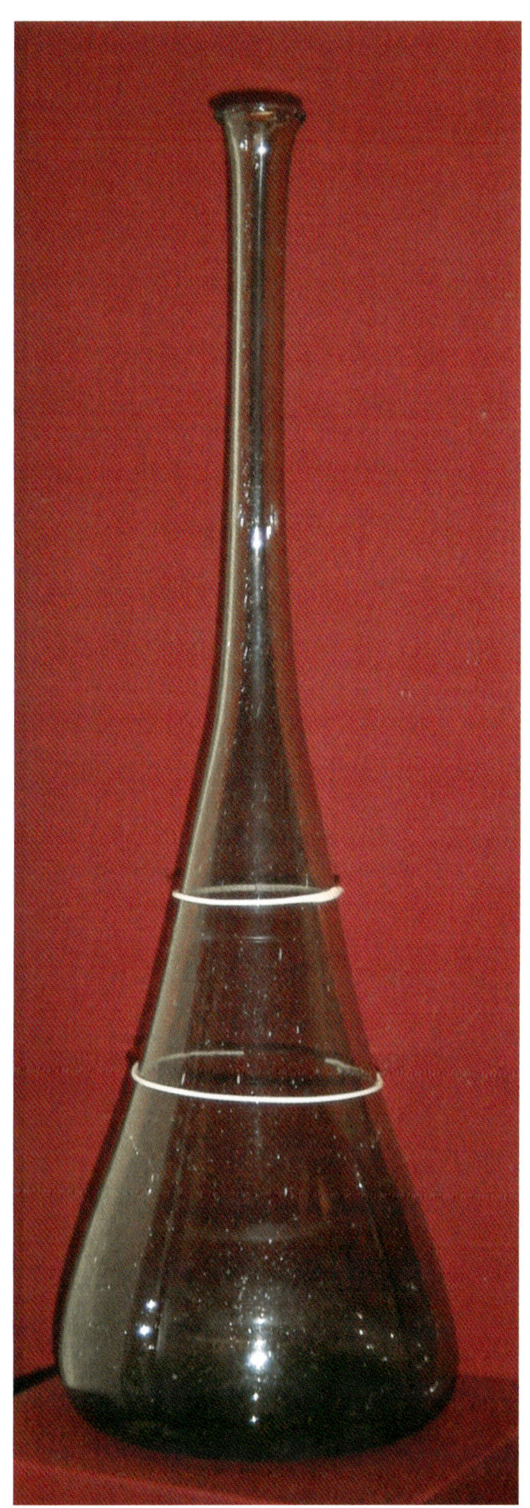

169 Bottle, sixteenth century. Green and milk glass. New York, The Metropolitan Museum of Art, Gift of James Jackson Jarves, 1881.81.8.35.

170 (*left*) Venetian goblet, ca. 1500–50. Clear glass with gilt and enamel decoration, height 17.2 cm, depth 12.1 cm. Richmond, Virginia Museum of Fine Arts.

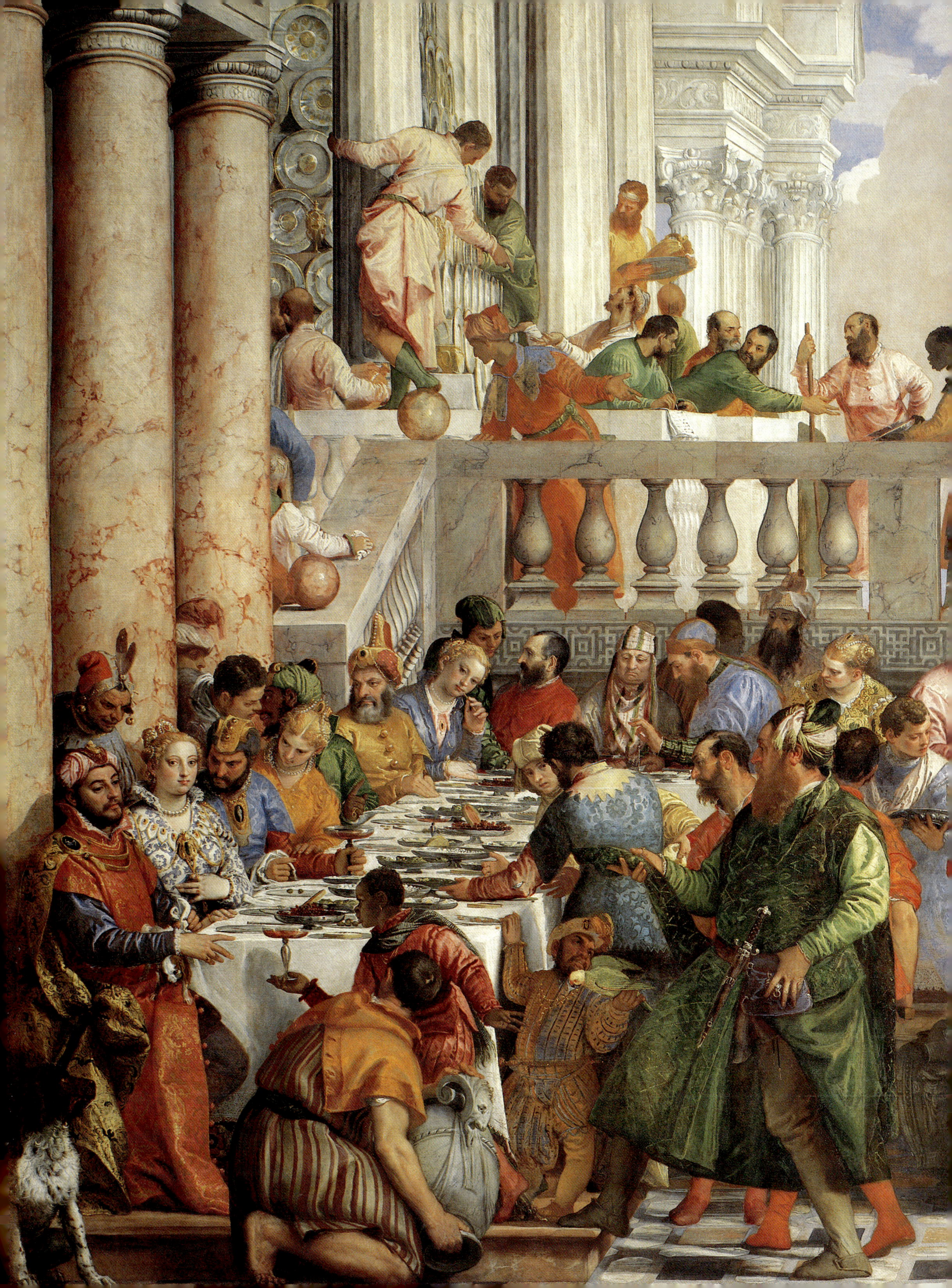

One unusual object that could have been made only in Venice is the *navicella*, a blown-glass water pitcher in the form of ship, complete with rigging (fig. 172). It was originally designed by a woman, Hermonia Vivarini, daughter of the painter Alvise and wife of a spinner.[59] According to Sanudo, in 1521 the Great Council granted Hermonia exclusive rights to produce it for ten years.[60] The early examples were blown in a yellowish *cristallo* glass called *giallino*, with the sides decorated with pastilles imprinted with crosses and lions' heads – that is, San Marcos – of aquamarine-colored glass. The little ships were a great success. At the feast of the Sensa in 1525, Sanudo marveled at the stalls of the Barovier, Serena, and Ballarin glass-making families, where he saw "a galley and a most beautiful large ship, as well as other vases and marvelous objects of glass."[61] In 1550 Leandro Alberti of Bologna cited one in his *Description of All Italy*, describing it as "a measured galley, one *braccia* [that is, about 23 inches] long, with all its furnishings." He exclaimed that it seemed to him impossible to make such an object so well proportioned from glass.[62]

171 (*facing page*) Paolo Veronese, *Marriage Feast at Cana* (detail), 1562–63. Oil on canvas, whole work 677 × 994 cm. Paris, Musée du Louvre.

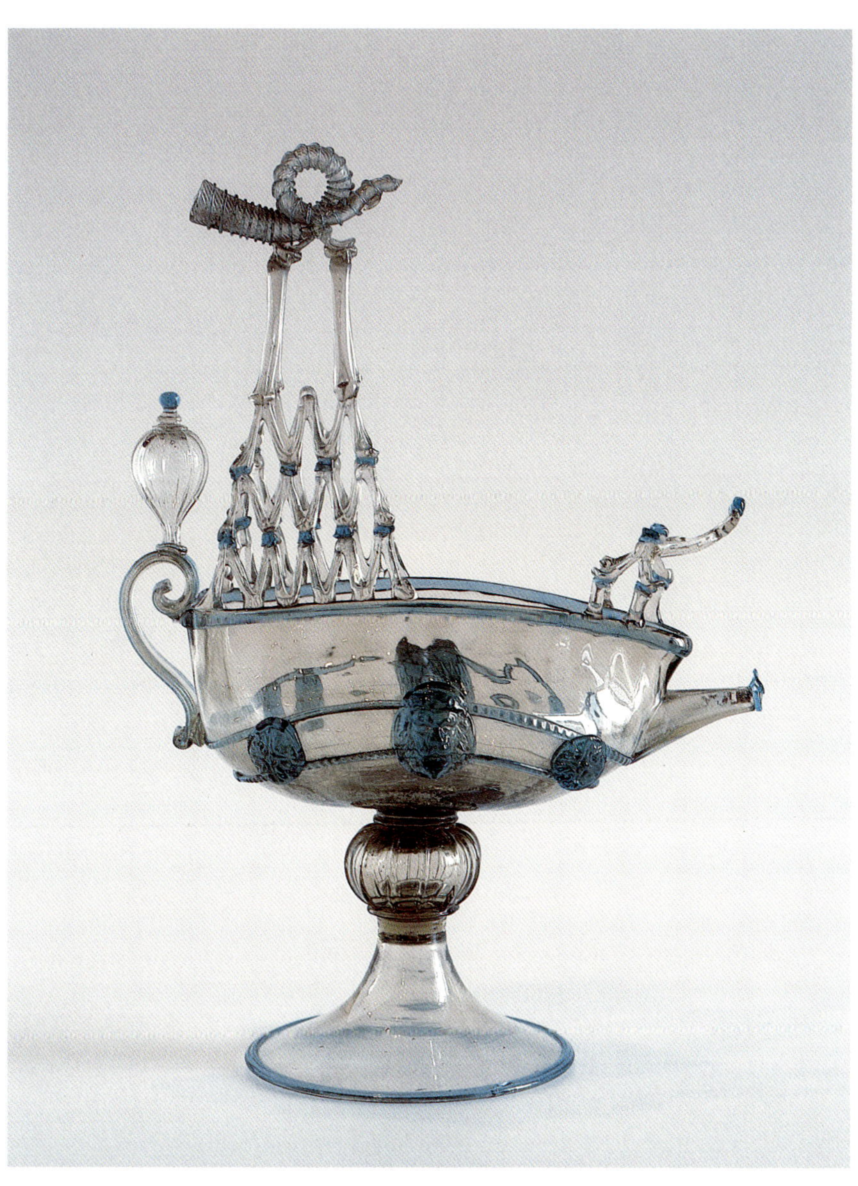

172 (*below*) *Navicella*, Venice, early sixteenth century. Glass ewer in the form of a ship, molded and blown stem, molded applied ornaments and foot, height 41 cm, length 29.5 cm. Venice, Museo del Vetrario.

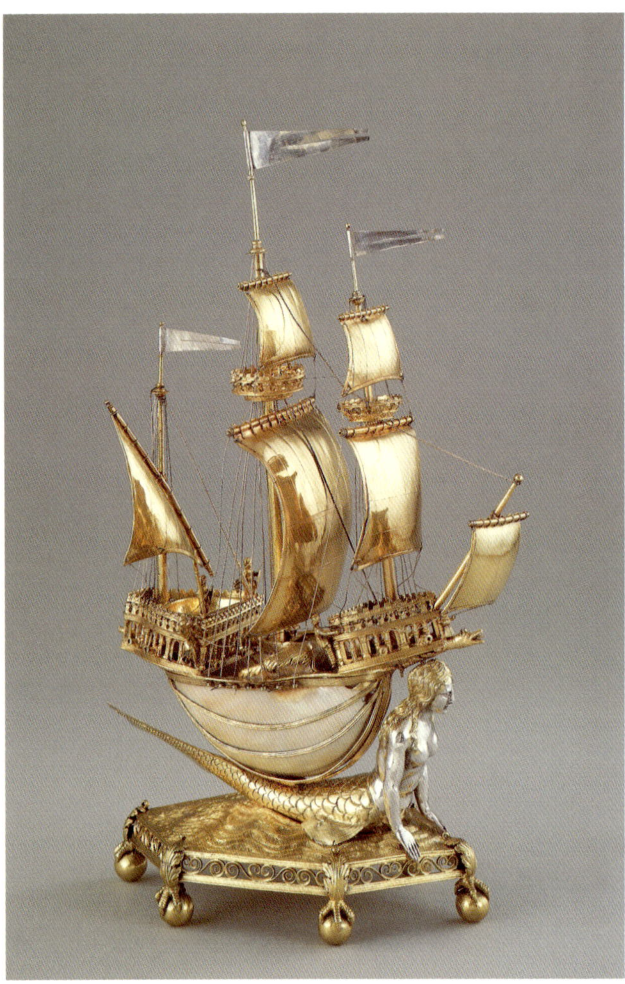

173 The Burghley *nef*, French, 1527–28. Nautilus shell mounted in silver parcel-gilt. Tiny figures of Tristan and Isolde sit playing chess in front of the main mast. London, Victoria and Albert Museum.

Although a definite connection cannot be proven, Hermonia may have been inspired to create her *navicella* after seeing or hearing of a *nef*, a ship crafted of metalwork that would have been placed in front of the host at a grand dinner as a receptacle for salt or dining utensils. And indeed, Sanudo records the gift of a silver ship that might well have been a *nef* at a Venetian wedding celebration in 1513.[63] These elegant vessels first appeared in Germany and France in the fifteenth century and were soon replicated on aristocratic tables throughout Europe. A particularly beautiful example called the Burghley *nef*, made of silver gilt with a nautilus-shell hull, was crafted in France in 1482 and is now in the Victoria and Albert Museum in London (fig. 173).[64]

In any case, gracing a cinquecento banquet table in Venice or elsewhere, Hermonia's *navicella* would have transformed, in a sense, the gritty mercantile activities that were the source of Venetian prosperity into an object of aesthetic delight. The piece embodies the *politia* – the refinement or civility – to which every aristocratic family aspired. It is moreover emblematic of the artistry and ingenuity of the Venetian craftsman – in this case craftswoman – who was adept at transforming objects from diverse provenances into pieces that were quintessentially Venetian.

Glassware typically appeared in the inventories of patrician families, even if they were not especially wealthy, but became increasingly rare in the homes of the popular classes by the end of the sixteenth century. Indeed, the demand for Venetian glass from abroad essentially priced it out of the market for much of the citizenry. And its preciousness was only enhanced by its vulnerability to breakage. A glassmaking treatise of 1540 made a moral point: "Considering the short life [of glass], due to its fragility, one cannot and must not give it too much love, and one must use it and understand it as an example of the life of man and of the things of this world which, though beautiful, are transitory and frail."[65]

Pewter drinking vessels were often used instead, and it is a rare inventory that does not include a full set of pewter dinnerware. Pewter is sometimes called "the poor man's silver," although it was found in the homes of the rich as well. A few figures from the inventories bespeak a capability for lavish entertaining: the estate of Donado Da Lezze listed 147 pieces of pewter "of diverse types and sizes"; and that of Pietro Gritti contained no less than 450 pieces, comprising 200 trenchers, 50 large dishes, and 200 platters. Silver and pewter were displayed as well as used, with services arranged on a steplike structure made to go on the top of a *credenza*, as in Tintoretto's *Marriage Feast at Cana* and even more impressively in Veronese's painting of the same subject (fig. 175). In the latter example, the display may be silver, as at the banquet described by Sanudo in 1521 where the silver on the sideboard was valued at 5,000 ducats.[66] A silver-gilt ewer and basin in the Victoria and Albert Museum is a fine example of the silversmith's art (fig. 174). Embossed with nudes, animals, and foliage, it features a gracefully shaped handle and small foot – elements influenced by the Mannerist aesthetic that dominated the decorative arts in Venice in the later sixteenth century but never really took hold in painting.

Cutlery was another matter. Even quite modest inventories had a few silver forks, spoons, and knives. And the great houses had enough for all but the largest banquets without having to rent or borrow. In the house of Domenico Cappello at the time of his death in 1532 there were a dozen spoons and forks described as decorated and gilded, another thirty spoons and forty-two forks that were presumably

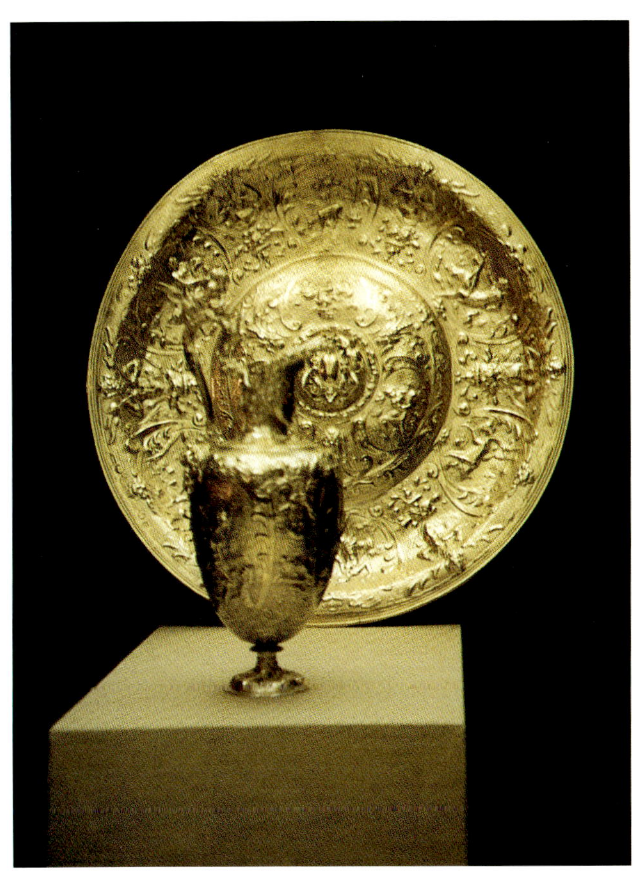

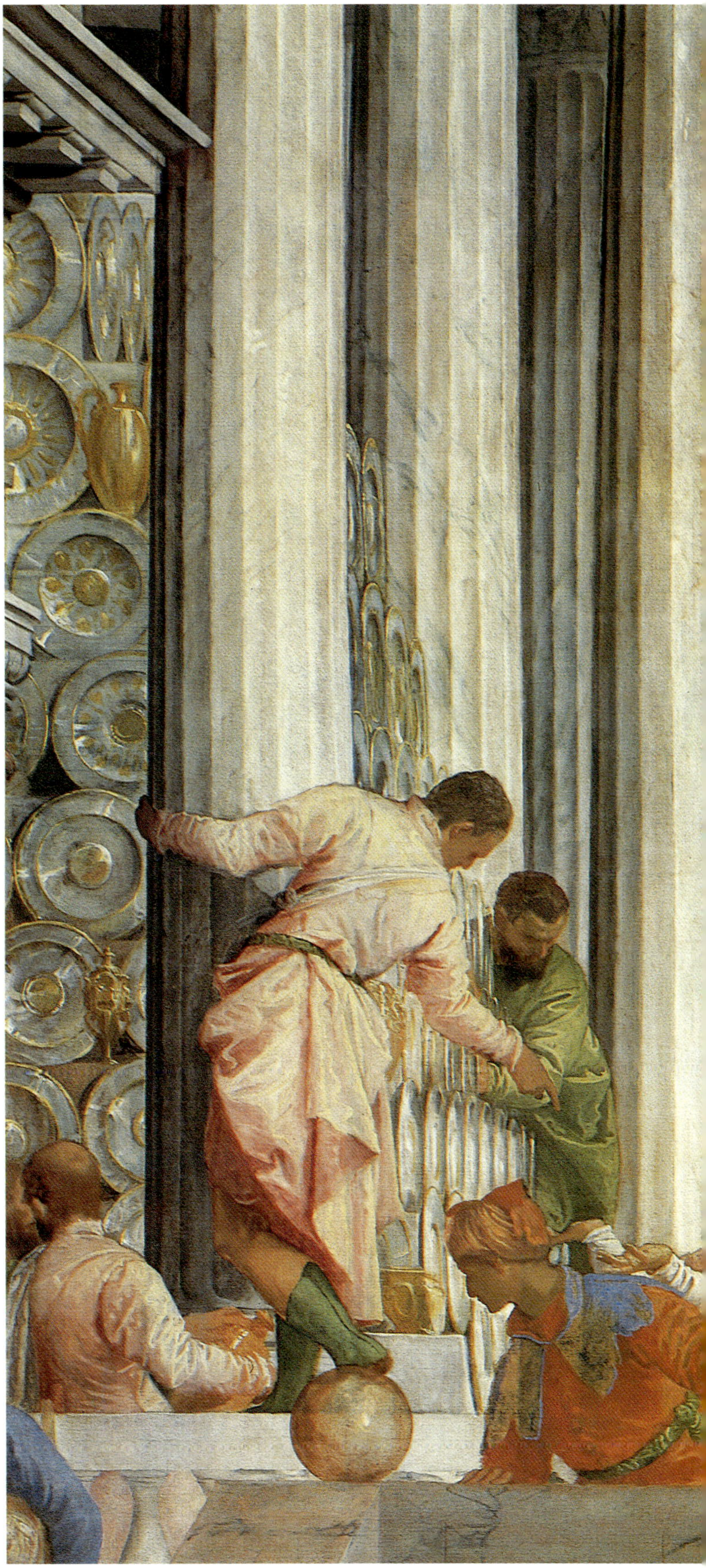

174 (*above*) Ewer and basin, Venice, ca. 1600. Silver-gilt; ewer cast and basin embossed and chased. The set was made for display and not use. London, Victoria and Albert Museum, cat. M237 and A-1956.

175 (*right*) Paolo Veronese, *Marriage Feast at Cana* (detail), 1562–63. Oil on canvas, whole work 677 × 994 cm. Paris, Musée du Louvre.

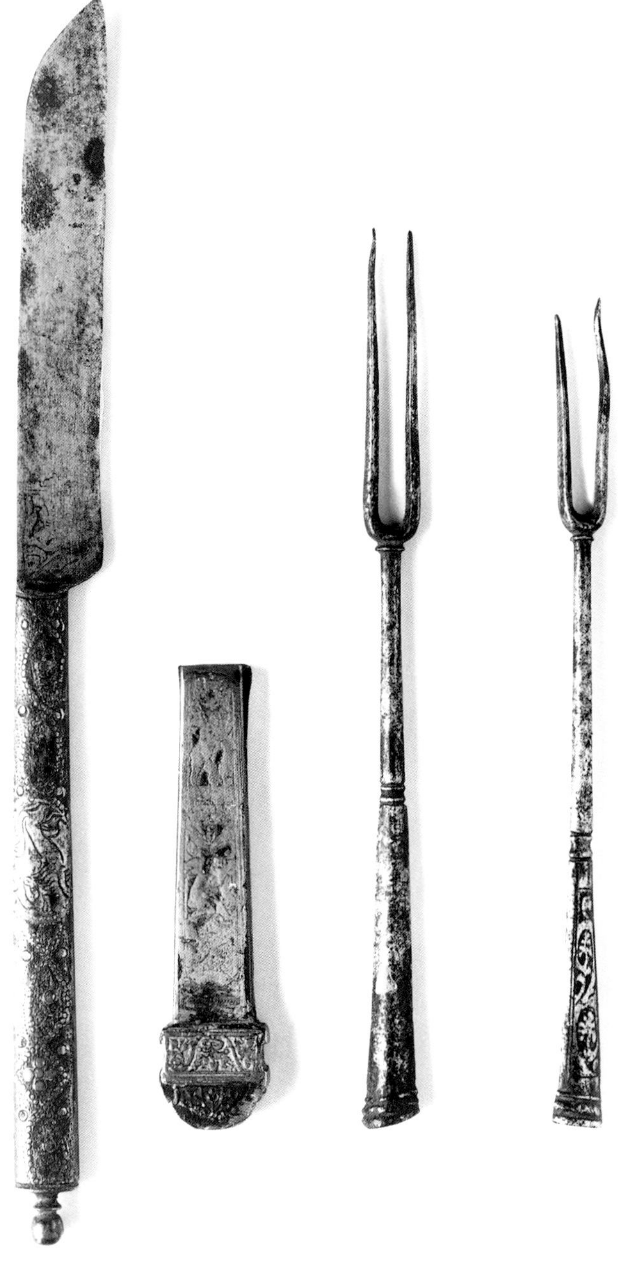

176 (*above*) Cutlery, Italian, sixteenth century. These remnants of a luxurious life-style consist of a carving knife, a dinner knife handle, and two dinner forks. Venice, Museo Civico Correr.

plainer and thirty-eight table knives with silver handles (fig. 176).[67] Forks were uncommon elsewhere in Europe in this period, and English travelers frequently remarked on their use in Italy. Coryat observed that the use of forks was: "a custome in all those Italian Townes and cities through . . . which I passed that is not used in any other country that I saw in my travels . . . [Italians] doe alwaies at their meales use a little forke when they cut their meat . . . The reason of this their curiosity is, because the Italian cannot by any means indure to have his dish touched with fingers, seeing all mens fingers are not alike cleane."[68] Personal utensil cases were common luxury items to keep toothpicks and eating utensils in good order. As noted in Chapter 4, ladies might carry their own cutlery around with them in a fitted case suspended from the belt (see fig. 140).

What else might be on the table? Sometimes the dowry itself. Sanudo thus wrote approvingly of a wedding banquet for Luca Da Lezze and the daughter of Zuan Battista Foscarini in 1507: "It should be noted that at the dinner hour, when I was present, about 4,000 ducats, part of the bride's dowry, was brought in in six basins. The first one contained gold [coins], the rest [silver] coins. Well done, for those who can afford it!"[69]

Immoderate Expenses

The potentially disruptive effects of ostentatious display had been of concern in Venice since the thirteenth century and attempts were made to control it, and this raises the subject of sumptuary legislation. The earliest such law, dating to 1299, focused – not surprisingly – on marriage celebrations. Limitations were put on gifts, the size of the bridal entourage, and the number of dinner guests at the wedding feasts. Similar injunctions were repeated with monotonous regularity over the centuries to come.[70]

Banquets, which eventually approached the elegance of Veronese's *Wedding Feast at Cana*, were frequent targets. By 1472, the state had entered the kitchen. The number of dishes was limited to three, not counting confections, and food was not to be gilded. Specifically forbidden were pheasants, francolins, peacocks, partridge, and doves. Nor would dinners in public – in *campi* and *cortili*, and on *fondamente* – be tolerated: "rather only private ones in the chambers as the ancients were accustomed to do, and only with small sweets [served]."[71]

The tendency toward state intrusion into the private spaces of Venetian palaces became even more pronounced in the sixteenth century. In January 1509, only months before the republic's humiliating defeat at Agnadello, the Senate spoke out once again on marriage banquets. It was a time for reassessment, or, to put it more precisely, retrenchment. It was reported that despite an earlier statute that allowed two banquets with only forty guests each to celebrate a wedding – about the number in Veronese's painting – such dinners were now being attended by 300 guests and more. The Senate declared that if the laws were less strict, "almost everyone would willingly observe them."[72]

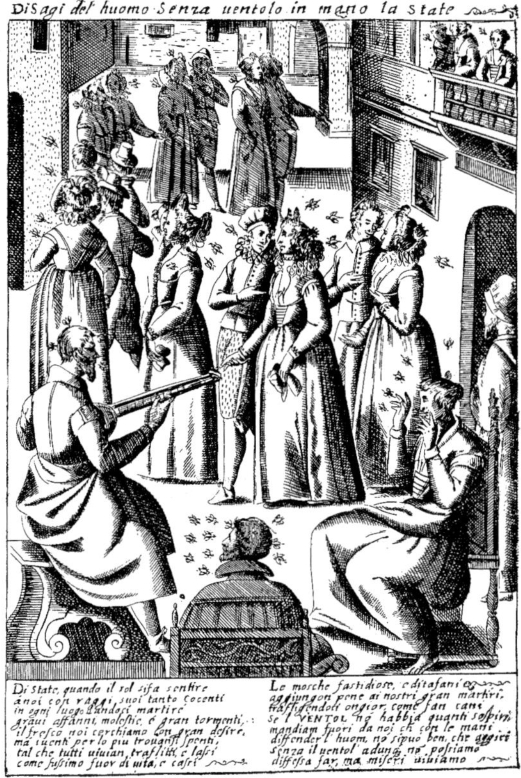

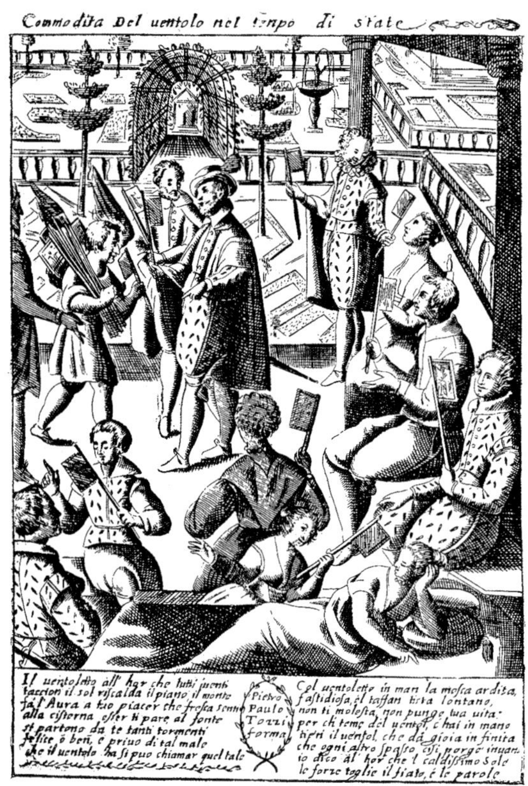

177a (*above left*) Pietro Paolo Tozzi, *Discomforts of Mankind without a Fan in the Hand in the Summer*, Venice-Padua, beginning of the seventeenth century. Engraving from Pompeo Molmenti, *La storia di Venezia nella vita privata dalle origini alla caduta della Repubblice*, (Bergamo, 1927–29; reprint, Trieste, Edizioni Lint, 1973), II: 291.

177b (*above right*) Pietro Paolo Tozzi, *Comforts of the Fan in the Summertime*, Venice-Padua, beginning of the seventeenth century. Engraving from Molmenti, *Vita privata*, II: 291.

The solution was ingenious: spread out the guests in an expanded number of dinners. Now, between the engagement and the marriage, there could be six small dinners of twenty-five guests each and two large dinners for fifty or less, and after the marriage itself, a dinner for up to eighty guests "because it is impossible to do it with [only] forty persons, as everyone knows."[73]

Ever larger reception parties were also a persistent problem. Whereas previously only the closest female relatives had been invited to receive the other guests, as many as fifty, eighty, a hundred and more ladies were now taking part, "so that there are more who receive than those who are received . . . [This], more than any other thing is the cause of great expense to our citizens, because in order to go to such offices and spectacles, everyone is forced to exceed the others with pomp and new fashions."[74] So it was now prohibited to have more than twenty ladies in the reception party, "whether in the *portego* or bedchamber or elsewhere" for marriages, childbirth celebrations, and election to state office.[75] How were these laws enforced? Slaves who reported on their masters were entitled to a share of the fines and manumission, while hired servants were granted full payment of unfilled contracts.[76] A permanent magistracy – the Magistrato alle Pompe – was set up in 1514 to ensure compliance. Sanudo referred to it as an *officio odioso* – an odious office – and it was generally ignored by those who could afford to pay the fines.[77]

Even the humble fan became an object of conspicuous display and a target for the sumptuary police. In 1522, "fans of lynx and ermine with handles of gold and silver encrusted with jewels and pearls" were forbidden. In 1525 it was further specified that only plain fans "of simple feathers with handles of black bone or ivory" would be permitted. In 1530, fans were to be plain "without any carving or working either of gold or silver."[78] That fans were there to stay is confirmed by two woodcuts from a book entitled *The Praises of the Fan*, published early in the seventeenth century, showing the discomforts of a summer without fans and the delight of a social occasion with them (figs. 177a and b). It must be admitted, however, that those depicted are very plain fans.

Sumptuary laws had a moral as well as an economic dimension. Theatrical performances and masquerades were incorporated into general sumptuary legislation for the first time in 1512. All such spectacles, whether public or private, whether tragedy or comedy or eclogue, were now to be banned as threats to public morals and incitements of the corruption of youth. Dancing was also targeted, with a certain *ballo del capello*, or "dance of the hat," strictly prohibited "and some other French dances full of lascivious and damnable gestures."[79]

And what was so threatening about the "dance of the hat"? According to a mid-sixteenth-century source, it went as follows. A woman would rise from her chair and invite a man to dance with her. As a sign that he agreed, he lifted his hat and put it on her head. She then lifted it from her head and kissed it and put it back on his, and then took it back and put it on hers again. Thus began the dance. The point of the dance was for the lady to outlast her male partner, and when he sat down to catch his breath, whether sincere or not, she continued to dance alone, amid applause, searching for another partner. Her demeanor was artfully flirtatious, her movements seductive. Pretending to choose one, she would then turn away and choose another. Often she stopped in front of a gentleman who was not paying attention and thinking of something else altogether. But plucking his cap from his head, she pulled him up firmly to dance, to the amusement of all. It is not surprising that moralists found the dance disturbing, for the control of the cap signified women's power to do what they pleased with their uncapped lovers and husbands.[80]

But Venetians continued to dance as a form of recreation, as is made evident in woodcuts from the later sixteenth century (fig. 178). Dancers aimed at dignified, graceful movements, and dancing then, as now, could be a form of art. As one sixteenth-century writer noted, rather churlishly, "recreation is made for beautiful women and beautiful women for recreation; for the ugly there is needlework and the rosary."[81] And despite all legislative attempts to control their leisure-time activities, Venetians continued to spend in a conspicuous manner. As one observer put it, "a Venetian law lasts but a week."[82] Inevitably, the laws were recast to follow practice.

By 1526, the permissible guest list for wedding feasts had expanded to six small suppers of twenty guests apiece to be given by the ring sponsors, two large meals by the families, "one of which may not exceed five hundred guests and the other eighty, including men, women, and close relatives," and two additional meals hosted by the groom of fifty and eighty guests each. A quick addition yields a possible 830 guests distributed among ten events. But coupled with this generous allotment for hospitality were the same old restrictions on the cuisine: no partridge, no pheasant, no peacocks, no francolins, no baby doves, and no more than three dishes, and these were not to be gilded.

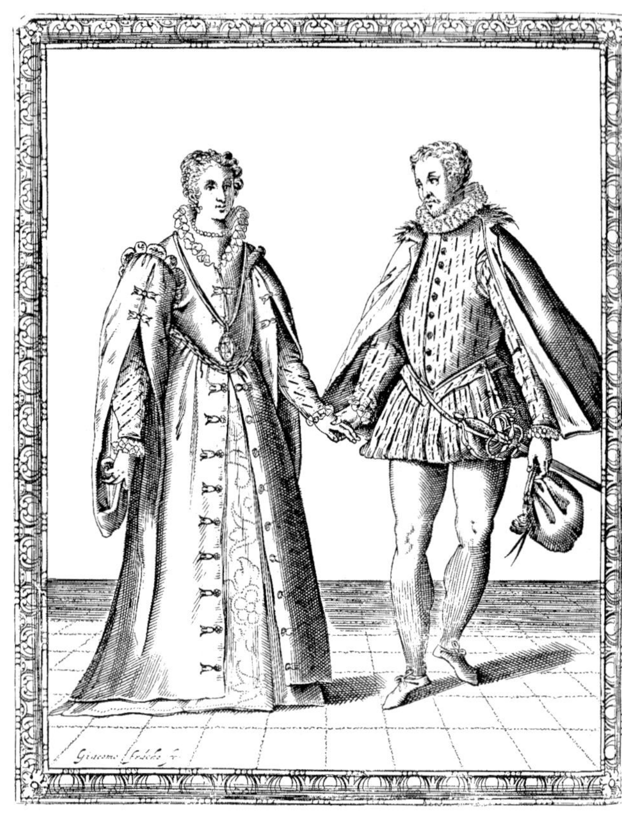

178 *Lady and gentleman dancing a pavaniglia.* Woodcut from Fabrizio Caroso da Sermoneta, *Della nobiltà di dame, nel quale s'insegnano varie sorti di Ballette, Cascarde, Tordiglione, Passo e Mezzo, Pavaniglia, Canario, & Gagliarde all uso d'Italia, Francia & Spagna* (Venice, 1600), 102. Height 25 cm. The dance is dedicated to the Dogaressa Morosina Morosini Grimani. By permission of the Folger Shakespeare Library.

As for dessert, no "large confections of pine-nut cakes, pistachios, round filled pastries, sweets of sugar and rosewater, confections, and sweet gums . . . molded meringues, sugared fruit, or any other type of large confection that one may make or imagine" were allowed. That each of these delicacies was lovingly listed with its own name suggests that they had been, and remained, standard fare on Venetian banquet tables. And an additional injunction by the Magistrato alle Pompe suggests that compliance was not enthusiastic: "And truly, those who would act so dishonorably as to throw bread or oranges at our employees, or push them or kick them out, will fall subject to a penalty of 50 ducats."[83]

The history of Venetian sumptuary law is a history of failure. Was such legislation merely an empty gesture, passed by a Senate wishing to make a point but knowing that it was doomed to fail? In Venice, for all the rhetoric on economics or morality, the bottom line was political. A proclamation of 1560 makes this clear: "We must in every respect give much consideration and use much study in conserving the equality between our nobles and citizens and in prohibiting those things that could give rise to any bad effect."[84]

And there were occasions that were another matter altogether, when the laws were suspended and ladies were not just allowed, but ordered, to wear their most sumptuous dresses and the costly pearl necklaces and other jewelry that were ordinarily forbidden by law: state receptions in the Ducal Palace and, in particular, the entertainment of a foreign dignitary in private homes. Perhaps the most spectacular such visit in the sixteenth century came in 1574, when Henry III, King of France, passed through Venice. After being greeted at the Lido, he was taken into the city on the Bucintoro, the Doge's triumphal barge, to temporary lodgings in Ca' Foscari, one of the city's most famous palaces (see fig. 25).

The facade was festooned with draperies, coats of arms, and banners, and the vestibule hung with tapestries and a temporary ceiling of star-studded blue cloth. Three chambers on the first *piano nobile* were specially furnished in a sumptuous manner and reserved for the king's use – and this for a stay of just seven nights. The rooms featured walls covered with gilded stamped leather and draperies of gold and crimson silk; marble mantlepieces; gilded beds with canopies of cloth of gold; hangings of sky-blue satin embroidered with fleur-de-lys and of gold-embroidered green brocade; tables of alabaster and of black marble; and a floor paved with mosaic work from designs by Veronese.[85] The apartments had a presence that was public as well as private. Before the arrival of the king, visitors were allowed into the palace to view the rooms, which were guarded by one hundred halberdiers. This was an extraordinary privilege and suggests the status of these decorated rooms as works of art.[86]

Where did these furnishings come from on such short notice? They might have been rented. Luxury goods were frequently hired from second-hand dealers for special occasions. Sanudo reported on the Holy League procession in 1511, when tapestries and wall hangings were rented from a Master Stefano to cover the entire Ducal Palace facade facing the Piazzetta. The merchant claimed that he had enough stock to furnish the entire palace, as he already had done for a similar occasion in 1495.[87]

There is no record of what happened to the special decorations at Ca' Foscari after Henry III's departure. And in any case, he seems to have spent little time at home. His apartments were equipped with a secret staircase for unofficial exits and entries, and his visit included such entertainments as regattas, banquets, fireworks displays, and an overnight stay with the famous courtesan Veronica Franco, where he presumably enjoyed a different sort of hospitality.[88]

"A Very Frugall Table"

But how does one account, then, for reports by visitors to the city who were not impressed with the graciousness of the Venetian household? After his visit to a childbirth celebration in a Venetian palace in 1495, Canon Pietro Casola observed: "After staying a good while and contemplating the room and the persons in it, every man departed fasting . . . I think the Venetians consider that the refreshment of the eyes is enough; and I like the idea, because the refections offered at Milan on such occasions are a great expense, and those at Venice cost nothing."[89] The Englishman William Thomas traveled through Venice in 1549 and spoke of the typical patrician as "proud, disdainful, covetous, a great niggard . . . spare of living, tyrant to his tenant, finally never satisfied with hoarding up of money. . . . He will go to the market himself and spend so miserably that many a mean man shall fare better than he. Of his 10,000 ducats a year, if he spend three or four hundred in his house he esteemeth it a wonderful charge."[90] As noted earlier, such observations were repeated a half-century later by Thomas Coryat, who would complain that the Venetian aristocracy "keepe no honourable hospitality, nor gallant retinue of servants about them, but a very frugall table, though they inhabit the most beautiful Palaces."[91]

In fact, the anomaly is more apparent than real, a point grasped by Coryat's countryman Sir Henry Wotton. He observed that Italians often put their kitchen and pantry in the basement (equivalent to the ground floor in Venice), "which besides the benefit of removing such Annoyes out of sight, and the gayning of so much more roome above doth also by elevation of the Fronte, adde Maiestie to the whole Aspect . . . yet by the naturall Hospitalitie of England, the Buttrie must be more visible, and wee neede perchance for our Raunges, a more spacious and luminous kitchen."[92] To the English observers, hospitality meant food and fine wine; to Venetians – although their kitchens were on the main living floors or on the mezzanines – it meant display.

Indeed, what is striking about Venetian feast scenes is the lack of emphasis on food. Looking once again at Veronese's *Marriage Feast at Cana*, costume overshadows comestibles

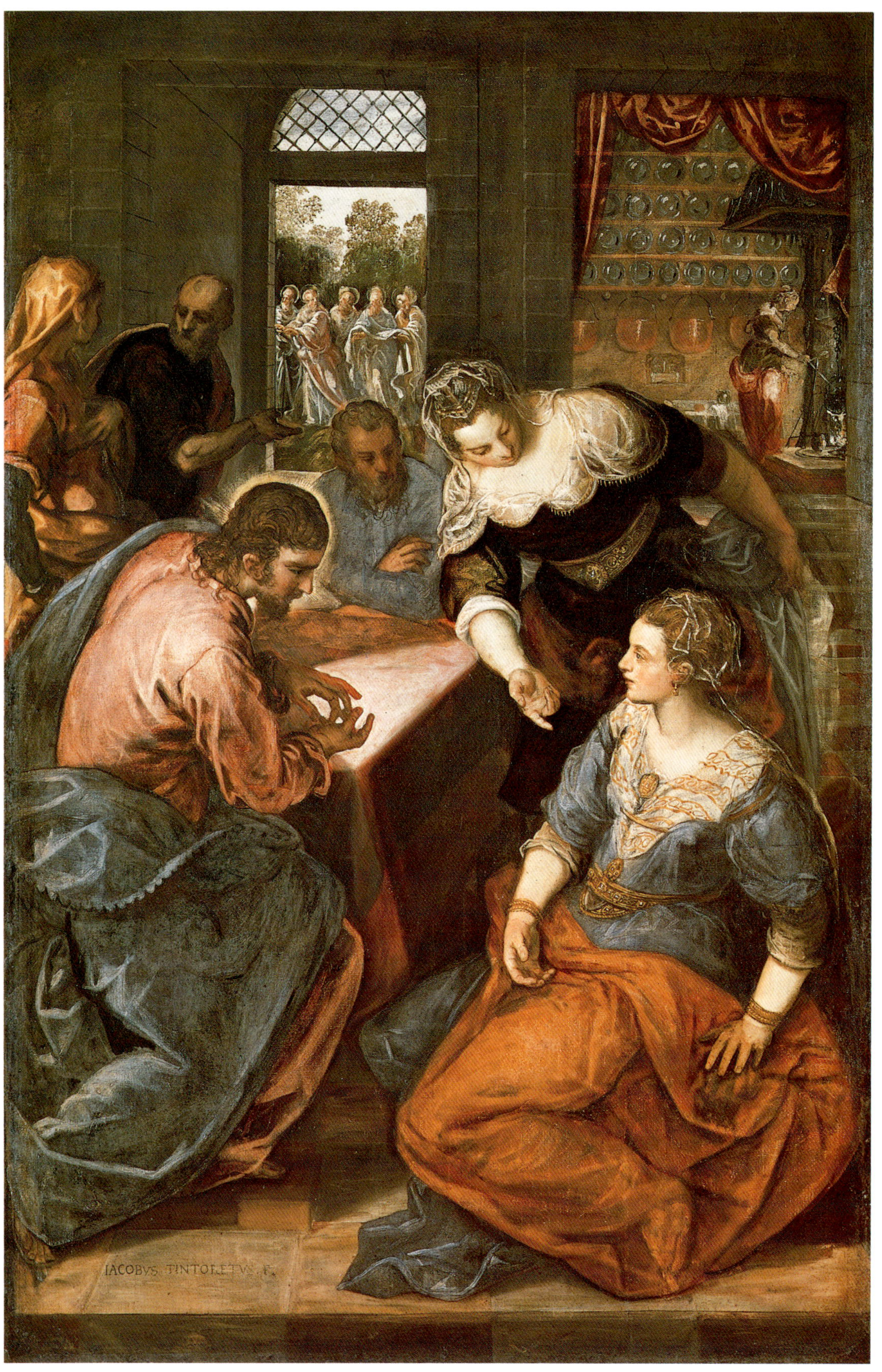
IACOBVS TINTORETVS F.

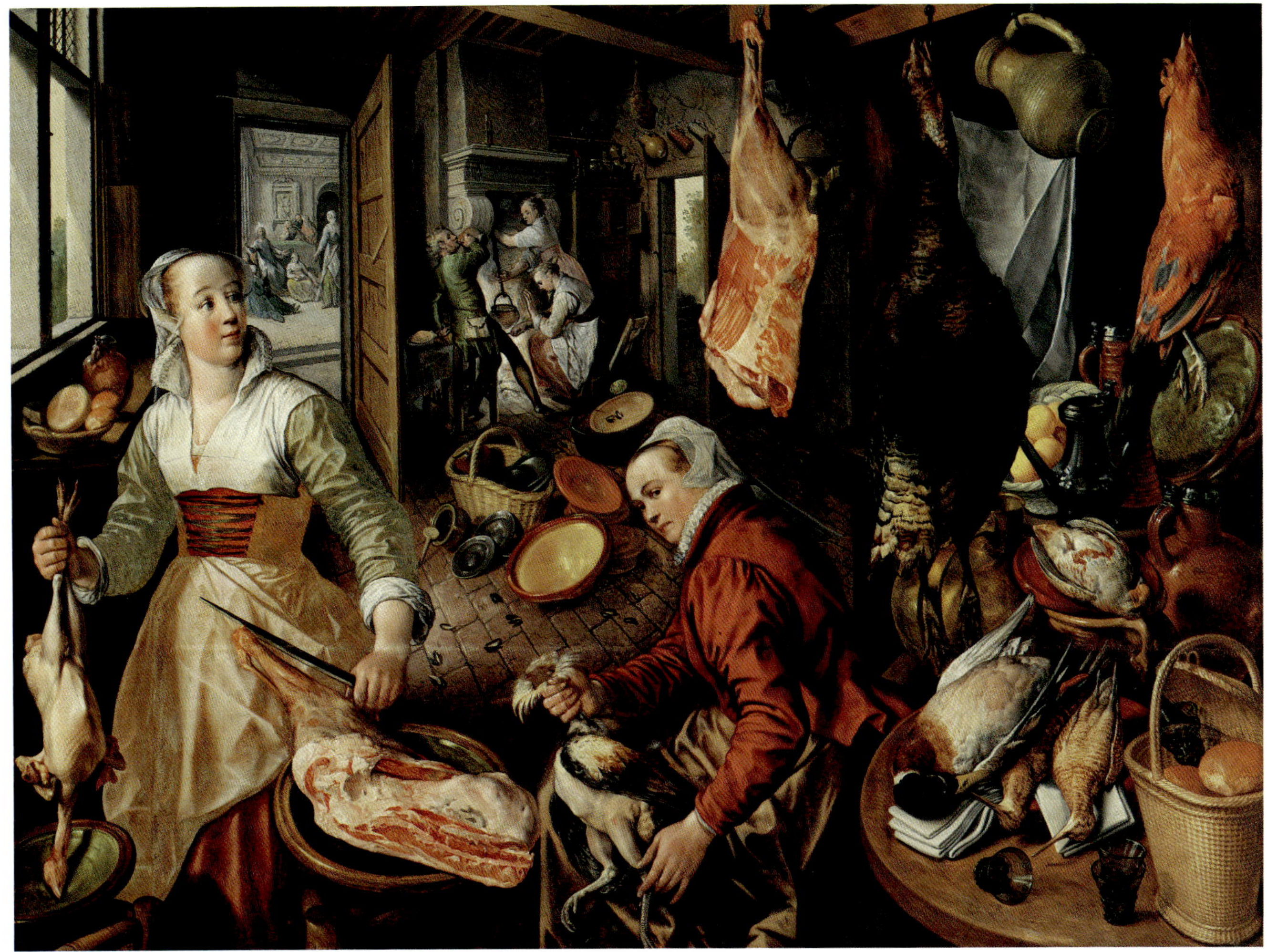

180 (*above*) Joachim Beuckelaer, *Christ in the House of Martha and Mary*, 1570. Oil on canvas, 157.5 × 215.5 cm. In this painting, the biblical episode is embedded in a scene that also symbolizes Fire in a set of four paintings representing the elements. Christ sits in the background in a room behind the kitchen. London, National Gallery.

179 (*facing page*) Jacopo Tintoretto, *Christ in the House of Martha and Mary*, 1567. Oil on canvas, 197.5 × 131 cm. In an episode recounted in Luke 10:38–42, Christ was welcomed into the house of two sisters, Mary and Martha. Busying herself in preparing the meal, Martha complained that her sister Mary was sitting idly by, simply listening to Christ's words. He responded: "Martha, Martha, you worry and fret about so many things, and yet few are needed, indeed only one. It is Mary who has chosen the better part, and it is not to be taken from her." Munich, Alte Pinakothek.

(fig. 181). If there is a focus other than Christ it is the musical performance and a conspicuous display of the material goods for which Venetian homes were famous: glassware, silver, pewter, fine textiles. A comparison between two canvases of *Christ in the House of Martha and Mary* painted in the same period tells all (figs. 179 and 180). For the Dutch artist Joachim Beuckelaer, the topic of the day is food. For the Venetian Jacopo Tintoretto, it is fashion: the kitchen itself is defined in terms of pewter and copperware and not an abundant table.

Coryat was also surprised to see the man of the house doing the shopping:

> I have observed a thing amongst the Venetians, that I have not a little wondred at, that their Gentlemen and greatest Senators, a man worth perhaps two millions of duckats, will come into the market, and buy their flesh, fish, fruits, and such other things as are necessary for the maintenance of their family: a token indeed of frugality,

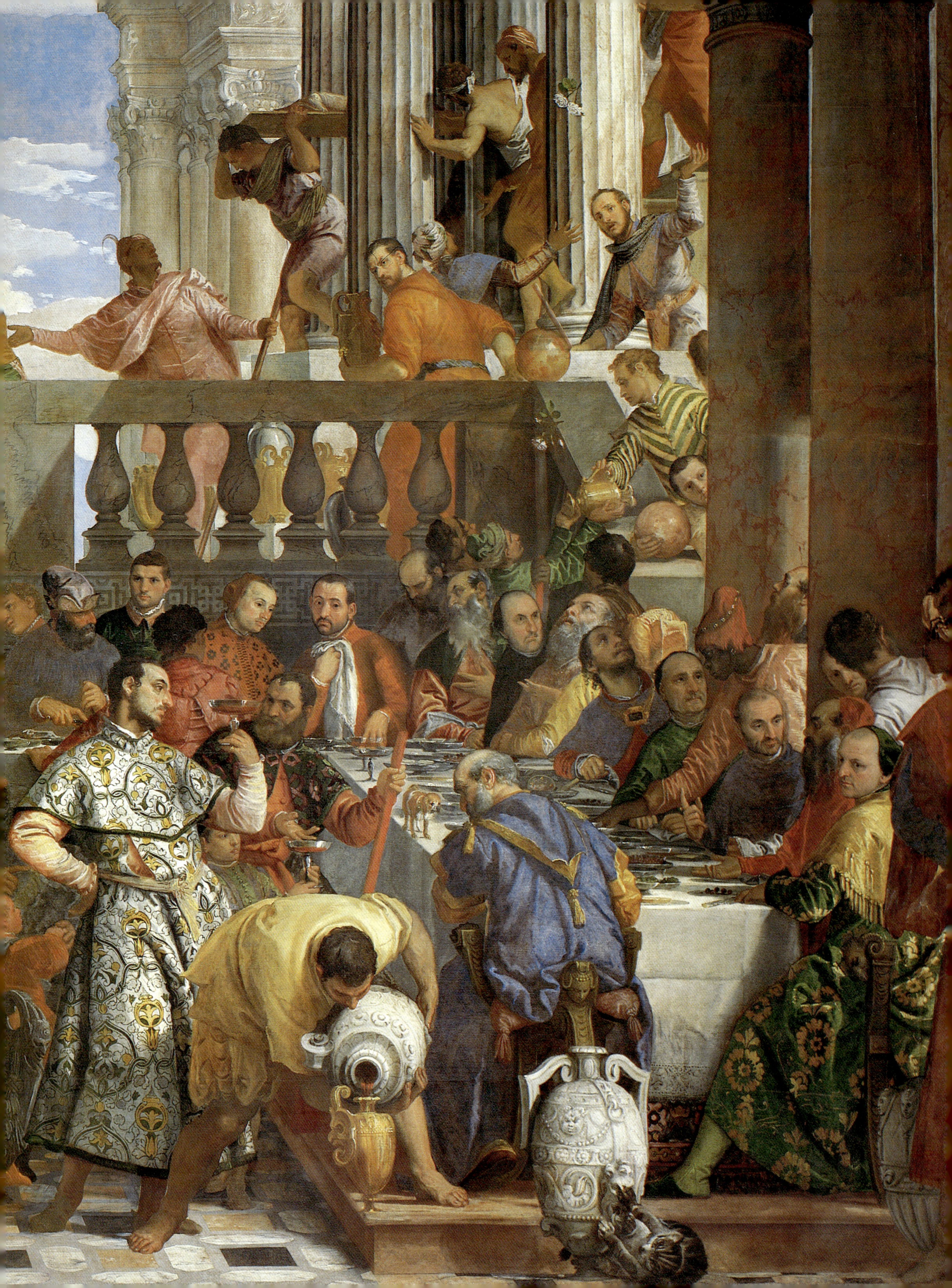

> which is commendable in all men; but me thinkes it is not an argument of true generosity, that a noble spirit should deject it selfe to these petty and base matters, that are fitter to be done by servants then [sic] men of a generose parentage.[93]

To present-day readers, it may not be the frugality that is surprising, nor the observation that servants did not do the grocery shopping, but the admirable fact that such "petty and base matters" were the concern of husbands and not wives. And why is this so? Venetian custom was grounded in two complementary truths: on the one hand, Venetian nobles had long been merchants in fact if not in name, and prided themselves on being good judges of the quality of merchandise, whether foodstuffs or luxury goods; on the other hand, noble women were part of the luxury goods kept out of the public eye except on special occasions. To use a phrase of Montesquieu's, women became "*objets de luxe*."[94] Those occasions when expense was no object and respectable women were on display outside the palace were the very times that the model of "the very frugall table" did not apply. These were events in which private and public interests were as one. Sumptuary laws were suspended not only when notable strangers arrived in town and women were commanded to wear their jewels and finest gowns, but also at the time of a wedding when the young bride left her parent's house and displayed herself in public space. If Coryat and other foreigners had been privy to this type of entertainment, their views of Venetian hospitality might have been quite different. Strictly speaking, a wedding was a family affair; but an extravagant wedding (or for that matter a princely reception) was, in Sanudo's words, "to the city's honor."[95]

181 (*facing page*) Paolo Veronese, *Marriage Feast at Cana* (detail), 1562–63. Oil on canvas, whole work 677 × 994 cm. Paris, Musée du Louvre.

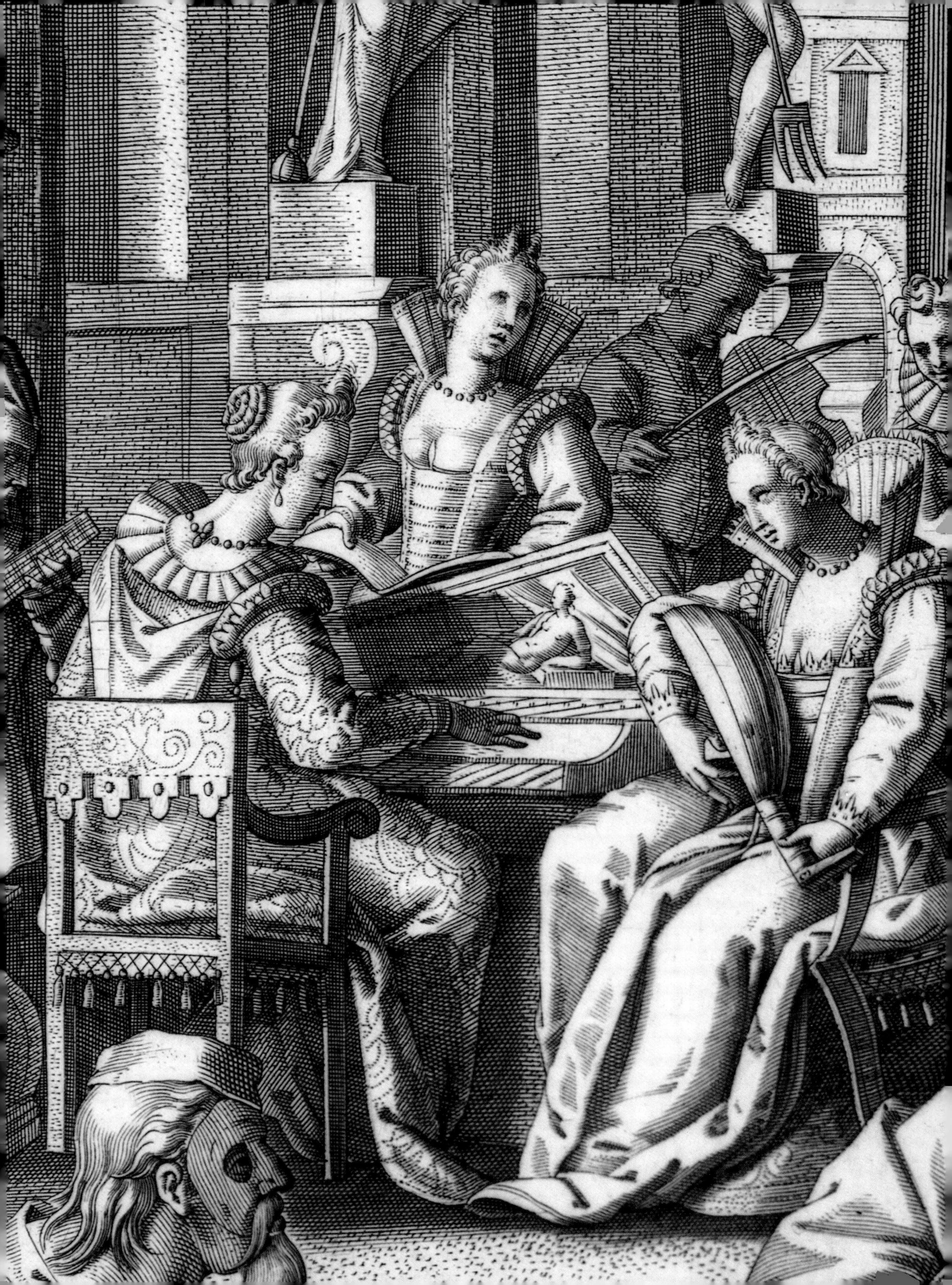

6

A Paradise of Venus

THE PREVIOUS TWO CHAPTERS HAVE touched upon the domestic space of the Venetian wife and the hospitality of the Venetian husband. Now we turn to women and entertainment of another sort: the household arrangements of the Venetian courtesan. The frontispiece of *Coryat's Crudities*, the travel account with which this book began, may serve to introduce the topic (fig. 182; cf. fig. 1).[1]

The capital letters accompanying the little vignettes are keyed to explanatory couplets in the pages that follow, most of which were written by no less than the playwright Ben Jonson. At issue are two images in the lower right-hand corner, marked E and F, which show Thomas Coryat fleeing in a Venetian gondola as a lady leans out a window and pelts him with eggs. Turning to the couplets there is an "explication" cast in elliptical terms. The first couplet applies to the letter E:

> Here to his Land-Friggat hee's ferried by Charon, He bords her, a service a hot and rare one. Or, Here to a Tutch-hole hee's row'd by his Gondelier, That fires his Linstocke, and empties his Bandolier.

In case the reader does not get the point, a gloss is provided in the margin: "That is, the beauty of her countenance, and sweet smatches of her lips did enflame his tongue with a divine & fierye enthusiasme, & emptyed the Bandolier of his conceipts & inventions for that time."[2]

The couplet for the letter F reads:

> Here his Friggat shootes egs at him empty of Chickens,
> Because shee had made his purse empty of Chiquins, or
> Here shee pelts him with egges, he saith, of Rose-water;
> But trust him not Reader, t'was some other matter.

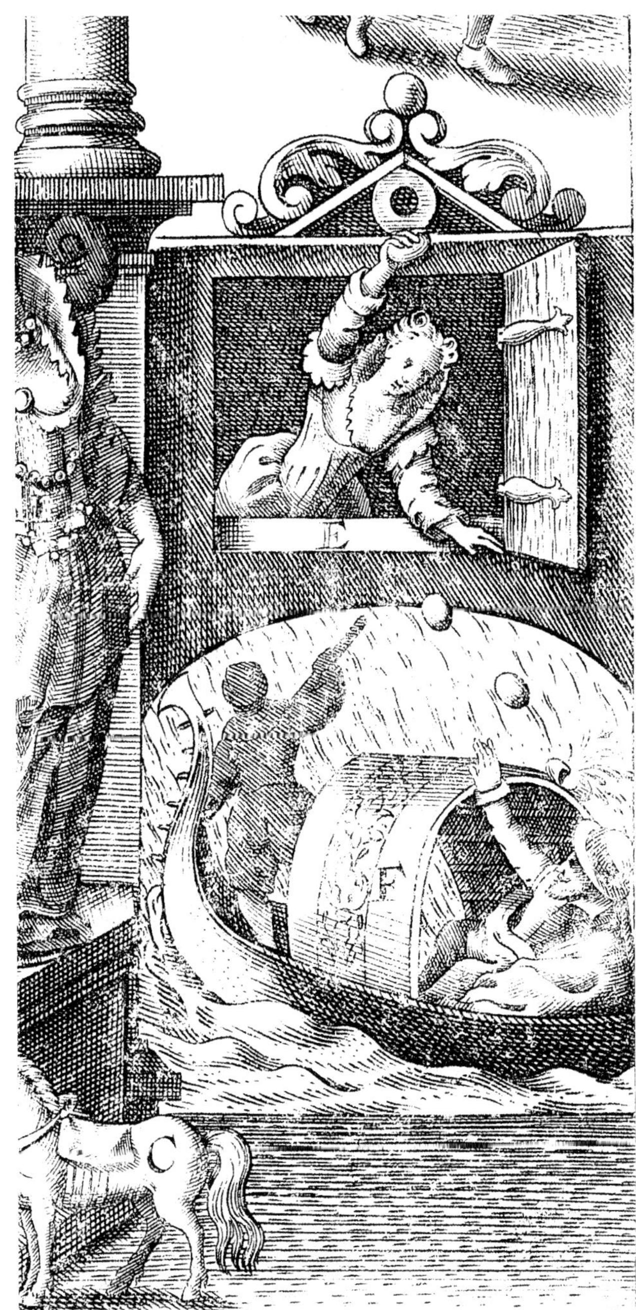

182 (*right*) Detail of the frontispiece from Thomas Coryat, *Coryat's Crudities: hastily gobled up in five moneths travels* (London: W. S[tansby], 1611). By permission of the Folger Shakespeare Library.

facing page Pieter de Jode the Elder, after Pozzoserrato , *A Venetian Carnival Scene on a Terrace* ca. 1595 or 1598 (detail of fig. 208).

But Ben Jonson is not finished yet, for over the pages a second set of verses amplifies the couplets. Under E it declares:

> A Punke here pelts him with egs. How so? For he did but kisse her, and so let her go.

And for F we learn:

> Religiously here, he bids, row from the stewes, he will expiate this sinne with converting the Jewes.[3]

Now who was this punke and what were the stews? The punke was a courtesan – one of the more renowned protagonists of sixteenth-century Venetian life. As to the stews, the *Oxford English Dictionary* states that they were "public rooms used for hot baths [and] often used for immoral purposes."[4] And turning back to Coryat's lady, what might we see if we were able to look through that window into the room beyond?

Indeed, one of the few descriptions of domestic space to be found in Coryat's account of Venice concerns the palace of a courtesan. Praising the courtesans' "infinite allurements," he adds that

> such is the variety of the delicious objects they minister to their lovers, that they want nothing tending to delight. For when you come into wone of their Palaces (as indeed some few of the principallest of them live in very magnificent and portly buildings fit for the entertainement of a great Prince) you seeme to enter into the Paradise of Venus. For their fairest roomes are most glorious and glittering to behold. . . .I have here inserted a picture of one of their nobler Cortezans, according to her Venetian habites, with my owne neare unto her, made in that forme as we saluted each other [fig. 183].

In the print, the beautiful Margarita Emiliana receives Coryat in what was probably the *portego* – the reception hall – shown devoid of furnishings. But Coryat observed "the walles round about being adorned with most sumptuous tapistry and gilt leather [. . . and also] the picture of the noble Cortezan most exquisitely drawen."[5]

The lady was dressed in a damask gown trimmed with a deep gold fringe, fragrantly perfumed, and "decked with many chaines of gold and orient pearle like a second Cleopatra." But Coryat cautions: "Though these things will at the first sight seeme unto thee most delectable allurements . . . shee will endevour to enchaunt thee partly with her melodious notes that she warbles out upon her lute, which shee fingers with as laudable a stroake as many men that are excellent professors in the noble science of Musicke; and partly with that heart-tempting harmony of her voice." He adds that she was also "a good Rhetorician, and a most elegant discourser, so that if she cannot move thee with all these foresaid delights, shee will assay thy constancy with her Rhetoricall tongue."[6]

Moreover, he continues: "And to the end shee may minister unto thee the stronger temptations to come to her lure, shee will shew thee her chamber of recreation, where thou shalt see all manner of pleasing objects, as many faire painted coffers wherewith it is garnished round about, a curious milke-white canopy of needle worke, a silke quilt embrodered with gold; and generally all her bedding sweetly perfumed." Amongst these "amiable ornaments," most surprising to Coryat was "a picture of our Lady by her bedde side, with Christ in her armes, placed within a cristall glasse."[7]

183 Thomas Coryat greeted by the courtesan Margarita Emiliana. Engraving from Coryat, *Coryat's Crudities*, 1611. By permission of the Folger Shakespeare Library.

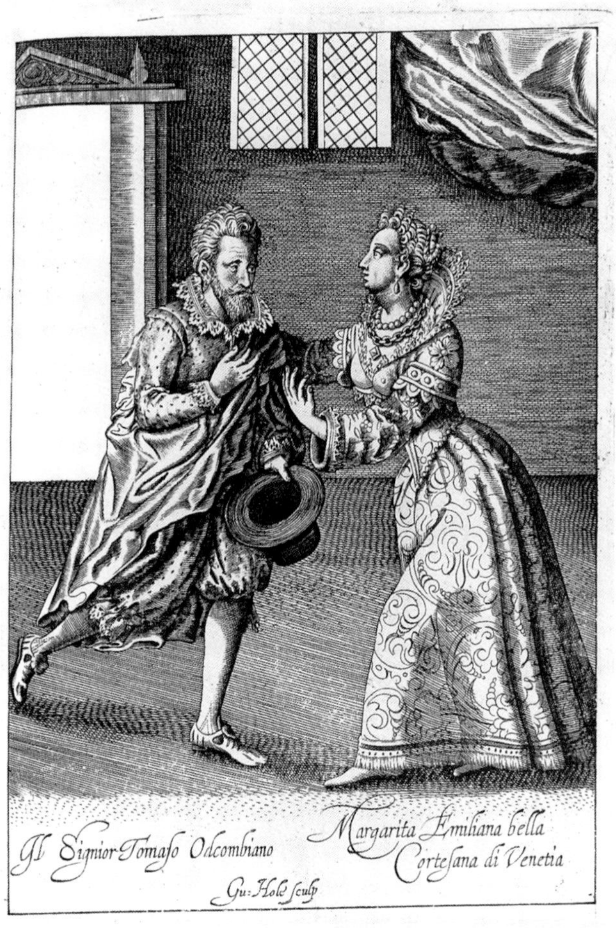

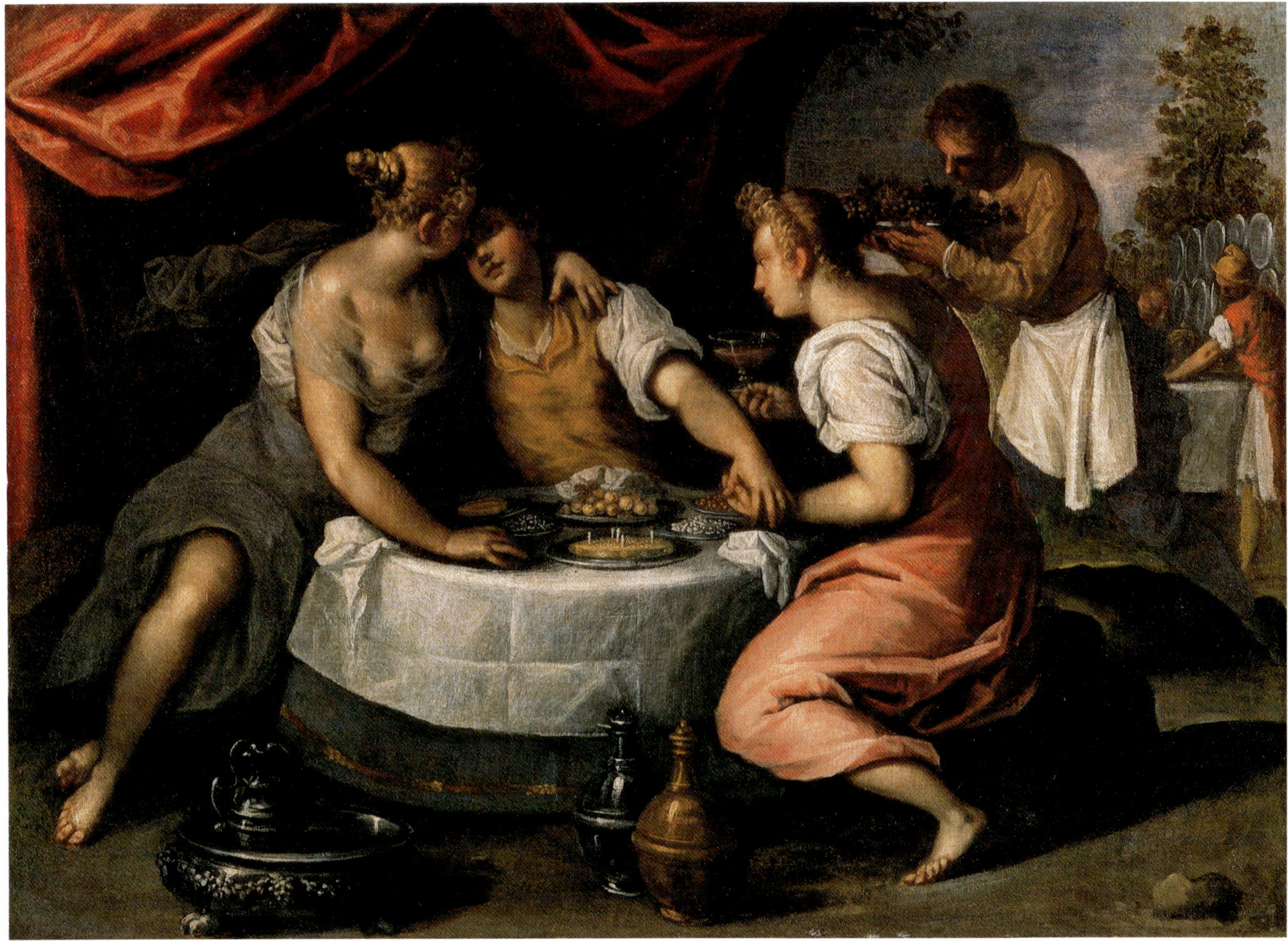

184 Jacopo Palma Giovane, *The Revels of the Prodigal Son*, ca. 1600. Oil on canvas, 83 × 118 cm. Venice, Accademia, cat. n. 634.

One Sort of Merchandise

According to Coryat, prostitution was one of the most profitable business enterprises in Venice, ministering to a clientele that was not just local but also foreign like himself. He estimated that the city, with a population of around 150,000, housed at least 20,000 courtesans, "whereof many are esteemed so loose, that they are said to open their quivers to every arrow."[8] He asked a Venetian how a Christian city could tolerate such a vice and was told that there were two rationales, one moral and the other economic: first, to avoid the greater danger that their own wives might otherwise be seduced or assaulted; and second, to profit from the taxes paid by courtesans, which were reputed to be enough to maintain a dozen galleys. Coryat's estimate was probably a little ambitious. And it failed to distinguish between bordello prostitutes, such as the harlots in Jacopo Palma Giovane's painting of the Prodigal Son, who were indeed available to all, and the fetching creature depicted in a print by Giacomo Franco – the courtesan who lived in her own home and chose her own lovers (figs. 184 and 185). The generic term for all such women was *meretrice* – a word with an ancient pedigree dating back to the Latin *meretrix*. The English word meretricious says it all.

Up to around the middle of the fifteenth century, most of the *meretrici* were comparable to Palma's tavern wenches. The state recognized that they were a necessary evil and attempted to confine them to certain neighborhoods in the Rialto area. Two houses were officially tolerated: the Castelletto, a state-run brothel in the parish of San Matteo di Rialto that opened in 1360 to control and protect prostitutes; and the Carampane, a private operation in the adjacent parish of San Cassiano that came under state scrutiny in 1421. Both institutions seem to have been organized in a similar manner with curfews, armed guards, and matrons who oversaw a common strongbox and distributed

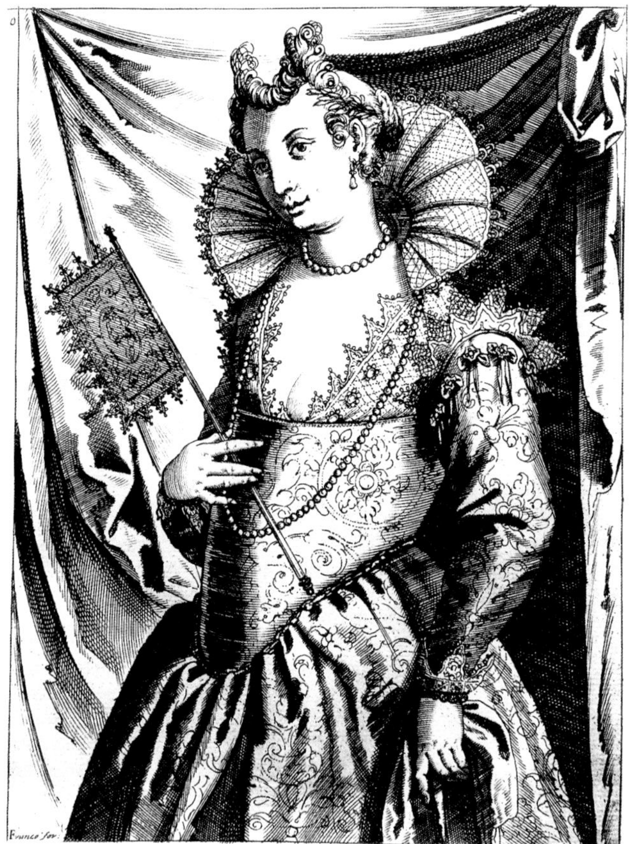

185 Giacomo Franco, *Courtesan*. Engraving from his *Habiti delle donne venetiane intagliate in rame nuovamente da Giacomo Franco*. Venice, Museo Correr.

monies received to the women. But it was impossible to keep prostitutes from settling elsewhere, and there were troublesome concentrations in two other zones: around San Marco, where there were a large number of hospices and taverns, and in the parish of San Samuele, where the Council of Ten ordered owners of the houses where the *meretrici* lived to wall up the doors and windows that fronted the main street between the Grand Canal and Campo San Stefano.[9]

In 1490 prostitutes were banned from the taverns near the bread and fruit markets, the law specifically naming the Osteria of the Capello, the shop sign of which is clearly visible in Gentile Bellini's *Procession in Piazza San Marco* of 1496 (fig. 187). The exotic array of ladies who fill the windows behind it suggests that the law, like most of those attempting to regulate public morals, was less than successful. But by that time, prostitution was diffused throughout the city. The poet Andrea Michieli, known as Strazzola, described the experience of his friend Alvise Contarini, who had been away from the city for a long time and returned to find many *landre* (prostitutes) calling to him from every corner:

> Venice seems to me to have been made a bordello,
> since I can not turn to any side
> without being called with voice or spit
> by some *landra* behind a little balcony [fig. 186]
> And one promises me her "ring,"
> the other a supply of muscat wine,
> in such a way that I find myself so befuddled.
> That I do not know where to spend my *marcello*.[10]

Three significant developments had taken place toward the end of the fifteenth century. First, a number of *meretrici* began to leave the brothels and to receive their clien-

186 *Prostitute Soliciting Two Gentlemen*, Venice, 1575. MS. 457, "Mores Italiae," fol. 72. This manuscript of 105 watercolor drawings of Italian costumes and scenes of daily life seems to have been compiled in Venice in 1575 for an unidentified member of the French De la Houssaye de la Morandais family as a memento of a trip to Italy. New Haven, Yale University, Beinecke Rare Book and Manuscript Library.

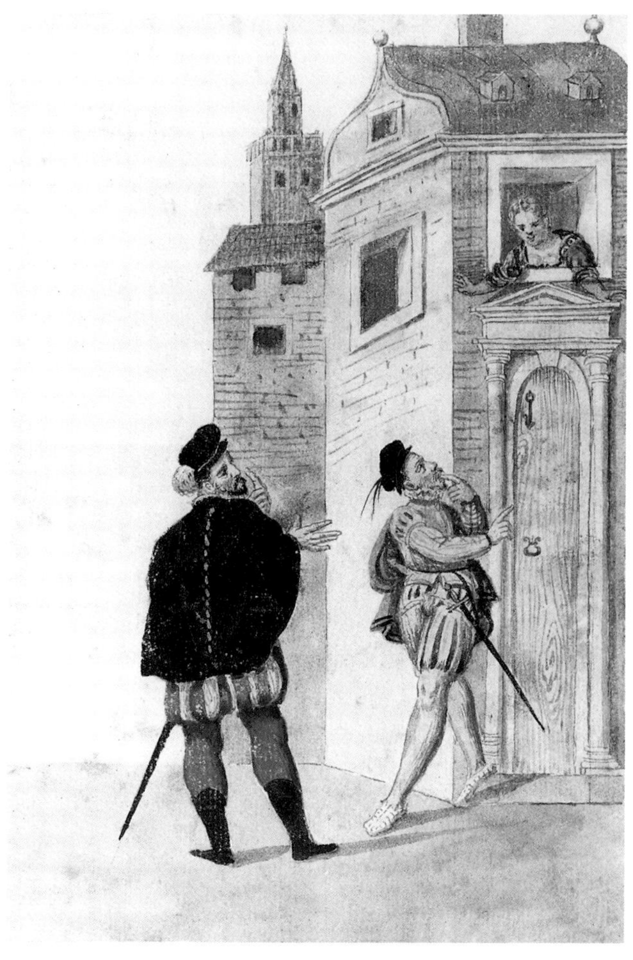

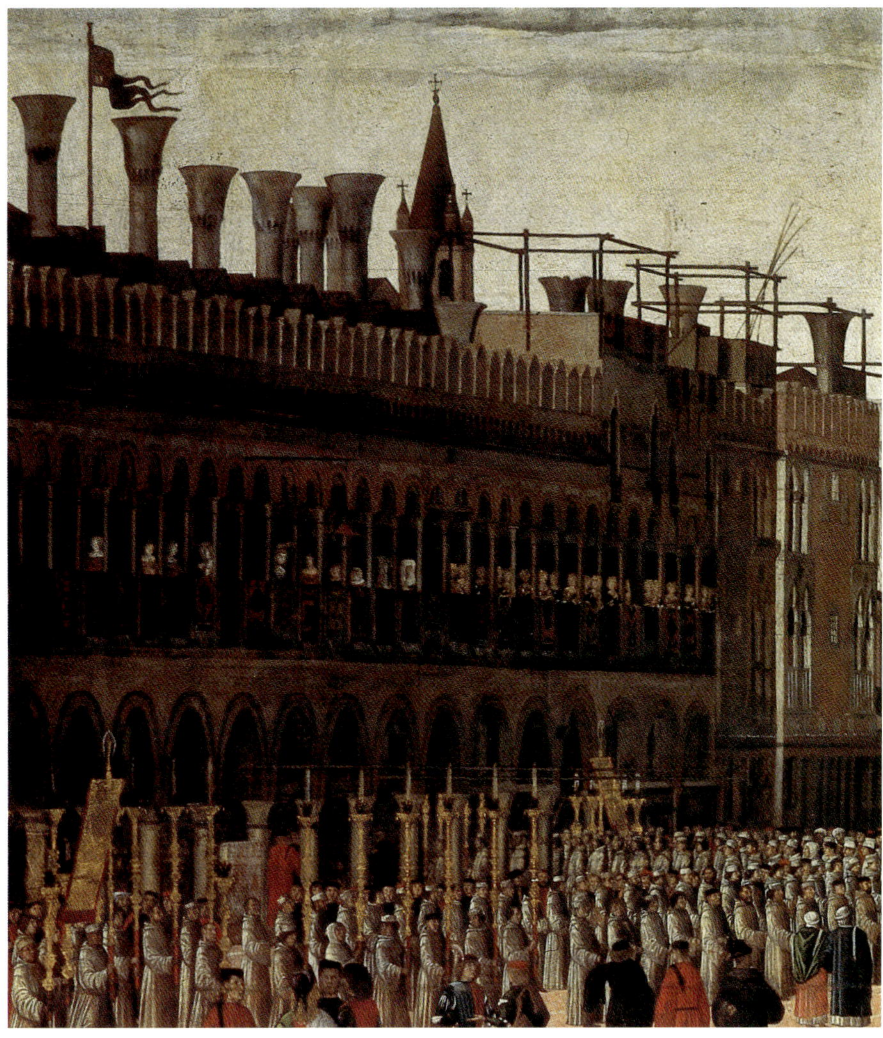

187 Gentile Bellini, *Procession in Piazza San Marco*, 1496 (detail of left side). Oil on canvas, whole work 367 × 745 mm. Venice, Accademia.

tele in their own homes. Second, a new hierarchy developed with the emergence of the courtesan, who was neither a common harlot nor a respectable woman; she was, strictly speaking, a prostitute, but one who enjoyed a special status because of exceptional beauty, charm, refinement, intellect, talent, or relationships with prominent men. And third, patrician males who once mingled with men of lower social ranks in the bordello or the tavern now socialized more often in the private homes of courtesans.[11]

An incident recorded by the diarist Marin Sanudo in 1500 is emblematic of the times. He wrote of a fight that involved six men, all from distinguished patrician families. One evening after dinner three young nobles had gone to the home of a certain lady called Anzola Chaga. She was already entertaining three others. A scuffle ensued and one of the intruders, named Zuan Moro, had his face slashed. Sanudo observes, "and so his face was marred, and much was spoken of it." He adds wryly: "All of them have very beautiful women for wives."[12] Fourteen years later, the name of Anzola Chaga appears again in Sanudo's diaries. Describing her now as an "honored and renowned *meretrice*," he reports that she has died and been buried in the church of the Frari.[13] A month later he records the death of a lady of similar reputation: "This morning Lucia Trivixan, who was an excellent singer, was buried at Santa Caterina. She was the consummate *cortigiana* of her day and was held in much esteem by musicians; all the virtuosi met at her house. She died last night and eight days from today, at Santa Caterina, the musicians will have a solemn funeral Mass and other offices said for her soul."[14] Note the use of the word *cortigiana* – one of its first appearances in the primary

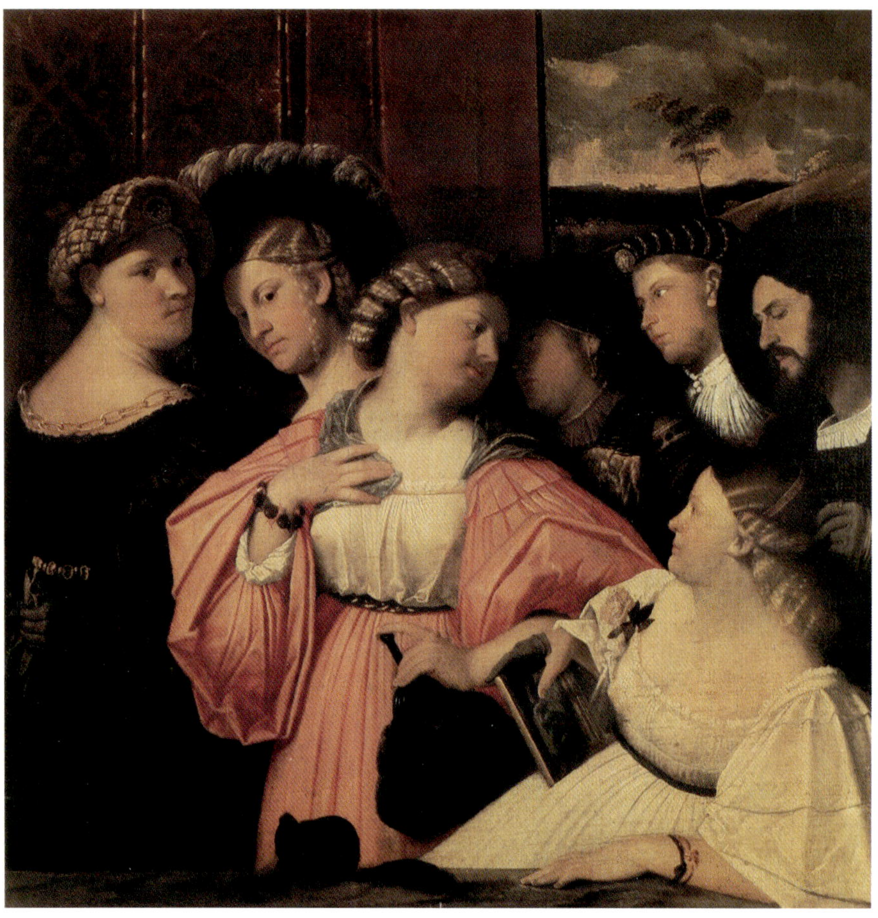

188 Giovanni Cariani, *Four Courtesans and Three Gentlemen*, 1519. Oil on canvas, 117 × 177 cm. Bergamo, private collection.

sources. Such women might live alone or with several others in what were sometimes called "scolete de donne" – little schools of ladies.[15]

A painting of four ladies and three gentlemen by Giovanni Cariani was once held to be a portrait of a noble family, but it is almost certainly something else (fig. 188). While the women may well be sisters, it is most unlikely that the exotically dressed men behind them are their brothers. The format is familiar from portraits, with the figures held inside a spatial envelope formed by a ledge in the foreground and a background of rich red cut-velvet draperies on one side and a window opening on to a deep landscape on the other. But the attitudes and gestures are not familial and not as casual as they appear at first glance. Consider the bearded man at the right who caresses the hair of the young blonde woman in front of him with his gloved hand. Consider the same woman's right hand. It grasps a mirror, which reflects not only her low-cut bodice but also her naked thumb, from which the glove has just been removed. And consider the woman on the left who holds her gloved hand behind her, grasping its mate. The mirror is a sign of vanity, often associated with courtesans; the squirrel on the ledge in the foreground a symbol of greed and lasciviousness; the plumed fan a sign of sensuality. The glances reveal a chain of relationships. The woman in the center observes the caress. The woman on the right – the object of the caress – looks back at her unaware. The men's attention is all on the women. But the two women on the left ignore them, and are more interested in the viewer. Taken together the work adds up to a subtle erotic metaphor of nudity and concealment, of seduction and restraint.[16]

In a portrait by Palma Vecchio, the sitter has been nicknamed Violante by modern scholars, because of the two violets tucked into her bodice (fig. 189). The flowers are symbols of pleasure – the word deflower sums up their meaning – and they, like the lady, may be available to the viewer. Indeed, there is a direct appeal here to the sense of

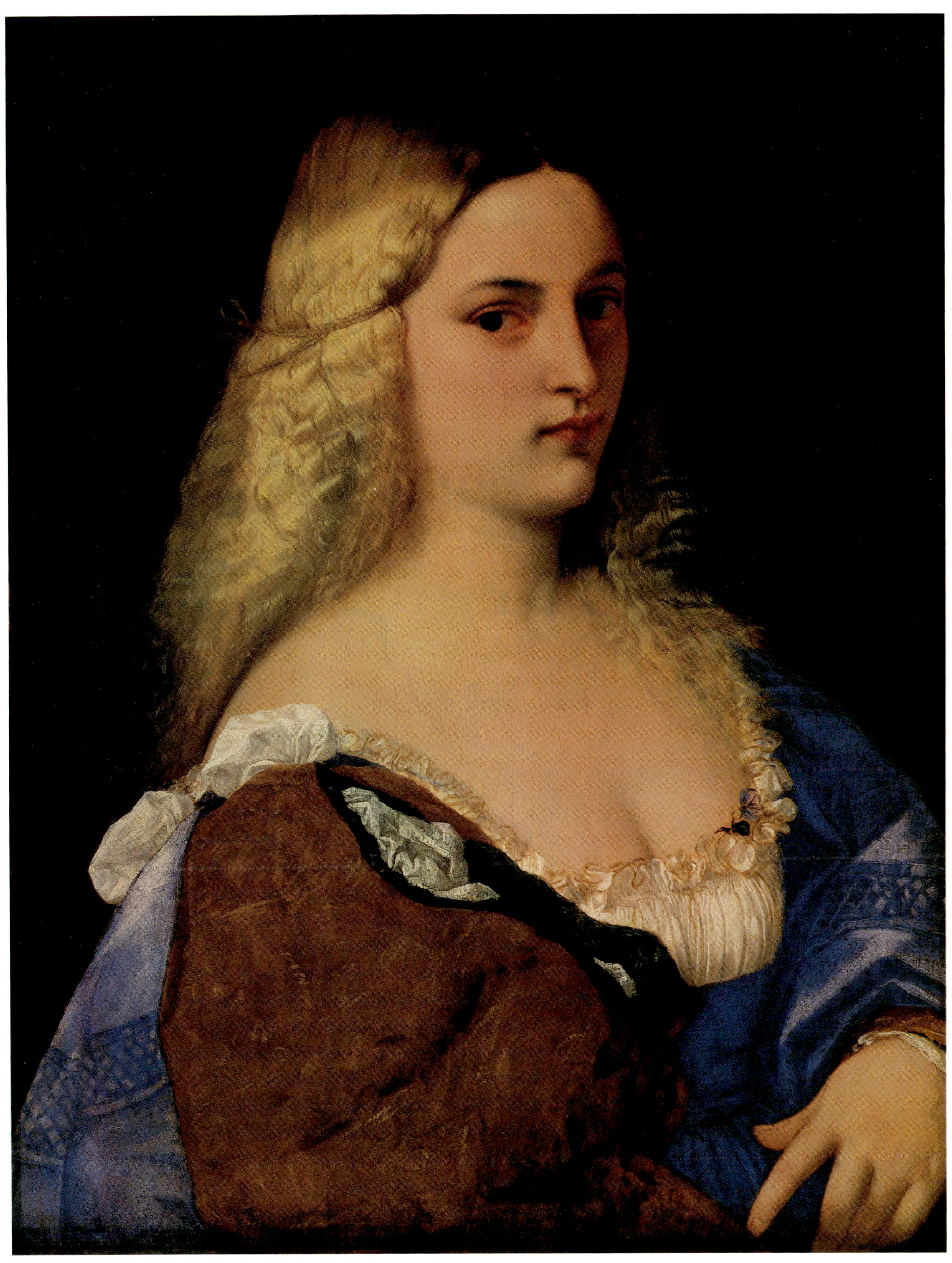

189 Palma Vecchio, *Portrait of a Woman, called "Violante,"* ca. 1515. Oil on panel, 64.5 × 50.8 cm. The painting has also been attributed to Titian. In an inventory of the paintings owned by Bartolomeo della Nave (before 1637), the painting was described as "A picture of a woman called the faire Catt a rare piece." Vienna, Kunsthistorisches Museum.

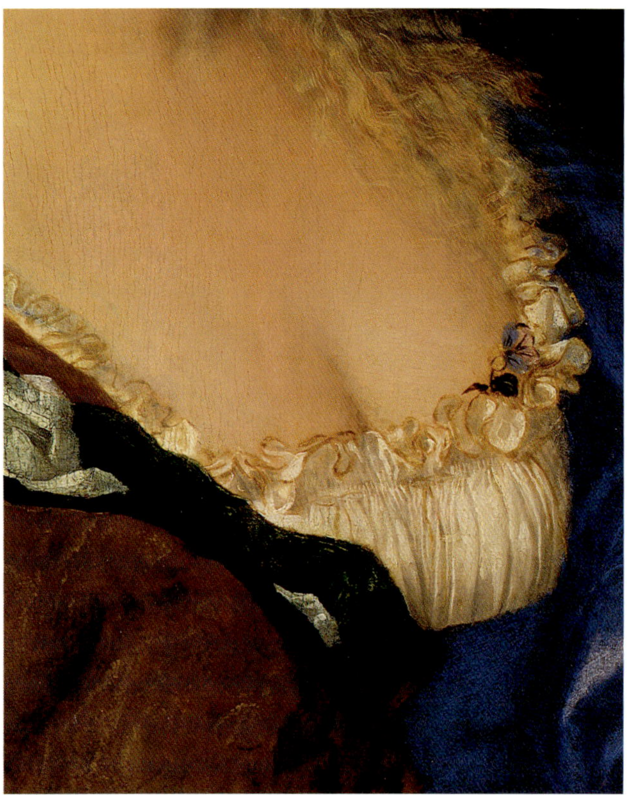

above Detail of fig. 189.

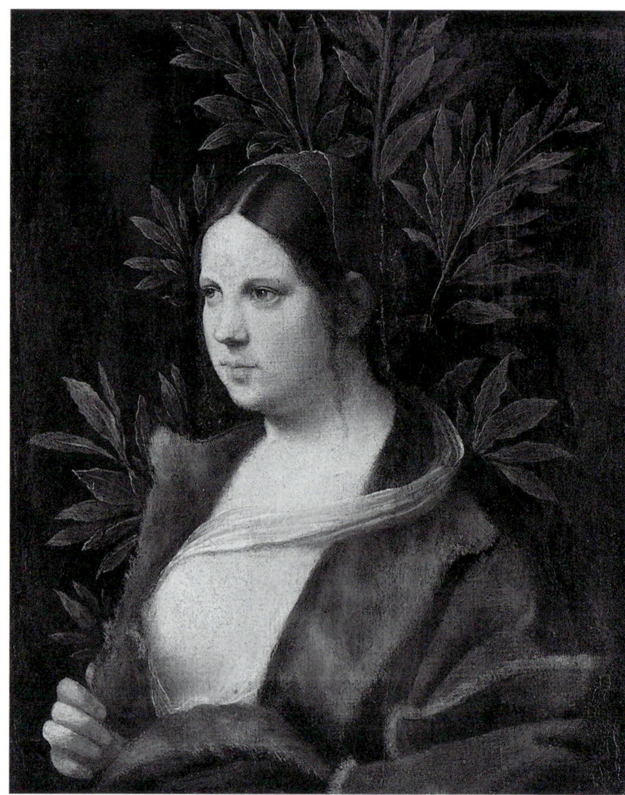

190 Giorgione, *Laura*, ca. 1506. Oil on wood, 41 × 33.6 cm. Vienna, Kunsthistorisches Museum.

touch with a whole range of textures, all of them soft. Her hair, in slight disarray, is like spun gold. Her skin is milk white and flawless, and it seems all the more bare by contrast to the filmy camisole and the huge taffeta sleeve. And yet the woman's status is not completely clear; her voluptuous sleeve serves as a barrier, and her steady gaze is tempered by a certain reserve.[17]

The use of the term *cortigiana* confirms the recognition of a new category of public women. Strictly speaking, of course, it simply means court lady – the female counterpart of *cortigiano* or courtier, which has no illicit sexual connotations. But the feminine noun *cortigiana* implies both availability and an elevated level of social graces. The terminology remained inconsistent. When Sanudo spoke of the beautiful Julia Lombardo in 1524 as a "somtuosa meretrize," he was referring to this new category of courtesan.[18]

In all likelihood, Giorgione's *Laura* was such a woman (fig. 190). As one scholar has argued compellingly, the mode of presentation is deliberately ambiguous. The key lies in Laura's gesture and her costume. She grasps her cloak, but the direction of her gesture is unclear. Is she concealing or revealing herself? It is not clear, but the point is that she is in control. As to her costume, it is a man's outer garment, a luxurious fur-lined coat that probably belonged to her protector. That she clothes herself in his garment and displays herself to him is a metaphor for her dependence and availability. But that she has the power to deny him access is a metaphor of her independence. The visual impact of this masterpiece of subtle eroticism thus depends on ambiguity and tension. Such a woman might have one or several patrons who supported her, but the point is that she seems to have had her own choice in the matter. So what was problematic about her was not her sexual morality *per se*, but her autonomy and independence.[19]

It was troubling to some, but so attractive to others that it posed a threat to the purity of the patrician bloodline. In April 1526, two decades after Laura's portrait was painted for an admirer whose identity is now unknown, Sanudo recorded an event that had lasting repercussions:

> Today one heard publicly about the wedding between Ser Andrea Michiel . . . of San Canziano, a widower, and a certain Cornelia Grifo, a most beautiful and sumptuous widowed prostitute. She is rich and has been publicly

> kept by Ser Ziprian Malipiero, and for a while she belonged to Ser Piero da Molin dal Banco, and to others, who have given her a dowry of . . . [several?] thousand ducats. The wedding was held at the monastery of San Zuan on Torcello and has cast great shame on the Venetian patriciate.[20]

Sanudo knew that memories were short, and that the male offspring of such a union might well claim noble credentials twenty years hence when they came of age. Official reaction was swift. Less than two weeks later, the Council of Ten met in secret session because, Sanudo reported, "many bastards have been accorded noble status" and "the doge and ducal council are incensed."[21] To guard against the possibility that a child of the likes of a notorious whore such as Cornelia Grifo, however sumptuous she may be, might some day claim the right to sit on the Great Council, the Ten passed a new law requiring the registration of all noble marriages with the State Attorney's Office within one month of the ceremony. These would be inscribed in the Libro d'Oro, the Book of Gold of the nobility, as a permanent record of incontestable respectability. At stake was "the honor, peace, and preservation" of the state, which rested on the "immaculacy and purity" of the "status and order of nobility."[22]

Domestic Arrangements

As to courtesans, they were considered commodities – luxury objects as it were. In 1531 Sanudo quoted from a letter written by a Venetian in Antwerp. It cited a conversation with the French ambassador, who praised the "perfection of one sort of merchandise" that he had found in Venice: "And he began to name Madonna Cornelia Grifo, Julia Lombardo, Bianca Saraton, [Elena] Balarine, and some others, but if your Lordship would have resided here for some days – being a merchant who would gladly attend to similar merchandise – I believe that you would have found some of these in abundance."[23] Accordingly, in 1535 the *Tariff of whores . . . in which is noted the price and the quality of all the Courtesans of Venice* was published, a satirical tract that purported to list the most famous public women of the city. Fashioned on the model of tariffs of merchandise, it portrays prostitutes as mercenary, vain, faithless, cunning, and deceitful.[24] But what about that sumptuous lifestyle that Cornelia Grifo and her colleagues enjoyed, which made them such attractively packaged merchandise? What is actually known about the living arrangements of the Venetian courtesan? There is little direct visual evidence.[25]

One of the few surviving images that appears to show a courtesan in a domestic environment is a puzzling painting now in Berlin depicting a nude couple in a bedchamber (fig. 192). It is datable to around 1500, the period in which Giorgione's *Laura* would have been painted. The locale must be Venice. The room features the classicizing architecture that began to replace the Gothic in the late fifteenth century and a characteristically Venetian built-in bed, adorned with the red and green draperies that fill the pages of Venetian inventories. The open door in the rear allows a glimpse of a palace with a cone-shaped Venetian-style chimney, a carpet suspended from a windowsill, and what appears to be a watery canal below. As with Cariani's courtesans, the young woman is psychologically detached – absorbed in herself as she contemplates her image in a small hand mirror. The youth, seeking to possess her, restricts her movement – his left leg extended in front of her, his right one behind, one hand on her breast and the other on her shoulder. She does not return his embrace. His attention is wholly on her; hers is wholly on herself. As in the painting of Laura, there is tension and ambiguity: this is a woman who is both independent and confined. It is a curious image – possibly the only one of its type. How might it be interpreted?

Turning it over reveals that it is the reverse of a double-sided panel (fig. 191). Both sides are painted in oil, each by a different hand, as yet unidentified. The main side features a picture of a young man with long blond hair, wearing a coat with a fur collar similar in style to that of Laura's, and undoubtedly a portrait. The young man's hairstyle, physiognomy, and dress suggest a German identity. Turning back to the bedchamber on the reverse and keeping the portrait in mind, we ask again what it might signify.

Several elements suggest an allegorical content: the mirror in the young woman's hand as a sign of vanity and, as noted earlier, associated with the courtesan; the glass in the foreground as a symbol of the fragility of human life; the sprig of laurel as a symbol of immortality; the partially open door as a sign of the passage from life to death. A recent exhibition catalogue interprets the sum of these features as a *memento mori* – a reminder of mortality.[26] But sometimes an open door is simply an open door, and the laurel branch has other possible associations – with literary or artistic genius, with victory, with the virtue of Petrarch's Laura. And what of that explicitly Venetian interior? And the unquestionably erotic pairing of male and female? It is most unlikely that this is a marriage portrait, but could it be a record of an experience similar to that of Thomas Coryat? That the dark-haired young man is different from the blond sitter on the reverse may be precisely the point. Moralizing

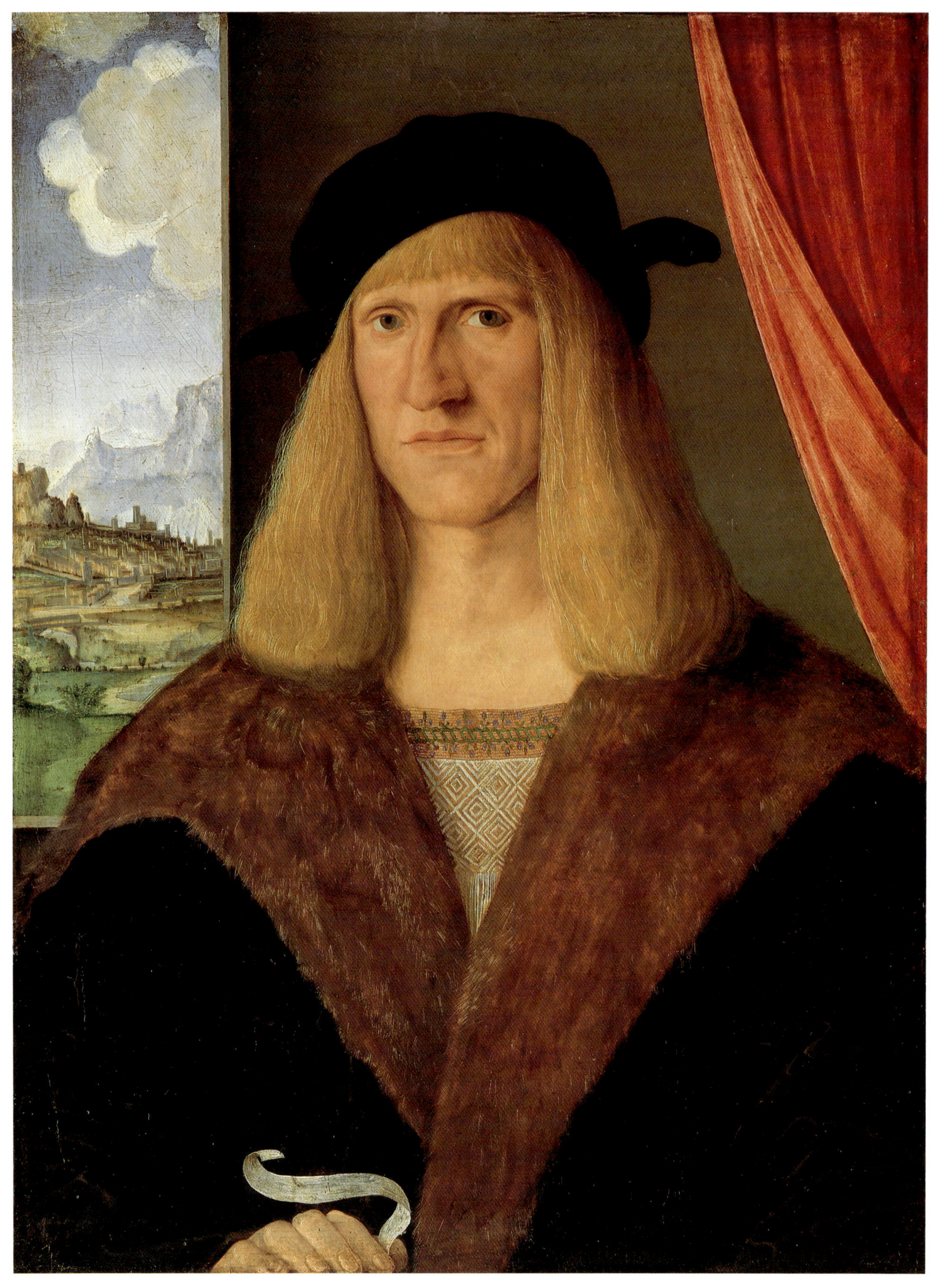

191 Anonymous German Painter, *Portrait of a Man*, ca. 1500. Oil on panel, 55 × 45 cm. Berlin, Staatliche Museen, Preussischer Kulturbesitz, Gemäldegalerie.

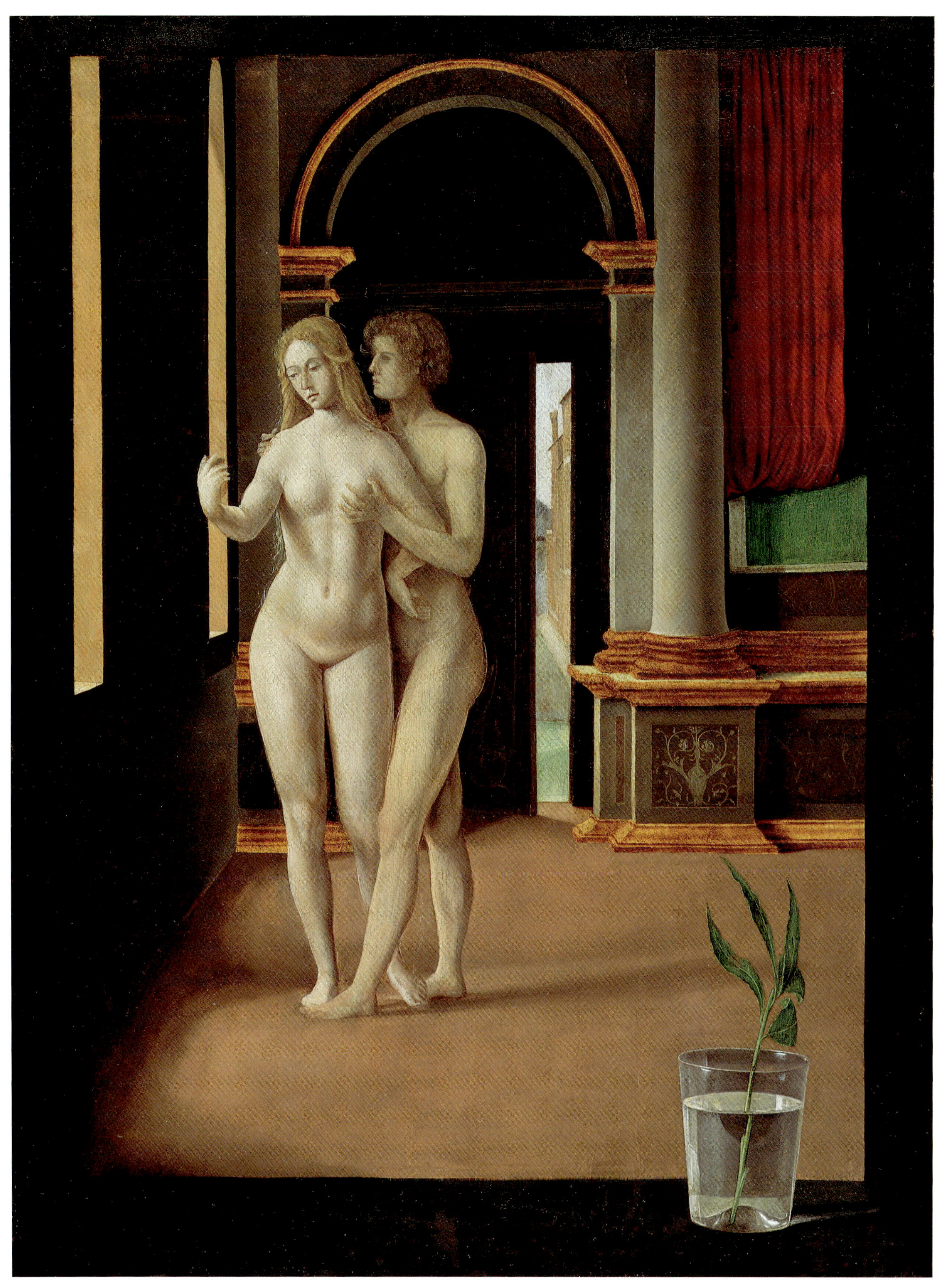

192 Anonymous Netherlandish or German painter, *A Pair of Lovers in an Interior*, ca. 1500. Oil on panel, verso of fig. 191.

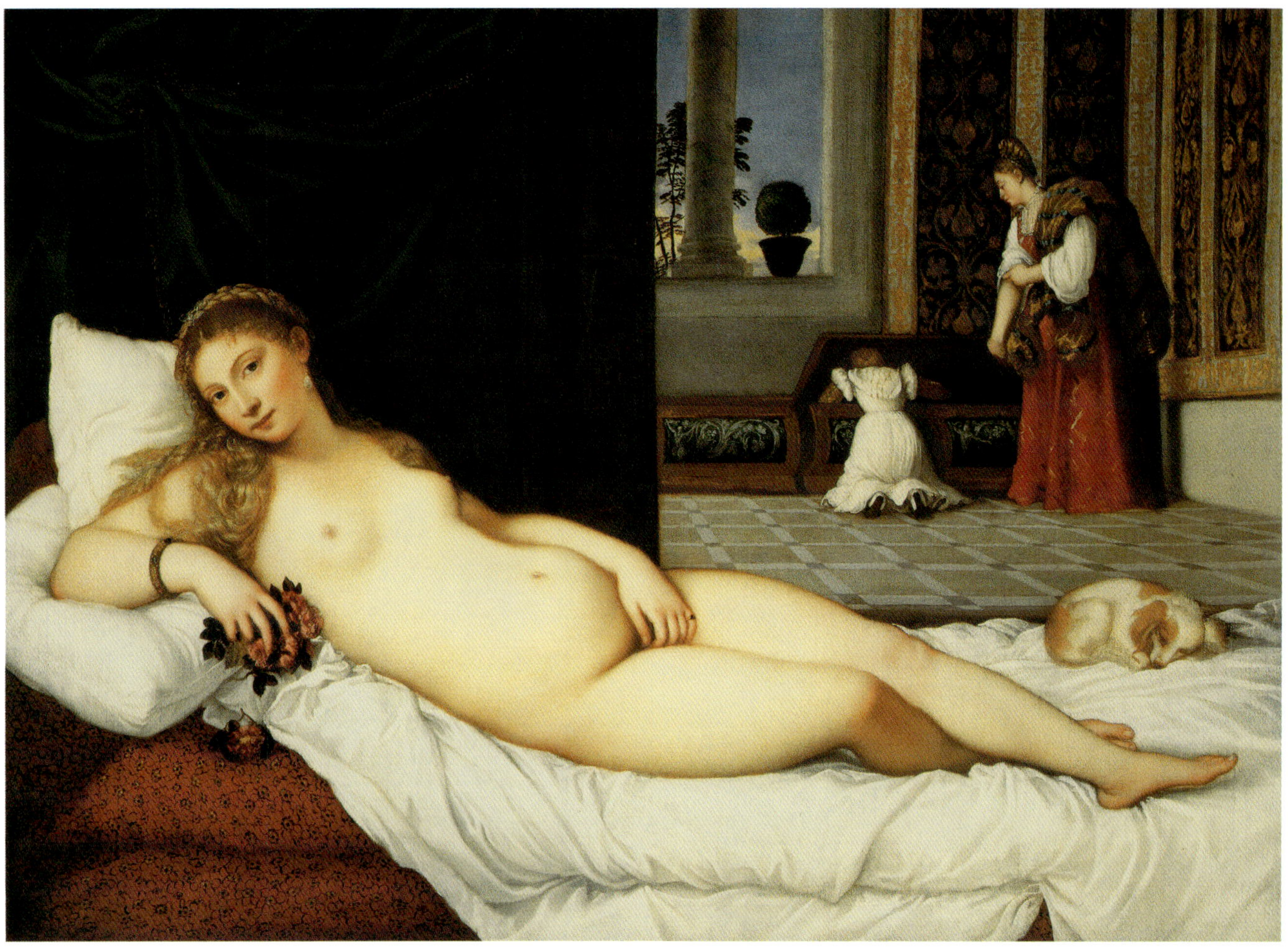

193 and 194 (*above and facing page*) Titian, *Venus of Urbino*, 1538. Oil on canvas, 119 × 165 cm. Florence, Galleria degli Uffizi.

to be sure, ambiguous to be sure, the reverse image may be regarded not as a portrait of a specific person, but as a portrait of a phenomenon – the culture of the courtesan (neither lady nor whore), for which the city of Venice was already becoming famous.

So perhaps this work provides an early glimpse of an *ambiance* that may fairly be called a "paradise of Venus." And what about that term, "paradise of Venus"? It suggests that artists may well have looked to the domestic arrangements of the courtesan's home to give credibility to their paintings of Venus, Danae, Leda, and other mythological ladies of dubious morals. How *did* Venus live in Venetian art? Titian's *Venus of Urbino* painted in the 1530s immediately comes to mind (figs. 193 and 194). But the lady's identity and character have been a matter of considerable discussion among scholars. Is she really Venus? Is she a courtesan? Is this a marriage painting – that is, one that was intended as an allegory of conjugal love? Or is this just a pin-up – one of the first?[27] As with so many paintings of beautiful young women of this period, the visual evidence is ambiguous.

It has been argued that the two chests in the background are marriage chests – an unambiguous symbol of marriage, since they were always made in pairs.[28] This may have been true in Florence but, as discussed earlier, Venetian inventories almost always place more than two *casse* or chests in the bedroom of a married couple and these chests rarely came in matched sets of two. More frequently there would be four, six, or more, all described as *simile*. Thus the fact that two chests are visible in Titian's painting may not be particularly significant. In any case, in all likelihood there were others along the wall behind the curtain, as there are at the end of the room in a painting by the Flemish artist Lambert Sustris (figs. 195 and 196).[29] He was inspired to copy Titian's work about a decade later, with another sumptuous nude reclining on snowy white but rumpled sheets.

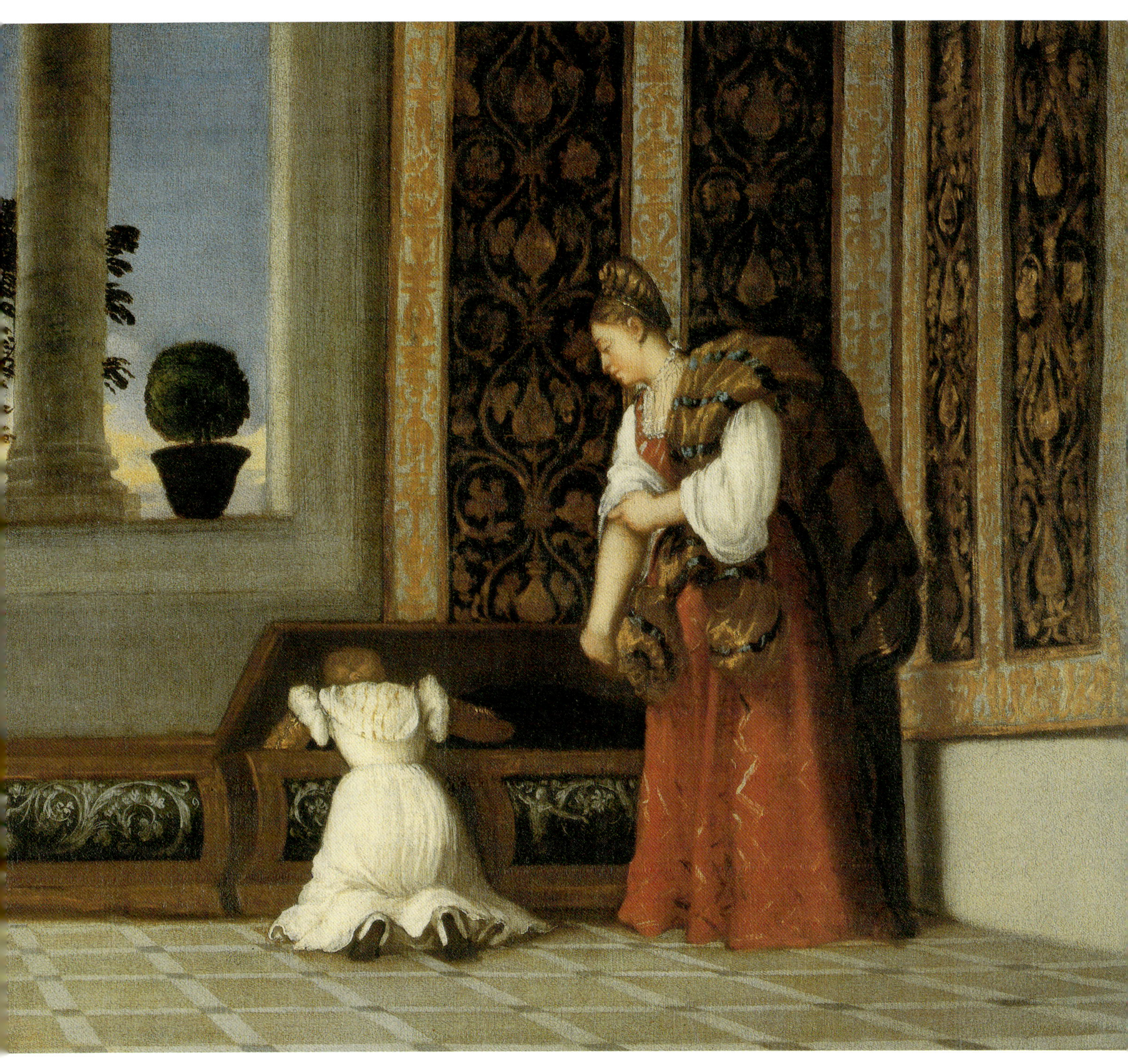

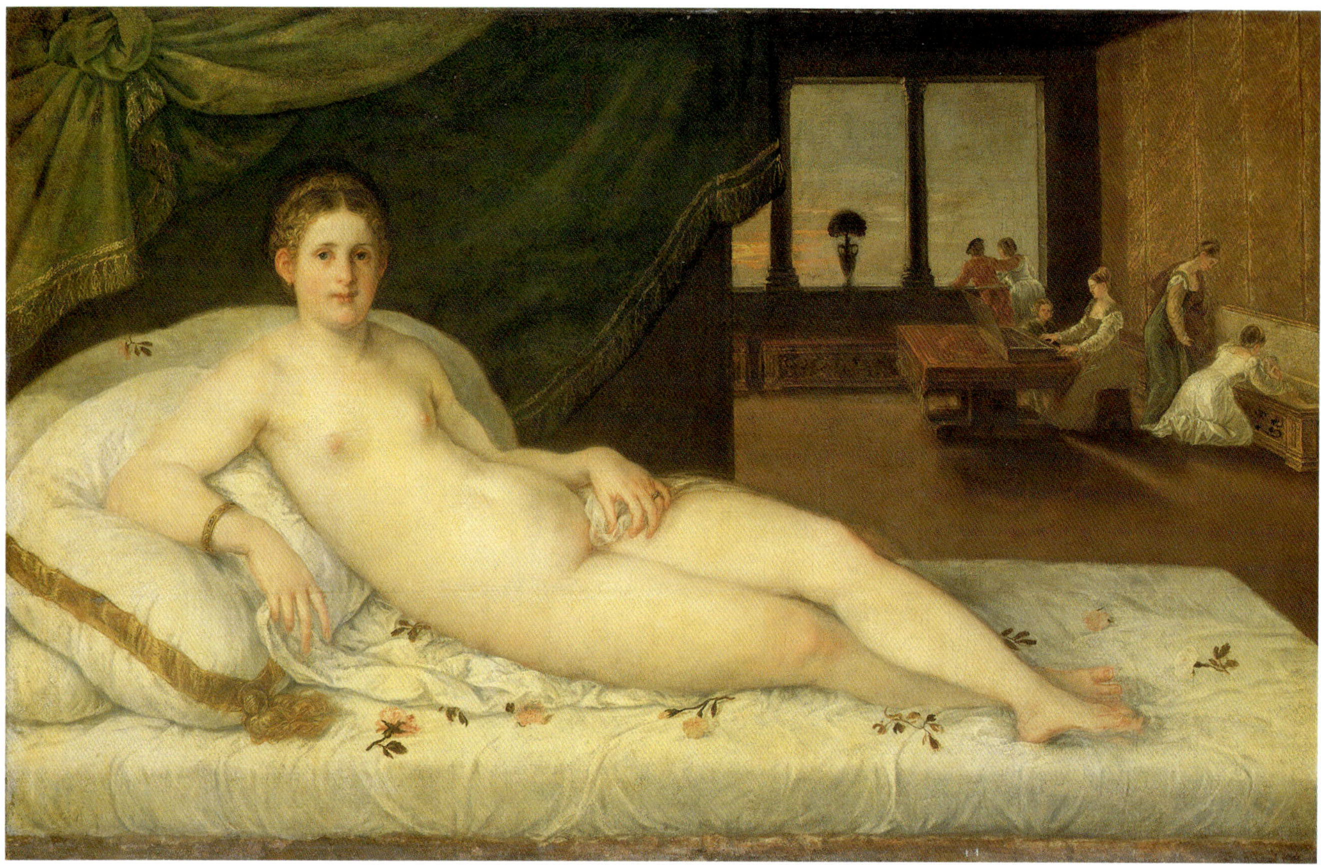

195 and 196 (*above and facing page*) Lambert Sustris, *Venus*, ca. 1548. Oil on canvas, 116 × 186 cm. Trained in Amsterdam, Sustris worked in Titian's studio in Venice in the 1530s, during which time he probably saw the *Venus of Urbino* before it was sent to the Duke of Urbino. Amsterdam, Rijksmuseum.

Turning to the Venus argument, in each of these works, wild roses – standard attributes of Venus as goddess of love – play a prominent role. While Titian's lady grasps a mass of them, in Sustris's painting the blossoms are scattered seductively around her on the bed. And beyond that, looking into the background of the latter work, the young woman playing the spinet is displaying one of the talents attributed to courtesans (fig. 196). But again, the evidence is ambiguous, for respectable wives played musical instruments as well. In fact, there was little difference in luxurious appointments between the home of a wealthy courtesan and her more respectable married counterpart.

In both venues the clothing would have been packed away in capacious storage chests and the walls covered with costly brocade or tapestry or gilded leather hangings. In both venues rich colors and patterned surfaces – whether of textiles, animal skins, woods, metals, or stone – would have created an environment to seduce the senses of sight and touch. What differentiated the two were the activities that took place in them and the centrality of the female and not the male in the residence of the courtesan.

Later in the century, several decades before Coryat would pay his respects to Margarita Emiliana, Lodewyck Toeput, a Flemish artist known in Italy as Pozzoserrato, betrayed his own familiarity with Venetian courtesan culture (fig. 197).[30] Here too the walls are hung with tapestries and a spinet holds center stage. The gentlemen, in northern attire, are visitors in a Venetian house. The ladies, dressed in the latest Venetian fashions, display those social graces for which courtesans were celebrated: dancing, music, and the art of conversation. These were the skills and talents that elevated them above the level of the common prostitute. The major piece of furniture in the room, a gilded bed partly hidden under a majestic canopy of silken draperies, is pushed into the background, a subtle allusion to another form of entertainment.

* * *

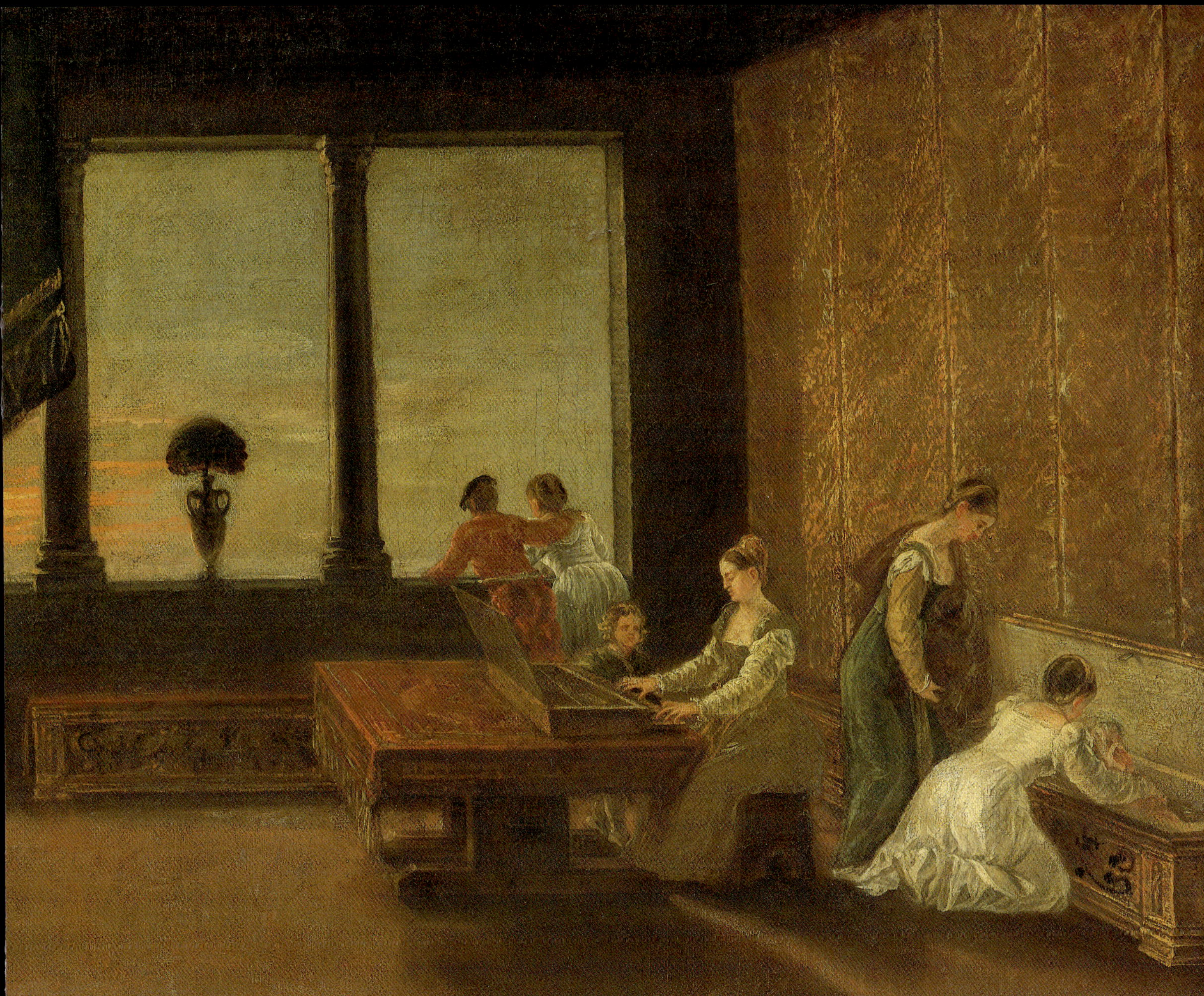

Elisabetta Condulmer

Is it possible to confirm the veracity of images such as these with more reliable evidence than idealized bedchambers, which were products of artistic license, or eyewitness accounts such as Coryat's, in which literary hyperbole played a role? A handful of inventories of household goods that can be linked convincingly to courtesans have been identified in the archives. The earliest may be that of Elisabetta Condulmer, who lived in the *contrada* of San Felice. We first make Elisabetta's acquaintance in her last will and testament, written 22 August 1538. She declares: "I, Elisabetta, daughter of Hieronimo Condulmer and wife of Gabriel di Angeli, healthy by the grace of the Lord God in mind and intellect, but infirm in body, being in bed, and wishing to order my possessions, have asked the Venetian notary Angelo da Canal to come to my home."[31] She continues: "And for my executors of this, my will, I wish messer Francesco da Sola, *mio signor*, messer Camillo Michiel . . . messer Vetor Trinchavilla, physician, and messer Nicolò Cocco, who lives in the house below me."[32] This immediately begs the question why her husband is not among them, but in the next sentence, the reason becomes apparent: "I declare that Hieronimo, Bernardin, Paula, and Laura, my sons and daughters, are of the said messer Francesco da Sola, *mio signor* [my lord]. And likewise, by my faith, I also swear that Cipriana and Condolmera, my daughters, are of the said Camillo Michiel [now also called *mio signor*], and that Julio, my son, is the son of messer Zuane Alvixe de Luca Varoter."[33]

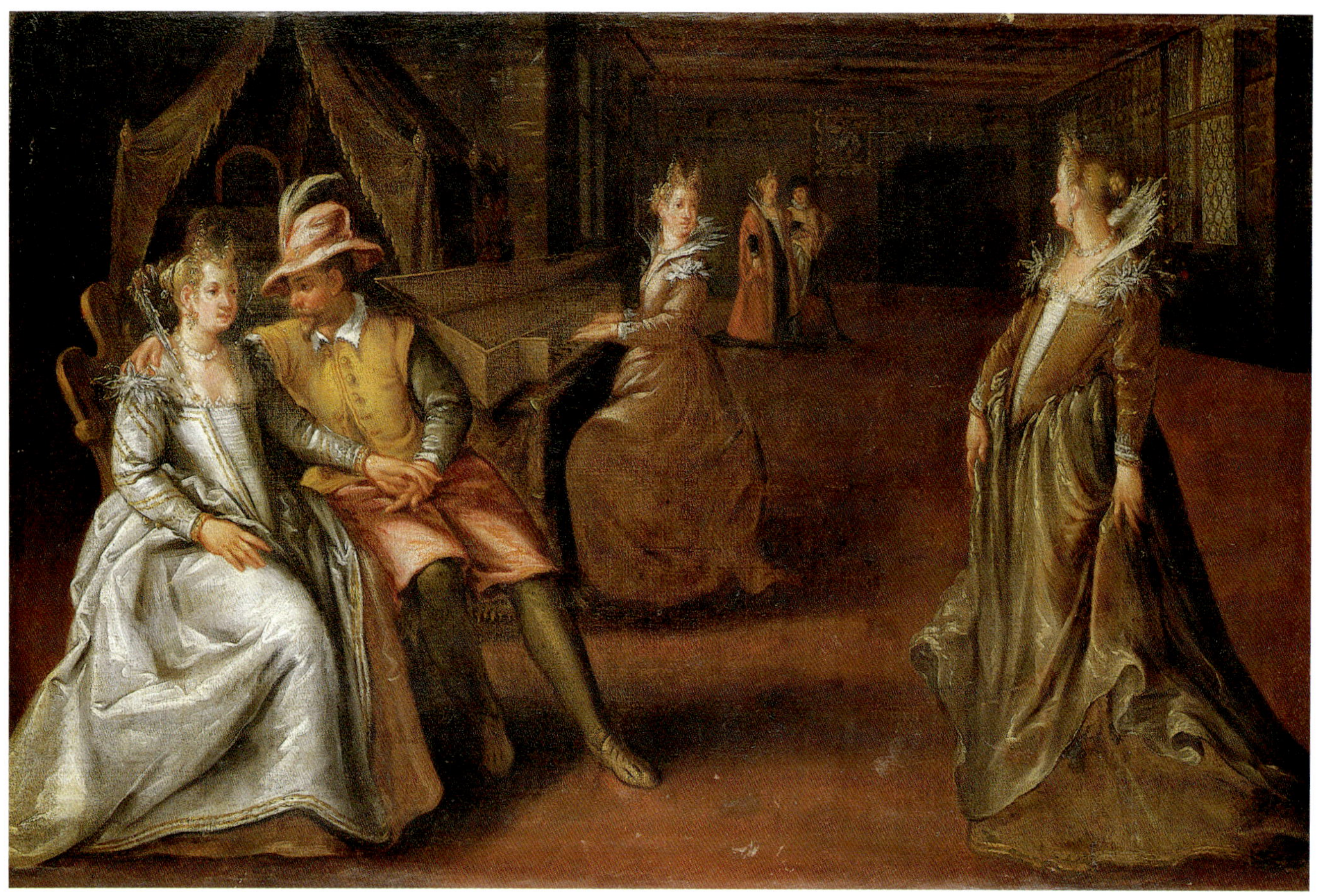

197 Ludovico Pozzoserrato (Lodwijck Toeput), *A Musical Evening*, late 1570s. Oil on canvas. Best known for his landscapes, Pozzoserrato also introduced a new kind of genre painting of festive gatherings, exemplified by the present work, anticipating the "merry company" pieces that became prominent in seventeenth-century Dutch art. Augsburg, Private Collection.

We have here a woman who is married to one man – Gabriel di Angeli – still living, and has seven children by three others, also living. Two of the latter – Francesco da Sola and Camillo Michiel, both designated as *mio signor* – are named as executors of her will and appear to have an ongoing relationship with her. Further on the will reveals that she is pregnant with an eighth child whose paternity is not stated. To her brother, Zuan Francesco, and her cousin, Pellegrina, she leaves 2 ducats each "in sign of love." To her cousin, Laura Fontana, she bequeaths 10 ducats and all the goods that she had lent her. Otherwise, all her worldly possessions go to her children. To her sons Hieronimo and Bernardin she leaves a house that she owns in the *contrada* of San Marcilian, and to her son Julio, 30 ducats. To provide for her daughters Paula, Laura, Cipriana, and Condolmera, she orders that all her other belongings – furniture, clothing, silver, rings, and jewels – be sold at the best price and the proceeds divided equally among them. It is significant that these funds are not designated for dowries, as they would be in a typical Venetian will. She further orders that her unborn child, whether male or female, should share equally in the bequest left to her daughters.[34]

In less than a month, Elisabetta would die, for on 13 September the notary Angelo da Canal drew up an inventory of all the goods that remained in her home at San Felice at the time of her death.[35] The executors appear to have changed somewhat. The patrician Nicolò Cocco, the gentleman downstairs, has taken charge. Vetor Trinchavilla is absent, and Camillo Michiel is replaced by the Reverend Giulio Michiel. They are joined by a certain Zuan Francesco de Torresani, who can be identified as Elisabetta's Francesco da Sola. Commonly known as Francesco d'Asola, his real name was Gian Francesco Torresani. He was the son of Andrea Torresani, who was associated with the famous printer Aldus Manutius by marriage and by profession. Aldus had married Gian Francesco's sister, Maria, in 1505

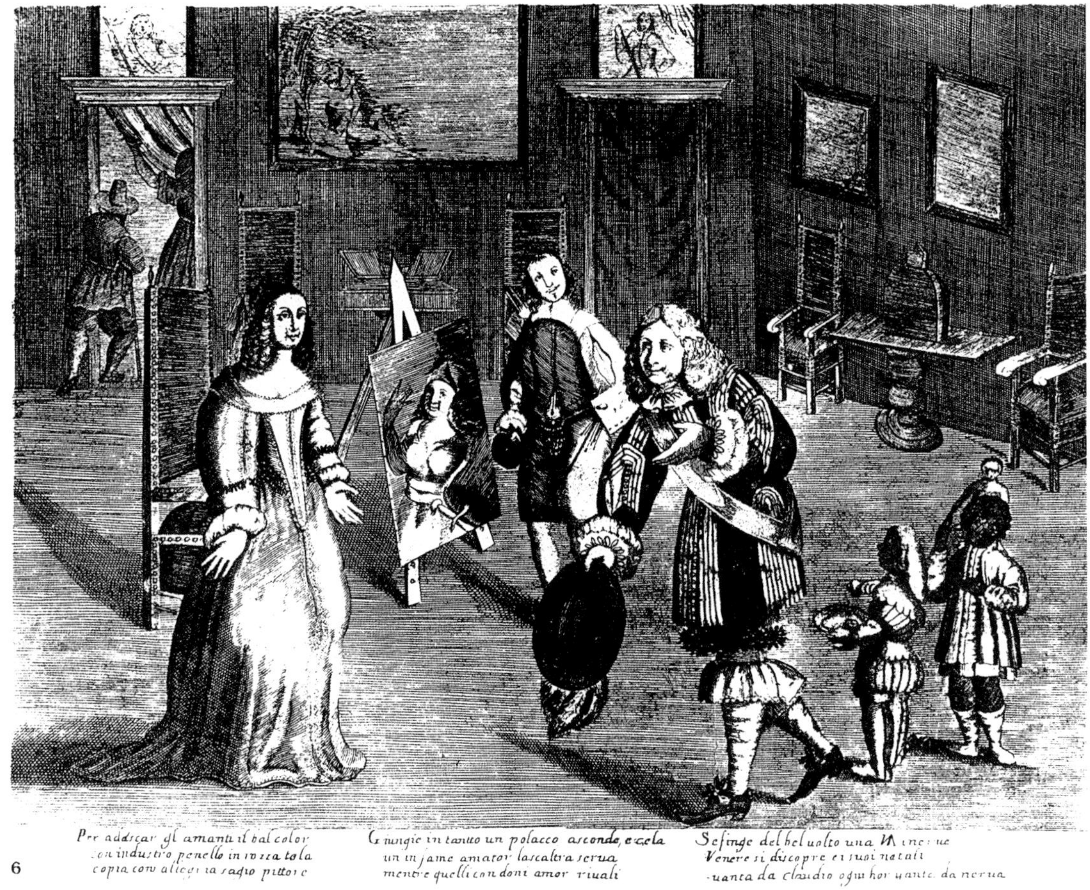

198 A courtesan having her portrait painted. Engraving from *Serie della Vita et miseranda fine della puttana* (Bologna: Giuseppe Longhi sotto alle scale, ca. 1650). Milan, Raccolta delle Stampe Achille Bertarelli.

and lived with the Torresani family until his death in 1515. Gian Francesco followed his father and brother-in-law into the printing business, and after their deaths opened a shop of his own.[36] Of that more later.

How did Elisabetta live? Comfortably, indeed, with her apartment comprising three chambers in addition to the *portego*, kitchen, and utility rooms. Let us walk with the notary through the house. Here the testimony is dry and unmediated – documentary as it were. Before the entrance to the *portego* there was a Flemish painting on canvas at the head of the stairs – a preface to the visual delights within. For the *portego* walls were covered with paintings featuring an eclectic range of subject matter. The first to attract Canal's attention was a large portrait of Elisabetta herself, complete with a *timpano* – a frame with a curtain that could be drawn across it. A seventeenth-century print may give a sense of the overall effect (fig. 198). There was also a framed map of the world, still unusual in Venetian homes, and probably a gift from her book-printer lover (see fig. 247). There were two more portraits, one described as *alla forestiera* – "in the foreign manner" – and the other *alla fiandrese* – in the Flemish style. Canal could not identify the subject of a second Flemish-style painting and simply described it as a man in a barrel.

But that is not all. There is also a painting of Pyramis and Thisbe, which Canal did recognize, another of a woman and a nude man, yet another of a nude woman tied to a tree (possibly Andromeda), and a painting of an old man with a cage, plus eight small ink drawings on paper in metal frames. These profane works were tempered by an Adoration of the Magi and a painting of the Magdalene, the latter in the Flemish style and described, like the portrait of Elisabetta herself, as large. In sum, there were ten paintings and eight drawings.[37] The number of works described as Flemish or foreign is worth noting. While at least some of these may have been imported despite protectionist legislation, they may well have been painted in Venice by immigrants from the north or by Venetian artists working in the Flemish manner.[38]

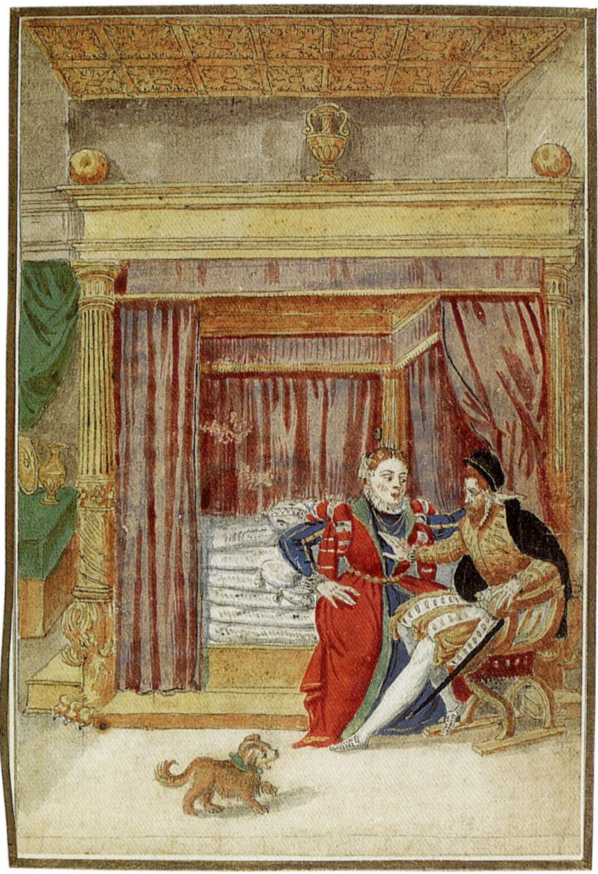

199 *A Courtesan in her Bedchamber with an Admirer*, Venice, 1575. Watercolor, 218 × 280 mm. Ms. 457, "Mores Italiae," fol. 17. New Haven, Yale University, Beinecke Rare Book and Manuscript Library.

200 (*facing page*) Coats of arms of the Condulmer and Canal families. Watercolor. According to the inscription, the Condulmer family originated in Pavia, and its members had been ancient tribunes of Venice. Because of outstanding service in the War of Chioggia of 1379, Jacopo Condulmer, was taken into the Great Council in 1381, and thus brought himself and his heirs into the hereditary nobility of Venice. Venice, Archivio di Stato, Misc. Cod. ser. 1, Storia Veneta, B. 37.

And how was Elisabetta's art gallery furnished? The inventory suggests an active social life: twenty-four chairs, a pinewood dining table, and three painted *banche da portego* – *portego* benches. There were also five black strongboxes with gilded fittings and the Condulmer coat of arms, as well as a walnut *credenza* with a broken door. The room was illuminated by a hanging lamp (a *cesendelo*) of brass and glass and, in all likelihood, wall sconces, although characteristically these were not listed because they were immovable. Was this room used only to receive guests in a formal manner? Probably not, for the notary also recorded "two cradles, one of walnut and one of pine."[39] These pieces were unusual furnishings for a formal room of presentation intended to impress visitors but not surprising, considering the size of Elisabetta's family.

The *camera granda de madona* – Elisabetta's paradise of Venus – was the major repository of her worldly goods. Here, as in the bedroom of Coryat's Margarita Emiliana, the artwork on the walls was sacred, not secular: a large painting of Our Lady with SS John the Baptist and Jerome and a half-length painting of a woman who, the notary observed, "appears to be Judith." There was also a gilded birdcage with a wire enclosure of silver; a large round basket with fifty-five pieces of majolica and other ceramics; and seventy-five pieces of glass of various sorts.[40]

But the room was dominated by a walnut bed with gilded columns. The bed, described as "alla cortesana" – courtesan-style – was well furnished with down-filled mattresses, coverlets, pillows, and cushions, all described as snowy white – an emphasis on pristine linens that recalls the bed of Margarita Emiliana as well as the two Venuses by Titian and Sustris. A manuscript dating to 1575 depicts a courtesan's bedchamber with a bed featuring elegant fluted columns resting on lion's paws and supporting a wooden tester. Furnished with a set of purple curtains, white sheets and bolsters, and at least six mattresses, it may well have been what was considered *alla cortesana* (fig. 199).[41]

As with the strongboxes in the *portego*, six gilded chests were decorated with the Condulmer arms. These were filled with linens and a considerable wardrobe. The Condulmer arms also appeared on a piece of wall tapestry, a little pine chest, and a straw fan. A locked walnut cabinet, or *scrigno*, held the household treasures: silver forks incised with the Condulmer arms; knives of Brescian iron, incised and gilded; spoons of silver and cups of silver gilt; a silver-gilt toothpick with a handle; carving knives; a bronze table bell; a small clock; and three large tassels of silk and gold. Elisabetta was also well provided with jewelry, including four crowns, two of amber and two of crystal, with strands that she would have woven into her hair for special occasions. A silver casket contained four gems, all in gold settings; a cameo and a sealing ring, both with the Condulmer arms; a gold ring with an inscription; a gold medal of the Madonna of Loreto; and an envelope containing little pearls and coral pieces to make a child's bracelet. In the kitchen, there was a second birdcage, this of walnut, another ninety-two pieces of majolica, and an abundance of pewter dinnerware and copper pots.[42] In sum, Elisabetta had all the appurtenances of a noble lifestyle, complete with a number of objects inscribed with her family coat of arms – insignia of a respectable lineage (fig. 200).

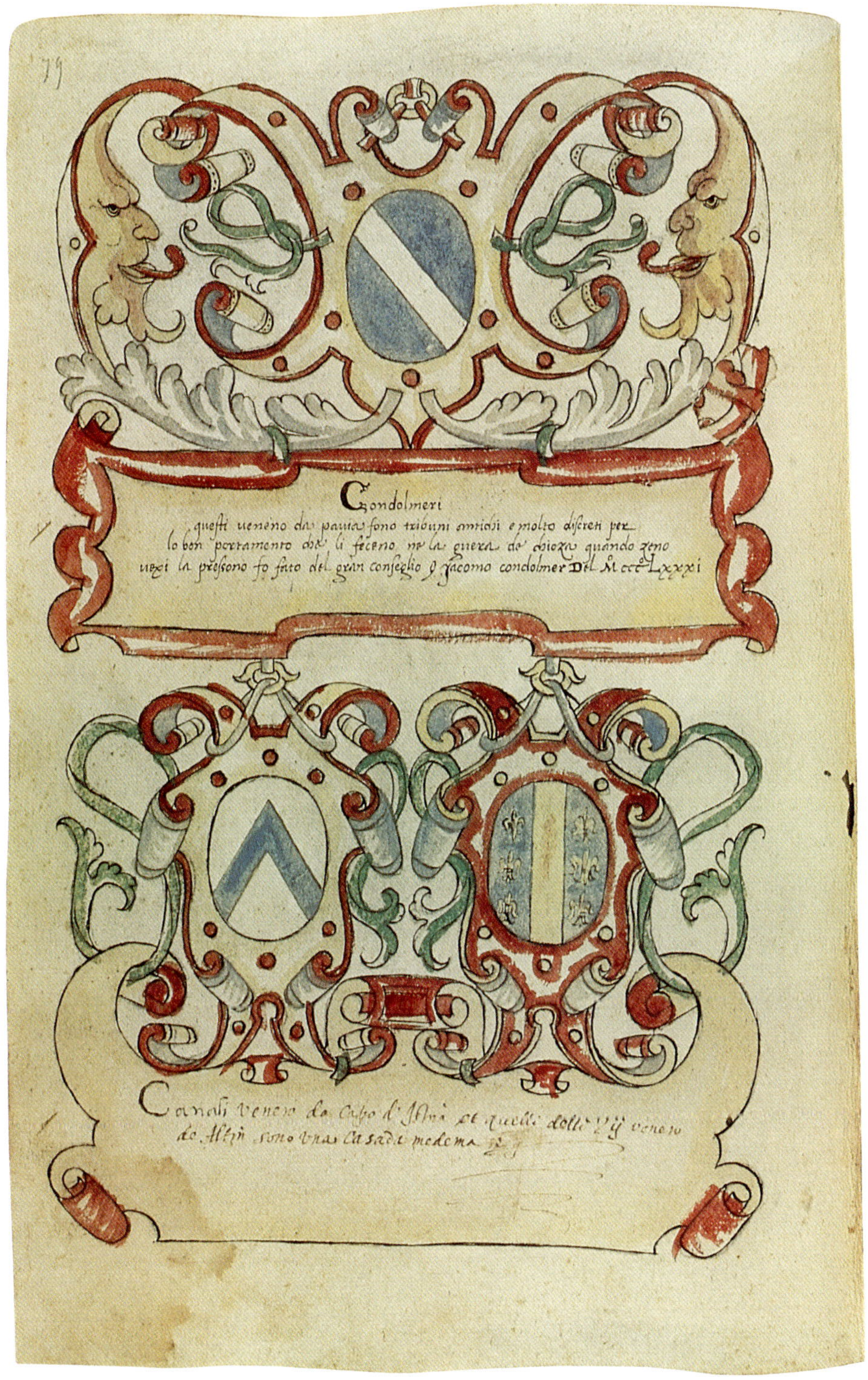

What did she do when she wasn't entertaining her *signori* or tending to the infants who occupied the cradles in the *portego*? Like any well-brought-up lady, she seems to have practiced needlework, for the inventory lists a spinning wheel, a good quantity of thread and yarn, and many fabric remnants. In the *mezzado* – a storage area on a mezzanine floor – was a prayer bench, seemingly no longer used, along with a broken *arzella*, an empty strongbox, also broken, and three shopping baskets.[43]

One of the smaller chambers held four lutes – evidence of the musical activities associated with the courtesan. A painting by Parrasio Micheli conveys the desired effect (fig.

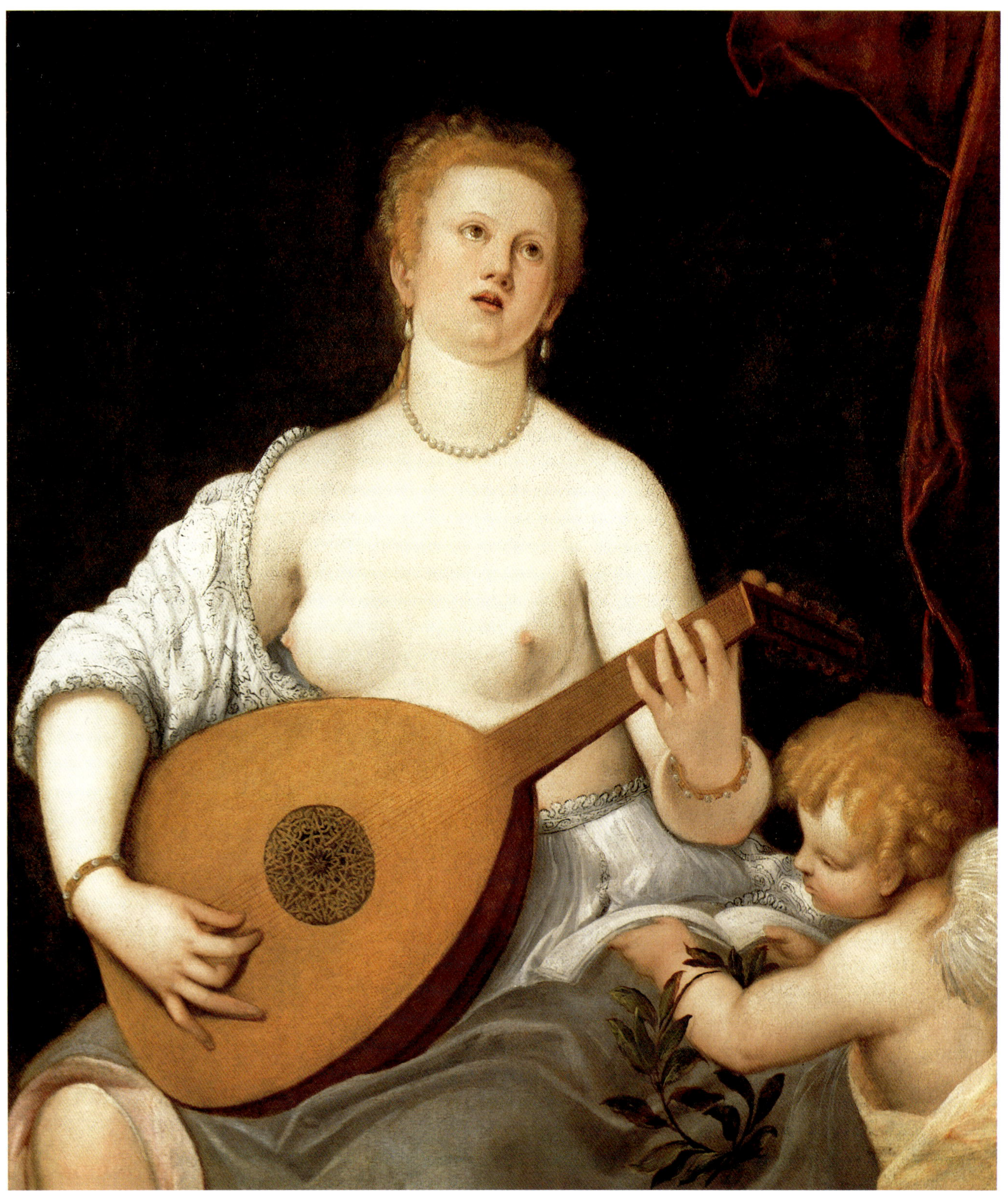

201 Parrasio Micheli, *Venus Playing a Lute*, mid-sixteenth century. Oil on canvas, 110 × 97 cm. Budapest, Szépmüvészeti Muzeum, no. 85.

201). Probably a portrait of an actual courtesan as Venus, accompanied by Cupid, who holds her sheet music, she plays a lute with seven strings instead of the usual eleven to thirteen, but with correctly positioned hands.[44] But was Elisabetta also a rhetorician, like Coryat's Margarita Emiliana? Most unlikely, for she was not much of a reader. Despite the fact that her *signore* Gian Francesco Torresani was a printer, there were, aside from a breviary, just four books in the house – three octavos and a quarto – in addition to some account books and documents relating to her property. There was little male presence revealed in the inventory. The only masculine apparel listed were three shirts of fine linen, two worked with black silk and the other with gold; and three pairs of men's shoes, two velvet and one leather. Gian Francesco may have lived elsewhere.

What else is revealed by the inventory? A pair of pine caskets were listed together, one with the Condulmer and the other with the Torresani coats of arms – evidence of a relationship with Gian Francisco Torresani that was close to a marriage, even though Elisabetta was the wife of another man. In fact, the notary writes that the documents and account books in her locked *scrigno* were immediately handed over to Torresani, along with a leather covered box for combs, a leather bag to hold jewelry, a writing cabinet, and a walnut table with its trestles. Indeed, there is evidence that Torresani laid claim to all Elisabetta's worldly possessions himself, including a number of items that she had lent to her sister, Ursia, a nun in the convent of Santa Caterina. These included four door curtains of scarlet cloth decorated with arms and foliage; a green and yellow striped satin cape lined with squirrel skins; a ten-piece bed ensemble of green and orange ormesino silk, described as new; and five figured *spallieri* wall hangings, decorated with arms with a yellow eagle who holds a lily to his breast. All this, Torresani argued, had been intended for Ursia's use only during Elisabetta's lifetime. Although the fate of Elisabetta's daughters is unknown, as well as that of her son by Zuane Alvixe de Luca Varoter, her sons Hieronimo [Gerolamo] and Bernardin [Bernardo] were fully accepted by their father, Gian Francesco Torresani, and went on to pursue successful careers as printers and book sellers themselves.[45]

Who was Elisabetta Condulmer? How could the daughter of Girolamo Condulmer – a Venetian nobleman – end up as a courtesan? To look for clues we must go back to 1501 and the testament of Elisabetta's father, Girolamo. Naming "Laura Fontana, my legitimate wife," as an executor, he left the bulk of his estate to be shared and shared alike by Zuan Gabriel and Zuan Francesco, "my legitimate and natural sons from the womb of the above cited Laura" (for the Condulmer family tree, see Appendix, p. 258). There are two conditions: first, if Laura remains a widow, she should be allowed to enjoy the residue of the estate as long as she lives; and second, that his sons should give 100 gold ducats to their sister Andriana at the time of her marriage or entry into a convent. If both sons should die without male descendants, the estate should revert to his wife Laura, and after her death be passed on to Girolamo's brothers, "the magnificent lords Bernardo and Jacopo in equal portions."[46]

There is a further declaration: "in order to remove every suspicion, I say and declare that in the year 1484 in the month of March, I accepted the above-cited Laura as my legitimate wife, being present ser Giovanni Polato who was the ring sponsor."[47] Now this is a most unusual attestation to find in a will and, as we shall see, Girolamo had good cause to be concerned. It may be noted that Elisabetta was not named. In all likelihood she was born during the decade after the will was written, putting her in her thirties at the time of her death, and in fact Girolamo would live another fourteen years. The tiny sum that he designated for his daughter Andriana's dowry at a time when 3,000 ducats for patrician daughters was common suggests that he was not a wealthy man. Indeed in 1508 Sanudo reported that Girolamo was convicted of selling his vote in the Great Council and deprived of all state offices for five years. The ban was rescinded a year-and-a-half later when the official who had bribed Girolamo paid a fine of 1,000 ducats.[48]

Condulmer was still alive in August 1514 when he made his tax declaration. He owned very little real property – only his house at San Marcilian, which was appraised at 300 ducats.[49] By February 1516 he was dead and his widow, identified as "the noble lady Laura Fontana," appeared in the State Attorney's Office and presented Zuan Francesco Condulmer as the legitimate son of the deceased Girolamo and herself. Girolamo's two brothers, Jacopo and Bernardo, both prominent patricians active in government affairs, attested to the truth of her declaration.[50] Now twenty years old, the young Zuan Francesco saw his name inscribed in the Libro d'Oro and was allowed to sit on the Great Council. But all was not well.

Moving ahead a decade to April 1526, we come once more to the marriage of the sumptuous *meretrice* Cornelia Grifo to a member of the nobility and to Sanudo's report that the ensuing scandal had prompted new legislation to ensure that the offspring of such ignoble alliances would not be allowed to claim the title of nobility. As part of the reform, he wrote, the *Capi* (heads) of the Council of Ten had summoned thirty patrician males to appear before them to offer new proof of their noble status. The legitimacy of their births had been called into question. Among them was Zuan Francesco Condulmer.[51]

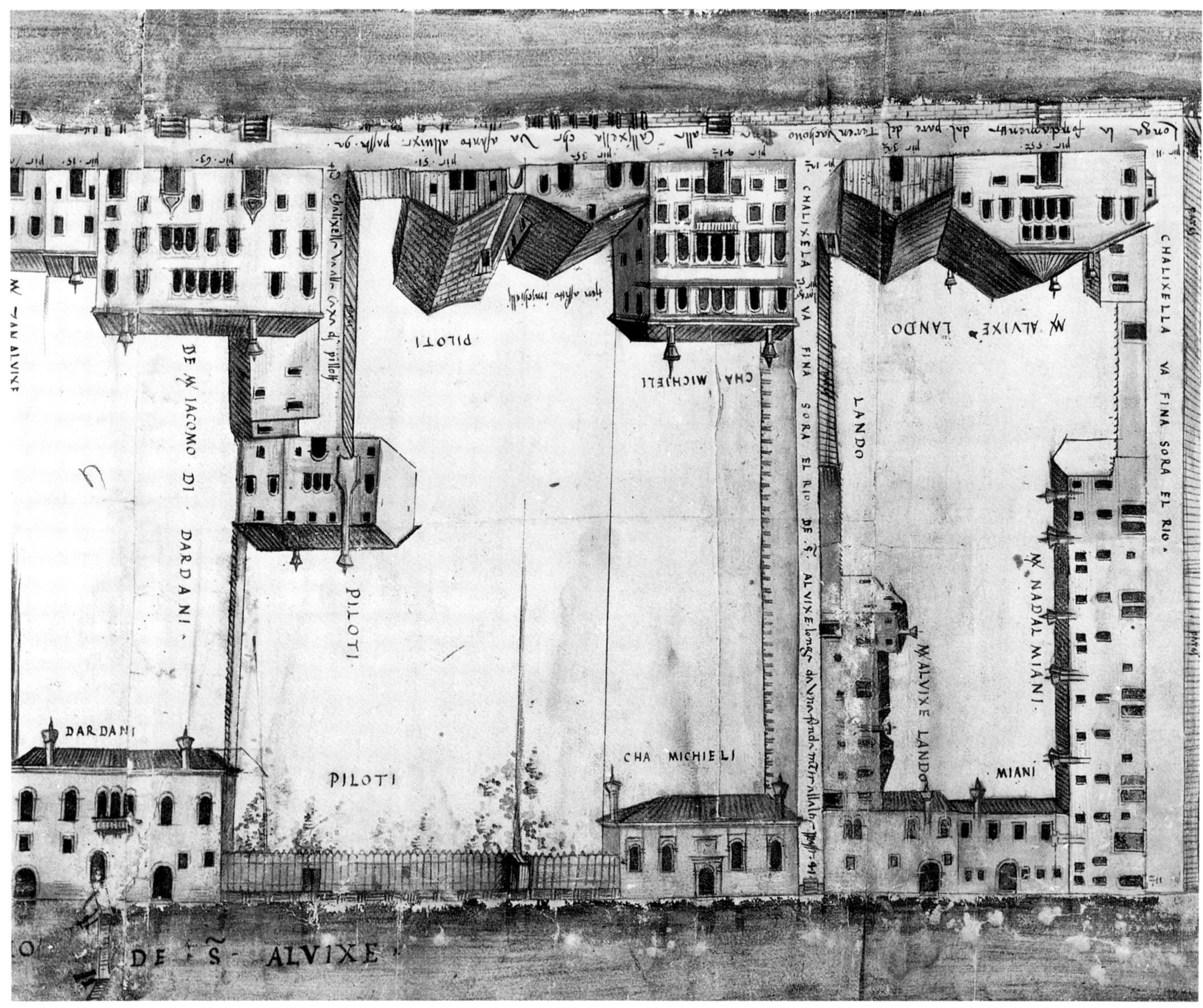

202 Nicolò Dal Cortivo, drawing of houses near the convent of Sant'Alvise in Cannaregio, 30 January 1538 m.v. (= 1539), where the Condulmer family *casa da statio* was located. According to the property deed, the house was situated between properties owned by the Foscari and Michiel families, was bordered on one side by the *callesella* (narrow *calle*) leading to Sant'Alvise, and had water frontage. Since the Foscari property is not indicated on the map, the precise location of the Condulmer house is uncertain. The map is oriented here with south at the top. Venice, Archivio di Stato, Miscellanea Mappe, dis 1216.

After two prolonged hearings, he was declared a bastard in January 1528 and his registration in the Libro d'Oro crossed out with a large X (see fig. 11).[52] The notation next to it on the left stated that he had failed to provide sufficient proof. His mother Laura – the primary witness – had already died, for the family home at San Marcilian was then owned jointly by Zuan Francesco, a brother, Eugenio, and their sister Elisabetta.[53]

In July 1528, Elisabetta bought the shares of both her brothers for 200 ducats to become sole owner of the house (fig. 202).[54] It is not difficult to imagine the source of her prosperity. And it may well be that her profession was one of the reasons that doubt had been cast upon the legitimacy of her brother's birth. So how did she come to pursue such a life? The judgment that Zuan Francesco was a bastard, long after their father had sworn to the propriety of his marriage, suggests that their mother's status was questionable. Perhaps she too had lived for a time as a courtesan and the death of her husband left her without adequate financial resources to supply a reasonable dowry for her daughters. To put the purchase of the house into perspective, it should

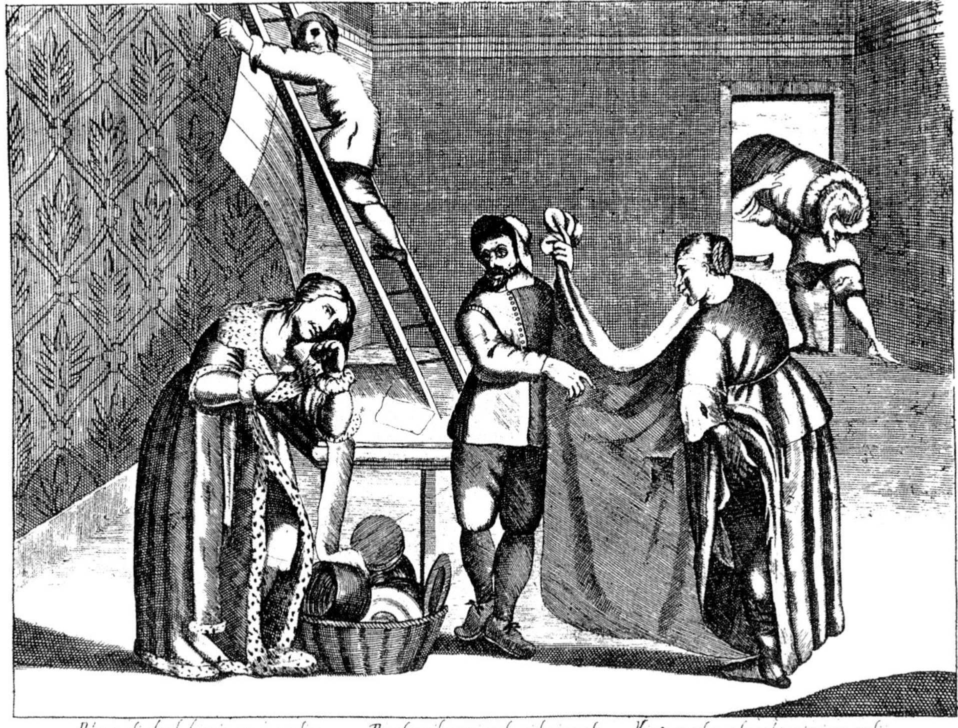

203 A once sumptuous but now abandoned prostitute sells her furnishings to survive. Engraving from *Serie della Vita et miseranda fine della puttana*, ca. 1650. The leather hangings are being stripped from the walls. Milan, Civica Raccolta delle Stampe, Achille Bertarelli.

be noted that when Elisabetta made her tax declaration ten years later, she stated that it was so old and in such bad condition that she had not been able to rent it out to tenants for several years. Once she had it "honorably restored," she planned to live in it herself.[55] It should be remembered, however, that property was often described as in poor condition in such declarations in order to pay lower taxes.

To Elisabetta, the perilous life of a courtesan may well have seemed preferable to her sister Ursia's secure but austere existence in a convent. It may seem surprising that she had a husband at all, but this was a common strategy of courtesans who wished to circumvent legislation aimed at curtailing their freedom of action.[56]

The Abundance of Necessary Things

Although Elisabetta lived well, she did not capture the attention of Marin Sanudo, and her name does not seem to appear in the *Tariffa*, that nasty little tract published in 1535 that purported to list the most famous public women of the city. One whose name did appear, however, was Julia Lombardo.[57] Described as "sumptuous and very beautiful" and endowed with a "subtle genius," she died in 1543. An inventory of her household goods portrays a lifestyle similar to that of Elisabetta Condulmer. She had not only two parrots, as indicated by two birdcages, but also a small dog, whose presence is revealed by a harness with eight little silver bells. And her level of education may be said to be superior – she owned a picture of Dante and eighteen books as opposed to Elisabetta's four, and a green harpsichord in contrast to Elisabetta's lutes. As is well known, several courtesans of the next generation – most notably Veronica Franco and Gaspara Stampa – exhibited considerable musical and literary talents. Veronica, whose poetry was legendary, arranged musical evenings in her home, and Gaspara's singing voice and proficiency with the lute were so celebrated that the composer Perissone Cambio dedicated a book of madrigals to her. Such women might be seen as poetesses and musicians who were also courtesans.[58]

But, as suggested by a print depicting painted leather hangings being stripped from the walls of a destitute prostitute, even a sumptuous courtesan like Julia Lombardo faced an uncertain future (fig. 203). If she managed to

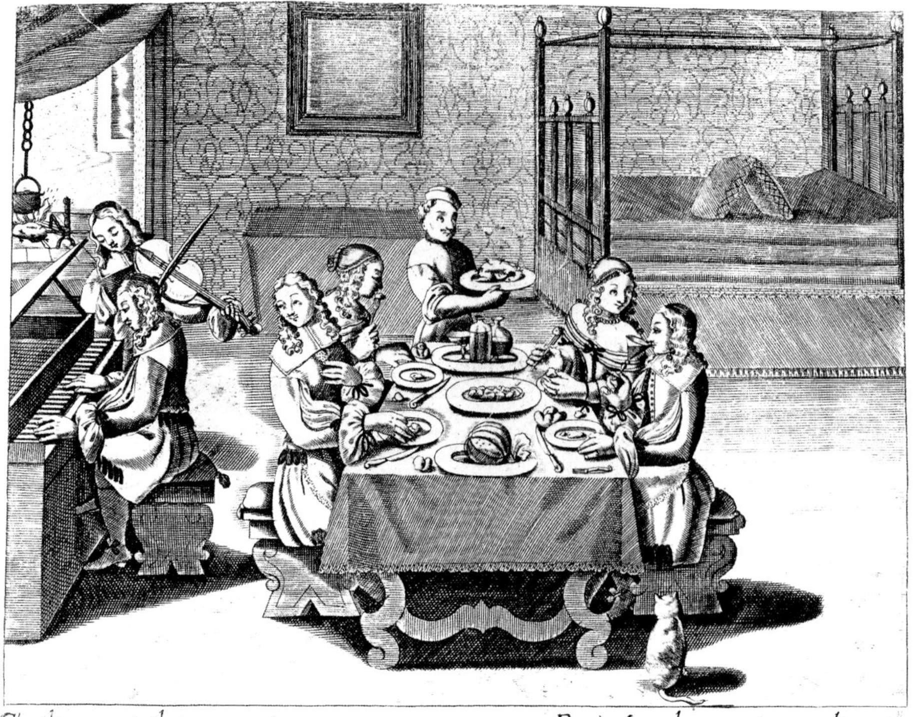

204 Courtesans entertain their guests at a dinner party. Engraving from *Vita del Lascivo* (Venice, seventeenth century). The New York Public Library, Astor, Lenox and Tilden Foundations, Print Collection, Miriam and Ira D. Wallach Division of Art, Prints and Photographs.

survive without dying in childbirth or contracting syphilis, she had to face the indignities of old age. In her tax declaration of 1542, Julia declared herself impoverished – an exaggeration belied by her death inventory – and now past "that age and all that flower that many could desire, from which came to me the abundance of necessary things."[59]

In the literary arena, the Venetian poet Niccolò Franco praised a courtesan's elaborate entertaining: "Not only have you revived a lost age, but you have brought it back in grand style, eliminating everything rustic and coarse. Instead of acorns, blackberries, and strawberries, you propose sumptuous platters and set elaborate tables covered with richly woven cloths appropriate for such delicate foods" (fig. 204).[60] But as courtesans became more accomplished and more affluent with that "abundance of necessary things," concern about them grew more pronounced. The writer Andrea Calmo addressed a letter to a Signora Brunella, "a lady full of jokes, deceits and traps and snares" on whom he had spent all his resources. Asking if she remembered from whom she had acquired her "paradise of delights," he continues: "One does not [even] speak of the tapestries, the carpets, the canopies of damask, the gilded bed, the painted chests, the Brescian draperies, and kitchen pewter; no, the dresses [piled] one above the other are nothing, the pearls are smoke; the rings a small thing . . . At least have a little conscience, seeing me a naked infant, seeing me derelict, and seeing me impoverished." Calmo concludes with an admonitory postscript: "However, he who spends his means luxuriating, sets himself up to go begging."[61]

The Mask of Decency

The high-living courtesan also attracted official attention. In 1543, the Venetian Senate declared:

> There are now excessive numbers of prostitutes in this our city; they have put aside all modesty and shame, and go about openly in the streets and churches, and furthermore are so well dressed and adorned that on many occasions our noble and citizen women have been confused with them, the good with the bad, and not only by foreigners but also by those who live here, because there

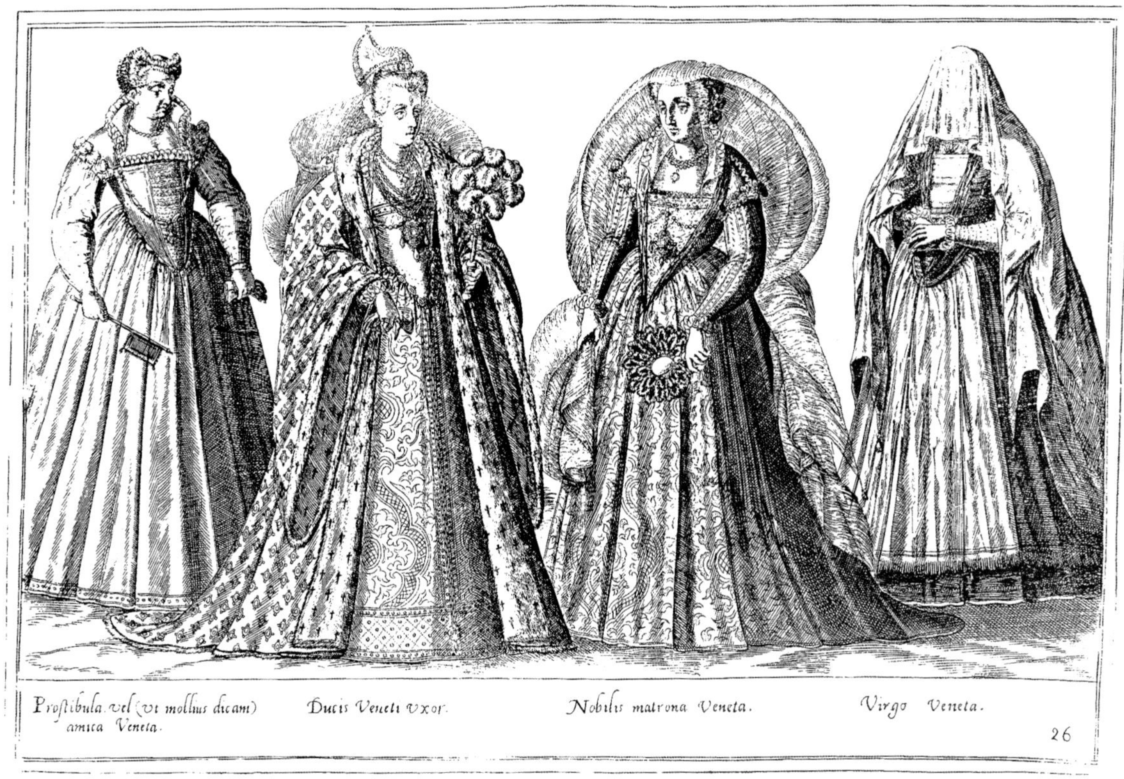

205 Four conditions of Venetian women. Engraving from Abraham de Bruyn, *Costumes civils & militaires du XVIe siècle* (facsimile of 1581 ed.: Brussels: G.A. van Trigt, 1872). The caption beneath the prostitute on the left states that in Venice such a woman might be called an *amica.* Next to her, from left to right, are the dogaressa, a noble matron, and a virgin. By permission of the Folger Shakespeare Library. ART Vol. f106, plate 26.

> is no difference of dress [fig. 205]. They set a bad example to women who enter and see their dwellings, and they cause no little discontent and scandal to everyone. Seeking to please the everlasting God, we must take steps to prevent these bad examples . . . and to curb the excessive expenditure of whores upon their own garments and upon the decoration of their houses.[62]

Accordingly, legislation was passed forbidding prostitutes from dressing in gold, silver, or silk and jewels of any kind. Nor in their houses were they to have "any furnishings of silk, or arrasses [tapestries], or upholstery, or bench-covers, or leathers of any kind, but only cloths of Bergamo or Brescia, and these must be plain and have no patterns cut upon them."[63] Sumptuary legislation had little lasting effect, however, and by the end of the century Coryat was not the only visitor to the city who would be awed by a paradise of Venus.

Another Englishman, Thomas Nashe, published a picaresque travel narrative entitled *The Unfortunate Traveler, or the Life of Jack Wilton* in 1594. Set in the 1530s, it was pure fiction, but contained references to historical events and was based upon observations in the present. The hero arrived in Venice, where he was immediately accosted by a well-dressed gentleman who "having half a dozen several languages in his purse, entertained us in our own tongue very paraphrastically and eloquently." But his new-found friend turned out to be

> a notable practitioner in the policy of bawdry. The place whither he brought us was a pernicious courtesan's house named Tabitha the Temptress, a wench that could set as civil a face on it as chastity's first martyr Lucretia. What will you conceit to be in any saint's house that was there to seek? Books, pictures, beads, crucifixes – why there was a haberdasher's shop of them in every chamber. I warrant you should not see one set of her neckercher perverted or turned awry, not a piece of a hair displaced. On her beds there was not a wrinkle of any wallowing to be found; her pillows bare out as smooth as a groaning wife's belly; and yet she was a Turk and an infidel, and had more doings than all her neighbors besides.[64]

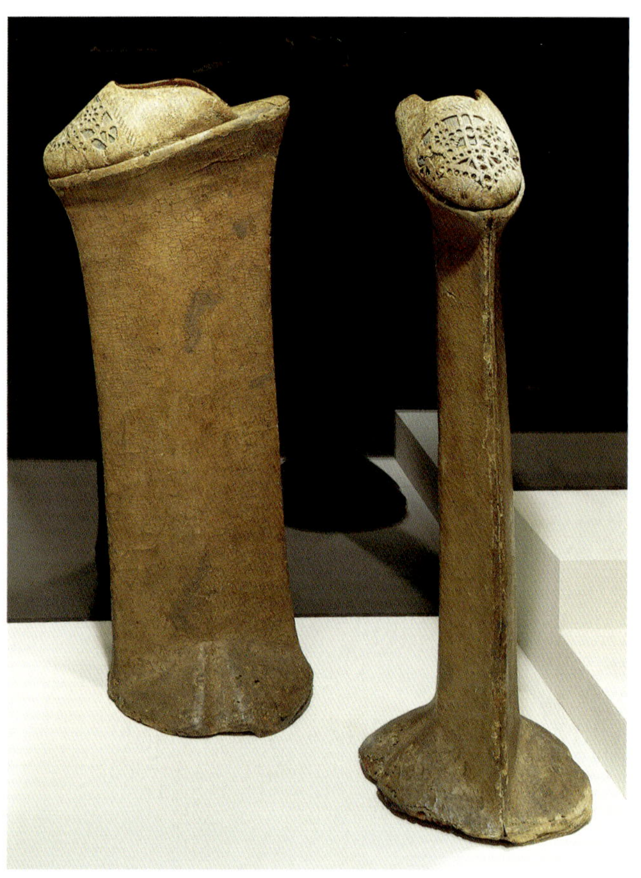

But of greater concern was the persistent problem of ambiguous or disguised identity, already decried in the Senate proclamation of 1543 cited above. Courtesans continued to make every effort to seem what they were not. For one thing, as numerous prints attest, the courtesan might attempt to pass as a respectable woman. As Pietro Aretino wrote to his mistress, the courtesan Angela Zaffetta: "Indeed, I give you the palm . . . for knowing how to put the mask of decency upon the face of lasciviousness; and hence it is, by your wisdom and discretion, you have procured money and praise."[65] In 1578 the Provveditori della Sanita complained that "in the churches of this city when the holy offices are celebrated, diverse *meretrici* and courtesans go . . . dressed like married women and widows, doing

206 (*left*) Platform shoes (also called *chopineys*, *calcagnetti*, *pianelle*, or *zoccole*), Venetian, late fifteenth century. Cut white leather and wood, height 52 cm. Venice, Museo Civico Correr, inv. cl. XXIV, n. 15.

207a (*below left*) Pietro Bertelli, *A Decorous Courtesan*. Engraving from his *Diversaru[m] nationum habitus*, 1589. 30.5 cm × 22.8 cm. London, British Library.

207b (*below right*) Pietro Bertelli, *A Courtesan with her Charms Revealed*. Engraving from his *Diversaru[m] nationum habitus*, 1589. 30.5 cm × 22.8 cm. London, British Library.

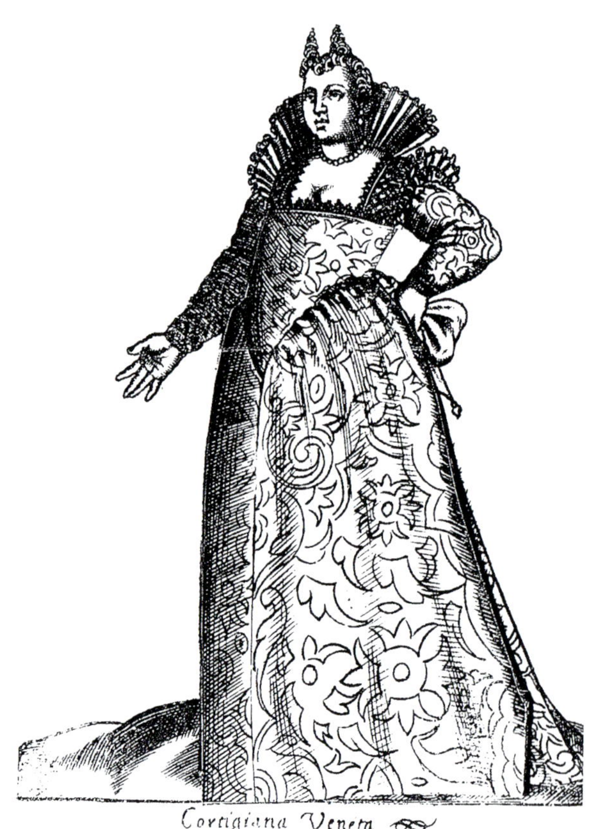

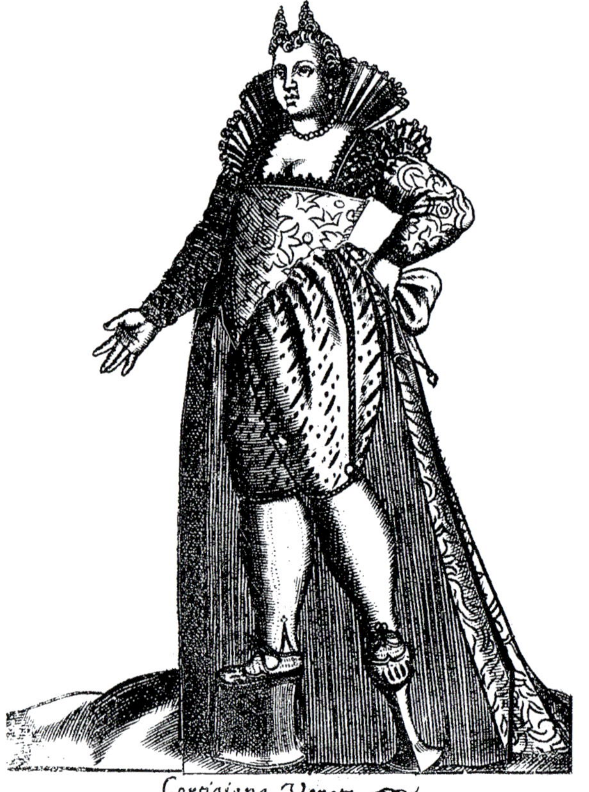

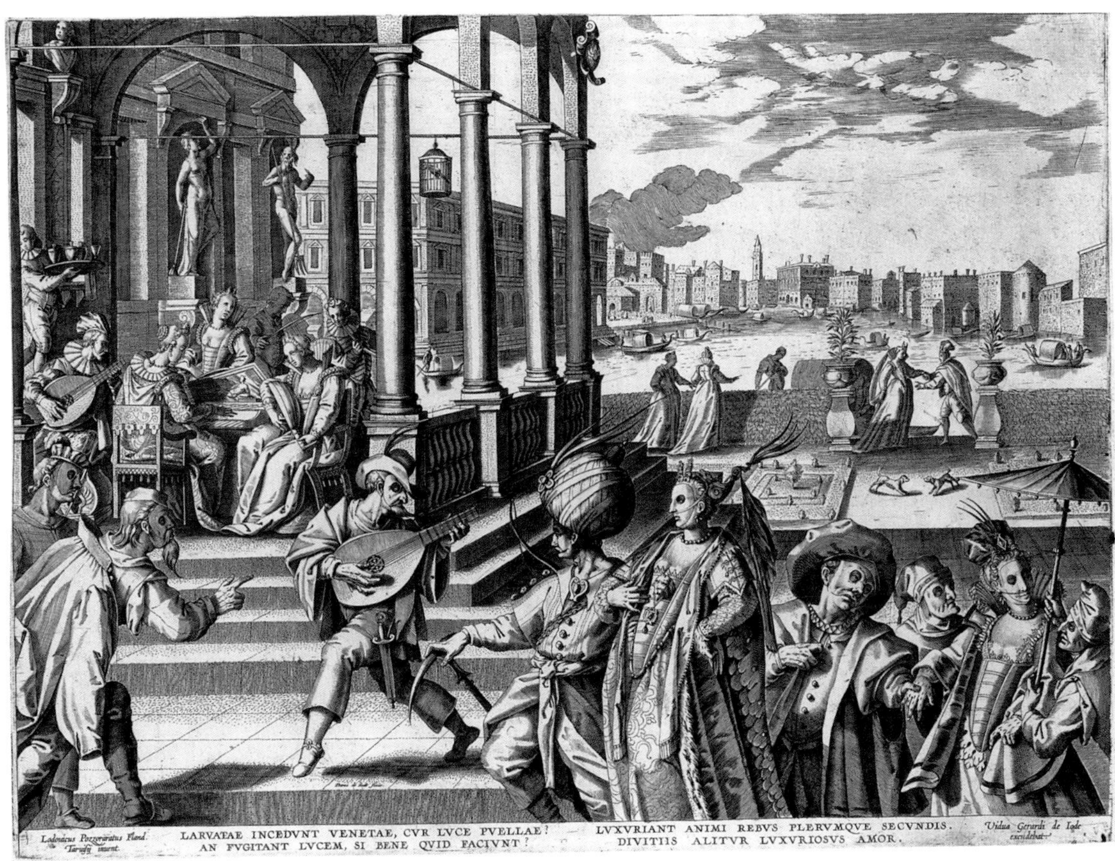

208 Pieter de Jode the Elder, after Pozzoserrato (Lodwijck Toeput), *A Venetian Carnival Scene on a Terrace*, ca. 1595 or 1598. Engraving, 374 × 502 mm. The birdcage suspended from the loggia is a feature often present in Dutch art, alluding to love and its dangers. Amsterdam, Rijksmuseum, Rijksprentenkabinet.

dishonorable acts, and setting a bad example with complaints by many, and many people who do not know them believe that they are respectable women, married and of good reputation."[66] In 1598 it was lamented that prostitutes had recently taken to "go out of the house often well covered with white veils of silk, a habit particular to young married ladies or nuns, noble as well as citizen, and others whom the custom of the city and their honor have reasonably been permitted to cover themselves in this manner." Even though married, if *meretrici* were not living with their husbands, they were strictly forbidden to dress in this manner.[67]

Or a courtesan might augment her height. Although many aristocratic women wore platform shoes called *pianelle*, courtesans were notorious for their exaggerated stilt-like footwear. One visitor to the city remarked that some of the women there appeared to be giants (fig. 206).[68]

Or she might obfuscate her gender. Cross-dressing was one more weapon in the courtesan's arsenal of seduction, and some wore men's clothing – perhaps a coat, in the manner of Giorgione's *Laura* or a shirt *alla mascolina* or even breeches concealed beneath their skirts, as revealed in an "interactive" print by Pietro Bertelli (figs. 207a and b) Aretino wrote to a courtesan called La Zufolina in 1547: "Twice my good fortune has sent your fair person into that house which is mine and others – the first time as a woman dressed like a man and the next time as a man dressed like a woman. You are a man when you are chanced on from behind and a woman when seen from in front."[69] In 1578 the Council of Ten heard a complaint that courtesans and prostitutes dressed in men's clothing and went on tour in gondolas through the canals. The cabins, closed front and back, became mobile paradises of Venus where impressionable youths were incited to engage in sodomy and other illicit activities.[70]

But sometimes the courtesan simply wore a mask (fig. 208). Elisabetta Condulmer's wardrobe included ten satin masks *da stravestir* – to disguise oneself – three of them described as with a beard.[71] Coryat would later write: "I was at one of their Play-houses where I saw a Comedie acted.

... Also their noble & famous Cortezans came to this comedy, but so disguised, that a man cannot perceive them. For they wore double maskes upon their faces, to the end they might not be seene ... [and] each of them wore a black short Taffata cloake."[72]

The paradise of Venus thus had its darker shadows. A print based upon a drawing by the Flemish artist Lodewyck Toeput, called Pozzoserrato, depicts a carnival celebration next to the Grand Canal (see fig. 208). In the foreground women in masks are joined by actors of the *commedia dell'arte*. In the loggia to the left, a concert is in progress. A caption on the pavement asks: "if they are fleeing the light, then what may they be up to?"[73]

An Adverse Fate

But there was also concern for the young women themselves. The beautiful and talented Veronica Franco (fig. 209) wrote to a friend to dissuade her from allowing her daughter to follow the life of a courtesan: "It is a most wretched thing ... to subject one's body and industriousness to a servitude whose very thought is most frightful ... to eat with another's mouth, sleep with another's eyes, move according to another's will, obviously rushing toward the shipwreck of one's mental abilities and one's life and body; What greater misery? What riches, what comforts, what delights can possibly outweigh all this?"[74]

Several refuges were founded during the Counter-Reformation period to address the problem. The Casa delle Zitelle or Convertite was established in 1559 to house and educate young women who were poor, attractive, and at risk of falling into sin.[75] And for those who already had, Veronica Franco herself petitioned the government in 1577 to found the Casa del Soccorso – a hospice for aged, indigent, and repentant prostitutes.[76] But these were no paradises of Venus.

It took another century before the Renaissance courtesan disappeared. One of the last was Paola Provesin, who died in 1638 in her apartment on Piazza San Marco. It had been rented from the procurators by the nobleman Tommaso Contarini back in 1600. He paid not only for her rent and living expenses, but also for her instruction by masters of music, painting, and poetry. The inventory made at the time of her death described rooms decorated with green and yellow flowered damask and gilded and lacquered leather, and a library of seventy-six books, including a Genealogy of the Gods.[77]

On the walls were thirty paintings, one described as "portraits in a concert of music" – perhaps as in a painting by Jacopo Tintoretto (fig. 210).[78] Indeed, the rooms were filled with books of music and a veritable orchestra of musical instruments: a spinet and a harpsichord, both painted with fillets of gold, six theorbos described as old, and another of ivory, as well as an ivory lute, and another theorbo and another lute, each with its case, and a large harp. In her will, Paola had ordered all of her worldly possessions to be sold and the proceeds given to charity.[79] Her music may have been profane, but her life was a testament to the capacity of music not only to enchant and to seduce, but also to enlighten and to elevate the soul. As Veronica Franco had written half a century earlier: "True wealth consists of peace and contentment, and the contentment of our soul is nothing else but the possession of virtue, easily recognized by its works, which in the face of all the hostile efforts of an adverse fate have the strength to give man happiness."[80]

And yet, it is all too easy to parody and stigmatize the Renaissance courtesan as Coryat and other writers did,

209 (*right*) *Portrait of Veronica Franco*, Venice, 1575. MS. 457, "Mores Italiae," fol. 6. New Haven, Yale University, Beinecke Rare Book and Manuscript Library.

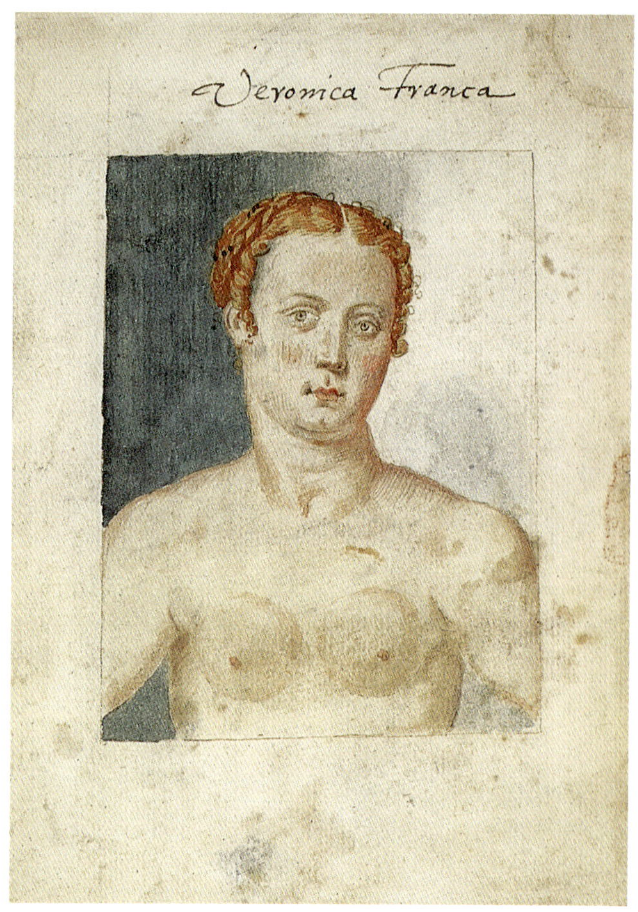

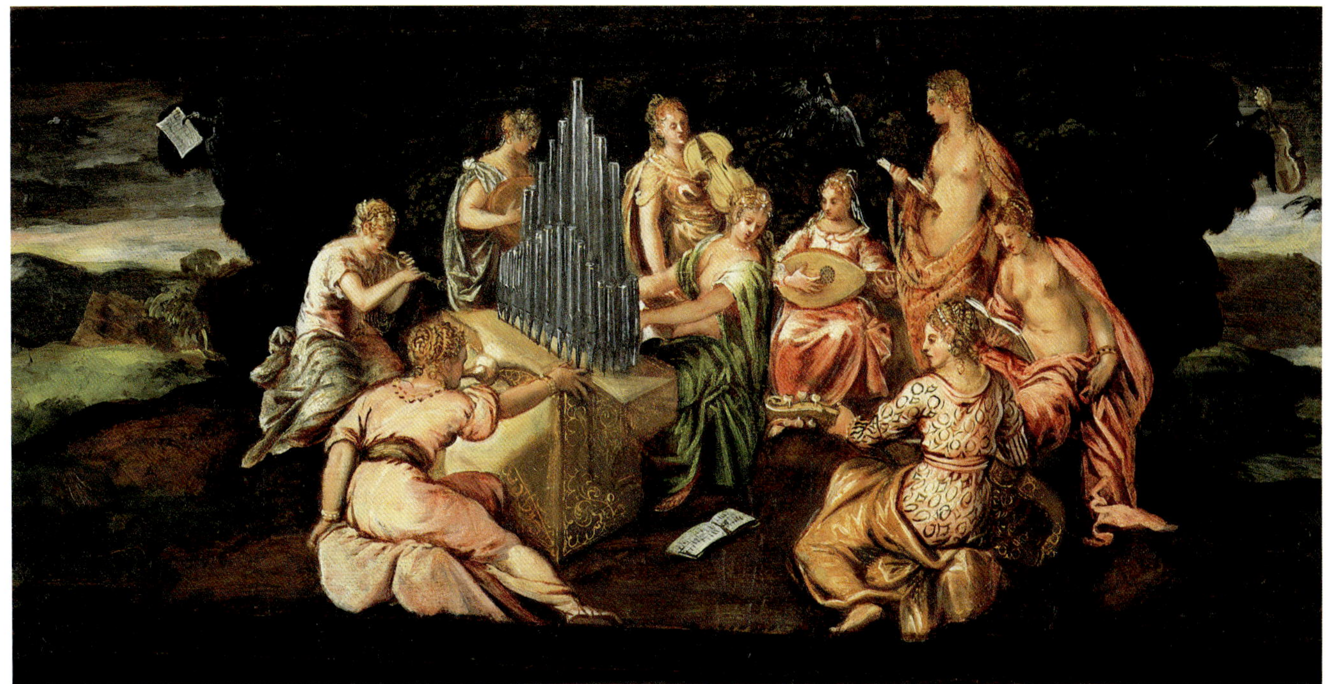

210 Jacopo Tintoretto, *Contest between the Muses and Pierides*, 1544–45. Oil on wood, 46 × 90 cm. In an episode recounted by Ovid (*Metamorphosis* v), the nine daughters of Pieris, called the Pierides, challenged the muses to a singing contest. Easily outsung by Calliope, who represented her sister muses, the Pierides did not concede defeat and as punishment were turned into chattering magpies, "the scandalmongers of the woods." In his painting, Tintoretto depicts the muses playing an organ, two lutes, a violin, a viol, a flared horn and a pipe, with two of them singing from sheet music. Three of the Pierides, already turned into magpies, fly away with sheet music, a reed pipe, and a violin. The work may originally have been painted on the inside lid of a spinet or harpsichord. Museo del Castelvecchio, Verona.

without considering the realities of life in a highly stratified society. Marriages in affluent families were increasingly restricted to one son to limit succession – and dispersion of the patrimony – to a single line of descent; the number of daughters marrying was also limited to a few because of extravagant dowry expectations. As Cornelia, a protagonist in Moderata Fonte's treatise, *Il merito delle donne*, published in 1600, asked: "How many fathers there are who do not provide for their daughters while they are alive and then finally, when they die, leave their whole estate or the greatest part of it to their sons, leaving their poor daughters to fall into all kinds of errors through no fault of their own?" Her friend Corinna agreed: "they are forced to provide for themselves by blameworthy and reprehensible means."[81]

The situation was that much worse when there were few resources to begin with. A young woman with a patrician, if tarnished, birthright, like Elisabetta Condulmer, with expectations of a refined lifestyle but without the means to achieve it through a good marriage, had few options other than the convent. In all likelihood, it was her beauty, charm, and enterprise that had allowed her to attain a level of considerable comfort with "an abundance of necessary things," and even the resources to buy out her brothers' shares in the family home, through a series of liaisons. Most importantly, it gave her a measure of autonomy and independence – those qualities that were so intriguing and yet so threatening to the order of things in a period when a writer could propose: "in a woman one does not look for profound eloquence or subtle intelligence, or exquisite prudence or talent for living or administration of the republic or justice or anything else except chastity . . . because in a woman this is worth every other excellence."[82]

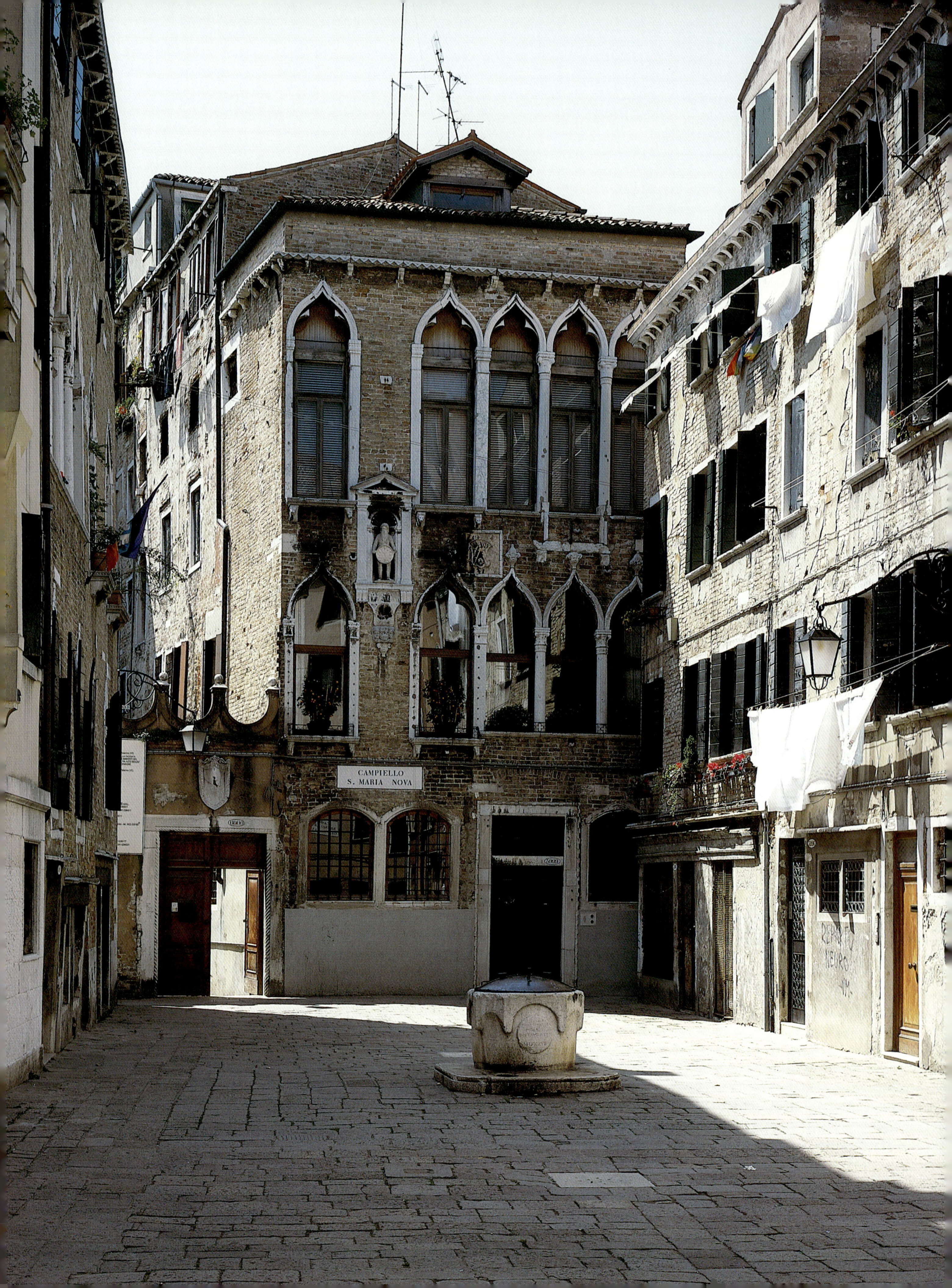
CAMPIELLO
S. MARIA NOVA

7

Not One but Many Separate Cities

IN 1581, FRANCESCO SANSOVINO spoke of "not one but many separate cities, all conjoined together." He was referring to the seventy-odd islands, surrounded by canals and linked by bridges, that make up Venice. What looked to be a single city was really an aggregation of separate islands, apparent only to "the subtle observer of things."[1] But turning Sansovino's metaphor on its side, framing it in social rather than physical terms, reveals yet another dimension of Venice's diversity within a seeming unity. Writing, as well, of the ornaments, the furnishings, and the incredible richness of the houses, he claimed that each householder shared in the city's refinements and wealth, "according to their quality and condition."[2] And, indeed, this must have seemed the case to a visitor rowing along the Grand Canal, admiring the marble-clad facades and peering through velvet-draped windows at sparkling chandeliers of Murano glass.

But the "subtle observer of things" who ventured into the narrow canals and dark streets would see a fuller picture that revealed, within each island city, many other cities yet. For while the city of the rich was one of spacious golden chambers and richly woven tapestries, the city of the poor was often one of sparsely furnished rooms at best, or the streets at worst. What made the situation perhaps more complex than in other places was Venice's rigid hierarchy of social orders. For Sansovino's reference to each householder's "quality and condition" alluded to the caste system created by the Serrata – the closure of the Great Council in 1297.[3] Since that time, as discussed in Chapter 1, the noble caste of patricians at the top held all the political power. This hereditary nobility included the doge, who was elected for life, and all the public officials – councilors, judges, senators, administrators – who rotated in and out of office for periods ranging from a few months to several years.[4] In the early days patricians were usually merchants; by the later sixteenth century, they increasingly lived off their rents and other investments. But a good number of them were poor and depended upon public offices to sustain themselves and their families.[5]

Just below the patriciate was the order of *cittadini*, an elite caste who came to be called *seconda corona* or second crown of the republic.[6] They were, for the most part, merchants or bureaucrats who staffed the state offices and provided continuity in a government run by noble amateurs.[7] The remaining 90 percent or so of the population – the *popolani* – included a broad miscellany of occupations and economic conditions, from wealthy merchants to the truly indigent.[8]

The republic used various strategies throughout its history to deal with these disjunctions of social caste and economic class and to ensure domestic peace: ideological tools, as exemplified by the ethos of *concordia* and *unanimitas* that prevailed within the ruling elite; political tools, such as a succession of regulations intended to discourage the formation of factions and nepotism within the patriciate; economic tools, including the provision of grain in times of famine; and legal tools, most notably sumptuary laws, which aimed to limit ostentatious display and to ensure the rule of *mediocritas* among the affluent.[9] This chapter explores ways in which attitudes and practices pertaining to real property and housing helped to fuse the city of the rich and the city of the poor into a well-functioning whole.

* * *

As the primary locus of family identity, the home was where the wealthy family, whether noble or not, displayed its taste,

211 *(facing page)* Ca' Bembo on Campiello Santa Maria Nova (Cannaregio 5999), late fourteenth century. Each *soler* (residential floor) of the late trecento facade features a pair of cusped windows on the left, flanking the aedicule, behind which is a chamber now used as a dining room. The right-hand window is separated by a pilaster strip from the columned triforate window further to the right, which defines the *portego*.

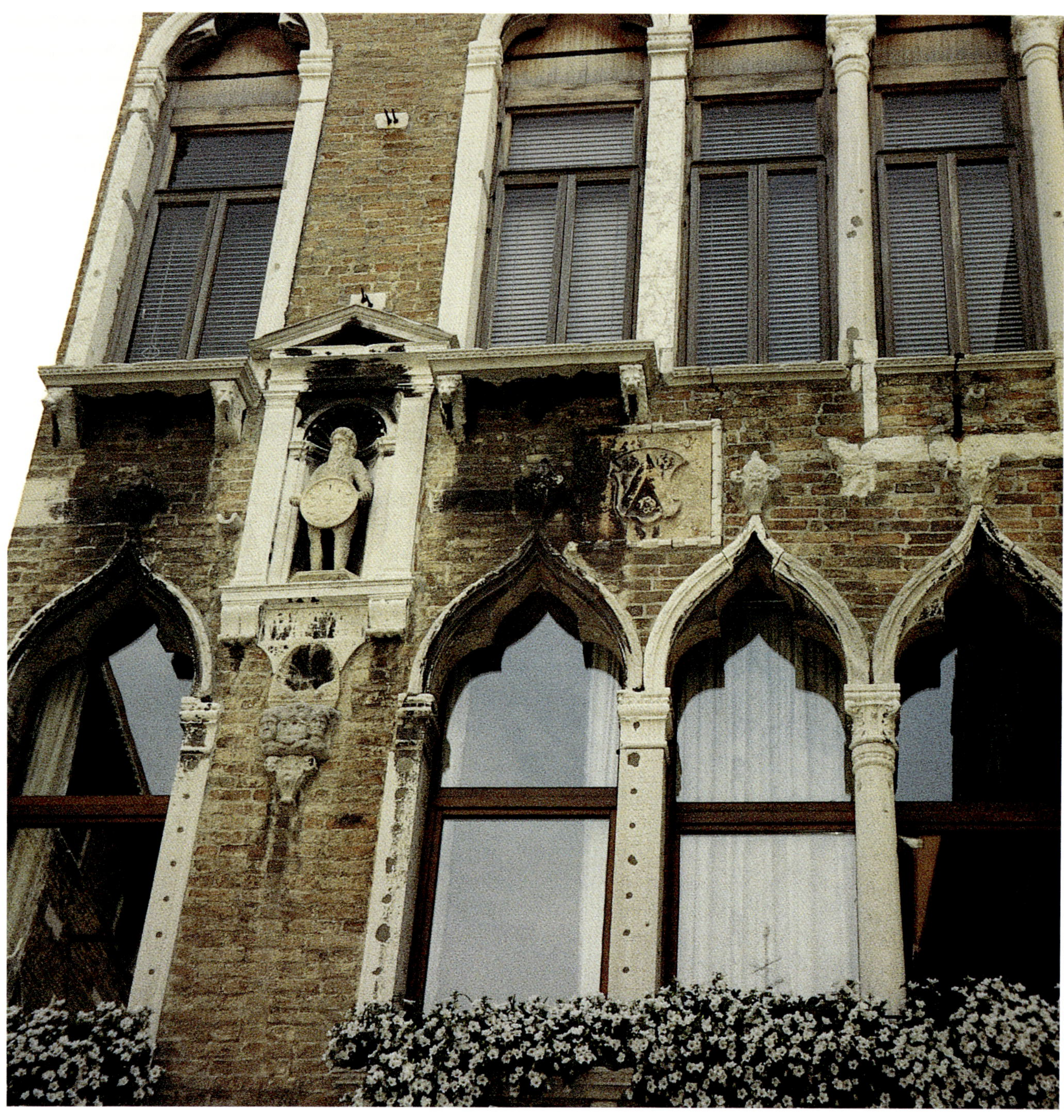

212 Facade detail from Ca' Bembo (see fig. 211). The coat of arms above the triforate window is a typical feature on Venetian facades. By contrast, the tabernacle to the left, containing a statue of a wild man who holds a solar disc and featuring an inscription praising the patron Zuan Matteo Bembo, is a unique example of self-definition in a city that valued patrician *mediocritas*. According to Girolamo Ruscelli, *Le imprese illustri* (1584), Bembo also had a personal *impresa* composed of an radiant sun above a vase containing an evergreen (*semper-vivum*) plant, with the motto "DVM VOLVITVR ISTE." Ruscelli explains: "I believe that this great senator wished to denote to himself, to his sons, to his posterity, and to the world, that his virtuous and illustrious deeds made under the splendor of the sun – that is, in the view of the world and under the light and grace of the highest God, truly the sun of Justice – will never perish, nor be lost or stolen by malice or envy, but live eternally green and most vigorous." He adds that Bembo vanquished the envy that plagued so many famous persons, "with virtue, with ingenuity, with patience, with love, and with generosity, showing everyone more by deeds, rather than by words or with superficial ways, cerimonious and simulated, as many are accustomed to do."

its prosperity, and its prominence. As shown in Chapter 2, the Corner family, for example, proclaimed its pre-eminent position as one of the wealthiest families in the city with the construction of Ca' Corner della Ca' Grande (see fig. 44). Designed in a classical style by Jacopo Sansovino in the middle decades of the sixteenth century, it was so massive as to dwarf all its neighbors and was praised as one of the four most outstanding palaces on the Grand Canal by Francesco Sansovino in 1581.[10] But the Corner family was at the high end of patrician affluence, and Ca' Corner was not a typical *casa da statio* – a Venetian term of dignity denoting the family palace, a residence that was one cut above an ordinary house.[11]

The Casa da Statio

The patrician Zuan Matteo Bembo, by contrast, lived with his family in the *sestiere* of Cannaregio in a *casa da statio* that might be considered more characteristic of the noble caste. Bembo was well connected. He has been mentioned already in Chapter 4 as the husband of Marcella Marcello, niece of the famous Cardinal Pietro Bembo (for the Bembo family tree see Appendix, p. 256). As well as maintaining a long and affectionate correspondence with Pietro,[12] Zuan Matteo was granted a copyright in 1530 to publish a number of his works in Latin and vernacular Italian.[13] He is interesting, however, not only as a man of affairs with a long career of service to the republic, but also as a homeowner.

Originally built in the late trecento, his modest Gothic palace faces Campiello Santa Maria Nova in Cannaregio (figs. 211 and 212).[14] The Bembo coat of arms in the center of the asymmetrical facade still marks the domus, but beyond that, Zuan Matteo demonstrated an innovative approach to the age-old Venetian tradition of embedding sculpted reliefs in the walls of the family home when he squeezed a classical tabernacle between the two residential floors in the wall to the left. Bembo's sculpture is really a time-spanning pastiche, the sixteenth-century aedicule containing a fourteenth-century statue of Chronos or Saturn in the form of a wild man holding a solar disc. An inscribed plaque below is supported by three male heads, carved in high relief and also datable to the fourteenth century.[15] The Latin inscription reads, in translation: "As long as this [the sun] rotates, the cities of Zara, Cattaro, Capodistria, Verona, Cyprus, and Candia [Crete] will give testimony to his actions."[16] The cities are those in which Zuan Matteo had served as *podestà* or *capitano* of the Venetian Republic. In all likelihood he had composed the assemblage as a personal *impresa* that spoke to posterity, possibly with a collateral function as totem to protect the house and its inhabitants.

Among Zuan Matteo's contributions to colonial life was a fountain constructed in Candia that also survives to this day (fig. 213).[17] It too was a sculptural pastiche. Incorporating a headless Roman statue, it testifies to his humanist credentials and to his awareness of the evocative power of sculpture, publicly displayed. Zuan Matteo's civic honors include his portrayal by Jacopo Tintoretto in one of the narrative paintings in the Great Council Hall of the Ducal Palace. These canvases were, as Sansovino later reported, "all consumed by the fire of 1577, bringing great displeasure to everyone, through the loss . . . of the memories of so many excellent persons, in which the world is rarely so abundant."[18]

Despite Zuan Matteo's frequent missions abroad, he and Marcella raised eight sons and two daughters in the house at Santa Maria Nova (figs. 214 and 215). By the time he wrote his last will and testament in 1570, three of the sons had

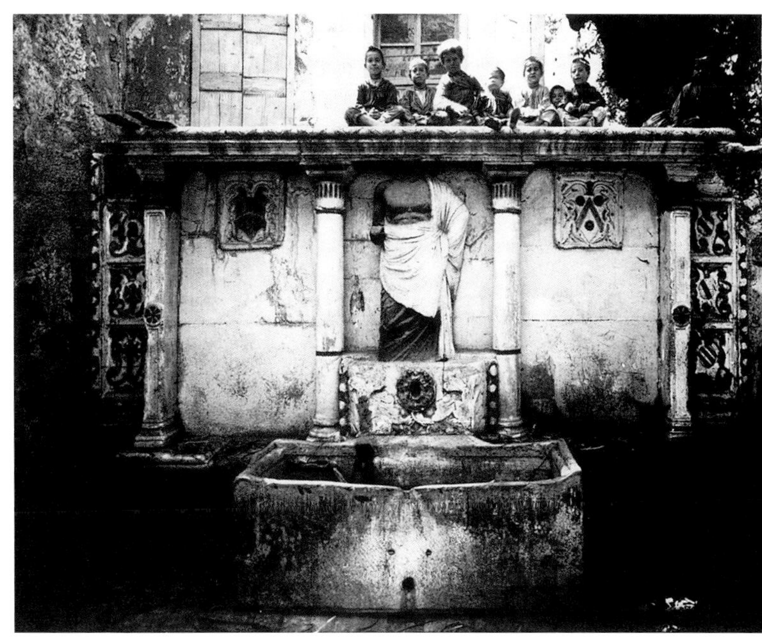

213 Fountain in Candia (now Heraklion), Crete, built by Zuan Matteo Bembo. A chronicle entry (BCV, MS. Cicogna 3558/III: Discretione dell'Isola di Candia. Author unknown.) with a description of Crete writes: "infinite columns of marble of various colors and likewise a great number of buried marble statues, some large and some small are found there together with fragments of statues of different sorts . . . and one of these statues without a head or the right hand was placed below the cubit of the fountain of San Salvatore in the city of Candia made by the Illustrious Lord Giovanni Matteo Bembo, who was Capitano of the Kingdom of Candia in the year 1553; these remains and fragments demonstrate that it was a very grand city."

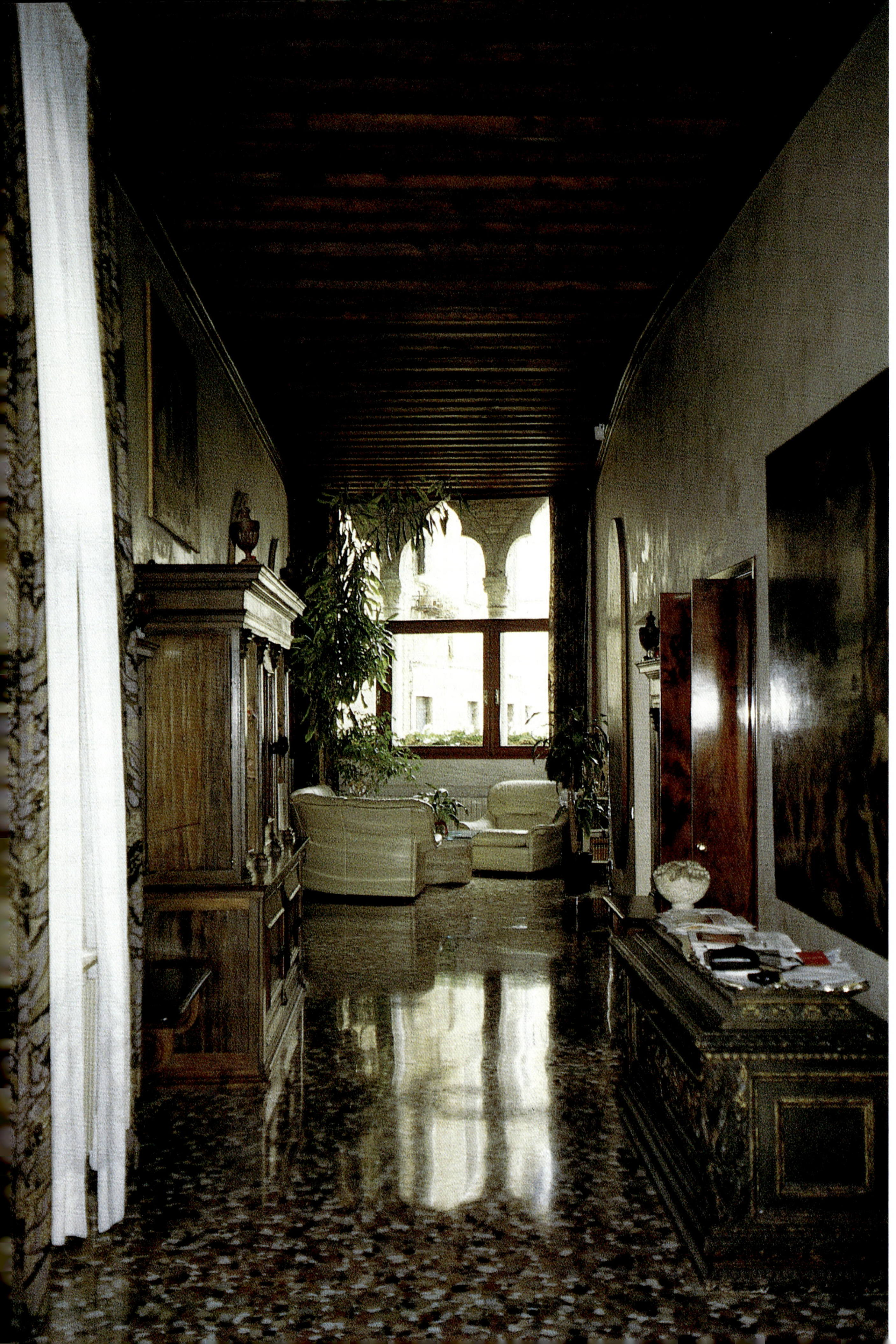

already died. The document offers a thumbnail sketch of Venetian attitudes about property and warrants a brief examination. He declares: "I wish that all my real estate, houses, and villa lands, and those few pieces of silver and furniture acquired with my money, would stay in perpetual *fedecommesso* for my four sons, Lorenzo, Alvise, Marc' Antonio, and David, and their legitimate male descendants," with each share to pass on from father to sons.[19] (His fifth surviving legitinate son, not mentioned in the testament, will enter the story later). Each male heir was allowed to leave his portion to his daughters, but only during their lifetimes, typically as part of their dowries, after which it would revert to the male descendants. If male descendants from all of Zuan Matteo's four sons were lacking, then the estate should revert to the descendants of his brother David, again to pass from father to sons. If these direct lines should die out, then a legitimate male member of the house of Bembo should be selected by the Procurators of San Marco to inherit the estate. If the Bembo line died out entirely, then the residue of the estate should be given to the hospital of San Giovanni e Paolo "for the use and aid of the poor."[20]

And what of Zuan Matteo's daughters? Augusta, he states, "is satisfied with the legacy of 100 ducats that was left to her and she had even been given 25 ducats more, by her mother."[21] Giulia was deceased by this time and was not mentioned. In any case, she had married into mainland nobility and would have received her share of the patrimony in her dowry. Indeed, their mother Marcella's will of 1547 had referred to both daughters and made plain that she was making the initial bequest of 100 ducats to Augusta "in sign of love, for a single time only, and more I do not leave her, who by grace of God is rich and is doing very well."[22] As to Giulia, her mother had declared,

> that if my daughter Giulia is not married or in a convent before my death, I wish that she would have 500 ducats from all my possessions, whether from my dowry or that of my sister Madonna Giulia, and any other properties that may come to me, with this condition: that she marry one of our Venetian gentlemen or an honorable foreigner with the consent of my magnificent consort and her brothers, and if she is married before my death I do not wish her to have anything, and if she becomes a nun I do not wish her to have those 500 ducats [since] it seems to me that she could enter a very good convent with the 400 ducats that her father is leaving her.

If none of Marcella's sons produced heirs, then her daughters were to receive her entire estate.[23]

In accordance with Venetian custom, the testaments of both parents made plain that the bulk of the family patrimony was to pass down through the male lineage. Moreover, Marcella's will stresses the importance of maintaining the purity of the bloodline: 'Declaring above all that if in due course, my sons would have bastards or a bastard, they can never leave them anything of mine.'[24]

The rules of the game were different, however, for men. While preserving the bulk of his estate for the legitimate progeny of his legitimate sons, Zuan Matteo also provided for a natural son, Ettor, probably born after his wife's death in 1555. He was to be "governed, taught, dressed, and shod, and the masters who will instruct him, to be paid" from the proceeds of the estate. At the time, the boy was in the care of a tutor, but he was given leave to move in with one of his half-brothers – Zuan Matteo's legitimate sons – if he chose. The latter were, in any case, collectively obliged to support the boy until he reached the age of eighteen years.[25]

Surprisingly, Zuan Matteo does not include his son Pietro among his heirs. Namesake of Cardinal Pietro Bembo, he had entered the Church and was now Bishop of Veglia. He was cited in the will only as "Monsignore, my son" in connection with a loan of 300 ducats, a favor that Zuan Matteo had also extended in various amounts to his other sons. And yet, in conformity with the Venetian legal principle of "absolute equivalence" among brothers, all surviving sons should have received the remainder in strictly equal portions.[26] So despite a legitimate will, the estate was open to question. The language of Zuan Matteo's will suggests not enmity toward Pietro but rather that he was concerned, first and foremost, with posterity – so much so that he did not feel the need to endow Pietro, a celibate son with a high position in the Church, with a share of his estate. But predictably, after Zuan Matteo's death, Pietro contested the will and the case went to arbitration. The dispute was between Pietro and his three surviving brothers since Alvise had already died without progeny. Because the inheritance was not made "pro indiviso" the court was allowed to divide the real estate among the four parties.[27]

Zuan Matteo had written in his will that the *casa da statio* at Santa Maria Nova consisted of the principal building, "that is the upper and lower *soleri*" – the Venetian term for full-sized stories above the ground floor – along with a

214 (*facing page*) Ca' Bembo on Campiello Santa Maria Nova, interior view of the upper *portego*. The long narrow space functions as a hallway that culminates in a sitting area, well illuminated by the triforate window in the front of the house. The reflections on the terrazza floor demonstrate the magical quality of light in a constricted living space.

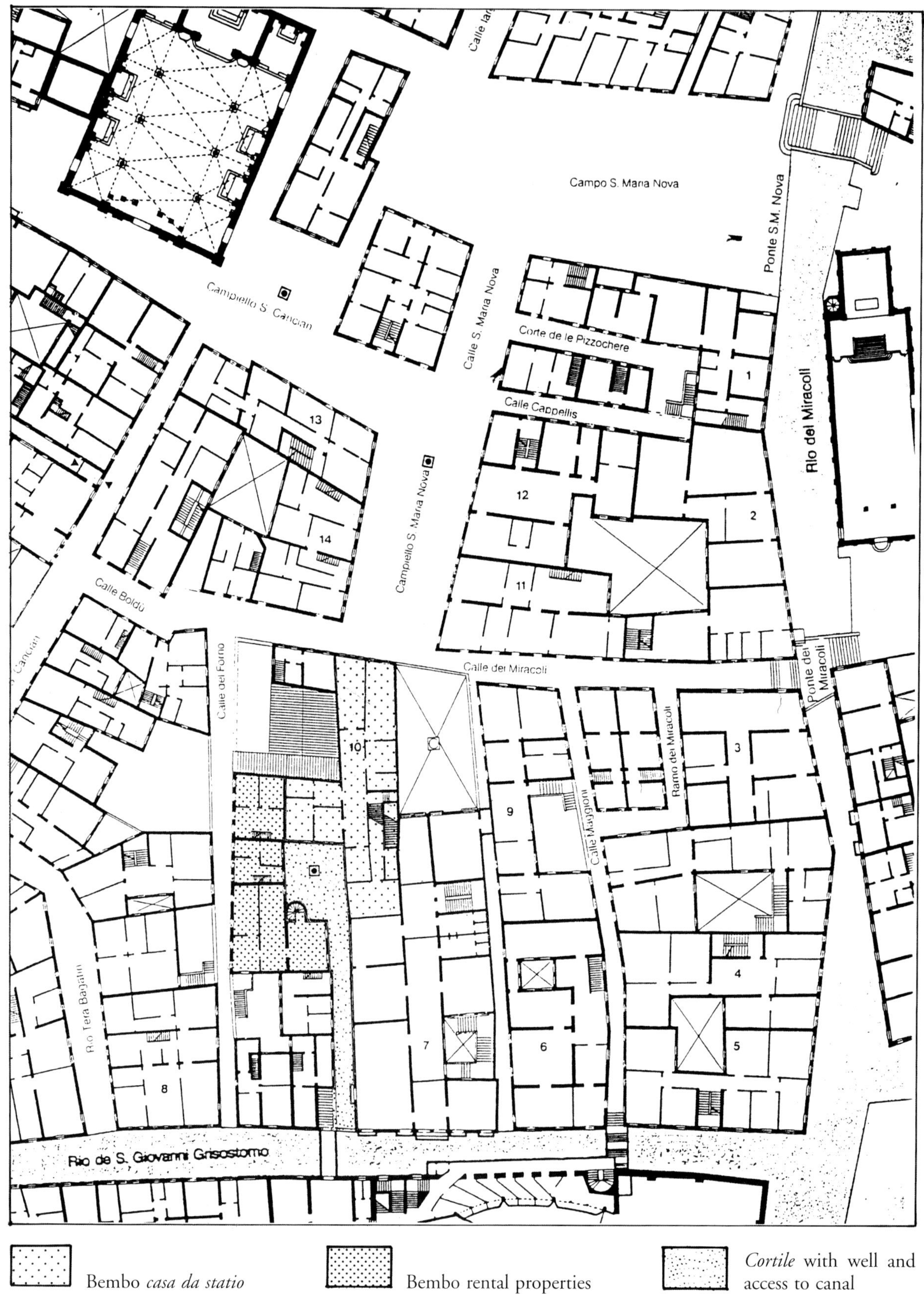

215 Ca' Bembo and the surrounding neighborhood in Cannaregio, adapted from Giuseppe Cristinelli, *Cannaregio: un sestiere di Venezia – la forma urbana, l'assetto edilizio, le architetture* (Rome: Officina Edizioni, 1987), tavola 71. The room added to the left side of the house by Zuan Matteo Bembo is partitioned to create four spaces, two of them chambers. Ca' Boldu (7), built in the sixteenth century with the main facade on Rio San Giovanni Crisostomo, was joined for a time to Ca' Bembo.

chamber that he had added to one side and a row of rental houses on Calle del Forno to the west (figs. 215 and 216). Each of the two *soleri* consisted of a long *portego* or *sala*, opening to the single large chamber that Zuan Matteo had added on the west side and to a row of smaller chambers, including a kitchen, on the east.[28]

The court determined that the family home could not accommodate four households and divided it into two living units. The lower *soler*, along with the *mezzado* or mezzanine floor between it and the *piano terra*, was assigned to the heirs of Zuan Matteo's eldest son, Lorenzo, who was now also deceased.[29] Their portion also included five houses – one *casa* and four *casette* – on Calle del Forno, which collectively brought in rents of 51 ducats per year. The entire upper *soler* was now given to Pietro, Bishop of Veglia, along with its own *mezzado* and the *soffitta* or attic. He also received two houses and three apartments on Calle del Forno, bringing in annual rents of 53 ducats. The courtyard with the well-head and catchment basin remained common to both properties (figs. 217 and 218). The two other sons, Marc'Antonio and David, divided up the remaining real estate. To David went two houses on Calle del Forno, bringing in rents of 52 ducats, plus an apartment not rented at the time. He was also given two houses, each described as a *casa da statio*, in the *contrade* of San Maurizio and San Pantalon, with rents unspecified, along with two smaller dwellings in the latter location that brought in 15 ducats of rent.[30] Marc'Antonio was given a villa and agricultural land in Ponte de Brenta, with the income that came from grain, wine, and tributes. He was also given two *case* and two *casette* on Calle del Forno yielding rents of 31 ducats, and was to be paid 2 ducats per year by each of the three other parties for sixteen-and-a-half years, for a total of around 100 ducats, an arrangement that led to further litigation.[31]

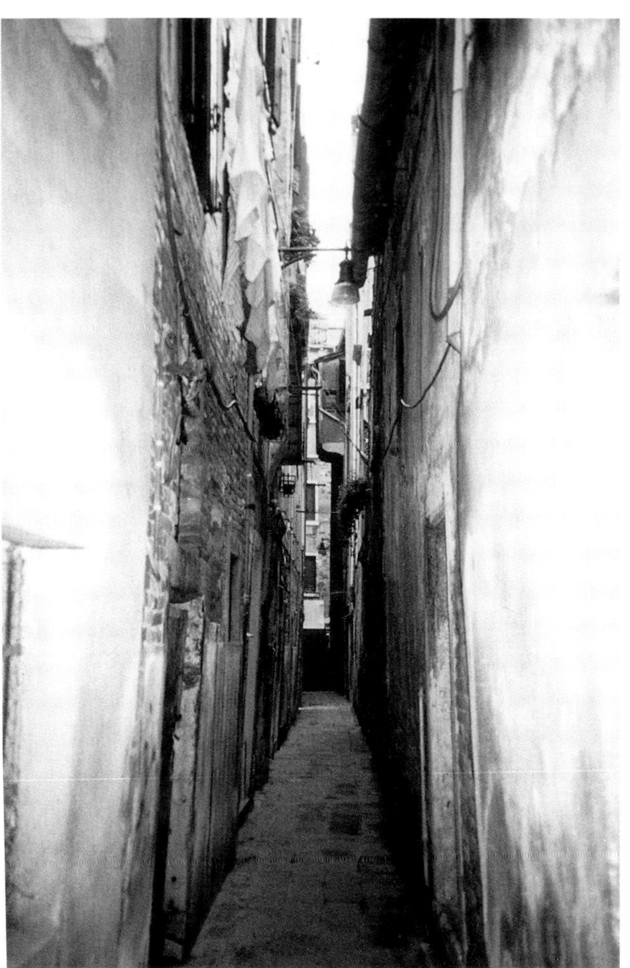

216 Calle del Forno at Santa Maria Nova. The entrance to the courtyard of Ca' Bembo is at the left. At the end of the alley is Rio San Giovanni Crisostomo.

Landlords and Tenants

Less than a decade later the *decime* (tax declarations) of 1582 show Lorenzo's three sons renting out the lower *soler* to another patrician, Alessandro Balbi, who paid a rent of 80 ducats per year.[32] And what of their three uncles? Pietro is out of town at the time, according to his nephew Andrea, but is keeping the *soler di sopra* "as his habitation."[33] Marc' Antonio had died and his widow, Lucietta, is living in the same *contrada* with five minor children. Although she had received several small properties from her husband's estate in restitution of her dowry, she declares herself poor and sick and unable to keep all of them in good repair while supporting her children on an income of more than 90 ducats per year. The rental value of her own home, called a *casetta* in the declaration, is given as only 16 ducats.[34] David, Zuan Matteo's youngest surviving son, is living in a rented *casa da statio* at San Barnaba, across the Grand Canal from Santa Maria Nova, in the *sestiere* of Dorsoduro. He is paying a rather substantial rent of 100 ducats per year to another nobleman, Gabriel Zorzi, who owns the property but is not living in it himself. David's rent is subsidized in part by his share in the rental units on Calle del Forno at Santa Maria Nova, which bring in 24 ducats a year, and income from a large *casa da statio* at San Boldù that was part of his wife's dowry. Like David's own family home, the latter property was divided into two living units, one on each floor, yielding a total of 160 ducats a year in rent. So although David was deprived of his ancestral home, he was ahead of the game, more than offsetting his own rent with proceeds from other properties in his possession.[35]

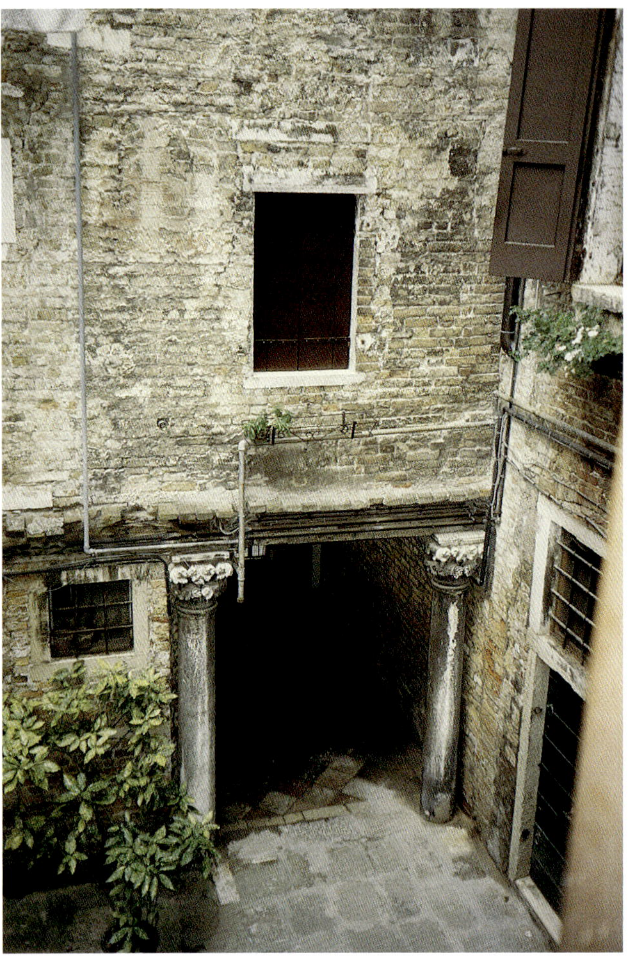

217 View from the courtyard of Ca' Bembo toward the entrance portal and rental properties on Calle del Forno. Zuan Matteo Bembo's addition to the original house is on the right.

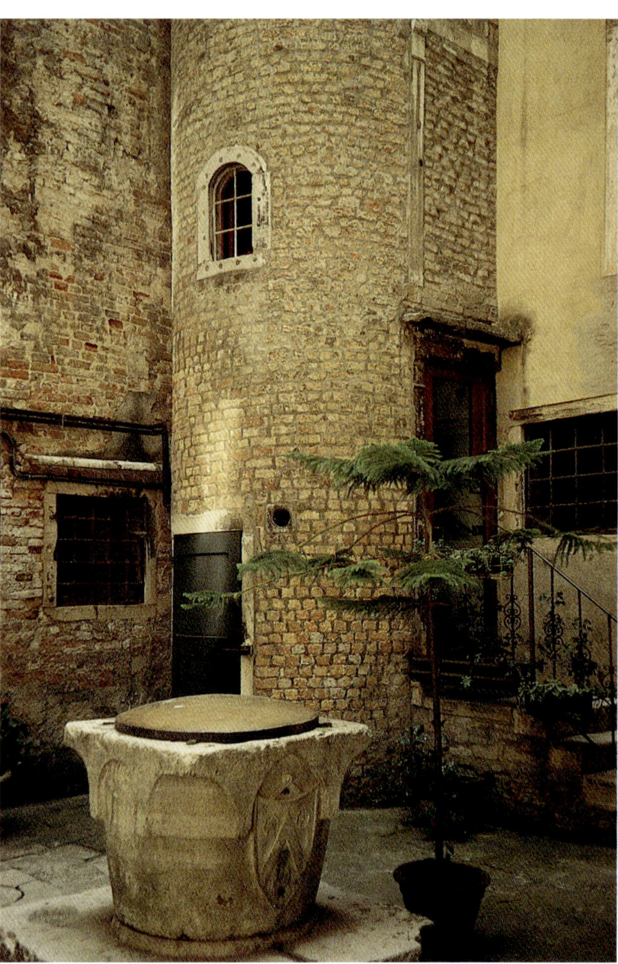

218 Well-head with the Bembo *stemma* in the courtyard of Ca' Bembo. The staircase *a chiccola* in the background was part of the sixteenth-century complex of rental buildings facing Calle del Forno.

It should be stressed that this was not an unusual situation. Tax records show that approximately half of the 1,230 patrician families in the city in 1582 lived in rental housing, and that the renters enjoyed the same broad spectrum of financial resources as those who lived in their own houses. Some could not afford to purchase or build a house, but others rented by choice, preferring to keep their capital liquid for investments or, as in the case of David Bembo, finding that the balance sheet showed a distinct advantage to renting. His rent of 100 ducats was around the eightieth percentile for patricians. Somewhat more than 20 percent paid 100 ducats per year or more, with the top 2.5 percent within that group paying more than 200 ducats.[36] A little more than 40 percent of patricians paid between 50 and 100 ducats and 33 percent paid less than 50.

Of those patricians who did live in their own homes, about one in eight were paying rent on part of the building to a sibling or someone else. An heir of a certain Zuan Barbarigo reported ownership in the tax rolls of 1537 of "two-thirds of one-half of a *casa da statio*." Another patrician, Giulio Balbi, lived in the old family home at San Zulian, which he owned jointly "with relatives of Ca' Balbi." These were his landlords, and he was obligated to pay rent to nine other parties.[37]

It was during this period that patrician families were encouraging only one or two sons to marry to prevent further fragmentation of the patrimony.[38] And, not surprisingly, many Venetians who had large estates with several pieces of property to divide among their heirs often still insisted that the primary family home – the *casa da statio* – remain intact, or at least they put limits on the subdivisions. Marco Giustinian was not atypical in ordering in his will that his *casa da statio* at San Leonardo, described as "very comfortable and honorable," was not to be divided upon his death. Revealing that it had cost him 4,000 ducats to build, plus another 400 to 500 in expenses from a lawsuit over the property, he cautioned his sons to have "an eye to saving," a credo that had allowed him to "never fail to be able to support the house and a family of five sons and three daughters with the added burdens of wife, male and female servants, obligations, repairs, and other very great expenses," including dowries of 4,000 ducats for each daughter. He admonished his sons that "every good comes from unity" and that "fraternal love" is the key to conserving the patrimony and augmenting the esteem of the house. If his sons did not wish to live together *in fraterna* – with the property held in common by two or more brothers – and preferred to divide up the estate instead, so be it, but they were expressly forbidden to divide up the *casa da statio* at San Leonardo. If his sons declined to keep the house for common use, they could rent it to a third party and divide the rent in equal shares. By 1582, the three surviving sons had crafted an ingenious solution of time-sharing. Each would live with his family in the *casa da statio* for ten years at a time in rotation, and then move out into one of the other properties they had received in the equitable division of the estate.[39] More typically adult families were dispersed. As with the Bembo family, two or more brothers or their heirs might still share a house, but married brothers just as often lived in neighborhoods that were quite distant from one another.

But if the palace was a major factor in family identity, was there a loss of dignity and honor for those who rented rather than living in the homes they owned? Not necessarily. For appearances and a noble style of living may well have been more important than a property deed. The model had been set at the highest level of Venetian political life. In addition to the doge, who resided in the Ducal Palace, the Procurators of San Marco were allowed to live in signorial residences on Piazza San Marco at public expense. Since other noble homes were banned from the *contrada* of San Marco, this was a special privilege. A procuratorship was a lifetime appointment and the highest office in the land next to that of the doge. Even though paid only a token salary, the procurators were highly esteemed, with duties that involved the administration of private estates and trusts and the handling of large sums of public money. By the end of the fifteenth century, there were nine elected procurators, but over the course of the sixteenth century, additional positions were added for those who could pay for the distinction.[40]

The apartments of the Procurators were in the Procuratie Nuove, the wing on the south side of the Piazza, extending across two very high-ceilinged floors above the arcade level (figs. 219 and 220). Probably dating back to the thirteenth century, the complex was rebuilt by Vincenzo Scamozzi in the late sixteenth century. The wing now houses the Museo Correr, which gives a sense of the original scale and grandeur of the interior spaces.[41] These noble tenants, although not renters *per se*, carried the dignity of the *casa* through the office and not through residence in the ancestral home. And yet, they were almost certainly property owners, whether they lived in their own houses or not. For patricians, consisting of less than 5 percent of the population, owned more than 70 percent of all real property in the city.[42]

Indeed, most patricians were landlords, a situation that had important ramifications. On the one hand, it helped to bridge the gap between rich and poor by encouraging direct contact between the landlord and his or her tenants; on the other, it had the potential for exacerbating class differences when properties were not kept up or tenants were evicted in hard times. Household inventories made at the time of a person's death often list account books and rental receipts attesting to the close personal involvement of the property owner in the managing of rental units, as do the *decima* tax declarations and assessments. *Decima* records survive from the sixteenth century in the form of large *buste*, each holding a mass of separate sheets, one or more for each taxpayer.[43] Declarations were either given verbally to the tax officials, who transcribed them, or written out by the property owners themselves with the name of each tenant listed meticulously, along with his or her rent.

The declaration proffered by the executors of the estate of Tomà Michiel in 1537 is typical of a landlord with large holdings (fig. 221).[44] Properties are listed according to parish, twelve in all, plus a house in Burano and country properties on the Terraferma. Under San Cassan (San Cassiano) at the top of the list is *una casa*, rented to a Battista di Zuane for a very modest 4 ducats, the lowest rent on the page; further down the column is a *magazen*, or warehouse, rented to Battista dal Capello for 14 ducats, and at the bottom of the same section *una camera* – simply a room – rented to Bernardo Marangon for 5 ducats. The most expensive home on the page is a *casa* in San Zuanne Novo, rented to Zorzi Balestrieri for 30 ducats. Such renters comprise the lower end of the economic spectrum but, as witness the reduced circumstances of the widowed Lucietta Bembo cited earlier, there might well have been a few patricians and *cittadini* among the *popolani*.

Anecdotal evidence drawn from the *decime* suggests that landlords were familiar with the tenants and their problems. The noblewoman Andriana Contarini, widow of the Magnificent Francesco, reported in her declaration that many of her rental properties "are in great ruin, so that they

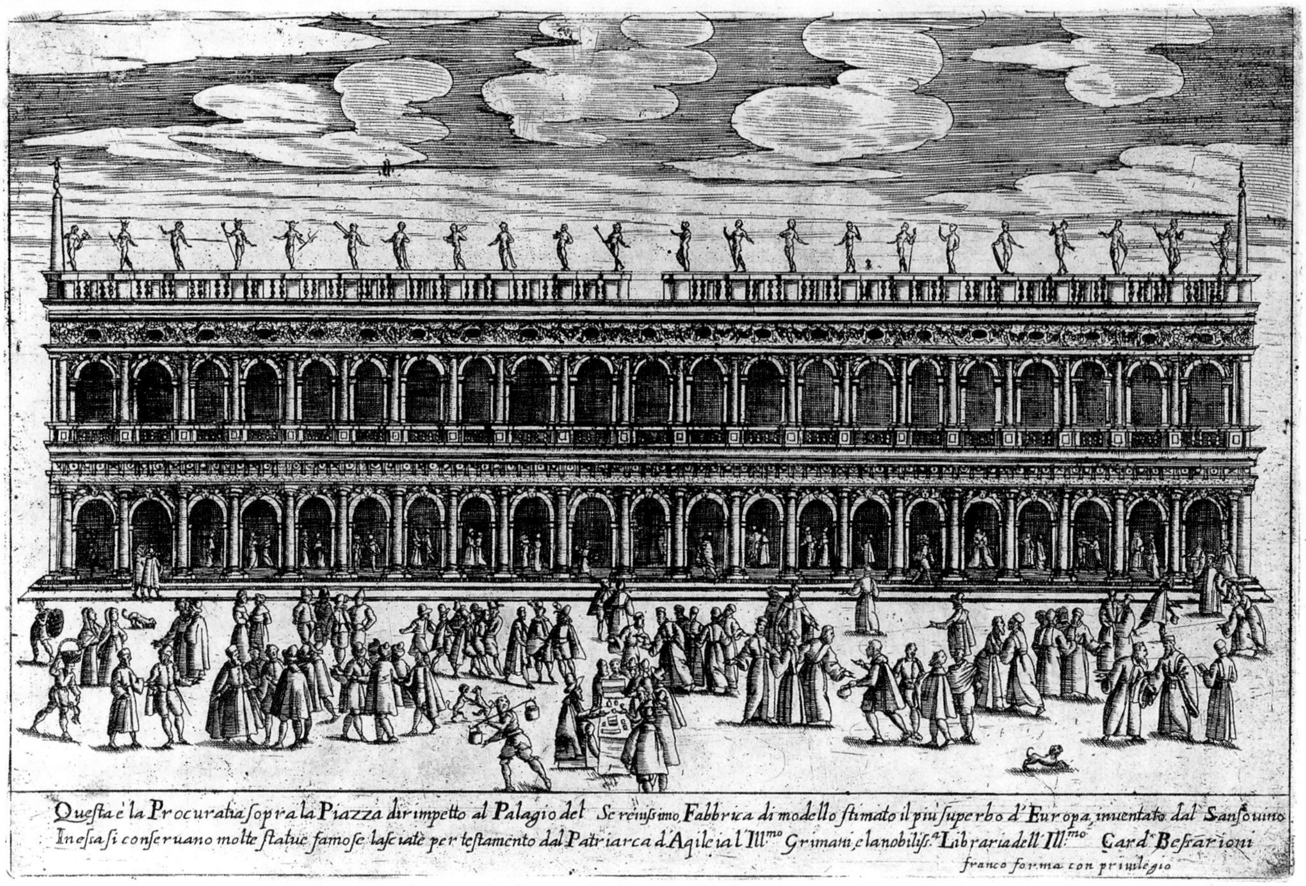

219 Giacomo Franco, *Procuratie Nuove*. Engraving from his *Habiti d'huomeni et donne* (Venice, 1626). By permission of the Folger Shakespeare Library.

220 Procuratie Nuove, plan.

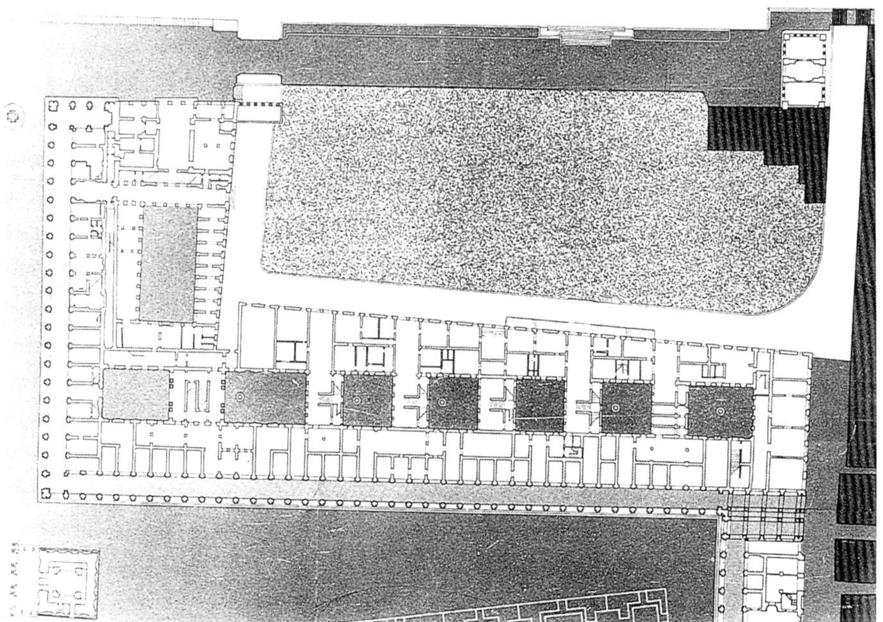

221 The first page of a tax declaration made by the executors of the estate of Tomà Michiel, 1537. Dieci Savi sopra le Decime (Redecima 1537), B. 97, no. 476, f. 1. Venice, Archivio di Stato.

need many repairs . . . and then one cannot recapture the expenses from all the rents because many of those living in them are poor people."[45] That her tenants were poor was probably accurate, but as stated earlier, a claim that the buildings were falling apart may have been a ploy to lower the tax assessment.[46]

Another point of contact between landlords and tenants was in their actual living arrangements. The Bembo complex at Santa Maria Nova was not unusual, with its row of little houses or apartments, sixteen in all, on Calle del Forno, next to the family palace, with a shared courtyard (see fig. 215). At the time of the property division in 1573, these units yielded about 187 ducats per year. The rents ranged from a low 4 ducats to a moderate 30, with the mean rent about 9.5 ducats – quite similar to those in the *decima* declaration of Tomà Michiel's estate. In the case of the Bembo properties, the tenants included a tailor, a dyer, a spicer, a beater of gold, and six single women – Isotta, Angelica, Chiara, Medea, Lucia, and Leandra – each living in a separate unit.[47] Thus the Bembo heirs residing in the *casa da statio* lived next door to – and shared their well with – a group of tenants, mostly women, whose rents put them at the low end of the economic spectrum of Venetian society.

The complex of Bembo properties along Calle del Forno might be considered an elongated variant of the public courtyard, wherein houses were arranged around an open space with a well-head in the center. The *decima* of 1582 lists about 270 such courtyards, a third of which carry a noble family name signifying the double aspect of residence and investment. The status of such areas as public spaces was ambiguous, with property owners asserting their hegemony through coats of arms and other signs of family dominance. Such patterns were repeated many times over throughout the city, with poor tenants often living in close proximity to their wealthy landlords.[48]

Charitable Strategies

In a society where real estate was beginning to compete with trade as a means to generate wealth, the home also became a major factor in charitable strategies. Zuan Matteo Bembo had named a hospital as his residuary heir in case every single Bembo in Venice should die without progeny, but he also used part of a house that he owned in the *contrada* of San Maurizio to endow a trust to benefit the poor immediately. The building was substantial enough for him to call it a *casa grande* in his will. The *mezzado* or mezzanine below the first *soler* was rented out for 10–12 ducats per year. Zuan Matteo stipulated that these funds be used by the Procurators of San Marco to ransom prisoners at Easter and Christmas. If any of his heirs wished to recover the use of that space, they would be allowed to buy it for 200 ducats and the funds invested by the Procurators for the same charitable purposes.[49]

In addition to the Procurators of San Marco, the Scuole Grandi served a fiduciary function in administering such legacies. The Scuole Grandi, a peculiarly Venetian type of religious lay confraternity, numbered six by the middle of the sixteenth century and played an important economic role in civic life. With memberships of 500–600 men each, drawn from all over the city, and governing boards made up of non-noble *cittadini*, the Scuole Grandi sought to maintain a balance of rich and poor members. The rich provided financial resources to help with the physical needs of the poor, while the poor marched in funeral processions and attended prayer services to support to the spiritual needs of the rich. Among the major sources of their wealth were bequests of real property that could be rented out to provide income or leased to poor members for little or no rent.[50]

In 1460, Tomaso Cavazza, a rich *cittadino*, named the officers of the Scuola Grande della Carità as executors of his will and ordered that his furniture and some property at Santa Marina be sold to build houses whose market-rate rents could be used by the Scuola for charitable purposes. It took another thirty years for his wishes to be executed. In 1491 the Scuola bought a house that was under construction with adjacent property on the Rio Santa Caterina and built a complex of two parallel rows of houses along the Calle dei Volti. Within a decade twelve houses were in place, renting for 24 to 25 ducats each. By 1566 the complex had been reorganized and fourteen houses were bringing in a wide range of rents, from 10 to 115 ducats per annum.[51]

On the rear facade of the complex facing the Rio Santa Caterina, a large relief sculpture of the Madonna della Misericordia sheltering two groups of kneeling *confratelli* under her cloak is embedded in the wall (fig. 222). On her breast is an emblem of the Scuola della Carità. A plaque below carries an inscription: "It was erected from the proceeds of the sale of the house of Tomaso Cavazza which he had left to the governors of the Scuola della Carità so that the profit would long be fruitful for the care of the poor."[52] Beneath the inscribed plaque is the Cavazza coat of arms. In contrast to most confraternity properties offered to the poor *pro amore dei* – that is, for the love of God – which were marked by a simple, discreet emblem, the relief at Calle dei Volti is a particularly ostentatious announcement. Why was the Cavazza plaque so elaborate? Perhaps to make clear that these homes were only to benefit the poor, and were not for the use of the poor.

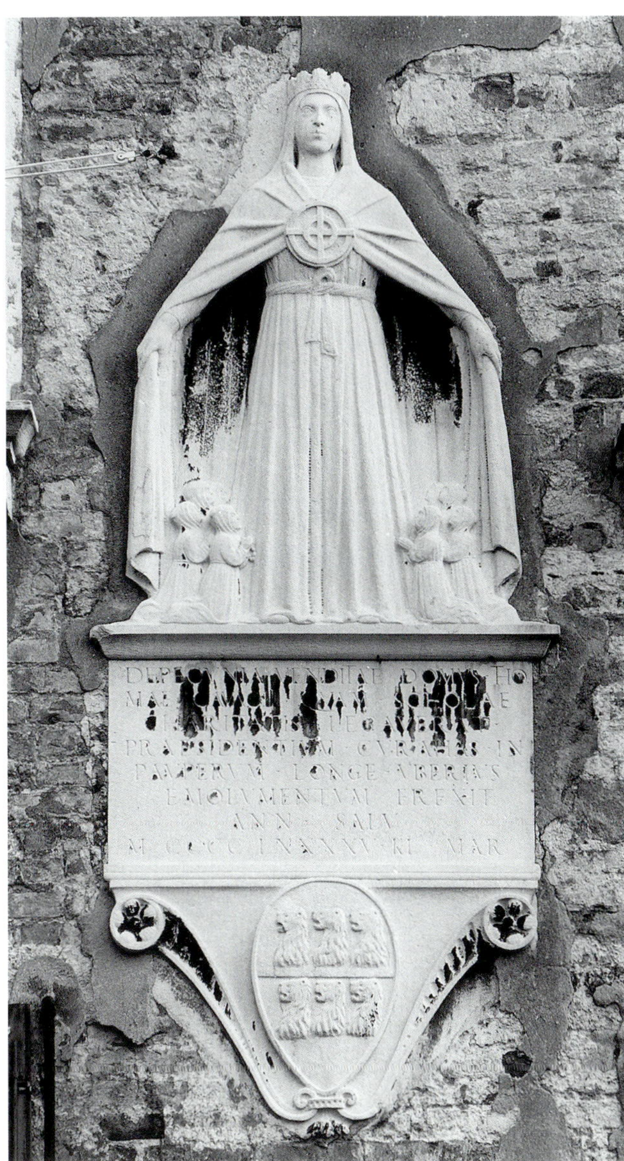

222 *Madonna della Misericordia*, emblem of the Scuola Grande di Santa Maria della Carità. Relief sculpture facing Rio Santa Caterina on the rear facade of Calle dei Volti.

The Working Poor

During the late Medieval and Renaissance period a number of housing projects were also built specifically as rentals, the more modest of them intended to house the working poor or those with some means to pay their own way – artisans, widows, the elderly.[53] Two architectural types predominated that distinguish them from the usual hodgepodge of random building: the diptych row house and the courtyard surrounded by apartments. The diptych model consists of a double row of attached houses with a wide alley in between, such as the Corte dei Preti located near the Arsenal (figs. 223 and 224). The project was owned by the hospital of SS Peter and Paul, an institution that dated back to the Middle Ages. Hospitals in that period were not just for the sick; this one was originally founded by a lay confraternity to shelter pilgrims en route to the Holy Land and the poor, as well as the infirm. In the best tradition of Venetian consensus, it was funded largely by private donations and bequests, administered by a prior and a governing board of three nobles and two *cittadini*, and enjoyed the special protection of the doge. Already in place in 1500, the complex was remodeled in the early sixteenth century. In 1564, thirty-nine units were occupied, with annual rents totaling 280 ducats, or around 7 ducats each.[54]

The complex has since been truncated, but the surviving structures show that it was ingeniously designed, with a balance between public and private spaces. Each row of the diptych now consists of six sections, each containing two living units stacked one above the other for a total of twelve

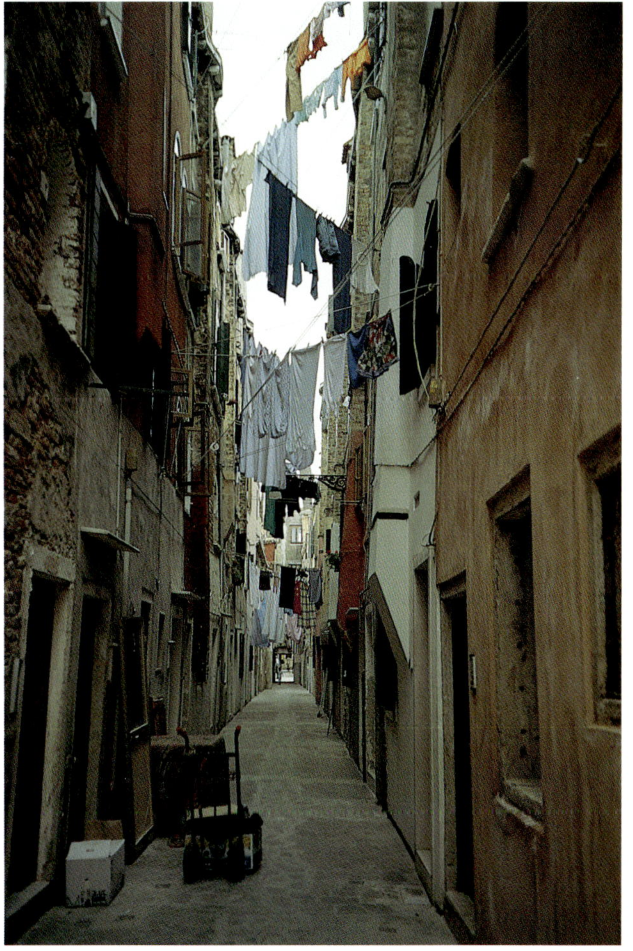

223 Corte dei Preti, Castello. View toward Via Garibaldi.

apartments (fig. 224). Each apartment featured a ground-floor entrance with a staircase leading up to a whole floor above, comprising two rooms for the unit on the *primo piano* and three for the unit on the *secondo piano*. Both units shared the same fireplace flues, one in front and the other at the back.

So, on the one hand, each unit had its own private entrance and staircase – still highly desirable features in Venice; and, on the other, each had windows that looked out on the *calle* or narrow courtyard in front, guaranteeing that no act went unobserved. The courtyard itself was like an open-air *portego*, with the double row of paired doorways ensuring social contact among the neighbors. Beyond that, the clothes lines that stretch across the narrow *calle* today suggest that those who looked directly into each others' windows might be closer than those who lived above one another in the same building. The apartments at Corte dei Preti were rented to low-paid workers at the Arsenal, so the complex should be considered affordable housing rather than an almshouse.

But there were also a number of initiatives in Venice whose sole aim was to provide housing for the poor that was either free or rented at considerably lower than market rate. This was housing offered *pro amore dei*. In most cases it came from private individuals who left houses or funding in their wills for such purposes and named the Procurators of San Marco or a confraternity, most often a Scuola Grande, as administrators of the bequest. Houses obtained by *scuole* in this way were then assigned to poor members in good standing.[55] Confraternity emblems marking the entrances of such houses are still visible throughout the city (fig. 225). Modern people might find this an unacceptable way of stigmatizing the poor, but in that period charitable gestures were supposed to be public and not hidden. Such signs fulfilled at least three functions. First, they rendered explicitly the mercy and benevolence of the republic and its citizens. Second, they testified to the symbiotic relationship between the rich and the poor and thus affirmed the social order.[56] Third, since houses offered *pro amore dei* were pre-

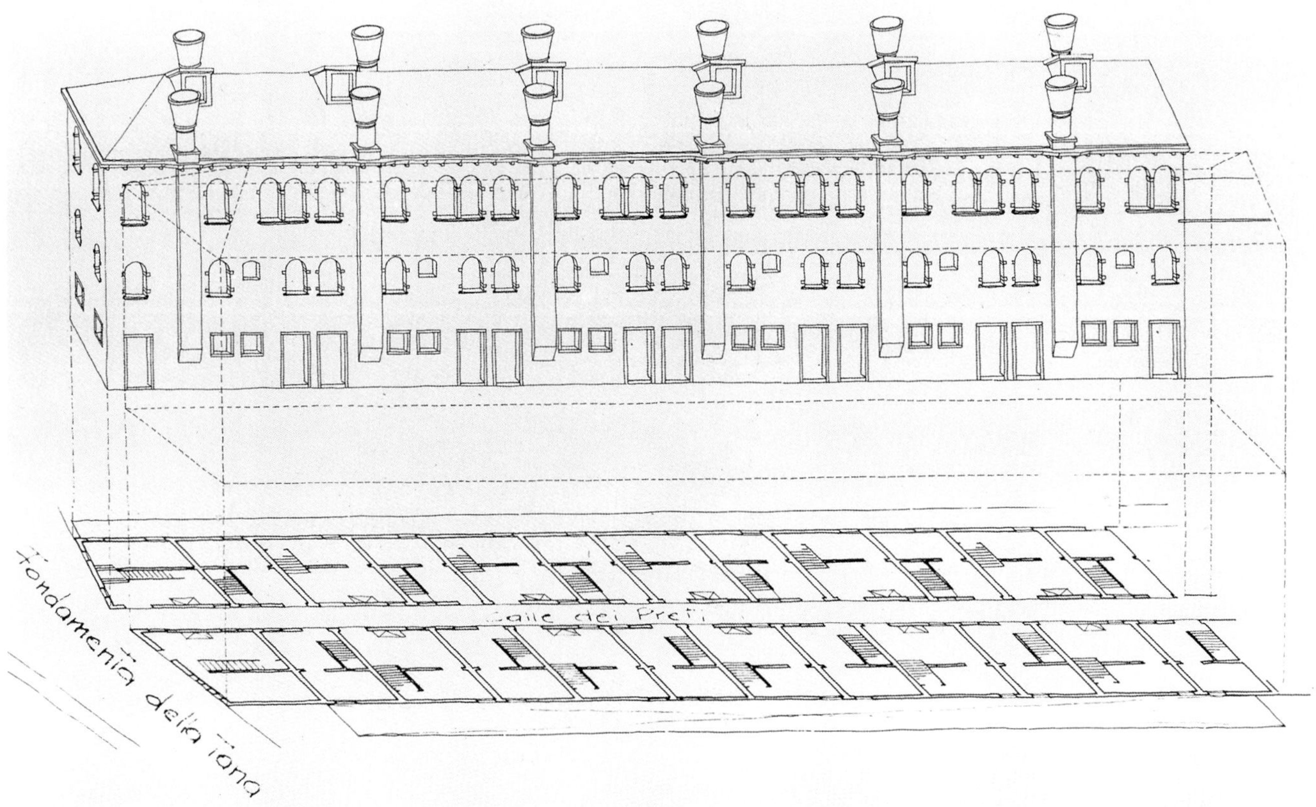

224 Corte dei Preti, Castello. Reconstruction drawing from Giorgio Gianighian and Paola Pavanini, *Dietro i Palazzi: Tre secoli di architetvra minore a Venezia 1492–1803* (Venice: Arsenale Editrice, 1984), 48.

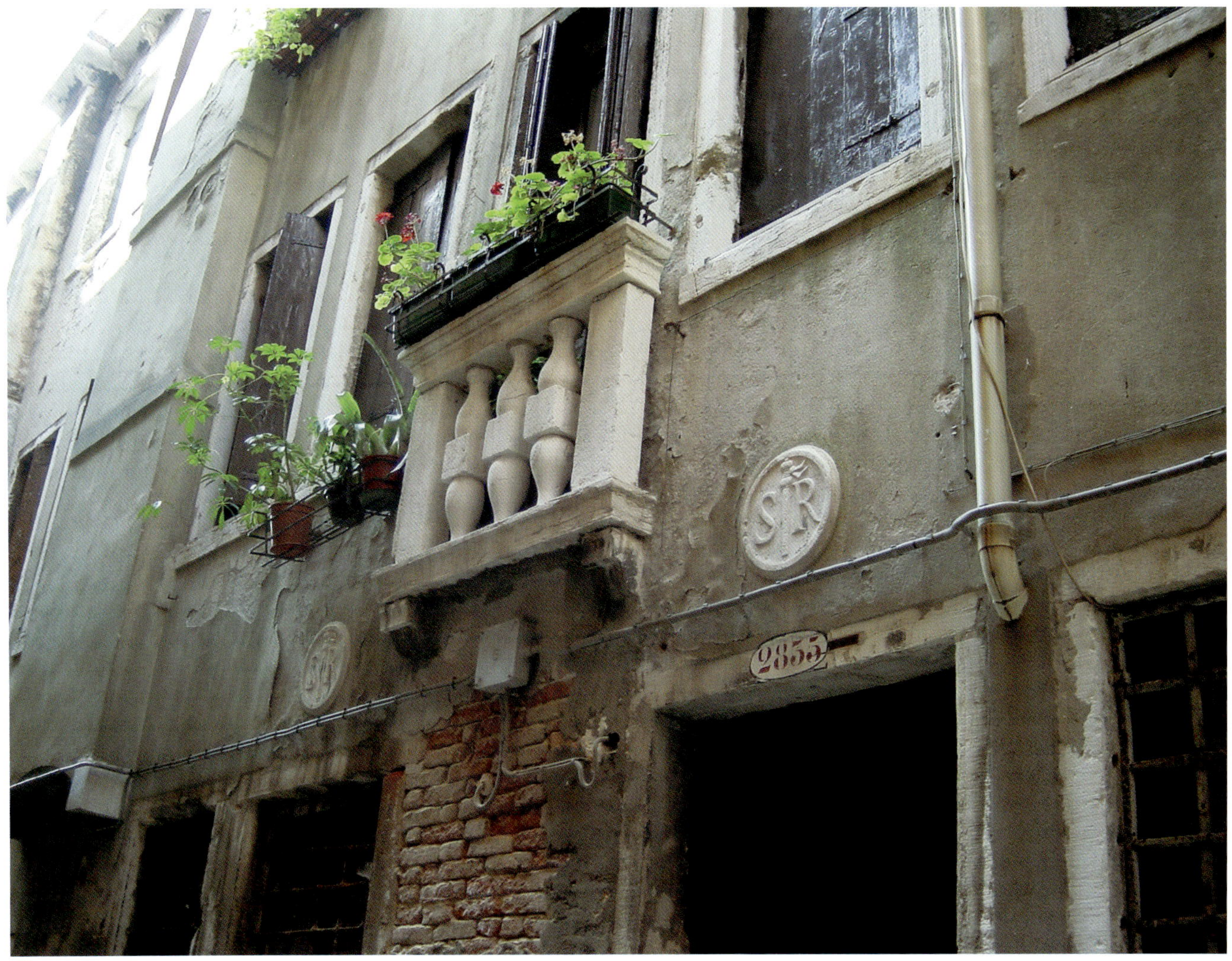

225 Emblems of Scuola Grande di San Rocco above doorways on Calle dei Corli at San Tomà.

sumably given only to persons of good reputation – that is, the worthy poor – possession of one of them offered testimony to good character and virtue.

Not surprisingly, reality often fell short of the ideal. The frailties of human nature were amply demonstrated at Corte San Marco, the second type of popular housing complex cited above (figs. 226 and 227). Featuring a large courtyard with a well in the center and bounded by twenty-four attached houses, it was built with funds from the estate of Pietro Olivieri. Naming the officers of the Scuola Grande di San Marco as his executors, he ordered them to purchase land on which they were to build very modest homes of a quality that normally rented for 5 to 6 ducats per year. These should be given gratis, *pro amore dei*, to "poor brothers of the Scuola di San Marco who above all should have children." The fortunate tenants would be entitled to enjoy the houses during their lifetimes, and when they died the units would be reassigned to other brothers of the Scuola. Olivieri himself seems to have died in 1529. It took some time for construction to get underway, but by 1542 the houses were finally built and distributed to the *confratelli*.[57]

Corte San Marco was a little world unto itself. The well in the center, suitably adorned with the insignia of the *scuola*, was the focal point of community life for the families who lived around it. All the homes opened only into the courtyard at that time, with access from the street outside through a single portal that could be closed off. But the complex was not closed off from attempts to regulate behavior, for with largesse came control. Dancing, gambling, swearing, and what were described as lascivious acts were banned by the Council of Ten in all such courtyards[58] – with little success, one suspects. And there were com-

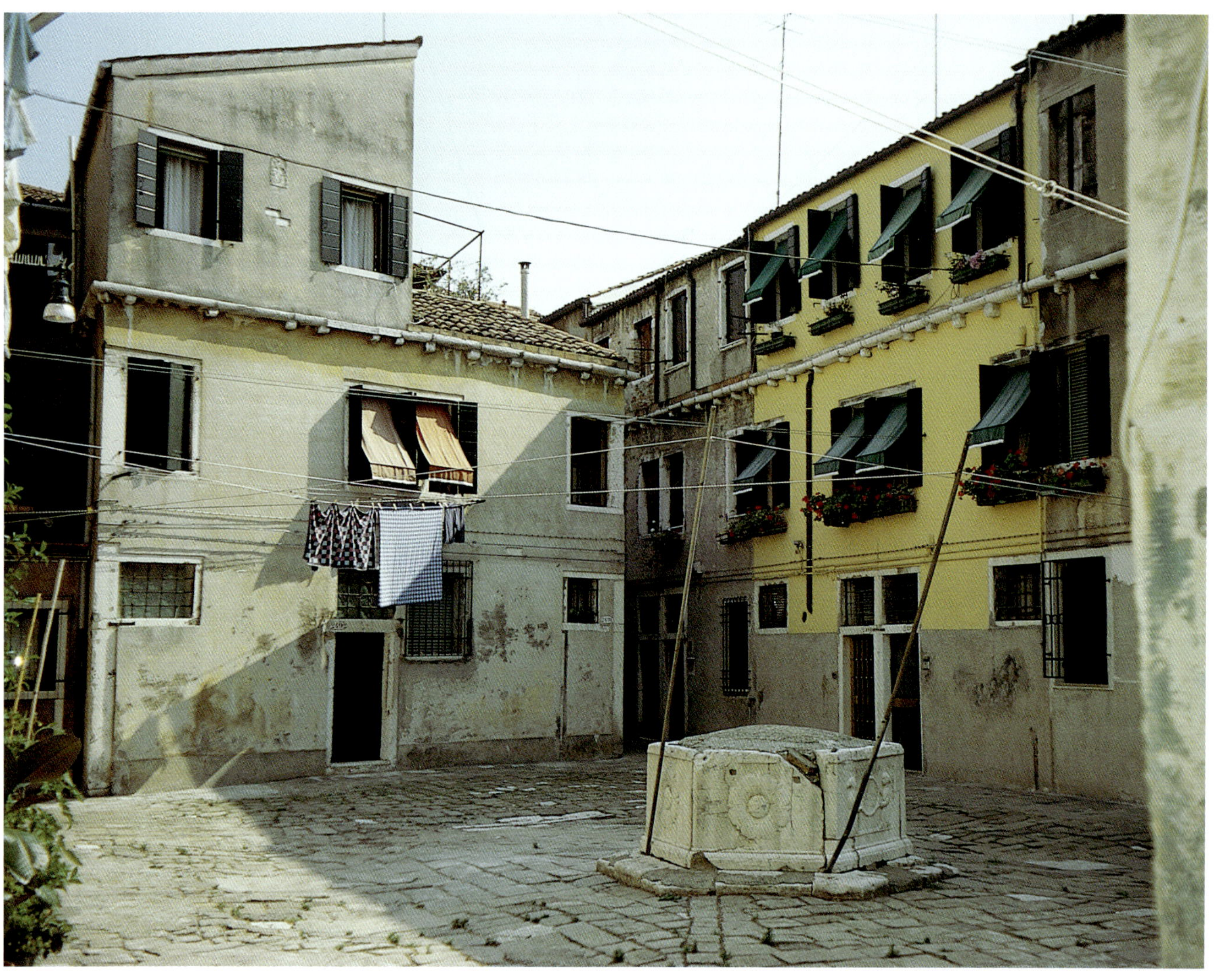

226 Corte San Marco, Dorsoduro.

plaints: that there had been favoritism in the selection process, that the beneficiaries had not been sufficiently screened, and that some were not worthy and honorable men. It was also charged that many of them failed to honor the quid pro quo for receiving such benefits and did not show up to march in confraternity processions.[59]

Equally troubling was the suggestion that the houses were too sumptuous for the poor and that they could easily rent for 12 to 14 ducats a year.[60] Indeed, in contrast to the flats at Corte dei Preti renting for around 7 ducats apiece, the units at Corte San Marco were floor-to-roof townhouses with attics and two floors of living space above the *piano terra*. Each had four rooms in all, and those on the corners had an extra, small room with windows. Aside from the all too human vice of envy – that others were getting more than they deserved – at play here was a notion, deeply ingrained at the time, that housing should correspond to one's social class more than one's economic circumstances.[61] For example, the family of a cobbler poor enough to live in housing offered *pro amore dei* should not be more comfortable than the families of arsenal workers of essentially the same "quality and condition" who were paying their own way.

Beyond that, tenants tended to think of the homes as their own property, and sub-letting was a common infraction. Some even joined apartments together and cut windows and doors in walls without permission.[62] Houses were generally offered at least partly furnished, and one *scuola* complained that relatives obliged to move out after the death of the beneficiary often stripped the houses, carrying away not only furniture such as "beds, benches,

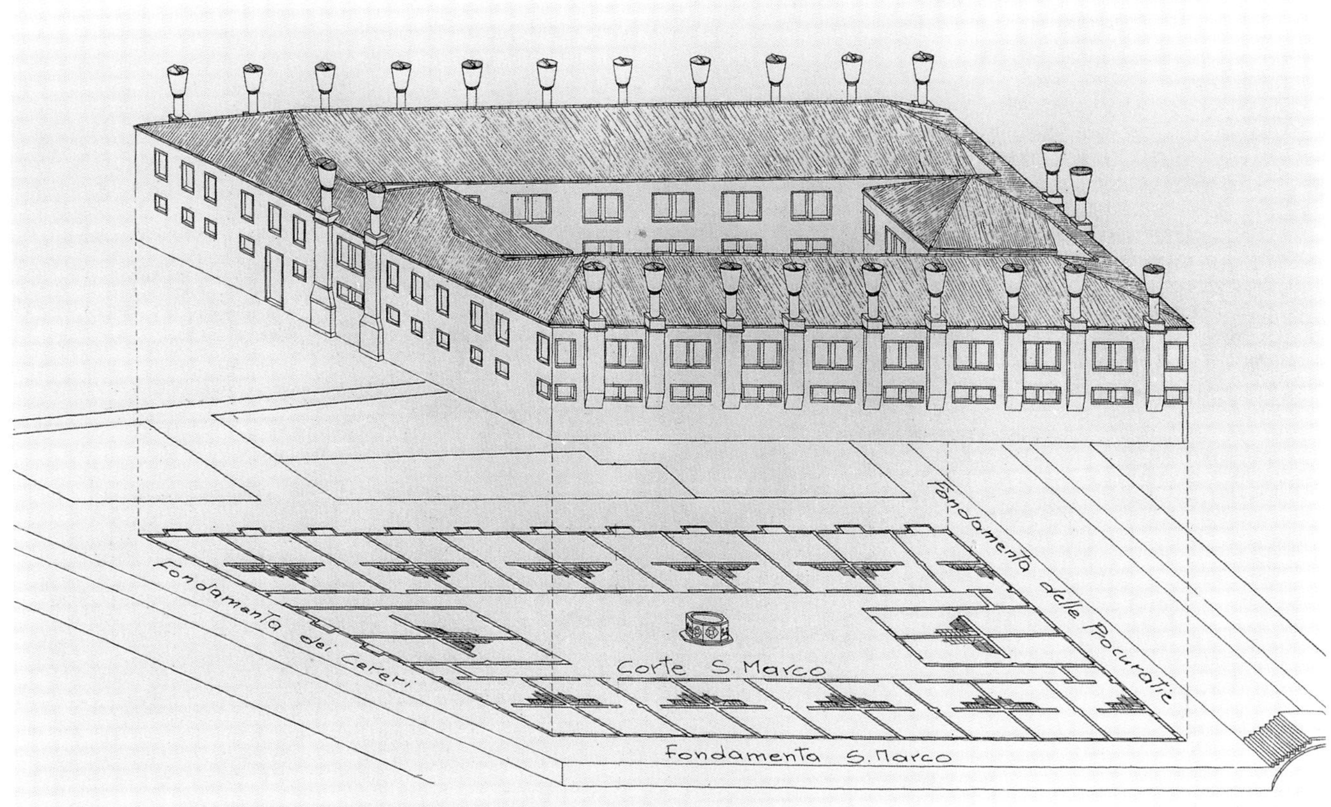

227 Corte San Marco. Reconstruction drawing from Gianighian and Pavanini, *Dietro e palazzi*, 110.

shelves, and other things," but also "window-panes, door locks, latches, keys, balconies, staircases, and cornices."[63] Who were the tenants? Artisans, such as shoemakers, dyers, weavers, barrelmakers, and the like. Some of them may even have owned property of their own – often outside Venice – from which they received small rents that were insufficient for subsistence.

The competition for such houses engendered creative strategies to secure them. Knowing that large families were favored, a certain woolworker named Hieronimo sought to tip the scales in his favor in the annual contest for free housing from the Scuola di San Rocco in 1583. He fraudulently obtained a certificate from the sacristan of his parish church and presented himself to the governors of the *scuola* with his wife "and six little children, barefoot and almost naked, and he and his wife too were poorly clad and, to outward appearances, weighed down by poverty and wretchedness, the better to move you to compassion, and he said that all six children really belonged to him, although only two were his children and he had brought the others with him for the purposes just mentioned."[64] He did not receive good marks for enterprise, nor, presumably, one of the apartments.

The Non-Working Poor

As to the dwellings of the truly poor, the most fortunate found homes in hospitals or hospices. Nearly a hundred such institutions can be documented at the end of the sixteenth century. These might have been run by Church, state, or confraternities, but the majority – about 60 percent – were private foundations. Private hospices were found in every sector of the city and were generally quite small. They were typically designated for specific categories, with the chosen groups changing over the centuries. In the thirteenth century, most were for pilgrims and were supported by the Church, but as lay bequests became more important in the fourteenth century, the emphasis shifted to the poor, the sick, the old, and particularly to women and orphans.[65]

While these establishments came in various sizes and configurations, the classic architectural type is exemplified by the Ospedale dei Crociferi. It was founded as a hostel for

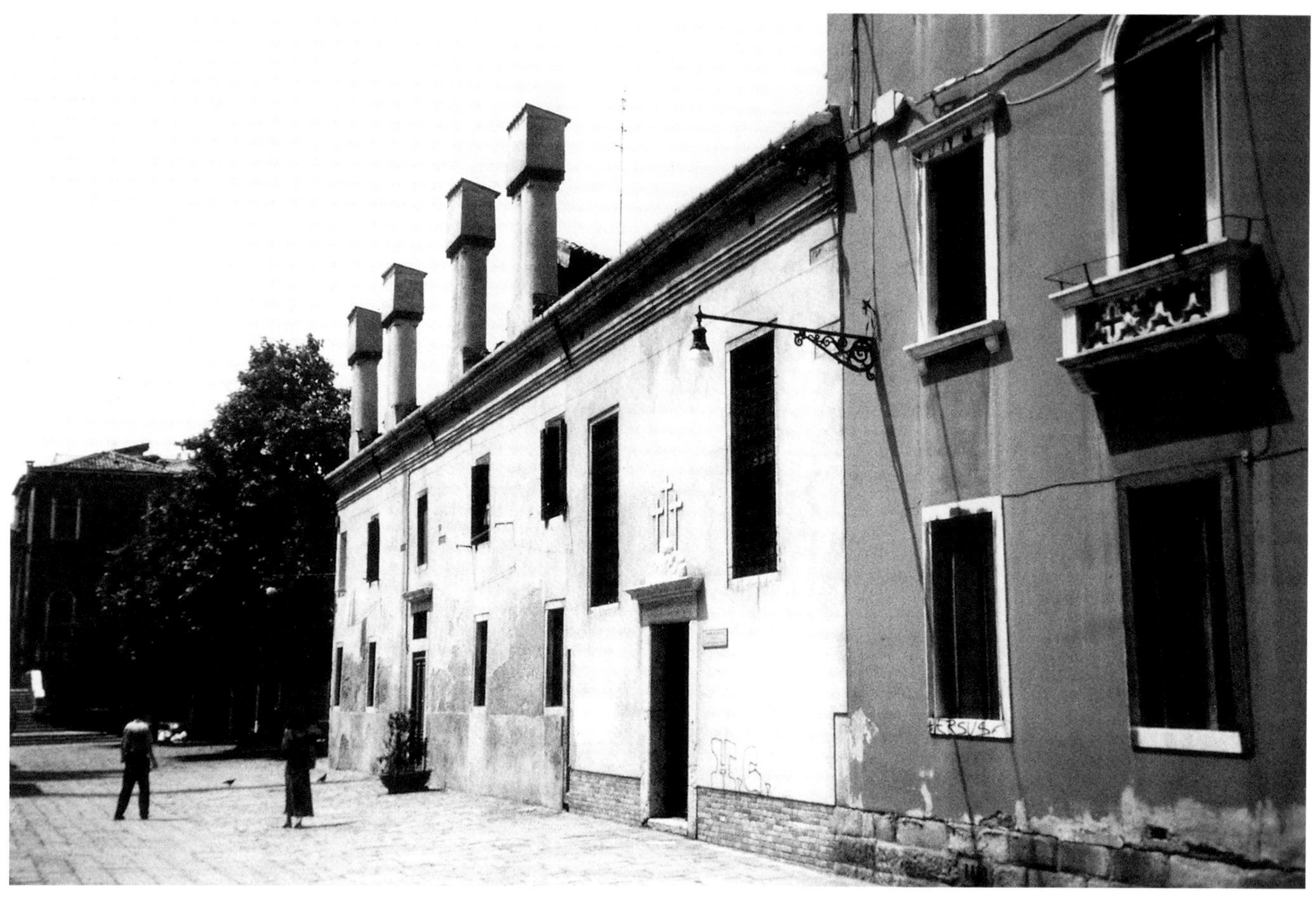

228 (*above*) Ospedale dei Crociferi, Campo dei Gesuiti, Cannaregio. The chimneys mark the bedrooms at the front of the building, four on each floor. As indicated on the floor plans, the door on the right leads to the chapel from the *campo*, while the women within entered it from a hallway outside their rooms. The doorway to the left provided direct access to the upper floor.

229 and 230 (*facing page*) Ospedale dei Crociferi. Plans of the present ground floor (top) and second floor (bottom) from France Semi, *Gli "Ospizi" di Venezia* (Venice: Edizioni Helvetia, 1983), 185.

pilgrims and the poor in the middle of the twelfth century by the Crociferi fathers next to their monastery in Cannaregio. In 1268, Doge Ranieri Zen left it a substantial bequest of land, houses, and capital and it became known as Ospizio Zen (figs. 228–31). At this point administration of the hospice passed from the monastery to the Procurators of San Marco and the emphasis changed from the pious traveler to the sick. In the fourteenth century it was housing forty to fifty sick men and women at one time, providing them with food, beds, linen, clothing, and shoes. By the early fifteenth century, the emphasis had changed again, and the hospital turned into a hospice, now housing just twelve poor women.[66]

Rebuilt several times, the hospice consisted of two floors, with six bedrooms on each level – four across the front and two at the back. The rooms were arranged along a common area, the equivalent of the *portego* in a palace, but here more of a hallway, with an oratory at the end. The ground floor – an area that a family of means would use for storage – was used for living space. Many of the poor lived then, and still live, on the *piano terra* – the least desirable location in a Venetian house, given the constant problem of damp and the periodic threat of flooding. The bottom floor was raised above the pavement at some time after the late nineteenth century, precisely because of this problem, and the building is still used as a hospice for the elderly.[67]

The hospital was organized like a religious community, the woman in charge being called *priora* – prioress – and the rooms called *celle* or cells. Each woman had her own apartment and received a small stipend at Christmas, Easter, and the feast of the Assumption of the Virgin. She was allowed to keep a cat in her room, but no other animals. There were duties both mundane and spiritual. Each

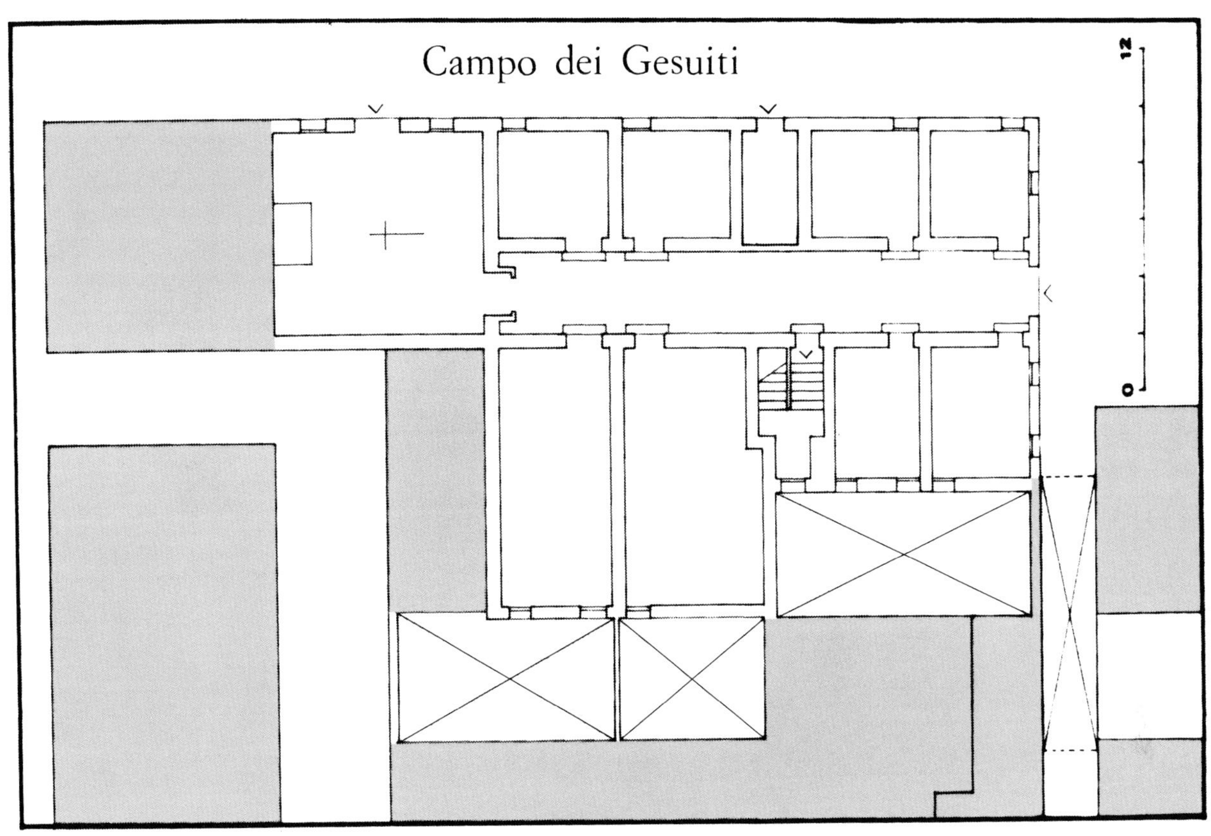
Campo dei Gesuiti
12
0

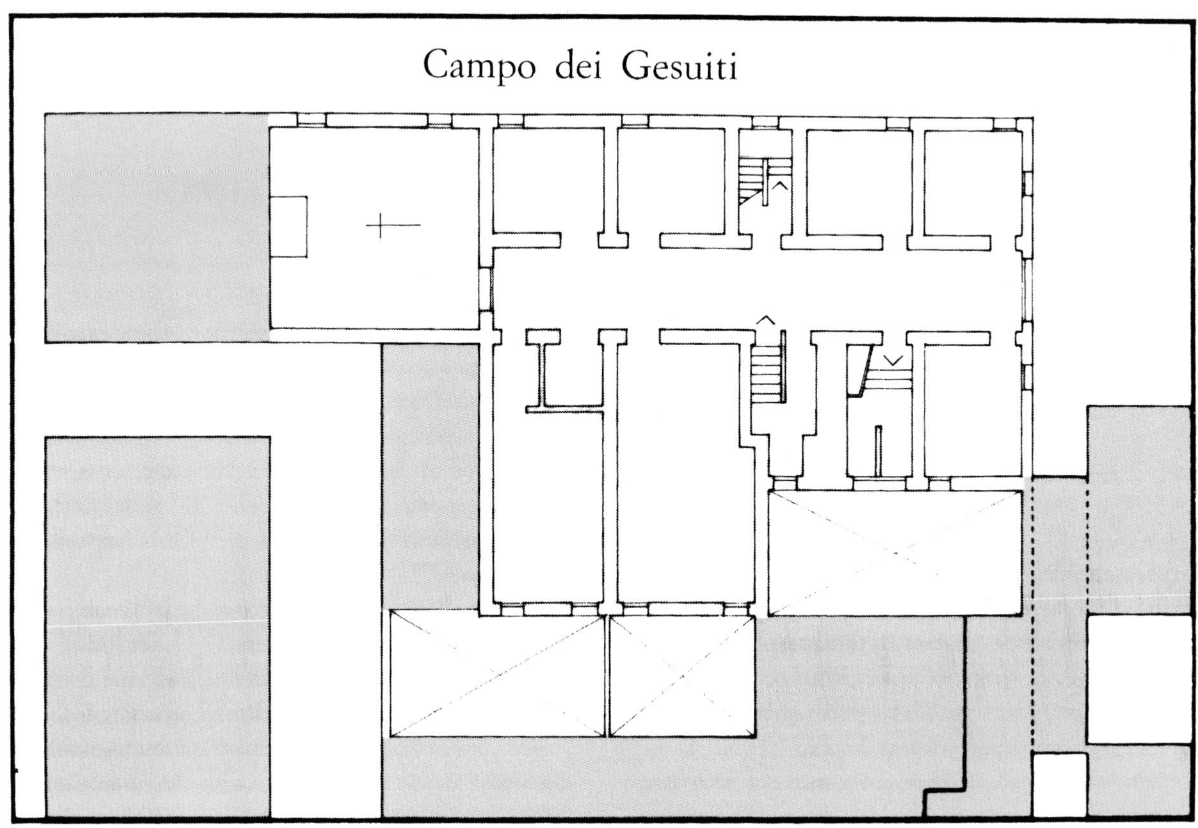
Campo dei Gesuiti

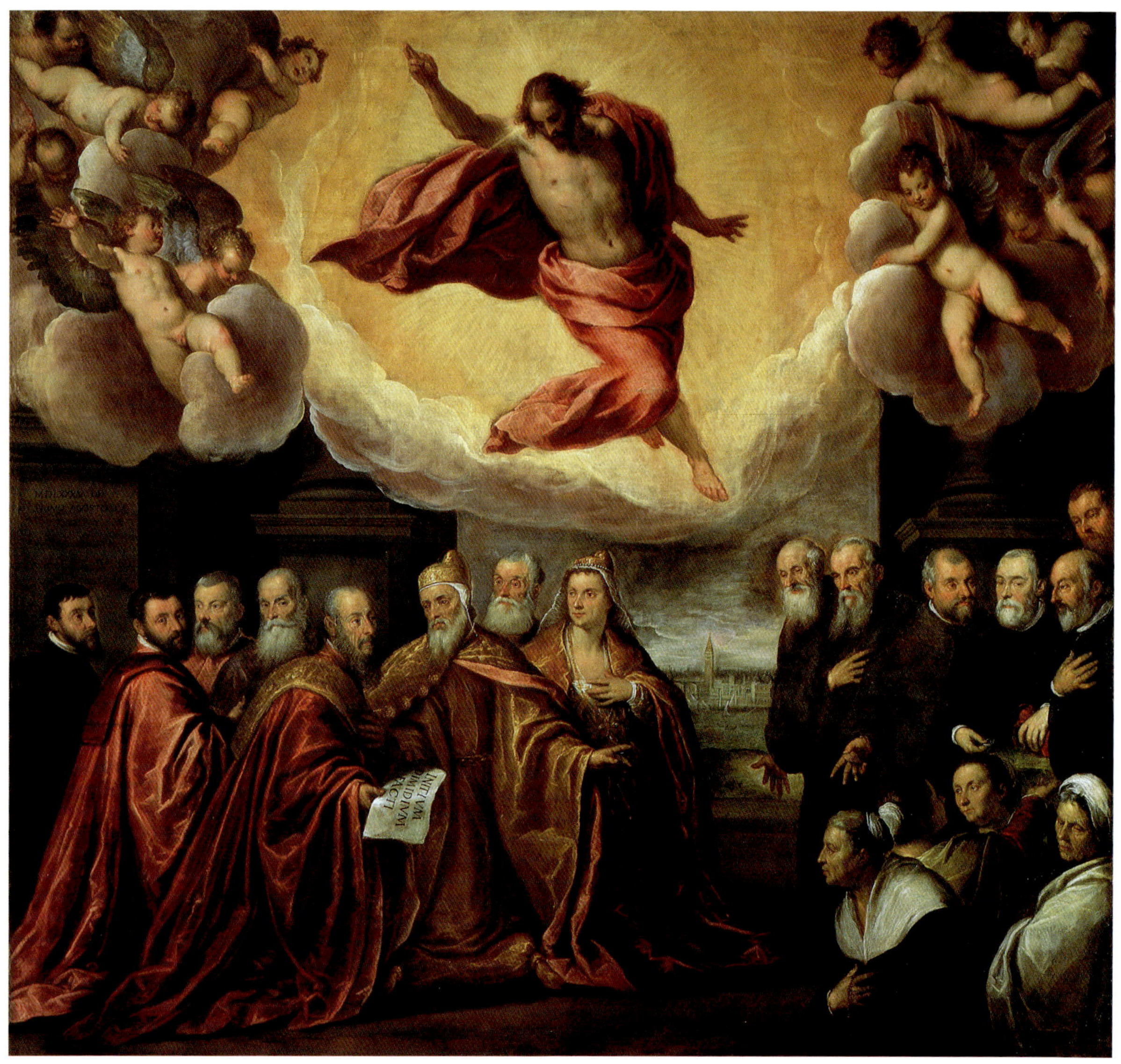

231 Jacopo Palma il Giovane, *Doge Ranieri Zen and the Endowment of the Crociferi*, 1585. Oil on canvas, 390 × 350 cm. The painting includes the Dogaressa at Zen's side, along with some elderly beneficiaries of his bequest at the lower right. Venice, Oratorio dei Crociferi.

woman was responsible for keeping her own rooms clean and orderly, and two were assigned to sweep and tidy the common hallways of the hospice, "from one door to the other," on a weekly or monthly basis, as the prioress determined. In addition, the residents were asked for their consent that all furnishings present in their rooms at the time of their death be passed on to the monastery. To ensure an "honorable and good example to the others," the women were not allowed to enter other parts of the adjacent church and monastery of the Crociferi. Aside from attending Mass on Sundays, they were required to kneel before the altar of the Madonna in the oratory each morning to "render thanks to her, and to pray to God for the state of our most illustrious Signoria, the freedom and conservation of the monastery, and for the souls of those who have given so much good."[68]

Ospizio Priuli (also called Ospizio de' Vecchi) was a male counterpart to the Ospedale dei Crociferi, but with a significant difference: it was run by a family and not a religious order. Founded by Lodovico Priuli, son of a doge, who left money in his will and explicit instructions to build a hospice dedicated to his name saint, Lodovico, it was intended to house twelve poor old men. Each would receive his own room and a stipend of 12 ducats and six cartloads of firewood per year, plus a measure of wheat each month. The hospice, built in Dorsoduro near the church of Sant'Angelo Raffaele in 1571, follows the dipytch model, with a double row of two-storied buildings flanking a blind alley (fig. 232). While the building has since been remodeled, the distribution of the bedrooms is essentially the same, and an oratory at the end of the right-hand wing remains intact.

Lodovico left little to chance. He specified that the oldest surviving Priuli male heir must serve as prior and would participate with the executors of the estate, who included Ludovico's wife Marietta, in choosing the residents. These should be persons, he declared, "of good life, and without sons or wives, and they must be Venetians or subjects, because I do not wish in any way that the [benefits] be given to persons of a foreign country; indeed, they must have lived for thirty years or more in Venice. And if any of them should marry or gain a bad reputation, he must be replaced immediately by someone else."[69] A chaplain, "of good life and example," would live on the premises to "care for the souls of these twelve old men," and to say the mass on every feast day, but the administration of the *scuola* was to remain strictly lay and secular and must not be interfered with by any priest or other ecclesiastic. Each year on the feast of the Conception of the Virgin, a solemn mass should be sung in the oratory and dinner given to the twelve residents, which should include "malvasia wine, *bussoli* [a kind of bagel], risotto, a main course of fish because it was Advent, and other dishes to be determined by the Prior from the house of Priuli, this being his duty."[70]

The Ospizio di Sant'Agnesina on the Rio San Barnaba was intended to serve a different population. It was founded in 1383 by Angelo Condulmer, father of Pope Eugenius IV, who left funds for it in his will. The hospice was run by the Scuola di Sant'Agnese and housed twelve orphaned girls of legitimate birth, noble or *cittadino*.[71] The number was reduced to six girls in 1527, when Marin Sanudo visited the church. He went there on the feast day of Saint Agnes, he reported, "to see a new thing, that is six girls, eight to nine years old, who each stood on a platform, daughters of *scuola* members, dressed half in white and half in red with their hair down to their shoulders and wearing crowns of leaves on their heads. They live together in the house at San Barnaba with a mistress who is given 40 ducats per year to maintain them and who teaches them to read and to work [probably needlework] until they reached the right age to marry," or enter a convent. These girls, he reported, "are elected by those of the *scuola* with a certain very fine order."[72] The hospice maintained its mission until at least the end of the sixteenth century. The Englishman Fynes

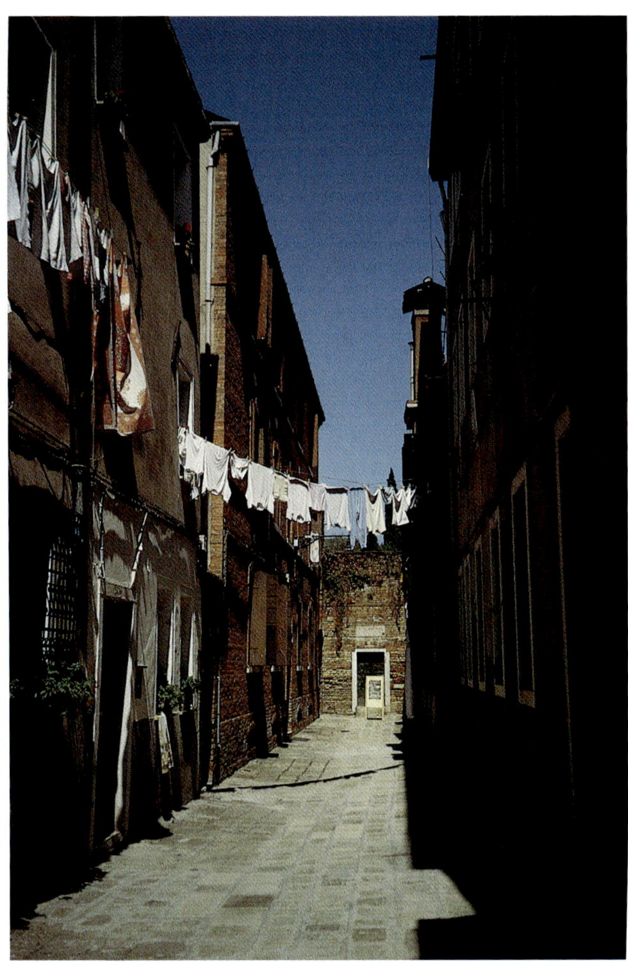

232 Ospizio Priuli [also called Ospizio de' Vecchi], Corte dei Vecchi, Dorsoduro 2551–2, 2568.

Moryson reported in 1595: "In the cloyster of Saint Agnes, the Prioresse bringeth up six Virgins, which being of ripe yeeres, are either married or made Nunnes, and sixe more of good families sent thither in their place."[73]

Such foundations are typical, and the message is consistent. Charity began at home, and some poor were more deserving than others. Relatives came before friends; neighbors before strangers; confraternity members before the unaffiliated; Venetians before foreigners. And virtue was rewarded. Charity normally came with strings attached, namely that the poor recipients be morally upright and that they pray for the souls of their benefactors. San Bernardino was not far from wrong when he said, "The rich are necessary to Republics; and the poor are necessary to the rich."[74] For the salvation of the rich depended on the prayers of the poor.[75]

* * *

The Shamefaced Poor

But poverty is a relative thing. Just as it was indecorous for the comfortable units of Corte San Marco to be given to humble cobblers, so too was it inappropriate for a poor nobleman to live in a hovel. "Poverty" could signify a loss of rank as much as a loss of financial resources, and perhaps the most troubling category of the needy was the *poveri vergognosi* – the shamefaced poor.[76] The Great Council articulated the mindset in a decree of 1544: "It is certainly a humane and pious duty to have mercy for the poor, and especially for those, who born of honorable parents and well endowed with the goods of fortune for some time, would then by diverse accidents be reduced to a state of poverty, of which there are a great number in this city, and they are called the shamefaced poor."[77] While it was appropriate for the widow of a boatman to beg for alms from passers-by and to lament openly about her hunger without embarrassment, it was a matter of civic shame for the destitute widow of a nobleman or *cittadino* merchant to do the same.

The Banca, or officers, of the Scuola Grande di San Rocco in 1591 thus listened with a sympathetic ear to an appeal from the widow of a former *Guardian Grande*:

> If ever there was a case deserving of the Christian charity of yourselves, honourable governors of the *Scuola*, it is mine, that of the wretched and unhappy Filomena Stella, widow of the late honourable Missier Paulo d'Anna . . . for I am reduced to such a parlous state by the misfortunes I have suffered, in which the late Ser Paulo left me. For it is well known that nothing remains to me but the hopes I have of God and of Catholic Christians, who must consider the rank to which I was born, the parents of whom I was born, and the husband to whom I was married, for your worships know all these things, and are aware that I am brought to such destitution that I have to beg for a living from those who will pity me.

Filomena requested that the *Scuola* give her one of its "small and lowly houses let at paltry rents of 4, 5, or at most 6 ducats a year," free of rent, or at half rent for as long as she lived, but the Banca did more. Its twenty-one members voted unanimously to offer her the first available house belonging to the *Scuola* that rented for 15 ducats or less, with Signor Bortolomio, a mercer, pledging to pay the rent on her behalf.[78] The situation was particularly poignant, given the fact that Paolo d'Anna had belonged to what was once one of the wealthiest *cittadino* families in the city.[79]

233 Tommaso Porcacchi, Venetian beggars. Detail of a woodcut from his *Funerali antichi* (Venice, 1574). By permission of the Folger Shakespeare Library.

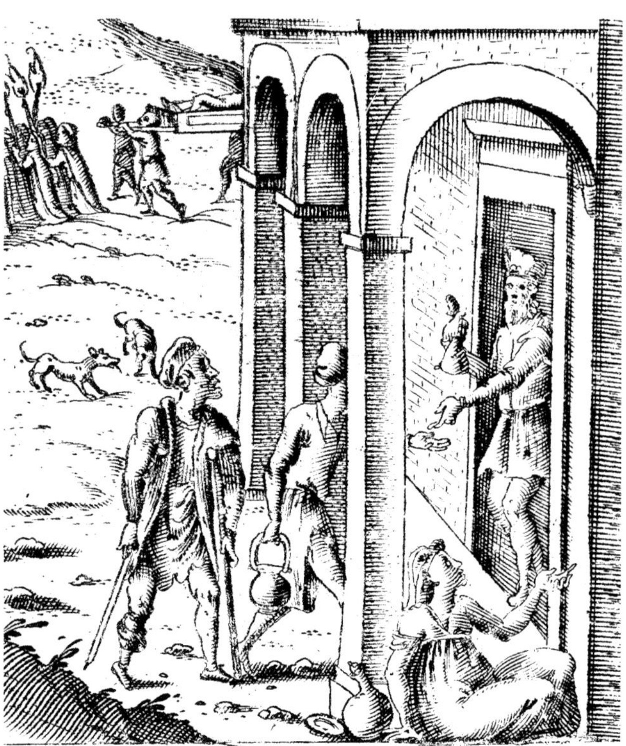

The Immigrant Poor

Nowhere is the principle of charity beginning at home more evident than in the laws passed in the midst of a famine in 1528 that brought droves of starving peasants into the city from the Terraferma (fig. 233). The high ideals of Christian charity were mixed with a desire to get beggars off the streets and out of public view. The Senate voted to select at least two or three sites where "all those poor who go through this city would be lodged, and there would be made rooms of wood with enough straw and other things to sleep on." Those who left the hostels and were found begging in public "would be arrested and put in prison and the following day flogged and sent outside the city." Those who returned "would be flogged again and taken outside, and so on each time." None of the poor who came into the city after this point was to be lodged in the places designated, "and all foreigners who are found begging must be arrested."[80]

The law of 1528 was an emergency measure, passed to deal with the crisis at hand and supported by a property tax surcharge to be paid by all those whose rents were 10 ducats per year or more. It was to end the following June, when any poor peasants who were still in the city would be loaded onto boats and sent back to the Terraferma. As harsh as the

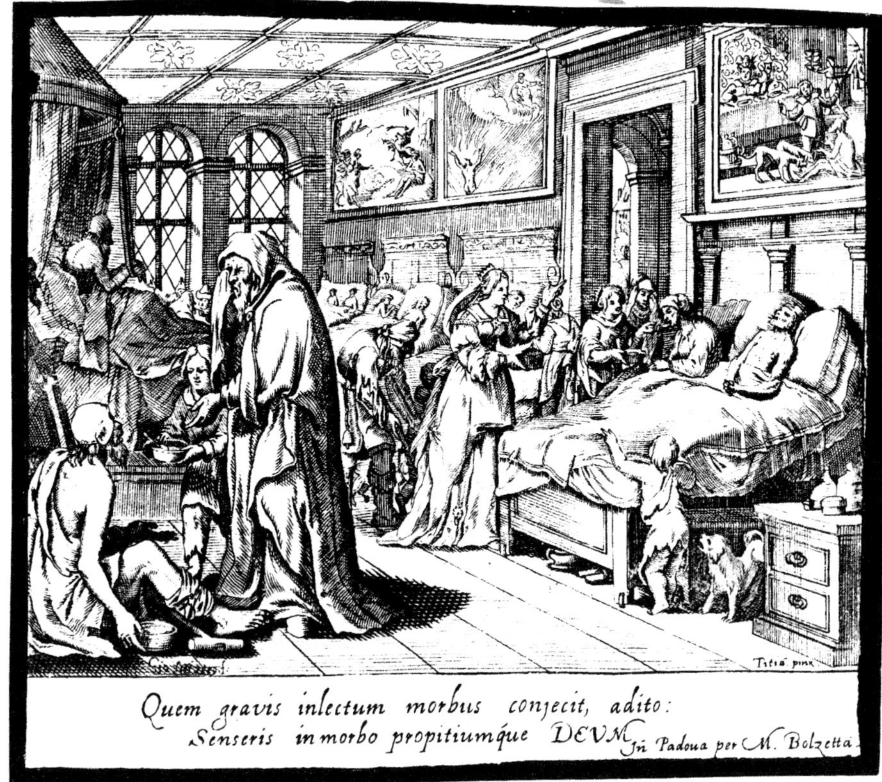

234 Hans Heinrich Schweitzer, *Visting the Sick in a Venetian Hospital*, seventeenth century. Engraving (after Titian?), Rome, Istituto Nazionale per la Grafica.

legislation may sound to us today, it marks an important shift to a collective social conscience, with the state assuming responsibility for what was formerly, for the most part, the initiative of individuals or groups such as confraternities.[81]

The Sick and Infirm

A French visitor at the end of the fifteenth century reported that there were three state hospitals in Venice with a fourth under construction. The Pietà, a foundling hospital that had been built on the Riva degli Schiavoni in 1346, later became famous for Vivaldi's musical orphans who were housed there. The Lazzaretto Vecchio (later the Mendicanti) was established on an island southeast of the city near the Lido in 1423 for plague victims, who stayed there until they recovered or died. And the Lazzaretto Nuovo, a quarantine hospital, was built in 1468 on an island next to Sant'Erasmo for those who had been exposed to, or were recovering from, the plague.[82] The Ospedale di Gesu Cristo di Sant'Antonio, begun in 1474 on the eastern tip of the city proper, "for the kindly reception and charitable treatment of the poor and other wretched persons who came to that hospital from every place," was completed around 1503 with financial support from a papal indulgence.[83] Two major foundations were added in the sixteenth century: the Incurabili, on the Zattere, created in 1523 to house those suffering from syphilis; and the Derelitti (also called the Ospedaletto) at SS. Giovanni e Paolo, founded as part of the reform of 1528 to shelter vagabonds and starving peasants.[84]

There was a general awareness that sickness and death were no respecter of persons, and of the interconnectedness of the different strata of the well-ordered republic. The equation is eloquently expressed in an engraving of a Venetian hospital by the Swiss artist Hans Heinrich Schweitzer (fig. 234). The room embraces the full range of humanity, from the rich man in a canopied bed to others across the room, two to a bed, to several beggars in rags, who sit on the floor. On the wall to the upper right is a painting of Lazarus and the Rich Man, a popular pictorial theme in this period that "aestheticized" a social problem by elevating it to the level of art.[85]

* * *

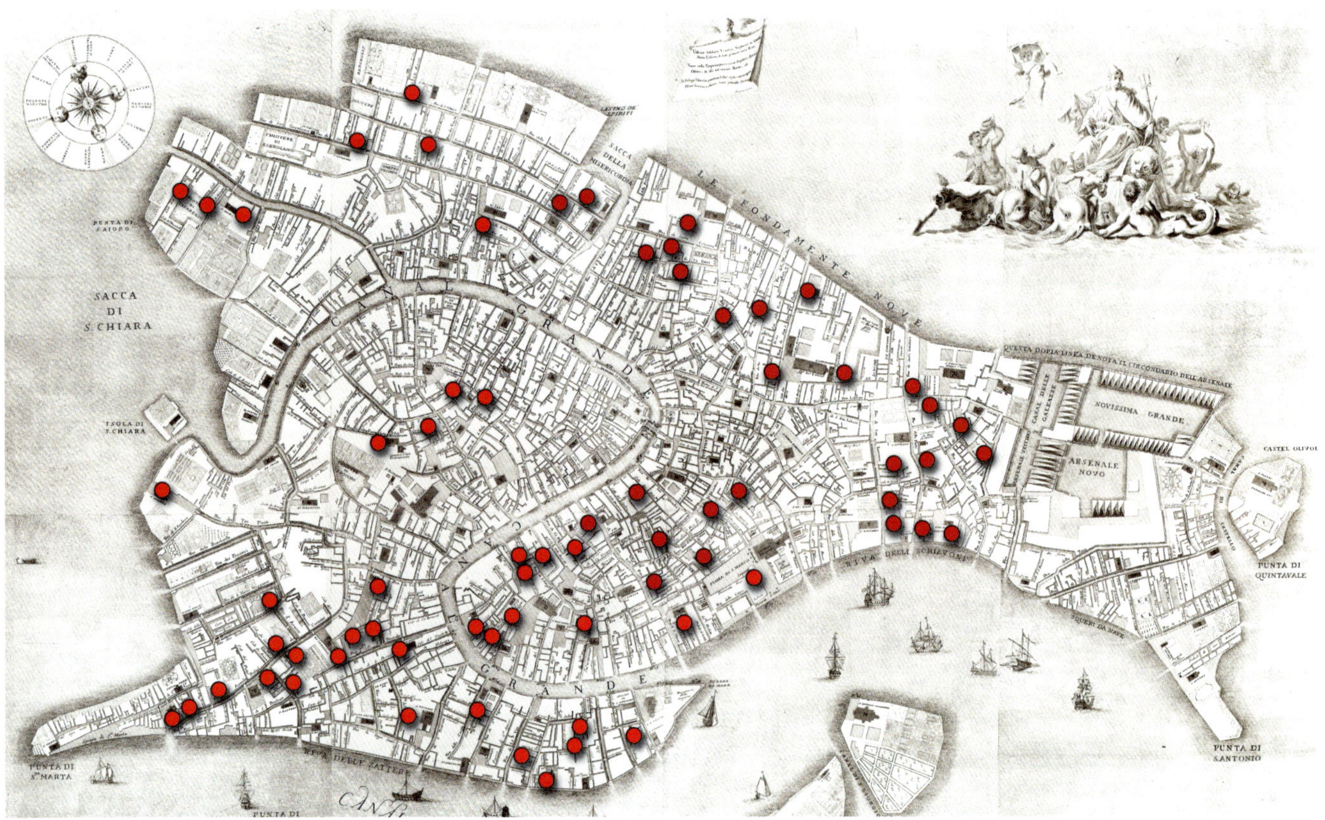

235 Hospices existing in Venice at the end of the sixteenth century, indicated on a detail of Ludovico Ughi's *Iconografica Rappresentazione della Inclita Città di Venezia al Reggio Serenissimo Domino Veneto*, 1729. Etching, eight sheets of ca. 640 × 435 cm each. This topographical map records the first full survey of Venice since Jacopo de' Barbari's *View of Venice* of 1500. A passage from the extensive inscription states: "She was born free, and kept herself so for so many centuries, the conception [*Idea*] of the great republic in the world is rendered." Less than seventy years later, the republic would be no more. London, British Library.

Distributing the Poor

The law of 1528 proclaimed:

> The poor people of Venice who are driven by want, and who cannot live by their own industry or manual labour on account of infirmity, shall be placed in and distributed among the hospitals or wherever it seems they can best get support. This measure shall be applied to those persons of either sex who have no fixed abode . . . Those who are feeble [*impotenti*] and yet have a dwelling place may on no account seek alms in the city. They must go or send to the priests in their parishes, who shall provide for their support . . . The poor of the city must be divided and distributed among the parishes in such a way that each parish has a number of poor appropriate to its wealth and standing.

Further, each parish was ordered to maintain a box for support of the poor – the priest and his deputies holding the

237 (*facing page*) Artist unknown, *Lighting the Sabbath Lights*. Woodcut from *Minhagim* (Venice, 1601), f. 63 verso. Opp.4_ 1004. A passage from the Venetian Rabbi Leone Modena's *Historia de riti hebraici, vita & osservanze degl'Hebrei di questi tempi* (1616), translated into English by an Oxford chaplain in 1650, explains: "The Jewes have the Sabbath in very great Veneration, and far above all the Other Feastivals; as being in so many several places of the Scripture made mention of, and commanded to be kept, even from the very Creation of the World . . . When the 23. hour then of Friday is now come, about half an hour before Sun-set, the Feast is understood to be begun; and then also the Forbearing from all Works that are Forbidden, begins to take place. And now the women are bound to set up a Lamp in the house lighted, which used to carry Four, or Six Lights at least; and this Lamp burneth the greatest part of the Night. They also spread the Table with a Clean Tablecloath, and set bread upon it; and over the Bread, they spread a long narrow Towel, which covers it all over: and this is done, say They, in Memorie of the Manna in the Wildernesse, which in like manner descended upon the Earth, being covered beneath, and having a Dew on top of it; and on the Sabbath, it fell not at all." Oxford, Bodleian Library.

keys – and the monies collected "must be spent solely upon the assistance of the poor." But, as in confraternity housing, with protection came control. The poor were not to move from one parish to another without a certificate from the parish priest.[86] This concern for the proper housing mix meant that Venetian hospices for the poor could be found side by side with the great palaces of the rich in every part of the city, except perhaps on the Grand Canal (fig. 235).[87]

Inventories indicate that families of this condition had few possessions of their own: the usual chests and chairs and beds, almost always of pine rather than walnut. They are often described as old and broken, if not *triste*, or sad. Absent from the lists are majolica, pewter, or silver. Very few items were decorated with carving, but chests were often painted, mostly red or green.[88] In all likelihood, they had been bought second-hand. And when money was short, they were pawned. Since the poor were often without money, these were the only things of value they had, and such goods were often taken forcibly from debtors.[89] In April 1583, the house of Paolo the Pole was entered by the authorities and a ragged garment, four small pieces of green cloth, and a chest full of rags were confiscated, along with candlesticks, a bed, and other items.[90] Indeed, with the second-hand trade, the lives of both rich and poor intersected with another group that had a distinctive living arrangement not of their own design – the Jews.

* * *

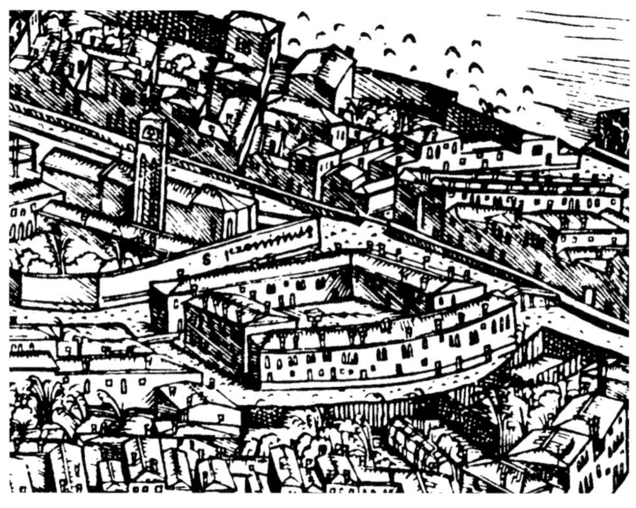

236 The Ghetto, detail from Jacopo de' Barbari, *View of Venice*, 1500. Woodcut.

Rich and Poor Within the Ghetto

Jews held an ambiguous status in Venetian society. Many had fled there during the War of Cambrai in 1509. Tolerated because of their usefulness to the city as bankers and taxpaying merchants and to the needy poor as moneylenders and second-hand dealers, they settled throughout Venice (fig. 237). But in 1516, concerned that the Jews were mixing too freely with Christians, the Venetian Senate

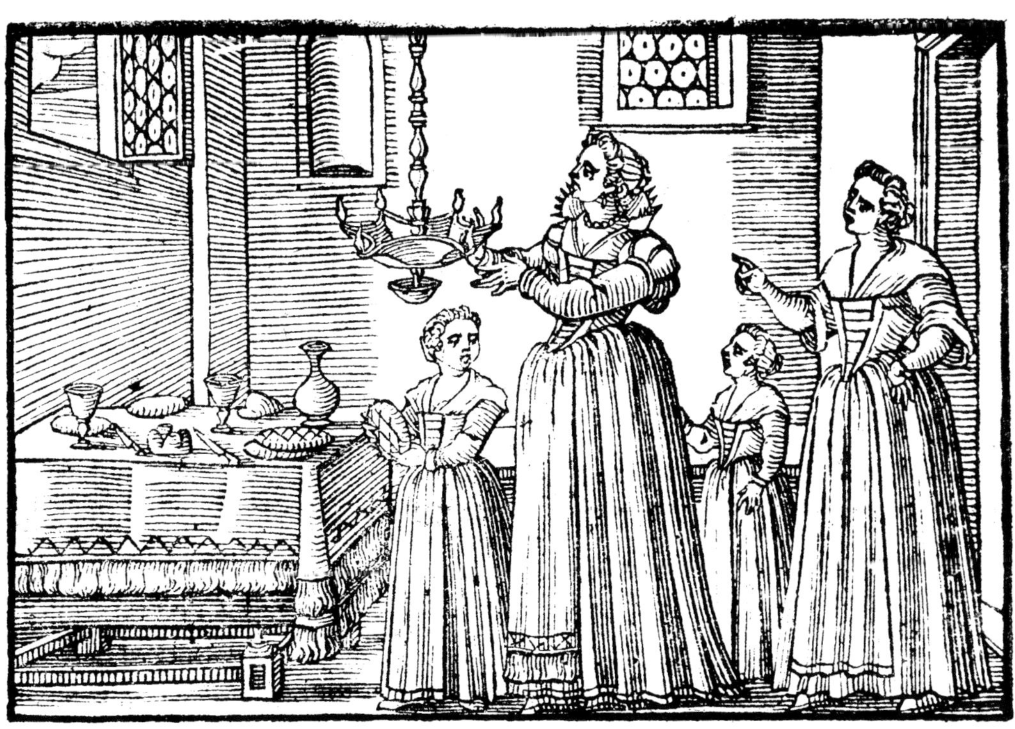

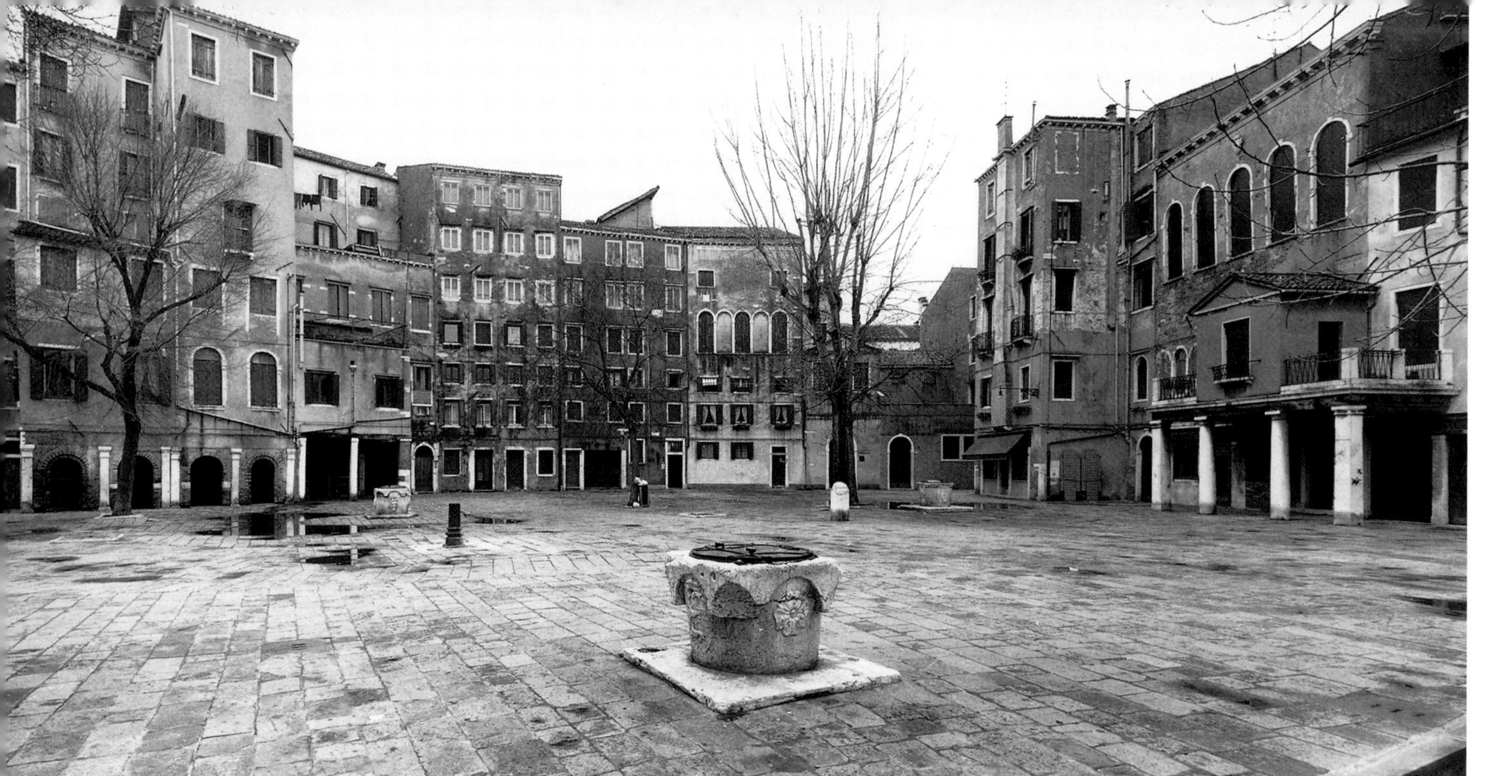

238 Present-day view of the *campo* of Ghetto Novo. The building on the far left, with white piers flanking four archways, was the Banco Rosso. Synagogues – called Scole, in the Venetian sense of brotherhood or congregation – with splendid prayer halls, were also inconspicuously integrated into the Ghetto fabric. Directly behind the well-head is the Scola Grande Tedesca, with the five arched windows (two of them bricked up) on an upper floor indicating the prayer hall; and on the right is the Scola Italiana, with a porch supported by an arcade of piers and columns and a prayer hall above denoted by five round-headed windows.

decreed: "The Jews must all reside together in the houses in the court within the Ghetto near San Girolamo, where there is plenty of room for them to live (fig. 236). And in order to prevent their roaming about at night, let there be built two gates."[91] The site was the Ghetto Novo, a trapezoidal island near the old public iron and brass foundries. The area, called "terren del Geto," had already been developed with rental housing around the middle of the fifteenth century by two merchant brothers, Costantino and Bartolomeo da Brolo. They constructed a cistern beneath the large *campo*, installed three well-heads, and built a two-story row of modest housing around the perimeter. It was not much different from other island parishes except that it lacked a church.[92] With the decree of 1516, the existing renters were moved out, the outside windows walled up, the Jews moved in, and rents raised by a third. The resettlement law applied to the rich as well as the poor, even to the affluent brother of Asher Meshullam, head of the Jewish community, who had rented Ca' Bernardo on the Grand Canal just the year before and was resented for flaunting his riches.[93]

The community was self-contained. Butchers' shops, bakeries, banks, pawnshops, and second-hand stores were installed on the ground floors with residences above (fig. 238). To accommodate the new concentration of population, houses with as many as nine stories were constructed on the foundations of the existing buildings – the standard elsewhere in Venice was only three or four stories at most. These very plain tenements, built primarily of wood to reduce weight, did not come close to the Gothic splendor of Ca' Bernardo. Their main exterior ornaments consisted of unadorned white Istrian stone frames on the door and window openings. But the interiors reflected the diversity of Venetian society at large, and inventories document not only the meager furnishings of the poor and dispossessed, but also the material comforts of the very rich.[94] All such homes were rental units, since Jews were forbidden from owning real estate. To compensate, the state granted them a special privilege: the rights to one's personal rental contract, which could be passed on to heirs, bestowed as dowry, given away, or sold – an early form of rent control.[95]

The Ghetto Novo was connected to the rest of the city by two bridges, which were locked at night (fig. 239).

239 (*facing page*) Ghetto Novo. View of exterior facades from Calle Farnese. The Ghetto tenements on the left are seven stories high. The bridge is one of three that join the Ghetto Novo to other islands.

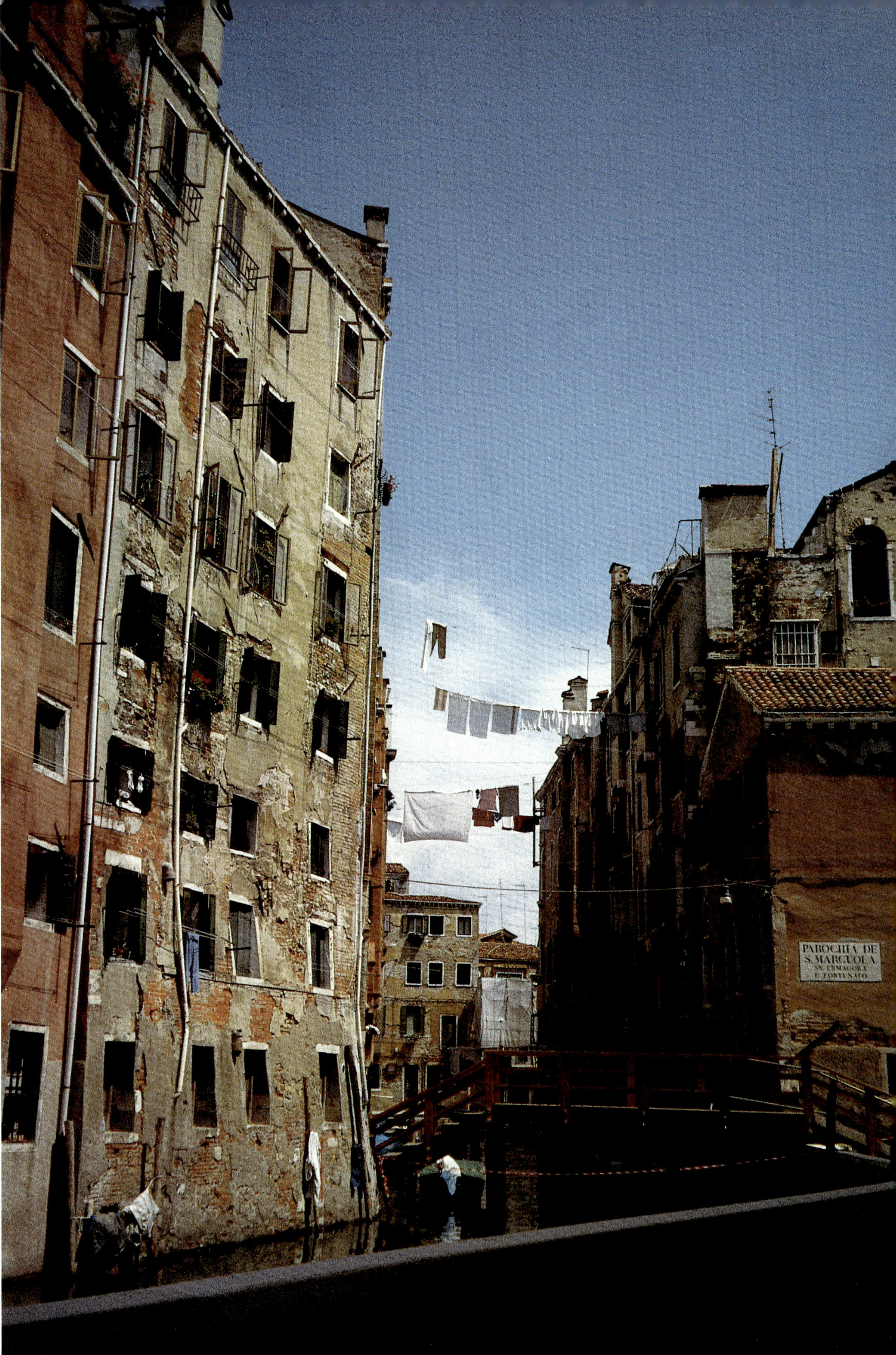
PAROCHIA DE
S. MARCUOLA

Indeed, it became a kind of open prison, with the Jews taxed to pay for boats to patrol the surrounding canals day and night, and for four Christian guards who imposed the curfew and controlled the access points.[96] From the outside it looked like a fortress. Forbidden to do manual labor and to engage in professional pursuits except for medicine, Jews were allowed to lend money and engage in the highly profitable second-hand trade. The Ghetto pawnshops were frequented by the rich as much as by the poor: to facilitate liquidation of debts and the settlement of estates, to tide people over in hard times, to fill the state coffers. Clothing and home furnishings could have considerable retail value and were commonly used as collateral or pawned to raise cash. Even the rags of the poor had their market. It is not by accident that the term for a second-hand dealer – *strazzaruol* – translates as "rag merchant."[97]

The Jews had immigrated to Venice in several waves. The first group to settle in the Ghetto Novo were the Ashkenazy or German Jews, including many Italian in origin. They were followed by refugees from Spain and Portugal, known as Ponentine or Western Jews. A third group, the Levantine Jews, was recognized as a separate entity by the republic in 1541, when an older area called the Ghetto Vecchio was built up to house them. Adjacent to the Ghetto Novo, it too was enclosed and guarded. The terms Vecchio and Novo thus related not to the Jewish settlements, which were established in reverse order, but to the foundries that originally gave these districts their characteristic names. Restricted to mercantile activity and forbidden to engage in moneylending or the second-hand trade, the Levantine Jews nonetheless became the wealthiest and most influential Jewish group. The community's physical space expanded again in 1633 when the Ghetto Novissimo – the name now corresponding to the order of Jewish settlement – was built to house twenty Sephardic families.[98]

In 1528 the Council of Ten dropped a ban against synagogues and allowed the Jews to build the equivalent of a parish church. By the end of the sixteenth century there were five major congregations, reflecting the diverse origins of the population.[99] In 1581, Francesco Sansovino would write optimistically that "as a result of trade, the Jews are extremely opulent and wealthy, and they prefer to live in Venice rather than in any other part of Italy. Since they are not subject to violence or tyranny here as they are elsewhere, and they are secure in all aspects of their business . . . reposing in most singular peace, they enjoy this city almost like a true promised land."[100]

* * *

Coexisting in Venice were a number of worlds, distinct from one another economically and socially, as well as spatially. And yet they were also overlapping, interlocking, side by side. It was a tight little island, its component parts fitting together as snugly as a jigsaw puzzle, and each sharing a common destiny. It should be stressed that the housing mix was characteristic of most late medieval cities.[101] But in Venice, large building blocks that housed the middling and even the poor could make it seem as if everyone was living in a palace – an illusion that helped to sustain the "myth of Venice" to foreigners and inhabitants alike. Not by chance was the city known throughout Europe as "la Serenissima". For all its many shortcomings, it was the strength and genius of the Venetian Republic and many generations of Venetians, both rich and poor, to cement this multifaceted mosaic together into a cohesive whole.

240 (*facing page*) Palazzo Grimani at Santa Maria Formosa, sixteenth-century facade. View from Rio San Severo with a Doric-style watergate in rusticated marble. Another water entrance to the palace, leading directly to the grand staircase, is around the corner facing Rio Santa Maria Formosa.

8

Theaters of the World

In this final chapter, Thomas Coryat, that keen observer of Venetian culture and society who has been an illuminating guide throughout this book, will be called upon once again. Like any cultivated gentleman of the period, he was, "a great admirer and curious observer of auncient monuments." In search of them he arrived at the Grimani palace near Santa Maria Formosa, "which is a very stately building . . . furnished with many notable antiquities (that is) statues . . . (but) the best and the greatest part are in chambers and higher roomes, whither I could not have accesse by reason of a sinister accident" (fig. 240).[1] The object of Coryat's thwarted intentions and the most

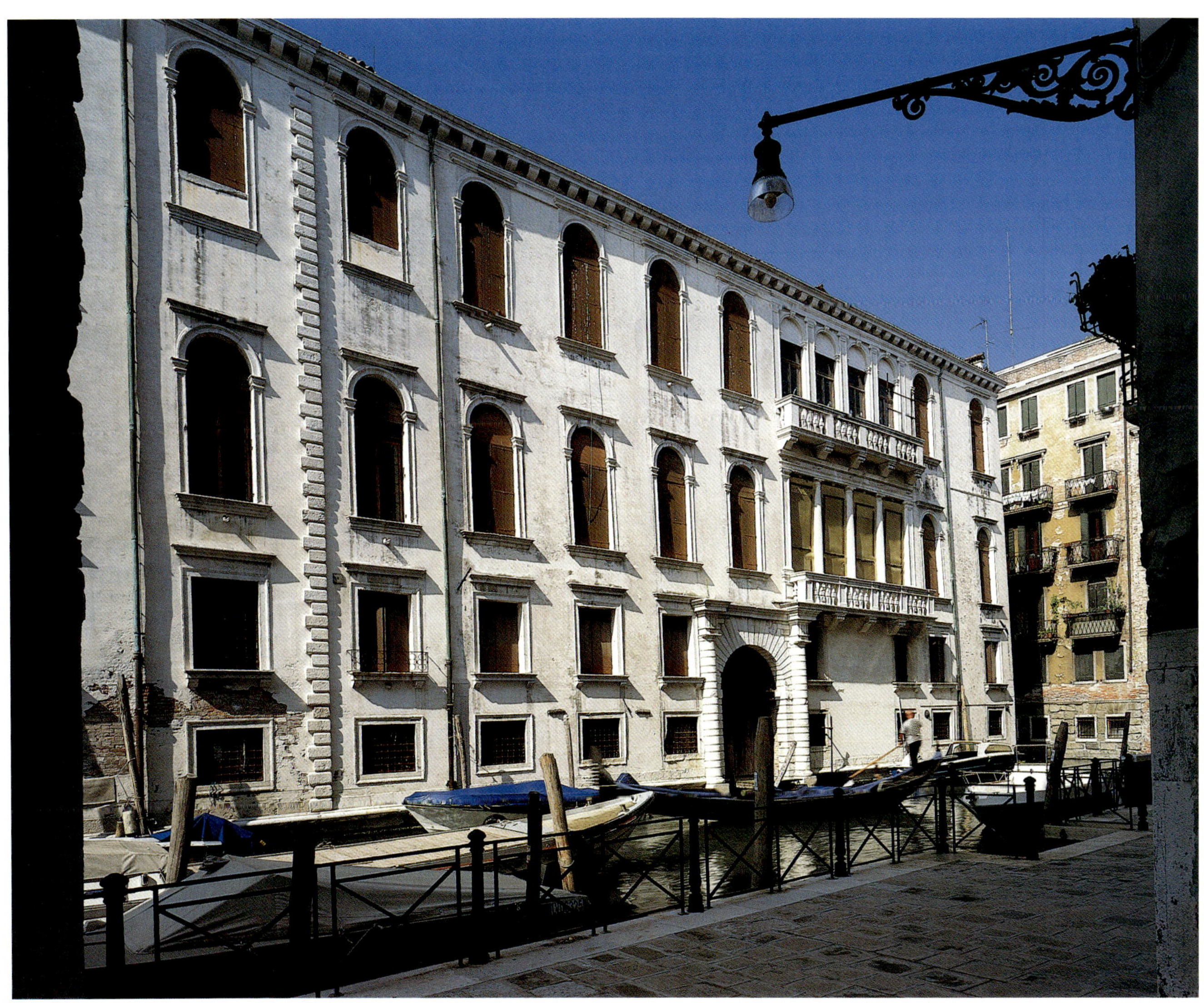

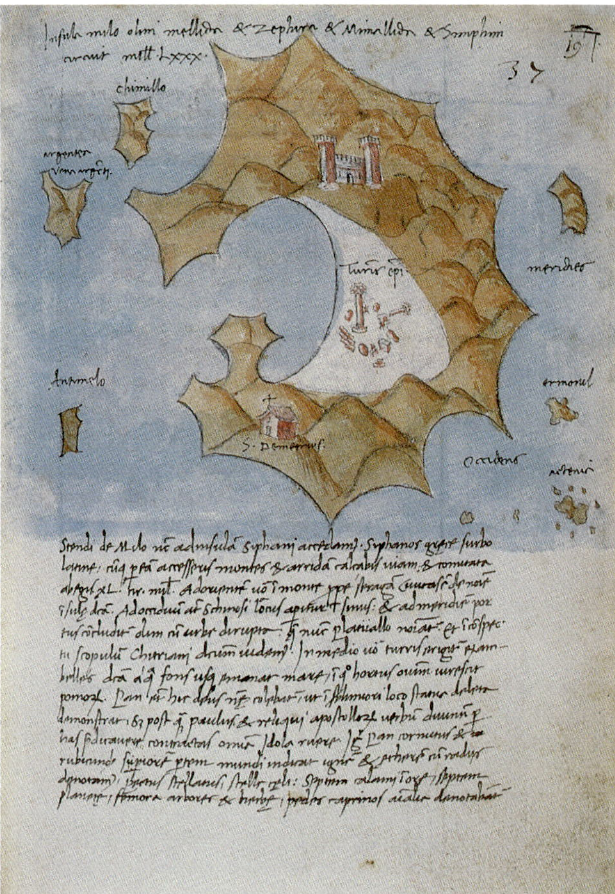

241 Bartolomeo delli Sonetti, *Map of Milos*, from his *Isolario*. The horseshoe-shaped island of Milos (Melos), one of the Cyclades, is the site of an ancient volcano whose crater is now filled with sea water to create a great bay. The map, oriented with east at the top, shows a castle built by the Venetians in the thirteenth century, the church of St. Demetrius, and scattered ruins of the ancient acropolis in the plain. The famous Venus de Milo, now in the Louvre, was discovered at the foot of the acropolis, near a Roman amphitheater, by a farmer in 1820. Venice, Biblioteca Nazionale Marciana, Cod. It. IX, 188 (6286).

renowned of these rooms was the *studio delle anticaglie*, also known as the *tribuna*, of Giovanni Grimani (see figs. 258 and 260 below).

As a space built especially to house a collection in a Venetian palace, Grimani's *studio* is an example of one of the most significant developments in sixteenth-century Venetian domestic architecture. For during this period there is a move away from multi-purpose rooms and the emergence of what might be called "dedicated spaces" to house specific objects and activities. Such spaces might serve as retreats for contemplation and escape from the burdens of daily life, or they might function as theaters of sorts – exhibition spaces to display the owner's acquisitions of the rare and the beautiful, thereby displaying his *politia* to an audience of friends and well-recommended strangers.

Expanding Horizons

The phenomenon is the culmination of a long trajectory that began in the early fourteenth century in the studies of scholars and not in the drawing rooms of the wealthy. But there is evidence that early collectors were not motivated solely by the pursuit of knowledge. Petrarch criticized manuscript collectors who "decorate their rooms with furniture devised to decorate their minds, and . . . use books as they use Corinthian vases or painted panels and statues and the like."[2] For most collectors in the Venetian milieu up to the end of the fifteenth century, the primary quest was for the ancient past: coins, medals, and sculpture, as well as inscriptions and classical manuscripts. Their trading activities gave them a privileged position from which to pursue such acquisitions. The shipowner Zuan Dolfin, for example, showed off his collection of coins and medals to Cyriacus of Ancona, an antiquarian and amateur archaeologist, in his ship's cabin in 1445.[3] The best source for manuscripts was monastic libraries. Some ancient marbles and coins were bought in Rome by Venetian collectors, where treasure-hunting had become an industry by this time, and others were dug up from newly appreciated ruins on the Terraferma, but most came from the Greek sphere, including Constantinople and the islands of the Aegean (fig. 241).[4]

The taste for collecting grew apace with the transformation of Venice's sense of its position in the world in terms of both time and space. Already in the early years of the fifteenth century, the republic had begun to pull back from the shores of the Adriatic Sea into the Terraferma for strategic reasons: to create a military buffer zone, to secure an agricultural hinterland, and to protect landward trade routes. This reorientation was further solidified by the Fall of Constantinople to the Ottoman Turks in 1453. For while trade with the Middle East continued, skirmishes on the seas made shipping more hazardous and Eastern ports less attractive.[5]

The discovery of new continents on the other side of the globe in the 1490s introduced a further element of dislocation. By the end of the century, the voyages of Columbus had opened up a whole new universe that had not existed before in the European mentality. The sense that Venetians would have shared with their contemporaries of an expanded awareness of a larger world is illustrated by the *mappamondo* painted in fresco by Donato Bramante in a house in Milan in that period (fig. 242).[6] While the New

World discovered in the voyages is not yet featured, and the depiction of the Indian Ocean as an enclosed sea still reflects Ptolemy's vision of the world, the sphere suggests a land mass that continues behind the curve at the upper right. Flanking the map are two Greek philosophers sitting in a study amid their books. Heraclitus on the left weeps, and Democritus on the right laughs, over the stupidity of mankind. Significantly, it is no longer a world defined essentially by the Mediterranean.[7]

The implications of these changes for people of the time, particularly for the seafaring merchants of Venice, were profound. Two tendencies are notable within the domestic sphere. On the one hand, as the Venetian mercantile world contracted, intellectual interest in the larger world expanded. Some Venetians, no longer satisfied with displaying only paintings and family arms in the *portego*, now sought out the antique, the rare, the exotic, the costly, the beautiful, the most wondrous works of nature and of man. The purpose was not to decorate but to possess.[8] The golden age of the collector was about to begin, and Venice would hold a central position with the emergence of the gallery or *studio delle anticaglie*, expressly intended for the study and display of art and artifacts.[9]

On the other hand, with patricians gradually withdrawing from active engagement in trade, a new leisure class was taking shape that turned increasingly away from the larger

242 (*below*) Donato Bramante, *Democritus and Theocritus*, ca. 1490–99. Detached fresco, 102 × 127 cm. The fresco, part of a cycle of famous men, was originally located over a doorway in a house owned by Gasparo Ambrogio Visconti, now known as Casa Panigarola, in Milan. The pseudo-antique frieze in the background depicts a triumphal procession on the left and a scene of submission on the right. Milan, Pinacoteca di Brera.

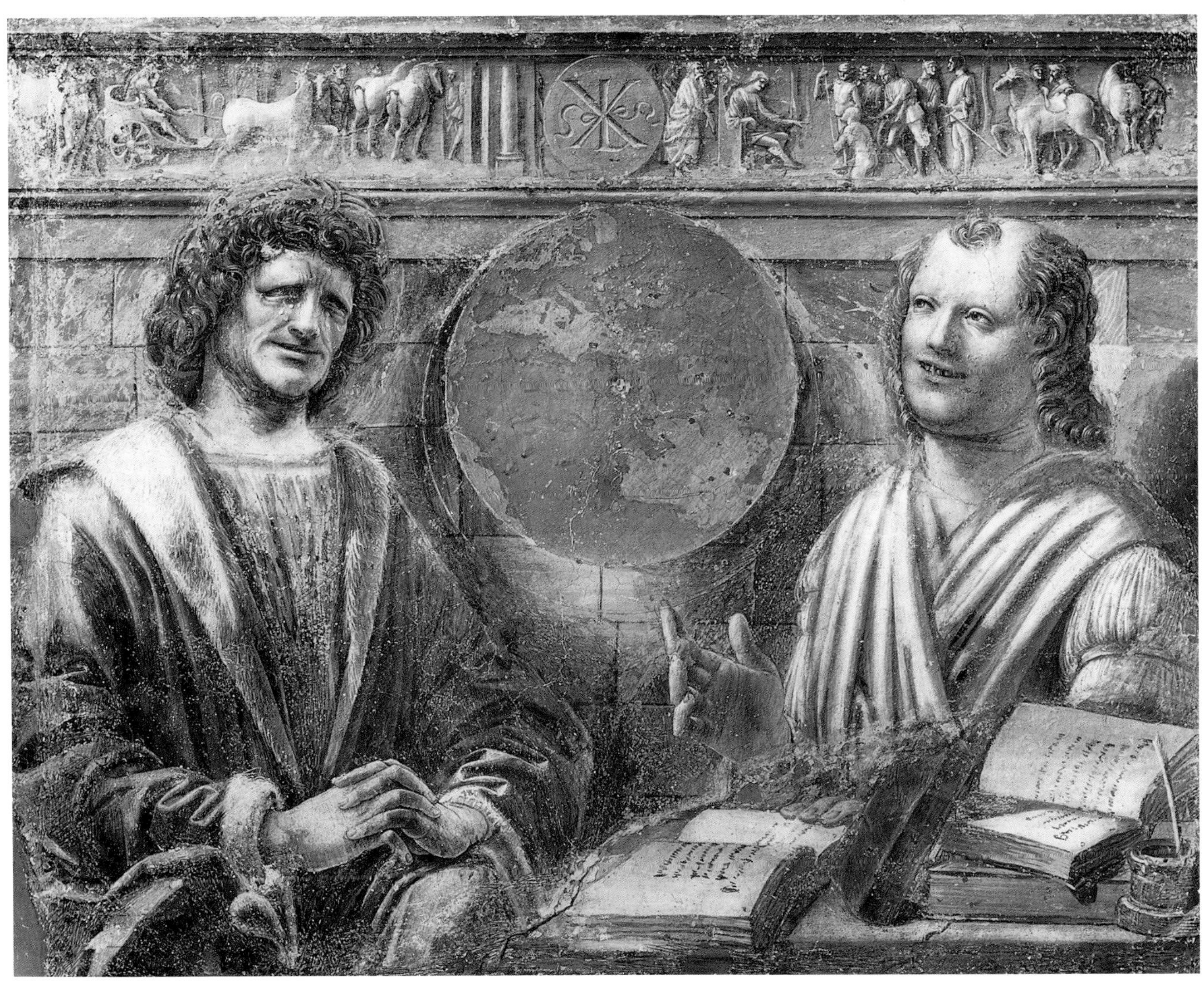

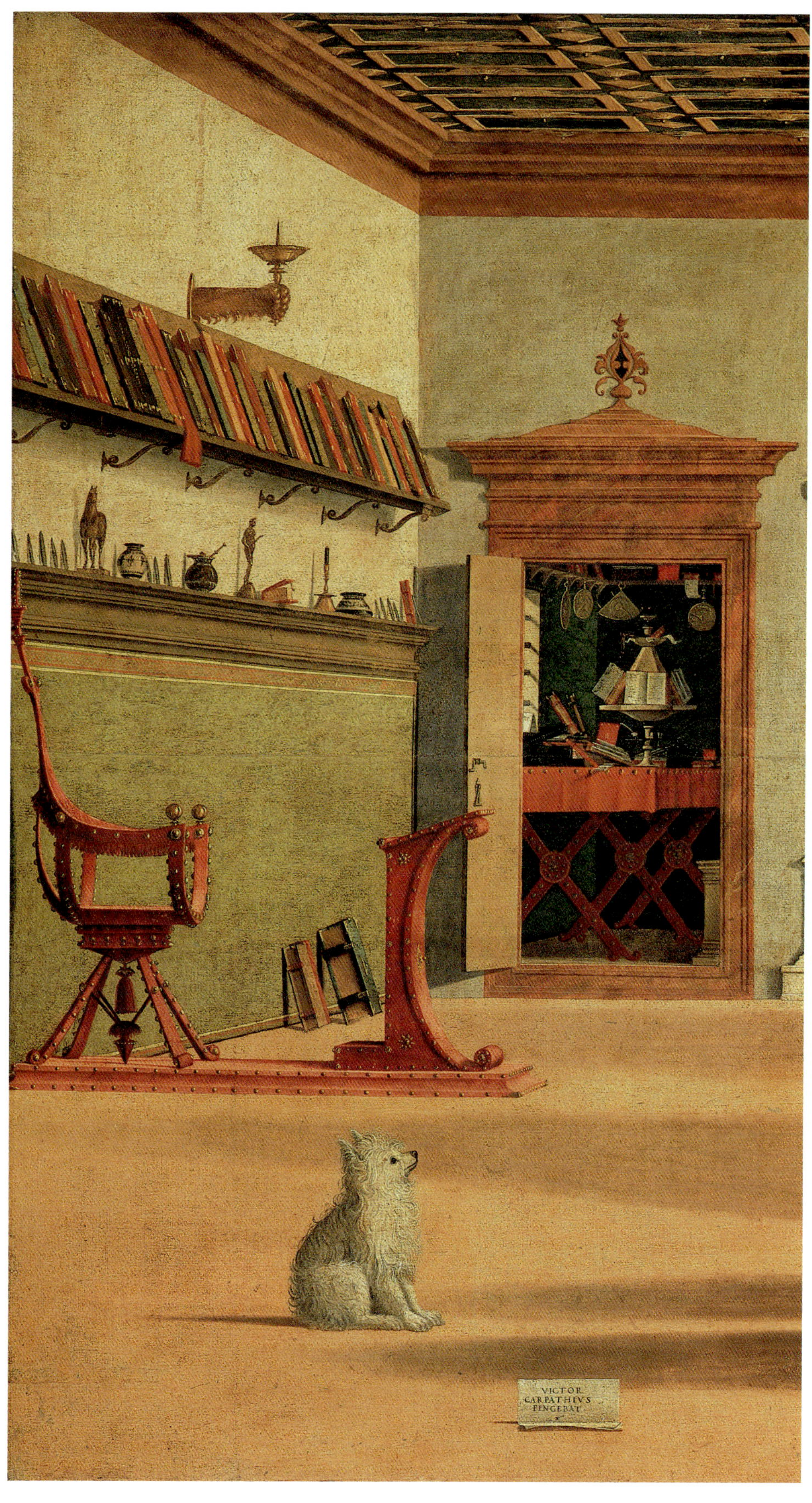

243 Vittore Carpaccio, *The Vision of St. Augustine* (detail), 1502. Oil on canvas, whole work 57.25 × 72.25 cm. Venice, Scuola di S. Giorgio degli Schiavoni.

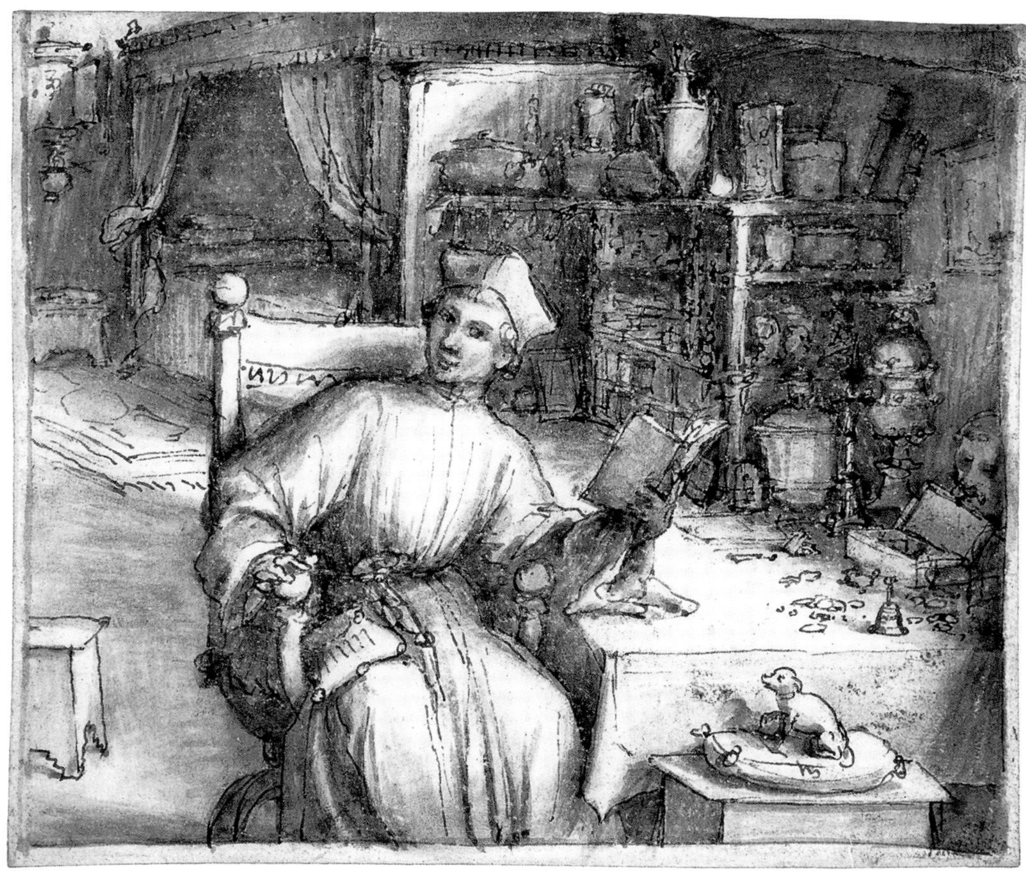

244 Lorenzo Lotto, *Ecclesiastic in his Study*, ca. 1530. Point of the brush and brown wash over traces of black chalk, 165 × 199 mm London, © British Museum (1951-2-8-34).

world and into itself, giving rise to different types of dedicated spaces within the home for private enjoyments, and sometimes even separate buildings – most notably the *casino*. As with the art gallery, such spaces might be considered "theaters of the world," the term theater being used in the sense given in John Florio's Italian–English dictionary of 1611: that is, a place where "men may sit, see and behold, or wherein one sheweth, plaieth or declareth."[10] These two tendencies, which were often intertwined, will be considered in turn.

Singular Objects

Vittore Carpaccio's well-known painting of *St. Augustine in his Study* portrays an ecclesiastic who had assembled a variety of objects in a harmonious dialogue between the sacred and the profane (fig. 243). A cornice running along the side walls serves as a display area for secular objects, some of antique provenance, such as painted Apulian vases, as well as counterfeit antiques of modern manufacture, such as the bronze statuettes of a female nude and a facsimile of one of the bronze horses on the facade of San Marco.[11] Astronomical instruments in the *camerino* in the background attest to an interest in the immediate physical world and not simply in the ancient past. The painting suggests that even those collectors with a very modest accumulation of treasures were beginning to think in terms of a coordinated ensemble in which artifacts of no utilitarian value, such as the statuettes, were an integral part. And yet, clutter had its own attractions, as demonstrated by Lorenzo Lotto's drawing *Ecclesiastic in his Study*, with shelves in the background piled high with vases and other objects (fig. 244). In either case, these studies were not secluded monastic cells; they were meant to be seen.

Likewise, the diarist Marin Sanudo was not content with simply collecting facts and gossip on life in the city. He also invited friends, acquaintances, and even strangers into his palace at San Zan Degolà to view a curious collection of

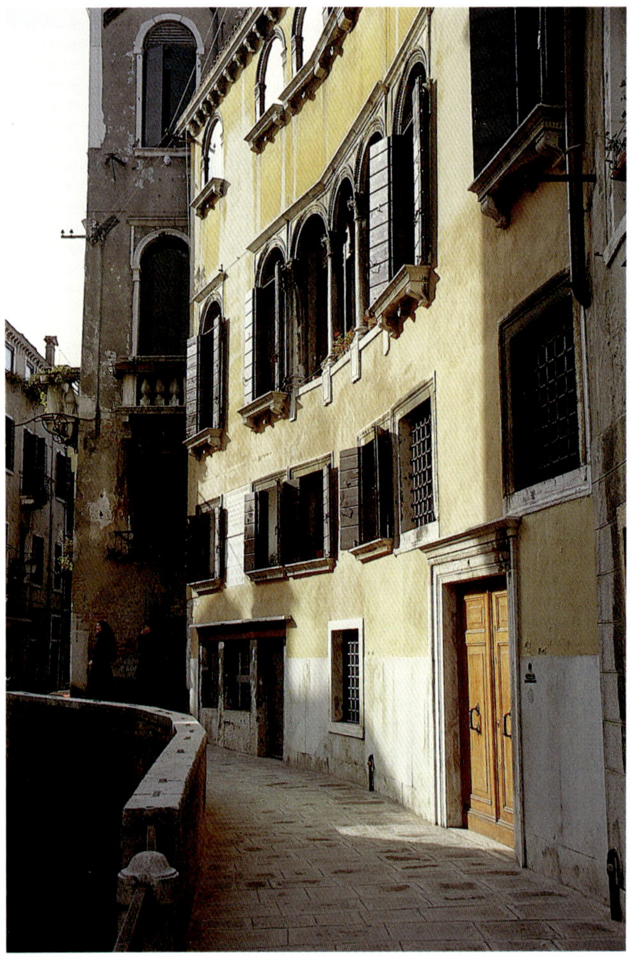

245 Ca' Sanudo on Fondamenta del Miglio at San Giacomo dall'Orio. Sanudo's *portego* is clearly demarcated by the five arched windows of the *piano nobile*.

books, images, and artifacts.[12] His *libreria* was reputed to be one of the three most popular tourist attractions for illustrious visitors to Venice in the early years of the sixteenth century – a distinction it shared with the Arsenale and the Treasury of San Marco.[13] Although the library has long been dispersed, the building still stands in the *sestiere* of Santa Croce, its curving Lombard-style facade following the line of the canal (fig. 245).[14] Federico da Porto, a visitor from Vicenza, wrote a thank-you note to Sanudo with a vivid account of his visit. Da Porto writes that having been greeted by his host at the doorstep

> Thence you commanded [me] to ascend the staircase of the palace; we moved upward little by little: a spacious *portego* stood open at the top. And here we entered a sea of singular objects; nor can a wall be seen anywhere: not any part is empty. Here you could see the various races of mankind, their outward features delineated; here you see a thousand new things . . . Here Spanish dress is seen, here Greek and Gallic, and every corner holds a different costume. What a wondrous thing to discern so many peoples on every side.[15]

Hanging in the center was a *mappamondo*, perhaps similar to the up-to-date map by Florentine engraver Francesco Rosselli, which incorporated the recent discoveries in the Americas (fig. 247).[16] To Da Porto, Sanudo's map was a revelation: "The immeasurable machine of the universe is opened up at last . . . I have seen what sustains the world, the seas, the heavens, the infernal regions, and those

246 Antonio Minello, *Mercury*, 1527. Marble, inlaid with bronze, height 76.8 cm. The rectangular relief above the horoscope contains a hieroglyph with a lyre, a caduceus, a money bag, a cock, a curved sword, and another bird. The planet Mercury, the patron of eloquence, was in conjunction with the Sun and Jupiter on 15 June 1527, an auspicious combination for Marcantonio Michiel, who had recently made a good marriage and was seeking to enter public life in that period. London, Victoria and Albert Museum (A.44-1951).

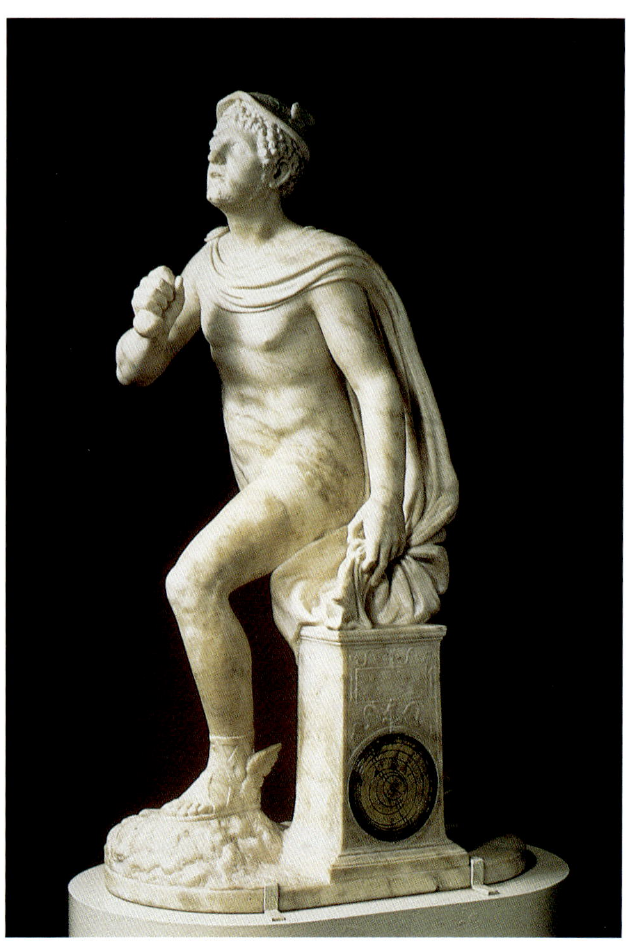

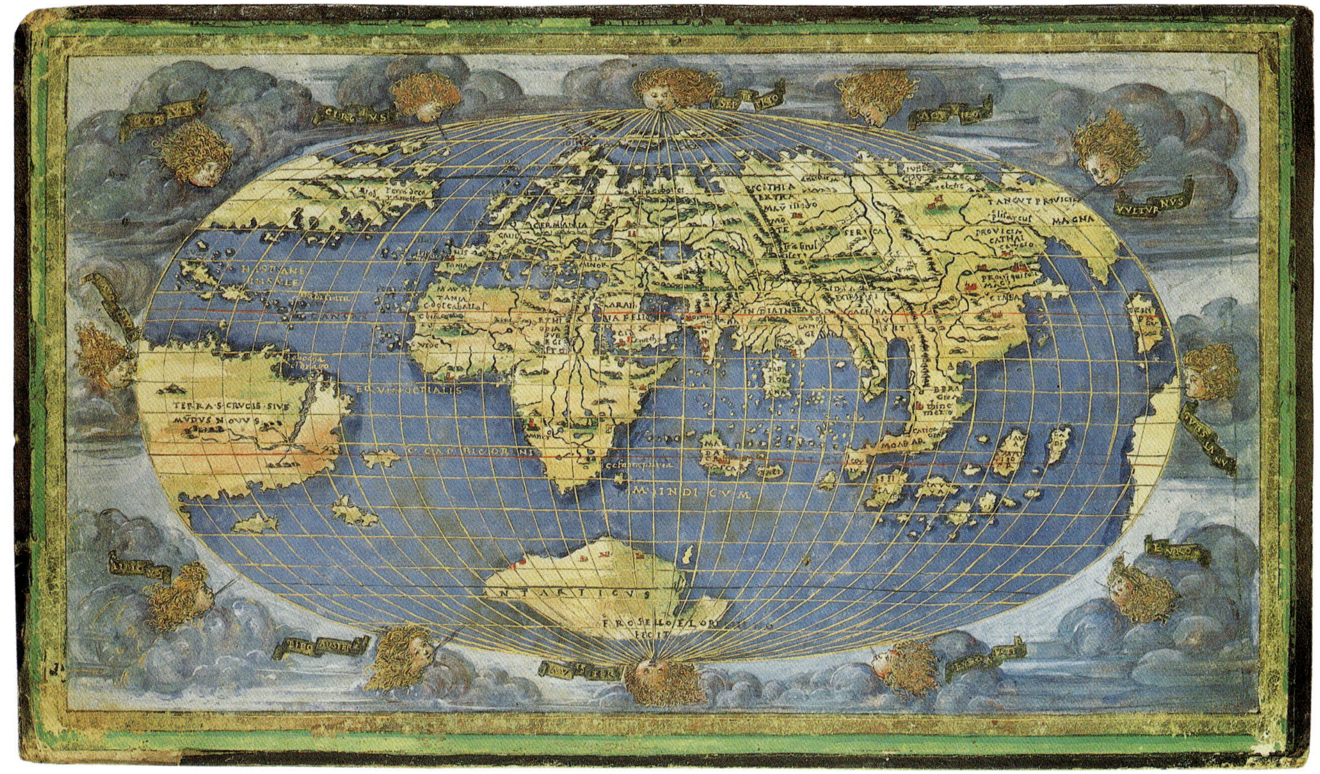

247 Franco Rosselli, *World Map*, ca. 1508. Hand-colored engraving, 21 × 35 cm. Rosselli, a Florentine cartographer known to have visited Venice in 1505 and 1508, made the map after a drawing by Giovanni Matteo Contarini (whose name suggests that he was a Venetian). This oval projection, which attempts to show the full globe in a single image, is the first printed map to show contemporary discoveries in the New World. At the upper left, Newfoundland, labeled Terra Nova, appears as the eastern tip of Asia in accordance with Columbus's belief that he had found the route to China. Below is the West Indies, labeled Hispane Insule, and further below is the large land mass of South America, called Terra S. Crucis or Mundus Novus. This map, the only one of three surviving prints to be hand-colored, was once thought to be a manuscript. London, National Maritime Museum.

who live on the other side of the earth . . . Whoever wishes to understand the sea, the earth, and the vast world, should behold this house of yours, learned Marino."[17] Sanudo was not a wealthy man, but he had transformed the *portego* of his home into what might be considered a theater of the world – a forerunner of the modern museum. It was a theater in which Venetians were increasingly involved more as spectators than as participants.

Like Sanudo, the patrician Marcantonio Michiel made up for a lack of wealth and political office with a prestigious collection. If he could not display riches, he could display his taste. And, like Sanudo, he did more, for he too kept a diary. His interests tended toward the cultural rather than the political, and his notes – brief as they are – remain the most valuable eyewitness record of Venetian collecting habits in the first half of the sixteenth century.[18] He was a collector of ancient marbles, such as statues of Diana, Apollo, Mercury, and Cleopatra valued at 10 ducats a piece, but also of modern paintings, including a *Pieta* by Giovanni Bellini.[19]

Michiel also owned what might be called modern fakes, meant to fool no one, such as a marble *Mercury* inlaid with bronze, a statuette based upon an antique original, complete with a circular bronze horoscope set into a small altar (fig. 246). An inscribed plaque in Latin on the reverse provides unusually full documentation on its manufacture and provenance, translating: "Simulacrum of Mercury, commissioned and consecrated by Marcus Antonius Michiel, Venetian Patrician. Begun by Antonio Minelli on 14 February and completed on 15 June 1527." The astronomical diagram on the face shows the motions of the planet Mercury on the date of the piece's completion.[20]

Indeed, Michiel seems to have had a penchant for establishing ownership of his objects, not just with the usual coat of arms, but with his name and the date of manufacture. One of his pieces, a bronze ewer decorated with Saracen-style engraving, has found its way into the corner of a

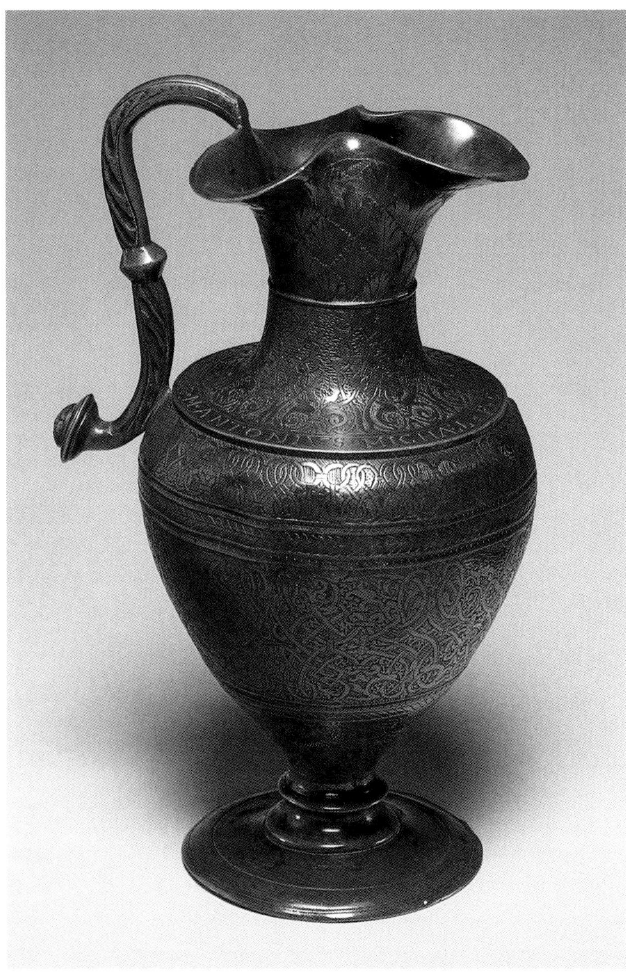

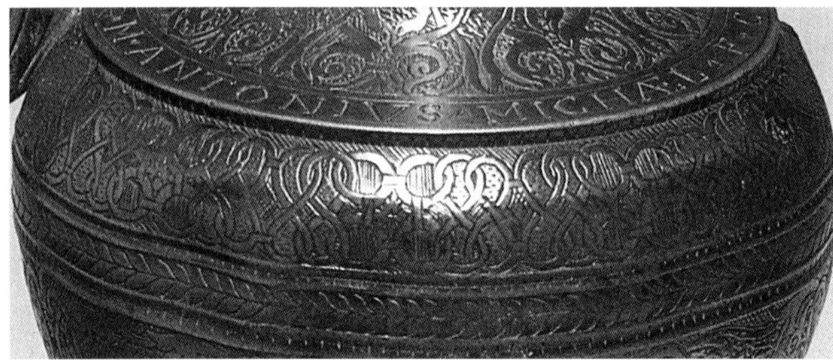

248 (*top*) and 249 Ewer, sixteenth century. Bronze. Cambridge, Fitzwilliam Museum.

display case in the Fitzwilliam Museum in Cambridge (figs. 248 and 249). An inscription running around the shoulder of the piece reads: "M. Antonius Michiel had it made in the year 1548."[21] Why is such a marking significant? The permanent labeling of expensive objects is characteristic of the collector mentality, where a distinguished provenance in and of itself bestows value on the object.[22]

During the 1520s and 1530s, Michiel made notes on collections in eleven homes in Venice and six in Padua. While his descriptions were often quite brief, he left a particularly good picture of the home of the wealthy *cittadino* Andrea Odoni. Located on Rio del Gaffaro in an unfashionable district on the edge of Venice near the present train station, Odoni's house was, nonetheless, an exercise in self-fashioning. All that remains are some carved panels from the balcony, now on a house across town (fig. 250).[23] Featuring fanciful sea creatures with bifurcated tails, the panels display an awareness of the antiquarian culture of the *Hypnerotomachia Poliphili* – that extraordinary illustrated romance, published by the Venetian printer Aldus Manutius in 1499. They were just one of many figural elements on the facade that would have announced to passers-by and first-time visitors that this was no ordinary *casa*. For the facade was further decorated with frescoes by Girolamo da Treviso, still visible in the seventeenth century when Marco Boschini described them as "a chorus of deities above and diverse statues in chiaroscuro below, along with Apollo and Diana in color." Once inside the courtyard, Odoni's guests were greeted by walls covered with more frescoes, there showing little *putti*, which Boschini termed *molto gentile* – "very fine." And they were also confronted with three modern and three antique statues, which they were implicitly invited to compare and contrast.[24]

This courtyard, which Odoni called his *antigaia*, led to a loggetta and garden beyond, containing additional pieces. In his written account of the collection, Michiel noted that one marble statue of a woman "without head and arms" had once been owned by the sculptor Tullio Lombardo and had been "portrayed by him many times in his works."[25] This observation is yet another early example of the value accorded provenance – comprising in this case ownership by a well-known artist – when appraising works of art.

Moving upstairs to the *portego*, the visitor found more antiques – most notably Roman portrait busts but also a number of modern paintings, including several by northern artists. Among the Venetian works was Titian's painting of the *Madonna and Child and St. Catherine* now in the National Gallery in London. It was in this room that Odoni's aristocratic pretensions were made clear, for he also had a *restelliera* with weapons, helmets, shields, and a banner with Orio and Odoni arms – trophies very rarely found in homes below the nobility no matter how affluent.[26]

Beyond that, the entire house was filled with works of art. The master bedroom was opulently decorated and furnished with gilded chests, a bed, and doors painted by a student of Titian. The study was full of bronze statuettes. And, like many patricians, Odoni had a golden room – a *camera d'oro*

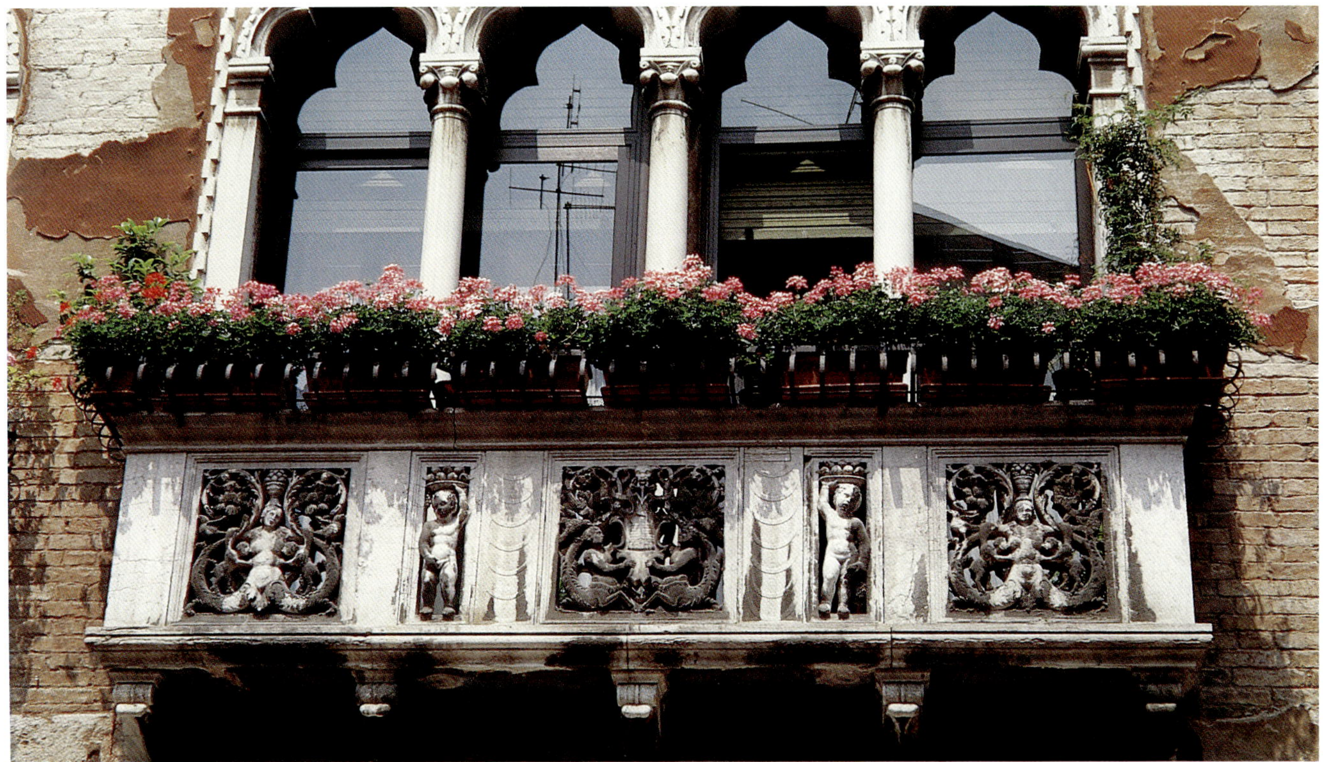

250 Balcony formerly on Ca' Odoni, now on the facade of a house at 1373 Rio Terrà San Leonardo, Cannaregio, early sixteenth century. The Odoni arms are still visible on the reverse side of the middle panel.

– with a studio containing all kinds of treasures, curiosities, and natural wonders: cups made of porphyry, crystal, and petrified wood; an illuminated breviary; petrified crabs, fish, and snakes; a dried chameleon; rare seashells; and "two pieces of amber with a butterfly and an ant inside them."[27]

Michiel described one of the paintings in the house as a "portrait of Messer Andrea himself, who contemplates antique marble fragments." This painting, by Lorenzo Lotto, initiated a new portrait type – the collector (fig. 251).[28] But as a recent study makes clear, the painting is not a document; it is, rather, a fiction. For only one of the objects depicted – Hadrian's head – can be found in the detailed inventory made of Odoni's possessions when he died in 1545. The other pieces in the painting are accessories – stage props, if you will – intended to construct an ideal image of the collector.[29] It has also been convincingly argued that Michiel's choice of the verb "contemplare" – to contemplate – is significant. Andrea is not sitting there passively, surrounded by his treasures; rather, he is actively thinking about them and even presenting them for our perusal. To intellectuals and other collectors in his circle, such activity would have been transparently a means to an end. According to Neoplatonic teachings current at the time, the contemplation of beautiful objects with one's own eyes was the first step toward the attainment of higher knowledge and, ultimately, the truth. Odoni's gesture to the viewer shows his desire to share that truth with his friends.[30]

A Theater of the Mind

But as rich and varied as Odoni's collection was, it paled in comparison to that which his contemporary, the patrician Gabriele Vendramin, had assembled in his palace at Santa Fosca. Like many collectors he had begun as a patron, and he began early. Born in 1484, he was probably just twenty-four years old when he commissioned Giorgione to paint the *Tempest* – often called the first true and proper landscape in Venetian art. By the time Gabriele was thirty-three, Sanudo reported that he was known as *el grando* or "the great."[31]

Vendramin had catholic tastes. Like Odoni, he was a collector not only of paintings and antiquities, but also of curiosities and natural wonders, and on the grand scale sug-

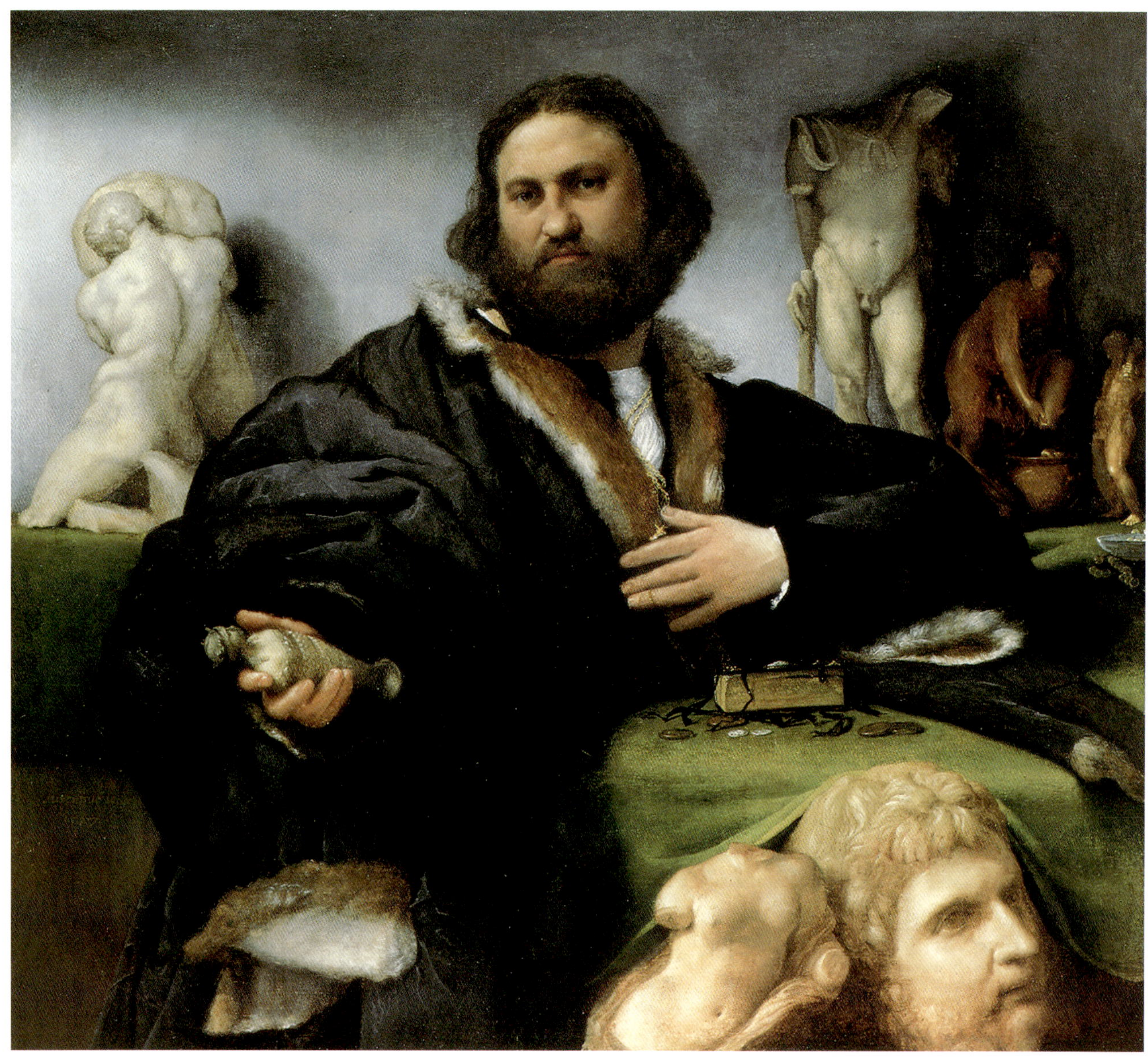

251 Lorenzo Lotto, *Portrait of Andrea Odoni*, 1527. Oil on canvas, 101 × 114 cm. Odoni proffers a statuette of the many-breasted Diana of Ephesus, a Renaissance symbol of Nature. His gesture may signify his dedication to nature, even though he is surrounded by culture, symbolized by antiquities and works of art. Hampton Court. The Royal Collection © 2003, Her Majesty Queen Elizabeth II.

gested by his nickname. Among the antiquities were statues, a rich series of marble heads inserted in gesso busts, and also reliefs, inscriptions, terracotta and glass vases, stucco heads (that were perhaps plaster casts from the antique), and numerous coins of gold, silver, and bronze.[32] The writer Anton Francesco Doni described Vendramin as "a Venetian gentleman of true courtesy, natural nobility, and admirable intelligence, manners, and goodness," and characterized his collection as "marvelous." He was particularly impressed with "divine drawings that his generosity had bought with great expense, and care, and ingenuity."[33] Among these were a copy of a preparatory sketch by Raphael for a fresco in the Vatican Stanze and Jacopo Bellini's large album of over 100 pencil drawings, now in the British Museum. It was during this period that collectors began to take drawings seriously and collect them as works of art, and Vendramin was one of the earliest in Venice to do so.[34] Doni was also impressed with what he called Vendramin's "rare antiques," and his description reveals that such prizes functioned not simply as objects of aesthetic delight, but also as conversation pieces:

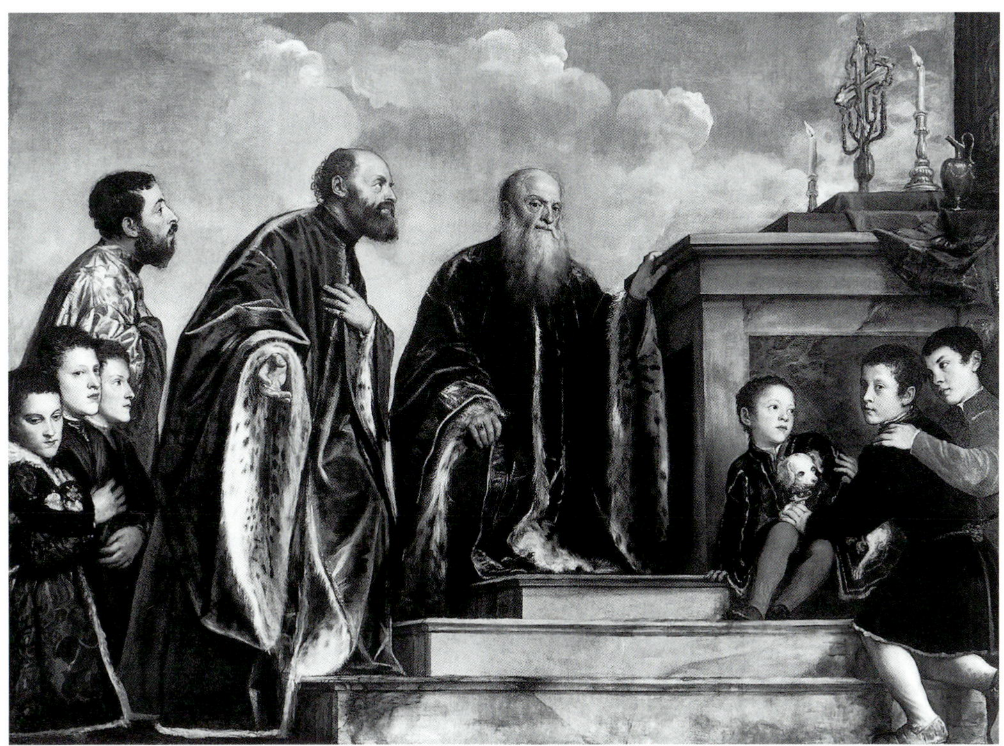

252 Titian, *The Vendramin Family and the Reliquary of the True Cross*, 1543–47. Oil on canvas, 206 × 301 cm. London, National Gallery.

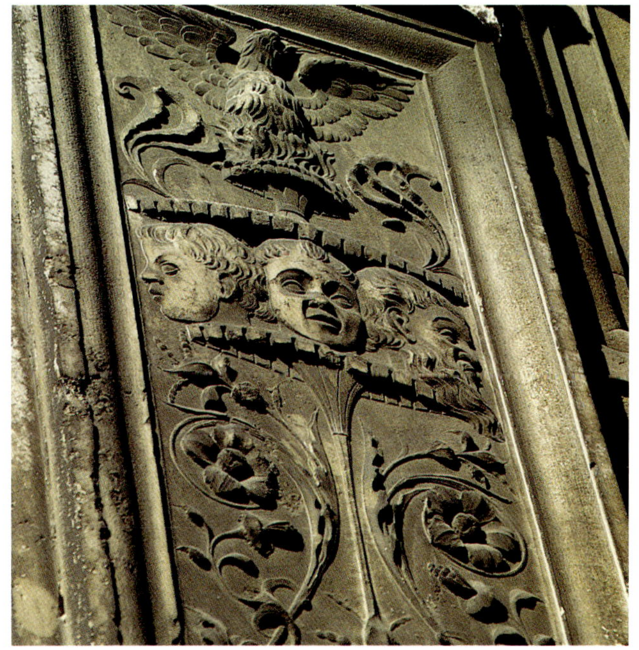

253 (*right*) Tricipitium (Three Ages of Man), early sixteenth century. Relief on pilaster to the right of the entrance portal of Palazzo Vendramin, S. Fosca.

"And among other objects he showed me a Lion with a Cupid on its back and we talked at length of the pleasing invention of the piece and we praised it for demonstrating that Love can conquer men's fierce and terrible nature."[35] Later in the century, Francesco Sansovino would look back on Gabriele's home as "once the meeting place of the *virtuosi* of the city."[36]

Titian depicted the white-haired Gabriele surrounded by his brother Andrea and nephews with the Reliquary of the Cross in a group portrait now in the National Gallery in London (fig. 252).[37] A patrician of the old school, Gabriele was a gentleman in name but not in fact according to Nicolò Machiavelli's definition, for the family were merchants first and foremost, having built up a great fortune in the soap trade.[38] Their ethos was proclaimed for all to see on the pilasters flanking the entrance to the *casa* at Santa Fosca, which feature a *tricipitium*, or cluster of three heads, of the young, the middle-aged and the old – that is, the *Ages of Man*, which signified Prudence in the emblematic language of the day (fig. 253).[39]

In his will, written in 1548, Gabriele left his entire estate of palaces, houses, lands, and a soap factory to the seven nephews portrayed in Titian's painting. He was particularly

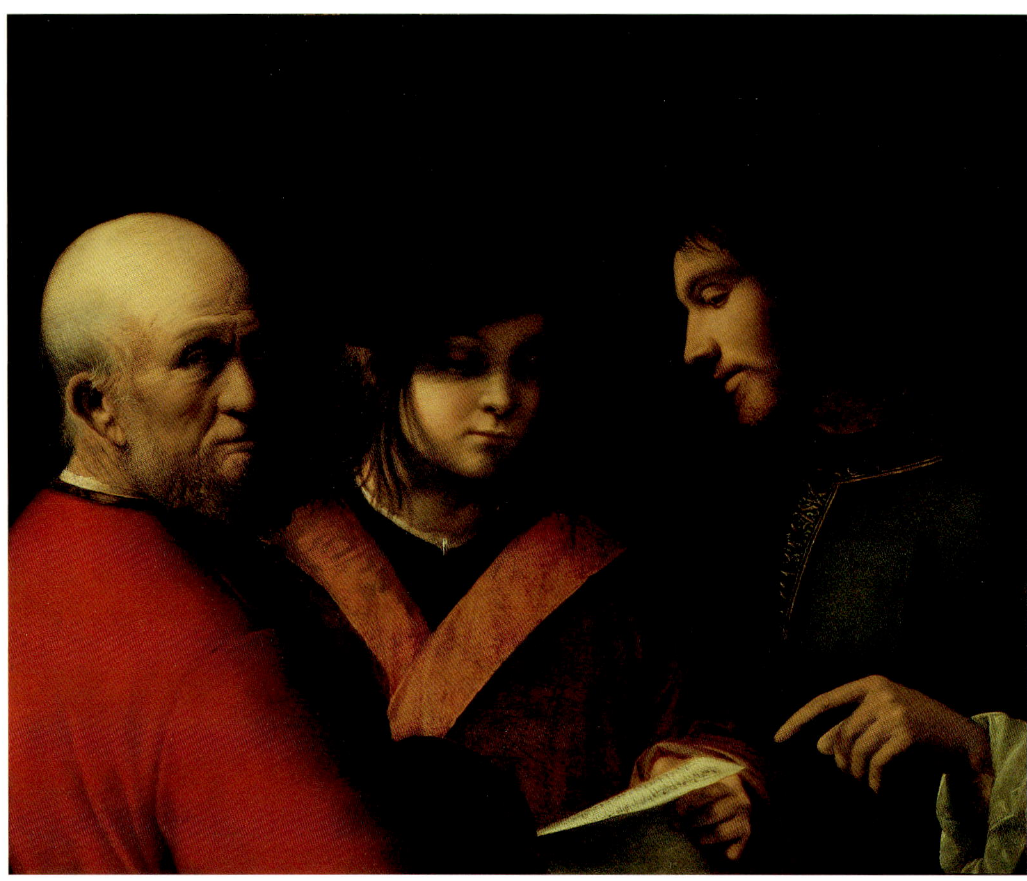

254 Giorgione, *The Ages of Man*, ca. 1500. Panel, 62 × 77 cm. The boy in the center holds a musical score, causing the work to be listed in an inventory of 1567–79 as "a painting with three who sing." But none of the figures open their mouths in song and in a 1666 inventory the work had become "Marcus Aurelius who studies between two philosophers." Only in 1698 was the work given its present title. It has recently been suggested that "A Singing Lesson" would be a more appropriate title, with Neoplatonic implications of a divine harmony achieved by the three voices and an ascent, underscored by the lighting, toward the wisdom and full illumination of old age. Florence, Palazzo Pitti.

concerned about a room in the *casa* at Santa Fosca that he called his *camerino delle antigaglie*, the latter word implying not just antiquities but all types of precious objects and works of art. After listing many pieces throughout the house, he writes:

> I declare that all the things that are found in this small room . . . both for their high quality and because of the many years' hard work taken to acquire them, and most of all because they have brought a little peace and quiet to my soul during the many labors of mind and body that I have endured in conducting the family business, are so pleasing and dear to me that I must pray and beseech those who inherit them to treat them with such care that they shall not perish.

For this reason, he ordered that they "never be sold, nor lent, neither in whole nor in part under any form."[40]

What were these works of which he was so fond? An inventory made around fifteen years later listed seventy-one paintings in Gabriele's *casa*, six of them in the *camerino* itself. Few are identifiable, but one was probably a painting of the *Ages of Man*, now in the Pitti Museum in Florence and attributed to Giorgione (fig. 254).[41] There were also 150 antiquities, now dispersed. How were these pieces arranged? The inventory states that the *camerino* featured a projecting cornice painted by Titian that held fifteen heads alternating with fourteen antique vases and some animal horns.[42] Another fifteen sculptures – heads, torsos, statues, vases, inscriptions, and *bas-reliefs* – were set on special bases along the walls. Placed on top of *armadi*, or cabinets, were bronzes, porcelains, terracottas, small paintings, and natural objects. The *armadi* themselves contained small paintings and other objects and were provided with drawers, divided into small compartments for medals and coins.[43] Gabriele, like Andrea Odoni, conceived of his acquisitions as an ensemble rather than as merely an accumulation of objects. And he had arranged the items with a spectator in mind.

For Gabriele Vendramin, his collection had two functions. On the one hand, it was a theater of the mind – a place of solace and meditation to which he might invite his friends upon occasion. On the other, it was a monument – to himself, for posterity. He was a collector in the modern sense, whose greatest desire was for his collection to remain intact after his death. In this he was, alas, thwarted. After Gabriele's death in 1552, his nephews divided up the estate, with the collection remaining in the *camerino* and adjoining rooms of the palace at Santa Fosca under the custody of his eldest nephew, Luca. For a time all was well. But in 1565 Luca's brothers Federigo and Filippo learned that he was selling off some of the drawings and antique coins to dealers in Venice and they filed a lawsuit, demanding that an inventory be made of the collection. Did they do this for love of scholarship and fine arts or to preserve the collection in accordance with their uncle's wishes? No indeed, for the art dealer Jacopo Strada was attempting to negotiate a sale of the collection on their behalf to the Duke of Bavaria. After prolonged litigation and even fist fights between the brothers, the inventory was finally drawn up from 1567 to 1569 by a commission of artists that included Jacopo Tintoretto, Jacopo Sansovino and Alessandro Vittoria. The sale was then blocked by Luca, who still wanted to sell objects piecemeal. The brothers were at a stand-off. In 1615, Vincenzo Scamozzi reported that the study was "still sealed, until there is someone in the family who will come and take delight in it."[44] It remained that way until the 1650s, when memories had dimmed and the paintings and antiquities were finally sold off in separate lots to various collectors.[45]

A Classical Setting

Domenico and Giovanni Grimani, uncle and nephew, would not made the same mistake. Their story begins in the early years of the sixteenth century in Rome, where the Venetian Cardinal Domenico Grimani began construction of a new palace on the Quirinale. As the foundations were dug, treasures were uncovered, and a collector was born. In 1505 Domenico invited the Venetian ambassador and his entourage to dinner at his residence. According to Sanudo they greatly admired the "library furnished with a great quantity of beautiful books and a great number of marble figures, and many other antiquities, all found underground at [Grimani's] *vigna* [vineyard on the Quirinal Hill] while excavating for the building of the palace he is erecting there."[46] By the time of his death in 1523, the cardinal had amassed a collection of more than 170 classical marbles and bronzes during his long residence in Rome. But Rome was just a starting point, for his guiding principle had been to obtain the best pieces from throughout the world, particularly the Aegean. He also built up a library of more than 15,000 volumes, probably the largest in Europe, and acquired hundreds of engraved gems, coins, and medals, as well as paintings by such artists as Raphael, Hans Memling, Hieronymus Bosch, Albrecht Dürer, and Antonello da Messina. Among his treasures were the famed Grimani Breviary and a small bronze copy of the *Laocoon* by Jacopo Sansovino. The latter was so finely crafted, Giorgio Vasari reported, that the cardinal considered it equal to a true antique.[47]

In his will, Grimani bequeathed twenty-two paintings and all his classical sculpture to the Venetian state, to be displayed "in his memory" in a specially fitted room in the Ducal Palace.[48] Significantly, the republic declined the paintings, but retained eleven busts and five statues – the rarest and choicest marbles in the collection – a decision revealing that antiquities were still more valuable than paintings in that period. The rest of the antiquities were eventually reconsigned to Grimani's heirs, his four nephews.[49] Over the next four decades, two of them – Vettore and Giovanni – would remodel and redecorate the family palace at Santa Maria Formosa especially to house the collection.[50]

The house was originally an L-shape, comprising just a north and an east wing (fig. 255; see also fig. 240). Focusing on the east wing, the first phase of reconstruction and decoration was completed around 1540. It involved the creation of a loggia facing an open courtyard in emulation of the peristyle of an ancient Roman house, and a refacing of the exterior facade on Rio San Severo. On the *piano nobile* above the loggia, three small chambers to house ancient treasures were specially decorated with classicizing decorations by Roman-trained artists.[51] Inspired by the baths at Hadrian's Villa, the Sala di Callisto featured a coved vault decorated by Giovanni da Udine, with compartmentalized stucco work and painted scenes from Ovid's story of the nymph Callisto. In the Sala di Apollo, the same artist created a stuccoed vault that was frescoed by Francesco Salviati with *grotteschi all'antica* inspired by the Domus Aurea or Nero's Golden House in Rome (fig. 256). This type of antique vault decoration, already adopted in the Vatican apartments by Raphael and now introduced into Venice, would have a

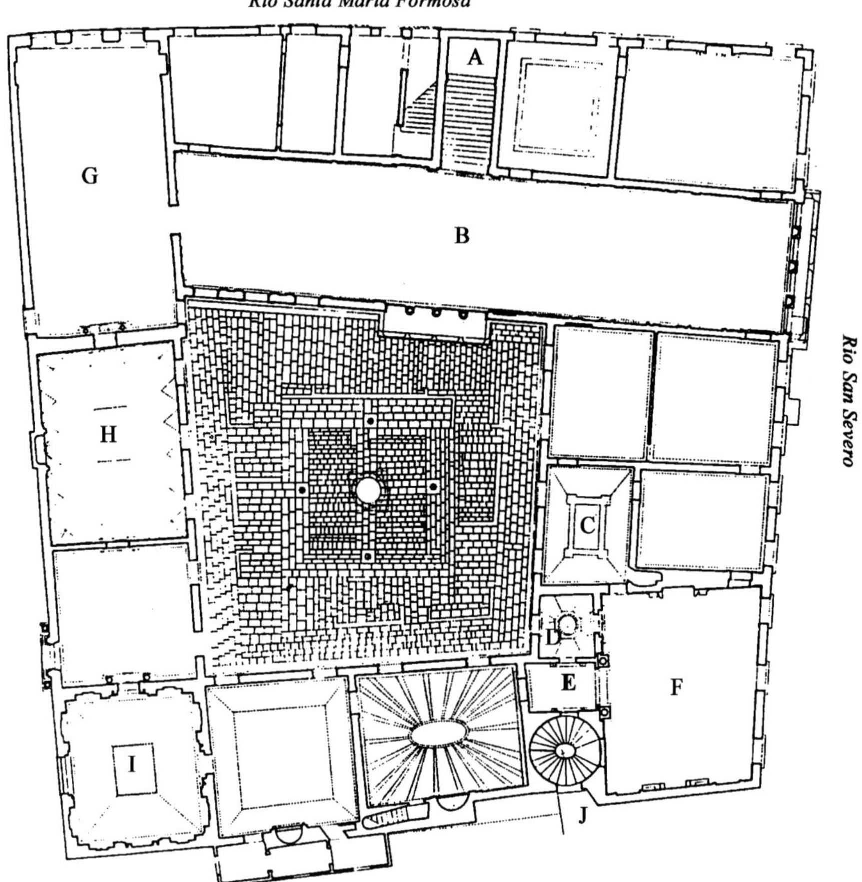

255 Palazzo Grimani at Santa Maria Formosa. Floor plan adapted from Irene Favaretto and Giovanna Luisa Ravagnan, *Lo Statuario pubblico della Serenissima: due secoli di collezionismo di antichità: 1596–1797* (Cittadella: Biblos, 1997). North is at the top. A: Main staircase from water entrance; B: Portego; C: Sala di Callisto; D: Sala di Apollo; E: Sala di Psyche; F: Sala di Antonio Grimani; G: Chameron d'Oro; H: Room with ceiling with arboreal decoration; I: Tribuna or Studio della Antichità; J: Land entrance off Ruga Giuffa.

long afterlife in Venetian villas on the Terraferma. The Sala di Psyche featured yet another scheme, with a ceiling by Salviati of painted panels of various sizes.[52] Judged by Vasari to be "the most beautiful work of painting in all of Venice," it is, ironically, the only room of the three not to survive.

What is the significance of these chambers, aside from their beauty and originality? They mark the first attempt by Venetian patrons to provide a proper *all'antica* – that is ancient Roman – setting in which to display classical objects: a unity of form and content that may be said to define the Renaissance aesthetic. In a definitive break with Venetian tradition, Rome had come to Venice along with Grimani's collection.[53]

By 1558 Giovanni Grimani, now Patriarch of Aquileia, had outlived his brothers. He had been adding to the collection all along and was the one most actively engaged in managing it. Denied his dearest wish to be named a cardinal like his uncle and two of his brothers, he threw himself into creating an even more suitable setting for the collection.[54] In the late 1560s, he began a second phase of construction and decoration. First he added two wings to the house on the west and south to create a large courtyard, again in the Roman manner. Here he installed classical statuary, as Andrea Odoni had done on a more modest scale several decades earlier. Then, on the *piano nobile* in the new west wing, he created a sequence of rooms to house the bulk of the collection. The palace exterior, visible only from two canals, was modest and unimposing, despite a rusticated basement and classical details that gave it a Roman look.[55] At Palazzo Grimani the taste for *Romanitas* would be pursued in private, for the most part, with a facade *alla veneziana* and an interior *alla moderna*.[56]

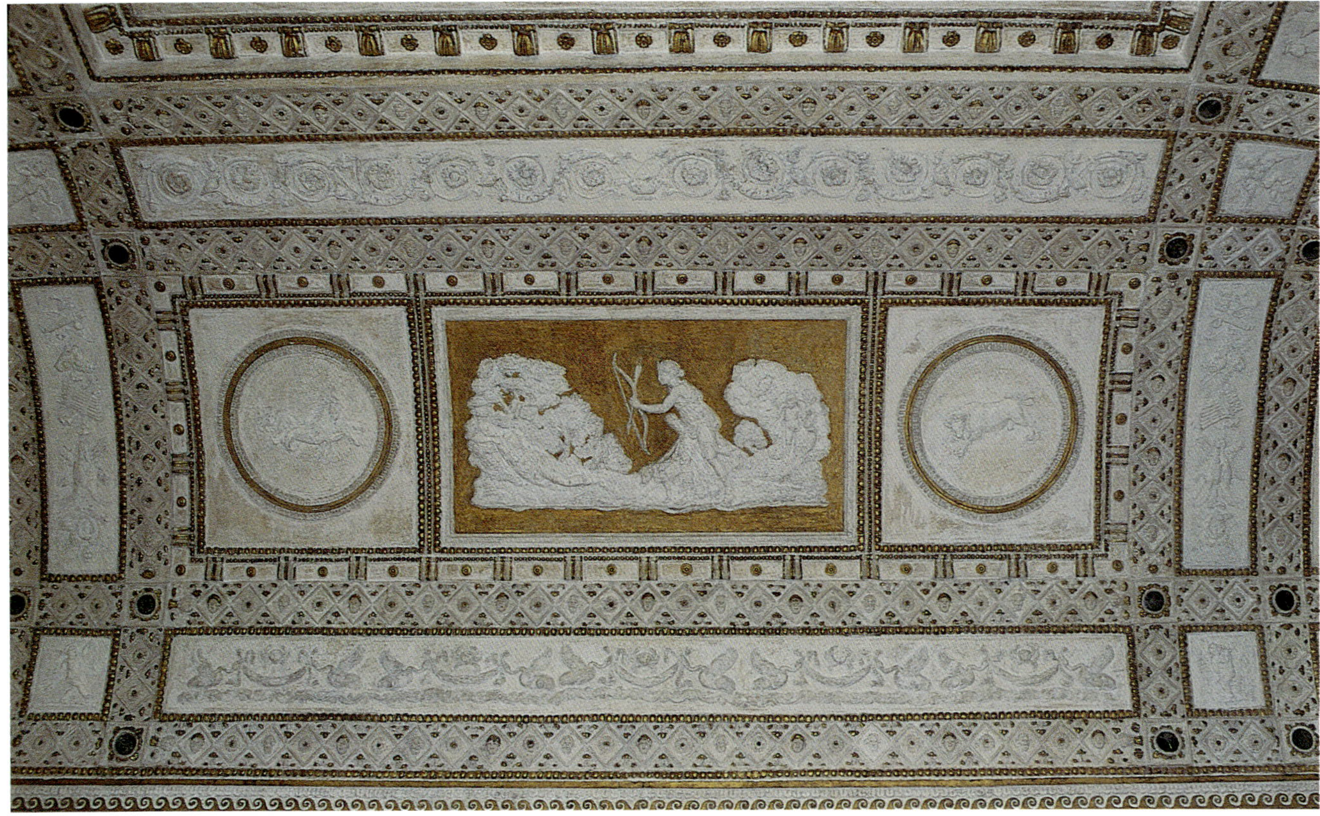

256 Giovanni da Udine and Francesco Salviati, vault frescoed with *grotteschi*, completed by 1540. Sala di Apollo, Palazzo Grimani at Santa Maria Formosa.

Only the land entrance, located at the end of a long, narrow alley, hinted at the extraordinary treasures within (fig. 257). The window above the portal was flanked by Corinthian columns, topped by an unusual curving pediment, and crowned with a Roman portrait bust. Two more busts were set on plinths at the sides, inscribed with a dedication making clear that this was a palace intended to be a true *casa aperta*: GENIO/ VRBIS/ AVG(usto)/ VSVIQ(ue)/ AMICO/RUM – "To the glory of the city and for the use of friends." While the first two words repeated the inscription on the palace of Giovanni Dario of the late fifteenth century (see Chapter 2), the remainder acknowledged the interior of a home as a place of representation as much as refuge.[57] Appropriately, the Grimani ensemble resembled nothing so much as a book frontispiece, a title page to the unique experience that awaited inside.

Visitors arriving by land had two options. They might ascend a spiral staircase directly behind the entrance. This gave direct access to a room commemorating Giovanni's grandfather, Doge Antonio Grimani, the paterfamilias whose bust originally graced the niche above the fireplace. It was he who had bequeathed the home to Giovanni and Vettore's father Girolamo and his brothers back in 1501. Furnished with classical statuary, the space was adjacent to the little jewel-box rooms decorated by Giovanni da Udine and Francesco Salviati in the 1530s. Probably designed by Giovanni himself, it is a virtual shrine – an extraordinary example of family *pietas* in emulation of the ancient Romans.

Alternatively, visitors could proceed directly to the main part of the collections by crossing the courtyard, populated with over-life-sized figures of Roman consuls and embellished with classical reliefs. Thence they would pass under the loggia, fashioned in the manner of a Roman peristyle, and join those arriving by boat to ascend the main staircase. With its splendid barrel vault stuccoed and painted by Federico Zuccari – another artist who had been summoned from Rome – the staircase was meant to impress. Its allegorical images were inspired by Roman cameos in the Grimani collection, and, in that age-old Venetian tradition of proclaiming family virtues at the entrance to the home, the central compartment featured the figure of Justice.

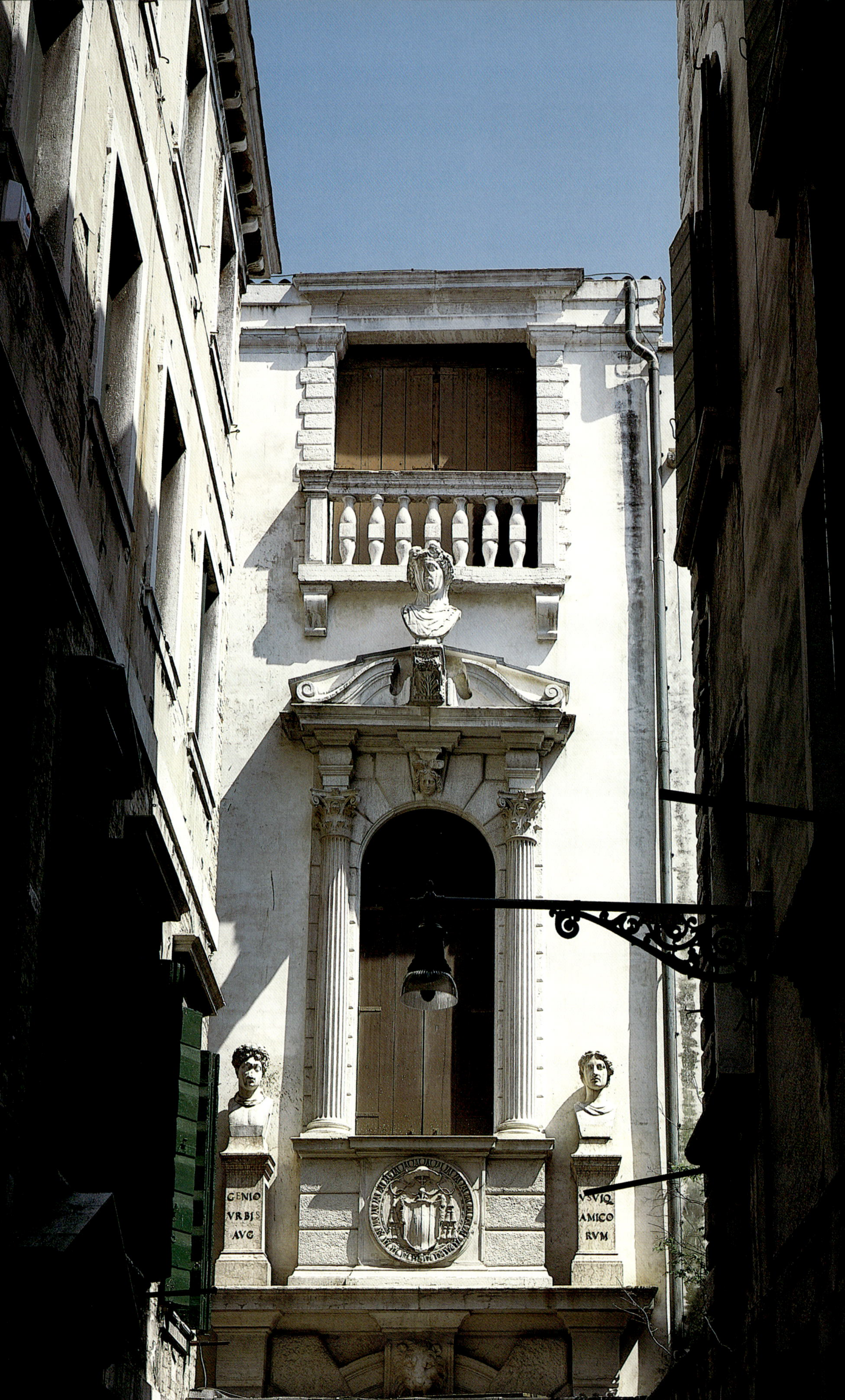
GENIO
VRBIS
AVG
VSVIQ
AMICO
RVM

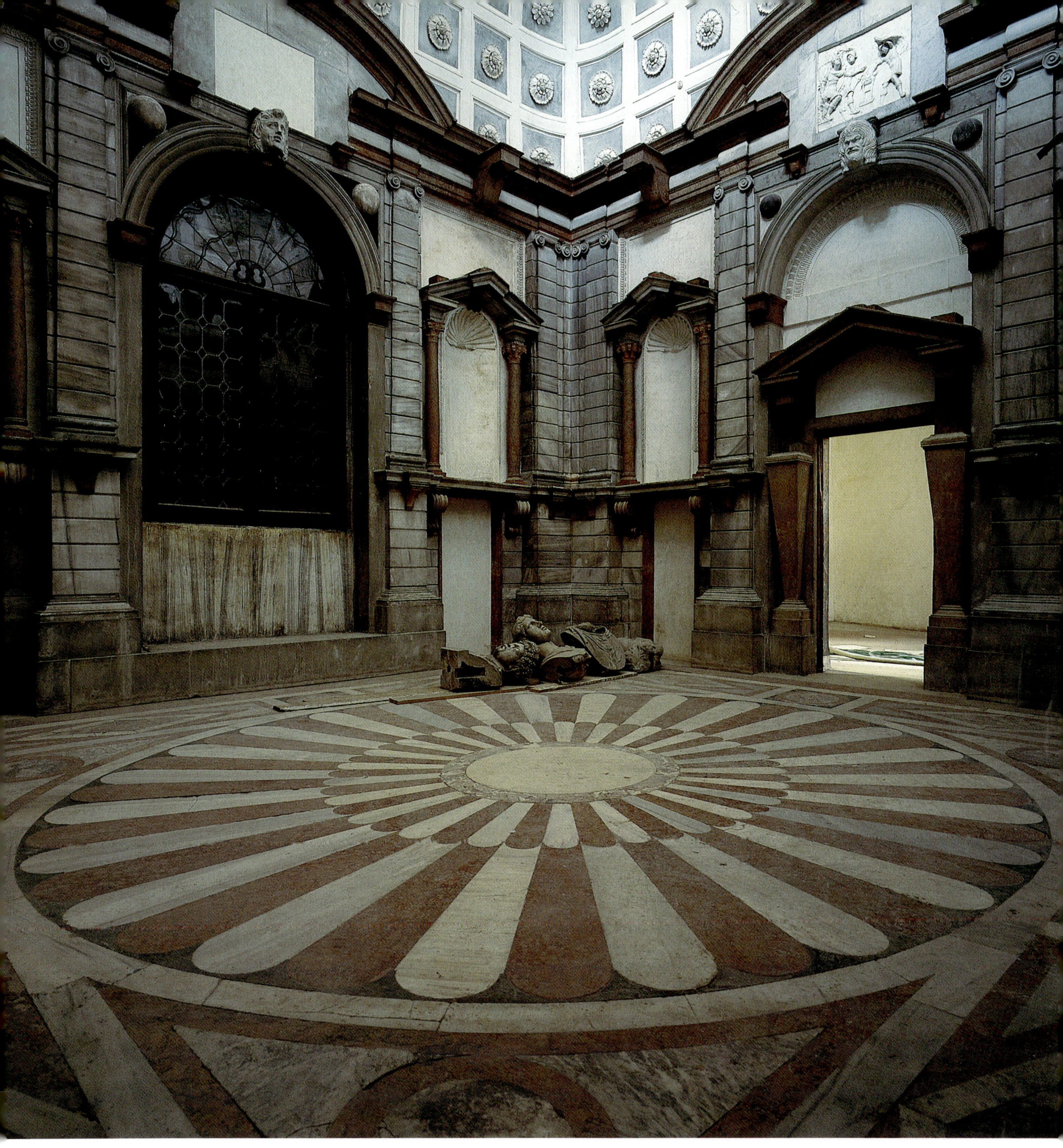

257 (*facing page*) Palazzo Grimani at Santa Maria Formosa, mid-sixteenth century. Facade above entrance portal. The portal is reached through a narrow alley off Ruga Giuffa.

258 (*above*) *Tribuna* or *studio delle anticaglie* in Palazzo Grimani at Santa Maria Formosa, 1560s. The room, illuminated by a cupola at the top of the pavilion vault, was designed to display around 130 antique sculptures. The Dutchman Nicolò Stoppio, in a letter to Johann Jakob Fugger in 1568, wrote that Giovanni Grimani had "consulted with the first architects of Italy" in designing the new studio. (See Manfredo Tafuri, *Venezia e il Rinascimento* (Turin: Giulio Einaudi, Editore, 1985). 16.

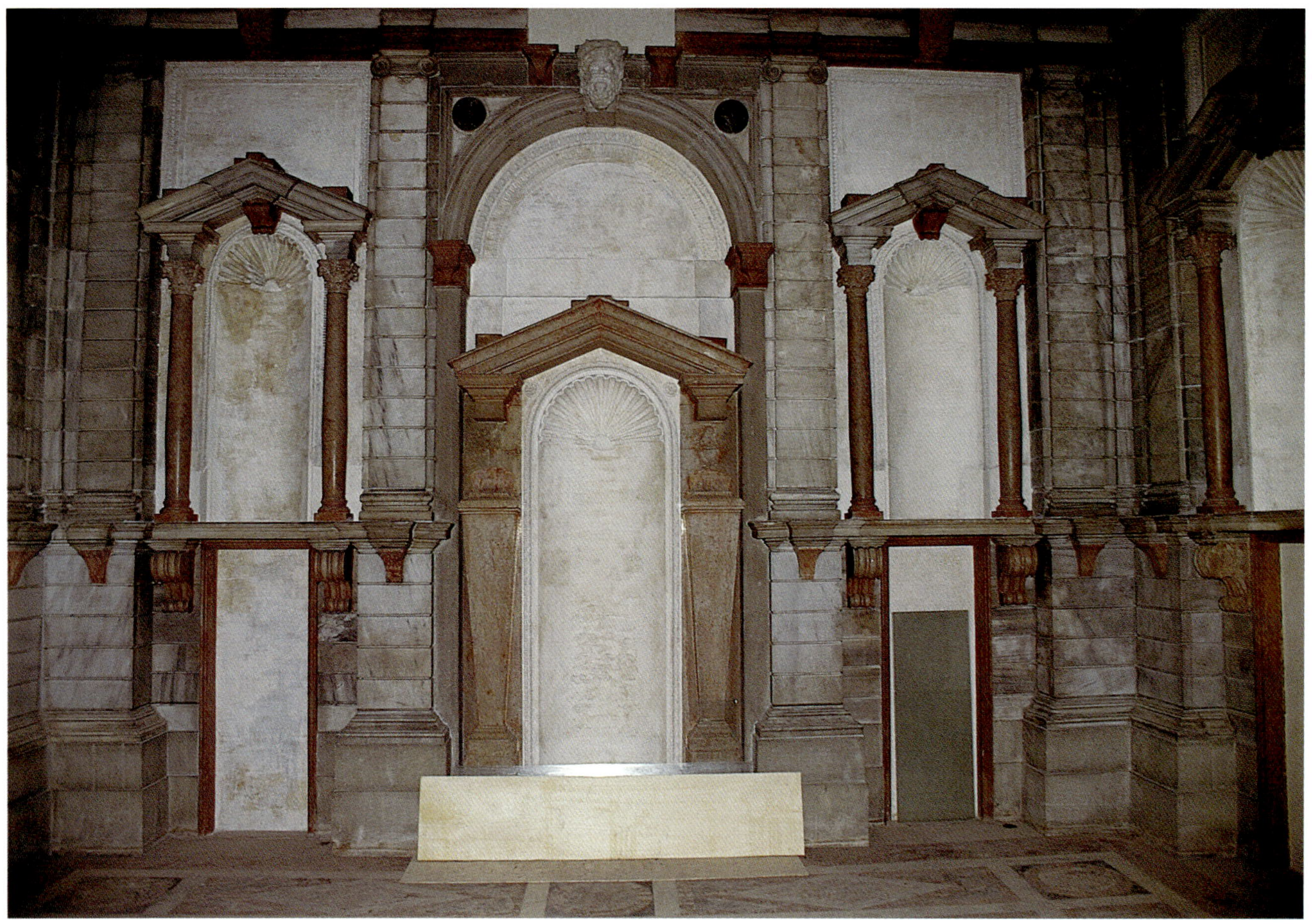

259 View of a side wall of the *tribuna* in Palazzo Grimani (fig. 258). Designed to display Grimani's best statuary, all four walls feature a tripartite scheme. The central bay contains a tabernacle with a broken pediment enclosing a shallow central niche within an arched surround of engaged rusticated pilasters which support a broken segmental pediment resting on the cornice above. At each side are elevated niches with columns and broken triangular pediments set on consoles. Statues were placed in the niches or on antique pedestals or set directly on the floor. *Bas-reliefs* were set into the cornice pediments above the keystone heads.

What made Grimani's collection particularly unique was the way in which it was presented as an itinerary in specially decorated rooms. Here, instead of art works being brought in to decorate the house, it was the house that was refashioned to frame the art. At the top of the stairs, visitors would pass through the end of the old *portego* to enter the first reception chamber, called the *chameron d'oro* – that is, the large chamber of gold. Turning left, they could look through three doorways perfectly aligned to provide an unobstructed view of the *tribuna* or *studio delle anticaglie* in the southwest corner of the building. As Sansovino put it, "one sees there in diverse rooms that open one into the other, entire and fragmented figures, torsos, and heads in unequaled abundance, and all select and praiseworthy."[58]

The ceiling of the central room in the sequence was frescoed, above spandrels filled with *grotteschi* and coats of arms, to simulate a great arbor, with fruit trees, vines, and birds in profusion – an elaborate example of the Venetian taste for bringing the garden inside the home. But the primary destination was the *studio dell'anticaglie* at the end, which Coryat never managed to see. It was there, in a costly stage set of pink and white marble walls and floor, that the treasures of the collection – some 130 sculptures – were displayed. Rising above the space was a coffered cupola, its lantern specially designed to illuminate the pieces with indirect light (figs. 258–260). In 1581 Sansovino cited eighteen studios of antiquities and medals in his *Venetia città nobilissima*, but singled out Grimani's as "the most principal not just of Venice but of almost any other city . . . a celebrated place, full of ancient beauties, and singular for quantity and quality and . . . most rare to see."[59]

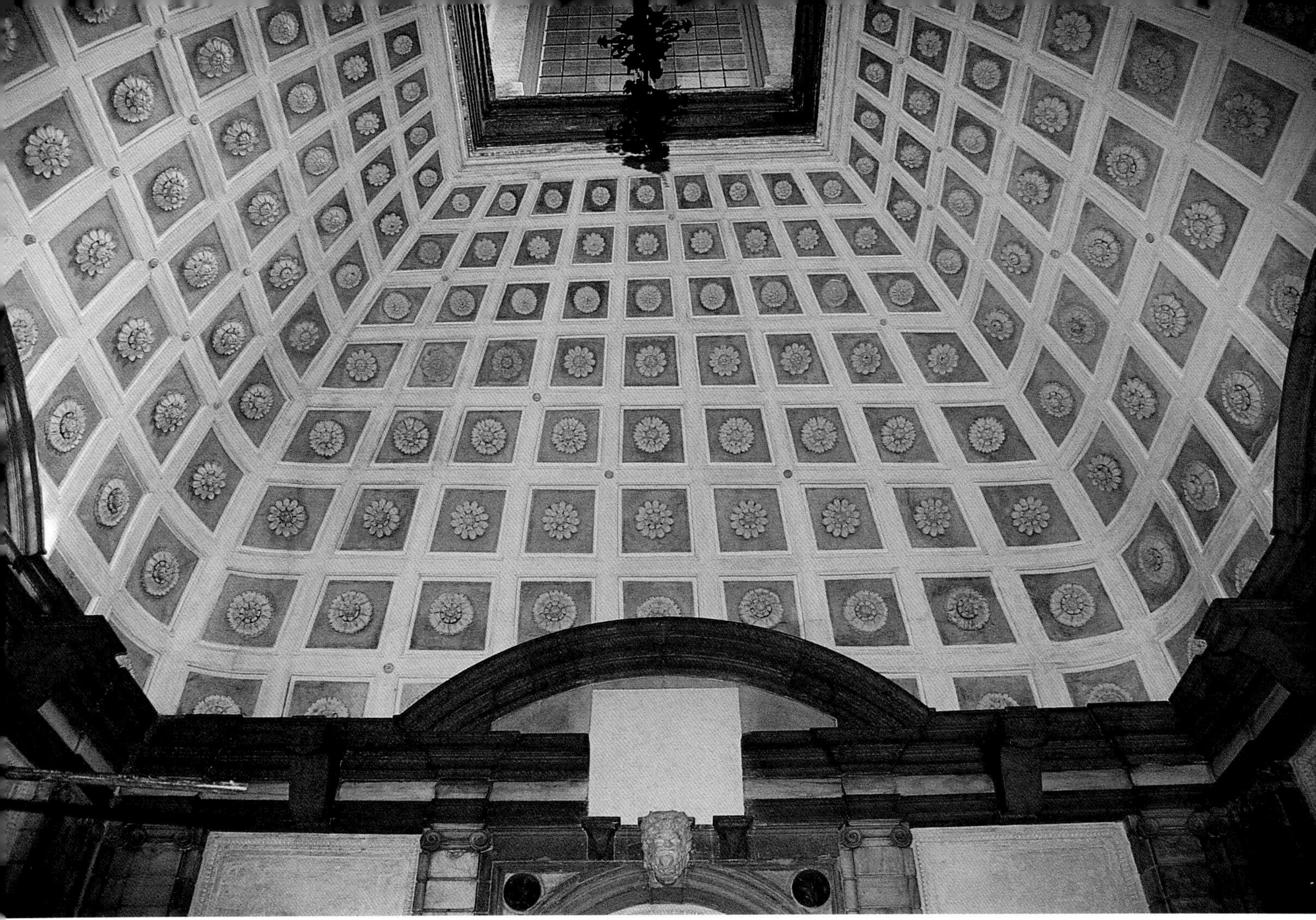

260 View of the vault and lantern of the *tribuna* in Palazzo Grimani (fig. 258). The architectural historian Manfredo Tafuri notes that the coffered pavilion vault recalled the work of the Mantuan architect Giovan Battista Bertani and observes, "Here, eccentricity reaches 'metaphysical' heights." (Tafuri, *Venezia e il Rinascimento*, 16).

It is perhaps here that the modern art museum was born, where the architecture is conceived primarily as a receptacle for works of art, with access provided to a specific public, and the problems of presentation, lighting, circulation of visitors, security, and climate control part of the equation.[60] The collection of Giovanni Grimani will be revisited further on, but first it is worth considering problems of display and presentation more generally.

The Order of Things

Early collections had been, arguably, forms of cultivated interior decoration. But as the number of accumulated objects grew, arrangement became an issue. In the early period a massed clutter of acquisitions was part of the aesthetic appeal of collecting, as Lotto's drawing of an *Ecclesiastic in his Study* reveals (see fig. 244). In any case, this gentleman's pursuit of the rare and the beautiful had clearly exceeded his capacity to arrange his treasures in a cogent manner. But as the example of Andrea Odoni attests, collectors became increasingly aware of the opportunity to define themselves through their artful presentation of their treasures.

The metamorphosis from accumulations like that of Lotto's prelate into organized displays led to the desire to classify and catalogue the pieces as objects of study rather than simply as ensembles of visual delight. This trend is exemplified by the collection of Andrea Vendramin, possibly a distant relative of Gabriele Vendramin of Santa Fosca. Scamozzi wrote in 1615 that in his palace on the Grand Canal near San Gregorio, Andrea "had arranged two rooms where with triplicate order are found not a few statues of various sizes, and 140 pieces of torsos, *bas-reliefs*, vases, and precious stones, and others petrified, and a good

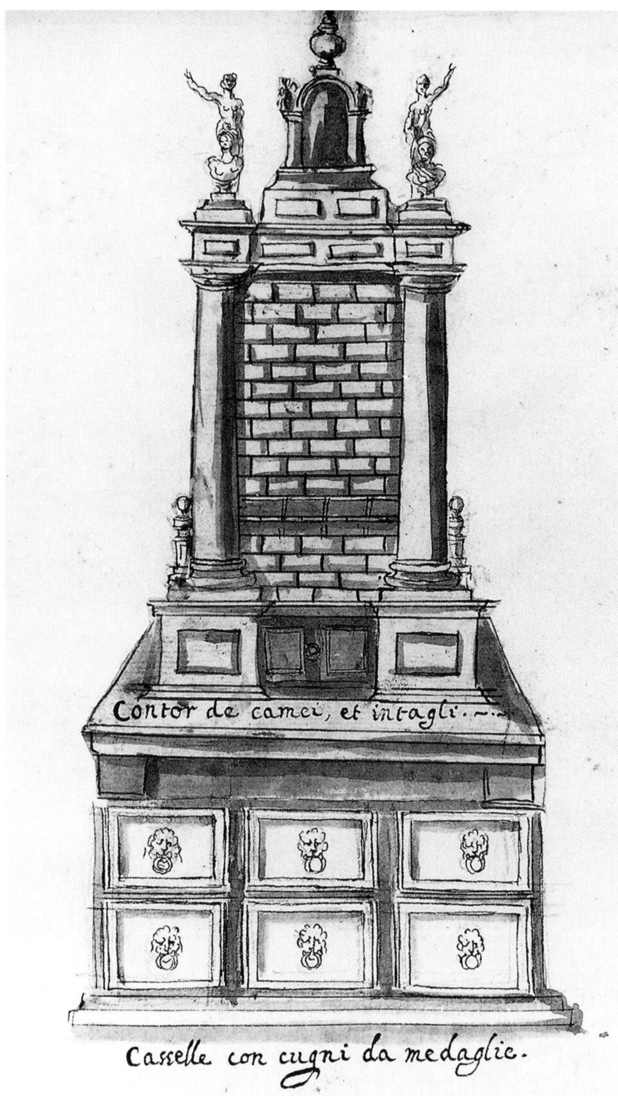

261 Cabinet for rings, gems, seals, and coins in the study of Andrea Vendramin, 1627. Ink sketch from a manuscript catalogue of his collection: *De Annulis & Sigillis Aegyptiorum Scarabaeis, Emblematibus ornatis et aliis signis & figuris in gemmis & lapidibus & incisis*. London, British Library, Sloane MS. 4005.

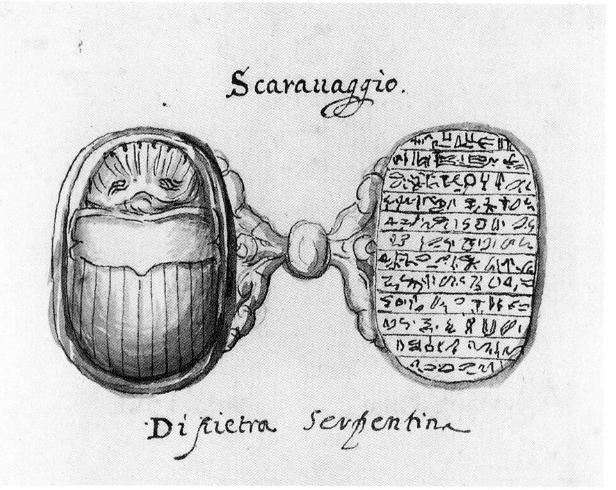

262 Scarab of serpentine in the collection of Andrea Vendramin, 1627. Ink sketch from a manuscript catalogue of his collection: *De Annulis et Sigillis Aegyptiorum*. London, British Library, Sloane MS. 4005.

number of antique medals, and . . . about 140 paintings large and small."[61] The operative word is "order," for Andrea was one of the first collectors to prepare a full catalogue of his pieces.[62]

As with other collectors of the period, Andrea's interests were diverse, but his collection is particularly notable for its encyclopedic scope, for it included minerals, gems, and other natural wonders, as well as the usual ancient marbles, paintings, and medals. He aimed to assemble the universe in microcosm, with specimens of every category of thing represented. Andrea was not unique. The cabinet of curiosities, known as a "Wunderkammer" in German-speaking countries, became a European fashion in the seventeenth century. No longer satisfied simply to collect the ancient past, these collectors wanted to capture the entire world within the walls of the study – a matter of Sanudo's *libreria* writ large.[63]

Andrea's catalogue consisted of sixteen volumes, with one book for paintings, another for sculpture, two for coins (one for Roman coins and another for Venetian), and yet others for vases, minerals, manuscripts, Egyptian rings and seals, as well as for other categories. When the collection was sold off, the catalogue was broken up and dispersed as well.[64] Among the four volumes that are now in the British Museum is one on rings, medals, gems, and Egyptian seals that includes a pen and wash drawing of a cabinet, custom-designed with drawers and a counter to hold cameos and intaglios, and compartmented drawers for medals (figs. 261–62). The catalogue of paintings consists of 86 folios containing 155 drawings of pictures in the collection, most with attributions (figs. 263–65).[65] Nearly all the paintings are held to be by Venetian artists, with nine attributed to Giovanni Bellini, five to Titian, and no less than thirteen, optimistically, to Giorgione. But Raphael was named as author of a self-portrait, and three works were attributed to Netherlandish artists. At the end of the catalogue is a listing of works not illustrated. These include "Medium and small-sized pictures in the studies, that have not been depicted because they are old and they are put in some places to fill the compartments" and "diverse portraits that are for

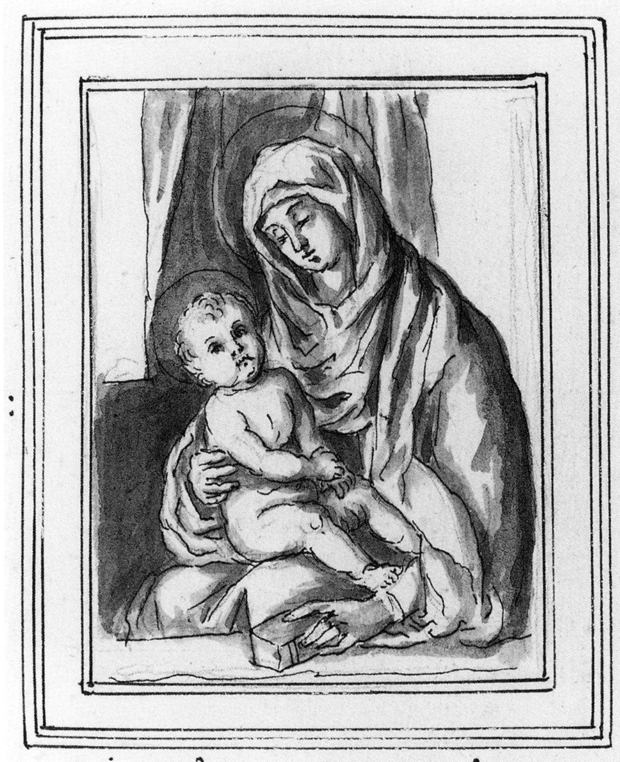

263 (*above*) Ink sketch from a manuscript catalogue of Andrea Vendramin's collection: *De Picturis*, 1627, showing a *Madonna and Child* attributed to Giovanni Bellini. The drawing is almost identical to a painting ascribed to the studio of Giovanni Bellini in the Fogg Art Museum, Cambridge, Mass., but there are numerous variants of the composition. London, British Library Sloane MS. 4004, fol 14.

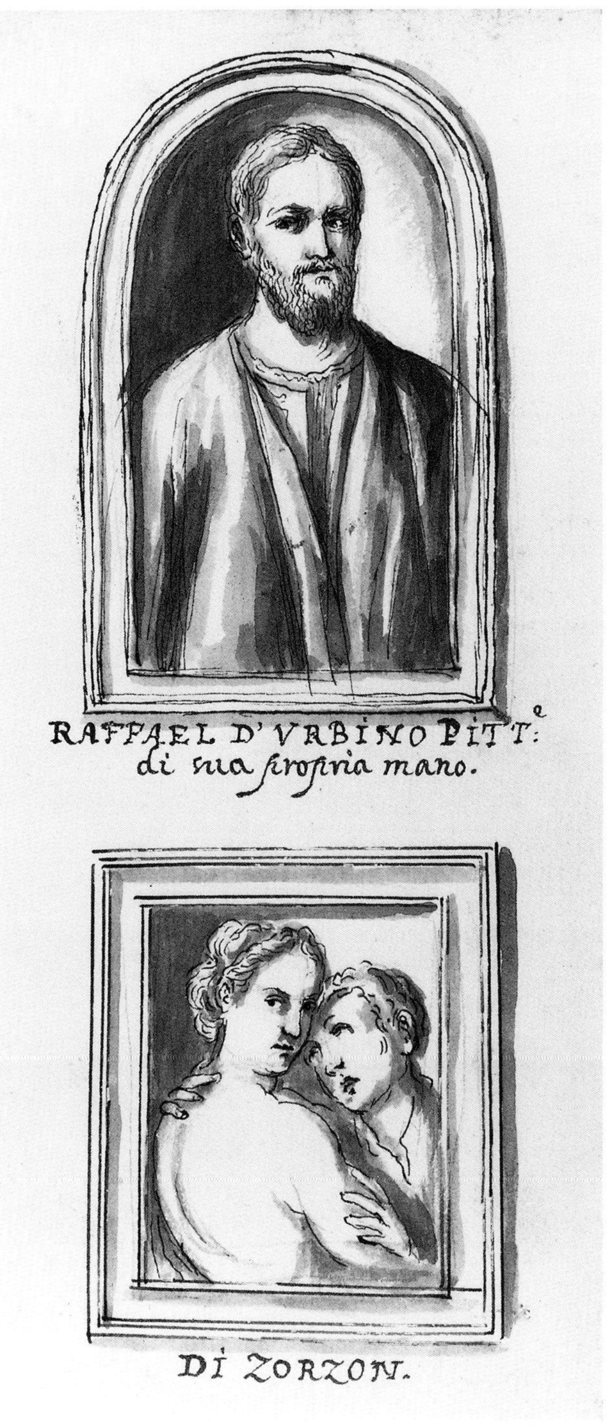

264 (*right*) Ink sketch from a manuscript catalogue of Andrea Vendramin's collection: *De Picturis*, 1627, showing a self-portrait of Raphael (alleged) and a painting of two lovers by Giorgione. The identification and attribution of the Raphael portrait are unlikely. The painting attributed to Giorgione is known in a number of variants by the seventeenth-century Venetian painter Pietro della Vecchia. London, Library Museum, Sloane MS. 4004, fol. 19.

adornment of the house."[66] Thus a distinction was made between works in the collection and those acquired for interior decoration or simply to fill empty spaces on the study walls.

Another part of the catalogue is in the Bodleian Library in Oxford. Entitled "Ancient instruments of sacrifice and triumph, including urns and lamps," it offers an invaluable illustration of how such objects might have been displayed, with a wash drawing showing a wall section divided into small compartments containing vases, urns, dishes, lamps, and small pieces of sculpture; two larger niches, each holding a large figural sculpture on a pedestal; and pre-

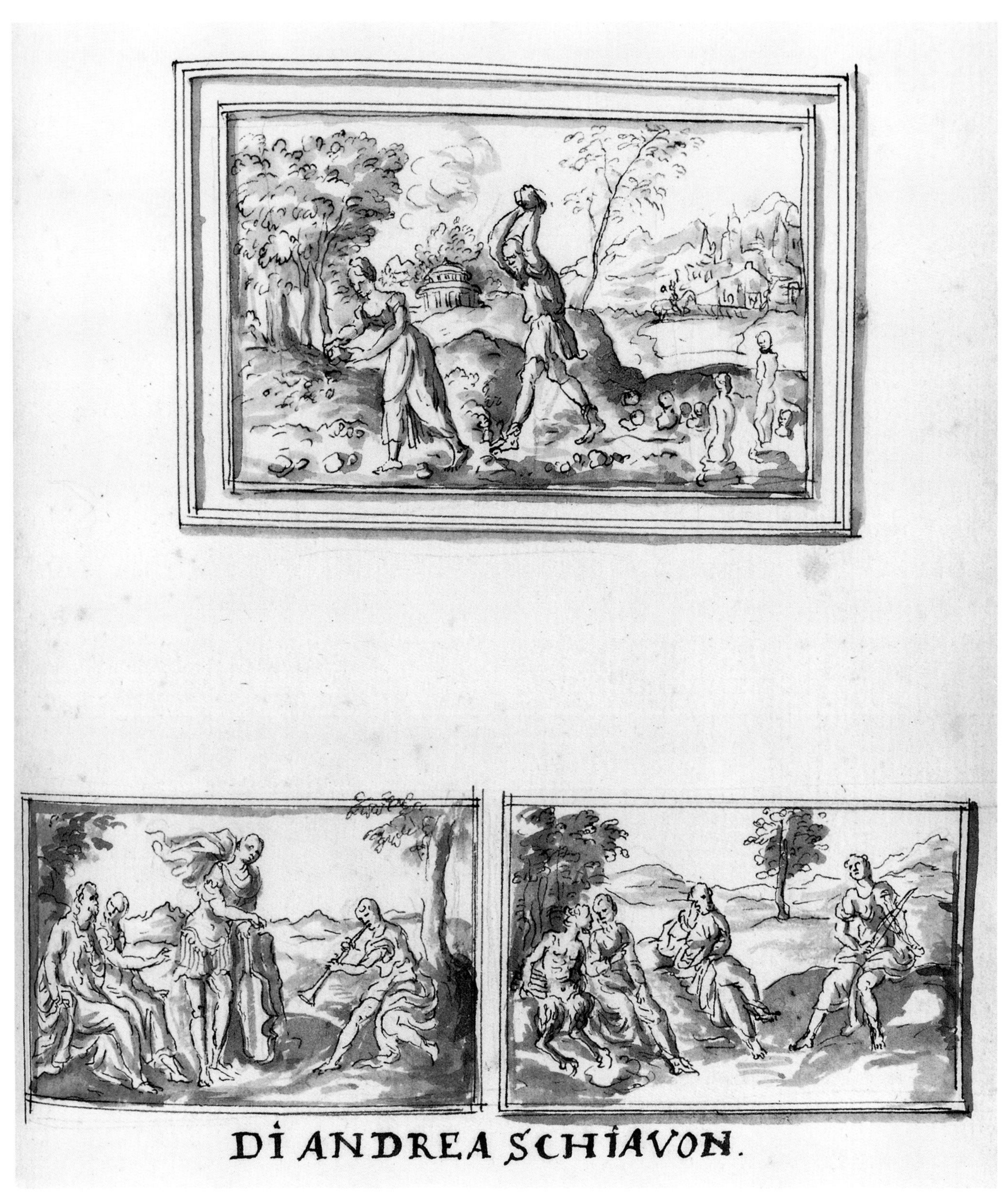

265 Ink sketch from a manuscript catalogue of Andrea Vendramin's collection: *De Picturis*, 1627, showing *Deucalion and Pyrrha* and *The Contest of Apollo and Marsyas* and *The Contest of Apollo and Pan* by Andrea Schiavone. Although only the latter two paintings carry an attribution to Andrea Schiavone, all three works recall his manner and were probably examples of the furniture painting for which he was renowned. See figure 114 for another version of *Deucalion and Pyrrha* by Schiavone. London, British Library, Sloane MS. 4004, fol. 71.

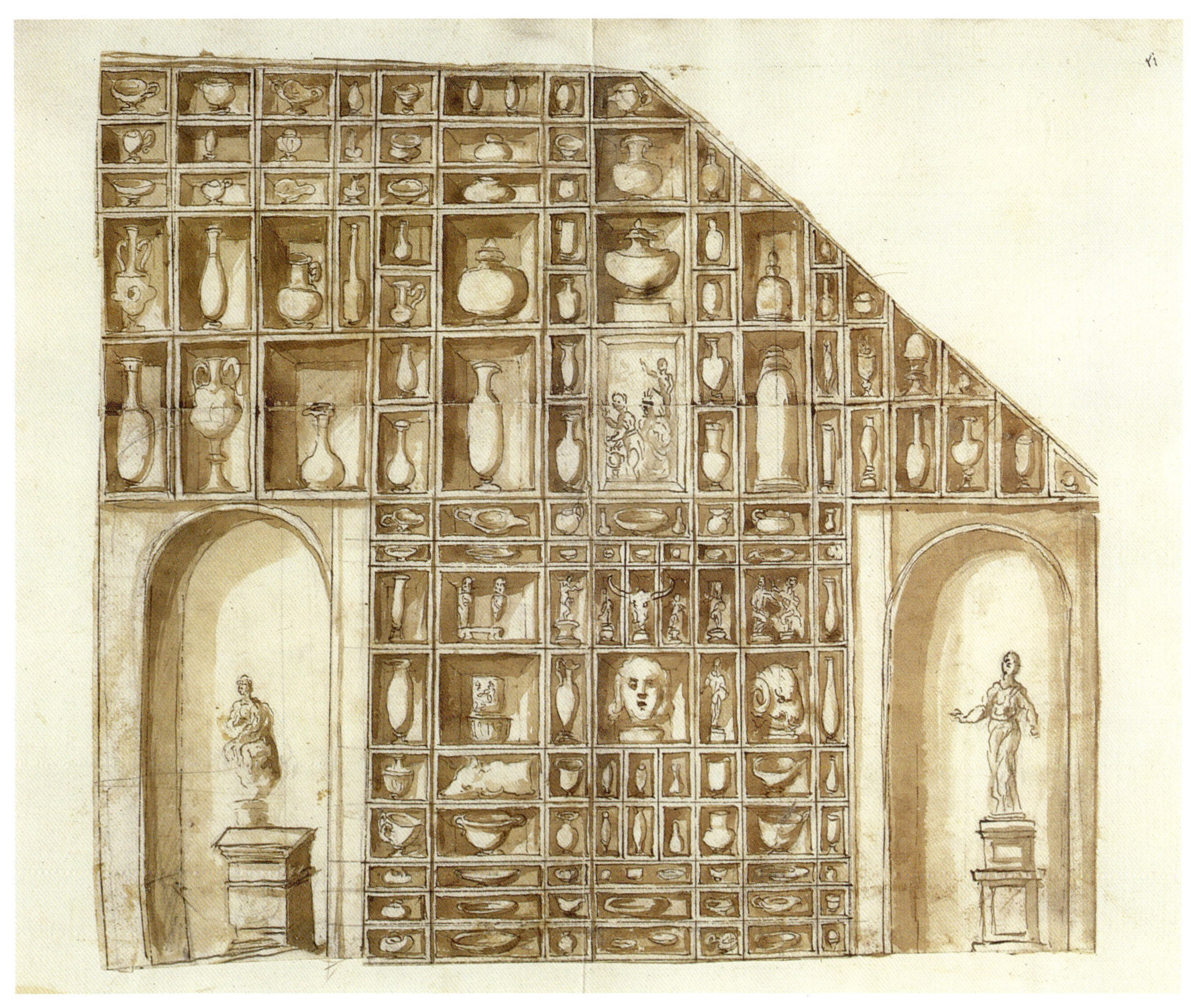

266 Ink sketch from a manuscript catalogue of Andrea Vendramin's collection: *De Sacrificiorum & Triumphorum vasculis, lucernisque Antiquorum, Urnis*, 1627, showing a wall of his study designed with compartments to display his collection of vases and antiquities. Oxford, Bodleian Library, MS. d'Orville 539, fols. Vv–VIr.

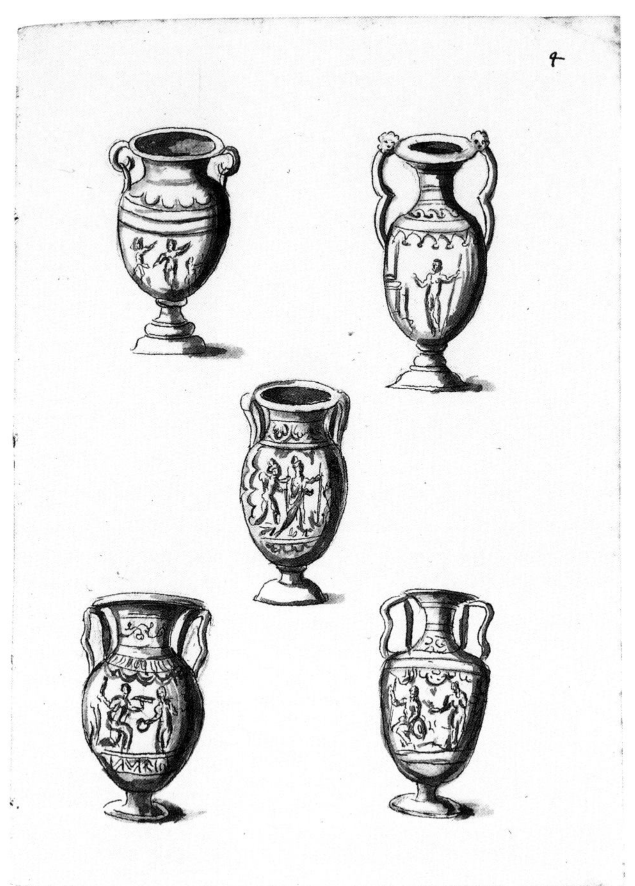

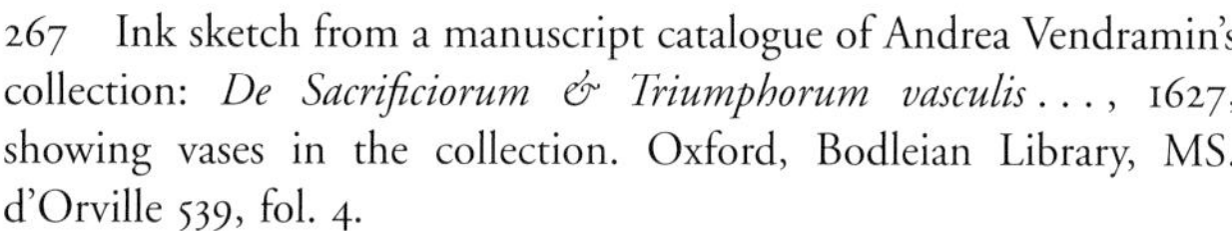

267 Ink sketch from a manuscript catalogue of Andrea Vendramin's collection: *De Sacrificiorum & Triumphorum vasculis . . .*, 1627, showing vases in the collection. Oxford, Bodleian Library, MS. d'Orville 539, fol. 4.

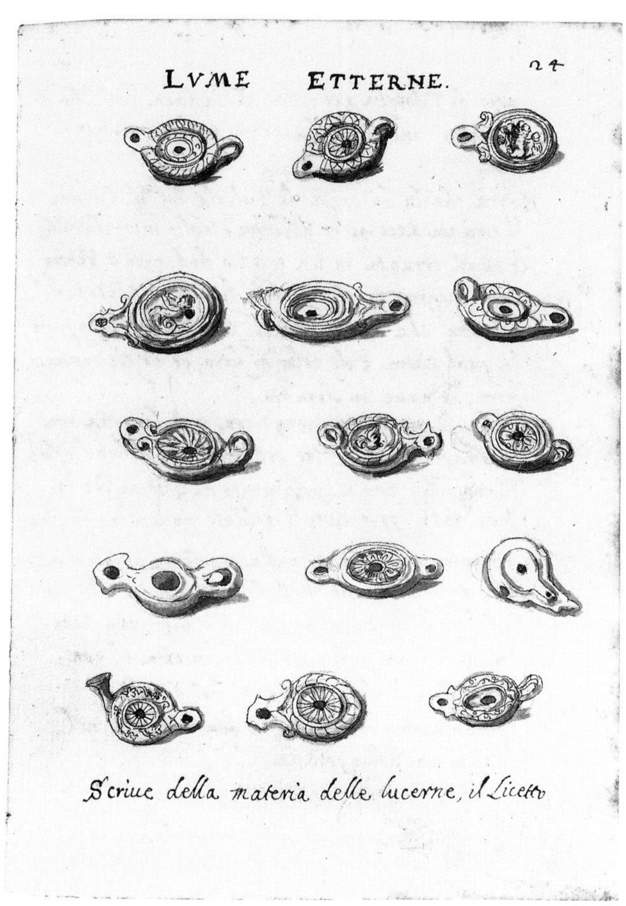

268 Ink sketch from a manuscript catalogue of Andrea Vendramin's collection: *De Sacrificiorum & Triumphorum vasculis . . .*, 1627, showing lamps in the collection. Oxford, Bodleian Library, MS. d'Orville 539, fol. 24.

sumably one of those pictures "put in some places to fill the compartments" (figs. 266–68).[67] As with Giovanni Grimani's *studio delle anticaglie*, this is a space contrived especially to hold a specific collection of pieces rather than the other way around.

The Englishman Fynes Moryson, who visited Venice in 1594, called such sites not museums but libraries:

> Also private Libraries may be found out by those that be curious, and will bee after the same manner easily shewed them, and are indeede most worthy to bee sought out for the rarenesse of many instruments, pictures, carved Images, Antiquities, and like rare things: For the Venetians being most sparing in diet and apparell, doe exercise their magnificence in these and the like deelights, and these precious Monuments, they will with great curtesie shew to any strangers, or to any loving antiquities, which my selfe found by experience, more specially at the hands of Signor. Nicolao Vendramini, a Gentleman dwelling in the Iland Giuedecca, who most curteously shewed mee and my friends, though being altogether unknowne to him, some rare clockes, admirable carved images, and a paire of Organs having strange varieties of sounds.[68]

* * *

facing page Detail of fig. 266.

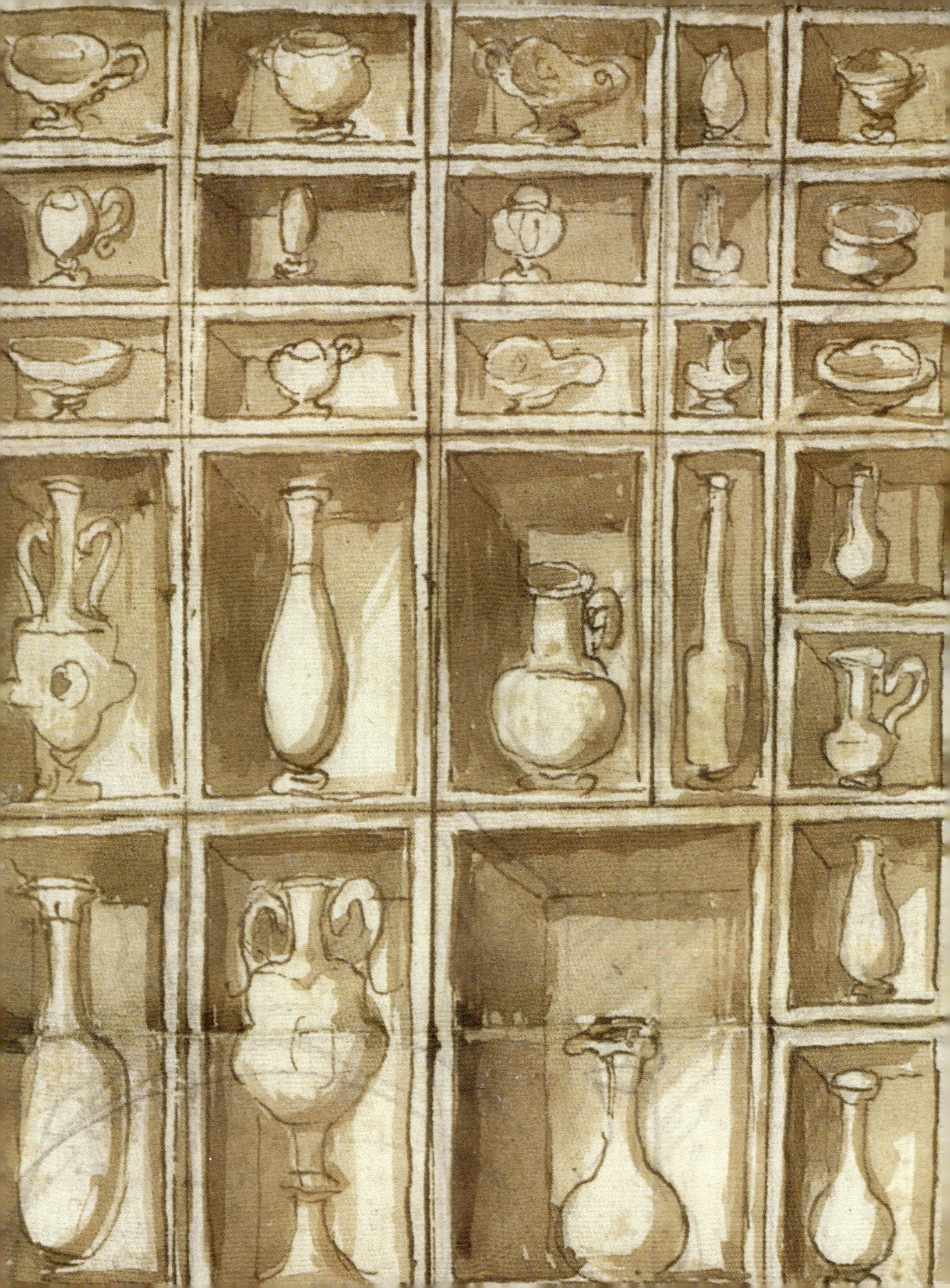

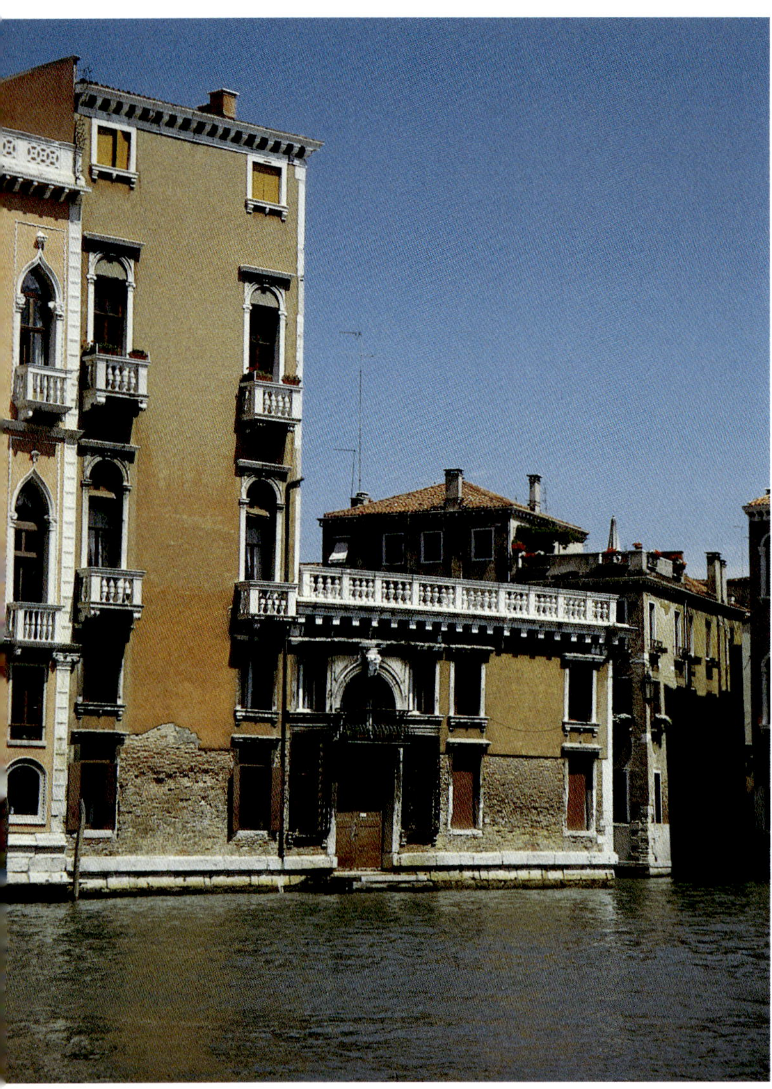

269 Palazzo Barbarigo della Terrazza on the Grand Canal, sixteenth century. The large terrace, measuring 14 × 24 square meters, is unique on the Grand Canal. It was originally a "hanging garden" with trees and ornamental shrubs. Behind it, the interior of the *portego* of the *piano nobile*, retains its sixteenth-century form and decoration, while that of the floor above is decorated in a neoclassical style. The building is presently the home of the Centro Tedesco di Studi Veneziani.

The Gallery of Paintings

Unfortunately Vendramin's catalogue does not tell us how the paintings were arranged, nor does it provide an illustration of a wall hung with them. However, a lithograph after a drawing by the English artist Lake Price, though made in the 1840s, offers a credible sense of what an early seventeenth-century gallery of paintings in a Venetian palace might have looked like. It depicts a room in Palazzo Barbarigo della Terrazza, an unusual palace that turns its face away from the Grand Canal to show off a large terrace or hanging garden at the side (figs. 269 and 270). The Sala del Caminetto, depicted by Price, was on the *piano nobile* of the narrow section of the palace, just one room wide, that faces the Grand Canal to the left of the terrace. The open door at the end of the room provides a glimpse of the library and beyond that a family chapel. It was in these rooms that the bulk of the family's painting collection was displayed.[69]

Price claimed that the palace preserved "the studio of the Great Titian . . . in its original state" and that many of the works remained "in the same splendid cinquecento frames in which they were placed during his lifetime."[70] The print shows an impressive array of over thirty paintings, many of them by Titian, hung floor to ceiling in the Baroque manner. Although there is a long tradition that the collection was begun by a Barbarigo, who purchased the contents of Titian's atelier along with his home after the artist's death in 1581, the evidence for this is thin. All that is certain is that the family owned four of Titian's works by the end of the sixteenth century. In all likelihood, this nucleus of acquisitions inspired successive generations to acquire more. A final inventory of the collection, made in the mid-nineteenth century, attributed sixteen paintings in the palace – a not insignificant number – to Titian.[71]

Lake Price's rendering of the sixteenth-century room, with its painted beamed ceiling supported by consoles bracketing cartouches filled with portraits of doges, is based upon first-hand observation, for the room survives in essentially that form today. But the scene is embellished with a large dose of artistic license. For the artist has recast the room as Titian's atelier, with the old painter presenting his *Entombment of Christ*, now in the Louvre, to a princely visitor.[72] The display of the paintings, covering the walls from wainscoting to ceiling, was, however, characteristic of the times and would undoubtedly have been close to the seventeenth-century arrangement. It is worth noting that the works are arranged according to size and shape to make a pleasing composition on the walls and not by subject or chronology. The *Toilette of Venus*, for example, hanging on the right-hand wall in an elaborately carved frame and now in the National Gallery of Art in Washington, D.C,, is displayed beneath a large *Madonna and Child with Saints* and flanked by two paintings of Christ.[73] The luxurious furnishings of a room meant to be lived in, as well as the floor-to-ceiling installation, suggest that the paintings were still perceived as interior decoration as much as works of art to be enjoyed individually for their excellence and aesthetic qualities.

* * *

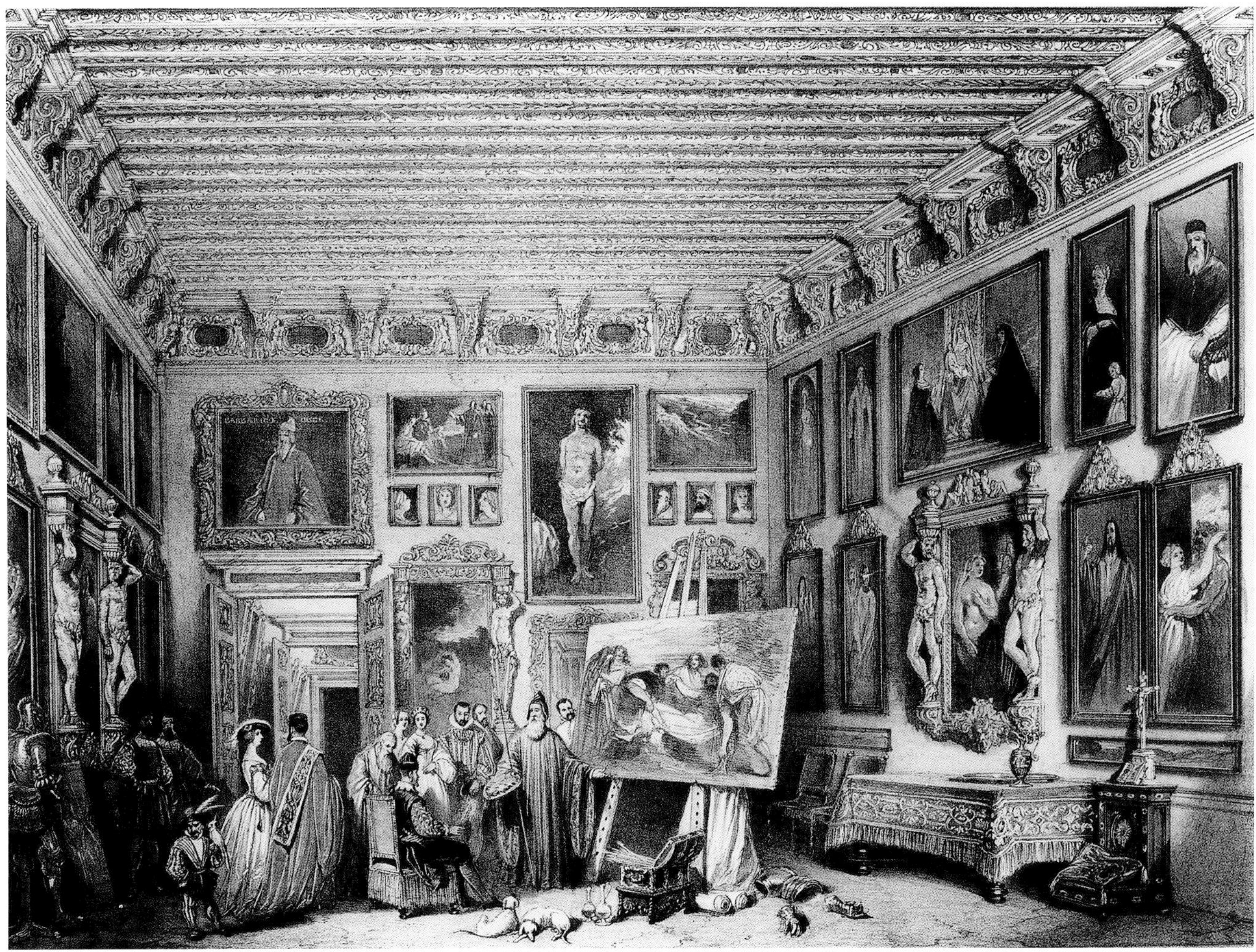

270 A room in Palazzo Barbarigo della Terrazza from Lake Price, *Interiors and Exteriors in Venice*, 1843. Lithographed by Joseph Nash from the original drawings. The room is found on the *piano nobile* to the left of the large terrace.

A Place of Noble Discourses

A similar bias can be noted in Sansovino's remarks in 1581 concerning private libraries. Judging twenty to be "of singular esteem and truly worthy of being recorded and seen," he singled out as particularly notable the library of the patrician Giacomo Contarini, housed in the *mezzado* of the classicizing Palazzo Contarini delle Figure on the Grand Canal at San Samuele (fig. 271; see also fig. 4).[74] Called "a new Archimedes" by the celebrated Paduan engraver Girolamo Porro in the dedication of Scamozzi's *Antichità di Roma*, Giacomo was a public man who applied his erudition and knowledge of the arts to the service of the state. After fulfilling several major political offices, such as *podesta* of Bergamo, he was put in charge of the decorations for the royal entry of Henry III at the Lido in 1574 and was appointed to the committee to plan the redecoration of the Great Council Hall after the devastating fire in the Ducal Palace of 1577. A protector of Galileo, as well as of Andrea Palladio – who left him his drawings of the antiquities of Rome – he filled his apartments with painters as well as intellectuals.[75]

Sansovino was impressed, as usual, with the cost of the collection, but also with its comprehensiveness. He wrote that Contarini

> with demonstrable expense, has put together almost all the histories that are printed and written by pen, not only universal but also particular of the cities, with various other books and a good number in the sciences. These are accompanied by drawings, mathematical instruments, and other things made by hand of the most outstanding

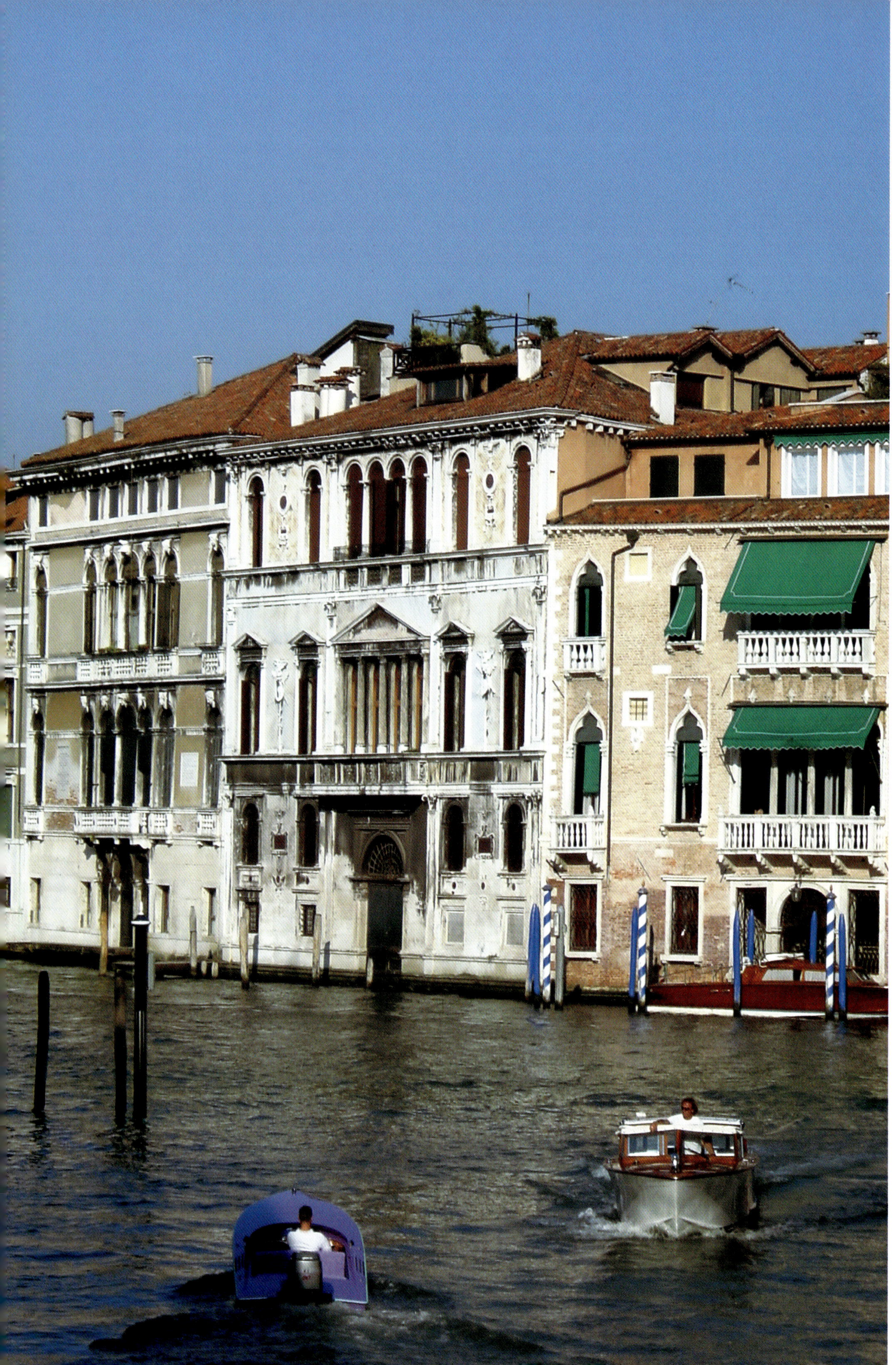

artists in painting, sculpture, and architecture of our age. These he has always, as a lover of men of talent, favored and cherished.[76]

It is significant that Sansovino placed the collection under the category of libraries rather than *Studi delle anticaglie.* Although Contarini owned dozens of paintings, including Veronese's *Rape of Europa*, now in the Palazzo Ducale, and works by Jacopo and Francesco Bassano, Tintoretto, and Giuseppe Salviati among others, they cannot be found in Sansovino's description. They are in the category of objects referred to simply as "other things made by hand."[77]

That the libraries of Contarini and others were cited in a guidebook to Venice suggests that such collections, like the *studi delle anticaglie*, were open to visiting scholars and intellectuals armed with appropriate letters of introduction. Indeed, Contarini's home was a true *casa aperta*. A contemporary observer reported that: "Many times I had the occasion . . . to find myself in his noble rooms, and of listening there to his various and important propositions [and] many noble discourses that were made many times every month on diverse most fertile subjects by many eloquent men of much erudition and the highest judgement, both nobles and foreigners, who came together to converse virtuously as in a very noble Academy."[78] It was perhaps inevitable that private collections would become public. In this regard, Giacomo was torn between duty to his family and to his country. In his last will and testament of 1585, he wrote:

One of the dearest things that I have had, and would have, is my studio, from which proceeded all the honors and esteem given my person. By this I mean not only the books, but all that which is contained in the four rooms of the *mezzadi* where I stay ordinarily, where there are exquisite things, such that whoever does not consider them well could not believe: printed books and manuscripts, mathematical and mechanical instruments, statues of marble as well as of bronze, paintings, minerals, stones, secrets, and other things, all of which have been collected by me with the greatest study and fatigue. Therefore I also wish that they would be conserved and augmented, so that our posterity can enjoy and experience the benefits of these my labors.

271 (*facing page*) Palazzo Contarini delle Figure on the Grand Canal. Jacopo Contarini's study was located on the mezzanine floor just beneath the piano nobile.

Ordering that the collection must be kept intact, never to be sold or given away, by his male heirs in succession, he ended with the proviso: "and lacking male heirs, I wish that it would go to my *patria*, since it has honored me beyond all my merit, and if there would not be the obligation that I owe to the blood, and the hope that I have in these sons . . . at present I would have left everything to the public."[79]

Giacomo was a man caught between the age-old tradition of loyalty to the clan in matters of inheritance and the new vision of public munificence pioneered by Cardinal Domenico Grimani, who had left his choicest marbles to the republic back in 1523. Domenico's nephew Giovanni Grimani, who had inherited and augmented the remainder of his collection, had no such qualms. In 1587, he had bequeathed the bulk of the collection not to his family but to the state. It was, he specified, to be installed in "a place proportioned [that is, arranged] to the end that foreigners after having seen both the Arsenal and other marvelous things of the city could also see as a notable thing these antiquities exhibited in a public place."[80] The government did not hesitate to accept the gift, determining that the "place proportioned" should be in the antechamber of the Biblioteca Marciana. Scamozzi was brought in to design the space, but the old Giovanni followed the work carefully, from the detailing of the walls to the design of pedestals to hold the pieces, until his death six years later at the age of ninety-two.[81]

By 1596, the family palace at Santa Maria Formosa was virtually stripped of its finest pieces and the treasures installed in the new Statuario Pubblico (fig. 272).[82] Fynes Moryson described the space soon after it opened:

On the inside, the arched roofes curiously painted, and the little study of ivory, with pillars of Allablaster, and rare stones, and carved Images (in which an old breviary of written hand, and much esteemed is kept) are things very remarkeable. The inner chamber is called the study; in which many statuaes and halfe statuaes, twelve heads of Emperors, and other things given to the State by Cardinall Dominicke Grimani, are esteemed precious by all antiquaries.[83]

Though frustrated in his efforts to gain entrance to the palace, the intrepid Thomas Coryat visited the public collection a decade later. There, he writes,

I observed a little world of memorable antiquities made in Alabaster, and some few in stone, which were brought thither by Cardinal Grimanus Patriarch of Aquileia . . . [thus bestowing upon Giovanni the cardinal's hat that had eluded him] . . . These antiquities are very highly

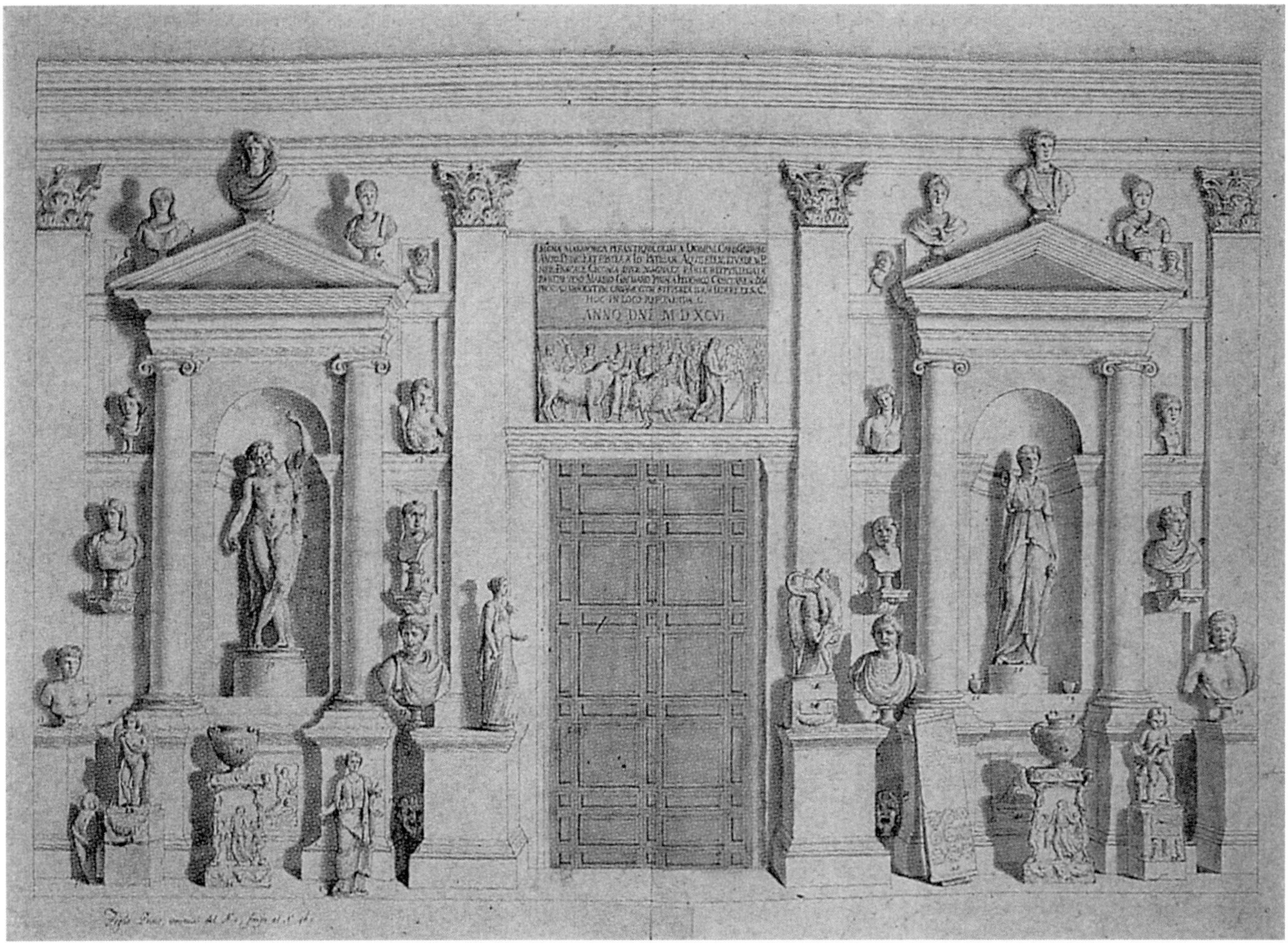

272 Anton Maria Zanetti, the entrance wall of the Statuario Pubblico, eighteenth century. Wash drawing from cod. Ital. IV, 123 (10040). "Rappresentazione in disegno delle Quattro facciate e piedestali isolati della Libreria, con le Statue, Busti, ed altri Marmi che ivi si veggono, divisa in cinque fogli." ("Representation in drawing of the four facades and free-standing pedestals in the library, with the statues, busts, and other marbles that one sees there, presented on five pages.") The Roman relief above the door, depicting a pagan sacrifice, was brought to Venice from Palazzo Venezia, Domenico Grimani's palace in Rome, where it had been in the garden. At the fall of the republic it was taken to Paris and remains in the Louvre. The figures in the large niches – *Silenus* and a female figure identified in the old inventories as Agrippina, mother of Caligula – remain in the Museo Archeologico in Venice, along with *Leda and the Swan* (fig. 273), to the right of the entrance in the drawing. Venice, Biblioteca Nazionale Marciana.

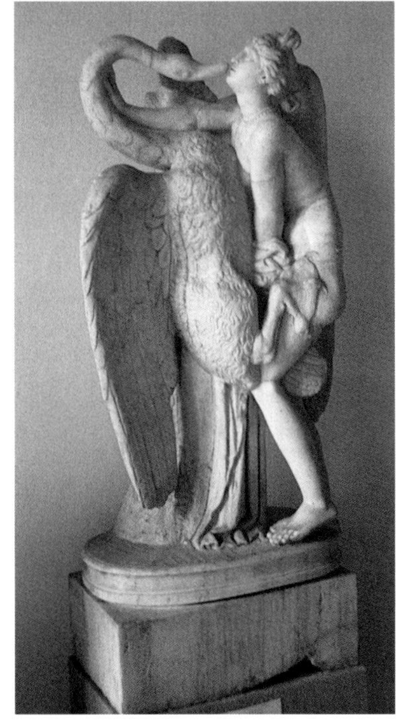

273 (*right*) *Leda and the Swan*, 2nd century A.D. (Roman copy of Greek 1st century B.C. original). Pentelic marble, height 74cm. Thomas Coryat described this work as "Jupiter againe in the forme of a Swanne, wantonly conversing and dallying with Leda." Venice, Museo Archeologico.

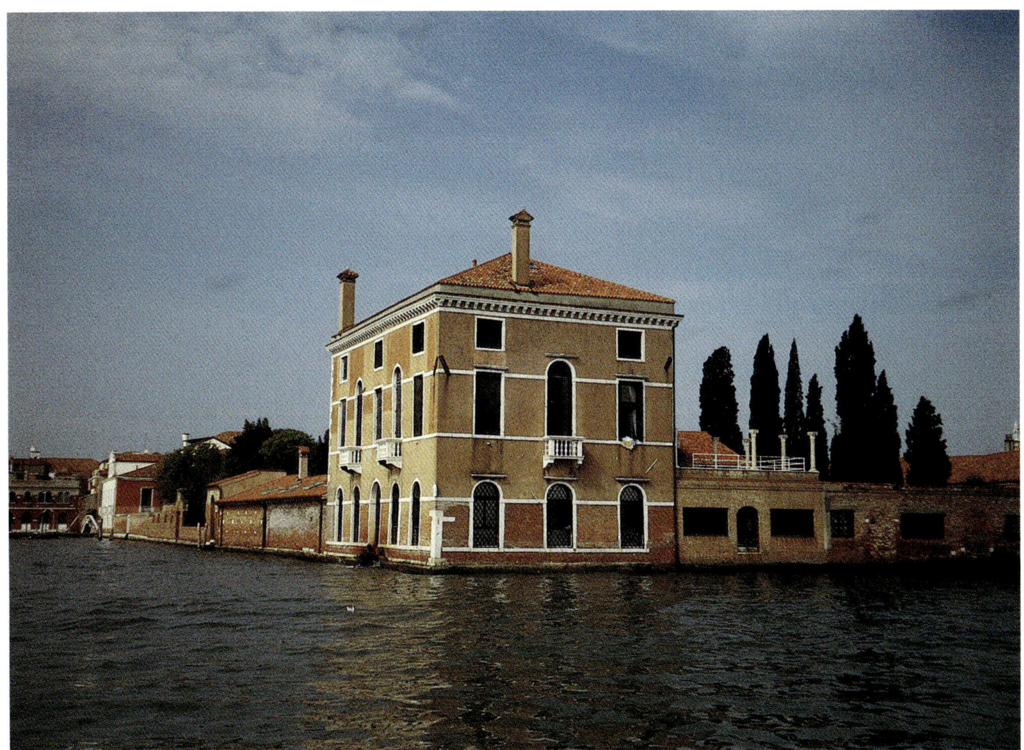

274 Casinò degli Spiriti, Sacca della Misericordia, Cannaregio, late sixteenth–early seventeenth century. Probably built by Tomasso Contarini, the *casinò* was on the property of Palazzo Contarini dal Zaffo, whose gardens were renowned (see fig. 55).

> esteemed in Venice; so that they are now no private and particular mans onely, but belong altogether to the State . . . who hath built a faire chamber that is assigned to no other use, but only to containe these auncient monuments.[84]

The collective bequests of Domenico and Giovanni Grimani constitute one of the earliest examples of a private (as opposed to a princely) collection turned over to public use in Renaissance Italy. A profound innovation, it marks the advent of the civic-minded collector, whose high social position obligates him to collect in the first place and whose sense of social responsibility moves him to dedicate the collection to the community after his death. It is no coincidence that the phenomenon appeared in Venice, with its long tradition of private collecting and its strong patrician ideology of public service.[85] Thanks to the binding effect of the bequest, virtually all the objects are still there today (fig. 273).[86]

Places of Delight

As Venetian patricians became nobles in fact as well as in name the less civic-minded tendency to turn inward mentioned above led to the creation of different types of "theaters of the world." Any family aspiring to a noble lifestyle would have a villa, no matter how modest, in the Terraferma, but there were also retreats closer at hand. For the sixteenth century saw the emergence of the *casinò*, a place of *delizie* – that is, of private delights and pleasures. The *casinò* was a kind of miniature urban villa within the city or on one of the islands, with one facade typically facing the water and the other opening into a garden. Originally it was a specially constructed building where friends gathered in the evening for literary or philosophical conversation. The Casinò degli Spiriti, still an imposing and evocative presence near the Misericordia on the northern edge of the city was characteristic (fig. 274). The name probably refers to the elevated "spirits" who once met there.[87]

Only a few of these early *casinì* survive today with the interior space reasonably intact. One of the exceptions is Casinò Mocenigo, built in the last decade of the sixteenth century on the island of Murano facing Venice across the lagoon. Long abandoned, it was used for years as a warehouse for a glass-making firm, but what remains was

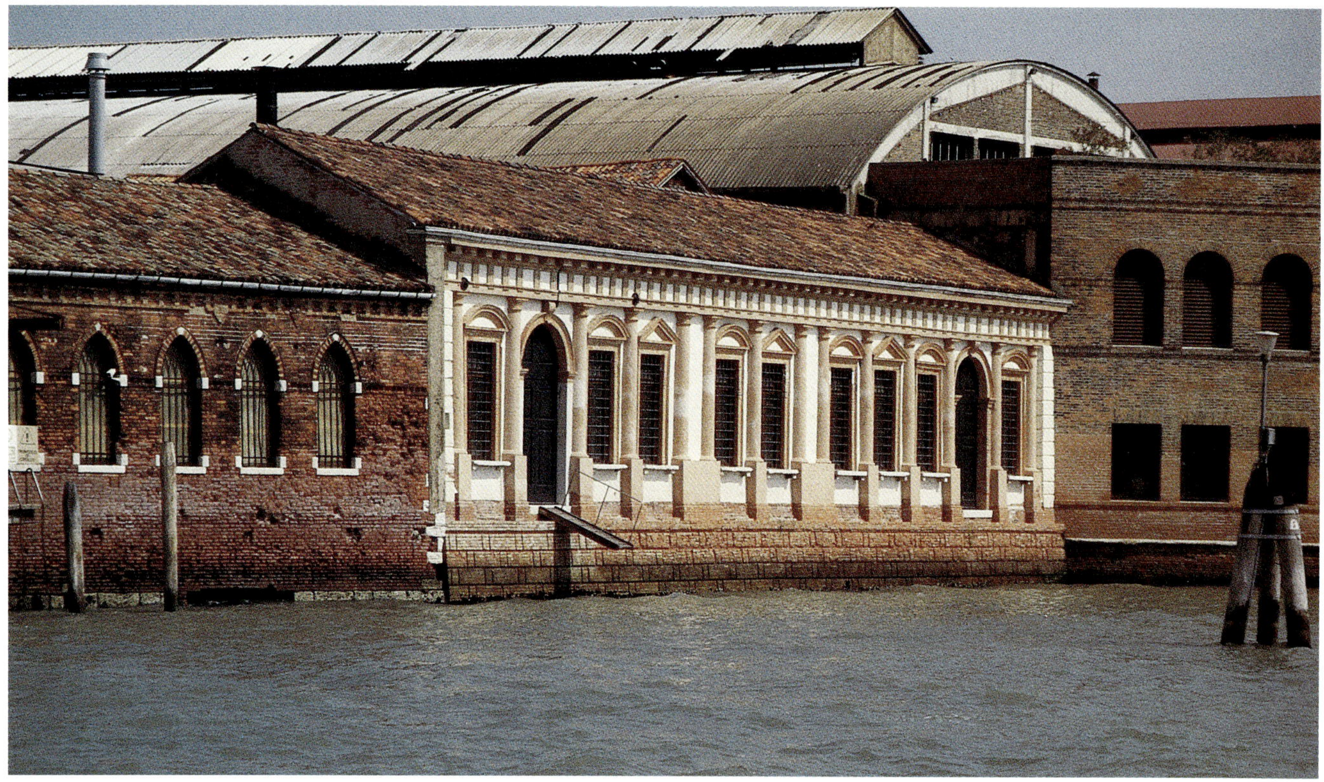

275 Casinò Mocenigo. The building was constructed between 1591 and 1617 by Gerolamo Morosini. Subsequently owned for a short period by the Pisani family, it was bought by Alvise Mocenigo IV in 1763, from whom it takes its present name. Murano, Fondamenta Manin.

recently restored (fig. 275).[88] With its elegant Doric columns flanking windows with alternating curved and pointed pediments, the exterior aspect of the long, one-story facade is opaque as to the building's character or function. It is clearly not a family palace and yet not a boathouse or factory either. The garden facade, by contrast, with a prominent coat of arms above the large entrance portal, is more transparent. It has the open look of a garden house – a place of retreat that recalls the writer Andrea Calmo's description of Murano, wherein he praised: "Those gardens full of lush greenery, and that canal so clear and clean with those beautiful houses so airy." These were, he declared, "true earthly paradises, because of the sweetness of the air and of the site, places of nymphs and semi-gods."[89] And indeed, the interior decoration of Casinò Mocenigo is a visual embodiment of such a concept. It consisted of three rooms, their vaulted ceilings frescoed in the manner of Paolo Veronese in *quadratura* painting – an illusionistic effect wherein a feigned architectural apparatus is contrived to look as if it were an extension upward of the walls.[90] A portion of the vault is virtually "painted away" and seemingly open to the sky.

The iconographic program was carefully worked out to create an itinerary moving the visitor through the rooms toward an ideal of celestial harmony.[91] The first room was dedicated to music. The figure of Apollo, unfortunately now badly damaged, floats in the center of the vault, silhouetted against the open heavens and surrounded by the nine muses, each playing a musical instrument (fig. 276). In the loggia below, human musicians are situated between spiral columns to complete the orchestra. Seeing this, the cultivated viewer would be reminded that the harmony of earthly music leads to, and is a reflection of, the celestial harmony of the spheres.

Moving on to the next, room the visitor looks up through a fictive rectangular opening supported by twelve cusped arches at Pegasus, the winged horse of Greek mythology, who caused the Hippocrene spring to gush forth with a kick of his hoof (fig. 277). Sacred to the muses, the spring was said to be the inspiration of poetry, the theme of the room and the next step above music toward the goal of divine harmony. Sixteen poets from biblical times to the sixteenth-century – several crowned with laurel and all holding their books – are dispersed between the paired columns of the

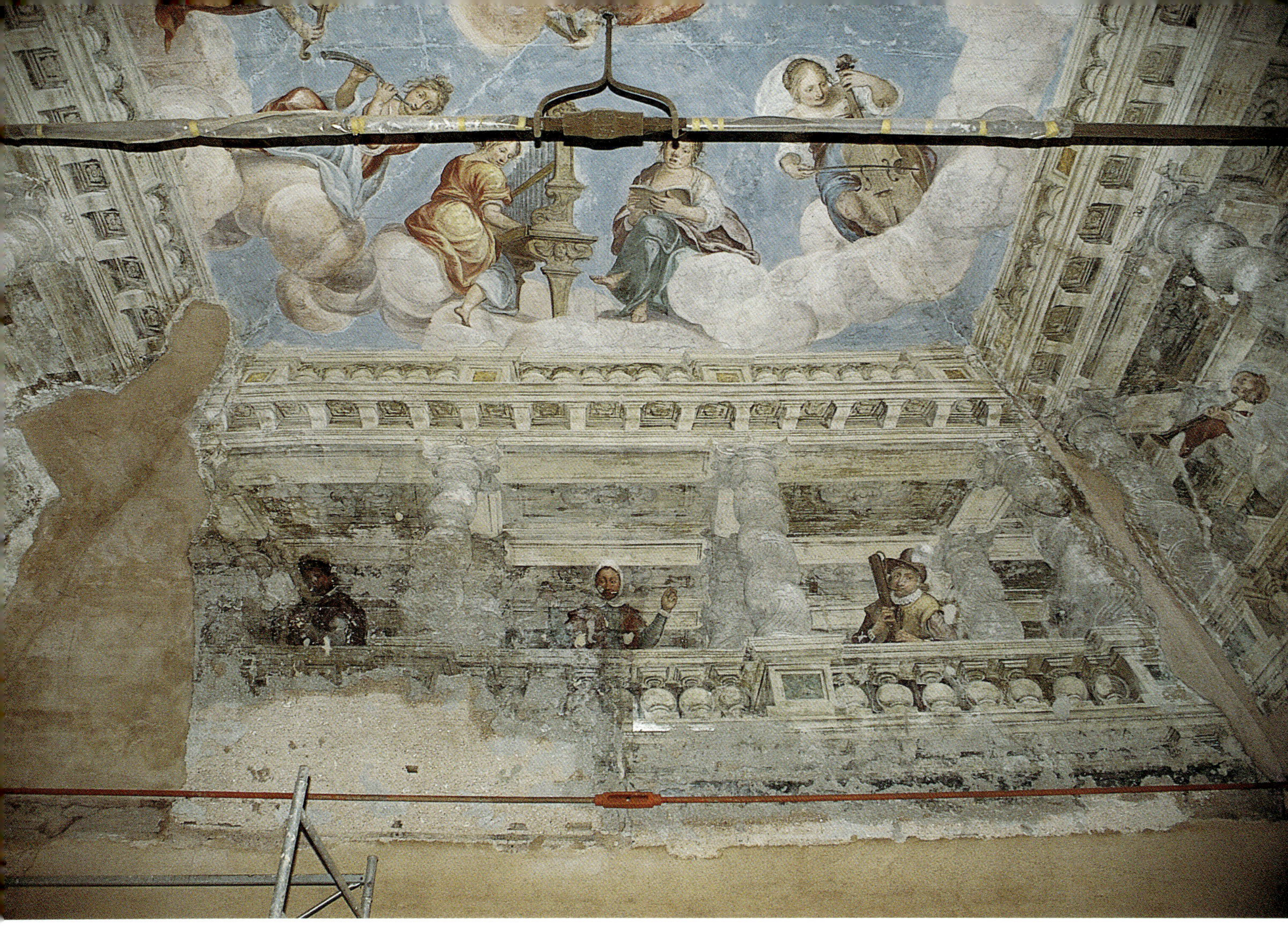

276 The frescoed vault of the Sala di Apollo (Music) in Casinò Mocenigo, late sixteenth–early seventeenth century. The figure in the central bay of the loggia appears to be the lady of the house, her arms raised in a gesture of welcome. Murano, Casinò Mocenigo.

loggia. The name of each was originally inscribed on the balustrade, but all that remain now are Petrarch, Tasso, Guarini, and Ariosto. Twelve of the poets hold a vase to be filled with the water of inspiration from the Hippocrene spring. The remaining four poets were Jews who received their inspiration directly from God.

The culmination of the program was found in the next room. With Cupid letting loose an arrow in the oval opening of the ceiling, this chamber is dedicated to love. Here the loggia openings are inhabited by twelve divinities of classical antiquity, including Vulcan, Jove, and Leda (fig. 278). Although they are gods or mythic beings, they are – like humans – subject to the caprices of love. The labors of the months, painted in small compartments above the loggia, indicate that there is no month or activity in which love does not exercise its power. Love, as mover and ruler of the universe, brings together the conflicting elements of concord and discord, and is the key to universal harmony.[92] The concept, quintessentially Venetian, had been articulated early on in the sixteenth century by Pietro Bembo and other Venetian writers. It was, of course, an illusion. In contrast to the theaters of the physical world assembled in the studies of Sanudo or Odoni or the Grimani or the Vendramin, who sought to collect the wondrous works of man and nature, this was a theater of the imagination.

* * *

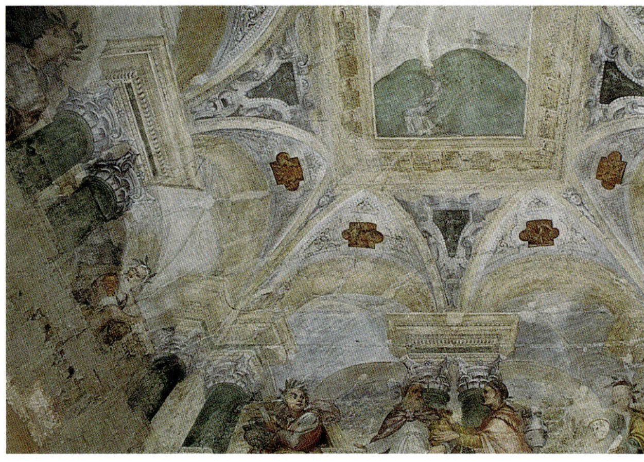

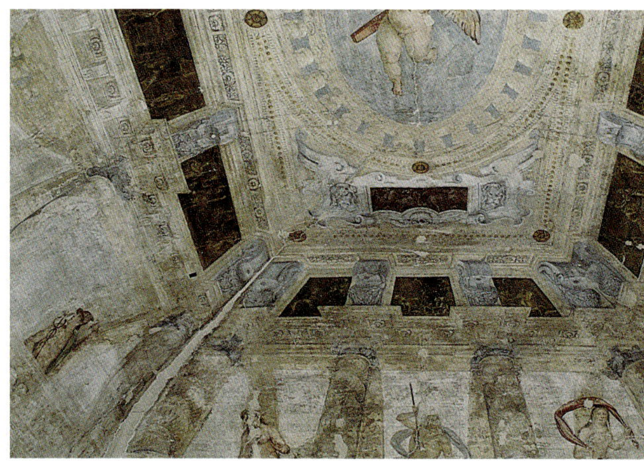

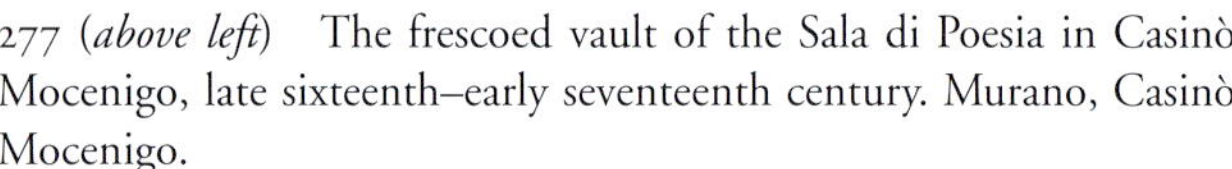

277 (*above left*) The frescoed vault of the Sala di Poesia in Casinò Mocenigo, late sixteenth–early seventeenth century. Murano, Casinò Mocenigo.

278 (*above right*) The frescoed vault of the Sala d'Amore in Casinò Mocenigo, late sixteenth–early seventeenth century. The badly damaged images of Venus, Neptune, and Thetis are still visible in the loggia on this side of the vault. Murano, Casinò Mocenigo.

Places of (Dis)honor

During the same period a less elevated type of theater had been developing in many *casinì*, and the term took on a new meaning that endures to the present day.[93] In 1609, the Council of Ten charged: "For some time many people have been renting Houses in groups, the houses are called *Casinì*. They were tolerable while they served for honest conversation, but because every day now new abuses are introduced there, with matters going from bad to worse, with the worst corruption of good manners, one sees in effect that these *Casinì* do not serve any more for honest and civil entertainment." The occasion was the prosecution of two noblemen for vandalism and inappropriate behavior in a gambling establishment at San Trovaso.[94]

The Ten were describing the consequences of a development that had been taking place for over a century. In the thirteenth and fourteenth centuries gambling had been a public activity, generally condemned but officially tolerated in specified places in the city – most prominently between the great columns of the Piazzetta – with the participation of nobles and commoners alike. But in the fifteenth century, gambling followed a trajectory parallel to prostitution and began to move into private houses, with a growing separation between the elite and the popular classes. Gambling soon spread throughout the city, albeit with more government regulation, and a group of nobles emerged who depended upon it for their livelihoods.[95]

A site where gambling took place was often called a *ridotto* – a term that initially meant any kind of meeting place or refuge and eventually came to refer to a place of entertainment and, most specifically, a gambling house, with associations of secrecy and privacy (fig. 279).[96] In 1567, the government banned *ridotti* of nobles, noting with dismay that certain places were given over to gambling on a daily basis.[97] The linguistic merging – or at least the interchangeability – of the terms *ridotto* and *casinò* in the later sixteenth century suggests that music and intellectual conversation in places of delight such as Casinò Mocenigo, were competing with activities more mercenary than literary among the privileged classes.

How, then, was gambling justified and how did it come to rival the study of humane letters as the recreation *par excellence* of the Venetian nobility? Perhaps it was a question of display. The shift from trade to investments in land by the patriciate in the sixteenth and seventeenth centuries brought a new emphasis on spending rather than earning. With Italy in general becoming more aristocratic, the importance of living *nobile* and displaying an ostentatiously noble lifestyle, whatever the financial means to support it, had gained currency, even in Venice with its long-standing ethos of *mediocritas*. Fynes Moryson lamented: "For howsoever this Common-wealth at the first founding, was tied by many lawes to mediocrity, and the equality among the Citizens, yet pride hath by degrees seised upon the same."[98]

As a modern scholar has observed, gambling "offered profits untainted by the sweat of physical labour and, if a noble failed to profit materially, he could profit morally by losing well."[99] Pietro Aretino's *Le carte parlanti*, a satirical treatise on gambling published in 1543, was – like most satire – based upon an incisive observation of contemporary

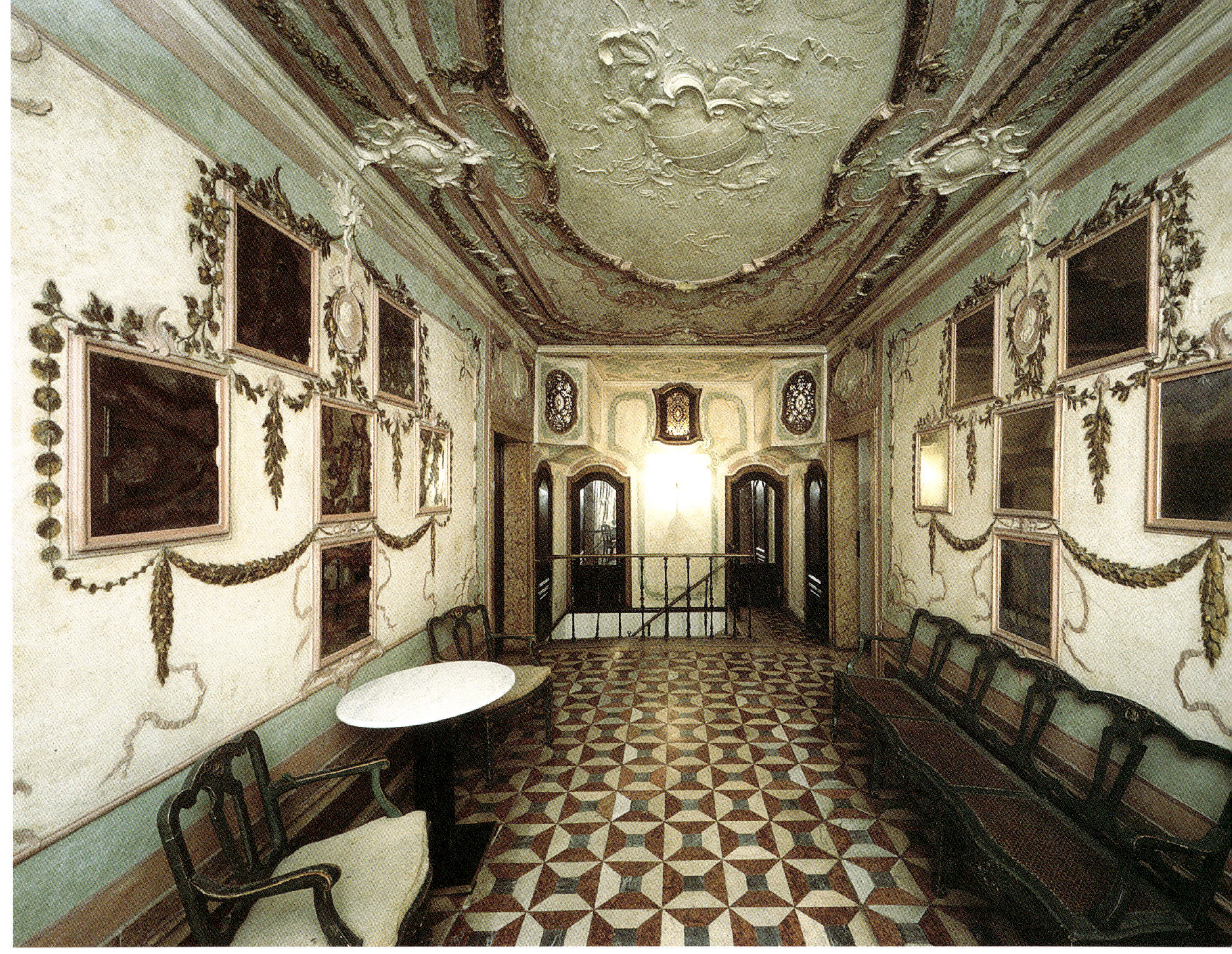

society. The writer compared card-playing to waging war. Profligate gambling, with substantial losses, was, in fact, he argued, the ultimate test of character and a means to display and assert one's honor through self-control and "studied carelessness" in the face of devastating losses.[100]

The legitimization of the *ridotto* and the *casinò* as sites where young nobles might be introduced into adulthood by their fathers and where they could make important contacts that would help them to obtain political office, led to predictably unhappy results.[101] By 1628, the Ten inveighed against those who gambled in "public *Ridotti*, *Casini*, their own Houses, or those of Prostitutes, Shops, Warehouses, Inns, and even in the *piazze* and public streets of the City, playing at Cards and Dice, [and who] disperse their means of support and the sustenance of their entire families, gambling often with what does not belong to them."[102]

In sixteenth-century Venice can thus be found the roots of both the museum and the *casinò* – dedicated spaces where, in the first instance, the world was bought in to contemplate and, in the second, it was shut out to escape. Taken together, they may be seen as a metaphor for a society that sought to achieve a lifestyle of refinement without equal and for its nobility to be gentlemen in fact as well as in name.

279 Casinò Venier, principal *sala*, with its eighteenth-century stucco and fresco decoration. Located at Ponte dei Baretteri (San Marco 4939–4970), the casinò consisted of a kitchen, storeroom, and two chambers in addition to the *sala* – a central hall equivalent to the old *portego*, which had a dual function as gaming room and place of conversation. The *casinò*, located on the *piano nobile*, had two entrances, one of them with a secret passageway for visitors who wished to enter and exit without being seen. Owned by the procurator Federico Venier and his wife Elena Priuli, the spaces were elegantly decorated. The *sala*, with mirrors set into the side walls, repeated the age-old iconography of the Venetian home, with stucco reliefs of the cardinal virtues – Fortitude, Justice, Temperance, and Prudence – above the side doors and the Venier *stemma* in the center of the ceiling.

Conclusion

THE REMARKABLE SUCCESS OF Venice, whose improbable survival in the sea was itself grounded in paradox, engendered a legendary reputation that came to be known as the "myth of Venice": a most perfect republic, with a political structure acclaimed (optimistically) as a consummate balance of monarchy, aristocracy, and democracy; an exemplary piety and loyalty to the Mother Church; a fabled economic prosperity built upon trade rather than feudalism; a relatively stable amalgam of rich and poor; and a fertile environment for the production of art, architecture, music, and literature. Modern scholars have labored both to substantiate and to debunk the myth. For the paradox of Venice encompassed more than its geophysical improbability; the myth masked an experience that had its imperfections and ambiguities. The government was not always just; its peoples were not all prosperous and happy; its homes were not all palaces; the poor noble might often compare himself with the rich commoner; modernity was seen by some as a threat to long-cherished tradition. While every society encompasses incongruities, the case of Venice is particularly intriguing because of the compelling success of the myth. When expectations are high, discrepancies are most provocative.

And yet perhaps the relevant question is not whether the myth was true or false, but rather how this enigma – this pastiche of polarities – was held together. There is no simple or single answer. Much has been written about a consciously fashioned civic image propagated by writers such as Marin Sanudo, Gasparo Contarini, and Francesco Sansovino, and reinforced by ceremonial and ritual, as well as by geographical circumstances that fostered a sense of community. As a further step toward answering this question, this book has focused on the material and visual culture of the home and the unique interplay between public and private in sixteenth-century Venice. Of paramount interest has been the role played by the domestic environment – the palace, or *casa*, along with the family and the furnishings that it housed – in expressing values and fostering the myth. We have seen how the tension between *magnificentia* and *mediocritas* manifest in palace building reflected a dialogue between tradition, in terms of a Byzantine–Gothic aesthetic, and modernity, expressed by an *all'antica* vocabulary. And yet the triumph of modernity, as witness the wholesale embrace of a romanizing style in new palace construction by the end of the sixteenth century, did not signal the end of *venezianità*. I would submit that this is precisely *because* of Venice's conservatism, which featured an extraordinary capacity to incorporate the new without rejecting the old.

Inside the palace walls such polemics were tempered for the most part and had a different dialectic. Here the dialogue was played out not so much in terms of style as in expense and ostentation. With imported wares abundant, and luxurious furnishings and clothing serving as signs of high status, the flourishing rental market allowed even families of middling resources to surround themselves with luxury goods. The Englishman Sir Henry Wotton put it well: "Every mans proper Mansion House and Home, being the Theater of his Hospitality, the Seate of Selfe-fruition, the Comfortablest part of his owne Life, the Noblest of his Sonnes Inheritance, a kinde of private Princedome; Nay to the Possessors thereof, an Epitome of the whole World: may well deserve by these Attributes, according to the degree of the Master, to be decently and delightfully adorned."[1]

Sumptuary laws intended to control display within the home, though earnestly put forth, were more a rhetorical stance than a practical remedy. While such legislation may have curbed the greatest excesses and allowed the poorer nobles to save face, they were only annoyances to the truly rich, who paid the fines as a form of luxury tax. Perhaps such laws, doomed from the start, were effective precisely *because* they did not work. Restraints imposed upon all,

facing page Detail of fig. 20.

regardless of rank, allowed the noble legislators to play out the political fiction of "conserving the equality between our nobles and citizens." Or, when aimed at courtesans, they gave voice to high-minded moral precepts, while doing little to curb a culture that fostered illicit liaisons. While noble rank – that most precious asset in an aristocratic society – was conferred only by bloodline and not to be bought, a noble lifestyle was possible for whoever could afford it. Tensions between the rich and the poor, of whatever rank, were further mitigated by a housing mix and a physical environment that kept them not only in close proximity, but also in an interdependent relationship required for survival. Unlike the landed aristocracy of the mainland, even old and wealthy families might live in – often opulent – rental housing. Appearances mattered; ownership less so.

In sum, Venetian domestic environments played many roles: places of reception and retreats of seclusion; cloisters of morality and arenas of pleasure; theaters of the nobility (in a public sense) and theaters of the world (in a private sense). Most importantly, they were an embodiment of the taste and values – the *politia* – not only of the families who lived in them, but of a society that valued both *magnificentia* and *mediocritas* – a paradox that made the myth so compelling, not only in its own time but also to us today.

Appendix
Family Trees

The reconstruction of Venetian family trees is a perilous operation, and any tree must be considered a work in progress. In the first instance, the archival records are not complete, particularly for the period up to the 1540s. Even in the later sixteenth century, some registers, such as the Necrologia dei Nobili – a list of noble deaths – have entire years missing.

Furthermore, the registration of noble births was instituted only in 1506, and even then the birth registers remain full of omissions for at least the first quarter of the sixteenth century. *Cittadino* births, as well as daughters and natural children born to noble fathers, were not registered at all. However, the existence of male nobles in the fifteenth and early sixteenth centuries can be confirmed, and their birth age estimated, albeit cautiously, from the registers of the Balla d'Oro, which survive for much of the fifteenth century and are fairly complete for the sixteenth century. Instituted in 1319, the Balla d'Oro, or Barbarella, was a register of noble males whose names were inscribed when they entered the Great Council at the age of twenty-five. In 1414 a new lottery system of selection was set up wherein youths were allowed to register at the age of eighteen, thus establishing their noble status, with the winners allowed to enter the Great Council at the age of twenty. In 1497[1] the minimum age for registration was raised to twenty years. It should be noted, however, that youths living abroad – in Cyprus, Corfu, or other Venetian possessions in the Aegean, for example – may well have been registered in the Balla d'Oro at a later date. The law required only that they have attained the statutory age, and frequently two or more brothers were registered at the same time, thus complicating the question of birth dates.

The problem is exacerbated by numerous homonyms in different branches of a family within the same generation, and testaments, marriage records, and birth records must be cross-checked to resolve ambiguous information. Typically, the oldest son was named after his paternal grandfather, with other children named after various family members on both side of the lineage. Thus, the use of patronymics attached to a first name (for example, Giovanni di Jacopo di Giovanni: Giovanni, son of Jacopo, grandson of Giovanni) was standard practice, and helps to sort out identities.

Finally, the name of an individual was often spelled in different ways, even in the same document, in Venetian dialect, or Italianized or Latinized, with alternate spellings for each. For example, the same man might be referred to as Hieronimo or Girolamo or Gerolamo; or Jacopo could also be cited as Jacobo or Giacomo; or Zuanne could be called Zuan, Giovanni or Ioannes; or Elisabetta might be shortened to Isabetta, or altered to Helisabeth, and so on.

* * *

The trees in this Appendix are based upon primary documents in the Archivio di Stato of Venice, the Biblioteca Nazionale Marciana, and Biblioteca del Museo Correr, and the genealogies compiled by Marco Barbaro: ASV, Miscellanea Codici 898: and BCV, Ms, Cicogna 516 (2504); as well as Girolamo Alessandro Capellari Vivaro Vicentino, "Il Campidoglio Veneto": BMV, MS. It. Cl. VII 16 (= 8305).

Bembo

Zaccaria Bembo (1405--)
m. 1436 Caterina Surian
Alvise Bembo
m. 1488 Pentesilia Michiel
di Zuan Matteo (–)
Zuan Matteo Bembo
(ca 1491–1570)
m. 1519 Marcella Marcello
di Sebastiano
(1496–1555)
Liaison
with
unnamed
woman
Quintilio Lorenzo
(1520-1570)
m. 1546 Laura
Foscarini di Alvise
(in casa at
San Ermagora)
Augusta
(1522–
aft 1570)
Alvise
(1523–1570)
m. (1) 1552
Maddalena
Pasqualigo
di Zuanne
(2) ca 1568
Cecilia Priuli
di Antonio
Marc'Antonio
(1524–1576)
m. 1557
Lucietta Bembo
di Gaspare
(--1612)
Sebastiano
(1528–1564)
Giulia
(1532–1562)
m. 1550
Girolamo
Della Torre
Piero
(1533–1589)
Bernardo
Andrea
(1534–
bef 1547)
Davide (1530–1611)
m. (1) 1563
Elisabetta Donado
(2) 1577
Marina Barbarigo
di Zuan Battista
Paolo
(--bef 1547)
Ettor
[natural]
Zuan Battista (1544–1564)
Alvise (1547–1613)
Andrea (1548–1618)
Bemardo (1549--)
Marcantonio (1550–1574)
Zuan Matteo (1551–1627)
Pietro (1553–1574)
Marcella
Zuan Matteo (1567–1629)
Gaspare (1572--)
Zuan Battista (1573–1610)
Piero (1575–1631)
Lodovico
Sigismondo
Tadea
Giulio
Marcella
Giovanni
Luigi
Ginevra
Helena
Giulia (1562--)
Alvise (1572--)
Zuan Matteo (1577–1618)

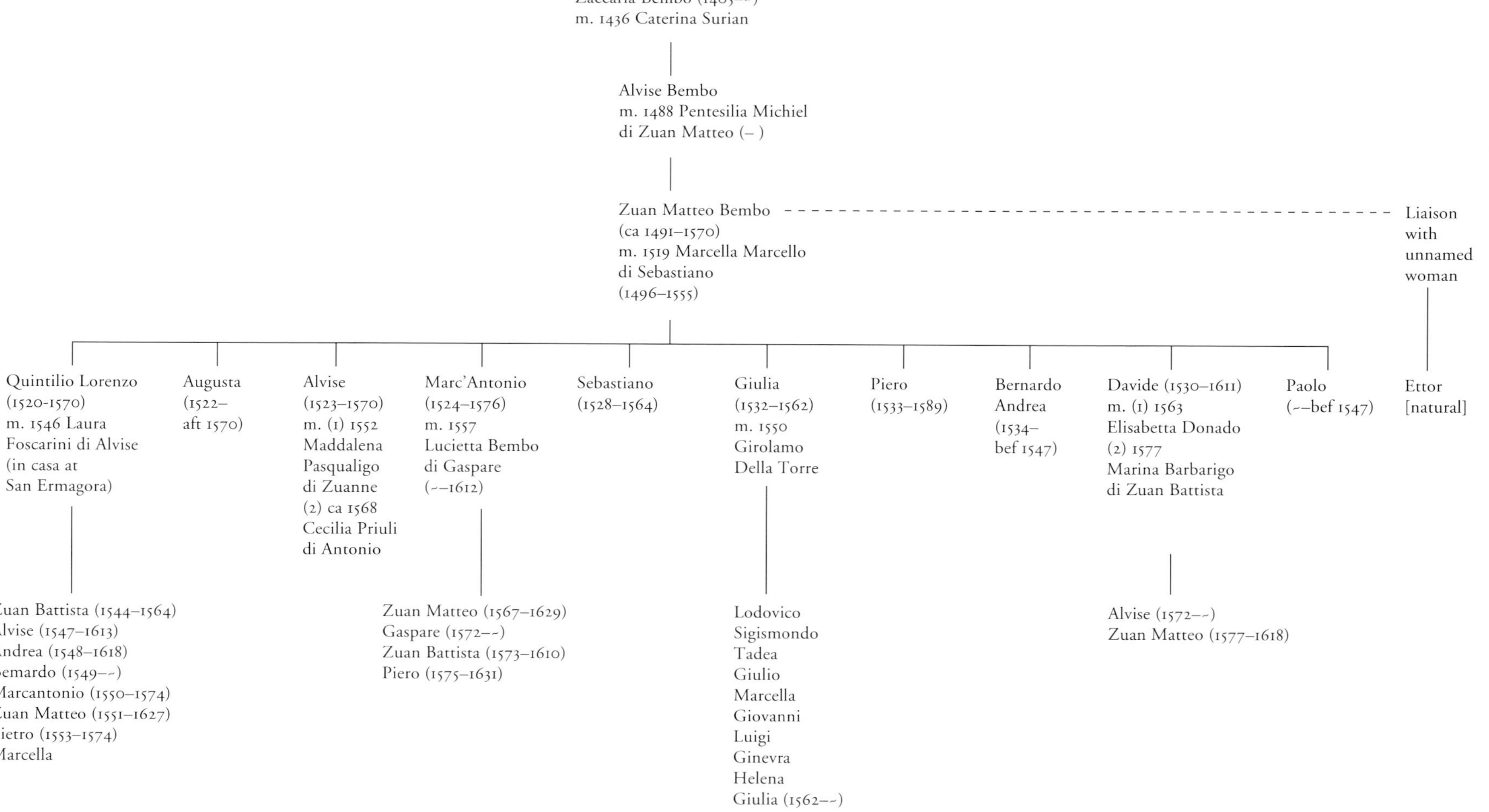

Bragadin

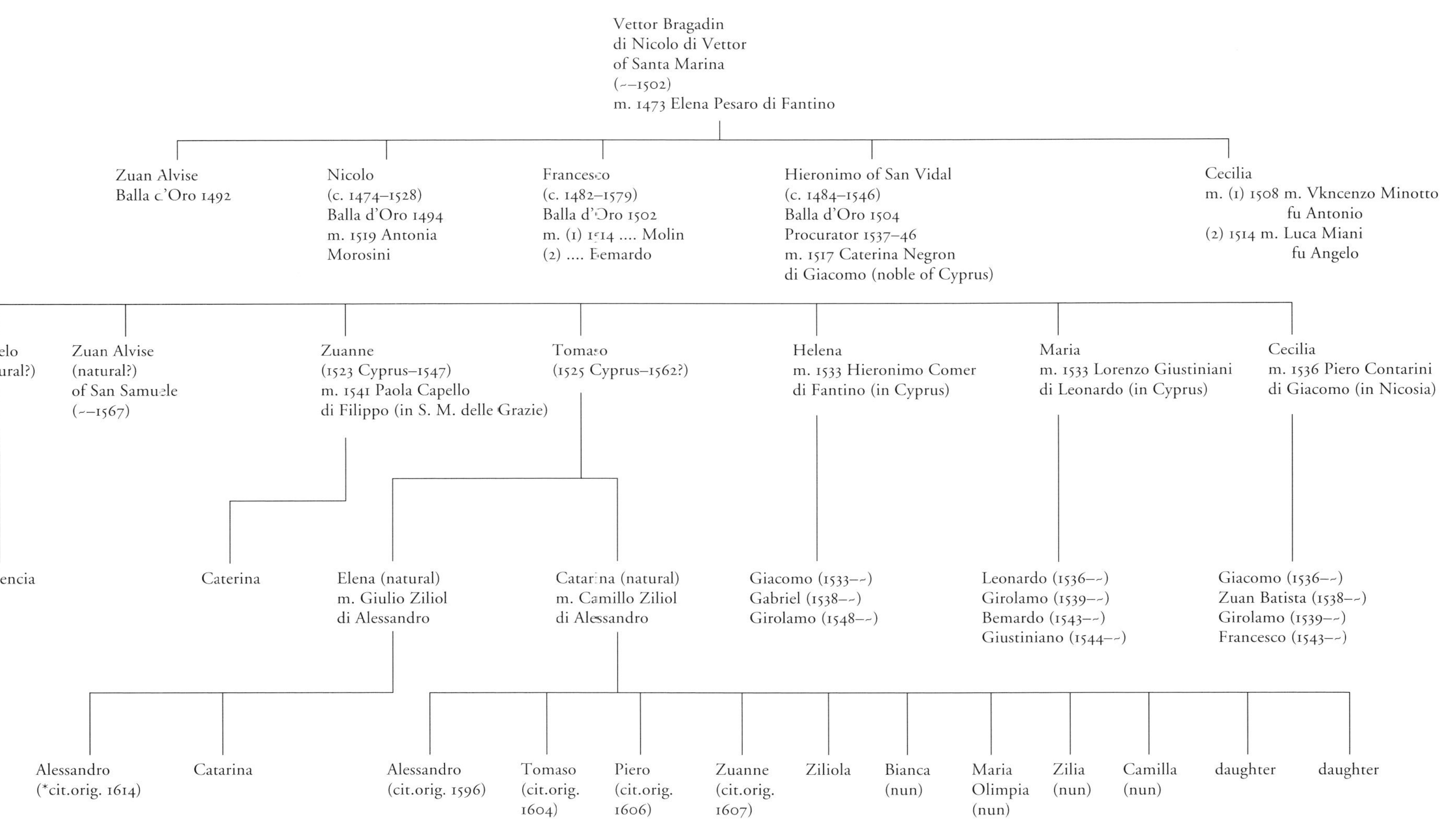

*cittadino originario
status proven (provato)

Condulmer

Antonio Condulmer
Bernardo
Zuan Francesco
m. 1461 Elisabetta Badoer
di Giovanni
di Andrea dalla Tana
Eugenio
Girolamo [Hieronimo]
(--1515)
Balla d'Oro 1497
m. 1484 Laura Fontana
di Alvise of Spalato
Bemardo
Balla d'Oro 1500
m. 1501 Elisabetta Da Mezzo
Giacomo [Jacobo]
Balla d'Oro 1500
m. 1499 Griseide Arborsani di Aurelio
Andriana
(bef 1501--)
Zuan Francesco
Balla d'Oro 1516
Failed proof of
nobility 1527
Zuan Gabriele
(bef 1501--)
Ursia
(nun)
Eugenio
Elisabetta
Condulmer
(aft 1501–1538)
m. Gabriel
di Angeli
Francesco
Luca
Zuan
Francesco
Aurelio
Carlo
Alvise
(1511–
1565)
Eugenio
[Nicoletto]
(1516--)
Antonio
(1521–
1562)
Zuan
Gerolamo
(1526–1563)
with Luca di Alvise Varoter
Julio
with Camillo Michiel
Cipriana
Condolmera
with Francesco d'Asola
(de Torresani)
Hieronimo (Girolamo)
(c. 1530–aft 1589)
Bemardino (Bemardo)
(c. 1532–aft 1589)
Paula
Laura.

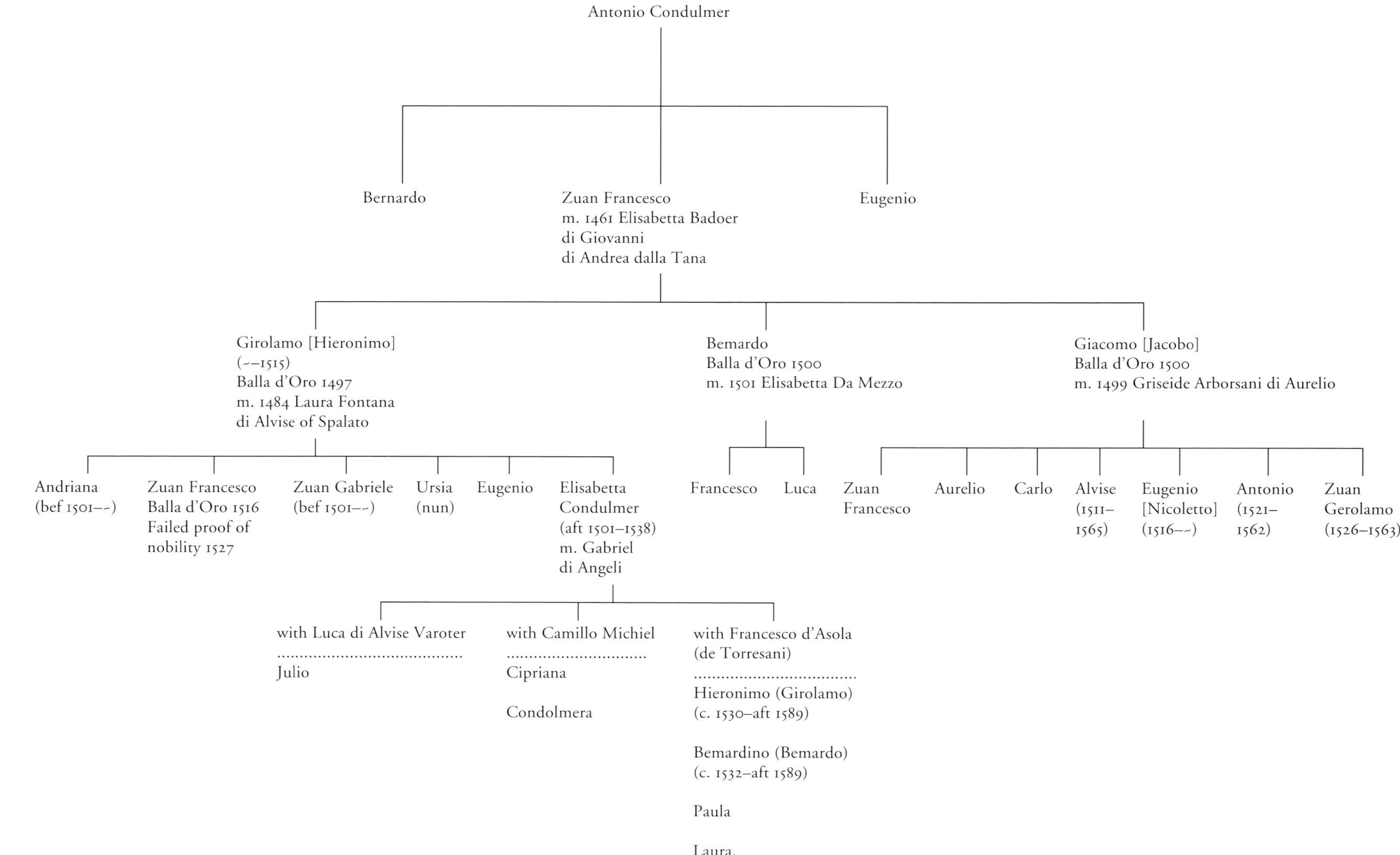

Da Lezze

Michiel Da Lezze
di Donato di Luca
(––1535)
Balla d'Oro 1469
m. 1474 Maria Marcello
di Antonio
Luca
(––1514)
Balla d'Oro 1503
m. 1507 Andriana Foscarini
di Giovanni Battista
Zorzi
(––1513)
Donado
(––1544)
m. 1503 Elena Foscarini
di Giovanni Battista
Zuanne
(––1575)
Balla d'Oro 1508
Procurator 1522–75
m. 1511 Maria Badoer di Benedetto
(widow of Alvise Foscari)
Francesco Maria
1514–1573
Giacomo
Michiel Gaspare Baldassare Melchiore
of San Vidal
1521–1552
m. 1545 Lucretia Contarini di Fantino
(in casa Da Lezze at San Stefano)
Zorzi
Luca Giacomo Bartolomeo
of San Vidal
1514–1551
Benedetto
1516–1571
Donado Da Lezze
1546–1582
m. 1573 Chiara Morosini
di Giacomo (in S. Agnese)
Lucrezia
Marietta
Michiel
(1577–)
Giacomo Martino
(1578––)
m. 1613 Cassandra Zen
di Bartolomeo
(in San Pantalon)
Helena
m. 1595 Marco Barbaro
di Francesco
(in S. Giacomo
della Giudecca)
Zorzi
(1580––)
Andriana
m. 1603 Giacomo Bembo
di Girolamo
(in San Luca)

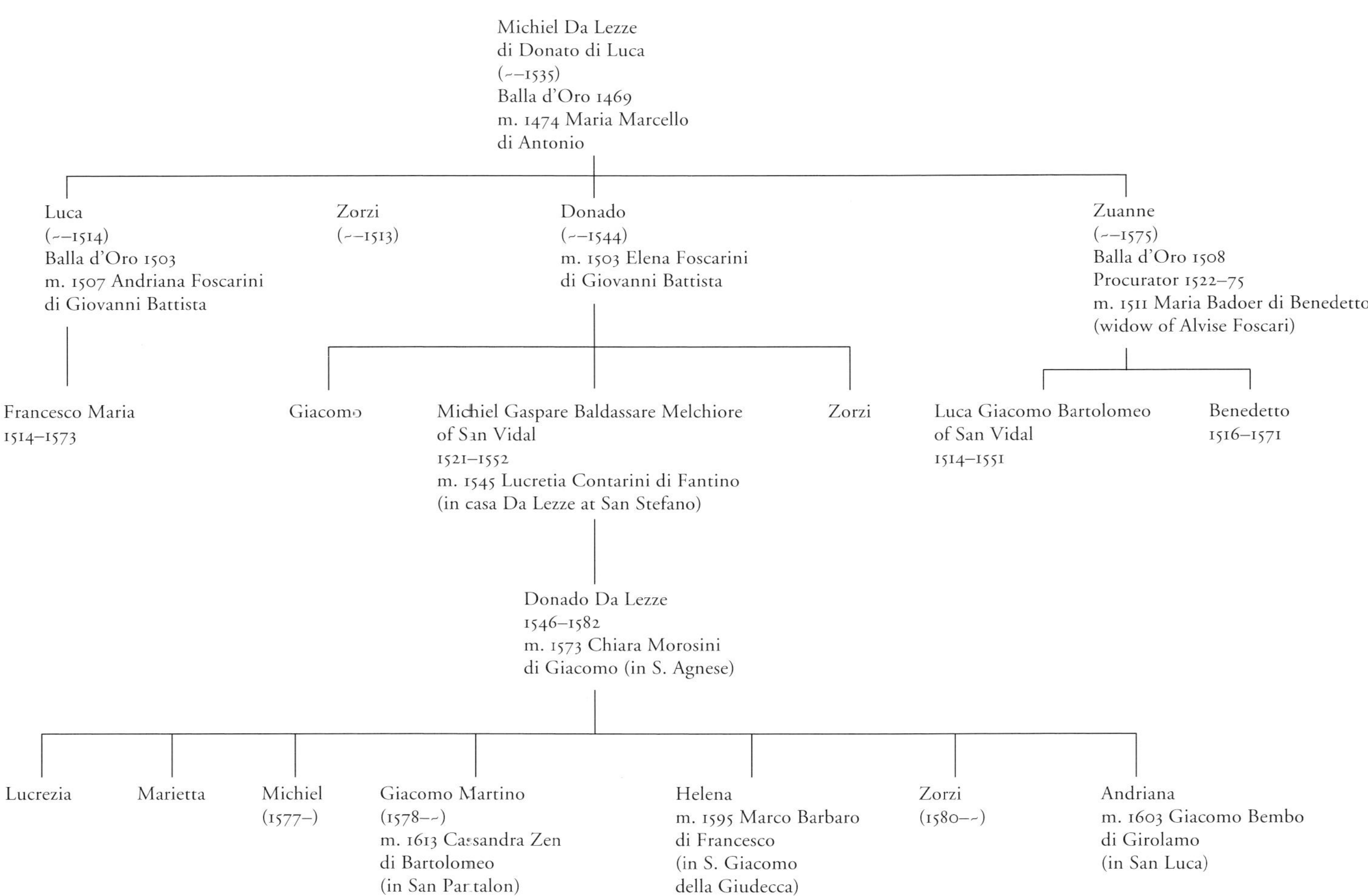

Soranzo

Francesco Soranzo
di Zuanne di Vettore
Balla d'Oro 1462
m. 1467 Catarina Foscari
di Giacomo
Jacopo
(1467–1551)
m. 1491 Francesca
Giustiniani di Lorenzo
Procurator 1522–
Francesco (called Forfetta)
(c. 1493–1562)
Balla d'Oro 1513
m. 1516 Chiara Capello
di Lorenzo
Jacopo
Gaspare
(1518–1599)
Procurator 51–51
Lorenzo
Giovanni Maria
Baldassare
(1519–1579)
m. 1548 Marina
Cappello di Filippo)
(in San Stae)
Jacopo (1549––)
Francesco (1550––)
Giovanni
Bartolomeo Melchiore
(1520–1603)
Procurator 1596–1603
m. 1555 Marietta Zane
di Girolamo (in casa)
Francesco (1557––)
Jacopo (1558––)
Jacopo (1559––)
Jacopo (1568––)
Girolamo (1569––)
Benedetto (1570––)
Lorenzo (1570––)
Lorenzo (1574––)
Cecilia
m. 1539
Marco Giustinian
di Antonio (1510–75)
(in S. Croce
alla Giudecca)
Antonio (1541––)
Giacomo Alvise (1543––)
Francesco (1550––)
Benedetto
Giovanni Francesco
Giovanni Maria
(1522–1571)
Bernardo
Natale
(1524––)
Bernardo
Caterino
(1530––)
Vettore
Vincenzo
(1532–1565)
Bemardo
Gaspare
(1534––)
Elisabetta
m. 1544
Giovanni
Vendramin
di Marco
(in casa)
Elena

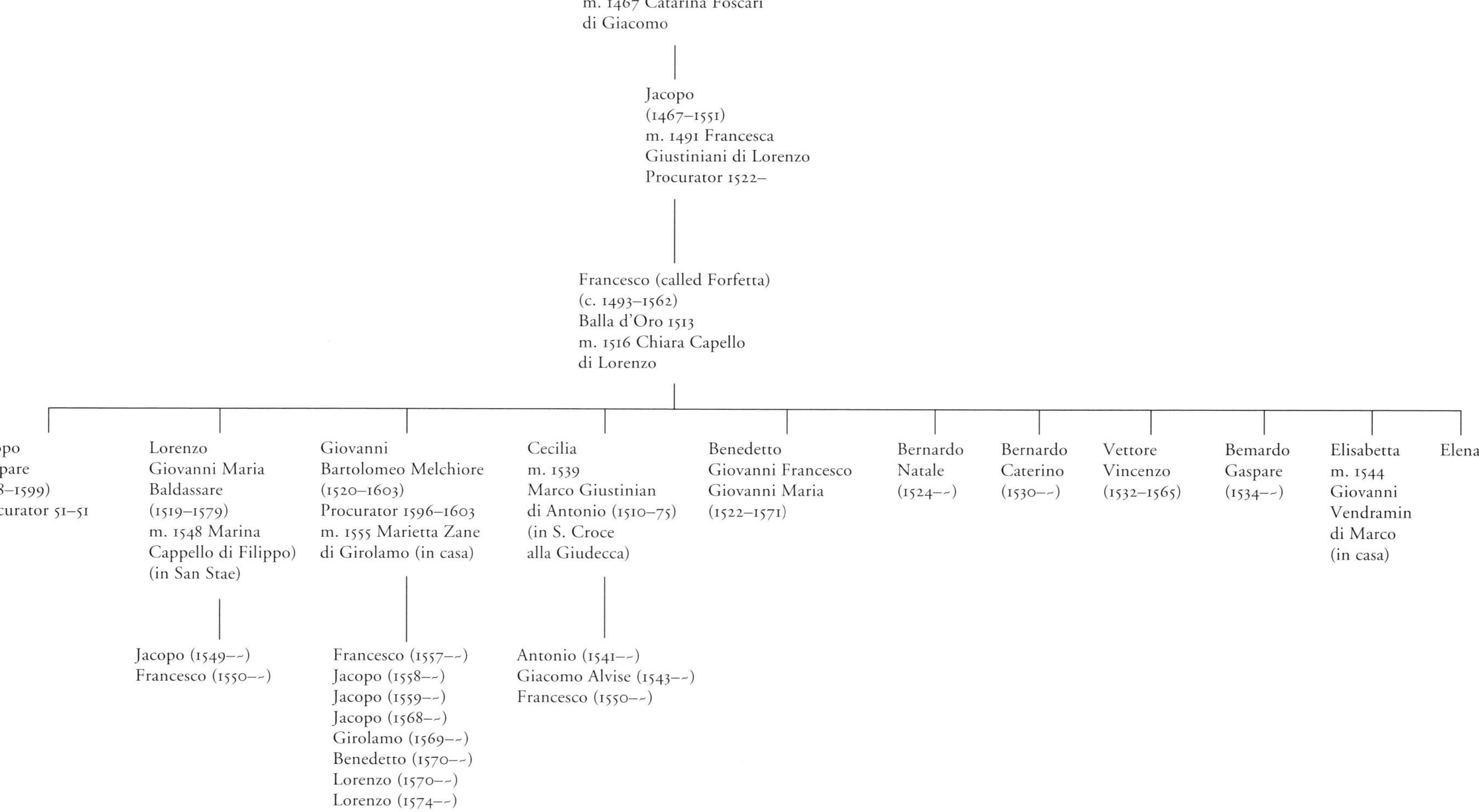

Notes

A note number attached to a figure citation in the text (e.g., [fig. 1][1]) denotes sources for information given in the relevant caption.

Preface

1 Among the exceptions are Luke Syson and Dora Thornton, *Objects of Virtue: Art in Renaissance Italy* (Los Angeles: The J. Paul Getty Museum, 2001); Dora Thornton, *The Scholar in his Study* (New Haven and London: Yale University Press, 1997); Peter Thornton, *The Italian Renaissance Interior 1400–1600* (London: Weidenfeld and Nicolson, 1991).

2 Marta Ajmar, "Introduction," *Journal of Design History* 15:4 (2002): 207, a special issue dedicated to Renaissance consumption. Two notable projects funded by the Arts and Humanities Research Board in London have broad-based interdisciplinary research programs and sponsor seminars and public symposia in this area: the Centre for the Study of the Domestic Interior in London – a collaborative effort of the Royal College of Art, the Victoria & Albert Museum, and the Bedford Centre for the History of Women at Royal Holloway, University of London; and the Material Renaissance project at the University of Sussex. An exhibition of the domestic interior in Italy, 1400–1600, will be held at the Victoria & Albert Museum in 2006.

3 Mario Praz, *An Illustrated History of Furnishing from the Renaissance to the 20th Century*, trans. William Weaver (New York: George Braziller, 1964), 51.

4 Francesco Sansovino, *Venetia città nobilissima et singolare descritta in* XIIII *libri*, with additions by Giustiniano Martinioni, 2 vols. (Venice: Steffano Curti, 1663; reprint, Venice: Filippi Editore 1968), 1: 393–94: "politura senza pari, & con mobigliamenti ricchi, & honorevoli quanto si possono desiderare in Casa privata." The book was first published as *Venetia città nobilissima et singolare descritta in* XIIII *libri* (Venice, 1581), and again as *Venetia città nobilissima ampliata da Giovanni Stringa* (Venice: Altobello, 1604). Sansovino's original text of 1581 remained unchanged in the 1663 edition, where Martinioni's contributions were clearly marked.

5 Richard Goldthwaite, *Wealth and the Demand for Art in Italy, 1300–1600* (Baltimore and London: The Johns Hopkins University Press, 1993); Lisa Jardine, *Worldly Goods: A New History of the Renaissance* (New York: Nan A. Talese, 1996); Simon Schama, *The Embarrassment of Riches: an Interpretation of Dutch Culture in the Golden Age* (New York: Knopf, 1987); Peter Burke, *Venice and Amsterdam: A Study of Seventeenth-Century Elites*, 2nd ed. (London: Polity Press, 1994); and idem, *The Historical Anthropology of Early Modern Italy: Essays in Perception and Communication* (Cambridge: Cambridge University Press, 1987); Katie Scott, *The Rococo Interior: Decoration and Social Spaces in Early Eighteenth-Century Paris* (New Haven and London: Yale University Press, 1995). Cf. Ingrid Rowland, "The Renaissance Revealed," *The New York Review of Books*, 6 November 1997; and Lauro Martines, "The Renaissance and the Birth of Consumer Society," *Renaissance Quarterly* 51 (1998): 193–203.

6 The work was first published in 1880 and went through several revisions and expansions. The most recent version is Pompeo Molmenti, *La storia di Venezia nella vita privata dalle origini alla caduta della Repubblica*, 3 vols. (Bergamo, 1927–29; reprint, Trieste: Edizioni Lint, 1973). For fuller details, see Chapter 3, n. 30.

7 Dennis Romano, *Housecraft and Statecraft: Domestic Service in Renaissance Venice, 1400–1600* (Baltimore and London: The Johns Hopkins University Press, 1996); Stanley Chojnacki, *Women and Men in Renaissance Venice: Twelve Essays on Patrician Society* (Baltimore and London: The Johns Hopkins University Press, 2000) and numerous articles; and Monica Chojnacka, *Working Women of Early Modern Venice* (Baltimore: The Johns Hopkins University Press, 2001).

Chapter 1

1 Michael Strachan, *The Life and Adventures of Thomas Coryate* (London: Oxford University Press, 1962), 1–13.

2 Thomas Coryat, *Coryat's Crudities*, 2 Vols. (Glasgow: James McLehose and Sons, 1905).

3 Ibid., 1:xv–xx.

4 Ibid., 1:2.

5 Ibid., 1:3. For Contarini's treatise, see below (nn. 34–35).

6 Coryat, *Coryat's Crudities*, 1:306. See Antonio Quadri, *Il Canal Grande di Venezia* (1828; reprint, Ponzano/Treviso: Vianello Libri, 1990); Umberto Franzoi, *The Grand Canal* (New York: Rizzoli, 2001); and Sandra Moschini Marconi, *Gallerie dell'Accademia di Venezia. Opere d'arte del secolo XV* (Rome: Istituto Poligrafico dello Stato, 1962), 238–39.

7 For plates of a few surviving Renaissance interiors, see Giuseppe Mazzariol and Attilia Dorigato, *Intérieurs Vénitiens* (Paris: Bibliothèque des Arts, 1991); and Cesare M. Cunaccia, *Venice, Hidden Splendors* (Paris and New York: Flammarion, 1994). For the Venetian *altana*, typically a wood platform with railings on the roof of a house, see Corrado Balistreri-Trincanato and Dario

Zanverdiani, *Jacopo de Barbari: Il racconto di una città*, 2nd ed. (Venice: Edizioni Stamperia Cetid, 2000), 31–38.

8 Vincenzo Scamozzi, *Dell'idea della architettura universale* (Venice, 1615), 243, observed of Venetians, "ne è meraviglia se non invitano nelle case loro i forastieri, se non di rado, ò molto famigliari." For Wotton's sojourn in Venice, see Logan Pearsall Smith, *The Life and Letters of Sir Henry Wotton* (Oxford: Clarendon Press, 1907), 1:60. For his views on Venetian homes, see Sir Henry Wotton, *The Elements of Architecture: A Facsimile Reprint of the First Edition (London, 1624). With Introduction and Notes by Frederick Hard* (Charlottesville: The University Press of Virginia, published for the Folger Shakespeare Library, 1968).

9 For Sansovino's background, see Paul Grendler, "Francesco Sansovino and Italian Popular History, 1560–1600," *Studies in the Renaissance* 16 (1969), 139–80; Bruce Boucher, *The Sculpture of Jacopo Sansovino* (New Haven and London: Yale University Press, 1991), 1:29; and Elena Bonora, "'Flânerie idéologique' dans la Venise du XVIe siècle: Francesco Sansovino et son guide, 1581," in *Les guides imprimés du XVIe au XXe siècle: villes, paysages, voyages* (Paris: Belin, 2000), 297–306.

10 Francesco Sansovino, *Venetia città nobilissima et singolare descritta in XIIII libri*, with additions by Giustiniano Martinioni (Venice: Steffano Curti, 1663; reprint, Venice: Filippi Editore 1968), 1:384–85. The translation is based upon David Chambers and Brian Pullan, eds., *Venice: A Documentary History, 1450–1630* (Oxford: Blackwell, 1992), 25.

11 For an early description of the Palazzo Trevisan frescoes see Carlo Ridolfi, *Le maraviglie dell'arte ovvero le vite degli illustri pittori veneti e dello stato*, ed. Detlev Freiherrn von Hadeln (Berlin, 1914–24; reprint, Rome: Società Multigrafica Editrice Somu, 1965), 1:322–23. See also Vincenzo Zanetti, *Guida di Murano e delle celebri sue fornaci vetrarie* (Venice, 1980; reprint, Venice: Arnaldo Forni Editore, 1984), 157–59. For the fireplace in Palazzo Contarini delle Figure, see Luisa Attardi, *Il camino veneto del Cinquecento: Struttiera architettonica e decorazione scultorea* (Costabizzara [Vicenza]: Angelo Colla Editore, 2002), 142–5.

12 Salvatore Battaglia, *Grande Dizionario della Lingua Italiana* (Turin: UTET, 1961–), 2:824: "Avere, tenere casa aperta: ricevere spesso e con molta cordialità molti ospiti. Anche: possedere una casa provvista di tutto ciò che occorre per potervi abitare." Cf. Vincenzo Giustiniani, "Discorso sopra la pittura (1610)," in his *Discorsi sulle arti e sui mestieri*, ed. A. Banti (Florence: Sansoni, 1981), 45: "in vero è cosa degna di maraviglia il considerare il gran numero dè pittori ordinari, e di molte persone che tengono casa aperta con molta famiglia;" and Torquato Alessandro, *Il cavalier compito* (Viterbo: Girolamo Discepolo, 1609), 9: "tenete casa grande aperta, e ben adobbata." The latter is translated by Guido Guerzoni, "*Liberalitas, Magnificentia*, Splendor: The Classic Origins of Italian Renaissance Lifestyles," in *Economic Engagements with Art*, ed. Neil De Marchi and Craufurd D. W. Goodwin (Durham and London: Duke University Press, 1999), 333, as "the maintenance of a large, well-furnished house always open to guests."

13 Sansovino, *Venetia città nobilissima* (1663), 1:384–85 (1581 ed., f. 142r). Part of the translation is based upon Chambers and Pullan, *Venice: A Documentary History*, 25.

14 *Vocabolario della Lingua Italiana* (Rome: Istituto della Enciclopedia Italiana, 1986–1994), 3.2:976: "politia, s. f. . . . sopratutto per rendere un partic. uso del termine greco, proprio di Aristotele nel trattato della *Politica*, dove indica la forma di costituzione nella quale il governo è in mano al popolo, che lo esercita in vista del bene comune." Ibid., 979: "polizia . . . Forma di governo; costituzione, ordinamento della città e dello stato; amministrazione, anche di istituzioni e di attività pubbliche; vita politica partecipazione alla vita pubblica; comportamento civile." Manlio Cortelazzo and Paolo Zolli, *Dizionario etimologico della lingua italiana* (Bologna: Zanichelli, 1979–1988), 4:950: "polizia, s. f. sistema col quale si governa bene una città (av. 1449, D. Burchiello)"; and Carlo Battisti and Giovanni Alessio, *Dizionario Etimologico Italiano*, IV (Florence: G. Barbèra Editore, 1950), 4:3002: "polizia f. (XVI–XVII sec) . . . forma di governo."

15 *Vocabolario della Lingua Italiana*, 3.2:976: "polizia . . . Forma ant. per *pulizia*, nel sign. proprio, e più spesso in quelli connessi con l'agg. *polito*, cioè finezza di modi e di comportamento, gentilezza e cortesia, raffinatezza, eleganza e anche probità." Battaglia, *Grande Dizionario della Lingua Italiana*, 13:772: "Polizia . . . Raffinatezza di modi, finezza di tratto, compitezza di contegno (talvolta puramente formale o osservata per opportunità o con affettazione); buona educazione, urbanità, cortesia, gentilezza; correttezza, scrupolosità – Anche: ostentazione di lusso." Battisti and Alessio, *Dizionario Etimologico Italiano*, 4:3001: "polito agg., XIV sec., *-ezza* (XVII sec., Redi); liscio, terso; 'pulito'; v. dotta, lat. *politus* adorno, elegante, fine."

16 Sansovino, *Venetia città nobilissima* (1663), 1:385 (1581 ed., f. 142r).

17 Coryat, *Coryat's Crudities*, 1:415. As an Englishman coming from a society with a more subtle hierarchical social system, Coryat distinguished between noblemen and gentlemen, or gentry, a distinction that would probably not have been made by Venetians.

18 Dennis Romano, *Housecraft and Statecraft: Domestic Service in Renaissance Venice, 1400–1600* (Baltimore and London: The Johns Hopkins University Press, 1996), 231 and passim.

19 Coryat, *Coryat's Crudities*, 1:415.

20 See, in particular, Mary Margaret Newett, "The Sumptuary Laws of Venice in the Fourteenth and Fifteenth Centuries," in *Historical Essays First Published in 1902 in Commemoration of the Jubilee of The Owens College Manchester*, ed. T. F. Tout and James Tait (Manchester: Manchester University Press, 1907); Giulio Bistort, *Il Magistrato alle Pompe nella Republica di Venezia* (Bologna: Forni Editore, 1912); and Pierogiovanni Mometto, "'Vizi privati, pubbliche virtù'. Aspetti e problemi della questione del lusso nella repubblica di Venezia (secolo XVI)", in *Crimine, giustizia e società veneta in età moderna*, ed. Luigi Berlinguer and Floriana Colao (Milan: Giuffrè, 1989).

21 See Victor Crescenzi, *Esse de Maiori Consilio: leggitimità civile e legittimazione politica nella repubblica di Venezia (secc. XIII–XVI)* (Rome: Istituto Storico Italiano per il Medio Evo, 1996); Stanley Chojnacki, "La formazione della nobiltà dopo la Serrata," in *Storia di Venezia dalle origini alla caduta della Serenissima. III. La formazione dello stato patrizio*, ed. Girolamo Arnaldi, Giorgio Cracco, and Alberto Tenenti (Rome: Istituto della Enciclopedia Italiana, 1997); idem, "Social Identity in Renaissance Venice: the Second Serrata," *Renaissance Studies* 8 (1994): 341–58; and James Grubb, "Memory and Identity: Why Venetians Didn't Keep *Ricordanze*," *Renaissance Studies* 8 (1994): 375–87.

22 The sitter was formerly identified as Francesco Savorgnan della Torre, but the recent discovery of a labeled copy confirms the present identification: Sandro Sponza, "Un dipinto di Tiziano riconosciuto: il ritratto di Nicolo Zeno a Kingston Lacy," in *Pittura veneziana dal Quattrocento al Settecento: Studi di storia dell'arte in*

onore di Egidio Martini, ed. Giuseppe Maria Pilo (Venice: Arsenale, 1999), 52–61. See also Charles Hope, Jennifer Fletcher and Jill Dunkerton, *Titian* (New Haven and London: Yale University Press, 2003), cat. 39. For Nicolo Zen, see Manfredo Tafuri, *Venice and the Renaissance*, trans. Jessica Levine (Cambridge, Mass., and London: The MIT Press, 1989) 1–5, and Chapter 2 below.

23 See Patricia Fortini Brown, "Behind the Walls: The Material Culture of Venetian Elites," in *Venice Reconsidered: The History and Civilization of an Italian City-State, 1297–1797*, ed. John Martin and Dennis Romano (Baltimore and London: Johns Hopkins University Press, 2000), 295–338, with additional bibliography.

24 See Margaret King, *Venetian Humanism in an Age of Patrician Dominance* (Princeton: Princeton University Press, 1986). For the "myth of Venice," from a vast literature see Elisabeth Crouzet-Pavan, *Venice Triumphant: Horizons of a Myth* (Baltimore: The Johns Hopkins University Press, 2002); and James Grubb, "When Myths Lose Power: Four Decades of Venetian Historiography," *Journal of Modern History* 58 (1986): 43–94.

25 James Grubb, "Elite Citizens," in *Venice Reconsidered: The History and Civilization of an Italian City-State, 1297–1797*, ed. John Martin and Dennis Romano (Baltimore and London: Johns Hopkins University Press, 2000), 339–64.

26 Carlo Bernardi with Pierluigi de Vecchi, *L'opera completa del Tintoretto* (Milan: Rizzoli Editore, 1970), 110–11. See also Philip Cottrell, "Corporate Colors: Bonifacio and Tintoretto at the Palazzo dei Camerlenghi in Venice," *Art Bulletin* 82 (2000): 671–72.

27 See Brian Pullan, *Rich and Poor in Renaisance Venice: the Social Institutions of a Catholic State, to 1620* (Cambridge, Mass.: Harvard University Press, 1971); and Patricia Fortini Brown, *Venetian Narrative Painting in the Age of Carpaccio* (New Haven and London: Yale University Press, 1988), 9–30.

28 For *broglio*, see Robert Finlay, *Politics in Renaissance Venice* (New Brunswick: Rutgers University Press, 1980), 22–23, 198–222; and Alvise Zorzi, *Venice 697–1797: City – Republic – Empire* (London: Sidgwick & Jackson, 1983), 158.

29 Claudio Donati, *L'idea di nobiltà in Italia, secoli* XIV–XVIII (Rome and Bari: Editori Laterza, 1995), 3–17.

30 Nicolò Machiavelli, *Discorsi sopra la prima deca di Tito Livio*, I:55. English translation from *Machiavelli: The Chief Works and Others*, trans. Allan Gilbert (Durham, N. C.: Duke University Press, 1965), 308–9. See also Donati, *L'idea di nobiltà*, 29–30.

31 Machiavelli, *Discorsi*, I, 34.

32 Ibid., I, 55; Gilbert trans., 310 (cited in n.30 above).

33 See Elisabeth G. Gleason, *Gasparo Contarini: Venice, Rome, and Reform* (Berkeley and Los Angeles: University of California Press, 1993).

34 Contarini composed the treatise in Latin between 1523 and 1531; it was first published in Paris in 1543. An Italian translation came out a year later in Venice: *La Republica e i Magistrati di Vinegia* (Venice: Girolamo Scoto, 1544). For the English translation, see Gasper Contareno, *The Commonwealth and Government of Venice*, trans. Lewes Lewkenor (London: John Windet, 1599; reprint, Amsterdam: Theatrum Orbis Terrarum, and New York: Da Capo Press, 1969), 16. See also Donati, *L'idea di nobiltà*, 56–58.

35 Contareno, *The Commonwealth and Government of Venice*, 16.

36 Ibid., 17–18.

37 ASV, Avogaria di Comun, Reg. 165 [Balla d'Oro, 1498–1544], f. 113v. For more on Zuan Francesco Condulmer, who lost his noble status, see Chapter 6 below.

38 Cited by Stanley Chojnacki, "Identity and Ideology in Renaissance Venice: The Third Serrata," in *Venice Reconsidered: The History and Civilization of an Italian City-State, 1297–1797*, ed. John Martin and Dennis Romano (Baltimore and London: Johns Hopkins University Press, 2000), 274. See also idem, "Marriage Regulation in Venice, 1420–1535," in *Marriage in Italy, 1300–1650*, ed. Trevor Dean and K. J. Lowe (Cambridge: Cambridge University Press, 1988), 142 (128–51); and Crescenzi, *Esse de Maiori Consilio*, 4–21 and passim.

39 Chojnacki, "Identity and Ideology in Renaissance Venice," 278–80. But cf. Grubb, "Elite Citizens," 339–64, who shows that some *cittadini* were more equal than others.

40 Giovambattista Nenna da Bari, *Il Nennio. Il quale ragiona di nobiltà* (Venice: Giovan Andrea Vavassore, 1543), III (no pagination). For another view, see John Martin "The Imaginary Piazza: Tommaso Garzoni and the Late Italian Renaissance," in *Portraits of Medieval and Renaissance Living: Essays in Memory of David Herlihy*, ed. Samuel K. Cohn Jr. and Steven A. Epstein (Ann Arbor: The University of Michigan Press, 1996), 439–54.

41 Contareno, *The Commonwealth and Government of Venice*, 18.

42 Federica Ambrosini, "Cerimonie, feste, lusso," in *Storia di Venezia dalle origini qalla caduta della Serenissima.* IV. *Il Rinascimento: politica e cultura*, ed. Alberto Tenenti and Ugo Tucci (Rome: Istituto della Enciclopedia Italiana, 1996), IV, 507, cites Marin Sanudo, *I diarii*, ed. Rinaldo Fulin et al. (Venice: F. Visentini, 1879–1903) 29:630 (11 February 1521), who quoted Marin Grimani, a very rich old nobleman who criticized a youth for wearing the *manege dogal* against the rules: "Poltron, meti zoso quella vesta, tu non è degno di portarla, tu non è stà mai di Pregadi." See also Stella Mary Newton, *The Dress of the Venetians, 1494–1534* (Aldershot, England and Brookfield, VT.: Scolar Press, 1988); Paul Hills, *Venetian Colour: Marble, Mosaic, Painting and Glass 1250–1550* (New Haven and London: Yale University Press, 1999), 173–92; and Paola Venturelli, "La moda come 'status symbol'. Legislazione suntuaria e 'segnali' di identificazione sociale," in Varese Ranieri and Grazietta Butazzi, *Storia della moda* (Bologna: Edizioni Calderini, 1995).

43 Girolamo Muzio, *Il gentilhuomo del Mutio Iustinopolitano* (Venice: Heredi di Luigi Valvassori, & Gio. Domenico Michieli, 1565), 1–55, cited by Donati, *L'idea di nobiltà*, 126–28.

44 See Patricia Fortini Brown: *Venice & Antiquity: The Venetian Sense of the Past* (New Haven and London: Yale University Press, 1996), 231–62.

45 Ibid., 262. See also Giacomo C. Bascapè and Marcello Del Piazzo, *Insegne e simboli. Araldica pubblica e privata medievale e moderna* (Rome: Ministero per i beni culturali e ambientali, 1983); and Maria Francesca Tiepolo, "Il linguaggio dei simboli: le arme de I Barbaro," in *Una famiglia veneziana nella storia: I Barbaro*, ed. Michela Marangoni and Manlio Pastore Stocchi (Venice: Istituto Veneto di Scienze, Lettere, ed Arti, 1996), 133–91.

46 Osvaldo Cavallar, Susanne Degenring, and Julius Kirshner, *A Grammar of Signs: Bartolo da Sassoferrato's "Tract on Insignia and Coats of Arms"* (Berkeley: Robbins Collection, University of California at Berkeley, 1994), 145–46. Cf. Maurice Keen, *Chivalry* (New Haven and London: Yale University Press, 1984), 143–61; and Cecil H. Clough, "Chivalry and Magnificence in the Golden Age of the Italian Renaissance," in *Chivalry in the Renaissance*, ed. Sidney Anglo (Woodbridge, Suffolk: The Boydell Press, 1990), 25–47.

47 Richard A. Goldthwaite, *Wealth and the Demand for Art in Italy, 1300–1600* (Baltimore and London: The Johns Hopkins University Press, 1993), 168–69. Cf. Lauro Martines, "The Renaissance and the

Birth of Consumer Society," *Renaissance Quarterly* 51 (1998): 193–203.

48 Alberto Rizzi, *Scultura Esterna a Venezia: Corpus delle Sculture Erratiche all'aperto di Venezia e della sua Laguna* (Venice: Stamperia di Venezia, 1987), 186–87, 208–9; Giannino Piamonte, *Venezia vista dall'acqua: Guida dei rii di Venezia e delle isole*, 3rd ed. (Venice: Stamperia di Venezia, 1992), 78.

49 Pompeo Molmenti, *La Storia di Venezia nella vita privata dalle origini alla caduta della Repubblica* (Bergamo, 1927–29; reprint, Trieste: Edizioni Lint, 1973), II:324. For Calle del Paradiso, see also Giuseppe Tassini, *Curiosità Veneziane* (Venice: Filippi Editore, 1970), 480–82; Egli Renata Trincanato, *Venezia Minore* (Milan: Edizioni del Milione, 1948), 136–45; Paolo Maretto, *L'ediliza gotica veneziana* (Venice: Filippi Editore, 1978), 108–10; and idem, *La casa veneziana nella storia della città dalle origini all'Ottocento* (Venice: Marsilio Editori, 1986), 345–47. For the sculptural reliefs, see Wolfgang Wolters, *La scultura veneziana gotica, 1300–1460* (Venice: Alfieri, 1976), 185 (cat. 68).

50 See ASV, Avogaria di Comun, Reg. 141, f. 133, for the contract made between Tommaso Michiel fu Francesco of San Canciano and Elisabetta Contarini fu Antonio of Sant'Angelo in 1516, with a typical preface: "In nome de la grandissima trinitade padre fiol et spirito sancto, et de la gloriosa verzene madre de Cristo madona sancta maria, et de tuta la celestial corte, che questo sanctissimo matrimonio possa haver bon principio, mior mezo, et perfectissimo fin cum salute de lanima et del corpo."

51 Both works were part of the Miracles of the True Cross cycle made for the Scuola Grande di San Giovanni Evangelista, ca.1494–1506 and now in the Accademia Galleries in Venice. See Brown, *Venetian Narrative Painting*, 135–64, 282–83; and Sandra Moschini Marconi, *Gallerie dell'Accademia di Venezia. Opere d'arte del secolo XIV e XV* (Rome: Istituto Poligrafico dello Stato, 1995), 96–97, 137.

52 ASV, Cancelleria Inferiore, Miscellanea Notai Diversi, B. 35, no. 27, ff. 2–4: "Una hora con sue colonelle, et l'arma Capella . . . uno bacin damascin con l'arma cappella et bernarda . . . tapezarie zoe spaliere nove a figure belle et altre con l'arma capella, et bernarda numero cinque."

53 John Florio, *Queen Anna's New World of Words 1611* (Menston, England: The Scolar Press Limited, 1968), 532–33.

54 See James C. Davis, *A Venetian Family and its Fortunes: 1500–1900* (Padua, 1975), 72–73.

55 Francesco Sansovino, *Vita delle illustre signora Contessa Giulia Bemba della Torre* (Venice: Domenico & Gio Battista Guerra, fratelli, 1565), 6v–8r. In Venetian dialect, Luigi and Alvise are versions of the name Ludovico.

56 For naming practices in Renaissance Tuscany see Christiane Klapisch-Zuber, *Women, Family, and Ritual in Renaissance Italy*, trans. Lydia Cochrane (Chicago and London: The University of Chicago Press, 1985), 283–309.

57 Giorgio Vasari, *Lives of the Artists*, trans. George Bull (Harmondsworth: Penguin Books, 1987), II, 68.

58 Tom Nichols, *Tintoretto: Tradition and Identity* (London: Reaktion Books, 1999), 51.

59 Paola Rossi, *Jacopo Tintoretto: Ritratti* (Milan: Electa, 1994), 90–95; see also Paola Rossi, *Jacopo Tintoretto. I: I Ritratti* (Venice: Alfieri, 1974), 31–32.

60 See Giuseppe Maria Pilo, "Il Procuratore di San Marco Jacopo Soranzo Jr. e il ritratto recuperato di Jacopo Tintoretto già in Procuratia 'De Supra'," in *Storia dell'arte marciana: i mosaici*, ed. Renato Polacco (Venice: Marsilio, 1997), 209–21; and idem, "Postilla a Jacopo Tintoretto," *Arte/Documenta* 5 (1991): 129–30. Unfortunately, Jacopo was disgraced for giving away state secrets in pursuit of a cardinal's hat and lost his procuratorship in 1584: Marco Barbaro (BCV, MS. Cicogna 516 (2504), VI:239) writes: "1584 28 luglio: fu bandito e private della Procuratia per aver rivelato a Principi secreti importanti per procurarsi con tali mezzi il Cardinalato, fu poi del 1586 17 dicembre liberato."

61 This analysis is based upon genealogical information drawn, in the first instance, from the family trees in ASV, Miscellanea Codici 898, Marco Barbaro. *Albori de' patritti veneti*: Soranzo alboro (L); and BCV, MS. Cicogna 516 (2504), Marco Barbaro, Discendenze patrizie, VI:238–239; and BMV, MS. It. Cl. VII 16 (= 8305), Girolamo Alessandro Capellari Vivaro Vicentino, "Il Campidoglio Veneto," Soranzo alboro [D], which contain, however, many omissions and errors. These sources are augmented, and corrected, by the following primary documents in the Archivio di Stato: Avogaria di Comun, R. 1 (Libro d'Oro, Nascite), cc. 245v–246v; Avogaria di Comun, R. 2 (Libro d'Oro, Nascite), cc. 250–251; Avogaria di Comun, R. 143 (Contratti di Nozze),cc. 268–9 (marriage of Cecilia); Avogaria di Comun, R. 145/6 (Contratti di Nozze), c. 310 (marriage of Elisabetta); Avogaria di Comun, R. 149/10 (Contratti di Nozze) c. 35v (marriage of Lorenzo); Avogaria di Comun, R 151/12 (Contratti di Nozze), c. 86 (marriage of Giovanni); and Notarile, Testamenti, B. 1245.498 (Lorenzo Soranzo di Francesco: 1 Feb. 1574 m.v.). There is no record of a marriage for Benedetto, although Marco Barbaro, Discendenze patrizie (BCV, MS. Cicogna 516 (2504), VI:238–239, Albero K), states that he had a natural son named Lazaro, who died in the Battle of Curzolari in 1574.

Cf. Rossi, cited in n. 59 above, who states incorrectly that Benedetto had married Paola Bernardo di Sebastiano at an uncertain date; in fact, she had married a Benedetto Soranzo di Bernardo (not di Francesco) on 28 April 1533 (ASV, Avogaria di Comun, Reg. 87, c. 288v). But Benedetto di Francesco did have a natural son, Lazzaro, to whom he left all his wordly possessions in his will, born to a Madonna Corona, (ASV, Notarile Testamenti, B. 1256, no. 130 (20 May 1562).

Although Rossi dates the painting to ca. 1550, the presence of spouses for all of Francesco and Chiara's married children as of 1555 suggests a mid-1550s date. This proposal supports Doretta Davanzo Poli's argument in *Architettura e utopia nella Venezia del Cinquecento* (Milan: Electa, 1980), 231, observing that the women's dress is more typical of the late 1550s.

For sumptuary legislation on the wearing of pearls, see ASV, Senato, Terra, Reg. 44, c. 55v (5 October 1562); and Giulio Bistort, *Il Magistrato delle Pompe*, 185–92, 373–77. The ban was subsequently applied to women beyond ten years of marriage.

62 Paolo Spezzani, "Riflettoscopia e raggi XC di alcuni ritratti di Jacopo Tintoretto," in *Jacopo Tintoretto: Ritratti*, 65–70.

63 Cited in the card file of noble family births in the Reading Room of the Archivio di Stato, Venice, all documented by records in the Avogaria di Comun.

64 For family portraiture see Blake de Maria, "The Merchants of Venice: A Study in Sixteenth-Century *Cittadino* Patronage" (Ph.D. diss., Princeton University, 2002), 243–81; and Grubb, "Memory and Identity," 384–87.

65 Palazzo Cappello, depicted in the plate, was owned by a different (albeit equally noble) branch of the Cappello family from the Domenico Cappello of Santa Maria Formosa.

66 Sanudo, *Diarii*, 17:246 (25 October 1513). Cf. Felix Gilbert, "Venice in the Crisis of the League of Cambrai," in *Renaissance Venice*, ed. J. R. Hale (London: Faber and Faber, 1973), 277, who must be incorrect in placing the portego on the ground floor of the palace.

67 Sansovino, *Venetia città nobilissima* (1663), 1:385. See also Isabella Palumbo-Fossati, "L'interno della casa dell'artigiano e dell'artista nella Venezia del Cinquecento," *Studi veneziani*, n.s. 8 (1984) 139.

68 ASV, Cancelleria Inferiore, Miscellanea Notai Diversi, B. 41, no. 48 (8 January 1572 m.v. [= 1573]), c. 3v.

69 See Palumbo-Fossati, "L'interno della casa dell'artigiano e dell'artista," 150; and Juergen Schulz, "The Houses of Titian, Aretino, and Sansovino," in *Titian: His World and His Legacy*, ed. David Rosand (New York: Columbia University Press, 1982), 89. However, there are exceptions. See de Maria, "The Merchants of Venice," 322–28, for the death inventory of Martino d'Anna, a *cittadino* merchant, which lists a wealth of weaponry; and Monika Anne Schmitter, "The Display of Distinction: Art Collecting and Social Status in Early Sixteenth-Century Venice" (Ph.D. diss., University of Michigan, 1997), 187, for the *cittadino* Andrea Odoni's collection of arms and banners.

70 See Lionello Venturi, *Le compagnie della calza, Sec. XV–XVI* (Venice: Istituto Venetodi Arti Grafiche, 1909; reprint, Venice: Filippi Editore, 1983); and Matteo Casini, *I gesti del principe: la festa politica a Firenze e Venezia in età rinascimentale* (Venice: Marsilio, 1996), 298–306.

71 For knights and chivalric orders in Venice, see Matteo Casini, "Gli ordini cavallereschi a Venezia fra Quattro e Seicento: problemi e ipotesi di ricerca," *Atti dell'Istituto Veneto di Scienze, Lettere ed Arti*, Classe di scienze morali, lettere ed arti, 156 (1997–98):179–99.

72 See A. D. Fraser Jenkins, "Cosimo de' Medici's Patronage of Architecture and the Theory of Magnificence," *Journal of the Warburg and Courtauld Institutes* 33 (1970): 162–70; David Thomson, *Renaissance Architecture: Critics, Patrons, Luxury* (Manchester and New York: Manchester University Press, 1993), 1–28; Guerzoni, "*Liberalitas, magnificentia*, Splendor," 332–78; and Evelyn Welch, "Public Magnificence and Private Display: Giovanni Pontano's *De splendore* (1498) and the Domestic Arts," *Journal of Design History* 15:4 (2002): 211–21.

73 See King, *Venetian Humanism*, 92–201.

74 Antonio Colluraffi da Librizzi, *Il Nobile Veneto* (Venice: Andrea Muschio, 1623). Cf. Muzio, *Il gentilhuomo*, 1–11, who makes essentially the same point.

75 See Peter Burke, *Venice and Amsterdam: A Study of Seventeenth-Century Elites*, 2nd ed. (London: Polity Press, 1994), 11–15, who speaks of three hierarchies within the patriciate: status (antiquity of the family); political power; and wealth. See also James C. Davis, *The Decline of the Venetian Nobility as a Ruling Class* (Baltimore: The Johns Hopkins University Press, 1962); and Giuseppe Trebbi, "La società veneziana," in *Storia di Venezia, VI. Dal Rinascimento al Barocco*, ed. Gaetano Cozzi and Paolo Prodi (Rome: Istituto della Enciclopedia Italiana, 1994), 129–52.

Chapter 2

1 Francesco Sansovino, *Venetia città nobilissima et singolare descritta in XIIII libri*, with additions by Giustiniano Martinioni (Venice: Steffano Curti, 1663; reprint, Venice: "Filippi Editore 1968), 1:381: "i quali noi chiamiamo case per modestia, non havendo nome di Palazzo."

2 Deborah Howard, *The Architectural History of Venice* (New Haven and London: Yale University Press, 2002), 107–9.

3 For an introduction to "home" as a concept, see Witold Rybczynski, *Home: A Short History of an Idea* (New York: Penguin Books, 1987). See also Olivier Marc, *The Psychology of the House* (London: Thames & Hudson, 1977); Fernand Braudel, *The Structures of Everyday Life: The Limits of the Possible* (New York: Harper & Row, 1979), 266–311; David Seamon and Robert Mugeraver, *Dwelling, Place and Environment: Towards a Phenomenology of Person and the World* (Dordrecht, Netherlands: Martinus Nijhoff, 1985); and Clare Cooper Marcus, *House as a Mirror of Self: Exploring the Deeper Meaning of Home* (Berkeley: Conari Press, 1995).

4 Samuele Romanin, *Storia documentata di Venezia* (Venice: Pietro Naratovich tipografo Editore, 1855), III:25–51.

5 As evidenced by a medal recorded by Giovanni Grevembroch in the eighteenth century (BCV, cod. Gradenigo 65, vol. I, c. XXXII), illustrated in Debra Pincus, *The Tombs of the Doges of Venice* (Cambridge: Cambridge University Press, 2000), 83.

6 Romanin, *Storia documentata di Venezia*, III:32: "libertà e morte al doge Gradenigo."

7 Dennis Romano, *Patricians and Popolani* (Baltimore and London: The Johns Hopkins University Press, 1987), 121.

8 Romanin, *Storia documentata di Venezia*, III:38–39. For the church, see Alvise Zorzi, *Venezia Scomparsa*, 2nd ed. (Milan: Electa, 1984), 262–63. For the reliefs, see Alberto Rizzi, *Scultura Esterna a Venezia: Corpus delle Sculture Erratiche all'aperto di Venezia e della sua Laguna* (Venice: Stamperia di Venezia, 1987), 460–61. For the procession, see Edward Muir, *Civic Ritual in Renaissance Venice* (New Brunswick: Rutgers University Press, 1981), 217–18.

9 Vittorio Lazzarini, "Aneddoti della congiura Quirini-Tiepolo," *Nuovo Archivio Veneto* 10:1 (1895): 87–88, citing ASV, Consiglio dei Dieci, Magnus, p. 9: on 22 August 1375, the Dieci reconfirmed the punishment, ordering the Signori di Notte to secure the *porta maggiore* with "good and thick chains of iron immured in the living stone," to make sure that it remained open day and night. If, despite such measures, it should ever be found closed the Balduin would be fined 25 lire each and every time. The order was finally revoked on 27 May 1422: ASV, Consiglio dei Dieci, Misti, Reg. 10, p. 41. The Balduin house was in the parish of SS. Simone e Giudia across the Grand Canal from the church of Santa Lucia (now the site of the railroad station). See also Pompeo Molmenti, *La storia di Venezia nella vita privata dalle origini alla caduta della Repubblica* (Bergamo, 1927–29; reprint, Trieste: Edizioni Lint, 1973), 66–69, and Romanin, *Storia documentata di Venezia*, III:38–40.

10 Molmenti, *Vita privata*, 66: "Di Baiamonte fo questo tereno / e mo per lo so iniquo tradimento / s'è posto in chomun per altrui spavento / e per mostrar a tutti sempre seno." The column is now in the Museo Civico Correr.

11 Ibid., 21–39.

12 Ibid., 460–61.

13 Patricia Fortini Brown, *Venice & Antiquity: The Venetian Sense of the Past* (New Haven and London: Yale University Press, 1996), 21–22.

14 Marin Sanudo, *De origine, situ et magistratibus urbis Venetae ovvero La città di Venetia (1493–1530)*, ed. Angela Caracciolo Aricò (Milan: Cisalpino – La Goliardica, 1980), 20. For an English translation of the first section of this treatise, entitled *Laus urbis Venetae* – originally written in Venetian dialect – from which these passages are

drawn, see David Chambers and Brian Pullan, eds., *Venice: A Documentary History, 1450–1630* (Oxford: Blackwell, 1992), 4–21.

15 Sanudo, *De origine*, 21.

16 Deborah Howard, *Jacopo Sansovino: Architecture and Patronage in Renaissance Venice* (New Haven and London: Yale University Press, 1975), 132–34; Elena Bassi, *Palazzi di Venezia: Admiranda Urbis Venetae* (Venice: Stamperia di Venezia Editrice, 1976), 88; Manuela Morresi, *Jacopo Sansovino* (Milan: Electa, 2000), 118–20.

17 Ennio Concina, *A History of Venetian Architecture*, trans. Judith Landry (Cambridge: Cambridge University Press, 1998), 104–6. See now Fabiola Sartori, ed., *La casa grande dei Foscari in volta de canal* (Venice: La Malcontenta, 2001).

18 Giuseppe Tassini, *Alcuni palazzi ed antichi edificii di Venezia* (Venice: M. Fontana, 1879; reprint, Venice: Filippi Editore, 1993), 60–67; Juergen Schulz, "Byzantine 'Continuity' and Western Romanesque: Secular Architecture," in *Venice: Art & Architecture*, ed. Giandomenico Romanelli (Cologne: Köhnemann, 1997), 80–90; Manfred Schuller, "Le facciate dei palazzi medioevali di Venezia. ricerche su singoli esempi architettonici," in *L'architettura gotica veneziana*, ed. Francesco Valcanover and Wolfgang Wolters (Venice: Istituto Veneto di Scienze, Lettere ed Arti, 2000), 290–304.

19 Richard J. Goy, *The House of Gold: Building a Palace in Medieval Venice* (Cambridge: Cambridge University Press, 1992); Schuller, "Le facciate dei palazzi medioevali di Venezia," 304–19; and Howard, *Architectural History of Venice*, 103–6.

20 Concina, *A History of Venetian Architecture*, 56–67; Howard, *Jacopo Sansovino*, 123–26; idem, *Venice & the East* (New Haven and London: Yale University Press, 2000), 134–40. Cf. Schulz, "Byzantine 'Continuity' and Western Romanesque," 87.

21 Ca' d'Oro, which retained elements from an earlier palace on the site, was an idiosyncratic exception. See Goy, *House of Gold*, 23–57.

22 Pietro Paoletti, *L'architettura e la scultura del rinascimento in Venezia* (Venice: Ongania-Naya, 1893–97), Part 1, 31; Roberta Martinis, "Su un fregio all 'antice. Un'ipotesi per Antonio Lombardo nel palazzo di Andrea Loredan a Venezia," *Arte Veneta* 56 (2000): 17–37.

23 Howard, *Venice & the East* 168–69.

24 See Juergen Schulz, "La critica di fronte al problema dei primi palazzi veneziani," in *L'architettura gotica veneziana*, ed. Francesco Valcanover and Wolfgang Wolters (Venice: Istituto Veneto di Scienze, Lettere ed Arti, 2000), 94–95.

25 Howard, *Venice & the East*, 153–54. For the palace, see Vittorio Sgarbi, *Ca' Dario: mito e storia di Giovanni Dario e del suo Palazzo tra Oriente e Venezia* (Milan: Franco Maria Ricci, 1966); and John McAndrew, *Venetian Architecture of the Early Renaissance* (Cambridge, Mass.: The MIT Press, 1980), 215–21. While the palace boasted a new facade and a Renaissance interior, the rear of the building reveals its Gothic origins.

26 Concina, *A History of Venetian Architecture*, 168; and Loredana Olivato Puppi and Lionello Puppi, *Mauro Codussi* (Milan: Electa, 1977), 203–6. Cf. McAndrew, *Venetian Architecture of the Early Renaissance*, 336–47. See also Manfredo Tafuri, *Ricerca del Rinascimento: i principi, città, architetti* (Turin: Giulio Einaudi Editore, 1992), 306–7, who argues that "Lombardesque" palaces in a variety of forms were accepted because they mediated between traditional Gothic models and a growing taste for more classical forms and a "modern" look. For Vasari's ceiling, see Juergen Schulz, "Vasari at Venice," *The Burlington Magazine* 103 (1961): 507.

27 Tassini, *Alcuni palazzi*, 89–92.

28 Marco Boschini, *Le ricche minere della pittura veneziana* (Venice: F. Nicolini, 1674), Cannaregio, 60; Bassi, *Palazzi di Venezia*, 196–202; Olivato Puppi and Puppi, *Mauro Codussi*, 221–25. As with Ca' Dario, the facade of Ca' Loredan-Vendramin-Calergi also represented an updating of a pre-existing structure: Roberta Martinis, "Ca' Loredan-Vendramin-Calergi a Venezia: Mauro Codussi e il palazzo di Andrea Loredan," *Annali di Architettura* 10–11 (1998–99): 43–61. Cf. McAndrew, *Venetian Architecture of the Early Renaissance*, 348–57.

29 Concina, *A History of Venetian Architecture*, 168–69; Martinis, "Su un fregio all 'antice," 17–24, sees the inscription as a confirmation that the palace is an offering to the city and notes that Loredan referred to it in his will as a gesture in "onor della patria."

30 Brown, *Venice & Antiquity*, 255, 260. Cf. John Onians, "The Last Judgement of Renaissance Architecture," *The Royal Society of Arts Journal* 128 (1980): 708–9, who describes the Latin inscription on Ca' Dario, as well as those on Ca' Malipiero, Ca' Loredan-Vendramin-Calergi, and Ca' Trevisan-Cappello, as "a sort of antidote to pagan ornament" and asserts: "It is worth emphasizing that these inscriptions are not simply here because the buildings are unusually grand or the patrons religious . . . It can only be the classical forms which require defense."

31 Tassini, *Alcuni palazzi*, 274.

32 From Psalms 30.2: Herbert Siebenhüner, *Der Palazzo Barbarigo della Terrazza in Venedig und seine Tizian-Sammlung* (Munich: Deutscher Kunstverlag, 1981), 10.

33 David Thomson, *Renaissance Architecture: Critics, Patrons, Luxury* (Manchester and New York: Manchester University Press, 1993), 161–63.

34 See, in particular, Manfredo Tafuri, *Venice and the Renaissance*, trans. Jessica Levine (Cambridge, Mass., and London: The MIT Press, 1989), Chapter 1. See also, Brown, *Venice & Antiquity*, 277–81.

35 For further discussion, see Brown, *Venice & Antiquity*, 273–84.

36 For Machiavelli's use of the term, see Chapter 1, n. 32.

37 Cassiodorus, *Variarum libri XII*, 12.24.

38 Tafuri, *Venice and the Renaissance*, 2, citing Nicolò Zen, *Storia della guerra veneto-turca del 1537*, BMV, MS. It., cl. 7, 2053 (= 7920).

39 Tafuri, *Venice and the Renaissance*, 3, citing Nicolò Zen, *Dell'origine de' barbari che distrussero per tutto 'l mondo l'imperio di Roma, onde hebbe principio la città di Venetia libri undici* (Venice: Marcolini, 1557), 194–95.

40 Ennio Concina, "Fra Oriente e Occidente: gli Zen, un palazzo e il mito di Trebisonda," in *"Renovatio urbis": Venezia nell'età di Andrea Gritti (1523–1538)*, ed. Manfredo Tafuri (Rome: Officina Edizioni, 1984), 265–90; and idem, *Dell'arabico. A Venezia tra Rinascimento e Oriente* (Venice: Marsilio Editori, 1994). Concina's analysis forms the basis for the discussion that follows.

41 Ibid.; Howard, *Venice & the East*, 146–47, 151.

42 Francesco Valcanover et al., *Pittura murale esterna nel Veneto. Venezia e Provincia* (Bassano: Ghedina & Tassotti Editori, 1981); David McTavish, "Roman Subject-Matter and Style in Venetian Facade Frescoes," *RACAR. Canadian Art Review* 12 (1985): 188–96; Corrado Balistreri-Trincanato and Dario Zanverdiani, *Jacopo de Barbari: Il racconto di una città*, 2nd ed. (Venice: Edizioni Stamperia Cetid, 2000), 25–30; Wolfgang Wolters, *Architektur und Ornament: venezianischer Bauschmuck der Renaissance* (Munich: C. H. Beck, 2000), 73–97.

43 Manfredo Tafuri, "Il pubblico e il privato. Architettura e committenza a Venezia," in *Storia di Venezia. VI. Dal Rinascimento al Barocco*, ed. Gaetano Cozzi and Paolo Prodi (Rome: Istituto della

Enciclopedia Italiana, 1994), 415; and Concina, *A History of Venetian Architecture*, 193.

44 Tafuri, *Ricerca del Rinascimento*, 300–15: They were preceded by Sansovino's attempt to design a palace for Vettor Grimani, also intended for a Grand Canal site, which ended in failure probably because of an uncompromisingly Roman vocabulary that was extraneous to the Venetian mindset.

45 Ibid., 315–27; Howard, *Jacopo Sansovino*, 126–46; Morresi, *Jacopo Sansovino*, 171–82.

46 See n. 20 above.

47 Tafuri, *Ricerca del Rinascimento*, 316–27, 338, defines it as a "hybrid" palace and describes the conflict between Sansovino's belief in the absolute universality of Donato Bramante's interpretation of the antique, and a difficult patron who wanted to be "modern" but also resisted challenges to patrician values of continuity and tradition.

48 Howard, *Jacopo Sansovino*, 126; Morresi, *Jacopo Sansovino*, 118–28; Giandomenico Romanelli, *Ca' Corner della Ca' Granda: Architettura e committenza nella Venezia del Cinquecento* (Venice: Albrizzi Editore, 1993); Tafuri, *Ricerca del Rinascimento*, 328–38. The surnames Corner and Cornaro refer to the same family and were often used interchangeably.

49 Howard, *Jacopo Sansovino*, 139–40.

50 Concina, *A History of Venetian Architecture*, 191.

51 Ibid., citing G. A. Oliva, *Ioanni Cornelio, Praetori Praefectoque Optimo et Humanissimo* (Venice, 1567). Tafuri, *Ricerca del Rinascimento*, 328, sees it as an example of "un superbo trionfalismo." For the Corner family as patrons, see Michel Hochman, *Peintres et commanditaires à Venise (1540–1628)* (Rome: Ecole Française de Rome, 1992), 219–29.

52 For a fine study of the entire tradition, see Daniela Frigo, *Il padre di famiglia. Governo della casa e governo civile nella tradizione dell "economica" tra cinque e seicento* (Rome: Bulzoni Editore, 1985). See also Romano, *Housecraft and Statecraft: Domestic Service in Renaissance Venice, 1400–1600* (Baltimore and London: The John Hopkins University Press, 1996), 3–42.

53 Sebastiano Serlio, *Regole generali di architettura* (Venice, 1537). The first five books were first published in Italian as *Tutte l'opere d'architettura et prospettiva* (Venice, 1584); and in English as *The Five Books of Architecture* (London: Robert Peake, 1611; reprint, New York: Dover Publications, 1982).

54 The original text is available in English translation in Xenophon, *The Estate Manager (Oeconomicus),* in *Conversations of Socrates* (London: Penguin, 1990), 269–359.

55 Alessandro Piccolomini, *Della institutione de la felice vita dell'huomo nato nobile e in città libera* (Venice: Hieronymum Scotum, 1545). See also Donati, *L'idea di nobiltà, secoli XIV–XVIII* (Rome and Bari: Editori Laterza, 1995), 60–61; and Mary Rogers, "An Ideal Wife at the Villa Maser: Veronese, the Barbaros and Renaissance Theorists of Marriage," *Renaissance Studies* 7:4 (1993): 385.

56 Frigo, *Il padre di famiglia*, Chapter 4.

57 See n. 20 above.

58 See Chapter 3, n. 31.

59 Sebastiano Serlio, *Sebastiano Serlio on domestic architecture; different dwellings from the meanest hovel to the most ornate palace. The Sixteenth-Century Manuscript of Book VI in the Avery Library of Columbia University*, ed. Myra Nan Rosenfeld (New York: Architectural History Foundation, 1978), 41–42.

60 Giovanni Maria Memmo, *Dialogo del Magn. Cavaliere M. Gio. Maria Memmo* (Venice: Gabriel Giolito de' Ferrari, 1563), 79, 81: "et sia ornato et fornito esso palagio secondo la conditione del patrono, et uso della Città."

61 Bassi, *Palazzi di Venezia*, 146–53; Lionello Puppi, *Michele Sanmicheli architetto: opera completa* (Rome: Caliban, 1986), 131–37; Deborah Howard, "Exterior Orders in Interior Planning in Sansovino and Sanmicheli," in *L'Emploi des ordres*, ed. Jean Guillaume (Paris: Picard, 1992), 183–92.

62 Sansovino, *Venetia città nobilissima* (1663), 1:384–85.

63 Ibid., 382: "Si legge che ne primi tempi, volendo i nostri mostrare unione & parità in tutte le cose loro, edificarono in virtù della legge Daula, le case tutte uguali in altezza. Ma cresciute poi le ricchezze per la mercatura che fu sempre il nervo di questa Republica, s'alzarono, & abbassarono secondo l'appetito de i fabricanti."

64 Ibid.: "palazzi & casamenti di molta grandezza." See also Thomson, *Renaissance Architecture*, 159–63.

65 Ibid., 387: "accennando à forestieri una parte, per la quale desiderosi di vedere ogni cosa, ricerchino il tutto" (in a section entitled "Palazzi" on pp. 385–89). In addition, one palace, Ca' d'Anna, formerly Talenti, was cited on p. 212 in relation to the church of Sant'Elena.

66 Ibid., 387–88: "di gran corpo, & di grand'altezza, & anteriore in tempo à gli altri, & quasi posto in isola è molto nobile, percioche oltre alla copia delle stanze di dentro, ha la faccia coperta di marmi Grechi, con gran finestroni tutti colonnati alla corinthia."

67 Ibid., 388: "che l'eccede di gran lunga di stanze reali, & d'ogni altra cosa, è ricchissimo di fatture, percioche gli intagli, i fogliami, & l'altre dilicature quasi fatte per fino alle fondamenta, sono con spesa eccessiva."

68 Ibid., 388: "primo dopò il Loredano, che fosse fabricato in Venetia con regole d'architettura, è degno di lode. Percioche occupando gran spatio di terreno, col cortile nel mezzo circondato di Loggie all'usanza Romana, è di fuori con bene intesa faccia, & di dentro ha larghissime & commode stanze."

69 Ibid., 388: "per sito, per magnificenza, per capacità, per ricchezze di pietre, per struttura, & per simmetria, e fra tutti gli altri memorando. . . . Et scuopre & è scoperto all'intorno per l'altezza sua, le Lagune. . . . apparisce a riguardanti piena di maestà."

70 Ibid., 388: "Ma tutti questi quattro, trapassa per sito, & per grandezza di machina, il Palazzo Foscaro, antico per fabrica & secondo l'uso Tedesco."

71 Ibid., 388: "antico, & fabricato in forma di castello con struttura Tedesca." See also Juergen Schulz, "The Restoration of the Fondaco dei Turchi," *Annali di architettura* 7 (1995): 19–38; and Howard, *Architectural History of Venice*, 31–4.

72 Sansovino, *Venetia città nobilissima* (1663 ed.), 1:389: "di maniera Tedesca, ma con forma durabile & soda."

73 Boschini, *Le ricche minere*, San Marco, 83–84: vi sono dipinti, di mano di Giorgione, molti fregi di chiaro oscuro, di rosso in rosso, di giallo in giallo, e di verde in verde, con varij capriccj de Puttini, nel mezo de' quali, vi sono dipinte quattro meze figure, cioè Bacco, Venere, marte, e Mercurio, coloriti al naturale.

74 Valcanover, *Pittura murale esterna*, 35, cat. 3; Boschini, *Le ricche minere*, Cannaregio, 55.

75 Cited in Mark W. Roskill, *Dolce's "Aretino" and Venetian Art Theory of the Cinquecento* (New York: New York University Press, 1968), 115.

76 Paul Hills, *Venetian Colour: Marble, Mosaic, Painting and Glass 1250–1550* (New Haven and London: Yale University Press, 1999), 68–79.

77 [Francesco Sansovino], *Delle cose notabili della città di Venetia. Libri II Ne' quali amplamente, e con ogni verità si contengono . . .* (Venice:

Heredi di Luigi Valvassori & Gio. Domenico Micheli, 1583), 71, which lists twenty palaces and one garden. It was originally published under the pseudonym of Anselmo Guisconi as *Tutte le cose notabili e belle che sono a Venezia* (Venice: 1556), with many later reprintings. See also Giuseppe Tassini, *Alcuni palazzi ed antichi edificii di Venezia* (Venice, 1879; reprint, Venice: Filippi Editore, 1993), 102–4.

78 Valcanover, *Pittura murale esterna*, 35, cat. 2; and Boschini, *Le ricche minere*, Cannaregio, 55.

79 Sebastiano Serlio, *Sebastiano Serlio on Architecture: Books I–V of Tutte l'opere d'architettura et prospettiva*, trans. Vaughan Hart and Peter Hicks (New Haven and London: Yale University Press, 1996), 378. For a penetrating analysis of Serlio's approach, see Wolters, *Architektur und Ornament*, 80–83.

80 Giorgio Vasari, *Le vite de più eccellenti pittori, scultori ed architettori*, ed. Gaetano Milanesi (Florence, 1906), v:115: "siccome é anco un Mercurio che vola in aria per ogni lato." For this program, see Charles E. Cohen, *The Art of Giovanni Antonio da Pordenone: Between Dialect and Language* (Cambridge: Cambridge University Press, 1996), I:392–99 and II:709–14 (cat. 79); and Blake de Maria, "The Merchants of Venice: A Study in Sixteenth-Century *Cittadino* Patronage" (Ph.D. diss., Princeton University, 2002), 68–83.

81 Serlio, *Sebastiano Serlio on Architecture*, 378.

82 Wolters, *Architektur und Ornament*, 84–85; Valcanover, *Pittura murale esterna* (as for 78), 54–55; and Bassi, *Palazzi di Venezia*, 528–43.

83 Serlio, *Sebastiano Serlio on domestic architecture* (1978), 30.

84 For wells and cisterns, see Giorgio Gianighian and Paola Pavanini, "Il tessuto gotico," in *L'architettura gotica veneziana*, ed. Francesco Valcanover and Wolfgang Wolters (Venice: Istituto Veneto di Scienze, Lettere ed Arti, 2000), 157–73. For Venetian gardens, see Gino Damerini, *Giardini di Venezia* (Bologna: Zanichelli, 1931); and Cristiana Moldi-Ravenna and Tudy Sammartini, *Secret Gardens in Venice* (Venice: Arsenale Editrice, 1996), the latter with beautiful photographs of Venetian gardens today.

85 Sansovino, *Venetia città nobilissima* (1663), I:369.

86 See Balistreri-Trincanato and Zanverdiani, *Jacopo de Barbari*, 165–70, 231–40; and Barbara Lynn-Davis, "*Landscapes of the Imagination in Renaissance Venice.*" (Ph.D. diss., Princeton University, 1998), 8–75.

87 Memmo, *Dialogo*, 80–81: "cerchi di havere una corte grande & spatiosa, & un bel giardino ornato di vari & delicati f rutti, herbe, & fiori di molte sorti, qualità & odori: perche stando il Cittadino una gran parte della vita sua nel palagio, di non poco giovamento & ricreatione gli saranno cotai cose, & massimamenta dilettandosi dell'agricoltura tanto locata, aprezzata, & usata da i saggi antiche: il giardino, la loggia, & la corte gli levaranno una gran parte de i pensieri, & delle noie, che apportano seco i negotij humani. Et dilettandosi de gli studi delle buone lettere, troverà una infinita ricreatione ogni fiata, che stanco dallo studio entrerà nel giardino, & con un coletellino in mano anderà scegliendo qualche odorifero & delicato fiore; coglierà una insalatuccia di sua propria mano, torrà un maturo frutto: & stando in tal diporti & ricreatione, farà altissimi & divine concetti: de' quali poi ritornando allo studio riempierà le dotte & honorate carte."

88 See Anthony Kurnata, "The Palazzo Loredan in the Campo Santo Stefano: Counter-Currents in Sixteenth Century Venetian Architecture" (Ph.D. diss., Boston University, 1976); Bassi, *Palazzi di Venezia*, 255–57.

Chapter 3

1 Mary Margaret Newett, ed., *Canon Pietro Casola's Pilgrimage to Jerusalem in the Year 1494* (Manchester: Manchester University Press, 1907), 129.

2 Sebastiano Serlio, *Il trattato di Architettura di Sebastiano Serlio. Sesto libro delle habitationi di tutti li gradi degli homeni*, with a commentary by Marco Rosci (Milan: I.T.E.C. Editore, 1966) 51v.

3 See Paolo Maretto, *L'edilizia gotica veneziana* (Venice: Filippi Editore, 1978), 80–81.

4 Bruce Boucher, *The Sculpture of Jacopo Sansovino*, 2 vols. (New Haven and London: Yale University Press, 1991), II:373, cat. 121, rejects the traditional attribution to Sansovino himself.

5 Andrea Bacchi, Lia Camerlengo, and Manfred Leithe-Jasper, eds., *"La bellissima maniera." Alessandro Vittoria e la scultura veneta del Cinquecento* (Trento: Castello del Buonconsiglio, Monumenti e Collezioni Provinciali, 1999), 350–51, cat. 77, attributes the work simply to a Venetian sculptor. However, Victoria Avery, "The Early Works of Alessandro Vittoria (ca.1540–ca.1570)" (Ph.D. diss., University of Cambridge, 1996), 523–26, makes a convincing argument for Vittoria.

6 Bacchi, Camerlengo, and Leithe-Jasper, eds., *"La bellissima maniera."* 350. See also Carlo Pedretti, *Leonardo: A Study in Chronology and Style* (New York and London: Harcourt Brace Jovanovich Publishers, 1982), 96 (fig. 24); and Carmen C. Bambach, *Leonardo da Vinci, Master Draftsman* (New York: The Metropolitan Museum of Art; and New Haven and London: Yale University Press, 2003), cat. 93, 512–15.

7 BCV, MS. Gradenigo 7, with watercolor copies by the Flemish artist Jan Grevembroch of eleven examples that existed in Venice at the end of the eighteenth century.

8 Paul Williamson, ed., *European Sculpture at the Victoria & Albert Museum* (London: Victoria & Albert Museum, 1996).

9 Richard J. Goy, *Venetian Vernacular Architecture: Traditional Housing in the Venetian Lagoon* (Cambridge: Cambridge University Press, 1989), 75–79; Peter Lauritzen and Alexander Zielcke, *Palaces of Venice* (London: Dorset Press, 1985), 121–22.

10 See Gaetano Cozzi, "Authority and the Law in Renaissance Venice," in *Renaissance Venice*, ed. J. R. Hale (London: Faber & Faber, 1973), 293–345.

11 See Chapter 2 above.

12 From the cinquecento onwards, many cisterns and well-heads were inside the *androne* on the ground floor rather than in open courtyards. See Giorgio Gianighian and Paola Pavanini, "Il tessuto gotico," in *L'architettura gotica veneziana*, ed. Wolfgang Wolters and Francesco Valcanover (Venice: Istituto Veneto di Scienze, Lettere ed Arti, 2000); and Corrado Balistreri-Trincanato and Dario Zanverdiani, *Jacopo de Barbari: Il racconto di una città*, 2nd ed. (Venice; Edizioni Stamperia Cetid, 2000), 285–90.

13 Giovanni Maria Memmo, *Dialogo del Magn. Cavaliere M. Gio. Maria Memmo* (Venice: Gabriel Giolito de' Ferrari, 1563), 80: "Et faccia oltra de questo che sopra ogni altra cosa sia abondante il suo palagio di dolce, chiare, & fresche acque, o per via di fontane, overo di cisterne."

14 Wolfgang Wolters, *La scultura veneziana gotica, 1300–1460* (Venice: Alfieri, 1976), 280–81, cat. 238, dated 1428. See also Richard Goy, *The House of Gold: Building a Palace in Medieval Venice* (Cambridge: Cambridge University Press, 1992), 133–36.

15 Francesco Sansovino, *Venetia città nobilissima et singolare descritta in*

XIIII libri, with additions by Giustiniano Martinioni (Venice: Steffano Curti, 1663; reprint, Venice; Filippi Editore 1968), 1:386 [1581 ed., c. 143r–v]: "con diverse bellezze, di ritratti & figure, di marmo, & di stucco, d'Alessandro Vittoria."

16 Pliny, *Natural History*, xxxv.ii.8, 6, cited by Douglas Lewis, "An Early Series of Dynastic Portrait Busts by Alessandro Vittoria," *Artibus et historiae* 35 [XVIII] (1997): 113.

17 Lewis, "An Early Series of Dynastic Portrait Busts," 113–34, who identifies these figures as, respectively, Alvise Zorzi and his wife Cristina (a very distant cousin and also a Zorzi by birth), and Cristina's parents, Antonio Zorzi (1504–65) and Angela Loredan. He attributes all four works to Alessandro Vittoria. For a different view, see Thomas Martin, *Alessandro Vittoria and the Portrait Bust in Renaissance Venice: Remodelling Antiquity* (Oxford: Clarendon Press, 1998), 127–29, 150–51, who offers a later dating and rejects Vittoria's authorship of the female bust in Washington. The bust of Antonio Zorzi, attributed to the workshop by Martin, was placed above his tomb in the Church of San Stefano in 1588. The other three busts were recorded in Palazzo Zorzi (later Carregiani) in 1854: Martin, *Alessandro Vittoria*, 127–29.

18 For this concept, see Patricia Fortini Brown, *Venice & Antiquity: The Venetian Sense of the Past* (New Haven and London: Yale University Press, 1996).

19 See Caterina Chiminelli, "Le scale scoperte nei palazzi veneziani," *Ateneo Veneto* 39:1 (1912): 209–53.

20 Samuel Putnam, *The Works of Aretino* (Chicago: Pascal Covici, 1926) II:180, Letter LXXX: To Messer Domenico Bolani.

21 Elena Bassi, *Palazzi di Venezia* (Venice: Stamperia di Venezia Editrice, 1976), 196–203.

22 For a summary of interior plans in the Gothic period, see Deborah Howard, *The Architectural History of Venice*, rev. ed. (London and New Haven: Yale University Press, 2002), 96–110; Goy, *Venetian Vernacular Architecture*, 121–71; and Edoardo Arslan, *Gothic Architecture in Venice*, trans. Anne Engel (London: Phaidon, 1971). For a fine general view of life in the home in this period, see Raffaella Sarti, *Europe at Home: Family and Material Culture, 1500–1800*, trans. Allan Cameron (New Haven and London: Yale University Press, 2002).

23 See Balistreri-Trincanato and Zanverdiani, *Jacopo de Barbari*, 185–96; Corrado Balistreri-Trincanato, *Case veneziane a loggia*, 2nd ed. (Venice: Cluva Università, 1988). It is equivalent, in a sense, to the English long gallery and French *gallerie*: Rosalys Coope, "The 'Long Gallery': Its Origins, Development, Use, and Decoration," *Architectural History* 29 (1986): 45–84.

24 James C. Davis, *The Decline of the Venetian Nobility as a Ruling Class* (Baltimore: The Johns Hopkins Press, 1962), 26. See also F. C. Lane, "Family Partnerships and Joint Ventures in the Venetian Republic," *Journal of Economic History* 4, 1944:2, 178–96.

25 See Vincenzo Scamozzi, *Dell'idea della architettura universale* (Venice, 1615), 243. For a specific example of shared living arrangements, see Fabiola Sartori, ed., *La casa grande dei Foscari in volta de canal* (Venice: La Malcontenta, 2001).

26 I owe this insight to Deborah Howard. For apartments and room layouts in general, see Peter Thornton, *The Italian Renaissance Interior 1400–1600* (London: Weidenfeld and Nicolson, 1991), 284–300; Jean Guillaume, ed., *Architecture et vie sociale: L'organisation intérieure des grandes demeures a la fin du moyen age et a la renaissance* (Paris: Picard, 1994).

27 It should also be kept in mind that inventories show that about 40 percent of the homes of artisans consisted of no more than two or three rooms, and this was true for a number of patricians as well: Isabella Palumbo-Fossati, "L'interno della casa dell'artigiano e dell'artista nella Venezia del Cinquecento," *Studi veneziani*, n.s. 8 (1984): 109–53.

28 Sir Henry Wotton, *The Elements of Architecture: A Facsimile Reprint of the First Edition (London 1624). With Introduction and Notes by Frederich Hard* (Charlottesville: The University Press of Virginia, published for the Folger Shakespeare Library, 1968), 73–74.

29 Andrea Palladio, *The Four Books of Architecture* (New York: Dover Publications, 1965), 38: Book II, Chapter II.

30 Obviously there were no inventories for the abject poor, although many of the lists have very few items indeed. Several inventories were published by Pompeo Molmenti, the first scholar to look at them analytically, in his groundbreaking study, *La Storia di Venezia nella vita privata dalle origini alla caduta della Repubblica*, first published in 1880 and expanded to three volumes in six subsequent editions. The first three editions were published in one volume. A second revised and expanded edition was published immediately in 1880, and a third in 1885. The book was expanded to three volumes in the fourth edition of 1905–8, which were presumably the basis for the English translation: Pompeo Molmenti, *Venice: Its Individual Growth from the Earliest Beginnings to the Fall of the Republic*, trans. Horatio F. Brown (Chicago: A. C. McClurg & Co., 1907). The work was again expanded and revised in three more editions. The final and seventh edition was published in Bergamo, 1927–29, and reprinted in Trieste: Edizioni Lint, 1973. Another important early study is Cesare Augusto Levi, *Le collezioni veneziane d'arte e d'antichità dal secolo XIV ai giorni nostri*, 2 vols. (Venice: F. Organia, 1906).

More recently, a major contribution was made by Isabella Palumbo-Fossati, "L'interno della casa dell'artigiano e dell'artista," cited in n. 27 above. Also valuable are idem, "Il collezionista Sebastiano Erizzo e l'inventario dei suoi beni." *Ateneo Veneto* 171:22, nos. 1/2 (1984): 201–18; idem, "Livres et lecteurs dans la Venise du XVIe siecle." *Revue francaise d'histoire du livre*, 54, n.s., no. 49 (1985): 481–513; idem, "La casa veneziana di Gioseffo Zarlino nel testamento e nell'inventario dei beni del grande teorico musicale." *Nuova Rivista Musicale Italiana*, 20:4 (1986): 633–49; Dora Thornton, *The Scholar in his Study* (New Haven and London: Yale University Press, 1997); and Wilfrid Brulez, *Marchands Flamands a Venise I (1568–1605)* (Brussels and Rome: Institut Historique Belge de Rome, 1965). For the seventeenth century, see Greta Devos and Wilfrid Brulez, *Marchands Flamands à Venise II (1606–1621)* (Brussels and Rome: Institut Historique Belge de Rome, 1986); and Simona Savini Branca, *Il collezionismo veneziano nel '600* (Padua: CEDAM, 1965).

31 Oddly, Serlio's Book VI is the only one in his treatise that was not published in the sixteenth century, although it had demonstrable influence in palace planning. Two manuscripts, as well as a set of printer's proofs of woodblock illustrations for a third version, survive. The earliest manuscript, made on paper from 1541 to 1549 by Serlio, is in the Avery Library of Columbia University, New York. It was published in facscimile in Sebastiano Serlio, *Sebastiano Serlio on domestic architecture; different dwellings from the meanest hovel to the most ornate palace. The Sixteenth-Century Manuscript of Book VI in the Avery Library of Columbia University*, ed. Myra Nan Rosenfeld (New York: Architectural History Foundation, 1978). This edition was republished with a valuable new preface that updates the scholarship, including Serlio's plates but not his text, as

Sebastiano Serlio, *Sebastiano Serlio on Domestic Architecture*, ed. Myra Nan Rosenfeld (Mineola: Dover Publications, Inc., 1996). A second revised version on parchment, made between 1547 and 1550, is in the Bayerische Staatsbibliothek in Munich (Codex Icon. 189). It was sold to Jacopo Strada and was known in Venice during the sixteenth century; Serlio, *Sebastiana Serlio on Domestic Architecture* (1996), 1–4. Proofs of the woodblocks for the third version (ca.1551–53) are in the Osterreichische Nationalbibliothek in Vienna (72P.20).

32 Serlio, *Sebastiano Serlio on domestic architecture* (1978 ed.), Plate LVI and text: "la maggior parte degli ornamenti delle case di questa città sono licenciosi: at anche le cose disordinate."

33 Bayerische Staatsbibliothek, Munich: Codex Icon. 189, Sebastiano Serlio, *Sesto libro delle habitationi di tutti li gradi degli homeni*, Project XV, ff. 51V-53. Cf. the earlier version in Serlio, *Sebastiano Serlio on Domestic Architecture* (1978 ed.), Plates LII–LII. Most notably, Serlio added an additional staircase from the ground floor that entered the portico where it joined the loggia in front. He also reduced the width of the large courtyard on each side to accommodate a "loggietta segreta" (G) between it and the outside wall. A terrace was added above the loggietta.

34 Serlio, *Il trattato di Architettura di Sebastiano Serlio* (Rosci ed., 1966), fol. 51V. For the analysis that follows, see also Marco Rosci's commentary in the companion volume to the facscimile, 80–81 (for which an English translation by Vaughan Hart and Peter Hicks is available on www.serlio.org).

35 Ibid.

36 Serlio, *Sebastiano Serlio on domestic architecture* (1978 ed.), text to Plan LII. He omits this information in the text to the Munich manuscript, but presumably the room would have had the same function.

37 Vincenzo Scamozzi, *Dell'idea della archittetura universale* (Venice: expensis auctoris, 1615), 307: "qui in Venetia usano certe stanze ammezate, le quali chiamansi sopraletti; accioche ad'un tratto si possono vedere, e dare gli ordini mentre, che sono sani, e sumministrare a' loro bisogni quando fussero amalati."

38 Serlio, *Il trattato di Architettura di Sebastiano Serlio* (Rosci ed., 1966), f. 51V: "si potra farne stua et bagno da basso." Kitchens seem to have had no standard location in Venetian homes in this period, and were even moved around from one generation to another. Designated rooms with huge fireplaces, common elsewhere in Europe in the period, were rare in Venice, and this may be related to the apparent lack of interest in cooking and everyday hospitality noted by Thomas Coryat and other visitors to the city. I am grateful to Deborah Howard, who notes as well that bathrooms also seem to have been unimportant, for this observation. Sartori, *La casa grande dei Foscari*, 49: in Ca' Foscari in 1520, there was a kitchen on each of the two *piani nobili*, which was entered directly from the *portego*. See also p. 43 below.

39 Ibid.: "uno andito segreto pel quale si passa di camera in camera senza passar per lo portico."

40 Ibid.: "In questa per non esser veduta da nessun lato stavano le figlie."

41 Ibid.: "Sopra questa et landito segreto sara uno tervazzo scoperto cosa molto commoda in queste case."

42 Scamozzi, *Architettura*, 307: "Le stanza coniugali . . . deono esser tra l'uno, e l'altro appartamento, come parte, che unisce insieme tutto il corpo; quelle de' figliuolini siano vicine à quelle delle madri di famiglia."

43 Giacomo Lanteri, *Della Economica. Trattato di m. Giacomo Lanteri gentilhuomo bresciano, nel quale si dimostrano le qualità, che all'uomo et alla donna separatamente convengono pel governo della casa* (Venice: Valgrisi, 1560), 102–3: "senza passare pel rimanente della casa, ove possano esser vedute." A document of 1520, referring to the lower *piano nobile* of Ca' Foscari, cites "tuti quelli loci in liquali se va per via la cusina de questo soler zoè camera da femene, salvarobba, luogo da buratar, caneva, luogo da lesiva . . .": Sartori, *La casa grande dei Foscari*, 47.

44 See Thornton, *Italian Renaissance Interior*, 284. For Florentine palaces and their use, see Brenda Preyer, "Planning for Visitors at Florentine Palaces," *Renaissance Studies* 12:3 (1998): 357–74. For Rome, see Elizabeth S. Cohen and Thomas V. Cohen, "Open and Shut: The Social Meanings of the Cinquecento Roman House," *Studies in the Decorative Arts* 9 (2001–2): 61–84.

45 ASV, Giudici del Proprio, Mobili, R. 66 (4 November 1582).

46 ASV, Dieci Savi alle Decime, Redecima 1582, B. 157, n. 277.

47 ASV, Notarile Testamenti (Girolamo Savina), B. 896, no. 38: Donado da Lezze q. Michele (2 October 1582).

48 Ibid. The inclusion of the daughters in the property division was not typical in Venice, and might be accounted for here by their very young age. Once they were of marriageable age they would usually be given their share of the family's patrimony in the form of a dowry, either for a marriage or entrance into a nunnery.

49 ASV, Cancelleria Inferiore, Miscellanea Notai Diversi, B. 42, no. 66: Donado da Lezze q. Michael (19 October 1582). For servant-keeping practices, see Dennis Romano, *Housecraft and Statecraft: Domestic Service in Renaissance Venice, 1400–1600* (Baltimore and London: Johns Hopkins University Press, 1996).

50 Jean Habert, *Une dame vénitienne dite la Belle Nani* (Paris: Musée du Louvre, 1996), makes a convincing case on the basis of portrait conventions, dress, and gesture that the work represents a respectable married woman, although not necessarily a member of the Nani family.

51 Sansovino, *Venetia città nobilissima* (1663), I:383: "in ben culta & polita Chiesa di Suore" and "lo homo può specchiarvisi dentro."

52 Scamozzi, *Architettura*, 243: "La pulitezza delle case de' Nobili, che non hà altretanto il mondo . . . I terrazzi nelle case si nettano ogni tratto dalle serve; di modo che paiono pietre lustre."

53 Paul Hills, *Venetian Colour: Marble, Mosaic, Painting and Glass 1250–1550* (New Haven and London: Yale University Press, 1999), 80–81: *Paston* (also known as *pastellon*) is a rusty red compound of crushed brick and lime with cinnabar added to an upper layer for color. Sanded smooth, it is finished with linseed oil and has a shiny surface. It may still be seen in Ca' Goldoni, birthplace of the famous Venetian playwright and now a public museum, library, and theater-studies center. *Terrazzo* floors, with chips of colored marble sprinkled into the bed of ground brick and lime, came into vogue by the end of the fifteenth century. See also Tudy Sammartini with Antonio Crovato, *Pavimenti a Venezia: The Floors of Venice* (Ponzano: Vianello Libri, 1999).

54 See Wolfgang Wolters, *Architektur und Ornament*: Venezianischer Bauschmuck der Renaissance (Munich: C. H. Bech, 2000), 237, Plate 225, for a surviving ceiling with papered beams.

55 Juergen Schulz, *Venetian Painted Ceilings of the Renaissance* (Berkeley and Los Angeles: University of California Press, 1968), 117–23, 142; and idem, "Vasari at Venice," *The Burlington Magazine* 103 (1961): 500–10.

56 Simone Chiarugi, in the scholarly catalogue of the Bagatti

Valsecchi Museum collections to be published by Electa, hypothesizes that the Milan chair essentially dates to the fifteenth century, but with heavy restorations made in the nineteenth century. For example, the pivot pins and the seat were remade, and some of the carving on the legs is freshly incised on top of the abrasions and worn surfaces.

57 ASV, Cancelleria Inferiore, Miscellanea Notai Diversi, B. 42, no. 66, ff 9 and 11v.

58 Scamozzi, *Architettura*, 243: "per poter ricevere i parentadi nel tempo delle nozze, e far conviti, e feste."

59 Marin Sanudo, *I diarii*, ed. Rinaldo Fulin et al (Venice: F. Visentini, 1879–1903): 22:346 (6 July 1516); cf. ibid., 28:135; and 37:415. The side of the palace, with frescoes, is visible in the left background of Gentile Bellini's *Miracle of the True Cross at the Bridge of San Lorenzo* (Venice, Accademia).

60 See Chapter 1 above; and Juergen Schulz,"The Houses of Titian, Aretino, and Sansovino," in *Titian: His World and His Legacy*, ed. David Rosand (New York: Columbia University Press, 1982), 89. The Da Lezze had a few such trophies as well as a sword, a Turkish bow, and an arquebus – but stored them in the chamber on the upper floor overlooking the *campo*. For the *portego* in general, see Palumbo-Fossati, "L'interno della casa dell'artigiano e dell'artista," 138–40.

61 Manfredo Tafuri, "Il pubblico e il privato. Architettura e committenza a Venezia," in *Storia di Venezia. VI. Dal Rinascimento al Barocco*, ed. Gaetano Cozzi and Paolo Prodi (Rome: Istituto della Enciclopedia Italiana, 1994), 367–70. See also n. 23 above.

62 Sansovino, *Venetia città nobilissima* (1663), 1:384: "si mettono le finestre della Sala nel mezzo della facciata, onde si comprende con facilità da i riguardanti, dove sia posta la Sala."

63 For a meticulous examination of this unusual piece, and observations on the Islamic sources for its design, see Anna Contadini, "Due pannelli di cuoio dorato nel Museo Civico Medievale di Bologna," *Annali di Ca' Foscari* 27:3 (1988): 127–42; and idem, "'Cuoridoro': tecnica e decorazione di cuoi dorati veneziani e italiani con influssi islamici," in *Venezia e l'Oriente Vicino*, ed. Ernst J. Grube (Venice: Edizioni l'Altra Riva, 1989).

64 Newett, *Canon Pietro Casola's Pilgrimage*, 339–40.

65 Ibid. Sartori, *La casa grande dei Foscari*, 49, refers to the completion of a new *camera* on the upper *piano nobile* with a "nappa letiera et altri adornamenti necessarii segondo è sta' facto el marchato."

66 See nn. 36–37 above.

67 Lionardo di Niccolò Frescobaldi in *Visit to the Holy Places of Egypt, Sinai, Palestine and Syria in 1384 by Frescobaldi, Gucci & Sigoli*, trans. Theophilus Bellorini and Eugene Hoade, Publications of the Studium Biblicum Franciscanum, no. 6 (Jerusalem, 1948), 33–34. I am grateful to Rosamond Mack for this reference.

68 Philippe de Commynes, *The Memoirs of Philippe de Commynes*, ed. Samuel Kinser (Columbia, SC: University off South Carolina Press, 1969–73), 11:490. Commynes stayed in Venice for about nine months (2 October 1494–31 May 1495).

69 Marcantonio Sabellico, *Del sito di Venezia Città (1502)*, ed. G. Meneghetti (Venice: Libreria Filippi Editrice, 1985), 32: "Niuna nuova casa si vede che non abbia dorate stanze et poco gli mancava che non si coprissero d'oro le case, se alla lussuria non provvedevano le leggi."

70 See Sansovino, *Venetia città nobilissima* (1663), 1:386.

71 ASV, Cancelleria Inferiore, Miscellanea Notai Diversi, B. 42, no. 66.

72 Palumbo-Fossati, "L'interno della casa dell'artigiano e dell'artista," 142.

73 ASV, Cancelleria Inferiore, Miscellanea Notai Diversi, B. 42, no. 66, 6v–8r. For Carpaccio's *Dream of St. Ursula* (fig. 87), see Sandra Moschini Marconi, *Gallerie dell'Accademia di Venezia. Opere d'arte del secolo XIV e XV* (Rome: Istituto Poligrafico dello Stato, 1995), 97–98, 103.

74 ASV, Cancellaria Inferiore, Miscellanea Notai Diversi, B. 42, no. 66, 12–13.

75 Ibid., f. 13v: "Una banca da predica con le sue banche attorno attorno." Although a "banca da predica" might signify a *prie-dieu*, a piece of furniture for individual prayer would not be accompanied by additional seating!

76 See Brown, *Venice & Antiquity*, 62–64. For the iconography of the virtues, see *Lexikon der Christlichen Ikonographie*, ed. Engelbert Kirschbaum (Rome: Herder, 1968), 4:364–80. For Prudence, see G. F. Hartlaub, *Zauber des Spiegels: Geschichte und Bedeutung des Spiegels in der Kunst* (Munich: R. Piper, 1951), 158–62; and Heinrich Schwarz, "The Mirror in Art," *Art Quarterly* 15 (1952): 104–5.

77 However, cf. Rona Goffen, *Giovanni Bellini* (New Haven and London: Yale University Press, 1989), 226–37, for Bellini's idiosyncratic group of four allegories from a *restello*, now in the Accademia Galleries. For *restelli*, see Chapter 4 below.

78 For Justice as a personification of Venice, see David Rosand, *Myths of Venice: The Figuration of a State* (Chapel Hill & London: University of North Carolina Press, 2001), 26–36 and passim.

79 As observed by Sandra Olivieri Secchi, "Il *De Nobilitate* di Sebastiano Venier una teoria per un modello," in *Non uno itinere. Studi storici offerti dagli allievi a Federico Seneca* (Venice: Stamperia di Venezia, 1993).

80 Thornton, *The Italian Renaissance Interior*, 288–90. See also Scamozzi, *Architettura*, 243.

81 Cited by Molmenti, *Vita privata*, 2:486. See Hills, *Venetian Colour*, 173–200; and Doretta Davanzo Poli and Stefania Moronato, *Le stoffe dei veneziani* (Venice: Albrizzi Editori, 1994).

82 ASV, Cancelleria Inferiore, Misecellanea Notai Diversi, B. 35, no. 4: Nicolo Duodo (1530–33): 1v.

83 ASV, Cancelleria Inferiore, Miscellanea Notai Diversi, B. 35, no. 27: Domenico Cappello (1532).

84 Wolters, *Architektur und Ornament*, 134; Goy, *Venetian Vernacular Architecture*, 216–27.

85 ASV, Cancelleria Inferiore, Miscellanea Notai Diversi, B.39, n. 59, f. 22: Piero Gritti q. Marco de Confinio San Salvador (March 1557).

86 Ibid., f. 9: "zambelotto pavonazo fodra de dossi."

87 Ibid. For oriental carpets as table coverings, see Patricia H. Labalme and Laura Sanguineti White, with translations by Linda Carroll, "How to (and How Not to) Get Married in Sixteenth-Century Venice," *Renaissance Quarterly* 52 (1999): 62–63 n. 58. For carpets in general, see Rosamond E. Mack, *Bazaar to Piazza: Islamic Trade and Italian Art, 1300–1600* (Berkeley: University of California Press, 2002), 73–93; Charles Grant Ellis, *Oriental Carpets in the Philadelphia Museum of Art* (Philadelphia: Philadelphia Museum of Art, 1988); Giovanni Curatola, "Tessuti e artigianato turco nel mercato veneziano," in *Venezia e i turchi: Scontri e confronti di due civiltà* (Milan: Electa, 1985), 186–95. For metal work see Chapter 4, n. 55.

88 ASV, Cancelleria Inferiore, Miscellanea Notai Diversi, B.39, n. 59.

89 Sansovino, *Venetia città nobilissima* (1663), 1:384: "secondo le stagioni de i tempi."

90 ASV, Cancelleria Inferiore, Miscellanea Notai Diversi, B. 42, no. 66: Donado da Lezze q. Michael (19 October 1582); ASV, Archivio di Proprio, Mobili, R. 66 (4 November 1582).

91 Sanudo, *Diarii*, 6:307 (5 March 1506). For mercers, see Richard

Mackenney, *Traders and Tradesmen: The World of the Guilds in Venice and Europe, ca.1250–ca.1650* (Totowa: Barnes & Noble Books, 1987), 90–110.

92 Patricia Anne Allerston, "The Market in Second-Hand Clothes and Furnishings in Venice, ca. 1500–ca. 1650" (Ph.D. diss., Florence: European University Institute, Department of History and Civilization, 1996), 217–19; Edward Muir, *Civic Ritual in Renaissance Venice* (Princeton: Princeton University Press, 1981), 119–34; Bianca Tamassia Mazzarotto, *Le feste veneziane: i giochi popolari le cerimonie religiose e di governo* (Florence: Sansoni, 1980), 189–91.

93 Allerston, "The Market in Second-Hand Clothes and Furnishings," 119–47, 196–213, 221–34. For the Ghetto, see also Chapter 7 below.

94 Allerston, "The Market in Second-Hand Clothes and Furnishings," 234–55 and passim; Idem, "L'abito come articolo di scambio nella società dell'età moderna: alcune implicazioni," in *Le trame della moda*, ed. Anna Giulia Cavagna and Grazietta Butazzi (Rome: Bulzoni Editore, 1995), 109–124; idem, "Le marché de l'occasion à Venise aux xvie–xviie siècles," in *Échanges et cultures textiles dans l'Europe pré-industrielle,* ed. Jacques Bottin and Nicole Pelegrin (Lille: Revue du Nord, 1996), 15–29; idem, "Wedding Finery in Sixteenth-Century Venice," in *Marriage in Italy, 1300–1650*, ed. Trevor Dean and K. J. Lowe (Cambridge, Cambridge University Press, 1998), 25–40; idem, "Clothing and Early Modern Venetian Society," *Continuity and Change* 15 (2000): 367–90. For auctions, see in particular, Jack Hinton, "By Sale, by Gift: Aspects of the Resale and Bequest of Goods in Late Sixteenth-Century Venice," *Journal of Design History* 15:4 (2002): 245–62. See also Evelyn Welch, "From Retail to Resale: the Second-Hand Market in Renaissance Italy," and other essays in Sara Matthews Grieco and Louisa Matthews, eds., *The Art Market in Italy, 1400–1600* (Florence: Olschki, 2002), 261–77.

95 Allerston, "The Market in Second-Hand Clothes and Furnishings," 205.

96 In his *Nichomachean Ethics*, in J. Barnes, ed., *The Complete Works of Aristotle* (Princeton: Princeton University Press, 1985), II:1772. See also Evelyn Welch, "Public Magnificence and Private Display: Giovanni Pontano's *De splendore* (1498) and the Domestic Arts," *Journal of Design History* 15:4 (2002): 214.

97 Welch, "Public Magnificence and Private Display," 214–15.

98 Sabba da Castiglione, *Ricordi* (Venice: Paolo Gerardo, 1560), 109, cited by Craig Clunas, *Superfluous Things: Material Culture and Social Status in Early Modern China* (Urbana and Chicago: University of Illinois Press, 1991), 22.

99 Daniela Frigo, *Il padre di famiglia: Governo della casa e governo civile nella tradizione dell "economica" tra cinque e seicento* (Rome: Bulzoni Editore, 1985).

Chapter 4

1 "Si come in beltà sete adornate, Donne gentil è di virtute amiche / Convien di ogn'hora le virtù cercate / Le ecco il specchio delle donne antiche. Lucretia illustre in fattura estate / Con le compagnie de l'otio nimiche, / Tal siate sempre accio per molti lustri / Il bel nome di voi, voi stesse illustre." See also Pompeo Molmenti, *La storia di Venezia nella vita privata dalle origini alla caduta della Repubblica* (Bergamo, 1927–29; reprint, Trieste: Edizioni Lint, 1973) II:314. On the use of ancient heroines as Renaissance exemplars and the exemplary role of such prints, see Marta Ajmar, "Exemplary Women in Renaissance Italy," and Sara Matthews Grieco, "Persuasive Pictures: Didactic Prints and the Construction of the Social Identity of Women in Sixteenth-Century Italy," in *Women in Italian Renaissance Culture and Society*, ed. Letizia Panizza (Oxford: Legenda, 2000).

2 Mary Margaret Newett, ed., *Canon Pietro Casola's Pilgrimage to Jerusalem in the Year 1494* (Manchester: Manchester University Press, 1907), 339–340.

3 Vincenzo Scamozzi, *Dell'idea della architettura universale* (Venice, 1615), 243: "I servi non vano mai ne gli appartamenti delle donne: intanto che non fano di certo, se in quella casa vi siano le figliuole dongelle: e parimente le serve giovani non comparono, se non di rado alla presenza de' loro padroni; ma servono ne gli appartamenti delle loro padrone . . . e vi si và per scale secretissime." See also Chapter 3 above.

4 On women in public and private, see Federica Ambrosini, "Toward a Social History of Women in Venice: From the Renaissance to the Enlightenment," in *Venice Reconsidered: The History and Civilization of an Italian City-State, 1297–1797*, ed. John Martin and Dennis Romano (Baltimore and London: Johns Hopkins University Press, 2000); Monica Chojnacka, *Working Women of Early Modern Venice* (Baltimore: The Johns Hopkins University Press, 2001), 103–5; Dennis Romano, "Gender and the Urban Geography of Renaissance Venice," *Journal of Social History* 23:2 (1989): 339–53; and Robert C. Davis, "The Geography of Gender in the Renaissance," in *Gender and Society in Renaissance Italy*, ed. Judith C. Brown and Robert C. Davis (New York: Addison-Wesley Publishing Company, 1998).

5 Augusto Gentili, "Painting in Venice: 1450–1515," in *Venice: Art & Architecture*, ed. Giandomenico Romanelli (Cologne: Köhnemann, 1997), 270–3; Patricia Fortini Brown, *Art and Life in Renaissance Venice* (New York: Harry N. Abrams, Inc., 1997), 130–32.

6 See Chapter 3, n. 90, above.

7 Stanley Chojnacki, *Women and Men in Renaissance Venice: Twelve Essays on Patrician Society* (Baltimore and London: The Johns Hopkins University Press, 2000). See also Monica Chojnacka, *Working Women of Early Modern Venice*, 26–49.

8 On unmarried men, see Stanley Chojnacki, "Subaltern Patriarchs: Patrician Bachelors," in *Women and Men in Renaissance Venice*, 244–56.

9 ASV, Notarile, Testamenti (Marcantonio Cavanis), B. 195, no 596: Zuan Alvise Bragadin fo del Clarissimo messer Hieronimo (22 Nov. 1566), which forms the basis for the paragraphs that follow.

10 Ibid., f. 7v: "Item a Zuane schiavo del q. messer Thomaso mio fradello dono la sua liberta & ordeno li sia dato el mio Cochio con li cavallj per sustentarsj."

11 ASV, Dieci Savi alle Decime, Redecima 1582, B. 157, n. 400.

12 ASV, Testamenti, B. 58 (Fabricio Beaciari), no. 350: Catterina Bragadin (13 April 1621): "et da quatro andate monache, per non voler star vecchie in casa."

13 ASV, Notarile, Testamenti, B. 87 (Michiel Barbaro), c. 10: Elena Bragadin relicta del quondam Clarissimo Signor Giulio Ziliol (19 June 1634).

14 Francesco Barbaro, "On Wifely Duties," trans. Benjamin G. Kohl, in *The Earthly Republic: Italian Humanists on Government and Society*, ed. Benjamin G. Kohl and Ronald G. Witt with Elizabeth B. Welles (Philadelphia: University of Pennsylvania Press, 1978). See also Margaret King, "Caldiera and the Barbaros on Marriage and the Family: Humanist Reflections of Venetian Realities," *The*

Journal of Medieval and Renaissance Studies 6 (1976): 19–50. See also Constance Jordan, *Renaissance Feminism: Library Texts and Political Models* (Ithaca and London: Cornell University Press, 1990), 68–85, and for later developments, 138–72, 250–69.

15 Pietro Bembo, *Nuove lettere famigliari . . . scritte a m. Gio. Mattheo Bembo suo nipote . . . ; nelle quali si commende particolarmente tutta la vita dell'autore, & qual fosse il suo stile nelle cose volgari in tutti i tempi* (Venice: Francesco Rampazetto, 1564).

16 Ibid., IV: "Mi piace che Marcella vostra sia entrata nelli nove mesi perche che tanto più tosto uscirà di quella fatica fastidiosa che le avanza. Il nome del fanciullo che nascerà, se sarà maschio, vorrei che fosse chiamato Quintilio, se femina Lucina."

17 Ibid., 2: "Di Marcella, che sia pregna, mi piace; in quanto non vi mancheranno figiuoli. Per lei m'increscе, che invechierà troppo presto. Ben vi so confortare ad haver cura di voi stesso, & à guardarvi da quelli disordini, che o ne togliono o ne abbreviano, et indeboliscono, & guastano la vecchiezza."

18 Ibid., passim.

19 Ibid., 5. One can imagine that by "those bad practices" he is referring to engaging in sexual activity too frequently. See Rudolph M. Bell, *How to Do It: Guides to Good Living for Renaissance Italians* (Chicago and London: The University of Chicago Press, 1999), 27–33, 38.

20 See Appendix II.

21 Bembo, *Nuove lettere famigliari*, 51: ". . . & attendete a star sano in questi caldi insieme con la mia Marcella, & la vostra brigatella."

22 Ibid., 62v: "che co'l corpo grande la die far male in quella sua prigione."

23 Ibid., 66: "Piace mi di Marcella che si sia alleggerita in bene, & anco che habbia partorito femina, che hoggimai de maschi ne havevate voi pur troppi."

24 Ibid., 101–101v: "Mi piace assai che Marcella si sia spedita in bene, & con poca noia del suo parto, & vi habbia a cresciuto il numero de i figliuoli maschi: I quali non sogliono mai esser troppi in mia casa."

25 Ibid., 108v (3 April 1537): "Ho inteso che Madonna la Contessa s'e sconciata d'un putto maschio di tre mesi. M'incresce per tema che ella non si risenta della sconciatura. La quale se sta bene, & non ha . . . [omissis in text] men male è, o pure poco male: essendo voi abastanza fornito, d'heredi, & di famiglia."

26 Ibid., 121–121v (22 June 1541).

27 Francesco Sansovino, *Vita delle illustre signora Contessa Giulia Bemba della Torre* (Venice: Domenico & Gio. Battista Guerra, fratelli, 1565), 3: "che nella vera Religione, & nelle virtù dell'animo fu molto eguale al marito, & di così felice ingegno dotata, che con molta sua lode apprese & la Greca, & la Latina favella."

28 Ibid., 2: "per grandezza di animo, per nobiltà di costumi, & per governo prudentissimo nelle cose famigliari, così la V. S. Illustre per vero zelo della santa Religione, & per nobile desiderio di virtù, & per altezza di spirito, è un chiaro essempio a giorni nostri." See also Chapter 1 for the naming of her children.

29 Ibid, 6: "Percioche avvenne che nessuna di quelle tre Signore proposte, di poi maritate non hebbe giamai gratia di far figliuli, diffetto si come principalmente infelice nel matrimonio."

30 From a vast bibliography on female portraiture in Renaissance Italy, see Paola Tinagli, *Women in Italian Renaissance Art: Gender, Representation, Identity* (Manchester: Manchester University Press, 1997), Chapters 2 and 3; and David Alan Brown, ed., *Virtue and Beauty: Leonardo's Ginevra de' Benci and Renaissance Portraits of Women* (Washington: National Gallery of Art and Princeton: Princeton University Press, 2001), particularly the essay by Joanna Woods-Marsden, "Portrait of the Lady, 1430–1520." 63–87.

31 David Rosand, *Painting in Cinquecento Venice: Titian, Veronese, Tintoretto* (New Haven and London: Yale University Press, 1982), 173–74. Cf. Terisio Pignatti and Filippo Pedrocco, *Veronese* (Milan: Electa, 1995), 1:135; and Richard Cocke, *Paolo Veronese: Piety and Display in an Age of Religious Reform* (Aldershot: Ashgate, 2001), 35.

32 See Blake de Maria, "The Merchants of Venice: A Study in Sixteenth-Century *Cittadino* Patronage" (Ph.D. diss., Princeton University, 2002).

33 Simone Chiarugi, in the scholarly catalogue of the Bagatti Valsecchi Musuem collections to be published by Electa, finds the *girello* (cat. 179) to be essentially authentic, datable to the late sixteenth to early seventeenth century, with restorations confined to the wheels beneath the base. I am grateful to the author and to the museum for making his manuscript available to me before publication. For baby walkers, see Peter Thornton *The Italian Renaissance Interior 1400–1600* (London: Weidenfeld and Nicolson, 1991), 253–57.

34 Simone Chiarugi, in the catalogue cited in n. 33, dates the *culla* (cat. 170) substantially to the sixteenth century, with the feet and several moldings and framing elements replaced in the nineteenth century. He considers the iron handles to be authentic and of high quality but probably readapted for this purpose. For cradles, see also Thornton, *The Italian Renaissance Interior*, 253–57. For furniture and accessories related to childbirth, see Jacqueline Marie Musacchio, *The Art and Ritual of Childbirth in Renaissance Italy* (New Haven and London: Yale University Press, 1999).

35 Although the *comoda per bambini* (cat. 129), was previously dated by the museum to the late sixteenth to early seventeenth century, Simone Chiarugi, in the catalogue cited in n. 33, determined that the piece was constructed in the nineteenth century from fragments datable to the sixteenth and seventeenth centuries. He suggests that the assemblage might have been inspired initially by the two side panels of the seat, decorated with carved arabesques and interwoven ribbons (not visible in the illustration), perhaps of Veneto provenance, datable to the sixteenth century. Giving a possible seventeenth-century dating to the candelabra pilasters, consoles, and volutes at the sides, he considers the backrest, with the conch shell, to be more recent. For commodes, close-stools, and latrines, see Thornton, *The Italian Renaissance Interior*, 245–49. See John Russell's *Boke of Nurture* in *Early English Meals and Manners*, ed. Frederick James Furnivall (London: Early English Text Society and Kegan Paul, Trench and Trübner, 1868), 180, lines 934–35.

36 Francesco Barbaro, "On Wifely Duties," 216. For the sixteenth century, see Mary Rogers, "An Ideal Wife at the Villa Maser: Veronese, the Barbaros, and Renaissance Theorists of Marriage," *Renaissance Studies* 7:4 (1993): 379–97.

37 For servants, see Dennis Romano, *Housecraft and Statecraft: Domestic Service in Renaissance Venice, 1400–1600* (Baltimore and London: Johns Hopkins University Press, 1996).

38 Sansovino, *Vita delle illustre signora Contessa Giulia Bemba della Torre*, 10v–11: "con bellissimo ordine mantenendo nella casa . . . Della nobile industria poi . . . nel procurar con vantaggio le provisioni di quello, che occorre in una casa, dove si veggono sempre effetti di molta magnificenza, & quale sia sempre piena di personaggi Illustri et del suo grande avedimento nell'adoperarle, & della diligenza nel conservarle, si può intendere non meno dall'ordine del vivere splendido, & dallo honoratissimo apparato di tutte le stanze

(benche molte, & in diversi luoghi fossero) cioè in Udine, in Ceneda, & in Villalta, ne' quai luoghi, tre Palazzi ha lasciati non solo ben forniti al commodo dello habitare, ma adornati di quei ricchi arnesi, che quanto piu si convengono alla grandezza della famiglia Torriana, tanto ben si veggono molto piu corrispondenti alla bella dispositione de predetti alloggiamenti; perche ella quando divenne sposa dello illustre Sig. Conte, trovò pochi, & invecchiati ornamenti così per esser stata la casa molti anni senza governo di donne, come per li gravi, & crudeli avenimenti delle discordie Civili, accompagnate da incendij, rapine, & da morti."

39 Barbaro, "On Wifely Duties," 204.

40 Alessandro Piccolomini, *Della institutione de la felice vita dell'hvomo nato nobile e in città libera* (Venice: Hieronymum Scotum, 1545), 259v–260: "E de i vestimenti poi altro luogho han d'haver quei de i fanciulli, altro quei del marito, e altro finalmente quei del istessa Consorta, per il cui ornamento, altro luogho si convien à le vesti, altro all'anella, o gioe, ò collane, ò maneglie, ò simil cose di pregio, le quali nel piu occulto luogho de la sua camera debba la donna havere."

41 Thornton, *The Italian Renaissance Interior,* 192–204.

42 ASV, Cancelleria Inferiore, Miscellanea Notai Diversi, B. 42, no. 66: Donado da Lezze q. Michael (19 October 1582). For the variety and uses of Renaissance chests, see Thornton, *The Italian Renaissance Interior*, 192–204, who states that in Venice the *cassa* was probably a large chest equivalent to the Florentine *cassone*.

43 Ibid., 100.

44 ASV, Cancelleria Inferiore, Misc. Not. Diversi, B. 35, no. 42: Tommaso Michael q. Francesco of Sant'Angelo (26 August 1532), ff. ff.1–4v, 6–7v: "un altra cassa de nogera tarsiado aquadretj . . . unaltra cassa vechia granda con due arme, una michiela et laltra Contarina, portado de la camera de sopra."

45 ASV, Cancelleria Inferiore, Miscellanea Notai Diversi, B. 35, n. 4: Nicolo Duodo (1530–33).

46 Clelia Alberici, *Il Mobile Veneto* (Milan: Electa, 1980), 24, no. 23. One *stemma* belongs to the family of Dondi dell'Orologio of Padua.

47 Alberici, *Il Mobile Veneto*, 33; Thornton, *The Italian Renaissance Interior*, 92–94 and 196–200.

48 For the influence of Islamic imports on Venetian decorative arts, see Rosamond E. Mack, *Bazaar to Piazza: Islamic Trade and Italian Art, 1300–1600* (Berkeley: University of California Press, 2002), particularly 95–147.

49 Cf. similar chests in Alberici, *Il Mobile Veneto*, 56–57.

50 Alberici, *Il Mobile Veneto*, 58 (fig. 69).

51 See ibid., 18–19.

52 Carlo Ridolfi, *Le maraviglie dell'arte ovvero le vite degli illustri pittori veneti e dello stato*, ed. Detlev Freiherrn von Hadeln (Berlin, 1914–24; reprint, Rome: Società Multigrafica Editrice Somu, 1965), 1:98.

53 Ibid., 1:248–49. See also Sandra Moschini Marconi, *Galleric dell'Accademia di Venezia. Opere d'arte del secolo* XVI (Rome: Istituto Poligrafico dello Stato, 1962), 190.

54 Marco Boschini, *Le ricche minere della pittura veneziana* (Venice: F. Nicolini, 1674), c.4. See also Jill Dunkerton, Susan Foister and Nicholas Penny, *Dürer to Veronese: Sixteenth-Century Painting in the National Gallery* (New Haven and London: Yale University Press, 1999), 87–135.

55 For Andrea Vendramin's collection, see Chapter 8 below.

56 Thornton, *The Italian Renaissance Interior*, 97.

57 See Luciana Martini, ed., *Bottega degli Embriachi: cofanetti e cassettine tra Gotico e Rinascimento* (Brescia: Musei Civici di Brescia, 2001); and Michele Tomasi, *La bottega degli Embriachi* (Florence: Museo Nazionale del Bargello, 2001). For betrothal gifts, see Luke Syson and Dora Thornton, *Objects of Virtue: Art in Renaissance Italy* (Los Angeles: The J. Paul Getty Museum, 2001), 37–76.

58 For metalwork *alla damaschina*, see Sylvia Auld, "Master Mahmud: Objects Fit for a Prince"; and J. W. Allan, "Venetian-Saracenic Metalwork: The Problems of Provenance," in *Arte veneziana e arte islamica,* ed. Ernst J. Grube (Venice: Edizioni L'Altra Riva, 1989). For *pastiglia*, see Patrick M. De Winter, "A Little-Known Creation of Renaissance Decorative Arts: the White Lead *Pastiglia* Box," *Saggi e memorie di storia dell'arte* 14 (1984): 7–42, 103–31; and Beth L. Holman, "Virtues of White Pastiglia", in *Tempting Pandora: A Selection of European Boxes 1200–1800*, ed. Helen Constantino Fioratti (New York: L'Antiquaire & the Connoisseur, Inc., 2000), 50–53.

59 Hans Huth, "A Venetian Renaissance Casket," in *Museum Monographs I: Papers on Objects in the Collections of the City Art Museum of Saint Louis* (St. Louis: City Art Museum of St. Louis, 1968), 42–50, citing Francesco Sansovino, *Venetia città nobilissima et singolave descritta in* XIIII *libri* (Venice, 1581), 134v.

60 ASV, Senato Terra, reg. 10, fols. 184–85 (10 Dec. 1488). See Patricia Fortini Brown, "Behind the Walls: The Material Culture of Venetian Elites," in *Venice Reconsidered: The History and Civilization of an Italian City-State, 1297–1797*, ed. John Martin and Dennis Romano (Baltimore and London: Johns Hopkins University Press, 2000).

61 Timothy J. Newbery, George Bisacca, and Laurence B. Kanter, *Italian Renaissance Frames* (New York: The Metropolitan Museum of Art, 1990), 48, fig. 18. See also Gustav Ludwig, "Venezianischer Hausrat zur Zeit der Renaissance: Restello, Spiegel und Toilettenutensilien in Venedig zur Zeit der Renaissance," in *Italianiesche Forschungen* 1 (Berlin: Kunsthistorischen Institut in Florenz and Verlag von Bruno Cassirer, 1908), 204. See also Thornton, *The Italian Renaissance Interior*, 234–41.

62 Alberici, *Il Mobile Veneto*, 62, nos. 76–77.

63 Ibid., 64, nos. 80–81; Hans Huth, *Lacquer of the West: The History of a Craft and an Industry, 1550–1950* (Chicago: University of Chicago Press, 1971), 5 ff; and idem, "A Venetian Renaissance Casket'; Ernst. J. Grube, "Le lacche veneziane e i loro modelli islamici," in *Arte veneziana e arte islamica*, ed. Ernst J. Grube (Venice: Edizioni L'Altra Riva, 1989). For metalwork *alla damaschina* see n. 58 above. For Islamic ornament, see Oleg Grabar, *The Mediation of Ornament* (Princeton: Princeton University Press, 1992).

64 See Grieco, "Persuasive Pictures," 299. For Doni, see q.v., *Dizionario biografico degli Italiani*, ed. Alberto M. Ghisalberti (Rome: Istituto della Enciclopedia Italiana, 1992), 41: 158–70.

65 Antonfrancesco Doni, *I marmi* (Florence: G. Barbèra, 1863), 168: "La sala sta ben così, perchè vi si riduce tutta la casa a un tratto dentro: le donne si stanno a piedi delle finestre, sì per veder lume a lavorare con l'ago le cose sottili e i ricami; sì per potere esser comode a farsi alla finestra; alla tavola in testa si mangia, a quella da lato si gioca: alcuni passeggiano, altri si stanno al fuoco; e così v'è luogo per tutti." Cf. Alison A. Smith, "Gender, Ownership and Domestic Space: Inventories and Family Archives in Renaissance Verona," *Renaissance Studies* 12:3 (1998): 375–91.

66 ASV, Cancelleria Inferiore, Misc. Notai Diversi, B. 41, No. 48 [8 January 1572 m.v.], ff 1–3v.

67 Ludovico Dolce, *Dialogo della institution delle donne* (Venice: Gabriel Giolito de Ferrari, 1547), 8v–9r: "consiglierei, che in iscam-

bio di quelle le si ponessero tra le mani gli strumenti di tutte le bisogne della casa, in certa picciola forma, come li veggiano, in legno, e in diversi metalli, ridotti. . . . che esse impareranno con diletto & il nome, & l'ufficio di ciascheduno." Other influential Renaissance treatises on the upbringing of young girls include Giovanni Dominici, *Regola del governo di cura famigliare*, ed. D. Salvi (Florence: Garinei, 1860); Giovanni Michele Bruto, *Institutione di una fanciulla nata nobilmente* (Antwerp: Bellere, 1555); and Juan Luis Vives, *De institutione foeminae christiane* (1523), in his *Opera omnia* (Valencia: Monfort, 1783), IV:78 (now published in English translation as *The Education of a Christian Woman: a Sixteenth-Century Manual*, ed. and trans. Charles Fantazzi [Chicago: University of Chicago Press, 2000]). See also Ajmar, "Exemplary Women," 244–64.

68 Dolce, *Dialogo*, 12: "O ventosa vanità, o delicatezza dannosa delle Nobili del nostro secolo. . . . Et certo i lavori di mano sono necessarij non solo alle Donne private, ma anchora alle Principesse et alle Reine: & tanto più a queste quanto manco sentono la gravezza delle cure famigliari percioche che faranno elle? consumeranno sempre le hore tra la moltitudine delle Damigelle & de' Cortegiani?"

69 Ibid., 12–12v: "Invero tutto il raccamare sia lavoro ingenioso & bello: non essendo quanto il cucire, necessario: non recarei a vergogna il non saperla: ma il diro bene, che il saper cucire a noi Donne tanto appartiene, quanto a voi huomini el saper scrivere."

70 Ibid., 12v: "nelle facende particolari della casa (che molte ne sono) si come in adornare una camera, acconciare un letto, far che tutte le massericie famigliari siano divisate con ordine & a luoghi loro, in modo, che paia, che tutta la casa da ogni parte goda, & sia piena d'allegrezza."

71 For the preparations she may have used to bleach her hair, see Giovanventura Rosetti, *Notandissimi secreti de l'arte profumatoria, Venezia 1555*, ed. Franco Brunello and Franca Facchetti (Vicenza: Neri Pozza Editore, 1973).

72 Alessandra Mottola Molfino, "Nobili, sagge e virtuose donne. Libri di modelli per merletti e organizzazione del lavoro femminile tra Cinquecento e Seicento," in *La famiglia e la vita quotidiana in Europa dal '400 al '600. Fonti e problemi* (Rome: Ministero per i beni culturali e ambientali, 1986); Arthur Lotz, *Bibliographie der Modelbücher* (Leipzig: Verlag Karl W. Hiersemann, 1933); Rosaria Campioni, "Libri di merletti e disposizioni suntuarie nel XVI secolo: alcuni indicazioni per l'Emilia romagna," in *Le trame della moda*, ed. Anna Giulia Cavagna and Grazietta Butazzi (Rome: Bulzoni Editore, 1995); Doretta Davanzo Poli, "Merletto ad ago e a fuselli," in *Storia di Venezia dalle origini alla caduta della Serenissima II, Temi: L'Arte*, ed. Rodolfo Pallucchini. See also Peter Thornton, *Form & Decoration: Innovation in the Decorative Arts, 1470–1870* (London: Weidenfeld and Nicolson, 1998), 31–34.

73 Giovanni Antonio Tagliente, *Essempio di recammi. Opera nuova che insenga alle Donne a cusire, a raccammare & a disegnar a ciascuno. Et la ditta opera sara di molta utilità ad ogni artista per essere il disegno ad ognuno necessario* (Venice, 1527).

74 Alessandro Paganino, *Libro primo De rechami per el quale se impara in diversi modi lordine e il modo de recamare, cosa non mai piu fatta ne stata mostrata, el qual modo se insegna al lettore voltando la carta. Opera nuova.* (Venice: Alessandro Paganino, 1527), fol. I: "E primo dico che tu pigli questo disegno che piu ti piace, e dipoi peglia uno ago sottile e va forendo tutto lorlo del disegno, facendo che il buco sia poco distante luno da laltro."

75 Nicolo d'Aristotile detto Zoppino, *Convivio delle belle donne* (Venice: Nicolo d'Aristotile detto Zoppino, 1532): "il piu polito libbro, che fusse mai a tempi nostri composto." See Lotz, *Bibliographie der Modelbücher*, 126–38, no. 68b, fig. 97.

76 Nicolo d'Aristotile detto Zoppino, *Gli universali de i belli Recami antichi, e moderni: ne i quali un pellegrino ingegno, si di huomo come di donna, potra in questa nostra etè con l'ago vertuosamente esercitar si. Non anchora da alcuni altri dati in luce* (Venice: Nicolo d'Aristotile detto Zoppino, 1537), fol. A (I) verso. As suggested by the use of the term *merletti* for the crowning elements of Venetian facades, such as those of Ca' d'Oro and the Palazzo Ducale, the relationship between lace patterns and architectural detail is also worth noting. See Doretta Davanzo Poli, *Il merletto veneziano* (Novara: Istituto Geografico, 1998), 17 and 40. In a personal communication, Deborah Howard has also called attention to the lace-like balconies on Ca' Contarini-Fasan and the surround on the entrance portal of Scuola di San Marco.

77 Ruth Kelso, *Doctrine for the Lady of the Renaissance* (Urbana: University of Illinois Press, 1956), 44, citing Federigo Luigi, *Il libro della bella Donna*, 1554.

78 Matteo Pagan, *L'Honesto Esempio del vertuoso desiderio che hanno le donne di nobil ingegno, circa lo imparare i punti tagliati a fogliami.* (Venice: per Matthio Pagan in Frezaria al segno della Fede, 1550).

79 Rozsika Parker, *The Subversive Stitch. Embroidery and the making of the Feminine* (London: The Women's Press, 1984), 64.

80 [Lucretia Romana], *Ornamento nobile per ogni gentil matrona, dove si contiene bavari, frisi d'infinita bellezza, Lavori, per Linzuoli Traverse, e Facuoli, Piena di Figure, Ninfe, Satiri, Grotesche, Fontane, Musiche, Caccie di Cervi, Uccelli, & altri Animali, con ponti in aria fiamenghi, et tagliati con Adornamenti bellissimi, da imparare, per ogni virtuosa Donna, che si diletta de perfettamente cucire.* (Venice: Appresso Lessandro de' Vecchi, 1620).

81 Doretta Davanzo Poli, "Merletto ad ago e a fuselli." For a good survey of Venetian lace, see idem, *Il merletto veneziano*.

82 Alessandro Piccolomini, *De L'Institutione di tutta la vita de l'homo nato nobile e in citta libera, Libri X. . . .* (Composti principalmente à beneficio del Nobilissimo Fanciullino Alessandro Colombini, pochi giorni innanzi nato, figlio de la immortale Mad. Laudomia Forteguerri) (Venice: Hieronymum Scotum, 1545), 254v.: "se la donna fusse à nobel Gentilhuomo congiunta in consorte, bruttissima cosa e odiosa saria di vedere, ch'ella con vesti apparisse fuore, più a Duchessa, o Regina, che a gran gentildonna si convenissero: come saria vestendo broccati, e tele d'oro, di perle e gemme riccamate e fregiate, e simili altri ornamenti a la sua condittion disdicevoli."

83 See Brown, "Behind the Walls."

84 Samuel Putnam, *The Works of Aretino* (Chicago: Pascal Covici, 1926), II:204: Letter XCV. To Messer Francesco Bacci [25 Nov 1537].

85 For dress as a sign in this period, see Paul Hills, *Venetian Colour: Marble, Mosaic, Painting and Glass 1250–1550* (New Haven and London: Yale University Press, 1999), 173–99; Stella Mary Newton, *The Dress of the Venetians, 1495–1525* (Aldershot, England and Brookfield, VT.: Scolar Press, 1988); Peter Stallybrass, "Worn Worlds: Clothes and Identity on the Renaissance Stage," in *Subject and Object in Renaissance Culture*, ed. Margreta de Grazia, Maureen Quilligan, and Peter Stallybrass (Cambridge: Cambridge University Press, 1996). For women's mobility, see Chojnacka, *Working Women of Early Modern Venice*, 103–20.

86 Thomas Coryat, *Coryat's Crudities* (Glasgow: James MacLehose and Sons, 1905), 399.

87 Ibid.

88 Ibid., 400.

89 Alexandre-Toussaint Limojon de Saint-Didier, cited by Charles Yriarte, *La vie d'un patricien de venise au seizième siècle* (Paris: E. Plon, 1874), 54.

90 Cited by Virginia Cox, "The Single Self: Feminist Thought and the Marriage Market in Early Modern Venice," *Renaissance Quarterly* 48:3 (1995): 552.

91 Cox, "The Single Self," 554, citing Arcangela Tarabotti, *Antisatira* (Venice, 1654), 142–43.

92 I owe this phrase to Kirsten Hammer, who made the observation in my graduate seminar, taught in the fall of 2000.

Chapter 5

1 Marin Sanudo, *I diarii*, ed. Rinaldo Fulin, et al. (Venice: F. Visentini, 1879–1903), 19:443 (19 February 1515), translation by Linda Carroll, taken from *"Cità Excelentissima": Renaissance Venice and its World, Excerpts from The Diaries (1496–1533) of Marin Sanudo*, ed. Patricia H. Labalme and Laura Sanguineti White, with translations by Linda Carroll, to appear. For early public theaters outside domestic space, see Eugene J. Johnson, "The Short, Lascivious Lives of Two Venetian Theaters, 1580–85," *Renaissance Quarterly* 55 (2002): 936–68.

2 See Pompeo Molmenti, *Venice: Its Individual Growth from the Earliest Beginnings to the Fall of the Republic*, trans. Horatio F. Brown (Chicago: A. C. McClurg & Co., 1907), II:28–43; idem, *La storia di Venezia nella vita privata dalle origini alla caduta della Repubblica* (Bergamo, 1927–29; reprint, Trieste: Edizioni Lint, 1973), II: 414–19. For a contemporary view of Venetian music, see Antonfrancesco Doni, *Dialogo della musica* (Venice: Scoto, 1543).

3 Isabella Palumbo-Fossati, "Livres et lecteurs dans la Venise du XVIe siecle," *Revue francaise d'histoire du livre* 54, n.s., no. 49 (1985): 481–513.

4 Edoardo Arslan, *I Bassano*, 2 vols. (Milan: Ceschina, 1960). See also Silvia Ferino-Pagden, ed., *Dipingere la musica: Strumenti in posa nell'arte del Cinque e Seicento* (Cremona: Skira, 2000).

5 Orazio Toscanella, *I nomi antichi e moderni delle provincie, regioni, città, castella, monti, laghi, fiumi, golfi, porti ed isole dell'Europa, dell'Africa et dell'Asia, con le graduazioni loro in lunghezza e larghezza*, etc. (Venice, 1567), 39: "È pur notissimo ch'ella s' è di musica in guisa dilettata che lungo tempo pagò la compagnia de' Fabbretti et Fruttaruoli, cantatori et sonatori eccellentissimi, I quali facevano in casa le musiche rarissime." See Molmenti, *Venice: Its Individual Growth*, 39; Molmenti, *Vita privata*, II:420.

6 James S. Ackerman, *The Villa: Form and Ideology of Country Houses* (Princeton: Princeton University Press, 1990), 117 and 131, citing Agostino Gallo, *Le dieci giornate della vera agricoltura e piaceri della villa* (Venice: Giovanni Bariletto, 1566), Day VIII, fols. 138–151v; and Alberto Lollio, *Lettere . . . nella quale . . . egli celebra la villa e lauda molto l'agricoltura . . .* (Venice, 1544), fol. v.

7 Marc-Henri Jordan and Francisca Costantini-Lachat, "Moorish Tracery," in *The History of Decorative Arts: The Renaissance and Mannerism in Europe*, ed. Alain Gruber (New York: Abbeville Press, 1994) particularly 342; Rosamond E. Mack, *Bazaar to Piazza: Islamic Trade and Italian Art, 1300–1600* (Berkeley: University of California Press, 2002), 136–37.

8 Hervé Oursel and Thierry Crépin-Leblond, *Musée National de la Renaissance. Chateau d'Écouen* (Paris: Réunion des Musées Nationaux, 1994), 95–96. For musical instruments in the home, see Peter Thornton, *Musical Instruments as Works of Art* (London: Victoria & Albert Museum, 1968; rev. ed. 1982); idem, The *Italian Renaissance Interior*, 1400–1600 (London: Weidenfeld & Nicolson, 1991), 272–74; and Francesca Costaperaria, "Gli strumenti musicali: la musica strumentale nel Cenedese tra Medioevo e Rinascimento," in *Interno Veneto: Arredamento domestico fra Trevigiano e Bellunese dal Gotico al Rinascimento*, ed. Vittorino Pianca and Federico Velluti (Vittorio Veneto: Città di Vittorio Veneto, 2002), 150–75.

9 Sabba da Castiglione, *Ricordi* (Venice: Paolo Gerardo, 1560), 56–56v.

10 Francesco Sansovino, *Venetia città nobilissima et singolare descritta in XIIII libri*, with additions by Giustiniano Martinioni (Venice: Steffano Curti, 1663; reprint, Venice: Filippi Editore, 1968) 1:379.

11 Palumbo-Fossati, "Livres et lecteurs," 492.

12 Sansovino, *Venetia città nobilissima* (1663) 1:370–71.

13 Palumbo-Fossati, "Livres et lecteurs," 481–513. The figure drops drastically in the popular classes below the *cittadino* level, comprising nearly 90 percent of the total population, but with only 12 percent owning books according to the inventories. For an earlier period, see Susan Connell, "Books and Their Owners in Venice 1345–1480," *Journal of the Warburg and Courtauld Institutes* 35 (1972): 163–86.

14 Paul Grendler, *Schooling in Renaissance Italy: Literacy and Learning, 1300–1600* (Baltimore and London: The Johns Hopkins University Press, 1989), 46–47, 93–102.

15 Sabba da Castiglione, *Ricordi*, 59.

16 Jonathan J. G. Alexander, ed., *The Painted Page: Italian Renaissance Book Illumination, 1450–1550* (New York: Prestel, 1994), 156–57, cat. 73. See also Patricia Fortini Brown, *Venice & Antiquity: The Venetian Sense of the Past* (New Haven and London: Yale University Press, 1996), 199–204.

17 Condulmer was the first cousin of, and bore the same name as, Zuan Francesco Condulmer, who was declared a bastard and expelled from the Great Council in 1528 (see Chapter 6, n. 51 below). The name Giovanni was the Italian equivalent of Zuan or Zuanne in Venetian dialect, and the same person was often referred to in all three ways; or he might even be called Ioanne, in a Latinized version.

18 Mack, *Bazaar to Piazza*, 134–35 and 213, nn. 45–46. See also Anna Contadini, "'Cuoridoro': Tecnica e decorazione di cuoi dorati veneziani e italiani con influssi islamici," and Anthony Hobson, "Islamic Influence on Venetian Renaissance Bookbinding," both in *Venezia e' l'Oriente Vicino*, ed. Ernst J. Grube, Atti del primo congresso internazionale sull'arte veneziana e l'arte islamica (Venice: Edizioni l'Altra Riva, 1989); Tammaro De Marinis, "L'influsso orientale sull'arte della legatura a Venezia," in *Venezia e l'Oriente fra tardo Medioevo e Rinascimento*, ed. Agostino Pertusi (Florence: Sansoni, 1966); Jordan and Costantini-Lachat, "Moorish Tracery," 284.

19 Sanudo, *Diarii*, 43:599 (7 January 1527), translation by Linda Carroll, taken from *"Città Excelentissima": Renaissance Venice and its World, excerpts from The Diaries (1496–1533) of Marin Sanudo*, ed. Patricia H. Labalme and Laura Sanguineti White (to appear).

20 See Jessie McNab Dennis, *Chess: East and West, Past and Present: A Selection from the G. A. Pfeiffer Collection* (New York: Metropolitan Museum of Art, 1968). For chess pieces, see Harold Osborne, ed., *The Oxford Companion to the Decorative Arts* (Oxford: Oxford University Press, 1985), 153–61.

21 Frate Jacopo da Cessole, *Opera nuova nella quale se insegna il vero*

regimento delli huomini et delle donne di qualunque grado, stato, e condition esser si voglia: Composta per lo Reverendissimo Padre Frate Giacobo da Cesole del ordine di predicatori sopra il giuoco deli Scacchi, Intitulata costume delli huomini, et efficii delli nobeli, nuovamente stampata (Venice: Francesco di Alessandro Bindoni et Mapheo Pasini Compagni, 1534). See Patricia Fortini Brown, *Art and Life in Renaissance Venice* (New York: Harry N. Abrams, Inc., 1997), 152–54.

22 See Clelia Alberici, *Il Mobile Veneto* (Milan: Electa, 1980), 75, figs. 95–96, who notes that Giustiniani–Emo marriages were recorded in 1507, 1508, 1515, and 1590.

23 Catherine Perry Hargrave, *A History of Playing Cards and a Bibliography of Cards and Gaming* (New York, Dover Publications, Inc., 1966), 221–46. On card playing in Venice, see Jonathan Walker, "Gambling and Venetian Noblemen, ca.1500–1700," *Past & Present* 162 (1999): 28–69.

24 Osborne, *The Oxford Companion to the Decorative Arts*, 625–30; Detlef Hoffman, *The Playing Card: An Illustrated History* (New York: New York Graphic Society Ltd, 1973; and Lucia Nadin Bassani, *Le carte da gioco a Venezia. L'Arte dei Cartoleri (1400–1700)* (Venice: Centro Internazionale della Grafica, 1989).

25 Lina Bolzoni, *The Gallery of Memory: Literary and Iconographic Models in the Age of the Printing Press* (Toronto: University of Toronto Press, 2001), 119, citing Emanuele Tesauro, *Cannochiale aristotelico* (Turin: Bartolomeo Zavatta, 1679; reprint, ed. A. Buck, Berlin and Zurich: Gehlen-Bad-Homburg, 1968), 58.

26 Gertrude Moakley, *The Tarot Cards Painted by Bonifacio Bembo* (New York: New York Public Library, 1966); Italo Calvino and Sergio Samek Ludovici, *Il mazzo Visconteo di Bergamo e New York* (Parma: Franco Maria Ricci, 1969); Osborne, *The Oxford Companion to the Decorative Arts*, 767.

27 Jay A. Levenson, Konrad Oberhuber, and Jacquelyn L. Sheehan, *Early Italian Engravings from the National Gallery of Art* (Washington, D.C.: National Gallery of Art, 1973), 81–89.

28 Alberto Fiorin, ed., *Fanti e denari. Sei secoli di giochi d'azzardo* (Venice: Arsenale Editrice, 1989), 155–57.

29 Cited by Leopoldo Cicognara, *Memorie spettanti alla storia della calcografia* (Prato: Giacchetti, 1831), 236–37.

30 Andrea Calmo, *Lettere*, ed. Vittorio Rossi (Turin: Ermanno Loescher, 1888), IV:22, 301, in a letter to a Signora Fulgentia: "el terzo che ve mando è quel piasevele libro de la Ventura, da star con le parente in berta e anche int'una compagnia de femene e de homeni; tragando quei tre dai se intende le pi gran stampie, le pi gran zanze, le pi gran busie del mondo." For Calmo, see *Dizionario biografico degli Italiani*, ed. Alberto M. Ghisalberti (Rome: Istituto della Enciclopedia Italiana, 1973), 16:775–81.

31 Lorenzo Spirito, *Libro de la ventura. Con somma diligentia revisto: et corretto: & nouanecche [sic] ristampate* (Venice: Mattio Pagan, 1557). The term book/game was coined by Bolzoni, *The Gallery of Memory*, 110. See also Fiorin, *Fanti e denari*, 145–46.

32 Sigismondo Fanti, *Triompho di Fortuna* (Venice: Agostino da Portese, 1527).

33 Bolzoni, *The Gallery of Memory*, 110–17; Robert Eisler, "The Frontispiece to Sigismondo Fanti's *Triompho di Fortuna*," *Journal of the Warburg and Courtauld Institutes* 10 (1947): 155–59. Cf. Leslie Thomsen, ed., *Fortune: "All is but Fortune"* (Washington, D.C.: The Folger Shakespeare Library, 2000), 85, cat. 95; and Geraldine A. Johnson, "Michelangelo, Fortune-Telling & the Formation of Artistic Canons in Fanti's *Triompho di Fortuna*," in *Coming About . . . A Festschrift for John Shearman*, ed. Lars R. Jones and Louisa C. Matthew (Cambridge, Mass.: Harvard University Art Museums, 2001), with further bibliography. For the belief in the prognostic significance of the frontispiece itself see Andre Chastel, *The Sack of Rome, 1527*, trans. Beth Archer (Princeton: Princeton University Press, 1983), 87–90.

34 Fanti, *Triompho di Fortuna*, f. 6r, cited by Bolzoni, *Gallery of Memory*, 112.

35 Fanti, *Triompho di Fortuna*, f. Bbv, "Domanda XXIIII: Quando si de cominciar una fabrica, Et per farla eccelentissima: quai sono le cose di che si de far provigione."

36 Ibid.: "Nella presente utilissima domanda dall'Auttore introdotta, il Fanti, non solamente da l'hora e'l punto quando ogni fabbrica si de principiare, Ma insegna anchora a conoscere & preparare tutte le cose necessarie. Et come per farla eccellentissima si debbano disporre."

37 Johnson, "Michelangelo, Fortunetelling & the Formation of Artistic Canons," 199–205.

38 Fanti, *Triompho di Fortuna:* "Felice fabricar almo thesauro / Ben spesso essendo Cintia e marte in faccia / Prima di Capricorno e nelle braccia / Di Vener bella e del candido Tauro." I am grateful to Professor Linda Carroll, Tulane University, for this interpretation.

39 As observed by Bolzoni, *Gallery of Memory*, 112.

40 For the wide variety of intellectual games played in this period, see ibid., 83–129; and Molmenti, *Vita privata*, II:376–78. Fiorin, *Fanti e denari*, 145–46, cites the following books in Venetian collections in addition to Spirito and Fanti: Innocenzo Ringhieri, *Cento Giuochi liberali, et d'ingegno, nuovamente da m. Innocentio Ringhieri . . . , ritrovati, et in dieci libri descritti* (Venice: Giovan Maria Bonelli, 1553); Francesco Marcolini, *Le ingeniose sorti composte per Francesco Marcolini . . . Intitulate Giardino di pensieri, nuovamente ristampate, et in novo et bellissimo ordine riformati* (Venice: Francesco Marcolini da Forlì, 1550).

41 Patricia H. Labalme and Laura Sanguineti White, with translations by Linda Carroll, "How to (and How Not to) Get Married in Sixteenth-Century Venice," *Renaissance Quarterly* 52 (1999): 56; Dino Coltro, *Sapienza del tempo contadino: lunario veneto* (Venice: Avsenale Cooperativa Editrice, 1980), 65.

42 Ibid., 119, citing Francesco Marcolini, *Le sorti* (Venice: Francesco Marcolini, 1550) f. 4.

43 Bolzoni, *Gallery of Memory*, 102.

44 Ibid., 117–19.

45 Sanudo, *Diarii*, 29:547 (16 January 1521, m.v = 1522). See Molmenti, *Vita privata*, II:382–83.

46 Labalme and White, "How to (and How Not to) Get Married in Sixteenth-Century Venice," 44–45.

47 Molmenti, *Vita privata*, 333; Sanudo, *Diarii*, 24:608 (26 August 1517).

48 Sansovino, *Venetia città nobilissima*, 400. Cf. Sanudo, *Diarii*, 41:167, reporting the marriage of Anzolo Badoer di Piero and the daughter of Zuan Francesco Morosini q. Piero (who lived in Ca' Loredan at San Polo on the upper *piano nobile*, sixty-three steps up from the ground floor) on 12 April 1526. "Et vidi cosa notanda, zà 20 anni non fatta, che vidi il novizo vestito di veludo cremexin al pè di la scala, et li soi Compagni vestitti di scarlato, che è la Compagnia di zoveni chiamati . . . I quali hanno cussi voluto si fazi a l'antica, et la noviza vadi in barca in trasto, come si andava zà alcuni anni, con felze di raso." This suggests that the custom was revived in the later sixteenth century.

49 Richard Judson, *Dirck Barendszen 1534–1592* (Amsterdam: Vangendt

& Co, 1970), cat. no. 61, 119–21; and Bernard Aikema and Beverly Louise Brown, *Renaissance Venice and the North: Crosscurrents in the Time of Bellini, Dürer and Titian* (Venice: Bompiani, 1999), 598–601.

50 See Patricia Fortini Brown, *Venetian Narrative Painting in the Age of Carpaccio* (New Haven and London: Yale University Press, 1988), for the "eyewitness style" popular in the late fifteenth and early sixteenth century.

51 Walter L. Strauss, ed., *Hendrik Goltzius 1558–1617: The Complete Engravings and Woodcuts* (New York: Abaris Books, 1977), cat. 182, 310–11, entitled "The Venetian Ball."

52 Brown, *Venice & Antiquity*, Chapter 1.

53 Sansovino, *Venetia città nobilissima* (1663), 1:399–400.

54 Thomas Coryat, *Coryate's Crudities* (Glasgow: James MacLehose and Sons, 1905), 1:425.

55 Patrick W. McCray, *Glassmaking in Renaissance Venice: The Fragile Craft* (Aldershot, England: Ashgate, 1999), 51.

56 Ibid., 66–95.

57 Reino Liefkes, ed., *Glass* (London: Victoria & Albert Museum, 1997), 53.

58 On the inventiveness and the reputation of Venetian glassmakers, see Luke Syson and Dora Thornton, *Objects of Virtue: Art in Renaissance Italy* (Los Angeles: The J. Paul Getty Museum, 2001), 182–200.

59 Rodolfo Gallo, *Contributi alla Storia dell'Arte del vetro di Murano* (Venice: Officine Grafiche F. Barzia, 1953), 5. See also *Mille anni di arte del vetro a Venezia* (Venice: Albrizzi Editore, 1982), 113.

60 Sanudo, *Diarii*, 30:45 (22 March 1521), supplemented by BMV, MS. It. Cl VII, n. 258, vol. 30, c. 27 verso: "Da poi disnar fo Pregadi . . . Fo posto, per li consieri, poi leto una gratia di una Armenia fo fia di Alvise da Muran depinse li quadri di Gran Consejo, et mojer di. . . . [sic], qual fa nave di vero, e dimanda di gratia per anni 10, altri che lei non possi far, soto pena, ut in parte; fu presa: 97, 27, 8." According to Armenia's will, dated 5 October 1569, her husband, Domenico, called Buscarino, de Calvi, was a *filatore*, or spinner. She also named three children – a son, Simone, and two daughters, Bernardina and Isabetta, as well as a brother-in-law, Zuan Giacomo: ASV, Notarile, Atti Antonio Contenio, B. 253 (published in Pietro Paoletti, *Raccolta di documenti inediti per servire alla storia della pittura veneziana* (Padua, 1895), fasc. II, n. 20).

61 Sanudo, *Diarii*, 38:346 (25 May 1525).

62 Leandro Alberti, *Descrittione di tutta Italia* (Bologna: Anselmo Giaccarelli, 1550), 468: "Io ho veduto quivi (fra l'altre cose fatte di vetro) una misurata galea, longa un Braccio, con tutti i suoi fornimenti, tanto misuratamente fatti, che par cosa impossibile (come dirò) che di tal materia tanto proporzionatamente si siano potuti formare oltra di questa Galea." According to Gallo, *Contributi alla Storia dell'Arte del vetro di Murano*, 5, Alberti had begun to collect notices in 1525 and his work was completed by 1536. It was published again in Venice in 1561. Alberti's critical vocabulary is limited to terms that deal with proportion: *misurata, misuratamente, proporzionatamente*. See also Syson and Thornton, *Objects of Virtue*, 159.

63 Sanudo, *Diarii*, 16:207 (2 May 1513). See also Labalme and White, "How to (and How Not to) Get Married in Sixteenth-Century Venice," 52–53.

64 Charles Oman, *Medieval Silver Nefs* (London: Her Majesty's Stationery Office, 1963), 11. For model ships as ex-votos in Venice, see Vittore Carpaccio's *Procession in the Church of Sant'Antonio* (Academia Galleries).

65 Vannoccio Biringuccio, *Pirotechnia* (Venice: Venturino Roffinello, 1540), 1540, cited by Liefkes, *Glass*, 50–51. Cf. the comments in the later fifteenth century of the German Friar Felix Faber, who praised Venetian glassmaking and remarked "Only the fragility of these vases makes them cheap and of low reputation, although they are most elegant in appearance, most beautiful to see." (cited by Creighton E. Gilbert, *Italian Art 1400–1500: Sources and Documents* (Evanston: Northwestern University Press, 1980), 154.

66 See note 45, above.

67 ASV, Cancelleria Inferiore, Miscellanea Notai Diversi, B. 35, no. 27, f. 2.

68 Coryat, *Coryate's Crudities*, 1:30. See also Fynes Moryson, *An Itinerary Containing His Ten Yeeres Travell through the Twelve Dominions of Germany, Bohmerland, Sweitzerland, Netherland, Denmarke, Poland, Italy, Turky [sic], France, England, Scotland & Ireland* (Glasgow: James MacLehose and Sons, 1907), IV:98.

69 Sanudo, *Diarii*, 7:161 (14 October 1507), cited with English translation in Labalme and White, "How to (and How Not to) Get Married in Sixteenth-Century Venice," 48.

70 See the fuller account of this section in Patricia Fortini Brown, "Behind the Walls: the Material Culture of Venetian Elites," in *Venice Reconsidered: The History and Civilization of an Italian City-State, 1297–1797*, ed. John Martin and Dennis Romano (Baltimore and London: Johns Hopkins University Press, 2000), 319–29. See also Mary Margaret Newett, "The Sumptuary Laws of Venice in the Fourteenth and Fifteenth Centuries," in *Historical Essays First Published in 1902 in Commemoration of the Jubilee of The Owens College Manchester*, ed. T. F. Tout and James Tait (Manchester: Manchester University Press, 1907); Giulio Bistort, *Il Magistrato alle Pompe nella Republica di Venezia* (Bologna: Forni Editore, 1912); Pierogiovanni Mometto, "'Vizi privati, pubbliche virtù'. Aspetti e problemi della questione del lusso nella repubblica di Venezia (secolo XVI)," in *Crimine, giustizia e società veneta in età moderna*, ed. Luigi Berlinguer and Floriana Colao (Milan: Giuffrè, 1989). For two excellent studies of sumptuary law, see Maria Giuseppina Muzzarelli, *Gli inganni delle apparenze. Disciplina di vesti e ornamenti alla fine del medioevo* (Turin: Scriptorium, 1996); and Alan Hunt, *Governance of the Consuming Passions: A History of Sumptuary Law* (New York: St. Martin's Press, 1996).

71 ASV, Senato, Terra, Reg. 6, c. 190v: "aza solamente privata in le chamere chome antiquitus far se voleva et de confecti menudi solamente." Cf. Newett, "Sumptuary Laws of Venice", 273; Bistort, *Il Magistrato alle Pompe*, 207.

72 ASV, Senato, Terra, Reg. 16, c. 69v (16 January 1508 m.v. [= 1509]): "Et perche imposibel è, che al sposar tal poco numero sia observato: et certa cossa, è Cadauno de questo Conseglio, per la prudentia sua molto ben lintende, che quando li ordenj & le lege non serani tanto strettissime quasi da ognj uno serano volentarie observate."

73 Ibid.: "Perche impossibel è farlo cum persone quaranta come ogniun intende."

74 Ibid.: "Ita che sono più che accetano cha tuti quelle sono acetade. . . . Il che più che ognj altra cossa è causa de gran spexa à li Citadinj nostri: perche ogniuna per andar a tal officij & spectaculj se sforza cum pompe & fozze nuove avanzar le altre."

75 Ibid.

76 Ibid.

77 Marin Sanudo, *De origine, situ et magistratibus urbis Venetae ovvero La Città di Venetia (1493–1530)*, ed. Angela Caracciolo Aricò (Milan: Cisalpino – La Goliardica, 1980) 250, cited by Labalme and White,

"How to (and How Not to) Get Married in Sixteenth-Century Venice," 64.

78 ASV, Senato, Terra, Reg. 18, c. 12v (8 May 1512); Reg. 24, c. 67v (25 Jan 1526); and Reg. 26, c. 5 (19 March 1530), cited by Molmenti, *Vita Privata*, 290.

79 ASV, Senato, Terra, Reg. 18, c. 14; cf. Bistort, *Il Magistrato alle Pompe*, 222–23. In this dance, the lady chose her male partner and danced around wearing his hat, a gender reversal that may have been particularly distasteful, if not threatening, to the elders of the Senate.

80 Bistort, *Il Magistrato alle Pompe*, 224, citing Simeone Zuccollo da Cologna, *La pazzia del ballo* (Padua, 1549), chapters 11 and 12, who quotes Doge Francesco Donà.

81 Molmenti, *Venice: Its Individual Growth*, Part II, II:118–21.

82 Girolamo Priuli, *I diarii (1494–1512)*, ed. Arturo Segre, in *Rerum Italicarum Scriptores*, ed. Roberto Cessi (Bologna: Zanichelli, 1921–41), XXIV.4:115.

83 Cited by Sanudo, *Diarii*, 40:751–52 (31 January 1526). See Labalme and White, "How to (and How Not to) get Married in Sixteenth-Century Venice," 63.

84 ASV, Senato, Terra, Reg. 42 (4 March 1559–13 August 1560], f. 109v (22 February 1559 m.v. [= 1560]).

85 Fabiola Sartori, ed., *La casa grande dei Foscari in volta de canal: Documenti* (Venice: La Malcontenta, 2001). See also Peter Lauritzen and Alexander Zielcke, *Palaces of Venice* (London: Dorset Press, 1985), 119.

86 Pierre De Nolhac and Angelo Solerti, *Il viaggio in Italia di Enrico III Re di Francia e le feste a Venezia, Ferrara, Mantova e Torino* (Turin: L. Roux, 1890), 108–10.

87 See Sanudo, *Diarii*, 13:131 (10 October 1495), cited by Patricia Anne Allerston, "The Market in Second-Hand Clothes and Furnishings in Venice, ca. 1500–ca. 1650" (Ph. D. diss., Florence: European University Institute, Department of History and Civilization, 1996), 176.

88 Margaret F. Rosenthal, *The Honest Courtesan: Veronica Franco, Citizen and Writer in Sixteenth-Century Venice* (Chicago: University of Chicago Press, 1992), 202–10.

89 Mary Margaret Newett, ed., *Canon Pietro Casola's Pilgrimage to Jerusalem in the Year 1494* (Manchester: Manchester University Press, 1907), 340–41.

90 William Thomas, *The History of Italy (1549)*, ed. George B. Parks (Ithaca: Cornell University Press, 1963), 80.

91 Coryat, *Coryat's Crudities*, I:415. See Chapter 1, note 17, above.

92 Sir Henry Wotton, *The Elements of Architecture. A Facsimile Reprint of the First Edition (London 1624). With Introduction and Notes by Frederick Hard* (Charlottesville: The University Press of Virginia, published for the Folger Shakespeare Library, 1968).

93 Coryat, *Coryat's Crudities*, I:396.

94 Cited by Molmenti, *Venice: Its Individual Growth*, II:110. See also Montesquieu, *The Spirit of the Laws*, trans. and ed. Anne M. Cohler, Basia Carolyn Miller, and Harold Samuel Stone (Cambridge: Cambridge University Press, 1989), 97–99.

95 Sanudo, *Diarii*, 18:299–300 (26 June 1514): "Tamen fu di honor al Stado." See also Labalme and White, "How to (and How Not to) get Married in Sixteenth-Century Venice," 54.

Chapter 6

1 Thomas Coryat, *Coryat's Crudities: hastily gobled up in five moneths travels* (London: W. S[tansby], 1611).

2 Ibid., a.1 verso.

3 Ibid., a.3 verso.

4 *Oxford English Dictionary Online*: "stew, n.[2] 3. A heated room used for hot air or vapour baths: hence, a hot bath. 4. A brothel. (Developed from sense 3, on account of the frequent use of the public hot-air bath-houses for immoral purposes. Cf. BAGNIO.) a. In plural (chiefly collect.; sometimes, a quarter occupied by houses of ill fame).

5 Coryat, *Coryat's Crudities* (Glasgow: James McLehose, 1905); I:401–3.

6 Ibid., I:405.

7 Ibid.

8 Ibid., I:402.

9 Giovanni Scarabello, "Le 'signore' della Repubblica," in *Il gioco dell'amore. Le cortigiane di Venezia dal trecento al settecento* (Milan: Berenice, 1990), 11–14; and Elizabeth Pavan, "Police des moeurs, société et politique à Venise à la fin du Moyen Age," *Revue Historique* 264 (1981): 241–88. See also Massimo Costantini, "Le strutture dell'ospitalità," in *Storia di Venezia dalle origini qalla caduta della Serenissima*, V. *Il Rinascimento Società e Economia*, ed. Alberto Tenenti and Ugo Tucci (Rome: Istituto della Enciclopedia Italiana, 1996).

10 Vittorio Rossi, "Il canzoniere inedito di Andrea Michieli detto Squarzòla o Strazzòla," *Giornale storico della letteratura italiana* 26 (1895): 45: "Parmi Vinegia esser fatta un bordello, poiché girar non posso in alcun lato, ch'io non sia a voce o con sputo chiamato da qualche *landra* drieto al balconcello. E l'una mi promette il proprio anello, l'altra la banda piena di moscato in modo ch'io mi trovo si impacciato che non so dove spendermi il marcello." Professor Linda Carroll interprets "anello," the Italian word for ring (as in wedding ring), to be a metaphor camouflaging an obscene reference to the lady's ass. This interpretation is supported by Giuseppe Boerio, *Dizionario del dialetto veneziano*, 2nd ed. (Venice: Giovanni Cecchini, 1856). In "L'indice Italiano Veneto," 9, a separately numbered section at the end of the volume, among the several definitions of "anello" is "*Detto per* Culo."

11 Giovanni Scarabello, "Le 'signore' della Repubblica," 15–18.

12 Marin Sanudo, *I Diarii*, ed. Rinaldo Fulin et al. (Venice: F. Visentini. 1879–1903), 3:133 (26 February 1499 m.v. = 1500): "Tutti tre hanno bellissime done per moglie, et cussì li fo vastà la faza, e si parlò assai."

13 Ibid., 19:25 (7 September 1514): "Etiam la matina fo sepulta una honorata e nominata meretrice, pur ai Frari, chiamata Anzola Caga in calle etc."

14 Ibid., 19:138 (16 October 1514): "In questa matina, fo sepulta a Santa Catarina Lucia Trivixan, qual cantava per excellentia. Era dona di tempo tuta coretesana, e molto nominata apresso musici, dove a caxa sua se reduceva tutte le virtù Et morite eri di note, et ozi 8 zorni si farà per li musici una solenne messa a Santa Catarina, funebre, e altri officii per l'anima sua." Translation by Linda Carroll.

15 Giovanni Scarabello, "Le 'signore' della Repubblica," 15–18.

16 See Enrico Maria Dal Pozzolo, "Sotto il guanto," *Venezia Arti* 8 (1994): 33–34 (29–36); Rodolfo Pallucchini and F. Rossi, *Giovanni Cariani* (Bergamo: Silvana, 1983), 112–13; Jane Martineau and Charles Hope, eds., *The Genius of Venice 1500–1600* (London: Wiedenfeld & Nicolson, 1983), 162; and Cathy Santore, "The Tools of Venus," *Renaissance Studies* 11 (1997): 179–205.

17 See Philip Rylands, *Palma Vecchio* (Cambridge: Cambridge University Press, 1992), 97–98, 172–73. Cf. David Rosand, *Titian* (New

York: Harry N. Abrams, Inc., 1978), 82; and Rona Goffen, *Titian's Women* (New Haven and London: Yale University Press, 1997), 45–106.

18 Sanudo, *Diarii*, 33:233 (9 May 1522).

19 Anne Christine Junkerman, "The Lady and the Laurel: Gender and Meaning in Giorgione's *Laura*," *Oxford Art Journal* 16 (1993): 49–58. See also Jaynie Anderson, *Giorgione: the Painter of Poetic Brevity* (Paris and New York: Flammarion, 1997), 208–17, 299–300. For possible portraits and other images of Venetian courtesans, see also Anne Christine Junkerman, "*Bellissima Donna*: An Interdisciplinary Study of Venetian Sensuous Half-Length Images of the Early Sixteenth Century" (Ph.D. diss. University of California, Berkeley, 1988); and Lynne Lawner, *Lives of the Courtesans: Portraits of the Renaissance* (New York: Rizzoli, 1987), 131–83.

20 Sanudo, *Diarii*, 41:166 (11 April 1526), translation by Linda Carroll from Patricia H. Labalme and Laura Sanguineti White, with translations by Linda Carroll, "How to (and How Not to) Get Married in Sixteenth-Century Venice," *Renaissance Quarterly* 52 (1999): 64.

21 Sanudo, *Diarii*, 41:201, 203 (20 April 1526).

22 Stanley Chojnacki, "Marriage Regulation in Venice, 1420–1535," in *Marriage in Italy*, 1300–1650, ed. Trevor Dean and K. J. Lowe (Cambridge: Cambridge University Press, 1988), 142; and idem, "Identity and Ideology in Renaissance Venice: The Third Serrata," in *Venice Reconsidered: The History and Civilization of an Italian City-State, 1297–1797*, ed. John Martin and Dennis Romano (Baltimore and London: Johns Hopkins University Press, 2000), 274–77; Alexander Cowan, "Love, Honour and the *Avogaria di Comun* in Early Modern Venice," Archivio Veneto Ser. 5, 179 (1995): 5–19.

23 Sanudo, *Diarii*, 54:421 (6 May 1531).

24 *La tariffa delle puttane di Vinegia Overo Ragionamento del Forestiero e del Gentilhuomo; nel quale dinota il prezzo e la qualità di tutte le Cortigiane di Vinegia col nome delle Ruffiane: Et Alcune Novelle piacevoli da ridere fatte da alcune di queste famose Signore a gli suoi amorosi* (Venice, 1535). Cf. Cathy Santore, "Julia Lombardo, 'Somtuosa Meretrize': A Portrait by Property," *Renaissance Quarterly* 41 (1988): 44–83.

25 See Monica Chojnacka, *Working Women of Early Modern Venice* (Baltimore: The Johns Hopkins University Press, 2001), 22–24, 54–55, for the homes of courtesans in the late sixteenth century.

26 Bernard Aikema and Beverly Louise Brown, *Renaissance Venice and the North: Crosscurrents in the Time of Bellini, Dürer and Titian* (Venice: Bompiani, 1999), 234–35 (entry written by Bernard Aikema).

27 For a range of interpretations, with further bibliography, see Rona Goffen, ed., *Titian's "Venus of Urbino"* (Cambridge: Cambridge University Press, 1997); and idem, *Titian's Women*, 146–57.

28 Ibid., 146.

29 Aikema and Brown, *Renaissance Venice and the North*, 532–33 (entry written by Bert W. Meijer).

30 Lawner, *Lives of the Courtesans*, 79. See also Bert W. Meijer, "A proposito della Vanità della ricchezza e di Ludovico Pozzoserrato," in *Toeput a Treviso: Ludovico Pozzoserrato, Lodewijk Topeut, pittore neerlandese nella civiltà veneta del tardo Cinquecento*, ed. Stefania Mason Rinaldi and Domenico Luciani (Asolo: Acelum Edizioni, 1988), 119; and idem, "Flemish and Dutch Artists in Venetian Workshops: The Case of Jacopo Tintoretto," in Aikema and Brown, *Renaissance Venice and the North*, 142.

31 ASV, Testamenti, Notarile, Antonio de Canali, B. 209: no. 172 (22 August 1538): "Io Elisabeta fiola del q. m. Hieronimo Condolmer, et moglier de S. Gabriel dj Agnolj. Et de la contrada al presente de S. Felixe, sana per gratia de messer domenedio de lo mente et de lo intelletto, ma del corpo inferma, essendo in letto, Et volendo ordenar lj mej benj ho facto chiamar per venir miss. Anzolo da Canal nodaro veneto." There is a copy of this document in ibid, B. 211, no. 25. (Protocolus testamentorum rogator et scriptor per q. ser. Angelum de Canali N. V. qui obijt die VI mensis Octobris MDLXXIII)

32 Ibid.: "Et per mie comissarij de questo mio testamento vogio che sia messer Francesco da Sola, mio signor, messer Camillo Michiel da S. Zuane di Furlanj, mess. Vetor Trinchavilla, medego, et mess. Nicolo Cocho che sta qua da basso de caxa mio."

33 Ibid: "Dechiaro che Hieronimo, Bernardin, Paula, & Laura, mie Fiolj, et fie, sono del ditto Mess. Francesco da Sola. Et cosj, e, per la fede mia, anchora zurigo che Cipriana et Condolmera, mie fie, sono del ditto mio signor Camillo Michiel, et che Julio, mio fio, è fiol de mess. Zuane Alvixe de Luca Varoter."

Cf. similar attestations in Veronica Franco's will: Margaret F. Rosenthal, *The Honest Courtesan: Veronica Franco, Citizen and Writer in Sixteenth-Century Venice* (Chicago: University of Chicago Press, 1992), 76–81. For Zuan Alvixe de Luca Varoter, see Gustav Ludwig, "Archivalische Beiträgen zur Geschichte der venezianischen Kunst," in *Italienische Forschungen* 4 (Berlin 1911), 72–73, citing ASV, Notarile, Testamenti, B. 1201:403 (Antonio Marsilio), the testament of Gabriele Vendramin of 3 Jan 1547 m.v. [=1548], for which one of the witnesses is "Zuan Alvixe varotter fo de ser Lucha."

34 ASV, Testamenti, Notarile, Antonio de Canali, B. 209: no. 172.

35 ASV, Cancelleria Inferiore, Miscellanea Notai Diversi, B. 37, n. 28 (13 Sept 1538 and 9 Feb 1540 m.v. [=1541]).

36 For Gian Francesco Torresani, see the meticulous biography by Annaclara Cataldi Palau, *Gian Francesco d'Asola e la tipografia Aldina: La vita, le edizionhi, la biblioteca dell'Asolano* (Genoa: Sagep, 1998), especially 36–50. Assuming that Gian Francesco was married, since he had sons, Cataldi Palau found no record of a marriage and was not aware of his alliance with Elisabetta Condulmer. See also BMV, MS. It. cl VII, 480 (=7785), f. 201=212, Testament of Andrea de' Franceschi, 1 March 1535–1 March 1541, cited by Michel Hochmann, *Peintres et commanditaires à Venise (1540–1628)* (Rome: Ecole Francaise de Rome, 1992), II:356–58, which refers to a "ser Francesco da Sola libraro quondam ser Andrea."

37 ASV, Cancelleria Inferiore, Miscellanea Notai Diversi, B. 37, n. 28, c. 12v.

38 See Aikema and Brown, *Renaissance Venice and the North*, particularly Louisa C. Matthew, "Working Abroad: Northern Artists in the Venetian Ambient"; Bernard Aikema, "The Lure of the North: Netherlandish Art in Venetian Collections"; Caterina Limentani Virdis, "Across the Alps and to the Lagoon: Northern Artists in Venice during the Sixteenth Century," and *passim*.

39 ASV, Cancelleria Inferiore, Miscellanea Notai Diversi, B. 37, n. 28, c. 12v, cc. 12r–13v.

40 Ibid., cc. 1r–8r.

41 Yale University, Beinecke Library MS. 457, "Mores Italiae." Cf. Peter Thornton, *The Italian Renaissance Interior 1400–1600* (London: Weidenfeld & Nicolson, 1991), 138–39.

42 ASV, Cancelleria Inferiore, Miscellanea Notai Diversi, B. 37, n. 28, cc. 11r–11v.

43 Ibid., c. 13v.

44 Marinella Laini, "Le cortigiane e la musica," in *Il gioco dell'amore Le cortigiane di Venezia dal trecento al settecento* (Milan: Berenice, 1990), 95–97, 115. See also Lawner, *Lives of the Courtesans*, 53.

45 Cataldi Palau, *Gian Francesco d'Asola e la tipografia Aldina*, 361–68. Gian Francesco also had an older son, Andrea, probably by another woman, since he is not mentioned in Elisabetta's will. Cataldi Palau suggests Gerolamo was born around 1530 and Bernardo around 1532.

46 ASV, *Notarile, Testamenti*, b. 1229, n. 299 (not. Cristoforo Rizzo): 16 Feb. 1500 m.v. (=1501); and ibid., b. 999, n. 229 (not. Marco de Tassis): 27 Apr. 1515: (a copy made at the proving of the testament after Girolamo's death).

47 Ibid.

48 Sanudo, *Diarii*, 7:606–7 (7 August 1508); ibid., 7:609 (13 August 1508): ibid., 7:611 (13 August 1508): and ibid., 10:51 (19 March 1510).

49 ASV, Dieci Savi alle Decime, B. 42, no. 79 (22 August 1514).

50 ASV, Avogaria di Comun, Reg. 165 (Balla d'Oro, 1498–1544), f. 113v.

51 Sanudo, *Diarii*, 41:241 (27 April 1526): "Et in questa sera, li Capi dil Conseio di X mandano a dir per li soi fanti a quelli è stà terminà che se reprovino, et li hanno quasi per non legiptimi, che damatina vengano a li Cai di x. Et sono numero 30, di quali 14 vien a Conseio et il resto non, ma ben provadi, li quali sono li infrascripti. Prima: Quelli vien a Conseio . . . (a list of fourteen names follows, including Sier Zuan Francesco Condolmer qu. sier Hironimo, qu. sier Zuan Francesco." Seven are "reprovato" at this time; two are not; and the others (including Zuan Francesco) are postponed, since they have no notation.

52 Ibid., 43:328–29 (25 November 1526); "In questo zorno, il Serenissimo con li Consieri et Capi di X fono per provar do zentilomeni, sier Alfonxo Valier di Sier Lorenzo, et leto iterum 1 processo, la pende. Ave: . . . Item, poi il processo di sier Zuan Francesco Condolmer qu. sier Hironimo, et aldito li testimoni, non fo expedito, la pende; and ibid., 43:670 (17 Jan 1527 m.v. = 1528): "Et il Serenissimo con li Consieri et Cai di x si reduseno per provar do zentilhomeni imputati esser bastardi, quali venivano a Conseio, videlicet che la sua cosa pendeva, sier Zuan Francesco Condolmer qu. sier Hironimo qu. sier Zuan Francesco di anni. . . . Et fu preso non fusse legiptimo. Et aldito il processo de sier Zuan Marcello di sier Andrea, qu. sier Zuanne, di anni 20, fu etiam lui preso che 'l non fusse legiptimo." For the revocation of noble status, see ASV, Avogaria di Comun, Reg. 165, f. 113v.

53 ASV, Cancelleria Inferiore, Miscellanea Notai Diversi, B. 37, n. 28, f. 8R: "Uno sacheto de canevaza con diverse scripture tra le qual erano uno instrumento de una caxa posta in S. Marcillian nel testamento de la soprascripta defuncta nominada. Scripto per man de S. Sebastian Pilloto sotto el 1537 adi 4 avosto. Et uno instrumento de quietancion fatta per messer Zuan Francesco Condulmer fratello di essa diffuncta per suo nome, et per nome de mess. Eugenio suo fradello. Ad essa sua sorella sotto lanno 1528 adj 29 lugio per man del q. m(esser) pre Alvixe Nadal piovan di S. Boldo et nodaro de Venetia. Et altre scripture pertinente alla dicta caxa quale altramente non forno viste ne notade"; and ASV, Giudici dell'Esaminador, Vendizion, R. 24, f. 73 (10 August 1537).

54 ASV, Giudici dell'Esaminador, Vendizion, R. 24, f. 73 (10 August 1537).

55 ASV, Dieci Savi sopra le decime, B. 97, no. 348 (30 January 1537 m.v. [=1538]): "Per obedire alla parte prexa nel eccellentissimo Conseglio de Pregadi sotto di xi ottobrio 1537, Magnifichi Signori X. Savij sopra lo Decime in execution della questa parte, io Isabetta Condolmor fo del magnifico Hieronimo fo de messer Zuan Francesco, denotto a vostro Ex.mo Signore esser pervenuto in mi una casa posta in la contrada de San Marzilian, la qual è malissima condicionata, et è voda za anno uno o più per haver bisogno di esser renovata tutta per esser antiquissima, la qual è allo eccellentissimo nel presento officio per dare 16 sudetto de fitto, ma fina non vien fabricata, non io atrova di affitarla, non trazo essa alcuna. Et quando che la sia honestamente conza, io medesima la voglio abitare, piaxendo al nostro Signor idio."

56 Rosenthal, *The Honest Courtesan*, 66; Joanne Ferraro, *Marriage Wars in Late Renaissance Venice* (Oxford: Oxford University Press, 2001), 114. See, for example, ASV, Senato, Terra, Reg. 32, 1542–1543, c. 125, which specified that legislation restricting the behavior of prostitutes applied to those with or without husbands: "Se intendino etiam meretrice quelle che havendo marito non habitano con sui mariti, ma stano separate et habino comercio con uno over piu homeni." See also Matteo Bandello, *Novelle*, ed. Francesco Flora (Milan 1966), II:31, who wrote of a custom in Venice whereby a courtesan would take six or seven lovers, "assigning to each a certain night of the week when she dines and sleeps with him. During the day she is free to entertain whomever she wishes so that her mill never lies idle and does not rust from lack of the opportunity to grind grain. . . . Each lover pays a monthly salary, and their agreement includes the provision that the courtesan is allowed to have foreigners as overnight guests." For the practice of concubinage with a focus on the seventeenth century, see Alexander Cowan, "Patricians and Partners in Early Modern Venice," in *Medieval and Renaissance Venice*, ed. Ellen E. Kittell and Thomas F. Madden (Urbana and Chicago: University of Illinois Press, 1999), 276–93.

57 *La tariffa delle puttane di Vinegia* (1535): "Credo che homai la fama è in tutto 'l mondo De la Lombarda, che d'oro e terreni / Ricca si fè con la virtù del tondo. / E tutti hebbé gli spron, e tutti i freni / Di voler e tener un amatore, / Si che giovando mai non si scateni. / Fu l'origine sua da un zappatore / Che stentando e soffiendo a l'ambra et al sole / Si guadagnava il pan con suo sudore. / Venne in Vinegia, come altra suole, Scalza, e con drappo di colore de' prati, / Raccamato di rose e di viole. / E s'altri annal di lei vi son mostrati, / Stimategli piu carchi d'heresie. / Che le vane talhor teste de' Frati. / Ch'io non vi venderei folle e bugie / Per città, per castella ne per oro, / In su 'l tenor de le parole mie. / Hor puossi dir la Fata del thesoro; / Ma solo per lo ingegno suo sottile, / Non per beltà che fosse in lei l'honoro. / Pur lassatela star, che fora vile / A comprar carne infracidita e vecchia / Di vacca, per cibar un huom gentile. / Dicon che venti scudi le apparecchia / L'huom che assagiar la vuole, e fanne acquisto / D'un mal che punge piu che vespe o pecchia / Importa anchor ch'aggiuntarebbe Christo, / E di cio dimandate a Gian Manenti, / Huomo per altro acccorto et assai provisto; / Ma in lei tanto non hebbe gli occhi intenti / De l'intelletto, che potesse trarne / Le spaliere prestate e gli altri argenti."

58 David and Ellen Rosand, "'Barbara Strozzi di Santa Sofia' and 'Il Prete Genoevese.' On the Identity of a Portrait by Bernardo Strozzi," in *The Art Bulletin* 63 (1981): 249–58.

59 Doretta Davanzo Poli, "Inventario delle cose di Giulia Leoncini, cortigiana in Venezia nel secolo XVI," in *Il costume nell'età del rinascimento*, ed. Dora Liscia Bemporad (Florence: Edifir, 1988), 273. See also Santore, "Julia Lombardo, 'Somtuosa Meretrize,'" 44–83.

60 Niccolò Franco, *Le pistole vulgari di M. Niccolò Franco* (Venice: Gardane, 1585), f. 223v.

61 Andrea Calmo, *Lettere*, ed. Vittorio Rossi (Turin: Ermanno Loescher, 1888), IV:16, 284–86.

62 *Leggi e memorie venete sulla prostituzione fino all caduta della republica* (Venice: Marco Visentini, a spese del Conte di Orford 1870–72), nos. 105, 108–9: ASV, Senato, Terra, Reg. 32, 1542–1543 Agosto,

c. 125. English translation from David Chambers and Brian Pullan, eds., *Venice: A Documentary History, 1450–1630* (Oxford: Blackwell, 1992). See also Rosenthal, *The Honest Courtesan*, 60–61; and Brian Pullan, *Rich and Poor in Renaissance Venice: The Social Institutions of a Catholic State, to 1620* (Cambridge, Mass.: Harvard University Press, 1971), 375–82.

63 *Leggi e memorie venete sulla prostituzione fino all caduta della repubblica*, no. 105, 108–9: ASV, Senato, Terra, Reg. 32, 1542–1543 (21 Feb. 1542 m.v.).

64 Thomas Nashe, *The Unfortunate Traveler, or the Life of Jack Wilton* (London: printed by T. Scarlet for C. Burby, 1594; reprint, New York: Greenberg, Publisher, 1926), 76–77.

65 Samuel Putnam, ed., *The Works of Aretino* (Chicago: Pascal Covici, 1926), 2:237, Letter 1, 291 (15 Dec 1537). See in particular Mary Rogers, "Fashioning Identities for the Renaissance Courtesan," in *Fashioning Identities in Renaissance Art*, ed. Mary Rogers (London: Ashgate, 2000).

66 *Leggi e memorie venete sulla prostituzione fino all caduta della repubblica*, no. 118, 122: ASV, Provveditori alla Sanitâ, Capitolare, II, 1574–1689, c. 37 (20 December 1578). Cf. Elizabeth S. Cohen, "Seen and Known: Prostitutes in the Cityscape of Late-Sixteenth Century Rome," *Renaissance Studies* 12:3 (1998): 392–409.

67 *Leggi e memorie venete sulla prostituzione fino all caduta della repubblica*, no. 124, 127: ASV, Provveditori sopra le Pompe, Capitolare, I, c. 46 (23 September 1598).

68 Mary Margaret Newett, ed., *Canon Pietro Casola's Pilgrimage to Jerusalem in the Year 1494* (Manchester: Manchester University Press, 1907), 144. Cf. Coryat, *Coryat's Crudities*, (1905), 1:400; *Il gioco dell'amore*, 169–70.

69 Pietro Aretino, *Letters*, VI, 249, trans. Thomas Chubb, cited in Lawner, *Lives of the Courtesans*, 23.

70 *Leggi e memorie venete sulla prostituzione fino all caduta della repubblica*, no. 117, 121–22: ASV, Consiglio de' Dieci, Comuni Reg. 33, 1577–78, c. 167v.

71 ASV, Cancelleria Inferiore, Miscellanea Notai Diversi, B. 37, n. 28, 9r: "Duj papafigi de ormesin negro . . . Voltj rassi da stravestir. no. sette, Voltj con barba da stravestir. no. tre."

72 Coryat, *Coryat's Crudities*, 1:386.

73 Bert Miejer, "A proposito della *Vanità della ricchezza* e di Ludovico Pozzoserrato," 115–16, in Aikema and Brown, *Renaissance Venice and the North*, 602 (cat.186). The caption reads: "Petrus de Iode fecit; larvatae incedunt venetae, cur luce puellae? / an fugitant lucem, si bene quid faciunt? / luxuriant animi rebus plerumque secundis / divitiis aliter luxuriosus amor."

74 Rosenthal, *The Honest Courtesan*, 133.

75 Monica Chojnacka, "Women, Charity and Community in Early Modern Venice: The Casa delle Zitelle," *Renaissance Quarterly* 51 (1998): 68–91; and idem, *Working Women of Early Modern Venice*, 121–37; Pullan, *Rich and Poor in Renaissance Venice*, 386–91.

76 See Bernard Aikema and Dulcia Meijers, *Nel regno dei poveri. Arte e storia dei grandi ospedali veneziani in età moderna 1474–1797* (Venice: IRE, 1989), 241–48; Franca Semi, *Gli "Ospizi" di Venezia* (Venice: Edizioni Helvetia, 1983), 282; and Pullan, *Rich and Poor in Renaissance Venice*, 391–93.

77 Giuseppe Ellero, "L'oro di ricchi e di poveri nei documenti degli ospedali veneziani," in *L'oro di Venezia. Oreficerie, argenti e gioelli di Venezia e delle città venete* ed. Piero Pazzi (Venice: Biblioteca Nazionale Marciana, 1996), 76, citing IRE, Derelitti, E 182, 6 (4 August 1638); see also Der. E. 182–85.

78 See Erasmus Weddingen, "Jacopo Tintoretto und die Musik," *Artibus et Historiae* 10 (1984): 67–119.

79 Ibid.

80 Rosenthal, *The Honest Courtesan*, 139.

81 Cited by Virginia Cox, "The Single Self: Feminist Thought and the Marriage Market in Early Modern Venice," *Renaissance Quarterly* 48:3 (1995), 544. See Moderata Fonte (Modesta Pozzo), *The Worth of Women: Wherein Is Clearly Revealed Their Nobility and Their Superiority to Men*, ed. and trans. Virginia Cox (Chicago: University of Chicago Press, 1997).

82 Lodovico Dolce, *Dialogo della institution delle donne* (Venice, 1543), cited by Junkerman, "The Lady and the Laurel," 49.

Chapter 7

1 Francesco Sansovino, *Venetia città nobilissima et singolare descritta in XIIII libri*, with additions by Giustiniano Martinioni (Venice: Steffano Curti, 1663; reprint, Venice: Filippi Editore 1968), 1:389.

2 Ibid., 1:384–85.

3 F. C. Lane, "The Enlargement of the Great Council of Venice," in *Florilegium Historiale: Essays Presented to Wallace K. Ferguson*, ed. J. G. Rose and W. H. Stockdale (Toronto: University of Toronto Press, 1971). For two recent views, see Gerhard Rösch, "The Serrata of the Great Council and Venetian Society, 1286–1323," and Stanley Chojnacki, "Identity and Ideology in Renaissance Venice: The Third Serrata," both in *Venice Reconsidered: The History and Civilization of an Italian City-State, 1297–1797*, ed. John Martin and Dennis Romano (Baltimore and London: Johns Hopkins University Press, 2000).

4 For the structure of the Venetian government, see Robert Finlay, *Politics in Renaissance Venice* (New Brunswick: Rutgers University Press, 1980).

5 For Venetian demographics, see Daniele Beltrami, *Storia del popolazione di Venezia dalla fine del secolo XVI alla caduta della Repubblica* (Padua: CEDAM, 1954), 72.

6 BCV, cod. Gradenigo 83, "Corona seconda della veneta republica."

7 Patricia Fortini Brown, *Venetian Narrative Painting in the Age of Carpaccio* (New Haven and London: Yale University Press, 1988), 13–16 and 23–26; and James Grubb, "Elite Citizens," in *Venice Reconsidered: The History and Civilization of an Italian City-State, 1297–1797*, ed. John Martin and Dennis Romano (Baltimore and London: Johns Hopkins University Press, 2000).

8 See Dennis Romano, *Patricians and Popolani: The Social Foundations of the Venetian Renaissance State* (Baltimore and London: The Johns Hopkins University Press, 1987); idem, *Housecraft and Statecraft: Domestic Service in Renaissance Venice, 1400–1600* (Baltimore: The Johns Hopkins University Press, 1996); and Ugo Tucci, "Carriere popolane e dinastie di mestiere a Venezia," in *Gerarchie economiche e gerarchie sociali: Secoli XII–XVIII*, ed. Annalisa Guarducci (Florence: Le Monnier, 1990).

9 For patrician ideology in the fifteenth century, see Margaret King, *Venetian Humanism in an Age of Patrician Dominance* (Princeton: Princeton University Press, 1986); for the sixteenth century see Manfredo Tafuri, *Venice and the Renaissance* (Cambridge, Mass.: MIT Press, 1989).

10 Sansovino, *Venetia città nobilissima* (1663) 1:387–88. See Deborah Howard, *Jacopo Sansovino: Architecture and Patronage in Renaissance*

Venice (New Haven and London: Yale University Press, 1975), 126–46; and Giandomenico Romanelli, *Ca' Corner della Ca' Granda: architettura e committenza nella Venezia del Cinquecento* (Venice: Albrizzi Editore, 1993).

11 For the term *casa da statio* (also spelled *casa da stazio*), see Wladimiro Dorigo, "Toponomastica urbana nella formazione della città medioevale," *Rassegna* 5, no. 22 (1985): 50–51; Elisabeth Crouzet-Pavan, *'Sopra le acque salse': Espaces, pouvoir et société à Venise à la fin du moyen âge* (Rome: Ecole Française de Rome, 1992), 1:509–14; and, in particular, Juergen Schulz,"The Houses of Titian, Aretino, and Sansovino," in *Titian: His World and His Legacy*, ed. David Rosand (New York: Columbia University Press, 1982), 83–84.

12 Pietro Bembo, *Nuove lettere famigliari . . . scritte a m. Gio. Mattheo Bembo suo nipote . . . ; nelle quali si commende particolarmente tutta la vita dell'autore, & qual fosse il suo stile nelle cose volgari in tutti i tempi* (Venice: Francesco Rampazetto, 1564). For Zuan Matteo's career, see Emmanuele A. Cicogna, *Delle iscrizioni veneziane* (Venice: Picotti, 1824–53), III:318–37; and "Giovanni Matteo Bembo," q. v., *Dizionario biografico degli italiani*, ed. Alberto M. Ghisalberti (Rome: Istituto della Enciclopedia Italiana, 1966) 8:124–25.

13 Marin Sanudo, *I diarii*, ed. Rinaldo Fulin et al. (Venice: F. Visentini, 1879–1903), 53:65 (22 March 1530): "Da poi leto le lettere, fo leto una suplication di sier Zuan Mathio Bembo qu. sier Alvise, qual vol far stampar do opere latine di suo barba reverendo missier Pietro Bembo, *videlicet, de Virgilii culice et Terentii fabulis*, et l'altra di *Guido Ubaldo et Elisabetta Gonzaga Urbini ducibus*, et un'altra volta far ristampar la *Ethna monte*, del ditto, et li *Asolani*, da lui reconzi et mutati in qualche parte, et che niun per anni 20 li possi far stampar, se non lui, *sub poena* etc. Et fo posto, per li Consieri et Cai di XL, di conciederli quanto el dimanda. Fu presa. Ave: 189, 6, 2."

14 See Paolo Maretto, *La casa veneziana nella storia della città dalle origini all'Ottocento* (Venice: Marsilio Editori, 1986), 115–20.

15 Alberto Rizzi, *Scultura Esterna a Venezia: Corpus delle Sculture Erratiche all'aperto di Venezia e della sua Laguna* (Venice: Stamperia di Venezia, 1987), 321: cat. CN 431, Cannaregio, no. 5999 (S. Canzian). Cf. ibid., 470–71, cat. DD 129, for a late Gothic *homo silvanus* on the facade of Ca' Brass, Campo S. Trovaso 1083. See also Giulio Lorenzetti, *Venice and its Lagoon*, trans. John Guthrie (Trieste: Edizioni Lint, 1975), 338 and 651; and Giuseppe Tassini, *Curiosità Veneziane* (Venice: Fuga, 1915; reprint, Venice: Filippi, 1988), 390. The lunette-shaped plaque above the relief with three male heads is badly defaced, but the details that remain suggest the symbol of San Marco as *leone in moleca*.

16 Cicogna, *Inscrizioni veneziane*, III:318: DVM. VOLVITVR. ISTE IAD. ASCR. IVSTINOP. VER. / SALAMIS. CRETA. IOVIS. / TESTES. ERVNT. ACTOR. / PA. IO. SE. M^{V}. See also Patricia Fortini Brown, *Venice & Antiquity: The Venetian Sense of the Past* (New Haven and London: Yale University Press, 1996), 285–86.

17 For the fountain, see BMV, cod. It. VII (14 (= 7418): Bernardo Bembo, *Cronica di tutte le case dell'inclitta Città di Venetia*, 68v; BCV, cod. Cicogna 3558/III: *Descritione dell'Isola di Candia*, ff. 9v-10; and Giuseppe Gerola, *Monumenti Veneti dell'isola di Creta* (Venice: Istituto Veneto delle Scienze, Lettere ed Arti, 1932).

18 Sansovino, *Venetia città nobilissima* (1663), 1:336. The paintings depicted the Story of Alexander III, a legendary event in Venetian history. See Brown, *Venetian Narrative Painting*, 272–79; and Brown, *Venice & Antiquity*, 285–86.

19 ASV, Notarile, Testamenti, B. 1259, n. 507 [Cesare Ziliol] (22 March 1570): "Tutti li mei beni stabeli, case, et terre, dalla villa et quelli, serrano aquistati col tratto di quelli pochi arzenti, et mobeli, con denari mei, voglio stiano sotto perpetuo fideicommisso in quattro mei figlioli mascoli, Lorenzo, Alvise, Marc'Antonio et Davit, et in loro descendenti mascoli legitimi." Cf. ASV, Procuratoria di San Marco de Citra, B. 48: *Commissaria di Zuan Matteo Bembo fu Alvise of Santa Maria Nova*. The practice of entail is the English equivalent of *fedecomesso*.

20 Ibid.: "in uso, et agiuto di quelli poveri."

21 Ibid.: "Item dechiaro che Augusta fu' satisfatta del legato delli ducati cento che li fu lassato, et ha havuto anche ducati vinticinque de piui da sua madre."

22 ASV, Notarile, Testamenti, B. 1210, n. 716 (Antonio Marsilio): "Volgio anche sia dato cento ducati delli miei beni a mia fiola Augusta per segnio de de amor per una volta sola, et piu non le lasso: che per la gratia a di Dio l'è richa: e sta molto bene."

23 Ibid.: "se mia filgiola Julia non sarà maridata o monacha avanti la mia morte, volgio che l'abbia ducati cinquecento de tutti li mei beni, si della mia dota come de mia sorella madonna Julia e de qualunque altri beni mi potessi pervegnir, con questa condizion che la se marida in zentilhomo nostro venetian: overo in honorevole forestier de consentimento del Magnifico mio consorte e sui fratelli, e se la fusse maridà avanti la mia morte non volgio la habia per niente cossa alcuna, e se la andara monaca non volgio la habia dicti ducatj cinquecento, che mi par la possa andar in bonissimo monestier con li quatrocento ducatj che lassa suo Padre."

24 Ibid.: "Dechiarando sopratutto che se mei filgioli averà bastardi o bastardo non possa mai lassarle in tempo alcuno niente del mio." Cf. Chojnacki, "Identity and Ideology," 268–80.

25 ASV, Notarile, Testamenti, B. 1259, n. 507: "Lasso che Ettor, mio fiol natural, sia governato, amaestrato, vestito, et calzato, et pagato li maestri che li insegnaranno."

26 Laura Megna, "Comportamenti abitativi del patriziato veneziano (1582–1740)," *Studi Veneziani*, n.s., 22 (1991): 285 and 294–96, who incorrectly assumed that Pietro was one of the original heirs and made no mention of Alvise.

27 BCV, Cod. P.D./C 2706; cf. Megna, "Comportamenti abitativi," 294–95.

28 ASV, Notarile, Testamenti, B. 1259, n. 507. For the layout, see Paolo Maretto, *L'edilizia gotica veneziana*, 2nd ed. (Venice: Filippi Editore, 1978), 74–77; Cf. Ca' Bollani, rented out to Pietro Aretino, which has a plan similar to that of Bembo's before the chamber was added on the west side: Schulz, "Houses of Titian, Aretino, and Sansovino," 83–86.

29 BCV, cod. P.D. C.2706/1, f.9; and ASV, Dieci Savi sopra le Decime, B. 131, no. 839: In his decima declaration of 25 June 1566, Zuan Matteo declared that he was living in the *casa da statio* at Santa Maria Nova, presumably in the *soler di sopra*, for he was renting the *soler di sotto* for 55 ducats annually until his son Lorenzo returned from Famagosta, where he was presently living. For earlier tax declarations see ASV, Dieci Savi sopra le Decime, B. 96, no. 39 (1537); and ibid., B. 107, no. 962 (1540).

30 BCV, cod. P.D.C.2706/2 lists a total annual rent of 109 ducats for these properties. See also Megna, "Comportamenti abitativi," 294–95, citing BCV, cod. P.D. C.2706/2 and cod. P. D. C.2706/3.

31 BCV, cod. P.D. C.2706/2, ff. 32–40; ibid., cod. P.D. C.2706/3; and ASV, Notarile, Atti, Marc'Antonio Cavanis, 1573:II, R. 3290, ff. 344–5, 376, 451, 455. Not only did Marc' Antonio engage in addi-

tional lawsuits against his brothers and nephews, but in 1605 a cousin, Dardi Bembo fu David (*fu* meaning son or daughter of), successfully contested the will of their great-grandfather, Alvise fu Zaccaria, by which Zuan Matteo fu Alvise Bembo had claimed the house in the first place. Dardi was given the *soler di sotto* while the heirs of Lorenzo fu Zuan Matteo were moved upstairs to the *soler di sopra*, once owned by Pietro di Zuan Matteo, Bishop of Veglia. The legal squabbling continued until 1686, when Girolamo and Francesco Bembo attempted, unsuccessfully as it happens, to claim one-fourth of the house from Pellegrina, the last surviving heir of Lorenzo Bembo.

32 ASV, Dieci Savi sopra le Decime, B. 164/971.

33 Ibid., B. 164/984.

34 Ibid., B. 164/1098.

35 Ibid, B. 170/794. Cf. Megna, "Comportamenti abitativi," 283.

36 Megna, "Comportamenti abitativi," 278–81.

37 Ibid., 285 and 287.

38 For marriage strategies in this period, see Stanley Chojnacki, "Subaltern Patriarches: Patrician Bachelors in Renaissance Venice," in his *Women and Men in Renaissance Venice: Twelve Essays on Patrician Society* (Baltimore and London: The Johns Hopkins University Press, 2000), 244–56; and idem, "Identity and Ideology," 269–70.

39 Megna, "Comportamenti abitativi," 290–91, citing ASV, Notarile, Testamenti, b. 1193, prot. 11, cc. 90v ff. For a similar agreement see Fabiola Sartori, ed., *La casa grande dei Foscari in volta de canal: Documenti* (Venice: La Malcontenta, 2001), 45–52.

40 Howard, *Jacopo Sansovino*, 8–9; and Finlay, *Politics in Renaissance Venice*, 248–50.

41 Ennio Concina, *A History of Venetian Architecture*, trans. Judith Landry (Cambridge: Cambridge University Press, 1998), 220–26. On the earlier building, see Juergen Schulz, "La piazza medievale di San Marco," *Annali di architettura* 4–5 (1992–93): 139–40, who notes that procurators had lived there since at least 1319, when the Maggior Consiglio provided two additional houses near the church of San Geminiano. See also Vincenzo Scamozzi, *Dell' idea della architettura universale* (Venice: expensis auctoris, 1615) 243, for an enthusiastic description of the apartments.

42 Megna, "Comportamenti abitativi," 271.

43 For the *decima*, see Luciano Pezzolo, *L'oro dello stato: società, finanza e fisco nella Repubblica Veneta del secondo '500* (Venice: Il Cardo, 1990), 43–45. The term *decima* comes from the 10 percent tax that was levied annually on the rental value of property, including the primary residence. See Megna, "Comportamenti abitativi," 286. Beginning in 1582, the family residence was appraised at one-half its rental value, giving a tax break to those who lived in their own homes; it was later lowered to one-third.

44 ASV, Dieci Savi sopra le Decime (Redecima 1537), B. 97, no. 476, f. 1.

45 ASV, Dieci Savi sopra le Decime, B. 110 [Aggiunte – 1540], no. 2116: "ne sono molto ruina, tali che hanno bisogno de molti concierj . . . E poi non si puol scuoder tutti li fittj per esser in quelle de molta povera gente."

46 See Chapter 6, n. 55.

47 Megna, "Comportamenti abitativi," 294–95. See also Monica Chojnacka, *Working Women of Early Modern Venice* (Baltimore: The Johns Hopkins University Press, 2001), for the varied domestic arrangements of single women.

48 Megna, "Comportamenti abitativi," 267–70. For a magisterial study of such an enclave, see Juergen Schulz, "The Houses of the Dandolo: A Family Compound in Medieval Venice," *Journal of the Society of Architectural Historians* 52 (1993): 391–415.

49 ASV, Notarile, Testamenti, B. 1259, n. 507.

50 For the Scuole Grandi, see Brian Pullan, *Rich and Poor in Renaissance Venice: The Social Institutions of a Catholic State, to 1620* (Cambridge, Mass.: Harvard University Press, 1971).

51 Giorgio Gianighian and Paola Pavanini, *Dietro i Palazzi: Tre secoli di architettura minore a Venezia 1492–1803* (Venice: Arsenale Editrice, 1984), 72–73.

52 Ibid.; Alberto Rizzi, *La scultura esterna a Venezia: corpus delle sculture erratiche all'aperto di Venezia e della sua laguna* (Venice: Stamperia di Venezia, 1987), 297–98, no. 324; and Giannino Piamonte, *Venezia vista dall'acqua: Guida dei rii di Venezia e delle Isole*, 3rd ed. (Venice: Stamperia di Venezia, 1992), 91 and 102.

53 See Wladimiro Dorigo, "*Exigentes, sigentes, sezentes, sergentes*: le case d'affito a Venezia nel Medioevo," *Venezia Arti* 10 (1996): 25–36; Giorgio Bellavitis, "Il linguaggio gotico diffuso nell'edilizia minore veneziana; *domos a statio*, *hospicii*, e *domos a sergentibus* nella Venezia medioevale," in *L'architettura gotica veneziana*, ed. Francesco Valcanover and Wolfgang Wolters (Venice: Istituto Veneto di Scienze, Lettere ed Arti, 2000), 175–88.

54 This discussion is based upon Gianighian and Pavanini, *Dietro i Palazzi*, 68–69. See also Egli Renata Trincanato, *Venezia Minore* (Milan: Edizioni del Milione, 1948), 156–58.

55 See, in particular, Pullan, *Rich and Poor in Renaisance Venice* 132–37; and idem, "Abitazioni al servizio dei poveri nella repubblica di Venezia," in Gianighian and Pavanini, *Dietro i Palazzi.*

56 Dennis Romano, "L'assistenza e la beneficenza," in *Storia di Venezia dalle origini alla caduta della Serenissima, V: Il Rinascimento: Società e Economica*, ed. Alberto Tenenti and Ugo Tucci (Rome: Istituto della Enciclopedia Italiana, 1996).

57 Gianighian and Pavanini, *Dietro i palazzi*, 110–13. See also Trincanato, *Venezia minore*, 306–9.

58 Gianighian and Pavanini, *Dietro i palazzi*, 113.

59 Ibid., 111–13.

60 Ibid.

61 See, for example, Giacomo Lanteri, *Della economica; nel quale si dimostrano le qualità, che all'huomo & alla donna separatamente convengono pel governo della casa* (Venice: Appresso Vincenzo Valgrisi, 1560), 14; and Sebastiano Serlio, *Sebastiano Serlio on domestic architecture; different dwellings from the meanest hovel to the most ornate palace. The Sixteenth-Century Manuscript of Book VI in the Avery Library of Columbia University*, ed. Myra Nan Rosenfeld (New York: Architectural History Foundation, 1978), 56–57. See also Brown, "Behind the Walls: The Material Culture of Venetian Elites," in *Venice Reconsidered: The History and Civilization of an Italian City-State, 1297–1797*, ed. John Martin and Dennis Romano (Baltimore and London: Johns Hopkins University Press, 2000), 317–19.

62 Pullan, "Abitazioni al servizio dei poveri," 39–44.

63 Paola Pavanini, "Abitazioni popolari e borghesi nella Venezia cinquecentesca," *Studi Veneziani*, n.s, 5 (1981): 109–11: "veri, serradure, chiave, cadenazzi, balconi, scale, sovaze, et ogn'altra cosa."

64 Pullan, "Abitazioni al servizio dei poveri," 41–42, citing Archivio di Scuola di San Rocco, Registro delle Terminazioni 3, ff. 71–75: "con sei creaturine picciole, scalce, et si può dire nude, et lui similmente insieme con sua moglie mal vestito, et pieno in apparenza di miseria et povertà per maggiormente concitar gli animi vostri a favorirlo, et moverli a compassione, affermando tutti sei quei figliolini esser suoi,

se bene dui soli d'essi erano suoi figlioli, et gl'altri menati secco per l'intentione sopradetta."

65 See Franca Semi, *Gli "Ospizi" di Venezia* (Venice: Edizioni Helvetia, 1983); Bernard Aikema and Dulcia Meijers, *Nel regno dei poveri. Arte e storia dei grandi ospedali veneziani in età moderna, 1474–1797* (Venice: IRE, 1989); David Chambers and Brian Pullan, eds., with Jennifer Fletcher, *Venice. A Documentary History, 1450–1630*, (Oxford: Blackwell, 1992), 295–322; and Romano, "L'assistenza e la beneficenza."

66 Romano, "L'assistenza e la beneficenza," 370. The hospice is located on Campo dei Gesuiti 4905, near Santi Apostoli. See Silvia Lunardon, *Hospitale S. Mariae Cruciferorum: L'ospizio dei Crociferi a Venezia* (Venice: IRE, 1984); and Semi, *Gli "Ospizi" di Venezia*, 184–86. The present layout is similar to that of the late sixteenth century, although two bedrooms have been added. For Palma il Giovane's painting, *Ranieri Zen and the Endowment of the Crociferi*, see Stefania Mason Rinaldi, *Palma il Giovane. L'opera completa* (Milan: Electa, 1984), 138.

67 Semi, *Gli "Ospizi" di Venezia*, 184–86. Jacopo Sansovino followed this time-honored typology for his Ca' di Dio in the mid-sixteenth century: Howard, *Jacopo Sansovino*, 112–19.

68 Dennis Romano, "L'assistenza e le beneficenza," 370–78.

69 Semi, *Gli "Ospizi" di Venezia*, 278–80, citing from Priuli's testament (3 May 1569), published in *Antichi testamenti, tratti dagli archivi della Congregazione di Carità*, ser. XI, 1883: "avvertendo di metter persone di buona vita, et senza fioi ne mugier, mache siano venetiani, over suditi, perchè in modo alcun non vogioche sieno dati (camera e ducati) a persone di paese alieno, abenchè fussero stati anni trenta et più in Venetia."

70 Ibid: "malavasia, buzolai, minestra de risi, per piatanza pesce per esser ne l'avento, et quel più che parerà al Prior da chà di Priuli, essendo questo carico suo."

71 Semi, *Gli "Ospizi" di Venezia*, 263–64, who names Pope Gregorio IV instead of Eugenius IV in error. See also Tassini, *Curiosità veneziane*, 302–3.

72 Sanudo, *Diarii*, 40:696–97 (21 January 1526 m v = 1527): "per veder cosa nova, *videlicet* sopra uno solereto le 6 pute di anni 8 in 9 l'una, fiole di quelle di la Scuola, qual e' vestite meze bianche e meze rosse, con caveli zò per spala e una zoia di verdure in testa. Stanno in una caxa a San Barnuba dedicata a questo, con una maistra a la qual se li dà ducati 40 a l'anno; e a queste vien fato le spese e insegnatoli lezer e la vorar fino siano a età perfeta di maridar o altro . . . si eleze da quelli di la Scuola con certo ordine bellissimo." See also Semi, *Gli "Ospizi" di Venezia*, 263–64.

73 Fynes Moryson, *An Itinerary Containing His Ten Yeeres Travell through the Twelve Dominions of Germany, Bohmerland, Sweitzerland, Netherland, Denmarke, Poland, Italy, Turky [sic], France, England, Scotland & Ireland* (Glasgow: James MacLehose and Sons, 1907), 183.

74 Cited by Romano, "L'assistenza e la beneficenza," 358.

75 Ibid., 355–406; and Pullan, "Abitazioni al servizio dei poveri," 39–44.

76 Romano, "L'assistenza e la beneficenza," 363; Pullan, *Rich and Poor in Renaisance Venice*, 372–74.

77 Romano, "L'assistenza e la beneficenza," 363: "è certo umano, et pietoso officio l'haver à poveri commiseratione, et massimamente à coloro, che nati di honesti parenti, e de' beni di fortuna per qualche tempo ben dotati, siano poi per varii et diversi accidente di quella, à povero stato ridotti, delli quali in questa città ne habbiano gran numero, et sono chiamati li poveri vergognosi."

78 Chambers and Pullan, *Venice: A Documentary History*, 319–20, citing Archivio della Scuola Grande de San Rocco, Registro delle Terminazioni 3, f. 230v (2 June 1593).

79 See Blake de Maria, "The Merchants of Venice: A Study in Sixteenth-Century *Cittadino* Patronage" (Ph.D. diss., Princeton University, 2002), 56–182.

80 Sanudo, *Diarii*, 47:81–82 (13 March 1528) "dove siano posti tutti ditti poveri che vanno per questa terra, et li siano fatte le stantie de tavola *cum* assai paglia et altro per dormir, nè de lì se possino partir sotto pena a chi sarà trovato fuora de ditti loci et andar per la terra mendicando et cridando la notte, da esser subito retenuto et messo in preson, et il giorno seguente fatto frustar et condutto fuora de la terra, et se'l ritornerà la seconda volta, sia *iterum* frustato et conduto fuora, et *hoc toties quoties*."

81 Semi, *Gli "Ospizi" di Venezia*, 33; Brian Pullan, "La nuova filantropia nella Venezia Cinquecentesca," in Bernard Aikema and Dulcia Meijers, *Nel regno dei poveri: Arte e storia dei grandi ospedali veneziani in età moderna, 1474–1797* (Venice: IRE, 1989).

82 Chambers and Pullan, *Venice: A Documentary History*, 114–15, 302–3; Semi, *Gli "Ospizi" di Venezia*, 33–45. Built on the island of Santa Maria di Nazareth, the Lazzaretto Vecchio was renamed the Mendicanti and moved to the Zattere at the beginning of the seventeenth century, when a new building was constructed to house orphans and beggars. For the Pietà and the Mendicanti, see Aikema and Meijers, *Nel regno dei poveri*, 197–214 and 249–71 respectively.

83 Chambers and Pullan, *Venice: A Documentary History*, 303, 307–8; Dulcia Meijers, "L'architettura della nuova filantropia," in Bernard Aikema and Dulcia Meijers, *Nel regno dei poveri Arte e steria dei grandi ospedali veneziani in età moderna, 1474–1797* (Venice: IRE, 1989).

84 Chambers and Pullan, *Venice: A Documentary History*, 308–15; Aikema and Meijers, *Nel regno dei poveri*, 131–95.

85 Patricia Fortini Brown, *Art and Life in Renaissance Venice* (New York: Harry N. Abrams, 1997), 107–9. Cf. Bernard Aikema, "L'immagine della 'carità veneziana'," in Aikema and Meijers, *Nel regno dei poveri*; Thomas Riis, "I poveri nell'arte italiana (secoli XV–XVIII)" in *Timore e carità: i poveri nell'Italia moderna*, ed. Giorgio Politi, Mario Rosa, and Franco Della Peruta (Cremona: Annali della Biblioteca Statale e Libreria Civica di Cremona, 1982).

86 Chambers and Pullan, *Venice: A Documentary History*, 303–6, citing ASV, Senato, Terra, Reg. for 1529, ff. 125v–127r, 3 April 1529.

87 The locations of the hospices shown in fig. 235 are taken from Semi, *Gli "Ospizi" di Venezia*. For Ludovico Ughi's topographical map of Venice, see Juergen Schulz, *The Printed Plans and Panoramic Views of Venice, 1486–1797* (Florence: Leo S. Olschki, 1970), 82–89; and Giocondo Cassini, *Piante e vedute prospettiche di Venezia (1479–1855)* (Venice: La Stamperia di Venezia Editrice, 1982), 140.

88 Isabella Palumbo-Fossati, "L'interno della casa dell'artigiano e dell'artista nella Venezia del Cinquecento." *Studi Veneziani*, n.s. 8 (1984): 109–53.

89 Patricia Anne Allerston, "The Market in Second-Hand Clothes and Furnishings in Venice, ca. 1500–ca. 1650" (Ph. D. diss., Florence: European University Institute, Department of History and Civilization, 1996), 69–71.

90 Ibid., 74, citing ASV, SNC, b. 216, Inventari d'asporti, Reg. 1, 21 April 1583.

91 Cited by Riccardo Calimani, *The Ghetto of Venice*, trans. Katherine Silberblatt Wolfthal (New York: M. Evans and Company, 1987), 1. For the word "ghetto," see Benjamin Ravid, "From Geographical

Realia to Historiographical Symbol: The Odyssey of the Word *Ghetto*," in *Essential Papers on Jewish Culture in Renaissance and Baroque Italy*, ed. David B. Ruderman, (New York: New York University Press, 1992), 373–84.

92 See, in general, Gaetano Cozzi, ed., *Gli Ebrei e Venezia, Secoli XIV–XVIII* (Milan: Comunita, 1987); E. Concina, U. Camerino, and D. Calabi, *La città degli ebrei. Il Ghetto di Venezia: architettura e urbanistica* (Venice: Marsilio, 1991); Donatella Calabi "The 'City of the Jews'," in *The Jews of Early Modern Venice*, ed. Robert C. Davis and Benjamin Ravid (Baltimore and London: The Johns Hopkins University Press, 2001); Richard Goy, *Venice: The City and its Architecture* (London: Phaidon, 1997), 86–93; and Gianighian and Pavanini, *Dietro i Palazzi*, 186–91.

93 Benjamin Ravid, "Curfew Time in the Ghetto of Venice," in *Medieval and Renaissance Venice*, ed. Ellen E. Kittel and Thomas F. Madden (Urbana and Chicago: University of Illinois Press, 1999); and Calimani, *The Ghetto of Venice*, 1–20. See also Calabi, "The 'City of the Jews'," 32, who notes that many of the tenants rebuilt their apartments, cutting prohibited windows into the outside walls.

94 See Umberto Fortis, *The Ghetto on the Lagoon: A Guide to the History and Art of the Venetian Ghetto (1516–1797)*, rev. ed., trans. Roberto Matteoda (Venice: Storti Edizioni, 1997), 82; and Leone Modena, *The History of the Rites, Customes, and Manner of Life, of the Present Jews, Throughout the World*, trans. Edmund Chilmead (London: J. L., 1650), 104–5, 111–12.

95 Calabi "The 'City of the Jews'".

96 Ravid, "Curfew Time in the Ghetto of Venice," 237–75.

97 Allerston, "*The Market in Second-Hand Clothes and Furnishings*," 120–55, 197–206, and passim.

98 Calimani, *The Ghetto of Venice*, 1–20.

99 Benjamin Ravid, "Christian Travelers in the Ghetto of Venice: Some Preliminary Observations," in *Between History and Literature: Studies in Honor of Isaac Barzilay*, ed. Stanley Nash (Bnei-Brak, 1997), 115–16.

100 Sansovino, *Venetia città nobilissima* (1663), 1:368. For life in the Ghetto, see the rich collection of essays in Davis and Ravid, *The Jews of Early Modern Venice*.

101 James S. Ackerman and Myra Nan Rosenfeld, "Social Stratification in Renaissance Urban Planning," in *Urban Life in the Renaissance*, ed. Susan Zimmerman and Ronald F. E. Weissman (Newark: University of Delaware Press; London and Toronto: Associated University Presses, 1989), 21–49.

Chapter 8

1 Thomas Coryat, *Coryat's Crudities* (Glasgow: James MacLehose and Sons, 1905), 1: 386.

2 Francesco Petrarch, *Petrarch: Four Dialogues for Scholars*, ed. and trans. Conrad H. Rawski (Cleveland: Press of Western Reserve University, 1967), 31, with a translation of his *De remediis utriusque fortunae* (begun in the 1350s and completed in 1366). See also Paula Findlen, "Possessing the Past: The Material World of the Italian Renaissance," *American Historical Review* 103 (1998), 91.

3 Deborah Howard, "Responses to Ancient Greek Architecture," *Annali di Architettura* 6 (1994): 31; Patricia Fortini Brown, *Venice & Antiquity: The Venetian Sense of the Past* (New Haven and London: Yale University Press, 1996), 83–91.

4 Kzrystof Pomian, *Collectors and Curiosities: Paris and Venice, 1500–1800*, trans. Elizabeth Wiles-Portier (Cambridge: Polity Press, 1990), 34: "in a most interesting process scrap was being turned into semiophores." See also Susan Connell, "Books and their Owners in Venice 1345–1480," *Journal of the Warburg and Courtauld Institutes* 35 (1972): 163–86; Roberto Weiss, *Renaissance Discovery of Classical Antiquity* (Oxford: Oxford University Press, 1973), 22–27; Marino Zorzi, ed., *Collezioni di antichità a Venezia nei secoli della Repubblica* (Rome: Istituto Poligrafico e Zecca dello Stato, 1988), 15–24; Irene Favaretto, *Arte antica e cultura antiquaria nelle collezioni venete al tempo della Serenissima* (Rome: "L'Erma" di Bretschneider, 1990), 31–62: and Brown, *Venice & Antiquity*, 75–98, 160–61. See also the facsimile edition: Bartolomeo dalli Sonetti, *Isolario* (Amsterdam: Theatrum Orbis Terrarum Ltd., 1972).

5 See Alberto Tenenti, "The Sense of Space and Time in the Venetian World of the Fifteenth and Sixteenth Centuries," in *Renaissance Venice*, ed. J. R. Hale (London: Faber and Faber, 1973).

6 Arnaldo Bruschi, *Bramante* (London: Thames & Hudson, 1977), 39–41.

7 Jay A. Levenson, ed., *Circa 1492: Art in the Age of Exploration* (New Haven and London: Yale University Press, 1992), 229; Franco Borsi, *Bramante* (Milan: Electa, 1989), 163–66.

8 See the perceptive essay by Findlen, "Possessing the Past," 83–114.

9 See Oliver Logan, *Culture and Society in Venice, 1470–1790* (London: B. T. Batsford Ltd, 1972), 148–81; Dora Thornton, *The Scholar in His Study* (New Haven and London: Yale University Press, 1997), 99–125.

10 John Florio, *Queen Anna's New Worlde of Words* (London: Melch Bradwood, 1611; reprint, London: Scolar Press, 1968), 562.

11 See Helen Roberts, "St. Augustine in St. Jerome's Study: Carpaccio's Painting and its Legendary Source," *Art Bulletin* 41 (1959): 293–95; Patricia Fortini Brown, "Carpaccio's *St. Augustine in his Study*: A Portrait within a Portrait," in *St. Augustine in Iconography, History and Legend*, ed. Joseph C. Schnaubelt and Frederick Van Fleteren (New York: Peter Lang Publishing, 1999); and Thornton, *The Scholar in His Study*, 161–63.

12 Marin Sanudo, *I diarii*, ed. Rinaldo Fulin et al. (Venice: F. Visentini, 1879–1903) 13:293 (5 December 1511): "Da poi disnar, noto, el signor Alberto da Carpi vene a veder il mio studio e il mapamondo." See also Thornton, *The Scholar in His Study*, 114.

13 Rawdon Brown, *Ragguagli sulla vita e sulle opere di Marin Sanuto detto il Juniore veneto patrizio e cronista pregevolissimo de secoli XV, XVI* (Venice: Alvisopoli, 1837–38), II: 65; and R. Fulin, "Diarii e diaristi," *Nuovo Archivio Veneto* 22:1 (1881): xix.

14 Brown, *Ragguagli*, I: 10. The house (Santa Croce 1757) had recently been subdivided from the principal body of the ancient family residence following a prolonged legal battle: Giorgio Bellavitis, "Il linguaggio gotico diffuso nell'edilizia minore veneziana; *domos a statio, hospicii*, e *domos a sergentibus* nella Venezia medioevale," in *L'architettura gotica veneziana*, ed. Francesco Valcanover and Wolfgang Wolters (Venice: Istituto Veneto di Scienze, Lettere ed Arti, 2000), 187.

15 BMV, It. cl. XII, cod. 211, cited by R. Fulin, "Diarii e diaristi," xix–xx.

16 Levenson, *Circa 1492*, 234–35, dates the map to around 1508; See also Jay A. Levenson, Konrad Oberhuber, and Jacquelyn L. Sheehan, *Early Italian Engravings from the National Gallery of Art* (Washington: National Gallery of Art, 1973), 47–59.

17 Federica Ambrosini, "'Descrittioni del mondo' nelle case venete dei secoli XVI e XVII," *Archivio Veneto* 112, ser. v, no. 152 (1981), 67–68. Cf. the epigram of Giovanni Perloto, BMV,. MS. It. cl. IX, cod. 364.

18 BMV, MS. It. xi, 67 (7351), transcribed in J. Morelli, *Notizia d'opere di Disegno*, rev. and ed. G. Frizzoni (Bologna, 1884); and Theodor Frimmel, *"Der Anonimo Morelliano (Marcanton Michiel's Notizia d'Opere del Disegno),"* in *Quellenschriften für Kunstgeschichte und Kunsttechnik*, I (Vienna: Verlag Carl Graeser, 1896). On this text, see Jennifer Fletcher, "Marcantonio Michiel: his Friends and Collection," *The Burlington Magazine* 123 (1981): 453–57; and Monika Anne Schmitter, "The Display of Distinction: Art Collecting and Social Status in Early Sixteenth-Century Venice," Ph.D. diss. (University of Michigan, 1997), 29–38.

19 See Jennifer Fletcher, "Marcantonio Michiel's Collection," *Journal of the Warburg and Courtauld Institutes* 36 (1973): 382–85; and Zorzi, *Collezioni di antichità a Venezia*, 47.

20 John Pope-Hennessy, *Catalogue of Italian Sculpture in the Victoria and Albert Museum* (London: Her Majesty's Stationery Office, 1964), II: Text, 510–12; Fletcher, "Marcantonio Michiel: his Friends and Collection," 463–64; J. C. Eade, "Marcantonio Michiel's Mercury Statue: Astronomical or Astrological," *Journal of the Warburg and Courtauld Institutes* 44 (1981): 207–9; Jane Martineau and Charles Hope, *The Genius of Venice, 1500–1600* (London: Weidenfeld & Nicolson, 1983), 367–68.

21 Fletcher, "Marcantonio Michiel: his Friends and Collection," 462.

22 See, for example, the name of Lorenzo de' Medici (typically by the abbreviation, LAVR. MED.) incised prominently on many of the antique gems in his collection: Nicole Dacos, ed., *Il Tesoro di Lorenzo il Magnifico: Repertorio delle gemme e dei vasi* (Florence: Sansoni Editore, 1980).

23 Identified by Schmitter, "The Display of Distinction," 171–72.

24 Marco Boschini, *Le ricche minere della pittura veneziana* (Venice: F. Nicolini, 1674), Sestiere of Dorsoduro, 52–53; Schmitter, "The Display of Distinction," 165–86.

25 Frimmel, *Der Anonimo Morelliano*, 82.

26 Schmitter, "The Display of Distinction," 187. Cf. Isabella Palumbo-Fossati, "L'interno della casa dell'artigiano e dell'artista nella Venezia del Cinquecento." *Studi Veneziani*, 8, n.s. (1984): 150.

27 Georg Gronau, "Venezianische Kunstsammlungen des 16 Jahrhunderts," *Jahrbuch für Kunstsammler* 4–5 (1924–25), 56–59; Schmitter, "The Display of Distinction," 209–13.

28 See John Shearman, *The Early Italian Pictures in the Collection of Her Majesty the Queen* (Cambridge: Cambridge University Press, 1983), 144–48.

29 Schmitter,"The Display of Distinction," 222–235.

30 Ibid., 252. Cf. Shearman, *Early Italian Pictures*, 146–47.

31 Salvatore Settis, *Giorgione's Tempest: Interpreting the Hidden Subject*, trans. Ellen Bianchini (Chicago: The University of Chicago Press, 1990), 142. For a rich collection of primary documents, see Donata Battilotti and Maria Teresa Franco, "Regesti dei committenti e dei primi collezionisti di Giorgione," *Antichità Viva* 17 (1978): 64–68.

32 Aldo Ravà, "Il 'camerino delle antigaglie' di Gabriele Vendramin," *Nuovo Archivio Veneto*, n.s., 39 (1920): 155–81; Favaretto, *Arte antica e cultura antiquaria*, 79–82.

33 Anton Francesco Doni, *I Marmi* (Venice, 1552), 400–1, cited with English translation in Settis, *Giorgione's Tempest*, 143.

34 Frimmel, *Der Anonimo Morelliano*, 108. Michiel listed only one other collector with drawings: Michiel Contarini at the Misericordia, who owned a drawing by Giorgione and a number of works in gouache painted by Contarini himself after other artists (ibid., 114–15).

35 See n. 33 above.

36 Francesco Sansovino, *Venetia città nobilissima, et singolare descritta in* XIIII *libri*, with additions by Giustiniano Martinioni (Venice: Steffano Curti, 1663; reprint, Venice: Filippi Editore, 1968) 387.

37 Settis, *Giorgione's Tempest*, 143. But cf. Jaynie Anderson, "A Further Inventory of Gabriel Vendramin's Collection," *The Burlington Magazine* 121 (1979): 642–43, who unconvincingly identifies Gabriele as the dark-haired man to the left.

38 For Machiavelli, see Chapter I.

39 Manfredi Tafuri, *Venice and the Renaissance* (Cambridge, Mass.: MIT Press, 1989), 11.

40 Gustav Ludwig, "Archivalische Beiträge zur Geschichte der venezianischen Kunst aus dem Nachlass Gustav Ludwigs," in *Italianische Forschungen* IV (Berlin: Verlag von Bruno Cassirer, 1911), 72–74. See also Settis, *Giorgione's Tempest*, 144–45.

41 Anderson, "A Further Inventory of Gabriel Vendramin's Collection," 643; Mauro Lucco, "Le cosiddette 'Tre età dell'uomo'," in Mauro Lucco, *Le tre età dell'uomo della Galleria Palatina* (Florence: Centro Di, 1989).

42 See Thornton, *Scholar in his Study*, 69.

43 Ravà, "Il 'camerino delle antigaglie' di Gabriele Vendramin," 161–79.

44 Vincenzo Scamozzi, *Dell'idea della architettura universale* (Venice: presso l'autore, 1615), 305–6.

45 Favaretto, *Arte antica e cultura antiquaria*, 81–82; and Emil Jacobs, "Das Museo Vendramin und die Sammlung Reynst," *Repertorium für Kunstwissenschaft* 46 (1925): 15–38.

46 Sanudo, *Diarii*, 6:172 (31 May 1505); Favaretto, *Arte antica e cultura antiquaria*, 84–85.

47 Marilyn Perry, "Cardinal Grimani's Legacy of Ancient Art to Venice," *Journal of the Warburg and Courtauld Institutes* 41 (1978): 215–44; Bruce Boucher, *The Sculpture of Jacopo Sansovino* (New Haven and London: Yale University Press, 1991), I: 9, II: 314–15.

48 Sanudo, *Diarii* 6:165–66 (6 May 1505) and 171–73 (31 May 1505): "Item lassa alla Signoria tutti li soi bronzi e marmi, da essere adornado una sala per sua memoria." See, in particular, Perry, "Cardinal Grimani's Legacy of Ancient Art."

49 See Perry, "Cardinal Grimani's Legacy of Ancient Art"; Zorzi, *Collezioni di antichità a Venezia*, 25–31; and Favaretto, *Arte antica e cultura antiquaria*, 84–89.

50 For the history of the house, see Annalisa Bistrot and Mario Piana, "Il Palazzo dei Grimani a Santa Maria Formosa," in *Lo Statuario pubblico della Serenissima: due secoli di collezionismo di antichità: 1596–1797*, ed. Irene Favaretto and Giovanna Luisa Ravagnan (Cittadella: Biblos, 1997): In 1500, Domenico's father, Antonio, had ceded the house to his three other sons: Vincenzo, Girolamo, and Pietro. After the deaths of Girolamo [1524?] and Pietro [1516], Vincenzo owned the property jointly with three of Girolamo's sons: Marco, Vettore, and Giovanni. A fourth son, Marino, had been named Patriarch of Aquileia in 1517 and would become a cardinal himself in 1528. In 1524, the palace was subdivided, with Vincenzo receiving the second *soler* and his nephews Marco, Vettore, and Giovanni the first *soler*. By 1532, both Vincenzo and his son Antonio had died, and his widow Isabetta ceded the second *soler* to Vettore. Marco and Giovanni now shared the first *soler*. In 1544, Marco died, with Giovanni taking over the first *soler*. Finally, in 1558, Vettore died, and his widow ceded her share to Giovanni, who took over the entire property.

51 Ibid.

52 Wolfgang Wolters, *Architektur und Ornament: venezianischer Bauschmuck der Renaissance* (Munich: C. H. Beck, 2000), 132–52.

See also Juergen Schulz, *Venetian Painted Ceilings of the Renaissance* (Berkeley and Los Angeles: University of California Press, 1968), 11 and 142–43; and Alain Gruber, "Grotesques," in *The History of Decorative Arts: The Renaissance and Mannerism in Europe*, ed. Alain Gruber (New York: Abbeville Press, 1994).

53 For Grimani's collecting and patronage, see also Michel Hochman, *Peintres et commanditaires à Venise (1540–1628)* (Rome: Ecole Française de Rome, 1992), 229–42.

54 Manfredo Tafuri, "Il pubblico e il privato. Architettura e committenza a Venezia," in *Storia di Venezia. VI. Dal Rinascimento al Barocco*, ed. Gaetano Cozzi and Paolo Prodi (Rome: Istituto della Enciclopedia Italiana, 1994).

55 For another family with Roman pretensions, see Michel Hochmann, "Tra Venezia e Roma: il cardinale Francesco Corner," *Saggi e memorie di storia dell'arte* 18 (1992): 97–110

56 Manfredo Tafuri, *Ricerca del Rinascimento: i principi, città, architetti* (Turin: Giulio Einaudi Editore, 1992), 315–16.

57 For the *casa aperta*, see Chapter 1, n. 12.

58 Sansovino, *Venetia città nobilissima* (1663), 372: "vi si veggono in diverse stanze ch'entrano l'una nell'altra, figure intere & spezzate, torsi, & teste in tanta abbondanza ch e nulla più, & tutte elette & di pregio."

59 Ibid.: "principalissimo non pur di Venetia, ma qusi di ogni altra città . . . un luogo celebre & ripieno di bellezze antiche & singolari per quantità & qualità . . . è rarissime da vedere." For the room, see Perry, "Cardinal Grimani's Legacy of Ancient Art to Venice," 220–21; and Tafuri, *Venice and the Renaissance*, 7–9.

60 Krzystof Pomian, "Collezioni, specchio della cultura," Ateneo Veneto, n.s., 22 (1984): 18–20.

61 Scamozzi, *Architettura* 305.

62 Cf. Irene Favaretto, "Memoria dell'immagine e immagine nella memoria: significato e valore del catalogo illustrato nella storia delle collezioni veneziane di antichità," in *Collezioni di anitchità a Venezia nei secoli della Repubblica (dai libri e documenti della Biblioteca Marciana)*, ed. Marino Zorzi (Rome: Istituto Poligrafico e Zecca dello Stato, 1988), who argues that for most Venetian collectors, the aesthetic unity of the whole collection – as opposed to singling out the individual pieces – was a primary goal, with works distributed throughout the home. This meant that an illustrated catalogue would make no sense, since direct vision was necessary to communicate the message.

63 See Paula Findlen, "The Museum: Its Classical Etymology and Renaissance Genealogy," *Journal of the History of Collections* 1 (1989): 59–78; idem, *Possessing Nature: Museums, Collecting, and Scientific Culture in Early Modern Italy* (Berkeley and Los Angeles: University of California Press, 1994); Katherine Park and Lorraine J. Daston, *Wonders and the Order of Nature, 1150–1750* (New York: Zone Books, 1998).

64 Anne-Marie S. Logan, *The 'Cabinet' of the Brothers Gerard and Jan Reynst* (Amsterdam and New York: Batsford, 1979), 67–75, lists six books that survive, with further bibliography: I. *De picturis*, British Museum: MS. Sloane 4004; V. *De Sacrificiorum & Triumphorum vasculis*, Bodleian Library, Oxford: MS. d'Orville 539; VIII. *De annulis et sigillis Aegyptiorum*, British Museum, MS. Sloane 4005; IX. *De rebus naturalibus*, British Museum, MS. Sloane 4006; XI. *De mineralibus*, British Museum, MS. Sloane 4007; XVII. *De Antiquorum Tumulis*, East Berlin, Deutsche Staatsbibiliothek, MS. Phill. 189. Two additional books were noted by Tancred Borenius, *The Picture Gallery of Andrea Vendramin* (London: The Medici Society, 1923), in the following libraries, but their present whereabouts is unknown: II. *De Sculpturis*, Berlin Staatliche Museen; and XIII. *De libris Chronologicorum universalium figuris & coloribus ornatis*, Warsaw, Zaluski Library. See also Jacobs, "Da Museo Vendramin und die Sammlung Reynst," 19–22; Zorzi, *Collezioni di antichità a Venezia*, 78–79.

65 British Museum, Sloane MS. 4004. Borenius, *The Picture Gallery of Andrea Vendramin*, contains reproductions of the drawings from the catalogue of paintings, with notes and tentative identifications of the few works that survive.

66 Borenius, *The Picture Gallery of Andrea Vendramin*, 21.

67 Bodleian Library, MS. d'Orville 539: *De Sacrificiorum & Triumphorum vasculis, lucernisque Antiquorum*. See also Thornton, *The Scholar in his Study*, 99–100.

68 Fynes Moryson, *An Itinerary . . .* (London, 1617; repr. Amsterdam, New York: Da Capo Press/Theatrum Orbis Terrarum Ltd., 1971), 88.

69 Herbert Siebenhühner, *Der Palazzo Barbarigo della Terrazza in Venedig und seine Tizian-Sammlung* (Munich: Deutscher Kunstverlag, 1981), 30.

70 Cited by Jaynie Anderson, "Titian's Unfinished 'Portrait of a Woman and her Daughter' from the Barbarigo Collection, Venice," *The Burlington Magazine* 14 (2002): 671.

71 Siebenhühner, *Der Palazzo Barbarigo della Terrazza in Venedig*, 26–32. But see now Anderson, "Titian's Unfinished 'Portrait of a Woman and her Daughter" from the Barbarigo Collection," 671–77.

72 Siebenhühner, *Der Palazzo Barbarigo della Terrazza in Venedig*, 30–31.

73 Anderson, "Titian's Unfinished 'Portrait of a Woman and her Daughter' from the Barbarigo Collection," 671, notes that the original frames were removed from all the paintings, save that of the Magdalen, when the collection was sold to Tsar Nicholas I of Russia in 1850.

74 See Michel Hochmann, *Peintres et commanditaires à Venise (1540–1628)* (Rome: Ecole Française de Rome, 1992), 254–62; idem, "La collection de Giacomo Contarini," *Mélanges de l'Ecole française de Rome: Moyen Age – Temps Modernes* 99:1 (1987): 447–89; and Paul Lawrence Rose, "Jacomo Contarini (1536–1595) a Venetian Patron and Collector of Mathematical Instruments and Books," *Physis, rivista internazionale di storia della scienza*, anno XVIII, fasc. 2 (1976): 117–30. For the palace, see Elena Bassi, *Palazzi di Venezia*, rev. ed. (Venice: Stamperia di Venezia Editrice, 1987), 382–85.

75 Paolo Gualdo, "Vita di Andrea Palladio, a cura di Giangiorgio Zorzi," *Saggi e Memorie di Storia dell'arte* 2 (1959): 93–94; and Hochmann, *Peintres et commanditaires à Venise*, 255–60. For Porro, see Manfredo Tafuri, *Venezia e il Rinascimento* (Turin: Giulio Einaudi, Editore, 1985), 197 and 255.

76 Sansovino, *Venetia città nobilissima* (1663), 370: "Il quale con spesa indicibile, ha posto insieme quasi tutte le historie stampate & le scritte à penna, non pure universali, ma particulari delle città, con diversi altri libri & in gran copia nelle scienze. Co quali sono accompagnati disegni, stomenti mathematici, & altre cose di mano de i più chiari artefici nella pittura, nella scoltura, e nell'architettura, che habbia havuto l'età. I quali tutti eglli ha sempte, come amante de i virtuosi favoriti & accarezzati."

77 Ibid. See Hochmann, "La collection de Giacomo Contarini," 457–58, who shows that Giacomo made an inventory of his collection, unfortunately lost by the eighteenth century.

78 ASV, Consultori in Jure, B. 28, fasc. no. 4, cited by Hochmann, "La collection de Giacomo Contarini," 456.

79 ASV, Notarile Testamenti (not. Galeazzo Secco), B. 1191, n. 350, cited by Tafuri, *Venice and the Renaissance*, 130; and Hochmann, "La collection de Giacomo Contarini," 457. See also Favaretto, *Arte antica e cultura antiquaria*, 94.

80 ASV, Procuratori di Supra, B. 68, proc. 151, fasc. 3/1, c. 1, cited by Favaretto, *Arte antica e cultura antiquaria*, 88–89.

81 Ibid. 88–93; Zorzi, *Collezioni di antichità a Venezia*, 30–33; and Irene Favaretto, "Un notabilissimo ornamento: la vita dello Statuario tra XVII e XVIII secolo," and Amalia Donatella Basso, "L'ambiente dello Statuario," in *Lo Statuario pubblico della Serenissima: due secoli di collezionismo di antichità: 1596–1797*, ed. Irene Favaretto and Giovanna Luisa Ravagnan (Cittadella: Biblos, 1997).

82 Zorzi, *Collezioni di antichità a Venezia*, 32–37.

83 Moryson, *An Itinerary*, 86.

84 Thomas Coryat, *Coryat's Crudities, reprinted from the edition of 1611, to which are now added his letters from India, etc.* [3 vols] (London 1776), 224–7.

85 See Pomian, "Collezioni, specchio della cultura," 17–36.

86 See Irene Favaretto and Giovanna Luisa Ravagnan, eds., *Lo statuario pubblico della Serenissima: due secoli di collezionismo di antichità: 1596–1979* (Cittadella: Biblos, 1997), 164–5.

87 Emmanuela Zucchetta, *Antichi ridotti veneziani: Arte e società dal Cinquecento al Settecento* (Rome: Fratelli Palombi, 1988), 29–30; Gino Damerini, *Giardini nella laguna* (Bologna N. Zanichelli, 1927), 37.

88 Zucchetta, *Antichi ridotti veneziani*, 88–90; Wolfgang Wolters, "Una villa cinquecentesca in pericolo a Murano," *Antichità Viva* 5:3 (1966): 27–33; Emanuela Zucchetta Benvenuti, "Gli affreschi del Casino Mogenico [sic] di Murano: tra armonia ed evasione," *Notizie da Palazzo Albani* 14:1 (1985): 54–62; Richard J. Goy, *Venetian Vernacular Architecture: Traditional Housing in the Venetian Lagoon* (Cambridge: Cambridge University Press, 1989), 234.

89 Andrea Calmo, *Lettere*, ed. Vittorio Rossi (Turin: Ermanno Loescher, 1888), 173.

90 See Wolters, "Una villa cinquecentesca in pericolo a Murano," 27–33; and idem, *Architektur und Ornament*, 140–45.

91 The interpretation that follows is based upon Vincenzo Zanetti, *Guida di Murano e delle celebri sue fornaci vetrarie* (Venice, 1980; reprint, Venice: Arnaldo Forni Editore, 1984), 50–53; and Zucchetta Benvenuti, "Gli affreschi del Casino Mogenico di Murano, 54–62.

92 Zucchetta Benvenuti, "Gli affreschi del Casino Mogenico di Murano," 62.

93 See Zucchetta, *Antichi ridotti veneziani*, 8–33; and Filippo Pedrocco, "Il luogo del gioco: il ridotto di Palazzo Dandolo a San Moisè," in *Fanti e danari: sei secoli di giochi d'azzardo*, ed. A. Fiorin (Venice: Arsenale, 1989). See also Jonathan Walker, "Gambling and Venetian Noblemen, ca.1500–1700," *Past & Present*, 162 (1999): 34–35; Elisabeth Crouzet-Pavan, "Quando la città si diverte. Giochi e ideologia urbana: Venezia negli ultimi secoli del Medioevo," in *Gioco e giustizia nell'Italia di Comune*, ed. Gherardo Ortalli: (Treviso: Fondazione Benetton/Viella, 1993).

94 Walker, "Gambling and Venetian Noblemen," 34–35, who appears to be citing ASV, Consiglio dei Dieci, Criminali, Reg. 26, ff. 132v–133v. See also ASV, Consiglio dei Dieci, Processi Criminali, Dogado, busta 1 (1607–20, 1726, 1739).

95 Crouzet-Pavan, "Quando la città si diverte."

96 Zucchetta, *Antichi ridotti veneziani*, 61–62, 95–96; Fiorin, *Fanti e danari*, 110–12.

97 Walker, "Gambling and Venetian Noblemen," 32.

98 Moryson, *An Itinerary*, 88.

99 Walker, "Gambling and Venetian Noblemen," 68.

100 Ibid., 49–52.

101 Ibid., 48–57.

102 Ibid., 37–38, citing ASV, Executori contro la bestemmia, B. 54, ff. 27–28v (29 December 1628).

Conclusion

1 Sir Henry Wotton, *The Elements of Architecture: A Facsimile Reprint of the First Edition (London, 1624). With Introduction and Notes by Frederick Hard* (Charlottesville: The University Press of Virginia, published for the Folger Shakespeare Library 1968), 82.

Appendix

1 ASV, Dieci, Misti R. 27, 171v–172v. See Stanley Chojnacki, "Measuring Adulthood: Adolescence and Gender," in his *Women and Men in Renaissance Venice: Twelve Essays on Patrician Society* (Baltimore and London: The Johns Hopkins University Press, 2000), 198.

Bibliography

Primary Sources

ARCHIVES

London, British Museum

MS. Sloane 4004: *Delineationes picturarum in musœo A. Vendrameni, Venetorum Ducis.* 1627.

MS. Sloane 4005: *De annulis, et sigillis Egyptiorum scarabeis, emblematibus ornatis, et alijs signis et figuris in gemmiss et lapidibus à natura delineatis, et incisis, in Museo Andreae Vendrameno repositus.* 1627.

MS. Sloane 4006: *De rebus naturalibus Pieris, mixtis, atque compositis et in omni genere petritus, in Musaeo Domini Andreae Vendrameno repositis.* 1627.

MS. Sloane 4007: *De mineralibus omnis generis, tam mallicis, et puris lapideis quam et gemmatis in musaeo D. Andreae Vendrameno positis.* 1627.

New Haven, Yale University, Beinecke Library

MS. 457, *Mores Italiae.* 1575.

Oxford, Bodleian Library

MS. d'Orville 539: *De Sacrificiorum & Triumphorum vasculis, lucernisque Antiquorum, Urnis, à liquoribus, lacrimis atque vaculis vitreis in Andreae Vendrameno musaeo repositis.* 1627.

Venice, Archivio di Stato [ASV]

Avogaria di Comun, registers 1, 2, 87, 89, 106, 107, 108, 111, 114, 115, 141, 142, 143, 145, 148, 149, 150, 151, 159, 164, 165, 205.

Cancelleria Inferiore, Miscellanea Notai Diversi, buste 34, 35, 37, 39, 40, 41, 42, 43, 44.

Dieci Savi sopra le Decime, buste 42, 48, 63, 83, 84, 85, 86, 87, 88, 93, 96, 97, 101, 102, 105, 106, 107, 108, 110, 131, 157, 161, 164, 167, 170, 172.

Giudici dell'Esaminador

Investizioni, registers 15, 16, 17.

Sentenze, busta 9.

Testificazioni, busta 17.

Vendizion, Alienazion, & Donazion, registers 16, 17, 18, 19, 20, 21, 22, 23, 24, 25, 26, 27, 28, 29, 30, 31, 32.

Giudici di Petizion, buste 371, 378, 444.

Giudici del Proprio, Mobili, registers 11, 12, 13, 14, 18, 19, 24, 31, 32, 33, 34, 37, 38, 66.

Miscellanea Codici 898, Marco Barbaro. *Albori de' patritti veneti.* 1536.

Notarile, Atti, register 3290.

Notarile, Testamenti, buste 58, 86, 87, 89, 125, 132, 133, 189, 195, 209, 211, 217, 220, 778, 896, 903, 938, 999, 1185, 1191, 1201, 1210, 1229, 1245, 1256, 1259.

Ospedale e luoghi pii diverse, buste 237, 238.

Procuratoria di San Marco de Citra, buste 48, 315.

Provveditore alle Pompe, buste 1, 3, 6.

Senato, Terra, registers 6–21, 25, 26, 40, 42–44.

Venice, Biblioteca del Museo Correr [BCV]

MS. Cicogna 516 (2504), Marco Barbaro, Discendenze patrizie, 6 vols.

MS. Cicogna 3558/III, *Descritione dell'Isola di Candia.*

MS. Gradenigo 65, Giovanni Grevembroch, *Monumenta Veneta.* 4 vols. Eighteenth century.

MS. Gradenigo 83, *Corona seconda della veneta republica.*

MS. Mariegola 56, Accademia degli Uniti. 1561.

MS. Provinenze Diverse, C 2706/I–2.

Venice, Biblioteca Nazionale Marciana [BMV]

MS. It. VII 15–18 (= 8304–7), Girolamo Alessandro Capellari Vivaro Vicentino, *Il campidoglio veneto.* 4 vols.

MS. It. VII 14 (= 7418): Bernardo Bembo, *Cronica di tutte le case dell'inclitta Città di Venetia.*

MS. It. VII 2053 (= 7920): Nicolò Zen, *Storia della guerra veneto-turca del 1537.*

Printed Primary Sources

Alberti, Leandro. *Descrittione di tutta Italia*. Bologna: Anselmo Giaccarelli, 1550.

Barbaro, Francesco. "On Wifely Duties." Translated by Benjamin G. Kohl. In *The Earthly Republic: Italian Humanists on Government and Society*, edited by Benjamin G. Kohl and Ronald G. Witt with Elizabeth B. Welles. Philadelphia: University of Pennsylvania Press, 1978.

Battilotti, Donata, and Maria Teresa Franco. "Regesti dei committenti e dei primi collezionisti di Giorgione." In *Antichità Viva* 17 (1978): 58–86.

Bembo, Pietro. *Nuove lettere famigliari . . . scritte a m. Gio. Mattheo Bembo suo nipote . . . ; nelle quali si commende particolarmente tutta la vita dell'autore, & qual fosse il suo stile nelle cose volgari in tutti i tempi*. Venice: Francesco Rampazetto, 1564.

Boschini, Marco. *Le ricche minere della pittura veneziana*. Venice: F. Nicolini, 1674.

Calmo, Andrea. *Lettere*. Edited by Vittorio Rossi. Turin: Ermanno Loescher, 1888.

Cassiodorus, *Variarum libri XII*.

Castiglione, Sabba da. *Ricordi*. Venice: Paolo Gerardo, 1560.

Cessole, Frate Jacopo da. *Opera nuova nella quale se insegna il vero regimento delli huomini et delle donne di qualunque grado, stato, e condition esser si voglia: Composta per lo Reverendissimo Padre Frate Giacobo da Cesole del ordine di predicatori sopra il giuoco deli Scacchi, Intitulata costume delli huomini, et efficii delli nobeli, nuovamente stampata*. Venice: Francesco di Alessandro Bindoni et Mapheo Pasini Compagni, 1534.

Chambers, David and Brian Pullan, with Jennifer Fletcher, eds. *Venice: A Documentary History, 1450–1630*. Oxford: Blackwell, 1992.

Commynes, Philippe de. *The Memoirs of Philippe de Commynes*. Edited by Samuel Kinser. 2 vols. Columbia, S.C.: University of South Carolina Press, 1969–73.

Contarini, Gasparo. *La Republica e i Magistrati di Vinegia*. Venice: Girolamo Scoto, 1544.

———. *The Commonwealth and Government of Venice*. Translated by Lewes Lewkenor. London: John Windet, 1599. Reprint, Amsterdam: Theatrum Orbis Terrarum, and New York: Da Capo Press, 1969.

Coryat, Thomas. *Coryat's Crudities: hastily gobled up in five moneths travels*. London: W. S[tansby], 1611.

———. *Coryat's Crudities*, 2 vols. Glasgow: James McLehose and Sons, 1905.

———. *Coryat's Crudities, reprinted from the edition of 1611, to which are now added his letters from India, etc.* 3 vols. London: printed for W. Cater [etc.], 1776.

Dolce, Ludovico. *Dialogo della institution delle donne*. Venice: Gabriel Giolito de Ferrari, 1547.

Doni, Antonfrancesco. *Dialogo della musica*. Venice: Scoto, 1543.

———. *I marmi del Doni, academico peregrino*. Venice: Francesco Marcolini, 1552.

———. *I marmi*. Florence: G. Barbèra, 1863.

Fanti, Sigismondo. *Triompho di Fortuna*. Venice: Agostino da Portese, 1527.

Florio, John. *Queen Anna's New World of Words 1611*. London: Melch Bradwood, 1611. Reprint, London: Scolar Press, 1968.

Grevembroch, Giovanni. *Gli abiti de veneziani di quasi ogni età con diligenza raccolti e dipinti nel secolo XVIII*. Introduction by Giovanni Mariacher. 4 vols. Venice: Filippi Editore, 1981.

Labalme, Patricia H., and Laura Sanguineti White, eds., with translations by Linda Carroll. *"Cità Excelentissima": Renaissance Venice and its World, Excerpts from The Diaries (1496–1533) of Marin Sanudo*. Forthcoming.

Lanteri, Giacomo. *Della Economica: Trattato di m. Giacomo Lanteri gentilhuomo bresciano, nel quale si dimostrano le qualità, che all'uomo et alla donna separatamente convengono pel governo della casa*. Venice: Valgrisi, 1560.

La tariffa delle puttane di Vinegia Overo Ragionamento del Forestiero e del Gentilhuomo; nel quale dinota il prezzo e la qualità di tutte le Cortigiane di Viegia col nome delle Ruffiane: Et Alcune Novelle piacevoli da ridere fatte da alcune di queste famose Signore a gli suoi amorosi. Venice, 1535.

Leggi e memorie venete sulla prostituzione fino all caduta della Republica. Venice: Marco Visentini, a spese del Conte di Orford, 1870–72.

Ludwig, Gustav. "Archivalische Beiträgen zur Geschichte der venezianischen Kunst." In *Italienische Forschungen* 4. Berlin: Kunsthistorischen Institut in Florenz and Verlag von Bruno Cassivir, 1911.

[Lucretia Romana]. *Ornamento nobile per ogni gentil matrona, dove si contiene bavari, frisi d'infinita bellezza, Lavori, per Linzuoli Traverse, e Facuoli, Piena di Figure, Ninfe, Satiri, Grotesche, Fontane, Musiche, Caccie di Cervi, Uccelli, & altri Animali, con ponti in aria fiamenghi, et tagliati con Adornamenti bellissimi, da imparare, per ogni virtuosa Donna, che si diletta de perfettamente cucire*. Venice: Appresso Lessandro de' Vecchi, 1620.

Machiavelli, Nicolò. *Machiavelli: The Chief Works and Others*. Translated by Allan Gilbert. Durham, N.C.: Duke University Press, 1965.

Memmo, Giovanni Maria. *Dialogo del Magn. Cavaliere M. Gio. Maria Memmo*. Venice: Gabriel Giolito de' Ferrari, 1563.

Modena, Leone. *The History of the Rites, Customes, and Manner of Life, of the Present Jews, throughout the World*. Translated by Edmund Chilmead. London: J.L., 1650.

Montesquieu, *The Spirit of the Laws*. Translated and edited by Anne M. Cohler, Basia Carolyn Miller, and Harold Samuel Stone. Cambridge: Cambridge University Press, 1989.

Moryson, Fynes. *An Itinerary Containing His Ten Yeeres Travell through the Twelve Dominions of Germany, Bohmerland, Sweitzerland, Netherland, Denmarke, Poland, Italy, Turky* [sic], *France, England, Scotland & Ireland*. Glasgow: James MacLehose and Sons, 1907.

Muzio, Girolamo. *Il gentilhuomo del Mutio Iustinopolitano*. Venice: Heredi di Luigi Valvassori, & Gio. Domenico Michieli, 1565.

Nashe, Thomas. *The Unfortunate Traveler, or the Life of Jack*

Wilton. London: printed by T. Scarlet for C. Burby, 1594. Reprint, New York: Greenberg, Publisher, 1926.
Nenna da Bari, Giovambattista. *Il Nennio. Il quale ragiona di nobiltà*. Venice: Giovan Andrea Vavassore, 1543.
Newett, Mary Margaret, ed. *Canon Pietro Casola's Pilgrimage to Jerusalem in the Year 1494*. Manchester: Manchester University Press, 1907.
Oliva, G. A. *Ioanni Cornelio, Praetori Praefectoque Optimo et Humanissimo*. Venice, 1567.
[Pagan, Matteo]. *L'Honesto Esempio del vertuoso desiderio che hanno le donne di nobil ingegno, circa lo imparare i punti tagliati a fogliami*. Venice: per Matthio Pagan in Frezaria al segno della Fede, 1550.
[Paganino, Alessandro]. *Libro primo De rechami per el quale se impara in diversi modi lordine e il modo de recamare, cosa non mai piu fatta ne stata mostrata, el qual modo se insegna al lettore voltando la carta. Opera nuova*. Venice: Alessandro Paganino, 1527.
Palladio, Andrea. *The Four Books of Architecture*. New York: Dover Publications, 1965.
Petrarch, Francesco. *Petrarch: Four Dialogues for Scholars*. Edited and translated by Conrad H. Rawski. Cleveland: Press of Western Reserve University, 1967.
Piccolomini, Alessandro. *De L'Institutione di tutta la vita de l'homo nato nobile e in citta libera, Libri x* . . . (Composti principalmente à beneficio del Nobilissimo Fanciullino Alessandro Colombini, pochi giorni innanzi nato, figlio de la immortale Mad. Laudomia Forteguerri). Venice: Hieronymum Scotum, 1545.
Putnam, Samuel, ed. *The Works of Aretino*, Chicago: Pascal Covici, 1926.
Ridolfi, Carlo. *Le maraviglie dell'arte ovvero le vite degli illustri pittori veneti e dello stato*. Edited by Detlev Freiherrn von Hadeln. Berlin, 1914–24. Reprint, Rome: Società Multigrafica Editrice Somu, 1965.
Rosetti, Giovanventura. *Notandissimi secreti de l'arte profumatoria, Venezia 1555*. Edited by Franco Brunello and Franca Facchetti. Vicenza: Neri Pozza Editore, 1973.
Roskill, Mark W. *Dolce's "Aretino" and Venetian Art Theory of the Cinquecento*. New York: New York University Press, 1968.
Ruscelli, Girolamo. *Le imprese illustri del Signor Ieronimo Ruscelli*. Venice: Francesco di Franceschi, 1584.
Sabellico, Marcantonio. *Del sito di Venezia Città (1502)*. Edited by G. Meneghetti. Venice: Libreria Filippi Editrice, 1985.
[Sansovino, Francesco]. *Delle cose notabili della città di Venetia. Libri ii. Ne' quali amplamente, e con ogni verità si contengono* . . . Venice, 1551. Reprint, Venice: Heredi di Luigi Valvassori & Gio. Domenico Micheli, 1583.
Sansovino, Francesco. *Venetia città nobilissima et singolare descritta in xiiii libri*. Venice, 1581.
———. *Venetia città nobilissima et singolare descritta in xiiii libri*. With additions by Giustiniano Martinioni. 2 vols. Venice: Steffano Curti, 1663. Reprint, Venice: Filippi Editore, 1968.
———. *Vita delle illustre signora Contessa Giulia Bemba della Torre*. Venice: Domenico & Gio Battista Guerra, fratelli, 1565.
Sanudo, Marin. *I diarii*. Edited by Rinaldo Fulin et al. 58 vols. Venice: F. Visentini, 1879–1903.
———. Marin. *De origine, situ et magistratibus urbis Venetae ovvero La città di Venetia (1493–1530)*. Edited by Angela Caracciolo Aricò. Milan: Cisalpino–La Goliardica, 1980.
Scamozzi, Vincenzo. *Dell'idea della architettura universale*. Venice: expensis auctoris, 1615.
Serlio, Sebastiano. *Regole generali di architettura*. Venice, 1537.
———. *The Five Books of Architecture*. London: Robert Peake, 1611. Reprint, New York: Dover Publications, 1982.
———. *Sebastiano Serlio on Architecture: Books i–v of Tutte l'opere d'architettura et prospettiva*. Translated by Vaughan Hart and Peter Hicks. New Haven and London: Yale University Press, 1996.
———. *Sebastiano Serlio on domestic architecture; different dwellings from the meanest hovel to the most ornate palace. The Sixteenth-Century Manuscript of Book vi in the Avery Library of Columbia University*. Edited by Myra Nan Rosenfeld. New York: Architectural History Foundation, 1978.
———. *Sebastiano Serlio on Domestic Architecture*, edited by Myra Nan Rosenfeld. Mineola: Dover Publications, Inc., 1996.
———. *Il trattato di Architettura di Sebastiano Serlio. Sesto libro delle habitationi di tutti li gradi degli homeni*. Commentary by Marco Rosci. Milan: I.T.E.C. Editore, 1966.
———. *Tutte l'opere d'architettura et prospettiva*. Venice, 1584.
Spirito, Lorenzo. *Libro della ventura, ovvero Libro delle sorti*. Brescia: Bonino de' Bonini, 1484.
———. *Libro de la ventura. Con somma diligentia reuisto: et corretto: & nouanecche [sic] ristampate*. Venice: Mattio Pagan, 1557.
Tagliente, Giovanni Antonio. *Essempio di recammi. Opera nuova che insenga alle Donne a cusire, a raccammare & a disegnar a ciuscuno. Et la ditta opera sara di motla utilità ad ogni artista per esere il disegno ad ognuno necessario*. Venice, 1527.
Tarabotti, Arcangela. *Antisatira*. Venice, 1654.
Tesauro, Emanuele. *Cannochiale aristotelico*. Turin: Bartolomeo Zavatta, 1679. Reprint, edited by A. Buck. Berlin and Zurich: Gehlen-Bad-Homburg, 1968.
Thomas, William. *The History of Italy (1549)*. Edited by George B. Parks. Ithaca: Cornell University Press, 1963.
Toscanella, Orazio. *I nomi antichi e moderni delle provincie, regioni, città, castella, monti, laghi, fiumi, golfi, porti ed isole dell'Europa, dell'Africa et dell'Asia, con le graduazioni loro in lunghezza e larghezza*, etc. Venice, 1567.
Vasari, Giorgio. *Lives of the Artists*. Translated by George Bull. Harmondsworth: Penguin Books, 1987.
———. *Le vite de più eccellenti pittori, scultori ed architettori*. Edited by Gaetano Milanesi. 9 vols. Florence, 1906.
Vecellio, Cesare. *Habiti antichi et moderni di tutto il mondo*. Paris: Firmin Didot, 1860.
Visit to the Holy Places of Egypt, Sinai, Palestine and Syria in 1384 by Frescobaldi, Gucci & Sigoli. Translated by Theophilus

Bellorini and Eugene Hoade. Jerusalem: Publications of the Studium Biblicum Franciscanum, 6, 1948.

Wotton, Sir Henry. *The Elements of Architecture: A Facsimile Reprint of the First Edition (London 1624). With Introduction and Notes by Frederick Hard.* Charlottesville: The University Press of Virginia, published for the Folger Shakespeare Library, 1968.

Xenophon, *Conversations of Socrates.* London: Penguin, 1990.

Zanetti, Antonio Maria. *Varie pitture a fresco de' principali maestri veneziani ora la prima volta con le stampe pubblicate.* Venice, 1760.

Zen, Nicolò. *Dell'origine de' barbari che distrussero per tutto 'l mondo l'imperio di Roma, onde hebbe principio la città di Venetia libri undici.* Venice: Marcolini, 1557.

[Zoppino, Nicolo d'Aristotile detto]. *Convivio delle belle donne.* Venice: Nicolo d'Aristotile detto Zoppino, 1532.

———. *Gli universali de i belli Recami antichi, e moderni: ne i quali un pellegrino ingegno, si di huomo come di donna, potra in questa nostra etè con l'ago vertuosamente esercitar si. Non anchora da alcuni altri dati in luce.* Venice: Nicolo d'Aristotile detto Zoppino, 1537.

Zuccollo da Cologna, Simeone. *La pazzia del ballo.* Padua, 1549.

Secondary Sources

Ackerman, James S. *The Villa: Form and Ideology of Country Houses.* Princeton: Princeton University Press, 1990.

Ackerman, James S., and Myra Nan Rosenfeld. "Social Stratification in Renaissance Urban Planning." In *Urban Life in the Renaissance,* edited by Susan Zimmerman and Ronald F. E. Weissman. Newark: University of Delaware Press; London and Toronto: Associated University Presses, 1989.

Aikema, Bernard. "The Lure of the North: Netherlandish Art in Venetian Collections," in Aikema and Brown, *Renaissance Venice and the North.*

Aikema, Bernard, and Beverly Louise Brown, eds. *Renaissance Venice and the North: Crosscurrents in the Time of Bellini, Dürer and Titian.* Venice: Bompiani, 1999.

Aikema, Bernard, and Dulcia Meijers. *Nel regno dei poveri: Arte e storia dei grandi ospedali veneziani in età moderna, 1474–1797.* Venice: IRE, 1989.

Ajmar, Marta. "Exemplary Women in Renaissance Italy." In *Women in Italian Renaissance Culture and Society,* edited by Letizia Panizza. Oxford: Legenda, 2000.

Alberici, Clelia. *Il Mobile Veneto.* Milan: Electa, 1980.

Allan, J. W. "Venetian-Saracenic Metalwork: The Problems of Provenance." In *Arte veneziana e arte islamica,* edited by Ernst J. Grube.

Allerston, Patricia Anne. "L'abito come articolo di scambio nella società dell'età moderna: alcune implicazioni." In *Le trame della moda,* edited by Anna Giulia Cavagna and Grazietta Butazzi. Rome: Bulzoni Editore, 1995.

———. "Clothing and Early Modern Venetian Society," *Continuity and Change* 15 (2000): 367–90.

———. "Le marché de l'occasion à Venise aux XVIe-XVIIe siècles." In *Échanges et cultures textiles dans l'Europe pré-industrielle,* edited by Jacques Bottin and Nicole Pelegrin. Lille: Revue du Nord, 1996.

———. "The Market in Second-Hand Clothes and Furnishings in Venice, ca. 1500–ca. 1650." Ph.D. diss., Florence: European University Institute, Department of |History and Civilization, 1996.

———. "Wedding Finery in Sixteenth-Century Venice." In *Marriage in Italy, 1300–1650,* edited by Trevor Dean and K. J. Lowe. Cambridge: Cambridge University Press, 1998.

Ambrosini, Federica. "Cerimonie, feste, lusso." In *Storia di Venezia dalle origini alla caduta della Serenissima. IV. Il Rinascimento: politica e cultura,* edited by Alberto Tenenti and Ugo Tucci. Rome: Istituto della Enciclopedia Italiana, 1996.

———. "'Descrittioni del mondo' nelle case venete dei secoli XVI e XVII," *Archivio Veneto* 112, ser. V, no. 152 (1981): 67–79.

———. "Toward a Social History of Women in Venice: From the Renaissance to the Enlightenment," in *Venice Reconsidered,* edited by John Martin and Dennis Romano.

Anderson, Jaynie. "A Further Inventory of Gabriel Vendramin's Collection." *The Burlington Magazine* 121 (1979): 642–43.

———. *Giorgione: The Painter of Poetic Brevity.* Paris and New York: Flammarion, 1997.

———. "Titian's Unfinished 'Portrait of a Woman and her Daughter' from the Barbarigo Collection, Venice." *The Burlington Magazine* 14 (2002): 671–79.

Armstrong, Lilian. "The Hand-Illumination of Printed Books in Italy 1465–1515." In *The Painted Page. Italian Renaissance Book Illumination, 1450–1550,* edited by Jonathan J. G. Alexander. New York: Prestel, 1994.

Arnaldi, Girolamo, Giorgio Cracco, and Alberto Tenenti, *Storia di Venezia dalle origini alla caduta della Serenissima. III. La formazione dello stato patrizio.* Rome: Istituto della Enciclopedia Italiana, 1997.

Arslan, Edoardo. *I Bassano.* 2 vols. Milan: Ceschina, 1960.

———. *Gothic Architecture in Venice.* Translated by Anne Engel. London: Phaidon, 1971.

Attardi, Luisa, *Il camino veneto del Cinquecento: Struttura architettonica e decorazione scultorea.* Costabizzara (Vicenza): Angelo Colla Editore, 2002.

Auld, Sylvia. "Master Mahmud: Objects Fit for a Prince." In *Arte veneziana e arte islamica,* edited by Ernst J. Grube.

Avery, Victoria. "The Early Works of Alessandro Vittoria (ca. 1540–ca. 1570)." Ph.D. diss., University of Cambridge, 1996.

Bacchi, Andrea, Lia Camerlengo, and Manfred Leithe-Jasper, eds. *"La bellissima maniera." Alessandro Vittoria e la scultura veneta del Cinquecento.* Trento: Castello del Buonconsiglio, Monumenti e Collezioni Provinciali, 1999.

Balistreri-Trincanato, Corrado, and Dario Zanverdiani. *Jacopo de Barbari: Il racconto di una città.* 2nd ed. Venice: Edizioni Stamperia Cetid, 2000.

Bascapè, Giacomo C., and Marcello Del Piazzo. *Insegne e simboli:*

Araldica pubblica e privata medievale e moderna. Rome: Ministero per i beni culturali e ambientali, 1983.

Bassi, Elena. *Palazzi di Venezia: Admiranda Urbis Veneta.* Revised edition. Venice: Stamperia di Venezia Editrice, 1987.

Bell, Rudolph M. *How to Do It: Guides to Good Living for Renaissance Italians*. Chicago and London: The University of Chicago Press, 1999.

Bellavitis, Giorgio. "Il linguaggio gotico diffuso nell'edilizia minore veneziana; *domos a statio, hospicii*, e *domos a sergentibus* nella Venezia medioevale." In *L'architettura gotica veneziana*, edited by Francesco Valcanover and Wolfgang Wolters.

Beltrami, Daniele. *Storia del popolazione di Venezia dalla fine del secolo XVI alla caduta della Repubblica*. Padua: CEDAM, 1954.

Bernardi, Carlo, with Pierluigi de Vecchi. *L'opera completa del Tintoretto.* Milan: Rizzoli Editore, 1970.

Bistort, Giulio. *Il Magistrato alle Pompe nella Republica di Venezia*. Bologna: Forni Editore, 1912.

Bistrot, Annalisa, and Mario Piana, "Il Palazzo dei Grimani a Santa Maria Formosa." In *Lo Statuario pubblico della Serenissima: due secoli di collezionismo di antichità: 1596–1797*, edited by Irene Favaretto and Giovanna Luisa Ravagnan.

Bolzoni, Lina. *The Gallery of Memory: Literary and Iconographic Models in the Age of the Printing Press*. Toronto: University of Toronto Press, 2001.

Bonora, Elena. "'Flânerie idéologique' dans la Venise du XVIe siècle: Francesco Sansovino et son guide, 1581." In *Les guides imprimés du XVIe au XXe siècle: villes, paysages, voyages*. Paris: Belin, 2000.

Borenius, Tancred. *The Picture Gallery of Andrea Vendramin*. London: The Medici Society, 1923.

Borsi, Franco. *Bramante*. Milan: Electa, 1989.

Boucher, Bruce. *The Sculpture of Jacopo Sansovino.* 2 vols. New Haven and London: Yale University Press, 1991.

Brown, Patricia Fortini. *Art and Life in Renaissance Venice*. New York: Harry N. Abrams, Inc., 1997.

———. "Behind the Walls: The Material Culture of Venetian Elites." In *Venice Reconsidered*, edited by John Martin and Dennis Romano.

———. "Carpaccio's *St. Augustine in his Study*: A Portrait within a Portrait." In *St. Augustine in Iconography, History and Legend*, edited by Joseph C. Schnaubelt and Frederick Van Fleteren. New York: Peter Lang Publishing, 1999.

———. *Venetian Narrative Painting in the Age of Carpaccio*. New Haven and London: Yale University Press, 1988.

———. *Venice & Antiquity: The Venetian Sense of the Past*. New Haven and London: Yale University Press, 1996.

Brown, Rawdon. *Ragguagli sulla vita e sulle opere di Marin Sanuto detto il Juniore veneto patrizio e cronista pregevolissimo de secoli XV, XVI*. Venice: Alvisopoli, 1837–38.

Brulez, Wilfrid. *Marchands Flamands a Venise I (1568–1605)*. Brussels and Rome: Institut Historique Belge de Rome, 1965.

Burke, Peter. *Venice and Amsterdam: A Study of Seventeenth-Century Elites*. 2nd ed. London: Polity Press, 1994.

Burns, Howard, Cristoph Luitpold Frommel, and Lionello Puppi. *Michele Sanmicheli: architettura, linguaggio e cultura artistica nel Cinquecento*. Milan: Electa and Vicenza: C.I.S.A. Andrea Palladio, 1995.

Calabi, Donatella. "The 'City of the Jews'." In *The Jews of Early Modern Venice*, edited by Robert C. Davis and Benjamin Ravid.

Calimani, Riccardo. *The Ghetto of Venice*. Translated by Katherine Silberblatt Wolfthal. New York: M. Evans and Company, 1987.

Calvino, Italo, and Sergio Samek Ludovici, *Il mazzo Visconteo di Bergamo e New York*. Parma: France Maria Ricci, 1969.

Campioni, Rosaria. "Libri di merletti e disposizioni suntuarie nel XVI secolo: alcuni indicazioni per l'Emilia Romagna." In *Le trame della moda*, edited by Anna Giulia Cavagna and Grazietta Butazzi. Rome: Bulzoni Editore, 1995.

Casini, Matteo. *I gesti del principe: la festa politica a Firenze e Venezia in età rinascimentale*. Venice: Marsilio, 1996.

———. "Gli ordini cavallereschi a Venezia fra Quattro e Seicento: problemi e ipotesi di ricerca." *Atti dell'Istituto Veneto di Scienze, Lettere ed Arti*, Classe di scienze morali, lettere ed arti, 156 (1997–98): 179–99.

Cataldi Palau, Annaclara. *Gian Francesco d'Asola e la tipografia Aldina: La vita, le edizioni, la biblioteca dell'Asolano*. Genoa: Sagep, 1998.

Cavallar, Osvaldo, Susanne Degenring, and Julius Kirshner, *A Grammar of Signs: Bartolo da Sassoferrato's "Tract on Insignia and Coats of Arms."* Berkeley: Robbins Collection, University of California at Berkeley, 1994.

Chiminelli, Caterina. "Le scale scoperte nei palazzi veneziani." *Ateneo Veneto* 39:1 (1912): 209–53.

Chojnacka, Monica. *Working Women of Early Modern Venice.* Baltimore: The Johns Hopkins University Press, 2001.

Chojnacki, Stanley. "La formazione della nobiltà dopo la Serrata." In *Storia di Venezia dalle origini alla caduta della Serenissima. III. La formazione dello stato patrizio*, edited by Girolamo Arnaldi, Giorgio Cracci, and Alberto Tenenti. Rome: Istituto della Enciclopedia Italiana, 1997.

———. "Identity and Ideology in Renaissance Venice: The Third Serrata." In *Venice Reconsidered*, edited by John Martin and Dennis Romano.

———. "Marriage Regulation in Venice, 1420–1535." In *Marriage in Italy, 1300–1650*, edited by Trevor Dean and K. J. Lowe. Cambridge: Cambridge University Press, 1988.

———. "Measuring Adulthood: Adolescence and Gender." In his *Women and Men in Renaissance Venice.*

———. "Social Identity in Renaissance Venice: the Second *Serrata*." *Renaissance* Studies 8 (1994): 341–58.

———. "Subaltern Patriarchs: Patrician Bachelors in Renaissance Venice." In his *Women and Men in Renaissance Venice.*

———. *Women and Men in Renaissance Venice: Twelve Essays on Patrician Society*. Baltimore and London: The Johns Hopkins University Press, 2000.

Cicogna, Emmanuele A. *Delle iscrizioni veneziane.* 6 vols. Venice: Picotti, 1824–53.

Cicognara, Leopoldo. *Memorie spettanti alla storia della calcografia*. Prato: Giacchetti, 1831.

Clough, Cecil H. "Chivalry and Magnificence in the Golden Age of the Italian Renaissance." In *Chivalry in the Renaissance*, edited by Sidney Anglo. Woodbridge, Suffolk: The Boydell Press, 1990.

Clunas, Craig. *Superfluous Things: Material Culture and Social Status in Early Modern China*. Urbana and Chicago: University of Illinois Press, 1991.

Cocke, Richard. *Paolo Veronese: Piety and Display in an Age of Religious Reform*. Aldershot: Ashgate, 2001.

Cohen, Charles E. *The Art of Giovanni Antonio da Pordenone: Between Dialect and Language.* 2 vols. Cambridge: Cambridge University Press, 1996.

Cohen, Elizabeth S. "Seen and Known: Prostitutes in the Cityscape of Late-Sixteenth Century Rome." *Renaissance Studies* 12:3 (1998): 392–409.

Cohen, Elizabeth S., and Thomas V. Cohen, "Open and Shut: The Social Meanings of the Cinquecento Roman House," *Studies in the Decorative Arts* 9 (2001–2): 61–84.

Coltro, Dino. *Sapienza del tempo contadino: lunario veneto*. Venice: Arsenale Cooperativa Editrice, 1980.

Concina, Ennio, Ugo Camerino, and Donatella Calabi, *La città degli ebrei: Il Ghetto di Venezia: architettura e urbanistica*. Venice: Marsilio, 1991.

Concina, Ennio. *Dell'arabico. A Venezia tra Rinascimento e Oriente.* Venice: Marsilio Editori, 1994.

———. "Fra Oriente e Occidente: gli Zen, un palazzo e il mito di Trebisonda." In *"Renovatio urbis": Venezia nell'età di Andrea Gritti (1523–1538)*, edited by Manfredo Tafuri. Rome: Officina Edizioni, 1984.

———. *A History of Venetian Architecture*. Translated by Judith Landry. Cambridge: Cambridge University Press, 1998.

Susan Connell. "Books and Their Owners in Venice 1345–1480." *Journal of the Warburg and Courtauld Institutes* 35 (1972): 163–86.

Contadini, Anna. "'Cuoridoro': Tecnica e decorazione di cuoi dorati veneziani e italiani con influssi islamici." In *Arte veneziana e arte islamica*, edited by Ernst J. Grube.

———. "Due pannelli di cuoio dorato nel Museo Civico Medievale di Bologna." *Annali di Ca' Foscari* 27:3 (1988): 127–42.

Costantini, Massimo. "Le strutture dell'ospitalità." In *Storia di Venezia dalle origini alla caduta della Serenissima*. v. *Il Rinascimento Società e Economia*, edited by Alberto Tenenti and Ugo Tucci. Rome: Istituto della Enciclopedia Italiana, 1996.

Costaperaria, Francesca. "Gli strumenti musicali: la musica strumentale nel Cenedese tra Medioevo e Rinascimento." In *Interno Veneto: Arredamento domestico fra Trevigiano e Bellunese dal Gotico al Rinascimento*, edited by Vittorino Pianca and Federico Velluti. Conegliano: Litografia C + D, 2000.

Cottrell, Philip. "Corporate Colors: Bonifacio and Tintoretto at the Palazzo dei Camerlenghi in Venice." *Art Bulletin* 82 (2000): 658–78.

Cowan, Alexander. "Love, Honour and the *Avogaria di Comun* in Early Modern Venice," *Archivio Veneto* 5, 179 (1995): 5–19.

———. "Patricians and Partners in Early Modern Venice." In *Medieval and Renaissance Venice*, edited by Ellen E. Kittell and Thomas F. Madden. Urbana and Chicago: University of Illinois Press, 1999.

Cox, Virginia. "The Single Self: Feminist Thought and the Marriage Market in Early Modern Venice." *Renaissance Quarterly* 48:3 (1995): 513–81.

Cozzi, Gaetano. "Authority and the Law in Renaissance Venice." In *Renaissance Venice*, edited by J. R. Hale.

Cozzi, Gaetano, ed. *Gli Ebrei e Venezia, secoli XIV–XVIII*. Milan: Comunita, 1987.

Crescenzi, Victor. *Esse de Maiori Consilio: leggitimità civile e legittimazione politica nella repubblica di Venezia (secc. XIII–XVI)*. Rome: Istituto Storico Italiano per il Medio Evo, 1996.

Crouzet-Pavan, Elisabeth. "Quando la città si diverte: Giochi e ideologia urbana: Venezia negli ultimi secoli del Medioevo." In *Gioco e giustizia nell'Italia di Comune*, edited by Gherardo Ortalli. Treviso: Fondazione Benetton/Viella, 1993.

———. *'Sopra le acque salse': Espaces, pouvoir et société à Venise à la fin du moyen âge*. 2 vols. Rome: Ecole Française de Rome, 1992.

———. *Venice Triumphant: Horizons of a Myth*. Baltimore: The Johns Hopkins University Press, 2002.

Cunaccia, Cesare M. *Venice, Hidden Splendors.* Paris and New York: Flammarion, 1994.

Curatola, Giovanni. "Tessuti e artigianato turco nel mercato veneziano." In *Venezia e i turchi: Scontri e confronti di due civiltà*. Milan: Electa, 1985.

Dacos, Nicole, ed. *Il Tesoro di Lorenzo il Magnifico: Repertorio delle gemme e dei vasi*. Florence: Sansoni Editore, 1980.

Dal Pozzolo, Enrico Maria. "Il bacile nell'Amor sacro e profano." *Critica d'arte* 64:4 (2001): 46–55.

———. "Sotto il guanto." *Venezia Arti* 8 (1994): 29–36.

Damerini, Gino. *Giardini sulla laguna*. Bologna: N. Zanichelli, 1927.

———. *Giardini di Venezia*. Bologna: Zanichelli, 1931.

Davanzo Poli, Doretta. *Il merletto veneziano*. Novara: Istituto Geografico, 1998.

———. "Merletto ad ago e a fuselli." In *Storia di Venezia dalle origini alla caduta della Serenissima. II. Temi: L'Arte*, edited by Rodolfo Pallucchini. Rome: Istituto della Enciclopedia Italiana, 1995.

Davanzo Poli, Doretta, and Stefania Moronato. *Le stoffe dei veneziani*. Venice: Albrizzi Editori, 1994.

Davis, James C. *The Decline of the Venetian Nobility as a Ruling Class*. Baltimore: The Johns Hopkins University Press, 1962.

———. *A Venetian Family and its Fortunes: 1500–1900*. Padua, 1975.

Davis, Robert C. "The Geography of Gender in the Renaissance." In *Gender and Society in Renaissance Italy*, edited by Judith C. Brown and Robert C. Davis. New York: Addison-Wesley Publishing Company, 1998.

Davis, Robert C., and Benjamin Ravid, eds. *The Jews of Early Modern Venice*. Baltimore and London: The Johns Hopkins University Press, 2001.

de Maria, Blake. "The Merchants of Venice: A Study in Sixteenth-

Century *Cittadino* Patronage." Ph.D. diss., Princeton University, 2002.

De Marinis, Tammaro. *La legatura artistica in Italia nei secoli* XV *e* XVI. Florence, 1960.

———. "L'influsso orientale sull'arte della legatura a Venezia." In *Venezia e l'Oriente fra tardo Medioevo e Rinascimento*, edited by Agostino Pertusi. Florence: Sansoni, 1966.

Dennis, Jessie McNab. *Chess: East and West, Past and Present: A Selection from the G. A. Pfeiffer Collection*. New York: Metropolitan Museum of Art, 1968.

De Nolhac, Pierre, and Angelo Solerti. *Il viaggio in Italia di Enrico* III *Re di Francia e le feste a Venezia, Ferrara, Mantova e Torino.* Turin: L. Roux, 1890.

Devos, Greta, and Wilfrid Brulez. *Marchands Flamands à Venise* II *(1606–1621).* Brussels and Rome: Institut Historique Belge de Rome, 1986.

De Winter, Patrick M. "A Little-Known Creation of Renaissance Decorative Arts: the White Lead *Pastiglia* Box." *Saggi e memorie di storia dell'arte* 14 (1984): 7–42, 103–31.

Dizionario biografico degli italiani. Edited by Alberto M. Ghisalberti. 49 vols. to date. Rome: Istituto della Enciclopedia Italiana, 1960–.

Donati, Claudio. *L'idea di nobiltà in Italia, secoli* XIV–XVIII. Rome and Bari: Editori Laterza, 1995.

Dorigo, Wladimiro." *Exigentes, sigentes, sezentes, sergentes*: le case d'affito a Venezia nel Medioevo." *Venezia Arti* 10 (1996): 25–36.

———. "Toponomastica urbana nella formazione della città medioevale." *Rassegna* 5, no. 22 (1985): 50–51.

Dunkerton, Jill, Susan Foister, and Nicholas Penny, *Dürer to Veronese: Sixteenth-Century Painting in the National Gallery.* New Haven and London: Yale University Press, 1999.

Eade, J. C. "Marcantonio Michiel's Mercury Statue: Astronomical or Astrological." *Journal of the Warburg and Courtauld Institutes* 44 (1981): 207–9.

Eisler, Robert. "The Frontispiece to Sigismondo Fanti's *Triompho di Fortuna*." *Journal of the Warburg and Courtauld Institutes* 10 (1947): 155–59.

Ellis, Charles Grant. *Oriental Carpets in the Philadelphia Museum of Art.* Philadelphia: Philadelphia Museum of Art, 1988.

Favaretto, Irene. *Arte antica e cultura antiquaria nelle collezioni venete al tempo della Serenissima*. Rome: "L'Erma" di Bretschneider, 1990.

———. "Memoria dell'immagine e immagine nella memoria: significato e valore del catalogo illustrato nella storia delle collezioni veneziane di antichità." In *Collezioni di anitchità a Venezia*, edited by Alvise Zorzi.

Favaretto, Irene, and Giovanna Luisa Ravagnan, eds. *Lo Statuario pubblico della Serenissima: due secoli di collezionismo di antichità: 1596–1797.* Cittadella: Biblos, 1997.

Findlen, Paula. "The Museum: Its Classical Etymology and Renaissance Genealogy." *Journal of the History of Collections* 1 (1989): 59–78.

———. *Possessing Nature: Museums, Collecting, and Scientific Culture in Early Modern Italy.* Berkeley and Los Angeles: University of California Press, 1994.

———. "Possessing the Past: The Material World of the Italian Renaissance." *American Historical Review* 103 (1998): 83–114.

Finlay, Robert. *Politics in Renaissance Venice.* New Brunswick: Rutgers University Press, 1980.

Fiorin, Alberto, ed. *Fanti e danari. Sei secoli di giochi d'azzardo.* Venice: Arsenale Editrice, 1989.

Fletcher, Jennifer. "Marcantonio Michiel: his Friends and Collection." *The Burlington Magazine* 123 (1981): 453–57.

———. "Marcantonio Michiel's Collection." *Journal of the Warburg and Courtauld Institutes* 36 (1973): 382–85.

Franzoi, Umberto. *The Grand Canal.* New York: Rizzoli, 2001.

Fraser Jenkins, A. D. "Cosimo de' Medici's Patronage of Architecture and the Theory of Magnificence." *Journal of the Warburg and Courtauld Institutes* 33 (1970): 162–70.

Frigo, Daniela. *Il padre di famiglia: Governo della casa e governo civile nella tradizione dell "economica" tra cinque e seicento.* Rome: Bulzoni Editore, 1985.

Frimmel, Theodor. "Der Anonimo Morelliano (Marcanton Michiel's Notizia d'Opere del Disegno)." In *Quellenschriften für Kunstgeschichte und Kunsttechnik.* vol I. Vienna: Verlag Carl Graeser, 1896.

Fulin, Rinaldo. "Diarii e diaristi." *Nuovo Archivio Veneto* 22:1 (1881): v–xxii.

Gallo, Rodolfo. *Contributi alla Storia dell'Arte del vetro di Murano.* Venice: Officine Grafiche F. Barzia, 1953.

Gentili, Augusto. "Painting in Venice: 1450–1515." In *Venice: Art & Architecture*, edited by Giandomenico Romanelli.

Gerola, Giuseppe. *Monumenti Veneti dell'isola di Creta.* 4 vols. Venice: Istituto Veneto delle Scienze, Lettere ed Arti, 1932.

Gianetto, Nella. *Bernardo Bembo: umanista e politico veneziano.* Florence: Leo S. Oschki, Editore, 1985.

Gianighian, Giorgio, and Paola Pavanini. *Dietro i Palazzi: Tre secoli di architettura minore a Venezia 1492–1803.* Venice: Arsenale Editrice, 1984.

———. "Il tessuto gotico." In *L'architettura gotica veneziana*, edited by Francesco Valcanover and Wolfgang Wolters.

Gilbert, Felix. "Venice in the Crisis of the League of Cambrai." In *Renaissance Venice*, edited by J. R. Hale. London: Faber and Faber, 1973.

Goffen, Rona. *Giovanni Bellini.* New Haven and London: Yale University Press, 1989.

———. *Titian's Women.* New Haven and London: Yale University Press, 1997.

Goldthwaite, Richard A. *Wealth and the Demand for Art in Italy, 1300–1600.* Baltimore and London: The Johns Hopkins University Press, 1993.

Goy, Richard J. *The House of Gold: Building a Palace in Medieval Venice.* Cambridge: Cambridge University Press, 1992.

———. *Venetian Vernacular Architecture: Traditional Housing in the Venetian Lagoon.* Cambridge: Cambridge University Press, 1989.

———. *Venice. The City and its Architecture*. London: Phaidon, 1997.

Grabar, Oleg. *The Mediation of Ornament*. Princeton: Princeton University Press, 1992.

Grendler, Paul. "Francesco Sansovino and Italian Popular History, 1560–1600," *Studies in the Renaissance* 16 (1969): 139–80.

———. *Schooling in Renaissance Italy: Literacy and Learning, 1300–1600*. Baltimore and London: The Johns Hopkins University Press, 1989.

Grieco, Sara Matthews. "Persuasive Pictures: Didactic Prints and the Construction of the Social Identity of Women in Sixteenth-Century Italy." In *Women in Italian Renaissance Culture and Society*, edited by Letizia Panizza. Oxford: Legenda, 2000.

Grieco, Sara Matthews, and Louisa Matthews, eds., *The Art Market in Italy, 1400–1600* Florence: Olschki, 2002.

Gronau, Georg. "Venezianische Kunstsammlungen des 16 Jahrhunderts." *Jahrbuch für Kunstsammler* 4–5 (1924–25), 56–59.

Grubb, James. "Elite Citizens." In *Venice Reconsidered*, edited by John Martin and Dennis Romano.

———. "Memory and Identity: Why Venetians Didn't Keep *Ricordanze*." *Renaissance Studies* 8 (1994): 375–87.

———. "When Myths Lose Power: Four Decades of Venetian Historiography." *Journal of Modern History* 58 (1986): 43–94.

Grube, Ernst J., ed. *Arte veneziana e arte islamica.* Atti del primo simposio internazionale sull'arte veneziana e l'arte islamica. Venice: Edizioni L'Altra Riva, 1989.

———. "Le lacche veneziane e i loro modelli islamici." In his *Arte veneziana e arte islamica*, edited by Ernst J. Grube.

Gruber, Alain, ed. *The History of Decorative Arts: The Renaissance and Mannerism in Europe*. New York: Abbeville Press, 1994.

Gualdo, Paolo. "Vita di Andrea Palladio, a cura di Giangiorgio Zorzi." *Saggi e Memorie di Storia dell'arte* 2 (1959): 91–104.

Guerzoni, Guido. "*Liberalitas, Magnificentia*, Splendor: The Classic Origins of Italian Renaissance Lifestyles." In *Economic Engagements with Art*, edited by Neil De Marchi and Craufurd D. W. Goodwin. Durham and London: Duke University Press, 1999.

Habert, Jean. *Une dame vénitienne dite la Belle Nani*. Paris: Musée du Louvre, 1996.

Hale, J. R., ed., *Renaissance Venice*. London: Faber & Faber, 1973.

Hargrave, Catherine Perry. *A History of Playing Cards and a Bibliography of Cards and Gaming*. New York, Dover Publications, Inc., 1966.

Hartlaub, G. F. *Zauber des Spiegels*: *Geschichte und Bedeutung des Spiegels in der Kunst*. Munich: R. Piper. 1951.

Hills, Paul. *Venetian Colour: Marble, Mosaic, Painting and Glass 1250–1550*. New Haven and London: Yale University Press, 1999.

Hinton, Jack. "By Sale, by Gift: Aspects of the Resale and Bequest of Goods in Late Sixteenth-Century Venice." *Journal of Design History* 15:4 (2002): 245–62.

Hobson, Anthony. "Islamic Influence on Venetian Renaissance Bookbinding." In *Arte veneziana e arte islamice* edited by Ernst J. Grube.

Hochmann, Michel. "La collection de Giacomo Contarini." *Mélanges de l'Ecole française de Rome: Moyen Age–Temps Modernes* 99:1 (1987): 447–89.

———. *Peintres et commanditaires à Venise (1540–1628)*. 2 vols. Rome: Ecole Française de Rome, 1992.

———. "Tra Venezia e Roma: il cardinale Francesco Corner." *Saggi e memorie di storia dell'arte* 18 (1992): 97–110.

Hoffman, Detlef. *The Playing Card: An Illustrated History*. New York: New York Graphic Society Ltd, 1973.

Hope, Charles, Jennifer Fletcher, and Jill Dunkerton. *Titian*. New Haven and London: Yale University Press, 2003.

Howard, Deborah. *The Architectural History of Venice*. Revised edition. New Haven and London: Yale University Press, 2002.

———. "Exterior Orders in Interior Planning in Sansovino and Sanmicheli." In *L'Emploi des ordres*, edited by Jean Guillaume. Paris: Picard, 1992.

———. *Jacopo Sansovino: Architecture and Patronage in Renaissance Venice*. New Haven and London: Yale University Press, 1975.

———. "Responses to Ancient Greek Architecture." *Annali di Architettura* 6 (1994): 23–38.

———. *Venice & the East*. New Haven and London: Yale University Press, 2000.

Hunt, Alan. *Governance of the Consuming Passions: A History of Sumptuary Law*. New York: St. Martin's Press, 1996.

Huth, Hans. *Lacquer of the West: The History of a Craft and an Industry, 1550–1950*. Chicago: University of Chicago Press, 1971.

———. "A Venetian Renaissance Casket." In *Museum Monographs*, I: *Papers On Objects in the Collections of the City Art Museum of Saint Louis*. St. Louis: City Art Museum of St. Louis, 1968.

Jacobs, Emil. "Das Museo Vendramin und die Sammlung Reynst." *Repertorium für Kunstwissenschaft* 46 (1925): 15–38.

Johnson, Eugene J. "The Short, Lascivious Lives of Two Venetian Theaters, 1580–85." *Renaissance Quarterly* 55 (2002): 936–68.

Johnson, Geraldine A. "Michelangelo, Fortunetelling & the Formation of Artistic Canons in Fanti's *Triompho di Fortuna*." In *Coming About . . . A Festschrift for John Shearman*, edited by Lars R. Jones and Louisa C. Matthew. Cambridge, Mass: Harvard University Art Museums, 2001.

Jordan, Constance. *Renaissance Feminism: Library Texts and Political Models*. Ithaca and London: Cornell University Press, 1990.

Jordan, Marc-Henri, and Francisca Costantini-Lachat, "Moorish Tracery." In *The History of Decorative Arts*, edited by Alain Gruber.

Judson, Richard. *Dirck Barendszen 1534–1592*. Amsterdam: Vangendt & Co, 1970.

Junkerman, Anne Christine. "*Bellissima Donna*: An Interdisciplinary Study of Venetian Sensuous Half-Length Images of the Early Sixteenth Century." Ph.D. diss., University of California, Berkeley, 1988.

———. "The Lady and the Laurel: Gender and Meaning in Giorgione's *Laura*." *Oxford Art Journal* 16 (1993): 49–58.

Keen, Maurice. *Chivalry*. New Haven and London: Yale University Press, 1984.

Kelso, Ruth. *Doctrine for the Lady of the Renaissance*. Urbana: University of Illinois Press, 1956.

King, Margaret. "Caldiera and the Barbaros on Marriage and the Family: Humanist Reflections of Venetian Realities." *The Journal of Medieval and Renaissance Studies* 6 (1976): 19–50.

———. *Venetian Humanism in an Age of Patrician Dominance*. Princeton: Princeton University Press, 1986.

Klapisch-Zuber, Christiane. *Women, Family, and Ritual in Renaissance Italy*. Translated by Lydia Cochrane. Chicago and London: The University of Chicago Press, 1985.

Kurnata, Anthony. "The Palazzo Loredan in the Campo Santo Stefano: Counter-Currents in Sixteenth Century Venetian Architecture." Ph.D. diss., Boston University, 1976.

Labalme, Patricia H., and Laura Sanguineti White, with translations by Linda Carroll. "How to (and How Not to) Get Married in Sixteenth-Century Venice." *Renaissance Quarterly* 52 (1999): 43–72.

Laini, Marinella. "Le cortigiane e la musica." In *Il gioco dell'amore. Le cortigiane di Venezia dal trecento al settecento*. Milan: Berenice, 1990.

Lane, F. C. "Family Partnerships and Joint Ventures in the Venetian Republic." *Journal of Economic History* 4 (1944), 2, 178–96.

———. "The Enlargement of the Great Council of Venice." In *Florilegium Historiale: Essays Presented to Wallace K. Ferguson*, edited by J. G. Rose and W. H. Stockdale. Toronto: University of Toronto Press, 1971.

Lauritzen, Peter, and Alexander Zielcke. *Palaces of Venice*. London: Dorset Press, 1985.

Lawner, Lynne. *Lives of the Courtesans: Portraits of the Renaissance*. New York: Rizzoli, 1987.

Lazzarini, Vittorio. "Aneddoti della congiura Quirini-Tiepolo." *Nuovo Archivio Veneto* 10:1 (1895): 81–96.

Levenson, Jay A., ed. *Circa 1492: Art in the Age of Exploration*. New Haven and London: Yale University Press, 1992.

Levenson, Jay A., Konrad Oberhuber, and Jacquelyn L. Sheehan. *Early Italian Engravings from the National Gallery of Art*. Washington, D.C.: National Gallery of Art, 1973.

Levi, Cesare Augusto. *Le collezioni veneziane d'arte e d'antichità dal secolo XIV ai giorni nostri*, 2 vols. Venice: F. Ongania, 1906.

Lewis, Douglas. "An Early Series of Dynastic Portrait Busts by Alessandro Vittoria." *Artibus et historiae* 35 (1997): 113–34.

Liefkes, Reino, ed. *Glass*. London: Victoria & Albert Museum, 1997.

Limentani Virdis, Caterina. "Across the Alps and to the Lagoon: Northern Artists in Venice during the Sixteenth Century." In Aikema and Brown, *Renaissance Venice and the North*.

Logan, Anne-Marie S. *The "Cabinet" of the Brothers Gerard and Jan Reynst*. Amsterdam and New York: Batsford, 1979.

Logan, Oliver. *Culture and Society in Venice, 1470–1790*. London: B. T. Batsford Ltd, 1972.

Lorenzetti, Giulio. *Venice and Its Lagoon*. Translated by John Guthrie. Trieste: Edizioni Lint, 1975.

Lotz, Arthur. *Bibliographie der Modelbücher*. Leipzig: Verlag Karl W. Hiersemann, 1933.

Lucco, Mauro. "Le cosiddette 'Tre età dell'uomo'." In his *Le tre età dell'uomo della Galleria Palatina*. Florence: Centro Di, 1989.

Ludwig, Gustav. "Venezianischer Hausrat zur Zeit der Renaissance: Restello, Spiegel und Toilettenutensilien in Venedig zur Zeit der Renaissance." In *Italienische Forschungen* Berlin: Kunsthistorischen Institut in Florenz and Verlag von Bruno Cassirer, 1908.

Lunardon, Silvia. *Hospitale S. Mariae Cruciferorum: L'ospizio dei Crociferi a Venezia*. Venice: IRE, Istituzioni di Ricovero e di Educazione, 1984.

Mack, Rosamond E. *Bazaar to Piazza: Islamic Trade and Italian Art, 1300–1600*. Berkeley: University of California Press, 2002.

Mackenney, Richard. *Traders and Tradesmen: The World of the Guilds in Venice and Europe, ca. 1250–ca. 1650*. Totowa: Barnes & Noble Books, 1987.

Maretto, Paolo. *La casa veneziana nella storia della città dalle origini all'Ottocento*. Venice: Marsilio Editori, 1986.

———. *L'ediliza gotica veneziana*. Venice: Filippi Editore, 1978.

Martin, John. "The Imaginary Piazza: Tommaso Garzoni and the Late Italian Renaissance." In *Portraits of Medieval and Renaissance Living: Essays in Memory of David Herlihy*, edited by Samuel K. Cohn Jr. and Steven A. Epstein. Ann Arbor: The University of Michigan Press, 1996.

Martin, John, and Dennis Romano, eds. *Venice Reconsidered: The History and Civilization of an Italian City-State, 1297–1797*. Baltimore and London: Johns Hopkins University Press, 2000.

Martineau, Jane, and Charles Hope, eds. *The Genius of Venice 1500–1600*. London: Wiedenfeld & Nicolson, 1983.

Martini, Luciana, ed. *Bottega degli Embriachi: cofanetti e cassettine tra Gotico e Rinascimento*. Brescia: Musei Civici di Brescia, 2001.

Martinis, Roberta. "Ca' Loredan-Vendramin-Calergi a Venezia: Mauro Codussi e il palazzo di Andrea Loredan." *Annali di Architettura* 10–11 (1998–99): 43–61.

———. "Su un fregio all'antica. Un'ipotesi per Antonio Lombardo nel palazzo di Andrea Loredan a Venezia." *Arte Veneta* 56 (2000): 17–37.

Matthew, Louisa C. "Working Abroad: Northern Artists in the Venetian Ambient." In Aikema and Brown, *Renaissance Venice and the North*.

Mazzariol, Giuseppe, and Attilia Dorigato. *Intérieurs Vénitiens*. Paris: Bibliothèque des Arts, 1991.

McAndrew, John. *Venetian Architecture of the Early Renaissance*. Cambridge, Mass.: The MIT Press, 1980.

McCray, Patrick W. *Glassmaking in Renaissance Venice: The Fragile Craft*. Aldershot, England: Ashgate, 1999.

McTavish, David. "Roman Subject-Matter and Style in Venetian Facade Frescoes." *RACAR. Canadian Art Review* 12 (1985): 188–96.

Megna, Laura. "Comportamenti abitativi del patriziato veneziano (1582–1740)." *Studi Veneziani*, n.s., 22 (1991): 253–323.

Meijer, Bert W. "Flemish and Dutch Artists in Venetian Workshops: The Case of Jacopo Tintoretto." In Aikema and Brown, *Renaissance Venice and the North.*

———. "A proposito della Vanità della ricchezza e di Ludovico Pozzoserrato." In *Toeput a Treviso: Ludovico Pozzoserrato, Lodewijk Topeut, pittore neerlandese nella civiltà veneta del tardo Cinquecento*, edited by Stefania Mason Rinaldi and Domenico Luciani. Asolo: Acelum Edizioni, 1988.

Mille anni di arte del vetro a Venezia. Venice: Albrizzi Editore, 1982.

Moakley, Gertrude. *The Tarot Cards Painted by Bonifacio Bembo.* New York: New York Public Library, 1966.

Molmenti, Pompeo. *La storia di venezia nella vita privata dalle origini alla caduta della Repubblica.* 3 vols. Bergamo, 1927–29. Reprint, Trieste: Edizioni Lint, 1973.

———. *Venice: Its Individual Growth from the Earliest Beginnings to the Fall of the Republic.* Translated by Horatio F. Brown. Chicago: A. C. McClurg & Co., 1907.

Moldi-Ravenna, Cristiana, and Tudy Sammartini. *Secret Gardens in Venice.* Venice: Arsenale Editrice, 1996.

Mometto, Pierogiovanni. "'Vizi privati, pubbliche virtù': Aspetti e problemi della questione del lusso nella repubblica di Venezia (secolo XVI)." In *Crimine, giustizia e società veneta in età moderna*, edited by Luigi Berlinguer and Floriana Colao. Milan: Giuffrè, 1989.

Morelli, Jacopo. *Notizia d'opere di Disegno.* Revised and edited by G. Frizzoni. Bologna, 1884.

Morresi, Manuela. *Jacopo Sansovino.* Milan: Electa, 2000.

Moschini Marconi, Sandra. *Gallerie dell'Accademia di Venezia. Opere d'arte del secolo XIV e XV.* Rome: Istituto Poligrafico dello Stato, 1955.

———. *Gallerie dell'Accademia di Venezia. Opere d'arte del secolo XVI.* Rome: Istituto Poligrafico dello Stato, 1962.

Mottola Molfino, Alessandra. "Nobili, sagge e virtuose donne: Libri di modelli per merletti e organizzazione del lavoro femminile tra Cinquecento e Seicento." In *La famiglia e la vita quotidiana in Europa dal '400 al '600. Fonti e problemi.* Rome: Ministero per i beni culturali e ambientali, 1986.

Muir, Edward. *Civic Ritual in Renaissance Venice.* Princeton: Princeton University Press, 1981.

Musacchio, Jacqueline Marie. *The Art and Ritual of Childbirth in Renaissance Italy.* New Haven and London: Yale University Press, 1999.

Muzzarelli, Maria Giuseppina. *Gli inganni delle apparenze: Disciplina di vesti e ornamenti alla fine del medioevo.* Turin: Scriptorium, 1996.

Nadin Bassani, Lucia. *Le carte da gioco a Venezia: L'Arte dei Cartoleri (1400–1700).* Venice: Centro Internazionale della Grafica, 1989.

Newbery, Timothy J., George Bisacca, and Laurence B. Kanter. *Italian Renaissance Frames.* New York: The Metropolitan Museum of Art, 1990.

Newett, Mary Margaret. "The Sumptuary Laws of Venice in the Fourteenth and Fifteenth Centuries." In *Historical Essays First Published in 1902 in Commemoration of the Jubilee of The Owens College Manchester.* Edited by T. F. Tout and James Tait. Manchester: Manchester University Press, 1907.

Newton, Stella Mary. *The Dress of the Venetians, 1494–1534.* Aldershot, England and Brookfield, VT.: Scolar Press, 1988.

Nichols, Tom. *Tintoretto: Tradition and Identity.* London: Reaktion Books, 1999.

Olivieri Secchi, Sandra. "Il *De Nobilitate* di Sebastiano Venier una teoria per un modello." In *Non uno itinere: Studi storici offerti dagli allievi a Federico Seneca*, edited by Mario De Biasi. Venice: Stamperia di Venezia, 1993.

Oman, Charles. *Medieval Silver Nefs.* London: Her Majesty's Stationery Office, 1963.

Onians, John. "The Last Judgement of Renaissance Architecture." *The Royal Society of Arts Journal* 128 (1980): 701–18.

Osborne, Harold, ed. *The Oxford Companion to the Decorative Arts.* Oxford: Oxford University Press, 1985.

Oursel, Hervé, and Thierry Crépin-Leblond. *Musée National de la Renaissance. Chateau d'Écouen.* Paris: Réunion des Musées Nationaux, 1994.

Pallucchini, Rodolfo, and F. Rossi. *Giovanni Cariani.* Bergamo: Silvana, 1983.

Palumbo-Fossati, Isabella. "La casa veneziana di Gioseffo Zarlino nel testamento e nell'inventario dei beni del grande teorico musicale." *Nuova Rivista Musicale Italiana* 20 (1986): 633–49.

———. "Il collezionista Sebastiano Erizzo e l'inventario dei suoi beni." *Ateneo Veneto* 171:22, nos. 1/2 (1984): 201–18.

———. "L'interno della casa dell'artigiano e dell'artista nella Venezia del Cinquecento." *Studi veneziani* n.s. 8 (1984): 109–53.

———. "Livres et lecteurs dans la Venise du XVIe siecle." *Revue francaise d'histoire du livre* 54, n.s., no. 49 (1985): 481–513.

Paoletti, Pietro. *L'architettura e la scultura del rinascimento in Venezia.* vol. 1. Venice: Ongania-Naya, 1893–97.

Park, Katherine, and Lorraine J. Daston. *Wonders and the Order of Nature, 1150–1750.* New York: Zone Books, 1998.

Parker, Rozsika. *The Subversive Stitch: Embroidery and the Making of the Feminine.* London: The Women's Press, 1984.

Pavan, Elisabeth. "Police des moeurs, société et politique à Venise à la fin du Moyen Age." *Revue Historique* 264 (1981): 241–88.

Pavanini, Paola. "Abitazioni popolari e borghesi nella Venezia cinquecentesca." *Studi Veneziani*, n.s., 5 (1981): 63–126.

Pedretti, Carlo. *Leonardo: A Study in Chronology and Style.* New York and London: Harcourt Brace Jovanovich, Publishers, 1982.

Pedrocco, Filippo. "Il luogo del gioco: il ridotto di Palazzo Dandolo a San Moisè." In *Fanti e danari*, edited by Alberto Fiorin.

Perry, Marilyn. "Cardinal Grimani's Legacy of Ancient Art to Venice." *Journal of the Warburg and Courtauld Institutes* 41 (1978): 215–44.

Pezzolo, Luciano. *L'oro dello stato: società, finanza e fisco nella Repubblica Veneta del secondo '500.* Venice: Il Cardo, 1990.

Piamonte, Giannino. *Venezia vista dall'acqua: Guida dei rii di Venezia e delle isole*, 3rd ed. Venice: Stamperia di Venezia, 1992.

Pignatti, Terisio, and Filippo Pedrocco. *Veronese*. Milan: Electa, 1995.

Pilo, Giuseppe Maria. "Postilla a Jacopo Tintoretto." *Arte/ Documenta* 5 (1991): 129–30.

———. "Il Procuratore di San Marco Jacopo Soranzo Jr. e il ritratto recuperato di Jacopo Tintoretto già in Procuratia 'De Supra'." In *Storia dell'arte marciana: i mosaici*, edited by Renato Polacco. Venice: Marsilio, 1997.

Pincus, Debra. *The Tombs of the Doges of Venice*. Cambridge: Cambridge University Press, 2000.

Pomian, Krzystof. *Collectors and Curiosities: Paris and Venice, 1500–1800*. Translated by Elizabeth Wiles-Portier. Cambridge: Polity Press, 1990.

Pope-Hennessy, John. *Catalogue of Italian Sculpture in the Victoria and Albert Museum*. 2 vols. London: Her Majesty's Stationery Office, 1964.

Praz, Mario. *An Illustrated History of Furnishing from the Renaissance to the 20th Century*. Translated by William Weaver. New York: George Braziller, 1964.

Preyer, Brenda. "Planning for Visitors at Florentine Palaces." *Renaissance Studies* 12:3 (1998): 357–74.

Pullan, Brian. "Abitazioni al servizio dei poveri." In Gianighian and Pavanini, *Dietro i Palazzi*.

———. *Rich and Poor in Renaisance Venice: the Social Institutions of a Catholic State, to 1620*. Cambridge, Mass.: Harvard University Press, 1971.

Puppi, Lionello. *Michele Sanmicheli architetto: opera completa*. Rome: Caliban, 1986.

Puppi, Lionello, and Loredana Olivato Puppi. *Mauro Codussi*. Milan: Electa, 1977.

Ravà, Aldo. "Il 'camerino delle antigaglie' di Gabriele Vendramin." *Nuovo Archivio Veneto*, n.s., 39 (1920): 155–81.

Ravid, Benjamin. "Christian Travelers in the Ghetto of Venice: Some Preliminary Observations." In *Between History and Literature: Studies in Honor of Isaac Barzilay*, edited by Stanley Nash. Bnei-Brak, 1997.

———. "Curfew Time in the Ghetto of Venice." In *Medieval and Renaissance Venice*, edited by Ellen E. Kittel and Thomas F. Madden. Urbana and Chicago: University of Illinois Press, 1999.

———. "From Geographical Realia to Historiographical Symbol: The Odyssey of the Word Ghetto." In *Essential Papers on Jewish Culture in Renaissance and Baroque Italy*, edited by David B. Ruderman. New York: New York University Press, 1992.

Riis, Thomas. "I poveri nell'arte italiana (secoli XV–XVIII)." In *Timore e carità: i poveri nell'Italia moderna*, edited by Giorgio Politi, Mario Rosa, and Franco Della Peruta. Cremona: Annali della Biblioteca Statale e Libreria Civica di Cremona, 1982.

Rizzi, Alberto. *Scultura Esterna a Venezia: Corpus delle Sculture Erratiche all'aperto di Venezia e della sua Laguna*. Venice: Stamperia di Venezia, 1987.

Roberts, Helen. "St. Augustine in St. Jerome's Study: Carpaccio's Painting and its Legendary Source." *Art Bulletin* 41 (1959): 283–97.

Rogers, Mary. "An Ideal Wife at the Villa Maser: Veronese, the Barbaros and Renaissance Theorists of Marriage." *Renaissance Studies* 7:4 (1993): 379–97.

Romanelli, Giandomenico. *Ca' Corner della Ca' Granda: Architettura e committenza nella Venezia del Cinquecento*. Venice: Albrizzi Editore, 1993.

———, ed. *Venice: Art & Architecture*. Cologne: Könemann, 1997.

Romanin, Samuele. *Storia documentata di Venezia*. 10 vols. Venice: Pietro Naratovich tipografo Editore, 1853–61.

Romano, Dennis. "L'assistenza e la beneficenza." In *Storia di Venezia dalle origini alla caduta della Serenissima. V. Il Rinascimento: Società ed economia*, edited by Alberto Tenenti and Ugo Tucci. Rome: Istituto della Enciclopedia Italiana, 1996.

———. "Gender and the Urban Geography of Renaissance Venice." *Journal of Social History* 23:2 (1989): 339–53.

———. *Housecraft and Statecraft: Domestic Service in Renaissance Venice, 1400–1600*. Baltimore and London: The Johns Hopkins University Press, 1996.

———. *Patricians and Popolani: The Social Foundations of the Venetian Renaissance State*. Baltimore and London: The Johns Hopkins University Press, 1987.

Rosand, David. *Myths of Venice: The Figuration of a State*. Chapel Hill and London: University of North Carolina Press, 2001.

———. *Painting in Cinquecento Venice: Titian, Veronese, Tintoretto*. New Haven and London: Yale University Press, 1982. Rev. ed. Cambridge and New York: Cambridge University Press, 1997.

Rösch, Gerhard. "The Serrata of the Great Council and Venetian Society, 1286–1323." In *Venice Reconsidered*, edited by John Martin and Dennis Romano.

Rose, Paul Lawrence. "Jacomo Contarini (1536–1595) a Venetian Patron and Collector of Mathematical Instruments and Books." *Physis, rivista internazionale di storia della scienza* 18, fasc. 2 (1976): 117–30.

Rosenthal, Margaret F. *The Honest Courtesan: Veronica Franco, Citizen and Writer in Sixteenth-Century Venice*. Chicago: University of Chicago Press, 1992.

Rossi, Paola. *Jacopo Tintoretto. I: I Ritratti*. Venice: Alfieri, 1974.

———. *Jacopo Tintoretto: Ritratti*. Milan: Electa, 1994.

Rossi, Vittorio. "Il canzoniere inedito di Andrea Michieli detto Squarzòla or Strazzòla." *Giornale storico della letteratura italiana* 26 (1895): 1–91.

Rybczynski, Witold. *Home: A Short History of an Idea*. New York: Penguin Books, 1987.

Rylands, Philip. *Palma Vecchio*. Cambridge: Cambridge University Press, 1992.

Sammartini, Tudy, with Antonio Crovato. *Pavimenti a Venezia: The Floors of Venice*. Ponzano: Vianello Libri, 1999.

Santore, Cathy. "Julia Lombardo, 'Somtuosa Meretrize': A Portrait by Property." *Renaissance Quarterly* 41 (1988): 44–83.

———. "The Tools of Venus." *Renaissance Studies* 11 (1997): 179–205.

Sarti, Raffaela. *Europe at Home: Family and Material Culture 1500–1800*. Translated by Allan Cameron. New Haven and London: Yale University Press, 2002.

Sartori, Fabiola, ed., *La casa grande dei Foscari in volta de Canal: Documenti, con un saggio di Antonio Foscari*. Venice: La Malcontentà, 2001.

Savini Branca, Simona. *Il collezionismo veneziano nel '600*. Padua: CEDAM, 1965.

Scarabello, Giovanni. "Le 'signore' della Repubblica." In *Il gioco dell'amore: Le cortigiane di Venezia dal trecento al settecento*. Milan: Berenice, 1990.

Schmitter, Monika Anne. "The Display of Distinction: Art Collecting and Social Status in Early Sixteenth-Century Venice." Ph.D. diss., University of Michigan, 1997.

Schuller, Manfred. "Le facciate dei palazzi medioevali di Venezia. ricerche su singoli esempi architettonici." In *L'architettura gotica veneziana*, edited by Francesco Valcanover and Wolfgang Wolters.

Schulz, Juergen. "Byzantine 'Continuity' and Western Romanesque: Secular Architecture." In *Venice: Art & Architecture*, edited by Giandomenico Romanelli.

———. "La critica di fronte al problema dei primi palazzi veneziani." In *L'architettura gotica veneziana*, edited by Francesco Valcanover and Wolfgang Wolters.

———. "The Houses of the Dandolo: A Family Compound in Medieval Venice." *Journal of the Society of Architectural Historians* 52 (1993): 391–415.

———. "The Houses of Titian, Aretino, and Sansovino." In *Titian: His World and His Legacy*, edited by David Rosand. New York: Columbia University Press, 1982.

———. "La piazza medievale di San Marco." *Annali di architettura* 4–5 (1992–93): 134–56.

———. "The Restoration of the Fondaco dei Turchi." *Annali di architettura* 7 (1995): 19–38.

———. "Vasari at Venice." *The Burlington Magazine* 103 (1961): 500–10.

———. *Venetian Painted Ceilings of the Renaissance*. Berkeley and Los Angeles: University of California Press, 1968.

Schwarz, Heinrich. "The Mirror in Art." *Art Quarterly* 15 (1952): 104–5.

Semi, Franca. *Gli "Ospizi" di Venezia*. Venice: Edizioni Helvetia, 1983.

Settis, Salvatore. *Giorgione's Tempest: Interpreting the Hidden Subject*. Translated by Ellen Bianchini. Chicago: The University of Chicago Press, 1990.

Shearman, John. *The Early Italian Pictures in the Collection of Her Majesty the Queen*. Cambridge: Cambridge University Press, 1983.

Siebenhüner, Herbert. *Der Palazzo Barbarigo della Terrazza in Venedig und seine Tizian-Sammlung*. Munich: Deutscher Kunstverlag, 1981.

Smith, Alison A. "Gender, Ownership and Domestic Space: Inventories and Family Archives in Renaissance Verona." *Renaissance Studies* 12:3 (1998): 375–91.

Smith, Logan Pearsall. *The Life and Letters of Sir Henry Wotton*. 2 vols. Oxford: Clarendon Press, 1907.

Spezzani, Paolo. "Riflettoscopia e raggi xc di alcuni ritratti di Jacopo Tintoretto." In Paola Rossi, *Jacopo Tintoretto: Ritratti*. Milan: Electa, 1994.

Sponza, Sandro. "Un dipinto di Tiziano riconosciueto: il ritratto di Nicolo Zeno a Kingston Lacy." In *Pittura veneziana dal Quattrocento al Settecento: Studi di storia dell'arte in onore di Egidio Martini*, edited by Giuseppe Maria Pilo. Venice: Arsenale, 1999.

Stallybrass, Peter. "Worn Worlds: Clothes and Identity on the Renaissance Stage." In *Subject and Object in Renaissance Culture*, edited by Margreta de Grazia, Maureen Quilligan, and Peter Stallybrass. Cambridge: Cambridge University Press, 1996.

Strachan, Michael. *The Life and Adventures of Thomas Coryate*. London: Oxford University Press, 1962.

Strauss, Walter L., ed. *Hendrik Goltzius 1558–1617: The Complete Engravings and Woodcuts*. New York: Abaris Books, 1977.

Syson, Luke, and Dora Thornton. *Objects of Virtue: Art in Renaissance Italy*. Los Angeles: The J. Paul Getty Museum, 2001.

Tafuri, Manfredo. "Il pubblico e il privato: Architettura e committenza a Venezia." In *Storia di Venezia dalle origine alla caduta della Serenissima. VI. Dal Rinascimento al Barocco*, edited by Gaetano Cozzi and Paolo Prodi. Rome: Istituto della Enciclopedia Italiana, 1994.

———. *Ricerca del Rinascimento: i principi, città, architetti*. Turin: Giulio Einaudi Editore, 1992.

———. *Venezia e il Rinascimento*. Turin: Giulio Einaudi Editore, 1985.

———. *Venice and the Renaissance*. Translated by Jessica Levine. Cambridge, Mass.: MIT Press, 1989.

Tamassia Mazzarotto, Bianca. *Le feste veneziane: i giochi popolari le cerimonie religiose e di governo*. Florence: Sansoni, 1980.

Tassini, Giuseppe. *Alcuni palazzi ed antichi edificii di Venezia*. Venice: M. Fontana, 1879. Reprint, Venice: Filippi Editore, 1993.

———. *Curiosità Veneziane*. Venice: Fuga 1915. Reprint, Venice: Filippi, 1988.

Tateo, Francesco, ed. *Umanesimo e culture nazionali europee: testimonianze letterarie dei secoli XV–XVI*. Palermo: Palumbo, 1999.

Tenenti, Alberto. "The Sense of Space and Time in the Venetian World of the Fifteenth and Sixteenth Centuries." In *Renaissance Venice*, edited by J. R. Hale.

Thomsen, Leslie, ed. *Fortune: "All is but Fortune"*. Washington, D.C.: The Folger Shakespeare Library, 2000.

Thomson, David. *Renaissance Architecture: Critics, Patrons, Luxury*. Manchester and New York: Manchester University Press, 1993.

Thornton, Dora. *The Scholar in his Study*. New Haven and London: Yale University Press, 1997.

Thornton, Peter. *Form & Decoration: Innovation in the Decorative Arts, 1470–1870*. London: Weidenfeld & Nicolson, 1998.

———. *The Italian Renaissance Interior 1400–1600*. London: Weidenfeld & Nicolson, 1991.

———. *Musical Instruments as Works of Art*. London: Victoria & Albert Museum, 1968 Rev. ed., London: Victoria & Albert Museum, 1982.

Tiepolo, Maria Francesca. "Il linguaggio dei simboli: le arme de I

Barbaro." In *Una famiglia veneziana nella storia: I Barbaro*, edited by Michela Marangoni and Manlio Pastore Stocchi. Venice: Istituto Veneto di Scienze, Lettere, ed Arti, 1996.

Tomasi, Michele. *La bottega degli Embriachi*. Florence: Museo Nazionale del Bargello, 2001.

Trebbi, Giuseppe. "La società veneziana." In *Storia di Venezia dalle origini alla caduta della Serenissima. VI. Dal Rinascimento al Barocco*, edited by Gaetano Cozzi and Paolo Prodi. Rome: Istituto della Enciclopedia Italiana, 1994.

Trincanato, Egli Renata. *Venezia Minore*. Milan: Edizioni del Milione, 1948.

Tucci, Ugo. "Carriere popolane e dinastie di mestiere a Venezia." In *Gerarchie economiche e gerarchie sociali: Secoli XII–XVIII*, edited by Annalisa Guarducci. Florence: Le Monnier, 1990.

Valcanover, Francesco et al. *Pittura murale esterna nel Veneto: Venezia e Provincia*. Bassano: Ghedina & Tassotti Editori, 1981.

Valcanover, Francesco, and Wolfgang Wolters, eds. *L'architettura gotica veneziana*. Venice: Istituto Veneto di Scienze, Lettere ed Arti, 2000.

Venturelli, Paola. "La moda come 'status symbol'. Legislazione suntuaria e 'segnali' di identificazione sociale." In *Storia della Moda*, edited by Ranier: Varese and Grazietta Butazzi. Bologna: Calderini, 1995.

Venturi, Lionello. *Le compagnie della calza, Sec. XV–XVI*. Venice: Istituto Veneto di Arti Grafiche, 1909. Reprint, Venice: Filippi Editore, 1983.

Walker, Jonathan. "Gambling and Venetian Noblemen, ca. 1500–1700." *Past & Present* 162 (1999): 28–69.

Weddingen, Erasmus. "Jacopo Tintoretto und die Musik." *Artibus et Historiae* 10 (1984): 67–119.

Roberto Weiss. *Renaissance Discovery of Classical Antiquity*. Oxford: Oxford University Press, 1973.

Welch, Evelyn. "From Retail to Resale: the Second-Hand Market in Renaissance Italy." In *The Art Market in Italy, 1400–1600*, edited by Sara Matthews Grieco and Louisa Matthews.

———. "Public Magnificence and Private Display: Giovanni Pontano's *De splendore* (1498) and the Domestic Arts." *Journal of Design History* 15:4 (2002): 211–21.

Williamson, Paul, ed. *European Sculpture at the Victoria & Albert Museum*. London: Victoria & Albert Museum, 1996.

Wolters, Wolfgang. *Architektur und Ornament: venezianischer Bauschmuck der Renaissance*. Munich: C. H. Beck, 2000.

———. *La scultura veneziana gotica, 1300–1460*. Venice: Alfieri, 1976.

———. "Una villa cinquecentesca in pericolo a Murano." *Antichità Viva* 5:3 (1966): 27–33.

Yriarte, Charles. *La vie d'un patricien de Venise au seizième siècle*. Paris: E. Plon, 1874.

Zanetti, Vincenzo. *Guida di Murano e delle celebri sue fornaci vetrarie*. Venice, 1980. Reprint, Venice: Arnaldo Forni Editore, 1984.

Zorzi, Alvise. *Venezia Scomparsa*, 2nd ed. Milan: Electa, 1984.

Zorzi, Marino, ed. *Collezioni di antichità a Venezia nei secoli della Repubblica*. Rome: Istituto Poligrafico e Zecca dello Stato, 1988.

Zucchetta, Emanuela. *Antichi ridotti veneziani: Arte e società dal Cinquecento al Settecento*. Rome: Fratelli Palombi, 1988.

Zucchetta Benvenuti, Emanuela. "Gli affreschi del Casino Mogenico [sic] di Murano: tra armonia ed evasione." *Notizie da Palazzo Albani* 14:1 (1985): 54–62.

Photograph and Text Credits

References are to figure numbers

Amsterdam, Rijksmuseum 195, 196, 208
Atlanta, High Museum of Art 89, 90
Author 2, 3, 14, 15, 16, 17, 21, 29, 32, 39, 41, 42, 47, 48, 54, 56, 57, 58, 63, 64, 66, 67, 70a, 70b, 80, 81, 82, 92, 93, 105, 111, 115, 147, 169, 174, 212, 214, 216, 217, 218, 219, 223, 225, 226, 228, 232, 239, 253, 269, 271, 273, 274, 275
Baltimore, Walters Art Museum 146
Berlin, Staatliche Museen Preussischer Kulturbesitz (Jörg P. Anders) 148, 191, 192
Bologna, Museo Civico Medievale (Maria Berardi) 83
Budapest, Szépmüvészeti Muzeum 201
Cambridge, Deborah Howard 245, 250
Cambridge, Fitzwilliam Museum 248, 249
London, British Library 124, 139, 145, 207a, 207b, 235, 244, 261, 262, 263, 264
London, British Museum 144, 244
London, National Gallery 180, 252
London, National Maritime Museum 246
London, National Trust Photographic Library (John Hammond) 5
London, © V&A Picture Library 57, 62, 91, 91, 107, 109, 173, 247
Milan, Castello Sforzesco, Pinacoteca/Foto Saporetti 20
Milan, Civica Raccolta delle Stampe Achille Bertarelli 96, 198, 203
Milan, Museo Bagatti Valsecchi 79, 100, 101, 102
Munich, Artothek (Jochen Remmer) 197
Munich, Bayerische Staatsbibliothek 74, 75,
New Haven, Yale University, Beinecke Rare Book and Manuscript Library 186, 199, 209
New York, Alinari/Art Resource 242, 254
New York, Erich Lessing/Art Resource 99, 171, 173, 181, 189
New York, © 2003 The Metropolitan Museum of Art 118, 119, 120, 122
New York, New York Public Library 204
New York, The Pierpont Morgan Library/Art Resource 153
New York, Réunion des Musées Nationaux/Art Resource 77, 112, 116, 117, 143
New York, Scala/Art Resource 73, 86, 98, 103, 104, 141, 179, 193, 194, 210
Offenbach, Deutsches Liedermuseum, (Monika Kotthaus) 140
Oxford, Ashmolean Museum 55
Oxford, Bodleian Library 237, 266, 267, 268
Paris, Musée Jacquemart André 149, 150
Princeton, John Blaszewski 72, 88, 177a, 177b, 229, 230, 255
Princeton, Princeton University Art Museum © Trustees of Princeton University 167
Princeton, Princeton University Library: General Collections 129, 130, 131, 132; Department of Rare Books and Special Collections 10, 84, 121, 123; Marquand Library 6, 12, 38, 50, 166
Richmond, Virginia Museum of Fine Arts 171
Rome, Antonio Ortolan 215, 224, 227
Rome, Istituto Nazionale per la Grafica 234
Venice, Archivio di Stato, Sezione di fotoriproduzione (su concessione del Ministero per i Beni e le Attività Culturali, Atti n. 39/2003, prot. 5610 V.12) 11, 13, 95, 200, 202, 221
Venice, Biblioteca Nazionale Marciana 40, 125, 126, 127, 241, 272
Venice, Cameraphoto Arte pages x and xi, 7, 8, 18, 24, 25, 27, 31, 33, 34, 35, 43, 44, 45, 46, 52, 68, 71, 85, 87, 94, 97, 110, 113, 114, 133, 142, 168, 172, 184, 187, 206, 210, 211, 231, 240, 243, 257, 269
Venice, Istituto Veneto delle Scienze, Lettere ed Arti 213
Venice, Mark Smith 4, 78, 106, 128, 279
Venice, Museo Civico Correr 19, 23, 26, 28, 151, 152, 185
Venice, Osvaldo Böhm 22, 30, 36, 37, 49, 53, 76, 108, 176, 222, 236, 238, 270
Vienna, Kunsthistorisches Museum 60, 69, 190
Washington, D.C., Folger Shakespeare Library 1, 59, 137, 138, 156, 157, 158, 159, 160, 161, 162, 163, 164, 165, 178, 182, 183, 205, 219, 233
Washington, D.C., National Gallery of Art 59, 154
Windsor, The Royal Collection © 2003, Her Majesty Queen Elizabeth II 61, 251

Chapter 7 will be published in a slightly different version as the following article: "Not One But Many Separate Cities: Housing Diversity in Renaissance Venice," in *Home and Homelessness in the Medieval and Renaissance Worlds*, ed. Nicholas Howe (South Bend: Notre Dame University Press, forthcoming).

Index

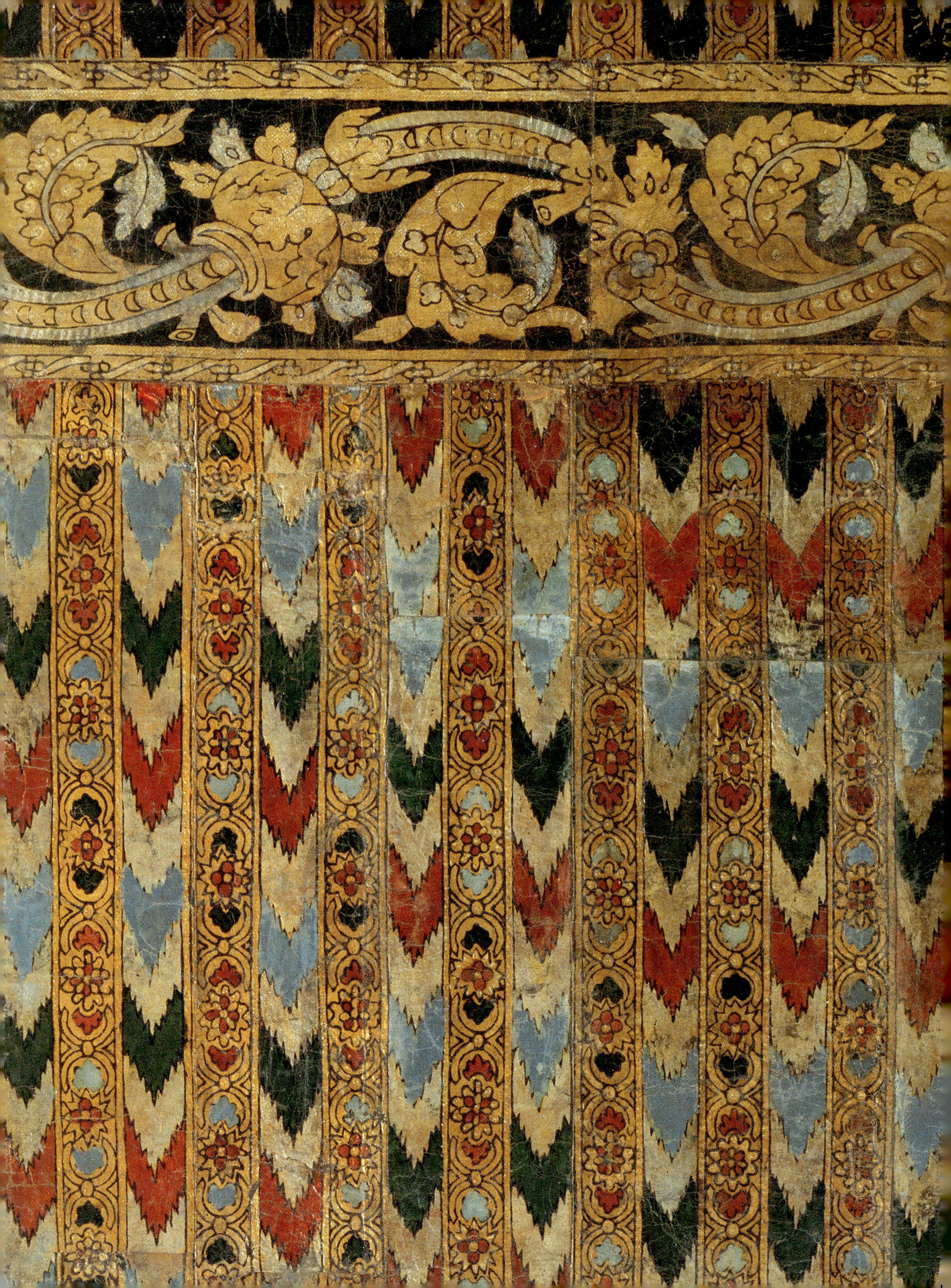